FINANCE

INTRODUCTION TO INSTITUTIONS, INVESTMENTS, AND MANAGEMENT
Ninth Edition

RONALD W. MELICHER
PROFESSOR OF FINANCE
UNIVERSITY OF COLORADO AT BOULDER

MERLE T. WELSHANS
EMERITUS PROFESSOR OF FINANCE
WASHINGTON UNIVERSITY, ST. LOUIS

EDGAR A. NORTON
ASSOCIATE PROFESSOR OF FINANCE
FAIRLEIGH DICKINSON UNIVERSITY

SOUTH-WESTERN College Publishing

An International Thomson Publishing Company

Acquisitions Editor: Christopher Will
Team Director: Jack C. Calhoun
Developmental Editor: Lois Boggs-Leavens
Production Editor: Sharon L. Smith
Production House: Lachina Publishing Services
Internal Designer: Debbie Leffert
Cover Design and Illustration: Photonics/Alan Brown
Cover Photos: (1) © Tony Stone/Mark Joseph
             (2) and (3) Images provided by © 1994 Photo Disc, Inc.
Photo Research: Jennifer Mayhall
Career Profiles: Words & Occasional Wisdom
Verification: Angela Bansal
Marketing Manager: Scott D. Person

Library of Congress Cataloging-in-Publication Data

Melicher, Ronald W.
  Finance : introduction to institutions, investments & management /
Ronald W. Melicher, Merle T. Welshans, Edgar A. Norton. — 9th ed.
  p. cm.
  Includes bibliographical references and index.
  ISBN 0-538-83993-7 (hardcover)
  1. Finance. 2. Finance—United States.   I. Welshans, Merle T.
II. Norton, Edgar.   III. Title.
HG173.M398   1996
332'.0973—dc20   96-8686
                                                              CIP

ISBN: 0-538-83993-7

1 2 3 4 5 6 7 8 D1 3 2 1 0 9 8 7 6

Printed in the United States of America

I(T)P
International Thomson Publishing

To my wife, Sharon, and our children,
Michelle, Sean, and Thor

Ronald W. Melicher

To the memory of my mother and father

Merle T. Welshans

To my best friend and wife, Becky,
and our gifts from God, Matthew and Amy

Edgar A. Norton

PREFACE

This ninth edition of *Finance: Introduction to Institutions, Investments, and Management* builds upon the successes of its earlier editions while maintaining a fresh and up-to-date coverage of the field of finance. A movement is growing across the United States to offer a more "balanced" first course in finance. The ninth edition was developed for this "new" first course. Its eighteen chapters cover the three major financial areas involving the financial system, investments, and business finance in three six-chapter parts. For the student who does not plan to take any more courses in finance, this book provides a valuable overview of the major concepts of the discipline. For the student who wants to take additional courses in finance, the overview presented in this text provides a solid foundation upon which future courses can build.

Finance is meant to be used in a course whose purpose is to survey the foundations of the finance discipline. As such, it is designed to meet the needs of students in a variety of programs. Specifically, *Finance* can be used in the following types of courses:

1. As the first and only course in finance for non-finance business students.
2. As the first course in finance at a college or university where the department wants to expose students to a broad foundational survey of the discipline.

3. With supplemental readings and articles, *Finance* can be used for a capstone finance course.
4. *Finance* is an appropriate text to use at a school which seeks to provide liberal arts majors with a business minor or business concentration. The writing level is appropriate to provide students with a good foundation in the basics of our discipline.
5. *Finance* can be used in a "lower division" service course whose goal is to attract freshmen and sophomores to business and to even attract them to become finance majors.

The philosophy behind this book is three-fold. First, we believe that a basic understanding of the complex world of finance should begin with a survey course that covers an introduction to financial institutions, financial markets (or, more broadly, "investments"), financial management, or business finance. Students can immediately gain an integrated perspective of the interrelationships between financial markets, financial institutions, and management. They will appreciate how businesses and individuals are affected by markets and institutions as well as how markets and institutions can be used to help meet individual or firm goals.

Second, as an introductory survey to the field of finance, we wrote the book with a readable and "user friendly" focus in mind. We seek to convey basic knowledge, concepts, and terms that will serve the non-finance major well into the future and that will form a foundation upon which the finance major can build. Finer points, discussions of theory, and complicated topics are best reserved for more advanced course work. We aim to make students using our text financially literate and cognizant of the richness of the field of finance.

Third, we focus on the practice of finance in the settings of institutions, investments, and financial management. We focus on the descriptive in each of these fields. We don't want students to be unable to see the forest of finance because the trees of quantitative methods obscure their view or scare them away. When we do introduce equations and mathematical concepts that are applicable to finance, we show step-by-step solutions.

This ninth edition of *Finance* represents a major revision. The prior edition's twenty-five chapters have been slimmed down to eighteen. This occurred by consolidating, streamlining, and integrating material as well as deleting some material that did not fit with this edition's mission of providing a foundational overview to the field of finance.

The first part of the book contains six chapters on The Financial System. Here we introduce the topic of finance and the role of the financial system to a nation's economy. Financial intermediaries are introduced as well as the functions of financial systems. Special attention is given to the U.S. monetary system, definitions of money, and the international monetary system. Different depository institutions are introduced and their functions in the U.S. economy explained. This part also introduces and reviews the role of the Federal Reserve System and the effects of monetary and fiscal policy on the economy. This part closes by discussing the international financial system, including exchange rates and the financing of international transactions.

Following this introduction of the financial system, Part 2 of the text focuses on investments and financial markets. We review the role of savings in an economy and how funds flow to and from different sectors. Interest rates are introduced and the discussion centers on making the student aware of the different influences on the level of interest rates and why they change over time. As interest rates measure the cost of moving money across time, this section reviews basic time value of money concepts with many worked out examples, including the keystrokes that students can use with financial calculators. The basic characteristics of bonds and stocks are reviewed. Students learn to apply time value of money concepts to find the prices of these securities. The fundamentals of investing risks and returns are discussed, as are the basics of investment banking and the operations of securities markets. Advanced classes may want to review the basics of financial derivatives which are explained in an appendix to Chapter 11's securities markets discussion.

Businesses raise funds in the institutional and market environment covered in Parts 1 and 2. In Part 3, the final six chapters of the text introduce students to business finance. Different ways in which to organize businesses are reviewed and the financial implications of each organizational form are highlighted. Accounting concepts such as the balance sheet, income statement, and statement of cash flows are introduced with simple examples. Financial ratios assist in the process of analyzing a firm's strengths and weaknesses. We also review their use as a means to help managers plan ahead for future asset and financing needs. Strategies for managing a firm's current assets and current liabilities are examined, as are the funding sources firms use to tap the financial markets for short-term financing. We introduce students to the basics of capital budgeting and to capital structure concepts.

By exposing students to institutions, markets, and management as the three major strands of finance, students will finish their course with a greater understanding of how these three fields interrelate. Financial institutions will be seen as facilitating the work of the financial markets by meeting the needs of different sets of borrowers and savers. Financial markets will be seen as the arena to which businesses and financial institutions go to raise funds and the mechanism through which individuals can invest their savings to meet their future goals. Financial management uses information it obtains from the financial markets and institutions to efficiently and profitably manage assets and to raise needed funds in a cost-efficient manner. This broad exposure to the discipline of finance will meet the needs of the non-major who needs to know the basics of finance so they can read *The Wall Street Journal* and other business periodicals intelligently. It will also help the non-finance major work effectively as a member of a cross-functional team at work, a team that will include finance professionals. This overview of the field of finance will also get the finance major started on the right foot. Rather than receiving a compartmentalized view of finance, probably viewed through the corporate finance lens that many texts use, the finance major will receive a practical introduction to the different disciplines of finance and will better appreciate their relationships to one another.

TEACHING AND LEARNING AIDS

The ninth edition of *Finance* has been reviewed and edited to improve readability and understanding. Each chapter begins with a list of learning objectives which the instructor can use to form the basis for in-class lecture or discussion. The student can use them to review each chapter's main points. Margin definitions of key terms are provided to assist students in learning the language of finance.

Each chapter provides end-of-chapter discussion questions that review chapter material. Each chapter contains problems for students to gather data for or to solve. Each chapter also ends with self-test questions and problems, as well as answers to reinforce learning.

Throughout the book boxes are used to focus on current topics or applications of interest. They are designed to demonstrate and illustrate concepts and practices in the dynamic field of finance.

A feature which is new to this edition are Career Profiles. These feature eighteen men and women (one per chapter) who, in an interview format, discuss their jobs and the skills needed to obtain positions in different areas of finance. Some of the positions reviewed are trust officer, business valuation analyst, money manager, collections manager, treasurer, and venture capitalist. Our hope is the Career Profile boxes will stimulate discussion and interest so students will consider pursuing a career in the finance area.

Several other features, new to this edition of *Finance*, are available to adopters. Videos from CNBC on financial topics can be used to initiate class discussion and facilitate learning by illustrating the relevance and practical use of the topics discussed in the textbook.

A set of Lotus- and Excel-compatible templates, developed by Robert Ritchey of Texas Tech University, are available with the text. Students can use the templates to help solve some of the end-of-chapter problems.

An interactive CD-ROM developed by Steve Wyatt of the University of Cincinnati is available at a discount to students using this text. This CD-ROM is an instructional and applications multimedia tool. It can also serve as an in-class presentation tool for the instructor.

An *Instructor's Manual* is available to those who adopt this text. It features detailed chapter outlines, lecture tips, and answers to end-of-chapter questions and problems. Transparency masters of many of the figures from the text are also provided in the manual. The manual includes an extensive test bank of over 1,500 true-false and multiple-choice examination questions with answers.

The test bank is also available for use with MicroSWAT III test generation software, which is available to instructors who adopt *Finance*. This easy-to-use, menu-driven software package allows an instructor to quickly and efficiently produce quality tests. It includes a word processor for entering, editing, and scrambling questions, and a grade book.

ACKNOWLEDGEMENTS

We wish to thank the South-Western *Finance* team of Christopher Will, acquisitions editor; Sharon Smith, production editor; and Lachina Publishing Services for helping to publish this ninth edition of *Finance*. We are especially grateful to the reviewers of prior drafts of the ninth edition for their comments and constructive criticisms:

Tim Alzheimer, Montana State University
Allan Blair, Palm Beach Atlantic College
Stewart Bonem, Cincinnati State University
Robert L. Chapman, Orlando College
David R. Durst, University of Akron
Irene M. Hammerbacher, Iona College
Kim Hansen, Mid-State Technical College
Ed Krohn, Miami Dade Community College
P. John Limberopoulos, University of Colorado-Boulder
Michael Murray, Winona State University
Michael Owen, Montana State University
Alan Questell, Richmond Community College
Amir Tavakkol, Kansas State University
Howard Whitney, Franklin University
David Zalewski, Providence College

Likewise, comments from students and teachers who have used prior editions of this book also are greatly appreciated, as is the assistance from the dozens of reviewers who have commented about the prior editions of *Finance*.

Finally, and perhaps most importantly, we wish to thank our families for their understanding and support during the writing of the ninth edition.

Ronald W. Melicher
Merle T. Welshans
Edgar A. Norton

Brief Contents

CONTENTS

PART 1
THE FINANCIAL SYSTEM

PART 2
INVESTMENTS

PART 3
BUSINESS FINANCE

14 Financial Analysis and Long-Term Financial Planning

FINANCE

INTRODUCTION TO INSTITUTIONS, INVESTMENTS, AND MANAGEMENT

PART 1

INTRODUCTION

Ask someone what they think about finance. You'll probably get a variety of responses: "It deals with money." "It is what my bank does." "The New York Stock Exchange has something to do with it." "It's how businesses and people get the money they need—you know, borrowing and stuff like that." And they'll all be correct!

Finance is a broad field. It involves national and international systems of banking and financing business. It also deals with the process you go through to get a car loan and what a business does when planning for its future needs.

Within the general field of finance, there are several areas of study. First is the area of financial institutions. **Financial institutions** collect funds from savers and lend them to or invest them in businesses or people that need cash. Examples of financial institutions are commercial banks, investment banks, insurance companies, and mutual funds. Financial institutions operate as part of the financial system. The financial system is the environment of finance. It includes the laws and regulations that affect financial transactions. The financial system encompasses the Federal Reserve System, which controls the supply of money in the U.S. economy. It also consists of the mechanisms that have been constructed to facilitate the flow of money and financial securities between countries. Part 1 of this book examines the financial system and the role of financial institutions in it.

A second area of study is the financial markets and investments. **Financial markets** are a framework or mechanism for bringing together those that have money to invest with those that need funds. A financial market can be a central location for the trading of financial claims, such as the New York Stock Exchange. It may also take the form of a communications network, as with the over-the-counter market, which is another means by which stocks and bonds can be traded. When people invest funds, lend or borrow money, or buy or sell shares of a company's stock, they are participating in the financial markets. Part 2 of this book examines the role of financial markets and the process of investing in bonds and stocks.

The third area of the field of finance is financial management. **Financial management** studies how a business should manage its assets, liabilities, and equity to produce a good or service. Whether or not a firm offers a new product or expands production, or how it invests excess cash are examples of decisions that financial managers are involved with. Part 3 discusses how financial concepts can help managers better manage their firms. Financial managers are constantly working with financial institutions and watching financial market trends as they make investment and financing decisions.

There are few clear distinctions or separations between the three areas of finance, as seen in the diagram on the following page. There is an overlap between each of three fields: institutions, markets, and financial management. Financial institutions operate in the environment of the financial markets and work to meet

The
Financial
System

the financial needs of individuals and businesses. Financial managers do analyses and make decisions based upon information they obtain from the financial markets. They also work with financial institutions when they need to raise funds and when they have excess funds to invest. Participants investing in the financial markets use information from financial institutions and firms to evaluate different investments in securities such as stocks, bonds, and certificates of deposit. A person working in one field must be knowledgeable about all three. Thus, this book is designed to give you a good working knowledge of all three areas of finance.

Part 1, The Financial System, presents an overview of the macro or global environment in which financial institutions operate. Financial institutions operate within the financial system to facilitate the work of the financial markets. For example, you can put your savings in a bank and earn interest. But your money just doesn't sit in the bank. The bank takes your deposit and the money from other depositors and lends it to Kathy who needs a short-term loan for her business, to Ron for a college loan, and to Roger and Maria who borrow the money to help buy a house. Banks bring together savers and those who need money, such as Kathy, Ron, Roger, and Maria. The interest rate the depositors earn and the interest rate that borrowers pay are determined by national and even international economic forces. Just what the bank does with depositors' money and how it reviews loan applications are determined to some extent by bank regulators and financial market participants, such as the Federal Reserve Board.

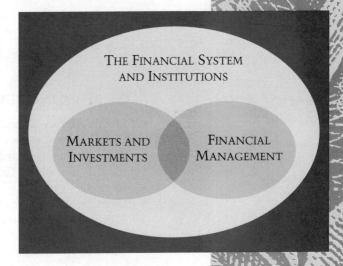

Chapter 1 introduces the topic of finance in more detail and discusses various types of financial institutions and the functions of a financial market. Chapter 2 presents an overview of the U.S. monetary system and how funds are transferred between individuals, firms, and countries. Depository institutions, such as banks and savings and loans, are the topic of Chapter 3. The Federal Reserve System, the U.S. central bank that controls the money supply, is discussed in Chapter 4. Chapter 5 places the previous chapters in perspective, discussing the role of the Federal Reserve and the banking system in helping to meet national economic goals for the United States, such as economic growth, low inflation, and stable exchange rates. Part 1 concludes with an explanation of international trade and the topic of international finance in Chapter 6.

CHAPTER 1

Role of Finance

AFTER STUDYING THIS CHAPTER, YOU SHOULD BE ABLE TO:

- Define *finance* at both the macro and micro levels.
- Explain what finance is about.
- Describe the basic requirements of an effective financial system.
- Identify the major financial intermediaries and their roles in the U.S. financial system.
- Identify and explain the types of claims to wealth that are traded in U.S. financial markets.
- Describe the financial functions in the U.S. financial system.
- Identify and discuss some career opportunities in finance.

We begin this chapter by asking the question, what is finance? While our answer is brief, we hope it will serve to initiate your understanding of the materials in this book.

We next discuss the basic requirements for an effective financial system along with the types of financial intermediaries operating in the U.S. system. Specific claims to wealth are identified and financial functions in the U.S. system are described. A modern market economy like ours needs an effective financial system to function properly. Intelligent participation in our system requires some knowledge of finance.

We conclude this initial chapter with a presentation of possible career opportunities available in the field of finance followed by the plan of study for this book. We hope that after studying the materials in this book, you will be better prepared for a business career, possibly even one in the field of finance.

WHAT IS FINANCE?

Finance can be defined at both the overall or macro level and the organization or micro level. **Finance** at the *macro level* is the study of financial institutions and financial markets and how they operate within the financial system in both the U.S. and global economies. Finance at the *micro level* is the study of financial planning, asset management, and fund raising for businesses and financial institutions.

finance
study of how institutions, markets, and individual firms operate within the financial system

Finance has its origins in economics and accounting. Economists use a supply-and-demand framework to explain how the prices and quantities of goods and services are determined in a free-market economic system. Accountants provide the record-keeping mechanism for showing ownership of the financial instruments used in the flow of financial funds between savers and borrowers. Accountants also record revenues, expenses, and profitability of organizations that produce and exchange goods and services.

Large-scale production and specialization of labor can exist only if there is an effective means of paying for raw materials and final products. Businesses can obtain the money needed to buy capital goods such as machinery and equipment only if a mechanism has been established for making savings available for investment. Similarly, federal and other governmental units, such as state and local governments and tax districts, can carry out their wide range of activities only if efficient means exist for raising money, for making payments, and for borrowing.

Financial markets, financial intermediaries, and financial management are crucial elements of well developed financial systems. Financial markets provide the mechanism for allocating financial resources or funds from savers to borrowers. **Financial intermediaries** are firms, such as banks and credit unions, that engage in financial activities to aid the flow of funds from savers to borrowers. Financial management in business involves the efficient use of financial resources in the production and exchange of goods and services. The goal of the financial manager in a profit-seeking organization is to maximize the owners' wealth. This is accomplished through effective financial planning and analysis, asset management, and the acquisition of financial capital. These same functions must be performed by financial managers in not-for-profit organizations to provide a desired level of services at acceptable costs.

financial intermediaries
firms that bring about the flow of funds from savers to borrowers

BASIC REQUIREMENTS FOR AN EFFECTIVE FINANCIAL SYSTEM

An effective financial system needs an efficient monetary system. It also must be able to allow capital formation by channeling savings into investment. Lastly, to complete the investment process, there must be markets in which to buy and sell claims to wealth, such as real estate or financial assets.

The monetary system must provide an efficient medium for exchanging goods and services. A way to measure prices, such as the dollar in the U.S. economy or the pound sterling in the British economy, is a basic requirement. This is called a *unit of account*. The unit of account must be universally accepted if exchange is to function smoothly. Its value must remain reasonably stable if it is to be used widely. And there must be convenient means to pay for goods and services purchased, whether the purchase is a pack of chewing gum or a business worth millions of dollars. This means that the monetary system must operate with monetary institutions, instruments such as stocks and bonds, and procedures geared to the needs of the economy.

capital formation
the creation of productive facilities such as buildings, tools, and equipment

A financial system must make possible the creation of capital on a scale large enough to meet the demands of the economy. **Capital formation** takes place whenever resources are used to produce buildings, machinery, or other equipment to be used in the production of goods for consumer or producer use. In a simple economy, such as a self-sufficient, one-person farm, this process takes place directly. For example, the farmer creates capital by building a new barn.

In a highly developed economy, capital formation takes place indirectly. If individuals, businesses, or governmental units do not need to spend all of their current income, they save some of it. If these savings are placed with some type of financial intermediary, they will be made available in the form of loans to others who use them to buy buildings, machinery, or equipment. The indirect process of capital formation can work only if the proper legal instruments and financial intermediaries exist. Then savers will feel secure transferring the use of their savings to businesses and other institutions who need them.

A third essential feature of the financial system is that it provides markets for the transfer of financial assets, such as stocks and bonds, and for the conversion of such assets into cash. Markets are necessary for capital formation. They encourage investment by providing the means for savers to quickly and easily convert their claims into cash when needed. For example, millions of people are willing to invest billions of dollars in AT&T, General Electric, and other companies because the New York Stock Exchange makes it possible to sell their shares to other investors easily and quickly.

FINANCIAL INTERMEDIARIES IN THE UNITED STATES

The current system of financial intermediaries that exists in the United States, like the monetary system, developed to meet the changing needs of our economy. Because the U.S. economy is closely tied to the economies of other nations, our financial intermediaries must continually respond to changes in the global economy as well. For example, today banks are willing to exchange foreign currencies for U.S. dollars and vice versa, as well as lend to foreign businesses.

FIVE TYPES OF FINANCIAL INTERMEDIARIES

The basic kinds of financial intermediaries that play active roles in the U.S. financial system are shown in Figure 1.1. First are the **depository institutions,** which are commercial banks, savings and loan associations (S&Ls), savings banks, and credit unions. These institutions play an important role in the channeling of individuals' savings into loans to governments (by purchasing their debt issues), loans to businesses, and home mortgages.

     The second category, *contractual savings institutions*, are so classified because they involve relatively steady inflows of money. Life insurance companies receive steady inflows in the form of insurance premium pay-

depository institutions commercial banks, savings and loan associations, savings banks, and credit unions

FIGURE 1.1   Major Intermediaries in the U.S. Financial System

DEPOSITORY INSTITUTIONS	FINANCE COMPANIES
Commercial banks	Sales finance companies
Savings and loan associations (S&Ls)	Consumer finance companies
Savings banks	Commercial finance companies
Credit unions	
CONTRACTUAL SAVINGS INSTITUTIONS	**SELECTED SECURITIES MARKET INSTITUTIONS**
Life insurance companies	Mortgage banking companies
Private pension funds	Investment bankers and brokerage companies
State and local government retirement funds	Organized securities markets
	Credit-reporting organizations
INVESTMENT INSTITUTIONS	Government credit-related agencies
Investment companies and mutual funds	
Real estate investment trusts (REITs)	
Money market funds	

ments. Likewise, pension funds for both private and government programs receive contributions on a regular basis. These institutions play an active role in supplying long-term funding by purchasing corporate stocks and bonds, mortgages, and government securities.

Investment institutions make up the third major category in our financial system. These institutions combine the relatively small amounts of savings from many individuals and invest the total in financial assets. Mutual funds purchase corporate stocks and bonds as well as government securities. REITs, or real estate investment trusts, invest in property and mortgages. Money market funds invest in short-term debt securities. While individual investors can invest directly in such securities, investment institutions offer small investors diversification and experienced management of their funds.

The fourth category consists of *finance companies*. These companies provide loans directly to consumers and businesses. Sales and consumer finance companies lend to individuals. Sales finance companies finance installment loan purchases of automobiles and other durable goods. Consumer finance companies provide small loans to individuals and households. Businesses that are unable to obtain financing from commercial banks often turn to commercial finance companies for necessary loans. Thus, finance companies play an important role in our financial system. They provide loanable funds to consumers and businesses that are not obtainable from depository institutions.

The fifth category consists of *securities market institutions* that are involved in the savings-investment process and/or the marketing and transferring of claims to wealth. (There are many kinds of securities market institutions so it is important to know that only selected ones are shown in Figure 1.1.) Creating or issuing new securities or other claims to wealth takes place in the **primary securities market.** The **secondary securities market** involves the transfer of existing securities from old investors to new investors.

Credit-reporting and credit-rating organizations aid lenders in deciding whether to extend credit to consumers and businesses. In recent years government credit-related agencies (such as the Government National Mortgage Association) have taken an increasingly active role in the marketing and transferring of real estate mortgages.

Among the listed institutions, mortgage banking firms play an important role in the origination of real estate mortgages by bringing together borrowers and lenders. Investment banking and brokerage firms are often involved in marketing new stock and bond securities issued by businesses. Brokerage houses, along with organized securities markets, handle the transfer of stocks and bonds among investors.

Few of today's financial intermediaries existed during the American colonial period. Only commercial banks and insurance companies (life and property) can be traced back prior to 1800. Savings banks and S&Ls began

primary securities market

market involved in creating and issuing new securities, mortgages, and other claims to wealth

secondary securities market

market for transferring existing securities between investors developing during the early 1800s. Investment banking firms and organized securities exchanges also can be traced back to the first half of the 1800s. No new major financial intermediaries evolved during the last half of the nineteenth century. Credit unions, pension funds, mutual funds, and finance companies began during the early part of the twentieth century. This was true for government involvement in credit-related agencies as well.

Financial intermediaries in other market economies are generally different in name and organizational structure from their U.S. counterparts. However, they carry out financial functions similar to those described in Figure 1.1. In addition, two international financial institutions exist to promote stability and growth in international finance and trade. Both the International Monetary Fund and the World Bank, which are affiliates of the United Nations, were founded at the end of World War II and have important roles in today's global economy.

The **International Monetary Fund (IMF)** focuses on maintaining orderly conditions in foreign exchange markets by providing facilities where member countries can borrow foreign currencies to correct temporary payment imbalances with other countries. The IMF is an outgrowth of the Bretton Woods agreements and will be discussed in Chapter 2. The **World Bank** encourages international trade by providing long-term loans to developing countries for basic capital projects designed to support their domestic development. Funds for loans made by the World Bank are obtained by selling bonds in developed countries.

International Monetary Fund (IMF)
provides means for United Nations' countries to borrow money

World Bank
provides loans to developing countries

FINANCIAL INTERMEDIATION

Intermediation is the process by which savings are accumulated in depository institutions and, in turn, lent or invested. During the 1970s and 1980s, the great bulk of all funds flowing into the credit markets was supplied by depository institutions. The role of depository institutions has increased significantly since the 1920s. At that time more than half the net increase in the financial assets of households was in the form of securities purchased directly in the credit markets. By the 1980s these purchases accounted for only a small amount of the financial savings of households. The remainder, except for net additions to currency holdings, flowed through depository institutions.

intermediation
the accumulation and lending of savings by depository institutions

The role of depository institutions has grown because they offer a variety of investment opportunities. Notes, bonds, and shares of stock offered by institutions seeking long-term funds are not the assets which most savers are willing to purchase and hold. Depository institutions offer savers safety of principal, easy access to funds, convenience, and availability in small amounts.

Small savers also prefer depository institutions because of the relatively high cost of making small transactions for securities. It is also more difficult to make transactions in securities markets than it is to put funds into a depository institution. Government guarantees of deposit safety through the Federal Deposit Insurance Corporation (FDIC) insurance and supervision has also made depository institutions attractive to small savers. Lastly, there are many choices among depository institutions, each competing for the saver's funds. This has led to a variety of services and conveniences for the saver as well as attractive rates of return.

In years of strong demand for credit and strong restraint on the money supply, such as the early 1980s, the percentage of funds moving through depository institutions to the credit markets has decreased significantly. These are referred to as periods of **disintermediation.** During these times, rapid shifts of sources of funds create difficulties in the economy by impeding the flow of funds to such sectors as housing, which rely heavily on loans from depository institutions.

disintermediation
periods of significant decrease in funds moving through depository institutions to the credit markets

CLAIMS TO WEALTH

Claims to wealth may be in the form of real assets or financial assets. **Real assets** would include the direct ownership of land, buildings, machinery, inventory, and even precious metals. **Financial assets,** also called *intangible assets* or *intangibles*, represent claims against the income and assets of those who issued them. Financial assets are claims against individuals, businesses, financial intermediaries, and governments in the form of obligations or liabilities. For example, a firm's debt obligations are financial assets to those who hold them but represent liabilities of that firm. Real assets in the form of inventory, machinery, and buildings often back the financial claims or liabilities issued by businesses.

real assets
land, buildings, machinery, inventory, and precious metals

financial assets
claims against the income or assets of others

Relatively few of the many types of financial assets actually require the use of financial markets. Checkable deposits, such as checking accounts and share drafts, and time deposits, such as savings accounts held in depository institutions, are also examples of financial assets. In fact, all kinds of promissory notes or IOUs represent financial assets to their holders. Also included is currency issued by the U.S. government. When held by the public, currency is a financial asset. At the same time, it is a financial liability to the government.

Only certain financial assets in the form of securities and debt instruments are marketed and traded in the financial markets. Financial markets are frequently divided into money and capital markets in addition to the previously mentioned primary and secondary markets. **Money markets** are the markets where debt instruments of one year or less are traded. **Capital markets** include longer-term debt securities such as notes and bonds, debt instruments such as mortgages, and corporate stocks.

money markets
markets where debt instruments of one year or less are traded

capital markets
markets for longer-term debt securities and corporate stocks

Figure 1.2 indicates the major types of financial assets that are traded in the financial markets. Since the U.S. government actively borrows through debt financing, its short- and longer-term financial claims, such as

FIGURE 1.2   Claims to Wealth Traded in U.S. Financial Markets

MONEY MARKET INSTRUMENTS	CAPITAL MARKET SECURITIES AND INSTRUMENTS
U.S. Treasury bills	U.S. Treasury notes and bonds
Negotiable certificates of deposit	U.S. Government agency bonds
Bankers' acceptances	State and local government bonds
Federal funds	Corporate bonds
Commercial paper	Corporate stocks
Repurchase agreements	Real estate mortgages

Treasury bills (T-bills) and notes and bonds, are very important in both the money and capital markets. Federal agencies, for example the Farm Credit Banks and Federal Home Loan Mortgage Corporation, and state and local governments generally issue longer-term financial claims that trade in the capital markets.

Businesses are active in both financial markets. Some businesses finance a portion of their needs by issuing debt instruments in the form of short-term unsecured promissory notes called **commercial paper.** Corporations also issue large amounts of stocks and bonds to meet their financing needs. Real estate mortgages, created to finance residential and other properties, are also traded in the capital markets.

Negotiable certificates of deposit are debt instruments issued by depository institutions to depositors.[1] They pay annual interest and at maturity pay back the original deposit. Negotiable certificates of deposit come in denominations of $100,000 or more and are readily exchangeable in the money markets. ***Bankers' acceptances*** are created as a result of international trade. They are a promise of payment at some future date, similar to a check, issued by a firm and guaranteed by a bank. Acceptances represent an obligation of the accepting or guaranteeing bank and are fully marketable. ***Federal funds*** are overnight loans between depository institutions of the deposits that these institutions maintain at their Federal Reserve Banks. ***Repurchase agreements*** are short-term loans in which Treasury bills serve as collateral. Each of these money market instruments and capital market securities and instruments will be described in detail in this book.

Markets for financial assets are also important for the continued development of international trade and finance in a global economy. An important element is a uniform worldwide currency. While U.S. currency has been readily available in many foreign countries for many years, most interna-

commercial paper
short-term unsecured promissory notes

negotiable certificates of deposit
debt instruments of $100,000 or more issued by banks that can be traded in the money markets

bankers' acceptances
a promise of future payment issued by a firm and guaranteed by a bank

federal funds
temporary excess reserves loaned by banks to other banks

repurchase agreements
short-term loans using Treasury bills as collateral

---

1.   These differ from the CDs that individuals obtain from banks, which are offered to individuals as a form of time deposit in which the depositor promises to keep his funds in the CD for a specified time frame. We discuss these CDs in more detail in Chapter 3.

tional trade involves the transfer of deposits between banks. Until the development of Eurodollars, deposits denominated in U.S. dollars were held only in U.S. banks. This situation hindered growth in international trade.

Eurodollars
U.S. dollars placed in foreign banks

Eurodollars are U.S. dollars deposited in banks outside the United States, usually in European banks. American banks can borrow these deposits from other banks or from their own foreign branches when they need funds. Eurodollars have become an internationally accepted currency denominated in U.S. dollars for conducting trade in a global economy. **Eurocurrencies,** a more broadly based term, refers to all foreign currency deposits held in banks outside the countries of origin.

Eurocurrencies
all non-U.S. currencies held by banks outside their country of origin

Bonds represent the primary method for raising funds in many countries. These debt instruments are traditionally denominated in the currency of the countries where they are sold. A more recent development in international bond markets is the issuance of **Eurobonds,** which are bonds denominated in currencies other than those of the countries in which they are marketed. The Eurobond market has expanded rapidly in recent years because the market is largely unregulated and interest on the bonds is generally tax-free. Eurobonds are unregistered and there is no record of ownership. Issuers of Eurobonds can move more quickly and with greater flexibility than can, for example, those in the U.S. bond market.

Eurobonds
bonds denominated in currencies other than that of the country where they are sold

FINANCIAL FUNCTIONS IN THE U.S. SYSTEM

In our economy, the government and private financial intermediaries of many kinds have developed instruments and procedures to perform the financial functions listed in Figure 1.3. These financial functions may, in turn, be viewed as characteristics of the financial system which evolved to support our modern market economy.

CREATING MONEY

money
anything that is generally accepted as payment

Money may be defined as anything that is generally accepted as payment for goods and services and for discharging debts. The value of money lies in its purchasing power. It is the most generalized claim to wealth, since it can be exchanged for almost anything else. Most transactions in a modern economy involve money, and most would not take place if money were not available.

One of the most significant functions of the financial system is creating money, which serves as a medium of exchange. In the United States, the Federal Reserve System has primary responsibility for the amount of money that is created, although most of the money is actually created by depository institutions. A sufficient amount of money is essential for economic activity to take place at an efficient rate. However, if too much money is made available, its value tends to fall and prices go up. When this happens, *inflation* occurs.

FIGURE 1.3   Characteristics of an Effective Financial System

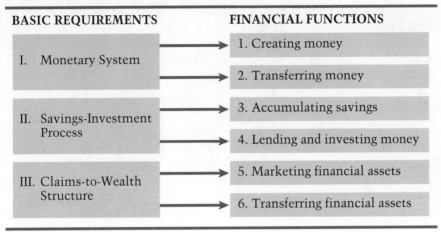

BASIC REQUIREMENTS	FINANCIAL FUNCTIONS
I. Monetary System	1. Creating money
	2. Transferring money
II. Savings-Investment Process	3. Accumulating savings
	4. Lending and investing money
III. Claims-to-Wealth Structure	5. Marketing financial assets
	6. Transferring financial assets

TRANSFERRING MONEY

Individuals and businesses hold money for purchases or payments they expect to make in the near future. One way to hold money is in checkable deposits at depository institutions. When money is held in this form, payments can easily be made by check. The check is an order to the depository institution to transfer money to the party who received the check. This is a great convenience, since checks can be written for the exact amount of payments, can be safely sent in the mail, and provide a record of payment. Institutions can also transfer funds between accounts electronically, making payments without paper checks. Funds transfers can be made by telephone or at remote terminals connected to a bank's computer.

ACCUMULATING SAVINGS

A function performed by financial intermediaries is the accumulation or gathering together of individual savings. Most individuals, businesses, and organizations do not want to take the risks involved in having cash on hand. Even if cash amounts are relatively small, they are put into a depository institution for safekeeping. When all the deposits are accumulated in one place, they can be used for loans and investments in amounts much larger than any individual depositor could supply. Depository institutions regularly conduct advertising campaigns and other promotional activities to attract deposits.

LENDING AND INVESTING MONEY

Another basic function of financial intermediaries is lending and investing. The money that has been put into these intermediaries may be loaned to businesses, farmers, consumers, institutions, and governmental units. It may be loaned for varying time periods and for different purposes, such as to buy equipment or to pay current bills. Some financial intermediaries make loans of almost all types. Others specialize in only one or two types of lending. Still other financial intermediaries invest all or part of their accumulated savings in the stock of a business or in debt obligations of businesses or other institutions.

MARKETING FINANCIAL ASSETS

A business may want to sell shares of ownership, called stock, to the general public. It can do so directly, but the process of finding individuals interested in investing funds in that business is likely to be difficult, costly, and time-consuming. A particular financial intermediary, an investment banking firm, can handle the sale of shares of ownership. The function of the investment banking firm is essentially one of merchandising.

TRANSFERRING FINANCIAL ASSETS

Several types of financial intermediaries facilitate or assist the processes of lending and of selling securities. If shares of stock are to be sold to the general public, it is desirable to have a ready market in which such stocks can be resold when the investor desires. The several stock exchanges serve this purpose. If lending is to be done effectively, it is necessary to have readily available up-to-date information on the applicants for loans. Various types of credit-checking agencies exist to meet this need.

CAREER OPPORTUNITIES IN FINANCE

Career opportunities in finance are generally found in five areas. The first area is business financial management. Larger firms typically divide their finance activities into treasury and control functions, while smaller firms often combine them. The treasurer is responsible for managing the firm's cash, acquiring and managing the firm's assets, and selling stocks and bonds to raise the financial capital necessary to conduct business. The controller is responsible for cost accounting, financial accounting, and tax record-keeping activities. Entry-level career opportunities might begin in cash management or asset acquisition activities in the treasurer's department or cost accounting activities in the controller's department.

A second job and career opportunity area is with financial intermediaries. For example, banks offer the opportunity to start a finance career in consumer or commercial lending. The entry-level job is usually as a *loan analyst* and involves evaluating loan applicants in terms of their credit worthiness and ability to repay. Successful analysts advance to assistant loan officer and then loan officer levels. Similar positions are available with savings and loans (S&Ls), credit unions, and other financial institutions.

A third area for a finance career is the securities markets field. At the entry level, one might begin as an account executive who sells stocks and bonds to individual and institutional customers. An account executive may also handle the management of client funds consistent with the client's risk-taking objectives. Careers in the securities area also include securities analyst or securities trader for brokerage firms. Other opportunities include managing securities portfolios for bank trust departments and life insurance companies.

A fourth area for a career in finance involves government or not-for-profit organizations. Finance opportunities at the federal or state government level include managing cash funds, making asset acquisition decisions, and obtaining borrowed funds. Not-for-profit organizations such as hospitals also need expert financial managers to manage assets, control costs, and obtain funds. Financial analysts and planners are hired both by government units and not-for-profit organizations to perform these tasks.

A fifth area for a career in finance involves personal financial planning. A personal financial planner or advisor helps individuals and families plan and manage their personal finances, helps them insure their resources, and helps them develop retirement and estate plans.

All of the above finance job opportunities can take place in an international as well as domestic setting. For example, many businesses engaged in producing and marketing products and services in foreign markets often offer employees opportunities for international job assignments. Large U.S. banks also offer international job experiences through their foreign banking operations. Furthermore, since worldwide securities markets exist, securities analysts and financial planners often must analyze and visit foreign-based firms.

An individual's "career profile" is provided in each chapter. In addition, several more detailed "career opportunities in finance" boxes are presented in later chapters. We hope that these materials provide a better understanding of some of the many career opportunities that currently exist in the finance field. We are also sure that new finance job opportunities will occur in the future as the field continues to develop and change.

THE PLAN OF STUDY

The subject matter of this book includes the entire scope of the financial system and its functions. You will learn about the markets in which funds are traded and the institutions that participate in and assist these flows of funds. And you will study the principles and concepts which guide these institutions in making sound decisions. International finance concepts and terms are integrated throughout the text.

Part 1 deals with the financial system in the U.S. economy and its role in the global economy. Financial functions, intermediaries, and instru-

CAREER ADVICE: IS IT DIFFERENT NOW COMPARED TO THEN?

Students are often advised today that they should prepare for several business careers during their working lifetimes. They may ask whether this is new advice, or what the experience of their predecessors has been. Let's take a look.

The Harvard College class of 1970 recently had its 25th reunion in Cambridge, Massachusetts. Prior to the reunion a survey was conducted with a response rate of about one-third of the 1970 graduates. Survey results indicated that nearly 60 percent of the respondents had worked for four or more employers and a little more than one-fourth had been fired (or in kinder terms were "involuntarily terminated"). Over one-half of the men and about 60 percent of the women had experienced at least two substantially different careers, with significant retraining required for one-half of these respondents.

A sub-sample of the male respondents was also compared with a similar sub-sample of male graduates from the Harvard class of 1945. About 30 percent of the respondents in each sample became lawyers or doctors, or had academic careers. For the 1945 graduates, about 40 percent worked for corporations, often in banking, insurance, and real estate. Only a small number were self-employed. In contrast, only 20 percent of the 1970 graduates had corporate employers. Relatively more of these graduates chose to be involved in the arts or are self-employed.

Given the continual restructuring in corporate America, it seems safe to say that graduates of today should plan to have multiple careers during their working lifetimes. Thus, remember as you read this book that even if you don't currently plan on a career in finance, learning about finance might become very important to you later in your personal and working lifetime.

Source: Thomas A. Stewart, "Navigating by Starlight: Career Guidance from the Class of 1970," *Fortune* (August 7, 1995), pp. 252–253.

ments have been considered briefly in this initial chapter. Chapter 2 describes the U.S. monetary system and Chapter 3 focuses on the role of depository institutions within the overall financial system. Chapter 4 discusses the Federal Reserve System. Chapter 5 discusses economic objectives, the role and actions of policymakers, and how money and credit are provided to meet the needs of the economy. We conclude Part 1 with a chapter on international trade and finance because of its importance in understanding market economies worldwide.

> *"We'll lose our entire investment in almost half of the companies we fund."*

DON PARSONS

Partner, Centennial Funds

BS Electrical Engineering
Northwestern
MBA Finance
University of Michigan

career profiles

Q: *You work in the venture capital industry. Please explain what that means.*

A: Our firm looks for entrepreneurial companies, especially in the high tech field, where we can make an equity investment and hopefully produce a high return on our investment over a 5 to 9 year period. We also take an active role with the entrepreneurs to help them succeed.

Q: *What kind of help do entrepreneurs need?*

A: Most entrepreneurs are experts in their specific fields—computers, electronics, whatever—but they're not experts in starting a business and making it profitable. We provide experience which can help a small company avoid common mistakes and improve its chance of survival.

Q: *But success is not guaranteed.*

A: Not at all. According to industry averages, we'll lose our entire investment in almost half of the companies we fund. And only a handful turn into huge successes like Microsoft or Intel, which started very small. In the case of a big success, we might make fifty times our original investment. But these few big successes must make up for the many that don't survive.

Q: *Describe an entry-level position in venture capital.*

A: I started as an investment analyst which is really an apprentice kind of position. I was assigned to a different partner every six months and I helped those partners evaluate potential investment in new companies. There's a lot of research involved—in the industry, the technology, the product, the management team of the company—and the investment analyst does a lot of that research. Then we compile our findings into a very comprehensive report which is used to make the investment recommendation.

Q: *How were you qualified to evaluate these start-up companies?*

A: I have an Electrical Engineering degree and worked with IBM during and after college. At IBM I was involved with the design of several of its early personal computers, so I learned a lot about the development process of new technology products. Not everyone brings a technology background into this business, but many do. It has helped me a lot. After IBM I got my MBA which enabled me to gain the financial skills necessary to evaluate investment opportunities.

Q: *What skills help you most in your job?*

A: There are many aspects to building a successful company, so it requires a broad set of skills. You have to understand the technology, the finances, tax considerations, the legal and securities aspects, negotiation, and whatever other issues arise. You must be able to successfully interact with many different people. And parallel thinking is also an absolute requirement. If you can't juggle multiple issues and multiple projects, you would find this a very frustrating business.

Q: *What's the toughest part of this job?*

A: It's difficult to evaluate your results. It may be four, seven, ten years before we can tell if a new company is going to survive, much less succeed. It keeps you humble.

15

Part 2 is concerned with the investments side of finance. Chapter 7 discusses the savings and investment process and its major role in our modern market economy. This is followed by Chapter 8 which describes the structure of interest rates. Time value of money concepts are covered in Chapter 9 and the characteristics and valuations of bonds and stocks are presented in Chapter 10. Chapter 11 discusses the characteristics and workings of the securities market. Part 2 concludes with Chapter 12 which describes financial return and risk concepts for a single asset or security, and for portfolios of securities.

Part 3 is concerned with business finance and how the business sector interacts with the financial system. We begin in Chapter 13 with an introduction and overview of the types of business organizations and follow with a review of basic financial statements and financial data important to the financial manager. Chapter 14 discusses the need for, and the way in which to conduct, financial analysis of past performance and concludes with a section on financial planning for the future. Chapter 15 covers the management of working capital, while Chapter 16 focuses on sources of short-term business financing. We then turn our attention in Chapter 17 to the process and methods for conducting capital budgeting analysis. We conclude Part 3 with Chapter 18 which provides a discussion of capital structure and cost of capital concepts.

We devote attention to business financing for several reasons. Firms typically use the financial markets for a large portion of the funds they need for current operations and capital investment. Because business profits are so sensitive to financial decisions, theories and concepts of financial management are carefully discussed. Business finance principles are also applicable to other areas of finance, including the management of financial institutions. In addition, a significant part of the financial system is involved in meeting the demands for funds in the business sector of the economy.

SUMMARY

Finance at the macroeconomic level focuses on the study of financial institutions and financial markets and how they operate within U.S. and global financial systems. At the microeconomic, or firm level, finance focuses on the study of financial planning, fund raising, and asset management for business and financial institutions.

An economy that provides a high standard of living for its inhabitants and one that can compete globally needs an effective financial system that includes an efficient monetary system. Conditions for capital formation must exist and be fostered through a process for channeling savings into investment. Markets where claims to wealth can be bought and sold need to be developed and a monetary system for efficiently exchanging goods and services must be created.

Five types of financial intermediaries play important roles in the operation of the U.S. financial system and the ability for Americans to compete internationally. They are: depository institutions, contractual savings institutions, investment institutions, finance companies, and securities market institutions. Claims to wealth may be real assets such as ownership of land, buildings, and equipment, or financial assets which are claims of obligations or liabilities. Financial asset claims may be traded in the money markets where maturities are one year or less or in the longer-maturity capital markets.

An effective financial system needs a monetary system for creating and transferring money. A savings-investment process also is necessary for accumulating savings and for lending and investing money. Finally, a claims-to-wealth structure is required to handle the marketing of financial assets and the transferring of financial assets.

KEY TERMS

bankers' acceptances	financial intermediaries
capital formation	intermediation
capital markets	International Monetary Fund (IMF)
commercial paper	money
depository institutions	money markets
disintermediation	negotiable certificates of deposit
Eurobonds	primary securities market
Eurocurrencies	real assets
Eurodollars	repurchase agreements
federal funds	secondary securities market
finance	World Bank
financial assets	

DISCUSSION QUESTIONS

1. What is finance? Provide a brief overview of the field.
2. What are the basic requirements of an effective financial system?
3. Identify and briefly describe the structure of financial intermediaries in the United States.
4. What is meant by the term *financial intermediation?*
5. How do real assets and financial assets differ?
6. Briefly describe the differences between the money and capital markets.

7. Identify and briefly describe the types of claims to wealth that are traded in U.S. financial markets.
8. Briefly explain the terms Eurodollars, Eurocurrencies, and Eurobonds.
9. Identify and describe the financial functions or characteristics of the financial system that evolved to support the U.S. economy.
10. Indicate some of the career opportunities in finance available to business students today.

PROBLEMS

1. Obtain a current issue of the *Federal Reserve Bulletin*. Identify recent "interest rates" in the money and capital markets for several of the instruments and securities presented in Figure 1.2. Indicate how much, if any, they have changed from two years ago.
2. Obtain a copy of a current issue of *Business Week*. Read and be prepared to discuss articles and issues under both the "Finance" and "International Business" sections that are usually included in this weekly magazine. Look specifically for articles that may relate to topics covered in this first chapter.

SELF-TEST QUESTIONS

1. The basic requirements for an effective financial system in a developed economy include:
   a. a monetary system
   b. a savings-investment process
   c. markets for the transfer of financial assets
   d. all of the above
2. Which one of these financial intermediaries focuses on maintaining orderly conditions in foreign exchange markets?
   a. commercial banks
   b. the World Bank
   c. International Monetary Fund
   d. commercial finance companies
3. Which of the following claims to wealth traded in U.S. financial markets is a money market instrument?
   a. commercial paper
   b. treasury notes and bonds
   c. corporate bonds
   d. real estate mortgages

4. Which of the following claims to wealth traded in U.S. financial markets is a capital market security or instrument?
   a. commercial paper
   b. treasury bills
   c. negotiable certificates of deposit
   d. corporate stocks
5. U.S.-dollar-denominated deposits held in banks outside the United States are referred to as:
   a. negotiable certificates of deposit
   b. bankers' acceptances
   c. federal funds
   d. Eurodollars
6. The financial functions of marketing and transferring financial assets are associated with which of the following basic requirements of an effective financial system:
   a. a monetary system
   b. a savings-investment process
   c. a claims-to-wealth structure
   d. all of the above
7. The savings-investment process involves which of the following financial functions:
   a. creating and transferring money
   b. accumulating savings and lending and investing money
   c. marketing and transferring financial assets
   d. all of the above
8. Career opportunities in finance involving both treasury and control functions are generally associated with:
   a. business financial management
   b. financial intermediaries
   c. securities markets
   d. government organizations

SELF-TEST PROBLEM

Identify the five types of financial intermediaries that are important to the efficient operation of the U.S. financial system. Identify specific examples of financial intermediaries that operated in the United States prior to 1800. Also, provide specific examples of financial intermediaries that first began operating during the early part of the twentieth century (i.e., 1900s).

SUGGESTED READINGS

Brooks, Donald E., and Robert H. Hertz. *Guide To Financial Instruments,* 3e. New York: Coopers and Lybrand, 1994.

Campbell, Tim S., and William A. Krakaw. *Financial Institutions and Capital Markets.* New York: HarperCollins College Publishers, 1993. Chap. 1.

Fabozzi, Frank J., Franco Modigliani, and Michael G. Ferri. *Foundations of Financial Markets and Institutions.* Englewood Cliffs, NJ: Prentice-Hall, 1994. Chap 1.

Johnson, Hazel J. *Financial Institutions and Markets: A Global Perspective.* New York: McGraw-Hill, 1993. Chap. 1.

Maxwell, Charles E. *Financial Markets and Institutions: The Global View.* St. Paul, MN: West Publishing Company, 1994. Part 1.

Rose, Peter S. *Money and Capital Markets,* 5e. Homewood, IL: BPI/Irwin, 1994. Chaps. 1 and 2.

Shapiro, Alan C. *Foundations of Multinational Financial Management,* 2e. Boston: Allyn & Bacon, 1994. Chap. 3.

ANSWERS TO SELF-TEST QUESTIONS   1. d, 2. c, 3. a, 4. d, 5. d, 6. c, 7. b, 8. a

ANSWER TO SELF-TEST PROBLEM

The five types of financial intermediaries are: depository institutions, contractual savings institutions, investment institutions, finance companies, and securities market institutions. Commercial banks and life and property insurance companies operated in the United States prior to 1800. Credit unions, pension funds, mutual funds, and finance companies were started in the United States during the early part of the 1900s.

CHAPTER 2

United States Monetary System

AFTER STUDYING THIS CHAPTER, YOU SHOULD BE ABLE TO:

- Describe the functions of money.
- Give a brief overview of the historical development of our monetary system.
- Define the bimetallic standard as used in the United States.
- Describe the history of paper money in the United States.
- Explain why it is important to have a monetary standard that serves as a standard of value.
- Explain what is important in defining the money supply and define the M1 money supply.
- Briefly explain the M2, M3, and L definitions of the money supply.

The essential role of a monetary system in the operation and development of a financial system was explained in Chapter 1. In this chapter the nature and functions of money are developed more fully. Also, the nature of the monetary system of the United States is described and analyzed. Consideration is also given to the monetary standard upon which the system is based and to the types of money currently used to meet the needs of the economy.

Although our focus is on the U.S. monetary system, today we operate in a global economy. Thus we must interact with other monetary systems. For example, a change in either the Japanese or German monetary systems will directly impact the U.S. monetary system. For example, when the Bundesbank (the German central bank) acts to increase interest rates in Germany, the value of the U.S. dollar weakens relative to the German mark. This increases the cost of products imported into the United States unless the Federal Reserve takes countering actions.

NATURE AND FUNCTIONS OF MONEY

medium of exchange
the basic function of money

In the preceding chapter, money was defined as anything generally accepted as a means of paying for goods and services and of discharging debts. This function of money is generally referred to as that of serving as a ***medium of exchange.*** This is the basic function of money in any economy. However, money also serves as a store of purchasing power and as a standard of value.

store of purchasing power
when money is held as a liquid asset

Money may be held as a ***store of purchasing power*** that can be drawn on at will. This may be done shortly after it is received or after it has been held for a period of time. While money is held, it is a liquid asset and provides its owner with flexibility. But the owner pays for this flexibility by giving up the potential return that could be earned through investment or the satisfaction that could be gained from spending it for goods and services. Furthermore, money can perform its function as a store of purchasing power only if its value is relatively stable.

liquidity
how easily an asset can be exchanged for money

The function of serving as a store of purchasing power can also be performed by an asset other than money if that asset can be converted into money quickly and without significant loss of value. We refer to this quality —the ease with which an asset can be exchanged for money or other assets —as ***liquidity.*** Money is perfectly liquid since it is a generally accepted medium of exchange. Other assets, such as savings deposits held at depository institutions, approach the liquidity of money. The existence of such liquid assets reduces the need for holding money itself as a store of purchasing power.

standard of value
a function of money that occurs when prices and debts are stated in terms of the monetary unit

The third function of money—as a ***standard of value***—means that prices and contracts for deferred payments are expressed in terms of the monetary unit. Prices and debts are usually expressed in terms of dollars without stating whether the purchase will be cash or credit. The function of money as a standard by which to judge value is circular. The value of money may be stated in terms of the goods it will buy; a change in prices generally reflects a change in the value of money. If money is to perform its function as a standard of value, it is essential that the value of the monetary unit be relatively stable.

DEVELOPMENT OF MONETARY SYSTEMS

We have answered the question of what money is, but we have not yet discussed what items serve as money. The answer to this may not be as simple as it seems at first. A look at the history of money reveals that the answer has changed over time, just as a monetary system changes to meet the changing needs of an economy. We can infer much about these developments from the available evidence and from practices still in use in more primitive economies.

BARTER

Primitive economies consisted largely of self-sufficient units or groups that lived by means of hunting, fishing, and simple agriculture. There was little need or occasion to exchange goods or services. Even in such economies, however, some trade took place.

As economies became more developed, the process of exchange became important. Some individuals specialized, to a degree at least, in herding sheep, raising grain, or as gold and silversmiths. To aid exchanges of goods for goods, called **barter**, tables of relative values were developed from past experience. For example, a table might show the number of furs, measures of grain, or amount of cloth agreed to equal one cow. This arrangement eased exchanges, but the process still had many serious drawbacks. For example, if a person had a cow and wanted to trade it for some nuts and furs, he or she would need to find someone who had an excess of both these items to trade. The need for a simpler means of exchange led to the development of money.

barter
exchange of goods or services without using money

EARLY DEVELOPMENT OF MONEY

The record of the early development of money is very sketchy. In all probability traders found that some items, such as furs and grain, were traded more frequently than others. Since these items could be easily traded, traders could afford to accept them in exchange when they did not need them. They probably also found it convenient to figure the value of less frequently traded goods in terms of more frequently traded items. This is because the system gave traders a familiar yardstick with which to value goods.

This system developed in much the same way in some prisoner of war camps in Germany during World War II. Cigarettes were used as a general medium of exchange since they could always be traded for other goods or services. Values of all types of goods were quoted in cigarettes even when there was no intention of exchanging them.

Records from early economies show that many items useful for food or clothing were used as a general medium of exchange and, to some degree at least, as a unit for measuring value. Included were grain, salt, skins, spices, tea, seeds, and cattle. Some early economies made use of such commodities as beads, ivory, bird feathers, gold, and silver because there was a general demand for personal ornaments. Objects that were used as tools or in making tools, such as animal claws, fishhooks, shark teeth, and stone discs, were also used. All of these items were generally accepted in exchange because they could be used for further exchange or as food, clothing, tools, or ornaments.

Traders accepted these items as long as they felt certain they could use them again in future trading. This meant that the supply of the item had to be limited in relation to the desires of individuals in the economy to have the item. In early economies this was generally true of items such as grains, cattle, and tools. Items of ornamentation could likewise be used as a general medium of exchange only if there was an unfilled demand for them. For example, Native Americans valued wampum beads as a decoration and were not able to get enough of them to meet the desires of everyone. Therefore, such beads served as a general medium of exchange.

USE OF PRECIOUS METALS AS MONEY

When commodities were used as a medium of exchange, goods could be valued in terms of the item used as money and could be exchanged for it. This process, however, was still clumsy and time-consuming. For example, if furs were used, they were bulky and difficult to carry. Furthermore, arguments could arise over the quality of the furs. It was also necessary to make a trade of goods equal to one, two, three, or more skins since furs lost value when cut into pieces.

The transition from the use of commodities like furs as money to the use of precious metals was probably a gradual one. The advantages of precious metals eventually led to their general usage. Gold and silver were in great demand for ornamentation because they were durable, beautiful, and could be shaped. The supply of these metals was limited enough so that very small amounts had great value. This made them easy to carry around as money. Furthermore, they could be refined into the pure metal rather easily, making their quality uniform. Various quantities could also be weighed out so that exchanges of varying values could be made. In time, coins with a certain weight of metal in them were developed. Because an unscrupulous trader could cover less valuable metals with gold or produce coins with short weight, the process of coinage needed regulation to make coins generally uniform. For that reason, coining money and determining its value has been a governmental function in some cultures for about 2,500 years.

Metal coins and other commodities that served as early forms of money are sometimes referred to as ***full-bodied money.*** They had a value equal to their value as commodities. Since they were money, they served as a standard of value—that is, the worth of other commodities was expressed in units of this monetary commodity. When governments undertook the function of coining money, they formalized the standard. They established by law the basic money unit in terms of the weight and fineness, or parity, of precious metals such as gold. This standardization also provided a convenient medium of exchange for trade between nations.

full-bodied money
coins that contain the same value in metal as their face value

REPRESENTATIVE MONEY

The earliest forerunners of private banks were goldsmiths, specialists in weighing, assaying, and storing precious metals. Individuals would pay these early banks to store their gold for safekeeping. The stored gold would be carefully evaluated, and a receipt issued verifying its weight and fineness. It was often more convenient to conduct a transaction by signing over the receipts rather than handing over the gold itself. Gold was cumbersome and dangerous to transport. Also, the recipients would often have more confidence in the expert evaluation of the gold's weight and fineness stated on the receipt than in their own evaluation. As the receipts or notes circulated more freely, they became the first representative full-bodied paper money.

Since early modern times, governments have also issued money in the form of paper. Gold and silver coins are difficult to protect and carry around for large transactions. To ease exchange, governments issued paper money to represent certain quantities of gold or silver that were kept on deposit by the government to back such paper. The paper was generally accepted as a medium of exchange because the persons accepting it knew they could get the precious metal when and if they wanted it.

After they were developed, banks also issued paper money backed by precious metals. At first this was done without specific authorization by governmental authorities. However, as time went on, governments regulated the issuance of paper money by the banks. Paper money backed by gold or silver circulated freely. As long as individuals felt certain they could exchange it for the precious metal behind it, they felt no need to do so.

These types of paper money were ***representative full-bodied money*** because such a government note or bank note represented a specific amount of gold or silver in storage in a government or bank vault. For localized transactions, the paper was exchanged freely. Holders of the paper rarely had a need to present the paper for redemption in metal. Gradually the paper circulated more widely, and eventually even merchants of different nations would accept the paper money issued by reputable

representative full-bodied money
paper money fully backed by a precious metal

banks and governments. Since only a small number of notes would be redeemed during a given period of time, there was relatively little turnover of the precious metal in the vaults. This situation led to the evolution of modern monetary systems.

CREDIT MONEY

As the paper circulated, the gold sat in vaults, with only a fraction of it being redeemed during any period of time. Like the goldsmiths before them, bankers went into the loan business, lending either gold itself or issuing additional receipts or notes. In so doing the bankers issued notes for more gold than they actually had in their vaults. As long as the bankers did not experience an unusually high number of customers presenting notes for redemption at the same time, they found this to be a safe and profitable way of doing business. And as long as the depositors were confident that the gold could be redeemed, they were usually content to leave it safely on deposit. This practice not only represents one of the earliest examples of credit money, but also describes the origins of our modern fractional reserve system of banking and money creation, which will be discussed in Chapter 5.

The general acceptance of paper money as a medium of exchange, with no intention of redeeming it for the precious metal behind it, made possible the issuance of paper money with no such backing. From time to time, money was issued based only on the general credit of a government and on the provision that such money was **legal tender,** acceptable to pay taxes and to fulfill contracts calling for payment in lawful money. This is the case today in the United States and in other countries. Since this money is proclaimed to be money by law or a decree known as a fiat, it is sometimes called **fiat money.**

Banks also issued paper money without metallic backing. As such issues were brought under regulation, the banks were required to have some metallic backing for their paper money. They also had to have some form of collateral, such as government bonds, for the remainder of the face value of the money they issued. The privilege of private banks to issue paper money of any type became more and more restricted and has been abolished in all countries in recent years. The only banks that issue any significant amounts of paper money today are central banks, which are owned or controlled by the national government of the country.

Any circulating medium which has little real value relative to its monetary value is called **credit money.** Almost all money circulating in the world today is some form of credit money—money which does not consist of or represent a specific valuable commodity. Rather, its value depends on its general acceptance based on the credit of its issuer.

legal tender
money backed only by government credit

fiat money
legal tender proclaimed to be money by law

credit money
money worth more than what it is made of

U.S. MONETARY SYSTEM

While barter was undoubtedly important in early U.S. history, the government moved swiftly towards a monetary system based on precious metals. Today the U.S. monetary system uses credit money, and money transfers are often conducted electronically.

EARLY LEGISLATION

The first monetary act in the United States was passed in 1792, and provided for a bimetallic standard. A ***bimetallic standard*** is one based upon two metals—in this case, silver and gold. The dollar, which was set up as the unit of value, was defined as 371.25 grains of pure silver or 24.75 grains of pure gold. Thus, the metal in the silver dollar was 15 times the weight of the metal in the gold dollar, making a ratio of 15 to 1 between the metals when minted. Provision was made for gold coins in denominations of $2.50, $5.00, and $10.00, and for silver coins in denominations of $1.00, 50¢, 25¢, 10¢, and 5¢. All of these coins contained silver equal to their full face value, the 10¢ piece one tenth as much as the silver dollar, and so on. In addition, provision was made for copper token coins in one-cent and half-cent denominations. Unlike full-bodied coins, ***token coins*** are worth more as money than the value of the metal they contain.

bimetallic standard
monetary standard based on two metals, usually silver and gold

token coins
coins containing metal of less value than their stated value

Prior to 1792, many foreign coins circulated in the United States. In addition to establishing a bimetallic standard, the Monetary Act of 1792 provided for the continued use of foreign coins until U.S. coins were produced in sufficient quantities. Spanish silver dollars were to be accepted as full legal tender. They weighed 415 grains nine-tenths pure, which gave them a silver content of 373.5 grains. They could be used legally to discharge debts, and creditors could not insist on payment in any other type of money if the debt was stated in Spanish dollars. All lighter Spanish dollars and all other foreign coins were to be accepted only for their actual value in metal. These provisions were unrealistic, since to carry them out meant weighing coins at every transaction. Most foreign coins were of short weight due to long periods of use, while the U.S. coins were of full weight. The result was that U.S. coins were hoarded and foreign coins were circulated. Therefore, the 1792 monetary act resulted in an early monetary system that relied almost exclusively on the use of foreign coins.

FOREIGN COINS IN THE EARLY AMERICAN ECONOMY

The bimetallic standard was difficult to maintain because the market ratio between silver and gold, which was about 15 to 1 in 1792, soon changed to about 15.5 to 1. Consequently, little gold was brought to the mint for coinage because it was found to be worth more in the open market. The few gold coins that were minted soon disappeared from circulation. In 1834 Congress changed the official mint ratio to 16 to 1. This reversed the situation rather than remedying it. Gold was now overvalued at the mint. Gold coins became abundant, but silver coins disappeared from circulation. Officially the bimetallic standard lasted until 1900, but the United States had in fact been on a gold standard since the 1830s. Full-bodied coins actually circulated until 1934, and the dollar was defined in terms of gold until the 1970s.

CREDIT MONEY IN THE UNITED STATES

Except for brief experiments beginning with the War of 1812, the federal government did not become a major issuer of credit money until the Civil War. However, twice during the early years of the country it chartered a national bank authorized to do so. During the years that the First and Second Banks of the United States existed, a reliable paper currency circulated nationally in significant quantities. However, each of these banks was chartered for only 20 years, and for political reasons, neither of the charters was renewed by Congress. Various state-chartered banks also issued bank notes. Except for the years that the national banks existed, the lack of uniform regulation made these state bank issues inconsistent and unreliable. They were frequently accepted only at a discount any distance from the issuing bank, and were sometimes not redeemable even there. Bank-issued money will be discussed in more detail in the next chapter.

greenbacks
money issued by the U.S. government to help finance the Civil War

To help finance the Civil War, Congress authorized the issue of paper money. It was officially known as United States Notes and popularly called **greenbacks.** This was fiat money; the notes were legal tender, but were not redeemable for gold or silver. In addition, in 1863 Congress established the National Banking System, which authorized nationally chartered banks to issue notes. The National Bank notes were carefully controlled and were backed by government securities. In effect, Congress allowed newly chartered banks to issue credit money and lend it to the Treasury. This helped finance the war, and it also provided another reliable source of credit money. At the same time, notes of state banks, which had been a source of confusion in the economy because of their unreliability, were taxed out of existence. Thus, for the first time, this country had a uniform national currency.

In 1878, the Treasury began issuing silver certificates backed by silver stored in its vault. These certificates continued to serve as the principal small-denomination currency in circulation until 1967. In 1914, the Federal Reserve System, known as the Fed, began operations, and Federal Reserve

Collectors of old coins and paper currency are referred to as *numis-matists*. Although authorized in 1792, the first U.S. silver dollar carried a 1794 mint date. As might be expected, the 1794 dollar is quite rare today and is very valuable even in worn condition. Minting silver dollars was stopped in 1804 before being resumed again in 1836. So-called liberty head or Morgan dollars were first minted in 1878 and continued into 1921. The peace-type silver dollar became available in 1921. It continued to be minted through 1935 when the production of silver dollars ceased. Eisenhower dollars were minted during 1971–78 and were followed by the ill-fated Susan B. Anthony dollars, which were minted from 1979 to 1981.

COLLECTING OLD U.S. COINS AND PAPER CURRENCY

The history of U.S. currency is as interesting as the history of U.S. coins. For example, the first paper money was issued by the U.S. government in the form of U.S. Treasury notes in conjunction with the War of 1812. U.S. large-size currency was much larger than that in use today. It came into circulation with the U.S. note series of 1862. Later, large-size currency also included silver certificates, gold certificates, and Treasury notes. Federal Reserve bank notes began with the series of 1918. National Bank notes were issued between 1863 and 1928. Large-size U.S. government currency and National Bank notes are avidly sought by collectors today. The smaller, current size U.S. currency began in 1929 (series of 1928) with the issuance of U.S. notes and silver certificates. It continues today in the form of Federal Reserve Notes.

Good information on U.S. silver dollars and other coins is provided in a variety of publications including: *A Guide Book of United States Coins* published annually by R. S. Yeoman (Racine, WI: Western Publishing Co.). Further information on U.S. paper currency is available in the *Standard Catalog of United States Paper Money* published periodically by Chester L. Krause and Robert E. Lemke (Lola, WI: Krause Publications) as well as many other sources.

notes replaced national bank notes. In 1967, Federal Reserve notes also replaced silver certificates and are the only paper currency of significance in the economy today.

DEMAND DEPOSITS

The process of making exchange more and more convenient did not stop with the widespread use of paper money. *Demand deposits* have a long history, but their growth was especially rapid after the national banking system was established and state banks could no longer issue bank notes.

Rather than issuing a note in a specific denomination, a bank allows the holder of a deposit to transfer ownership of that deposit by means of a check—an order to the bank to make payment to another party. Today most transactions for any but small amounts are made by checks drawn on banks or other depository institutions. Demand and checkable deposits take the advantages of paper money one step further. Demand deposits are issued only by commercial banks and do not earn interest. Today, there are many forms of checkable deposits issued by all types of depository institutions that earn interest. They currently make up the bulk of our money supply. With these deposits, the holder does not physically hold, or risk losing, anything. Checks can be safely sent in the mail and can be used to make payments in any specific amounts.

ELECTRONIC FUNDS TRANSFER SYSTEMS

electronic funds transfer systems (EFTS)
electronic method of receiving and disbursing funds

Though not actually a form of money, ***electronic funds transfer systems (EFTS)*** greatly enhance the efficiency of the payments mechanisms used in our economy. They can be considered another evolutionary step in our monetary system. With EFTS, individuals, businesses, and governments can receive and disburse funds electronically instead of through the use of checks. Transfers can be made between deposit accounts even nationwide, potentially reducing or eliminating the physical handling of checks.

Several EFTS applications are currently in use. Employers can have their employees' wages deposited directly in their checking accounts, rather than issuing payroll checks. Individuals can have regular payments such as mortgage payments or insurance premiums automatically deducted from their accounts. Electronic funds transfers by telephone, for payment of utility bills, credit card balances, and so forth, are increasingly in use. The automated teller machine (ATM), which accepts deposits, arranges transfers between accounts, and dispenses cash, is also commonplace.

MONETARY STANDARD AND THE VALUE OF MONEY

One of the functions of money is that it serves as a standard of value. Prices are stated in units of money, and an individual's wealth is frequently expressed in monetary terms. But the value of money is its purchasing power. When money was full-bodied, this was clear, at least in terms of a commodity with widely recognized value. This is quite different from the case today, when the monetary unit is not fixed in terms of any commodity.

When gold coins made up the money supply, the value of money was constant in terms of gold. This, of course, did not guarantee a constant purchasing power of gold. For instance, after the discovery of America, tons of gold flowed into Europe; and prices there rose sharply in terms of gold. Nevertheless, this sudden increase in the availability of gold was an exceptional case. Throughout most of history, the value of gold has been stable enough to provide a useful standard of value. Silver has also served as a monetary standard in the past.

When representative full-bodied paper money was issued, the standard remained the precious metal which the paper represented. Paper money that is easily redeemable for metal retains the value of that metal as its standard. Until 1900 the United States was officially on a bimetallic standard. However, differences between the official values and the market values of the two metals made it difficult to keep them both in circulation at the same time. For this reason, first silver and later gold served as the accepted monetary standard. As long as people were confident that the paper money issued by the banks was redeemable for gold or silver, it retained the value of a certain weight of metal, and people were willing to hold and circulate the paper.

However, during the Civil War the government printed paper currency and temporarily suspended redemption in metal. We were in effect on an inconvertible paper standard. Although there was an implied promise to redeem these notes at some time in the future, no time was specified, and the U.S. notes became the standard money. National Bank notes could be exchanged for U.S. notes, so these had equal purchasing power. However, metal coins virtually disappeared from circulation, and prices in terms of paper money rose dramatically. Since the money in circulation could not be exchanged for gold or silver, its value became dependent on its acceptability in trade: the amount of goods and services it could be exchanged for. This in turn depended on people's confidence in the monetary authority—confidence in both its restraint in maintaining the relative scarcity of the money and its ability to maintain the money's status as legal tender. The dollars of both the Confederacy and the Union lost value as paper money was printed and prices rose during the Civil War. Over time, however, the U.S. notes regained their prewar purchasing power while the value of Confederate money fell to zero.

The *de facto*, or actual, gold standard was restored after the Civil War. However, after a century of monetary experiments, both gold and silver have now been completely removed from any monetary role in our economy. The Treasury does own some gold and silver, but there is no minimum reserve of these metals backing any of our money. They are traded freely in markets just as are other commodities. Our monetary standard is the paper dollar, issued by the Fed. No one doubts the ability of our government to enforce the legal status of the paper dollar; however, its purchasing power, and thus its value, depends on its relative scarcity. It is one of the responsibilities of the Fed to regulate the supply of money to maintain its purchasing power. Some level of growth in the money supply is necessary to support and sustain real (adjusted for inflation) economic growth in our free-enterprise system. At the same time, a too-rapid growth in the money

inflation
a rise in prices not offset by increases in quality

supply is believed to be inflationary. **Inflation** is a rise or increase in the prices of goods and services that is not offset by increases in their quality. An increase in the general price level of all goods and services in our economy leads to a decline in the purchasing power of money.

INTERNATIONAL MONETARY SYSTEM

The international monetary system was historically tied to the gold standard. During the early seventeenth century, Great Britain returned to the gold standard. Many other countries then followed Great Britain's lead. This caused an international gold standard to dominate international trade during the 1880–1914 period. A breakdown in the gold standard occurred during World War I, and less formal exchange systems continued during the worldwide depression of the 1930s and during World War II.

In 1944, many of the world's economic powers met at Bretton Woods, New Hampshire. They agreed to an international monetary system which was tied to the U.S. dollar or gold via fixed or pegged exchange rates. One ounce of gold was set equal to $35. Each participating country then had its currency pegged to either gold or the U.S. dollar. This system of fixed exchange rates became known as the Bretton Woods System and was maintained through 1971.

By early 1973, major currencies were allowed to float against each other, resulting in a flexible or floating exchange rate system. While free market forces are allowed to operate today, central monetary authorities attempt to intervene in exchange markets when they believe that exchange rates between two currencies are harming world trade and the global economy. This actually makes the current international monetary system a managed floating exchange rate system.

Virtually all international transactions now involve the exchange of currencies or checkable deposits denominated in various currencies. Exchanges occur either for goods and services, for financial claims, or for other currencies. The value of one currency relative to another, or their

exchange rate
value of one currency in terms of another

exchange rate, depends on the supply of and demand for each currency relative to the other. The supply of a currency in international markets depends largely on the imports of the issuing country, that is, how much of their currency they spend in world markets. Demand for a currency depends on the amount of exports that currency will buy from the issuing country. Demand also depends on the confidence of market participants in the restraint and stability of the monetary authority issuing the currency. If demand for a particular currency falls relative to its supply, the exchange rate falls and the international purchasing power of that nation's money supply drops. This can be caused by domestic inflation, political instability, or an excess of imports over exports. On the other hand, if a currency is widely accepted, the demand for it may be increased by the desire of people worldwide to hold it as an international medium of exchange. Such is the case of the U.S. dollar. It is widely held by foreigners because of its general acceptance and ability to hold its value. International finance is discussed in detail in Chapter 6.

U.S. MONEY SUPPLY

No full-bodied or representative full-bodied money is in use in the United States today. All of our money is credit money. The Treasury issues token coins, and the Fed issues paper currency. The rest of the money supply is issued by depository institutions, and is held in checking accounts and similar deposits. As we have seen, the composition of the stock of money has changed over the years. In fact, some of the most dramatic changes have occurred quite recently. Because of the large number of deposit accounts and other financial instruments, the question of how much money there is no longer has a simple answer. Before we can count the money supply, we must know what to count.

DEFINING THE MONEY SUPPLY

There are two things we want to keep in mind when defining the money supply. First, we want to include in our definition only those things that perform the functions of money. Second, we want the definition to be useful. We have already discussed the effect the money supply has on economic activity and the importance of controlling it. Our definition should correspond to some measurable quantity that is clearly related to economic activity. This implies that it should consist of a set of categories we can actually measure; it would do us no good to include components which cannot be counted or separated from accounts we want to exclude.

Money serves three functions: it is a standard of value, a medium of exchange, and a store of purchasing power. The standard of value in our system is the dollar. Many assets, including many financial assets, are evaluated in dollar units, but not all are money. However, anything not measured in dollar units is disqualified—for example, gold is not money in our system. Many things also serve as a store of value, including financial assets and many real assets. Many of these are preferable to money as long-term stores of wealth, either because they earn interest or otherwise increase in value, or because they provide a flow of services to the owner. However, if we hold an asset as a store of purchasing power, we need to consider its liquidity, or the ease with which it can be converted into other assets. No other asset is as liquid as money, because money is itself a medium of exchange. Money does not need to be converted into anything else before it can be spent or used to make a payment. It is this liquidity of money that is the most helpful in narrowing our definition of the money supply.

**HOW THE
DEFINITION
OF THE MONEY
SUPPLY HAS
CHANGED**

In a simple economy in which metallic coins were used, it was easy to define money, because only one form of generally accepted medium of exchange was in use. As forms of payment increased to meet the needs of the U.S. economy, defining money became more complex. Differences of opinion developed about the items that should be included in the money supply.

One definition of the money supply that evolved included currency and coin in the hands of the public plus demand deposits held by the public in commercial banks. By the mid-1970s, this definition of the money supply was denoted as M1 by the Fed. The M2 measure added time deposits and savings deposits held by the public in commercial banks to M1 but did not include certificates of deposit with denominations of $100,000 or more. At that time, M3 included all of the items in M1 and M2 plus deposits at savings banks and S&Ls. By the beginning of the 1980s, credit union shares had been added to the M3 definition and the Fed even had M4 and M5 definitions of the money supply. By the mid-1980s, the Fed had carefully defined the money supply for the M1, M2, M3, and L measures. In the 1990s, only occasional small modifications in these definitions were taking place.

However, even liquidity is not completely clear in today's sophisticated financial system, where so many financial assets, such as various accounts at depository institutions, are so readily interchangeable. And when we consider that our definition of money includes a measurable set of assets which can be used in the economy, our choice becomes less certain. Very generally, our reasoning goes like this. The money supply is a measure of purchasing power in the economy. We expect the amount of purchasing power to have some correspondence with the volume of transactions actually made, and this should correspond with other measures of economic activity. Historically we have observed this to be generally true: too much money in circulation has led to an excessive amount of spending and has been inflationary; too little has restrained the economy and led to recession. Thus we need to define the money supply to include those stores of purchasing power which have a close relationship with spending and other measures of economic activity.

We look to the Fed as the ultimate authority in defining the money supply. It has responsibility for controlling the money supply and is also the source of most monetary data. Using the considerations discussed here, the Fed has come up with several alternative definitions of the money supply. The basic definition, M1, corresponds to the strict functional criteria above. It comprises those assets which are themselves

WHY NEW UNITED STATES PAPER CURRENCY?

For the first time since 1929, United States currency is being changed. A newly redesigned $100 bill began circulating in March 1996. Although most Americans don't usually carry $100 bills with the portrait of Ben Franklin, the new bill uses brighter ink and "Ben's" likeness is much larger and contains more detailed features. Is this an effort to celebrate an important American founding father? Unfortunately, no! Rather, the makeover was designed to counter high-tech counterfeiters. The development of high-quality color copiers and laser printers made it fairly easy to produce convincing fakes of the old U.S. bills. U.S. Treasury statistics show that on average about nine in every one million bills are fake. Counterfeit U.S. currency is actually more prevalent overseas, where the U.S. dollar circulates widely. In fiscal 1995, over $200 million in fake U.S. currency was seized outside the United States.

Some of the other changes in the new $100 bill include adding a security thread that is visible under bright light and that glows under ultraviolet light, microprinting "USA 100" on several areas of the bill to make it hard to duplicate, adding a watermark portrait that is visible when held up to a bright light, and using color-shifting ink on the lower right-hand corner of the bill that switches between green and black depending on the viewing angle.

About ten years were needed to decide on the redesign of U.S. paper currency. Extensive durability testing of the new security features was conducted. The government also launched an educational campaign prior to issuing the new bills to make sure that they would be accepted here and abroad. Current plans are to make over all denominations of U.S. paper money by the year 2001.

Source: Sandra Block, "The Unveiling of the New $100 Bill," *USA Today* (March 22, 1996), p. 4B.

acceptable in exchange and are normally held with the intention of spending them in the immediate future.

The second definition, M2, includes all of M1 plus a number of assets which may be held primarily as savings for some future expenditure. At the same time, these savings are readily convertible into M1 and thus may be held by some individuals or firms for immediate expenditure. In other words, M2 is a broader definition than M1 and is designed to be a more accurate measure of purchasing power. Although M1 more closely defines what has been traditionally considered money, some observers find M2 to be more consistently related to measures of economic activity.

M3 is a still broader measure than M2. A fourth measure is so broad and so far removed from our functional definition of money that the Fed designates it L, setting it off as a measure of liquid assets. L is a very broad measure of purchasing power, including everything in the other definitions plus a number of assets which can easily be sold to provide money for expenditures.

MEASURING THE MONEY SUPPLY

Even if the Fed did not define and publish measures of the money supply, it would collect most of the data necessary to do so in performing its central banking functions. Figures collected from depository institutions are totaled according to the definitions established, and money stock measures are published and released weekly. Since not all depository institutions report to the Fed every week, some estimation is necessary. These figures are then revised and adjusted as more complete information becomes available. A summary of the definitions of the money stock measures and their relationships is shown in Figure 2.1.

M1 Money Supply

The basic definition of the money supply, and the one referred to here unless stated otherwise, is M1. It measures transactions balances. These are sums of money that can be spent without first converting them to some other asset, and which are held for anticipated or unanticipated purchases or payments in the immediate future. These include currency, such as coin and Federal Reserve Notes; checkable deposits at banks, S&Ls, savings banks and credit unions; and travelers' checks. Essentially, only those amounts that represent the purchasing power of units in our economy other than the federal government are counted. Specifically excluded are vault cash and deposits of other depository institutions, the Fed, the federal government, and foreign banks and governments. The vault cash and deposits belonging to depository institutions do not represent purchasing power and therefore are not money. However, they serve as reserves, an important element of our financial system which will be discussed in the next several chapters. Adjustment is also made to avoid double counting of checks which are being processed.

As shown in Figure 2.1, the M1 stock of money in June 1995 was $1,144 billion. Although demand deposits at commercial banks currently comprise about 34 percent of the M1 total, the demand deposits share has declined since other checkable deposits were authorized nationwide by the Depository Institutions Deregulation and Monetary Control Act of 1980. Demand deposits took a particularly sharp dip, and other checkable deposits a sharp jump, in the first few months of 1981, as depositors shifted

FIGURE 2.1
Definitions of Money Supply Measures and Seasonally Adjusted Totals for June 1995

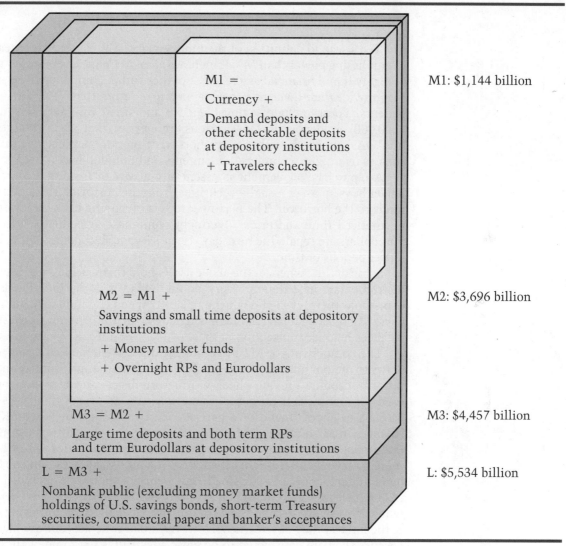

M1 =

Currency +

Demand deposits and other checkable deposits at depository institutions

+ Travelers checks

M1: $1,144 billion

M2 = M1 +

Savings and small time deposits at depository institutions

+ Money market funds

+ Overnight RPs and Eurodollars

M2: $3,696 billion

M3 = M2 +

Large time deposits and both term RPs and term Eurodollars at depository institutions

M3: $4,457 billion

L = M3 +

Nonbank public (excluding money market funds) holdings of U.S. savings bonds, short-term Treasury securities, commercial paper and banker's acceptances

L: $5,534 billion

Source: *Federal Reserve Bulletin* (October 1995): A14.

funds to the newly authorized accounts. In June 1995, other checkable deposits accounted for about 33 percent of M1. They include negotiable order of withdrawal (NOW) accounts, automatic transfer service (ATS) accounts, credit union share draft accounts, and demand deposits at S&Ls, savings banks, and credit unions. The other important component, currency, makes up about 32 percent of the M1 money measure. Travelers checks account for less than one percent of the total.[1]

M2 Money Supply

The Fed's second definition of the money stock, M2, is a broader measure of purchasing power than M1. It includes all of M1 plus several other types of highly liquid financial assets. Most of these other components are assets that provide their owners with a higher rate of return than would M1 components. These include savings deposits and small time deposits (under $100,000) at depository institutions, money market deposit accounts (MMDAs), and some other very short-term money market instruments, such as overnight repurchase agreements and Eurodollars.

A repurchase agreement is essentially a way of making a loan. The lender buys an asset, usually securities, from the borrower, thus providing funds to the borrower. The borrower repays by buying back the asset at a prearranged time and price. Overnight repurchase agreements (RPs) and Eurodollars are repaid the next day. Term RPs and Eurodollars are held for longer periods of time.

Some of the owners of the above assets hold them as long-term savings instruments. Since they are very liquid, however, some individuals and firms hold them even though they plan to spend the funds within a few days. M1 thus understates purchasing power by the amount of these M2 balances held for transaction purposes.

The components of M2 illustrate the difficulties the Fed has faced in drawing the boundaries of these definitions. For example, money market deposit accounts provide check-writing privileges, and can therefore be used for transaction purposes. Some analysts argue on this basis that MMDA balances should be a part of M1. The Fed has included MMDA balances in M2 but not in M1. This is because they are different from our traditional money components, and because they are believed to be used more as savings instruments than as transactions balances. On the other hand, it can be argued that small time deposits should be excluded from M2 because they are not, in practice, very liquid. Holders of these deposits who wish to cash them in before maturity are penalized by forfeiting some of the interest they have earned. However, small time deposits are included because they are considered to be close substitutes for some of the other savings instruments included in M2. As Figure 2.1 shows, M2 is over three times as large as M1. Savings deposits (including MMDAs) at depository institutions are approximately equal to the M1 total.

---

1.   *Federal Reserve Bulletin* (October 1995): A14.

M3 and L Money Supplies

M3 includes all of M2 plus large time deposits (over $100,000), term repurchase agreements and term Eurodollars, and institution-only money market funds. These instruments are frequently held by corporations and wealthy individuals, allowing them to earn market rates of interest on large cash balances while still maintaining their liquidity.

L is the Fed's broadest measure of money that is available to the public. It adds to M3 a variety of liquid assets, including the public's holdings of U.S. savings bonds, short-term Treasury securities, commercial paper, and bankers' acceptances. All of these represent stored purchasing power of their owners and are thus potentially related to economic activity. The relationship is an uncertain one, because some of the owners will hold these liquid assets for years, while others will convert them to cash and spend the funds within a few days. One reason the Fed defines so many measures of money and liquid wealth is that economists have different opinions as to which measure is most consistently related to spending and other economic activity.

MONEY SUPPLY GROWTH

We will see later that a major objective of the Fed is to regulate and control the supply of money and the availability of credit. The Fed sets target growth rates for M1, M2, and M3, but not for L, and attempts to keep actual growth of these money stock measures close to the targets. This task, however, is not an easy one since the banking system has the capacity to expand or contract the money supply. Furthermore, we will see that there are other factors affecting the money supply which are not under the control of our central bank.

Figure 2.2 illustrates the growth of M1, M2, and M3 during the period 1987–95. As mentioned earlier, some growth of the money stock or supply is necessary to support and sustain real growth in our economy. However, a too rapid rate of money supply growth may be inflationary. In fact, most economists agree that rapid rates of growth of the money supply contributed to the high rate of inflation during the 1970s and early 1980s.

The M1 measure grew at an unsteady pace since the mid-1980s, while the other two measures grew more smoothly. Part of the reason for this is decreasing regulation and increasing competition among financial institutions, which has led to the growth of new types of accounts. This evolution of the financial system makes it increasingly difficult to define consistent measures of the money supply.

The M1 growth was relatively flat during the 1988–90 period before increasing rapidly over the 1991–93 period. This increased growth was

FIGURE 2.2   Money Supply Growth, 1987–95

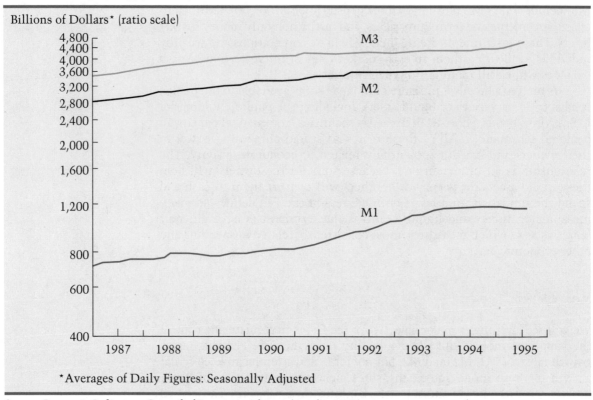

Billions of Dollars* (ratio scale)

*Averages of Daily Figures: Seasonally Adjusted

Source: *Economic Indicators,* Council of Economic Advisers (October 1995).

attributable in large part to the rapid growth in the use of other checkable deposits. Almost no growth occurred in M1 during 1994–95. We should now understand that different growth rates of the money supply measures may result from the way they are defined. This is another reason why the Fed keeps track of several measures of the money supply.

> *"I really act as more of a consultant than a true salesperson."*

COMFORT WENDEL

Trust Officer
Fifth Third Bank

BA Economics
Smith College

Q: You're a trust officer at Fifth Third Bank. What does your job entail?
A: I help companies select, set up, and manage retirement plans for their employees.

Q: If I owned or managed a company, what would you do for me?
A: First, I would take the time to learn about your firm and help you choose the kind of retirement plan that makes sense for your company's workforce, budget, and growth prospects. I would work directly with your upper management to ensure the plan is set up properly. I would then conduct enrollment seminars to help employees understand and hopefully participate in the plan.

Q: So you're involved during the sales process and afterward.
A: Right. I spend approximately 30 percent of my time working with prospects. During the sales process I really act as more of a consultant than a true salesperson. The rest of my time is spent working with the approximately forty existing client plans I am responsible for. I am considered the "relationship officer" so I address not only retirement plan issues, but other customer service needs that the client may have. I also spend a considerable amount of time selling the retirement plan to the employees.

Q: What does the employee education entail?
A: Since most of the plans we manage are 401(k) plans which involve employee contributions through payroll deduction, we explain the importance of saving for retirement. We often have to convince people that they can afford to save. Second, we focus on investment basics. We explain stocks, bonds, and mutual funds, and help them select the investment strategy appropriate for their risk tolerance and age.

Q: How did you end up in this job?
A: When I got out of college I looked into several bank training programs. I liked Fifth Third's because it included two- to three-month "rotations" in different areas of the bank. That's how I learned about the department I work in now.

Q: What skills help you most in your job?
A: It's definitely a people-oriented job. I have continual contact with clients, prospects, and employees and also manage a team of people who do all the day-to-day detail work for our clients. People skills and communication skills are very important. Obviously financial and analytical skills are important, but oddly enough, I've found that my ability to write has been a big help too. I am constantly sending letters to clients and attorneys, and preparing proposals and employee presentation materials. Thinking on your feet and public speaking help too.

Q: You went to Smith, an all women's college. Now you work in banking which historically has been a male-dominated business. Has it been a difficult adjustment?
A: Smith was a great preparation for the business world. At Smith all of the student leadership positions are held by women. Smith gave me the self confidence to assert myself and move forward. I wasn't afraid to take responsibility and speak my mind when I got to Fifth Third because that was standard procedure at Smith.

career profiles

41

SUMMARY

A working knowledge of the U.S. monetary system is essential to understanding the broader U.S. financial system and how businesses and financial institutions operate within the financial system. Of course, the U.S. monetary system does not operate in isolation but rather must interact with other monetary systems throughout the global economy.

Money must provide several functions for a monetary system to be successful. Money must serve as a medium of exchange, a store of purchasing power, and as a standard of value. Prior to the development of money, barter was used for purposes of exchanging goods and services. Early money began with the use of commodities and then was replaced with precious metals. Early paper money fully backed by a precious metal was termed representative full-bodied money. Then, over time paper money became credit money whereby it does not consist of or represent a specific valuable commodity. Money today is legal tender in that it is backed only by government credit.

The U.S. monetary system moved from a formal bimetallic standard (silver and gold) to a gold standard and then to a credit money standard. Historically, the international monetary system was tied to the gold standard. In 1944, the exchange rates between the currencies of most industrialized countries were fixed relative to the U.S. dollar or gold. However, by the early 1970s exchange rates between major currencies were allowed to float against each other.

As the U.S. monetary system became more complex, definitions of the money supply changed as forms of payment increased to meet the needs of the economy. Today, the money supply is measured in terms of M1, M2, M3, and L which adds a variety of liquid assets to more traditional measures of the supply of money.

KEY TERMS

barter
bimetallic standard
credit money
electronic funds transfer
    systems (EFTS)
exchange rate
fiat money
full-bodied money
greenbacks

inflation
legal tender
liquidity
medium of exchange
representative full-bodied money
standard of value
store of purchasing power
token coins

DISCUSSION QUESTIONS

1. What are the basic functions of money?
2. Briefly describe the development of money, from barter to the use of precious metals.
3. What is meant by a bimetallic standard?
4. Describe the development and use of paper money in the United States.
5. What is credit money? What is fiat money?
6. What are some examples of current electronic funds transfer systems?
7. Describe the historical relationship between monetary standards and the value of money in the United States.
8. Briefly describe the development of the international monetary system.
9. What factors are important in defining the money supply?
10. Describe the M1 definition of the money supply and indicate the relative significance of the M1 components.
11. How does M2 differ from M1? Which measure is probably more closely related to economic activity?
12. Describe the M3 and L measures of the money supply.

PROBLEMS

1. Obtain a current issue of the *Federal Reserve Bulletin.* Compare the present size of M1, M2, M3, and L money stock measures with the June 1995 figures presented in this chapter. Also find the current sizes of these M1 components: currency, travelers checks, demand deposits, and other checkable deposits. Express each component as a percentage of M1 and compare your percentages with those presented at the end of the chapter.
2. Obtain access to several recent issues of *Business Week.* Review the "Economic Analysis" section for articles relating to developments in the U.S. monetary system. Also examine the "International Business" section for possible developments occurring in terms of foreign monetary systems.

SELF-TEST QUESTIONS

1. The three functions of money are:
   a. medium of exchange, store of purchasing power, and measure of liquidity

    b.   conduit for international trade, store of purchasing power, and standard of value

    c.   medium of exchange, store of purchasing power, and standard of value

    d.   inflation hedge, measure of liquidity, and medium of exchange

2. Metal coins that have intrinsic value equal to their value as commodities are referred to as:
    a.   full-bodied money
    b.   token coins or money
    c.   credit money
    d.   fiat money

3. Money referred to as legal tender is money backed by:
    a.   precious metals
    b.   commodities
    c.   government credit
    d.   gold or silver

4. An increase in the general overall prices of goods and services that is not offset by increases in the quality of those goods and services is termed:
    a.   liquidity
    b.   inflation
    c.   full-bodied goods and services
    d.   store of purchasing power

5. The U.S. Monetary Act of 1792 provided for a:
    a.   gold standard
    b.   copper standard
    c.   bimetallic standard (gold and copper)
    d.   bimetallic standard (gold and silver)

6. The current international monetary system is a:
    a.   gold standard system
    b.   fixed exchange rate system
    c.   free-market floating exchange rate system
    d.   managed floating exchange rate system

7. Which one of the following items is not part of the M1 definition of the U.S. money supply?
    a.   currency
    b.   demand deposits at depository institutions
    c.   savings and small time deposits at depository institutions
    d.   checkable deposits at depository institutions

8. The definition of money used by the Fed that includes money market deposit accounts (MMDAs) is:
    a.   M1
    b.   M2
    c.   M3
    d.   L

SELF-TEST PROBLEM

Identify the components of the M1 definition of the money supply. Indicate the relative importance of each component, as a percentage of the total M1 money supply, by ranking the components in descending order.

SUGGESTED READINGS

Friedman, Milton, and Anna J. Schwartz. *A Monetary History of the United States, 1867–1960.* Princeton, NJ: Princeton University Press, 1963.

Johnson, Hazel J. *Financial Institutions and Markets: A Global Perspective.* New York: McGraw-Hill, 1993. Chap. 2.

Kaufman, George G. *The U.S. Financial System,* 5e. Englewood Cliffs, NJ: Prentice-Hall, 1992. Chap. 2.

Kidwell, David S., and Richard L. Peterson. *Financial Institutions, Markets, and Money,* 5e. Hinsdale, IL: The Dryden Press, 1993. Chap. 1.

Laurent, Robert D. "Is There a Role for Gold in Monetary Policy?" *Economic Perspectives,* Federal Reserve Bank of Chicago (March/April 1994): 2–14.

Rose, Peter S. *Money and Capital Markets,* 5e. Homewood, IL: BPI/Irwin, 1994. Chap. 2.

Shapiro, Alan C. *Foundations of Multinational Financial Management,* 2e. Boston: Allyn & Bacon, 1994. Chap. 3.

Thornton, Daniel L. "Targeting M2: The Issue of Monetary Control." *Review,* Federal Reserve Bank of St. Louis (July/August 1992): 23–35.

ANSWERS TO SELF-TEST QUESTIONS   1. c, 2. a, 3. c, 4. b, 5. d, 6. d, 7. c, 8. b

ANSWER TO SELF-TEST PROBLEM

The components of M1 are: currency, travelers checks, demand deposits, and other checkable deposits. The components in descending order of importance as of mid-1995 are: demand deposits (34%), other checkable deposits (33%), currency (32%), and travelers checks (1%). Notice that the first three components are approximately equal in size.

CHAPTER 3

*Depository
Institutions*

AFTER STUDYING THIS CHAPTER, YOU SHOULD BE ABLE TO:

- Describe the early history of the nation's depository institutions.
- Discuss the significance of recent legislation as it relates to the operation of the nation's depository institutions and the implications for businesses and individuals.
- Explain how our banking system obtains funds for operations and how these funds are committed to use.
- Evaluate the significance of trends in concentration within the banking system.
- Understand the development of interstate banking.
- Describe how banking is becoming an increasingly international business.

The financial services industry encompasses virtually every aspect of the financial mechanisms that serve our competitive enterprise economy. This book describes the major financial services of the nation's depository institutions, as well as investment banking and consumer financing. We will also touch on lesser-known financial services such as leasing, trade credit, and factoring, all of which depend upon our depository institutions. The four types of depository institutions are commercial banks, savings and loan associations (S&Ls), savings banks, and credit unions. The nature and functions of these institutions are described in the following pages.

Depository institutions play an integral part in the management of the monetary system. They accumulate and lend idle funds, handle the transfer of money, and provide for its safekeeping. These institutions provide the bulk of short-term loans to businesses for day-to-day working capital purposes. In addition, they provide part of the long-term financing required by industry, commerce, and agriculture. They play an important part in financing the construction of millions of homes and are an important source of personal loans. Depository institutions also provide loans to the federal government as well as to state and local governments.

HISTORY OF THE U.S. BANKING SYSTEM

The structure of the modern **banking system** includes commercial banks, savings and loans, mutual savings banks, and credit unions. It is the result of historical forces as well as of current banking requirements. Banking, like most forms of economic activity, is subject more to the forces of tradition than to those of innovation. Yet, despite the great influence of early banking practices and legislation on today's banking, the evolution of banks to meet the requirements of the modern industrial economy has been effective and successful. We must not assume, however, that the present structure of banking is here to stay. To meet the requirements of a dynamic economy, changes are constantly taking place in banking practices, regulation, and legislation. An understanding of banking in the United States today, therefore, requires an understanding of the development of the banking system in the economic history of the country.

banking system
commercial banks, savings and loans, savings banks, and credit unions

BEFORE THE CIVIL WAR

Until the Civil War banking in the United States developed under circumstances that explain much of the apparent confusion and difficulty that accompanied its development. The population lived for the most part on farms. Families were self-sufficient, and transportation and communications were poor. The friction between those who supported a strong central government and those who did not existed in the early years of our history as it does today. The country had little experience in money and financial management, and much controversy raged over the power to charter and regulate banks.

Early Chartered Banks
During the colonial period there were small unincorporated banks that were established to ease the shortage of capital for businesses. Their operations consisted largely of issuing their own paper money. Outside of the

larger towns, deposit banking was of minor significance. It was not until 1782 that the first incorporated bank, the Bank of North America, was created. It was established in Philadelphia by Robert Morris to assist in financing the Revolutionary War. This bank set a good example for successful banking—its notes served as a circulating monetary medium, it loaned liberally to the U.S. government, and it redeemed its own notes in metallic coins upon demand. Two years later the Bank of Massachusetts and the Bank of New York were established. These three incorporated banks were the only such banks until 1790.

The First Bank of the United States

Alexander Hamilton was the first Secretary of the Treasury of the United States. For several years he had harbored the idea of a federally chartered bank that would adequately support the rapidly growing economy and would give financial assistance to the government during its crises. His recommendations were submitted to the House of Representatives of the United States in 1790, and in 1791 a 20-year charter was issued to the First Bank of the United States. This bank served the nation effectively by issuing notes, transferring funds from region to region, providing useful service to the government, and curbing the excessive note issues of state banks by presenting such notes periodically for redemption. However, strong opposition existed to the renewal of its charter, and it ceased operations in 1811. The antagonism of state banking interests was an important cause of the demise of the First Bank.

Following the expiration of the charter of the First Bank of the United States, the number of state banks increased rapidly, as did the volume of their note issues. Abuses of banking privileges were extensive. The capital of many banks was largely fictitious, and there was a flood of irredeemable notes issued to the public.

The Second Bank of the United States

The Second Bank of the United States was chartered primarily to restore order to the chaotic banking situation that had developed after the First Bank of the United States ceased operations. Like the First Bank of the United States, it received a 20-year federal charter. It began operations in 1816 and, after a short period of mismanagement, set upon a course of reconstructing sound banking practices. It ably served individuals, businesses, and the government. It accepted deposits, made loans, and issued notes. Furthermore, it restrained the note-issuing practices of state banks by periodically presenting their notes for redemption. The Second Bank of the United States also played a most important and efficient role as fiscal agent for the government. As fiscal agent it received all deposits of government funds and reported regularly on all government receipts and expenditures.

In 1833 President Andrew Jackson and many of his associates began such a vigorous campaign against the Second Bank of the United States that it became apparent its charter would not be renewed when it expired in 1836. President Jackson claimed that the Bank was being run to benefit private interests and was operated in such a way as to weaken government policies. Like the First Bank of the United States, it became a victim of political pressure. Not until 1863 was another bank in the United States to receive a federal charter.

State Banks from 1836 to the Civil War

When the Second Bank's charter expired, the excesses that had plagued the period between 1811 and 1816 began again. This period is characterized as one of wildcat banking. Although many state banks operated on a conservative and very sound basis, the majority engaged in risky banking practices through excessive note issues, lack of adequate bank capital, and insufficient reserves against their notes and deposits.

Because the notes of even the well established banks were often of inferior quality, it was easy for skillful counterfeiters to increase the denomination of notes. Also, because of the poor communications that existed between various sections of the country, it was often quite difficult for a banker to be certain whether notes presented for payment were real. Skillfully prepared counterfeit notes frequently circulated with greater freedom than did the legitimate notes of weak and little known banks.

In spite of the many abuses of state banks during this period, New York, Massachusetts, and Louisiana originated highly commendable banking legislation, much of which provided the basis for the establishment of the National Banking System in 1863.

ENTRY OF THRIFT INSTITUTIONS

The chaotic banking conditions of the early 1800s left individuals with few safe institutions in which they could place their savings. The lack of safe depository institutions, in turn, inhibited the effective development of home financing. The rapidly growing population depended to a large extent on individual financial arrangements to meet its need for housing. The accumulated savings of most individual home buyers, then, as now, was simply not enough to buy a house. In response to this problem, two new forms of depository institutions, known as **thrift institutions,** came into being: savings banks and S&Ls. Credit unions developed later.

*thrift institutions
savings and loans,
savings banks, and
credit unions*

Savings Banks

Savings banks made their appearance in 1812, emphasizing individual thrift savings and safety of principal. The accumulation of funds by these savings banks was invested primarily in home mortgages. Very often the trustees of these banks were prominent local citizens, serving without pay, who regarded their service as an important civic duty. Although the approximately 500 savings banks now in operation are confined almost entirely to the New England area, New York State, and New Jersey, their contribution to both savings accumulation and home financing has been enormous. Today they have assets of nearly $500 billion, most of which is invested in mortgage loans.

Savings and Loan Institutions

S&Ls first came on the scene in 1831. First known as building societies, then as building and loan associations, their basic mission was to provide home mortgage financing. While home financing was important to the savings banks, it was the fundamental purpose of savings and loan operations. In distinguishing between these two important forms of depository institutions, it might be said that originally the savings banks' emphasis was on thrift and the safety of savings while the emphasis of the S&Ls was on home financing. In contrast with the limited geographic expansion of savings banking, savings and loan activity spread throughout the United States. The number of S&Ls peaked at about 4,000 at the beginning of the 1980s. However, because of financial difficulties the total number of associations has declined by over one-half since then. S&L assets peaked at over $1.0 trillion during the latter part of the 1980s before declining sharply since then.

Credit Unions

Credit unions, which now have assets of approximately $200 billion, came on the American scene much later than the other thrift institutions. As cooperative nonprofit organizations, they exist primarily to provide member depositors with consumer credit. They are made up of individuals who possess common bonds of association such as occupation, residence, or church affiliation. These institutions derive their funds almost entirely from the savings of their members. It was not until the 1920s that credit unions became important as a special form of depository institution.

LEGISLATION TO GOVERN THE BANKING SYSTEM

National Banking Act

In 1864 the National Banking Act made it possible for banks to receive federal charters. This legislation provided the basis for our present national banking laws. As in the cases of the First and the Second Bank of the United States, the reasons for federal interest in the banking system were to provide for a sound banking system and to curb the excesses of the state banks. An important additional purpose of the National Banking Act was to provide financing for the Civil War. Secretary of the Treasury Salmon P.

Chase and others believed that government bonds could be sold to the nationally chartered banks, which could in turn issue their own notes based in part on the government bonds they had purchased.

Through the National Banking Act, various steps were taken to promote safe banking practices. Among other things, minimum capital requirements were established for banks with federal charters, loans were regulated with respect to safety and liquidity, a system of supervision and examination was instituted, and minimum reserve requirements against notes and deposits were established. In general, these reform measures were constructive. However, in some instances they have been regarded as altogether too restrictive. For example, loans were forbidden against real estate. Much of the criticism of the national banking system, in fact, was caused by the inflexibility of its rules. Many of its limitations were either modified or eliminated in 1913 with the establishment of the Federal Reserve System.

The National Banking Act did not establish a system of central banks. It only made possible the chartering of banks by the federal government. The Federal Reserve Act of 1913 brought to the American economy a system of central banks. The Federal Reserve System was designed to eliminate many of the weaknesses that had persisted under the National Banking Act and to increase the effectiveness of commercial banking in general. It included not only strong central domination of banking practices but also many services for commercial banks. The influence of the Fed is described in the next chapter.

Depository Institutions Deregulation and Monetary Control Act

In 1980 President Jimmy Carter signed into law the Depository Institutions Deregulation and Monetary Control Act. This act represents a major step toward deregulating banking in the United States and improving the effectiveness of monetary policy. We will generally refer to this legislation as the Monetary Control Act throughout the text and will here describe the two main provisions of the Act: deregulation and monetary control.

Depository Institutions Deregulation. This major part of the Monetary Control Act was designed to reduce or eliminate interest rate limitations imposed on the banking system, increase the various sources of funds, and expand the uses of the funds of S&Ls. One significant change affected the Fed's Regulation Q, which established interest rate ceilings on time and savings deposits. Most provisions of Regulation Q were phased out by March 31, 1986. Furthermore, state-imposed interest rate ceilings were substantially modified, and existing state restrictions on deposit interest rates for insured institutions were eliminated.

To enable depository institutions to compete effectively for funds that were flowing in large amounts to money market mutual funds, NOW accounts (negotiable orders of withdrawal) were authorized. Money market mutual funds became available in large numbers as sponsored and promoted primarily by investment banks and mutual funds groups. The NOW accounts had interest rates more competitive with those of the money market mutual funds but continued to be subject to Regulation Q during the phase-out period. Credit unions were permitted to issue draft accounts which, for all intents and purposes, were the same as the NOW accounts. Federal deposit insurance was increased from $40,000 to $100,000 for each account. This large increase in deposit protection, although politically popular at the time, is now described as an undue expansion of protection. The U.S. Treasury has stated that it undermined market discipline and enabled depository institutions to make high-risk loans for which the taxpayers in the long run have become liable.

In order to enhance competition among depository institutions, Title IV of the Monetary Control Act amended the Home Owners' Loan Act of 1933. Federally chartered S&Ls were permitted to invest up to one-fifth of their assets in corporate debt securities, commercial paper, and consumer loans. Prior residential mortgage loan restrictions relating to geographical areas and first mortgage lending requirements were removed. Greater authority was also permitted for granting real estate development and construction loans by federally chartered S&Ls. In addition, federal savings banks were allowed to make a small number of commercial loans and accept some checkable deposits.

Monetary Control. The Monetary Control Act was designed to extend the Fed's control to thrift institutions and to commercial banks that are not members of the System. This was accomplished by extending both reserve requirements and general controls to these institutions. Because the Fed had more stringent regulations than many state regulatory agencies, many commercial banks had given up their membership in the System to become state-chartered nonmember banks. The Monetary Control Act, therefore, has had the effect of halting the declining System membership by transferring much regulatory control from the state to the federal level.

In the past, reserve requirements imposed by the Fed applied only to member banks. The requirements were based on a complicated formula involving size, location, and type of charter. These differential reserve requirements have now been eliminated. Even foreign banks and offices operating in this country have been included in these simplified reserve requirements. Along with the broadening of control by the Fed, there has also been a broadening of privileges to those institutions brought under its control. All depository institutions may now borrow from the Fed on the same basis, and the fee schedule for services rendered by the Fed applies to all regulated depository institutions.

To summarize, the Monetary Control Act permits both greater competition for deposits and more flexibility in the holding of assets by depository institutions. Thus, as institutions become more alike, similarities in their financial management are likely to increase.

Garn-St. Germain Depository Institutions Act

There had been high hopes that the Monetary Control Act would have a quick and beneficial effect on the banking system as well as on the effectiveness of monetary control by the Fed. However, this was not the case. Of special significance was the dramatic increase in interest rates in late 1980 and 1981. S&Ls and savings banks were faced with heavy increases in their cost of funds as depositors shifted from low-interest passbook savings to the higher yielding NOW accounts and savings certificates. Furthermore, since the NOW accounts continued to be subject to ceiling rates under Regulation Q, money market mutual funds had a clear competitive advantage in attracting funds. Rapidly increasing federal deficits and troubles in the automobile and housing industries added to the demand for legislation to address these problems. The Garn-St. Germain Act of 1982 resulted.

Although the Garn-St. Germain Act had many provisions, its principal focus was to assist the savings and loan industry, which had deteriorated to dangerous levels. Depository institutions in general were authorized, among other things, to issue a new money market deposit account with no regulated interest rate ceiling; S&Ls were authorized to make nonresidential real estate loans, commercial loans, and to issue variable-rate mortgages.

PROTECTION OF DEPOSITORS' FUNDS

The various legislative measures described above were all designed to enable depository institutions to adjust to the changing circumstances confronting them. Some of the measures, however, became the sources of critical problems.

THE SAVINGS AND LOAN CRISIS

Authorization in the early 1980s to invest funds in a wide range of higher yielding investments permitted many savings and loan associations to run wild by supporting speculative office buildings and other such ventures. This resulted not only in overbuilding at inflated costs but, as the promoters were unable to honor the terms of their loan contracts, many S&Ls became insolvent. Because the deposits of these associations were largely protected by the Federal Savings and Loan Insurance Corporation (FSLIC), the federal government was obliged to provide a safety net for the depositors at a cost of $500 billion or more to taxpayers. The Federal Savings and Loan Insurance Corporation had insured the deposits of most S&L depositors since the early 1930s. Federal financial assistance to the FSLIC was made possible through legislation approved by Congress in 1988. Legislators created the Resolution Trust Corporation (RTC) to take over and liquidate the assets of failed associations. As depositors withdrew funds for investment in other institutions, high interest rates continued to burden S&Ls in their attempt to remain solvent.

Additional legislation came in 1989 under the title Financial Institutions Reform, Recovery, and Enforcement Act (FIRREA). This legislation included numerous provisions and financial resources designed to strengthen the nation's depository institutions and their federal deposit insurance programs. Special features of this legislation included stronger capital standards for thrift institutions and enhanced enforcement powers for the federal government.

Figure 3.1 shows reductions in the number of insured savings institutions during the 1984–94 period. Some reductions were the result of savings institutions being voluntarily liquidated or placed in Resolution Trust Corporation conservatorships. In other cases, financially weak S&Ls were merged into financially stronger S&Ls or merged into commercial banks. Government agencies frequently assisted in bringing these mergers to completion. Up until 1989 S&Ls were either liquidated or merged into other S&Ls. Beginning in 1989 most failed S&Ls were placed in RTC conservatorship or assisted by the RTC in merging into other savings institutions. Other reductions occurred because savings institutions merged into commercial banks. In some instances, savings institutions had their charters transferred to commercial banks.

FIGURE 3.1   Reductions of Insured Savings Institutions, 1984–94

YEAR	VOLUNTARY LIQUIDATIONS AND ASSISTED PAYOUTS	FAILURES PLACED IN RTC CONSERVATORSHIPS	MERGED INTO OTHER SAVINGS INSTITUTIONS	MERGED INTO COMMERCIAL BANKS
1994	3	0	46	81
1993	9	6	52	74
1992	6	50	67	56
1991	6	123	72	64
1990	1	203	58	37
1989	9	316	48	6
1988	31	0	251	1
1987	32	0	123	3
1986	18	0	92	2
1985	14	0	82	2
1984	3	0	55	1

Source: *Statistics on Banking,* Federal Deposit Insurance Corporation, 1995.

Commercial banks have suffered some of the same difficulties as the S&Ls. However, losses from international loans, agricultural loans, and loans to the petroleum industry, have been more significant for commercial banks—many banks had to be merged with other banks. Savings banks and credit unions experienced some difficulties as well but to a lesser extent.

INSURANCE FOR DEPOSIT AND SHARE ACCOUNTS

Insurance protection for deposits at depository institutions was started during the Great Depression to restore the confidence of depositors. The Federal Deposit Insurance Corporation (FDIC), the Federal Savings and Loan Insurance Corporation (FSLIC), and the National Credit Union Share Insurance Fund (NCUSIF) were established under federal legislation to protect deposits in banks, S&Ls, and credit unions—in that order. Over the years the limitation on deposit account insurance was increased until by 1980 it had been set at $100,000 per account.

The financial difficulties discussed above resulted not only in the failure of many S&Ls but also the bankruptcy of the FSLIC. The reserves held by the FSLIC were not enough to meet the claims of depositors of bankrupt S&Ls, and its functions were transferred to the FDIC in 1989. The Treasury has transferred huge amounts of capital to the FDIC to cover the losses of S&L depositors. Furthermore, capital has been needed to cover losses from a significant increase in commercial bank failures.

One of the special problems of insuring bank losses has been the practice and assumption that some banks are "too big to fail"; too big in the sense that the problems created by losses may extend far beyond the failed bank. It is on this basis that all depositors have received 100 percent coverage of their funds even though coverage of only the first $100,000 deposited is guaranteed by law. This practice tended to reduce the incentive for large depositors to exercise market discipline and created an incentive for large deposits to be shifted to "too big to fail" banks. Congress addressed this issue as part of its deposit insurance bill, the Federal Deposit Insurance Corporation Improvement Act of 1991 (FDICIA). This act generally requires that failed banks be handled in such a way as to provide the lowest cost to the FDIC. Limited exceptions, however, were provided for in the act if very serious adverse effects on economic conditions could be expected as a result of failure of big banks.

There is little doubt that deposit insurance will continue to exist. It is also obvious that radical changes will have to be made if, after the resolution of the present crisis, we are to avoid future burdens on taxpayers resulting from deposit insurance programs. Suggestions for solving these problems include eliminating all deposit insurance, reducing insurable deposits limits to protect only the small deposits, levying higher premiums on depository institutions for the insurance, and having more strict regulatory and supervisory control.

Field: Financial Intermediaries

Opportunities:
Financial intermediaries, such as banks, savings and loans (S&Ls), and credit unions, assist businesses and individuals with the flow of funds between borrowers. Financial intermediary jobs provide the chance to work with individuals, small businesses, and large corporations on a variety of financial matters, and therefore provide invaluable business world experience. In addition, individuals interested in finance may find numerous entry-level jobs with strong advancement opportunities.

Jobs:
Loan Analyst
Loan Officer
Financial Economist

Responsibilities:
A *loan analyst* evaluates loan applicants in terms of their creditworthiness and ability to repay. Since these types of loans are usually for one or more years, the loan analyst must monitor and re-evaluate outstanding loans on a periodic basis.

A *loan officer* is responsible for generating new loan business and managing existing loans. As such, a loan officer must have the ability to address the needs of existing clients while at the same time identify and actively pursue new clients.

A *financial economist* analyzes business conditions over time and prepares forecasts of economic activity and employment trends. This information is crucial for lending institutions so that they do not make unwise loans.

Education:
The level of education needed varies among different jobs. However, all of these jobs require a solid background in economics and finance, as well as experience with computers, statistics, and communication.

FUNCTIONS OF THE BANKING SYSTEM

Modern depository institutions perform six functions. The most basic functions are (1) accepting deposits and (2) granting loans. In accepting deposits, banks provide a safe place for the public to keep money for future use. Individuals and businesses seldom wish to spend their money as it becomes available; without depository facilities such funds may lie idle.

The banking system puts the accumulated deposits to use through loans to persons and businesses having immediate use for them. The result of this pooling of funds is their more effective use.

Along with accepting deposits and granting loans, depository institutions provide (3) safekeeping for depositors, (4) efficient and economical transfer of payments through check-writing procedures, and (5) record keeping for depositors through regular reporting procedures.

When granting personal or business loans, the banking system carries out its function of (6) risk selection. A banker's refusal to finance an ill-conceived venture protects assets. It may also be in the best interest of the prospective operators of the new venture, by preventing them from engaging in an activity that will result in loss. The objective in business risk selection is the careful distribution of loan funds to those businesses with the best chances of success, which makes possible the most efficient development of the nation's resources.

ASSETS AND SOURCES OF FUNDS FOR DEPOSITORY INSTITUTIONS

Types of depository institution assets and the sources of the funds with which these assets are acquired are shown in Figure 3.2.

ASSETS

The principal assets of all depository institutions are cash, securities, and loans.

Cash
Cash includes funds in the depository institution's vault and deposits at its Reserve Bank or other banks. A certain minimum of vault cash is needed to meet the day-to-day currency requirements of customers. The amount of cash required may be small compared to total resources. This is because the typical day's operation will result in approximately the same amount of cash deposits as cash withdrawals. A margin of safety, however, is required to take care of those periods when for one reason or another withdrawals greatly exceed deposits.

The appropriate amount of cash a depository institution should carry depends largely upon the character of its operations. For example, a bank that has some very large accounts might be expected to have a larger volume of unanticipated withdrawals (and deposits) than a bank that has only small individual accounts. An unpredictable volume of day-to-day withdrawals requires, of course, a larger cash reserve.

The second cash item, designated reserves at Federal Reserve Bank, is considerably greater than vault cash. Depository institutions are required

FIGURE 3.2   Depository Assets and Sources of Funds

ASSETS	SOURCES OF FUNDS
CASH	**DEPOSITS**
Vault cash and cash due from banks	Checkable deposits
Reserves at the Federal Reserve Bank	Savings and time deposits
Deposits at other banks	**OTHER LIABILITIES AND DEFERRED CREDITS**
SECURITIES	Discounts and fees collected but not yet earned
U.S. government securities	Funds borrowed from Federal Reserve Bank or Federal Home Loan Bank
State and local government securities	
Other securities	**OWNER'S EQUITY**
Capital stock of the Federal Reserve Bank or Federal Home Loan Bank	Common and preferred stock
	Surplus
LOANS	Share accounts (for credit unions)
Secured loans	
Unsecured loans and discounts	
Real estate mortgages	
OTHER ASSETS	
Interest receivable	
Buildings and furniture	
Prepaid expenses	

to keep a percentage of their deposits as reserves either with the Reserve Bank in their districts or in the form of vault cash. The Monetary Control Act requires uniform reserve amounts for all depository institutions in order to enhance monetary control and competitive fairness. As withdrawals are made and total deposit balances decrease, the amount of the required reserves also decreases. The vault cash reserves that have been freed may then be used to help meet withdrawal demands.

Cash in other banks refers to the common practice used by smaller banks of keeping substantial deposits with banks in large cities. These correspondent relationships with other banks speed the clearing of drafts and other credit instruments by routing such instruments through their large city correspondents. They also provide immediate access to information regarding the money markets of the large cities.

Securities

Securities are the second major group of assets. Securities include those of the U.S. government, state governments, and municipalities. Also included are other securities and capital stock of the Federal Reserve Bank and Federal

Corporate America has been undergoing "reengineering," or restructuring, for several years in an effort to make firms more profitable. Terms like *down-sizing, right-sizing,* and *out-sourcing* are often used. Now, banks also need to reengineer.

REENGINEERING COMMERCIAL BANKS

High profit margins on loans to businesses were expected, and often realized, in the past. These margins were adequate for many banks to absorb customer defaults and still make profits.

Today's competitive environment has resulted in tighter profit margins. To be successful, commercial banks will need to streamline their lending activities. Banks will have to win customers through improved marketing skills. Banks also will have to keep lending costs low.

Banks traditionally have been tightly regulated. New managerial skills, including entrepreneurial skills, now are needed to be competitive. Bankers even may find it advantageous to learn marketing skills from industrial firms with successful marketing programs in place, as well as to learn state-of-the-art manufacturing skills to control and reduce "back office" costs. For example, Cherine Chalaby from Andersen Consulting in London indicates that several leading banks have hired managers skilled in "just-in-time production and quality at source" techniques to help them manage better their back office activities.

Source: Brian Caplen, "Time for a Cultural Revolution," *Euromoney* (December 1995), p. 38.

Home Loan Bank, held as investments. Holding the capital stock of its Reserve Bank is a requirement for all member banks of the Fed. The same is true for S&Ls that are members of the Federal Home Loan Bank System.

Loans

The third group of asset items includes several classifications of loans: first, secured loans that are payable on demand; second, secured loans that have definite maturities; third, unsecured loans and discounts with definite maturities; and, finally, real estate mortgages.

In a **secured loan**, specific property is pledged as collateral for the loan. In the event the borrower fails to repay the loan, the lending institution will take the assets pledged as collateral for the loan. In all cases, the borrower is required to sign a note specifying the details of the indebtedness; but unless specific assets are pledged for the loan, it is classified as unsecured.

An **unsecured loan** represents a general claim against the assets of the borrower. The interest rate charged by banks for short-term unsecured

secured loan
loan backed by collateral

unsecured loan
loan that is a general claim against the borrower's assets

prime rate
interest rate on short-term unsecured loans to highest quality business customers

loans to their highest quality business customers is referred to as the ***prime rate.*** This represents the lowest business loan rate available at a particular point in time and is sometimes called the *floor rate.* Less qualified business borrowers will be charged a higher rate; for example, prime plus two percentage points. If the prime rate is 8 percent, then the financially weaker business borrower would be charged 10 percent (8 percent prime plus 2 percent more).

Figure 3.3 shows changes in the prime rate over the 1975–94 period. Both the average annual and end-of-year prevailing rates are graphed. Notice that the prime rates during the middle of the 1970s were similar to those during the early 1990s. However, in between the beginning and end of the 20-year period, the prime rate fluctuated widely. For example, at the end of 1980 the prime rate reached a record high level of 21.50 percent. The prime rate continued to be historically high during 1981 when the average annual rate was 18.87 percent. The prime rate then continued to decline until lows were reached in single-digit levels during 1986 and 1987. Another peak occurred in 1989 before the prime rate declined all the way to the 6 percent level by 1993. In Chapter 8 we will discuss the factors that cause interest rates to rise or fall over time.

FIGURE 3.3   Bank Prime Rate Changes, 1975–94

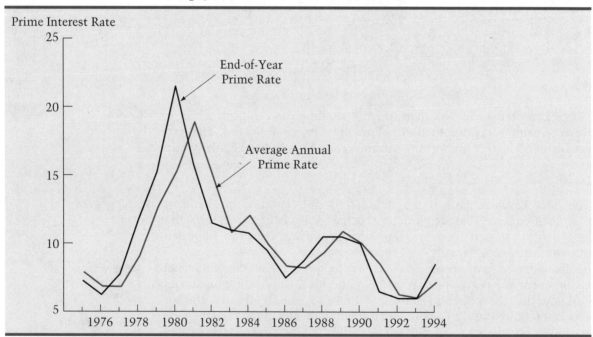

Source: *Federal Reserve Bulletin,* various issues.

A loan customarily includes a specified rate of interest such as the prevailing prime rate, or prime plus some percentage point amount. For short-term loans, the interest often is paid along with the principal amount of the loan when the loan contract matures. In some instances, a discount loan or note is offered. With a discount loan, the interest is deducted from the stated amount of the note at the time the money is loaned. The borrower receives less than the face value of the note, but repays the full amount of the note when it matures.

A given discount rate results in a higher cost of borrowing than an interest loan made for the same rate. This is true because under the discount arrangement less actual money is received by the borrower, although the amount paid for its use is the same. For example, if $5,000 is borrowed on a loan basis at an interest rate of 10 percent for one year, at maturity $5,000 plus $500 interest must be repaid. On the other hand, if the $5,000 is borrowed on a discount basis and the rate is 10 percent, a deduction of $500 from the face value of the note is made and the borrower receives only $4,500. At the end of the year, the borrower repays the face amount of the note, $5,000. In the first case, the borrower has paid $500 for the use of $5,000; in the second case, $500 has been paid for the use of only $4,500. The effective rate of interest, therefore, on the discount basis is approximately 11.1 percent compared with the even 10 percent paid when the $5,000 was borrowed on a loan basis.

Other Bank Assets

The remaining assets are less important than those previously discussed. They include interest that has been earned on bonds and notes but not yet received, bank buildings and furniture, office supplies, and prepaid expenses such as insurance premiums paid in advance.

Almost 60 percent of the assets of commercial banks are in the form of loans. However, in contrast with S&Ls and savings banks, less than one-quarter of all loans are for real estate mortgages. S&Ls and savings banks, on the other hand, have nearly three quarters of their assets in the form of real estate mortgages and mortgage-backed securities. The assets of credit unions are largely consumer loans with a small percentage in government securities. Some credit unions also make home mortgage loans, although such mortgage financing typically constitutes a small percentage of their total assets.

SOURCES OF FUNDS

There are two major sources from which depository institutions acquire their capital funds and liabilities. Owners' equity represents the initial investment and retained earnings of the owners of the institutions. Liabilities represent the funds owed to depositors and others from whom the bank has borrowed. The most important liability of a depository institution consists of its deposits of various kinds, but the other liabilities should be understood also.

Deposits

Several types of deposits—traditionally grouped as checkable, savings, and time deposits—make up the principal liabilities of all depository institutions. Checkable deposits are the checking accounts of individuals, businesses, and other institutions. These deposits may be withdrawn on demand, that is, the institution agrees to pay the depositor immediately when requested to do so. The depositor normally utilizes a check to request the bank to make payment.

In practice, depository institutions also make savings deposits immediately available to depositors on demand. However, they are legally permitted to require written notification up to thirty days in advance of withdrawal. All savings deposits and time deposits earn interest. Most time deposits are **certificates of deposit (CDs),** which have a stated maturity and either pay a fixed rate of interest or are sold at a discount. A smaller category of time deposits is special club accounts which includes Christmas and vacation savings clubs.

certificates of deposit (CDs)
time deposits with a stated maturity

Although records reveal that commercial banks issued certificates of deposit as early as 1900, a major innovation in the early 1960s resulted in a tremendous growth in their importance. Large denomination CDs for deposits of $100,000 or more were issued in negotiable form, which meant they could be bought and sold. The vastly increased use of negotiable CDs in the 1960s caused a secondary market for them to develop. Today, CDs issued by depository institutions are purchased and sold in the money markets as readily as most forms of debt obligations. The depository institutions of the nation have used negotiable CDs as a means of attracting much larger deposits from businesses and other institutions.

Other Liabilities and Deferred Credits

The second category of liabilities is represented by items having a far smaller dollar significance than that of deposits. In brief, these include liabilities not yet payable—such as accrued taxes, interest, and wages—and the receipt of fees and other charges for which service has not yet been rendered. Funds borrowed from a Reserve Bank or Federal Home Loan Bank or other banks are also reflected here.

Owners' Equity

The owners' equity category includes stock, surplus, and retained earnings. At the time a bank is formed, stock is purchased by the owners of the bank or by the public. In the case of credit unions, the members buy shares. From time to time additional stock may be sold to accommodate bank expansion. The surplus account is an accounting convenience to which the excess from the sale of stock at a price above its par or stated value per share is credited. When dividends are paid, the retained earnings account is reduced. These accounts constitute the primary equity of a depository institution.

On the balance sheets of many depository institutions today, there may be an item designated as capital notes in the equity section. These notes, always placed below the claims of bank depositors, reflect long-term borrowing on the part of the bank for purposes of bolstering the equity section. Although, like deposits, they are liabilities of the depository institutions that issue them, reserve requirements do not apply to them.

The owners' equity section of the balance sheet for all depository institutions is of special interest to various groups. Losses from operations are reflected immediately in this section. It would be expected that this would create a strong incentive for prudent management. Yet it is also true that the smaller the owners' investment relative to a given level of revenues and profits, the larger the percentage return per dollar of owners' investment. If the owners' investment is quite small compared to the total assets of the firm, the owners may consider their risks to be negligible relative to large potential profits. For this reason, all regulatory authorities have emphasized the importance of an adequate ratio of the owners' equity to deposits or assets.

Agencies that insure deposits have a critical interest in the safety of the institution. The losses previously recorded by many of the nation's S&Ls not only exhausted their equity accounts but also destroyed the agency that insured their depositors. Depositors, too, have an interest in the adequacy of the owners' equity or capital account. Although it is expected that the federal government will make good on the insured liabilities of the failed S&Ls, there is no absolute guarantee that it will be done now or in the future. The financial well-being of the entire nation depends upon a stable and thriving system of depository institutions. For this reason much attention is directed not only to the quality of a firm's loans and investments but also to its capital-to-deposits ratio. The size of adequate ratio percentage differs for each class of assets. For example, federal government obligations among a firm's assets would require a small percentage. A commercial real estate investment, on the other hand, may require a much higher ratio. A composite of these various risk categories is developed to obtain a single percentage figure described as the firm's *risk-based capital ratio.*

In late 1988 the three bank regulatory bodies—the Federal Deposit Insurance Corporation, the Fed, and the Office of the Comptroller of Currency—adopted new capital adequacy standards for commercial banks; minimum 8 percent risk-based capital ratio. These revised standards were arrived at in cooperation with the monetary authorities of eleven industrialized countries. Their goal was to bring foreign banking offices in this country into conformity with the requirements of domestic banks. For many years foreign banking offices had a competitive advantage over domestic banks since they were not subject to domestic requirements. With lower capital ratios they could offer better loan terms and still provide an adequate return on their capital accounts. The added risk for the low capital ratios of these foreign banking offices was borne by their home offices.

CONCENTRATION IN COMMERCIAL BANKING CONTROL

Concentration in banking control has taken a number of forms because banks, like other businesses, have increased their scope and volume of operations to accommodate the growing economy. The change in structure of the U.S. banking system has been especially significant since 1970. Since then there has been a strong trend toward branch banking and bank holding company arrangements.

BRANCH BANKING

branch banks
bank offices under a
single bank charter

Branch banks are those banking offices that are controlled by a single parent bank. One board of directors and one group of stockholders control the home office and the branches. Some of our branch banking systems are very small, involving perhaps only two, three, or four branches. Others are quite large, extending over an entire state or several states and having many branches. The laws of some states prevent the operation of branch banking. Other states permit the operation of branch offices only within limited areas, and still others permit branch operation on a statewide scale.

One of the particular merits of branch banking is that these systems are less likely to fail than independent unit banks. In a branch banking system, a wide diversification of investments can be made. Therefore, the temporary reverses of a single community are not as likely to cause the complete failure of an entire banking chain. This is true primarily of those branch systems that operate over wide geographical areas rather than in a single metropolitan area.

The independent bank cannot rely on other banks to offset local economic problems. It is on this point that branch banking operations appear to have their strongest support. The record of bank failures in the United States is one of which the banking system as a whole cannot be proud. However, opponents of branch banking have pointed out that failure of a system of banks, although less frequent, is far more serious.

There are also conflicting points of view on the pros and cons of branch banking among bank customers. The placement of branches in or near shopping centers, airports, and other centers of activity is convenient for consumers. The ability to make deposits or to withdraw funds at a branch

Removal of legal barriers to interstate branching would benefit consumers of banking services. Consumers in multistate areas would gain more convenient access to their accounts. In addition it would increase competition and provide lower interest rates. Also, interstate branching may increase the importation of funds into areas where credit demand is particularly strong. Concerns regarding the domination of local banks by large multistate banks is unfounded. Evidence indicates that as long as there is sufficient demand for credit services of local banks, such banks will continue to occupy an important niche in their communities.

AN ARGUMENT FOR INTERSTATE BRANCH BANKING

Source: Calem, Paul S. "The Proconsumer Argument For Branch Banking." *Business Review*, Federal Reserve Bank of Philadelphia (May/June 1993): 27.

is a special advantage for the elderly. Businesses may satisfy very large borrowing requirements by dealing with a bank that has been able to grow to a substantial size through its branch operations. In certain unit-banking states, though, it is common for the largest businesses to maintain their basic banking operations with banks located in money centers such as New York, Chicago, or San Francisco. This is because local banks cannot provide the variety of services and the amount of credit available from the very large banks. On the other hand, businesses may find an advantage in the highly competitive actions of many unit banks. Branches, of course, will not compete with each other, which means that a rejected loan application by one branch is a rejection by all of the branches of the bank. Small businesses especially may find it helpful to be able to shop among unit banks.

The resistance to branch banking has come primarily from small unit banks located in rural areas. The political power of these banks was used effectively for many years to prevent competition from the branches of urban financial center banks. S&Ls, on the other hand, have enjoyed far more flexibility in establishing branches. This advantage of the S&Ls has eroded some commercial bank opposition to branch banking. Since 1970, the number of states permitting branch banking has increased significantly. Currently, 35 states allow unlimited statewide branching or statewide expansion through acquisition of existing banks. Fifteen states allow only limited branching, but two of these have passed legislation that will permit statewide branching in the future.

Figure 3.4 shows the number of insured banks and branches for the 1950–94 period. At year-end 1950, branches provided only 26 percent of all bank offices. By the end of 1994, branches accounted for 84 percent of all banking offices.

FIGURE 3.4   Insured Banks and Branches, 1950–94

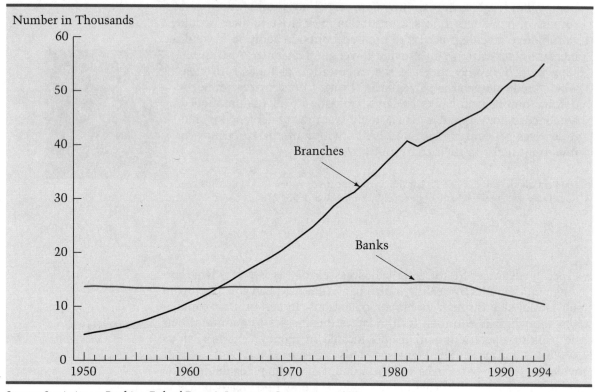

Source: *Statistics on Banking,* Federal Deposit Insurance Corporation, 1995.

Bank Holding Companies

bank holding company
company that holds voting power in two or more banks through stock ownership

The **bank holding company** is a device whereby two or more individual banks are controlled through one company that has voting control. The policies of banks thus controlled by such a holding company are determined by the parent company and coordinated for the purposes of that organization. The holding company itself may or may not engage in direct banking activities. The banks that are controlled by the holding company may operate branches.

Little control was exercised over bank holding companies until the depression years of the early 1930s. Bank holding companies did not come under the jurisdiction of either state or federal control unless they also engaged directly in banking operations themselves. The Banking Act of 1933 and the Securities Acts of 1933 and 1934 imposed limited control on bank holding companies, but it remained for the Bank Holding Company Act of 1956 to establish clear authority over these operations.

The Bank Holding Company Act defined a bank holding company as one which directly or indirectly owns, controls, or holds the power to vote 25 percent or more of the voting shares of each of two or more banks. The Bank Holding Company Act Amendments of 1966 established uniform standards to evaluate the legality of bank holding company acquisitions. But it remained for the Bank Holding Company Amendments of 1970 to provide the basis for modern bank operations. These amendments provide that bank holding companies can acquire companies having activities closely related to banking, such as credit card operations, insurance, and data processing services.

BANKS AND WALL STREET

Banks are currently spending billions of dollars to get into Wall Street. Many bankers view banking, at least the money lending function, as a mature business. In contrast, Wall Street, in the eyes of at least some bankers, offers potentially large profits through security trading revenues and money-management fees. (We will discuss securities markets and participants in Chapter 11.)

Pittsburgh's Mellon Bank, for example, has made a major move into Wall Street. In 1993, the Boston Company, with a large investment and trust business, was purchased from American Express for $1.45 billion. Then, in 1994, Dreyfus, with a large mutual funds operation, was purchased for $1.8 billion.

However, rather than large profits, Mellon has found its ventures into Wall Street to be risky endeavors—at least in the short-run. The previously high fees the Boston Company charged on its mutual fund administration business have been reduced due to increased competition and other developments.

Furthermore, the values of fixed-interest-rate debt securities declined when interest rates rose in 1994. (We will see why this relationship exists when we get to Chapter 10.) Dreyfus was particularly hard hit because most of its assets were in debt instruments with fixed interest rates. The resulting decline in values, along with investor withdrawals, resulted in a decline in assets under management and lower profits.

Evidence suggests that Wall Street is different from banking. Whether the combining of banks and Wall Street firms is advantageous from a profitability standpoint remains to be seen.

Source: Terence P. Pare, "A Bitter Lesson for Banks," *Fortune* (August 21, 1995), pp. 54–55.

A major development of the last few years has been the merging of financially troubled S&Ls with bank holding companies. Among the largest of these mergers is that of Western S&L of Phoenix, Arizona, which was acquired by BankAmerica Corp. The collapse of the real estate market in Arizona has resulted in the bankruptcy of virtually every S&L in that state, including Western. S&Ls in the southwestern part of the United States have been especially hard hit by the boom-and-bust in the real estate market. Bank holding companies have acquired financially distressed commercial banks as well as S&Ls. Each monthly issue of the *Federal Reserve Bulletin* lists approved mergers of S&Ls and commercial banks with bank holding companies.

The liberalization of regulations relating to interstate banking is as significant as the liberalization of branch banking within states. At this time 48 states permit the acquisition of banks by out-of-state bank holding companies. In contrast, only one state permitted interstate banking before 1982. Although the majority of state laws still limit entry to banking organizations from nearby states, called regional reciprocal, some states are beginning to permit entry on a nationwide basis, known as national reciprocal or open-entry. Recent congressional actions have paved the way for passage of a nationwide banking bill. In anticipation, large banking mergers have been occurring in an effort to establish nationwide empires.

INTERNATIONAL BANKING

The growth of international banking in recent years has been just as dramatic as the growth of interstate banking. The United States has long maintained banking facilities on either a branch or agency basis in foreign countries, and other countries have had banking representation in the United States. However, the burst of expansion in these facilities in recent years now gives banking a strongly international character. Foreign interests have been attracted to commercial banking in the United States just as they have been attracted to business firms in general. The growing financial strength of certain foreign nations and the attraction of competitive lending opportunities in the United States are among the factors generating this interest. Foreigners found special opportunity for commercial banking in the United States because they were not subject to the same restrictions as domestic banks. For example, foreign banks were able to engage in interstate banking long before domestic banks.

A "level playing field" for all banks, both domestic and foreign, was largely achieved through the passage of the International Banking Act of 1978. On December 19, 1991, Congress strengthened regulations relating to foreign banks by enacting the Foreign Bank Supervision Enhancement Act. This act was intended to fill gaps in supervision and regulation of foreign banks and to insure that the banking policies established by Congress were implemented in a fair and consistent manner.

The level playing field for commercial banks in the United States has not meant level banking interests throughout the world. Japan, as well as other countries, continues to offer regulatory resistance in those countries to U.S. banking interests. Further, Japan's favorable balance of trade has made it necessary to invest abroad to accommodate its large accumulation of foreign wealth. That nation's high savings rate adds to this need for foreign investment. Japanese banks have invested heavily in commercial banking throughout the world as they have in nonbanking enterprises. To a lesser extent European banking interests, especially those of Great Britain and West Germany, have also moved into U.S. banking. Hong Kong and British banks have established important positions in the U.S. commercial lending market. Commercial banking in the United States is now truly international. By 1993 foreign banks held approximately 30 percent of all U.S. loans and securities.

NONBANK FINANCIAL CONGLOMERATES

In competition with the large bank holding companies are **nonbank financial conglomerates.** These financial supermarkets have now become dominant in many areas of financial service. Without the regulatory constraints of the banking system, there is virtually no limit to the scope of their activities.

nonbank financial conglomerates
large corporations that offer various financial services

Sears Roebuck & Company at one time owned virtually every form of significant financial service, including mortgage insurance, real estate management, consumer finance, leasing, commercial banking, auto and fire insurance, and investment banking. Of special interest was the acquisition and later disposition of the investment banking firm of Dean Witter Reynolds, Inc. Other investment banking firms have been acquired by financial conglomerates. For example, Prudential Insurance Company purchased the Bache Group Securities, Inc., and Travelers Insurance purchased Dillon Reed and Company. Other major conglomerates include General Electric Company, Primerica, and American Express Company.

Firms such as General Motors, Ford Motor Company, International Harvester, and others have for many years owned financial subsidiaries to support sales. However, the supermarket conglomerates of today come close to creating their own financial universes. Early in this chapter we saw that one of the purposes of the Monetary Control Act and the Garn-St. Germain Act was to enable banks, S&Ls, savings banks, and credit unions to compete on equal terms with the money market mutual funds of the conglomerates. These acts have provided help in the competitive race with the nonbank conglomerates, but depository institutions continue to operate at a distinct disadvantage.

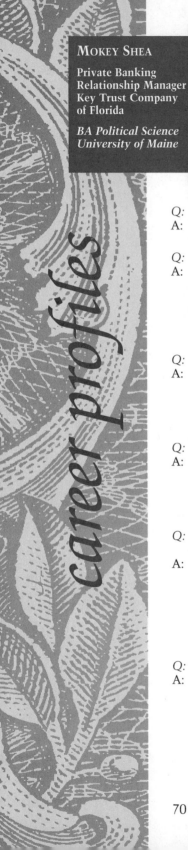

MOKEY SHEA

Private Banking Relationship Manager Key Trust Company of Florida

BA Political Science University of Maine

"The whole basis for this service is that I become very familiar with the personal finances of the client."

Q: *What is Private Banking?*

A: Private Banking means providing very personalized and specialized services to high net worth individuals and families.

Q: *What kind of services are involved?*

A: We use a team approach to meet the needs of these clients. I supply the checking, savings, and mortgage instruments, the normal retail banking pieces. There is a brokerage officer on the team who provides investment services. Then we have a trust officer who deals with issues such as estate planning. It's not unusual for a bank or other financial services company to provide all of these functions. What's new about private banking is that we all work as a team rather than independently.

Q: *How high does a client's net worth need to be to qualify?*

A: There are several criteria we look for, but in general we look for investible assets of $250,000. This would be above and beyond whatever they have invested in real estate. We're located in Naples, Florida, which has an unusual number of wealthy retirees that fit the profile we look for. There are other banks in town that require even higher net worth to qualify for their private banking services.

Q: *You're a "Relationship Manager." What is that?*

A: The whole basis for this service is that I become very familiar with and involved in the personal finances of the client. The more I know about their financial situation and needs, the better our team can meet those needs. It really is a relationship. I get to know their families, learn about their lifestyles, discuss their futures, including what happens after they die. So the term Relationship Manager is very accurate.

Q: *You were a branch manager for Key Bank before you took your current position. How would you describe that experience?*

A: I ran a branch in Maine with about a dozen employees. In that setting you need to be a true jack-of-all-trades. At nine o'clock I might open a savings account for a 12-year-old who has a paper route. At ten o'clock I might discuss a $100,000 business loan. At eleven o'clock I might open a checking account for a small business. So I was dealing with every imaginable kind of client. Plus I had the management and operations responsibilities. I was essentially running a small bank. I had profitability targets I needed to meet and other requirements set at our main office.

Q: *Do you miss anything about that job?*

A: It was a tough job because it combined the sales and management roles. Either one of those roles is plenty of work. Doing both demands a lot. The thing I miss the most is working with new businesses and watching them grow from ideas into successes. Most of my private banking clients are past the point of starting a new business. But what I like about my current job is that I get so involved with my clients. I can be much more focused on them and spend more time with them compared to the branch environment where it's a continuous stream of different people all day long.

70

SUMMARY

This chapter began with a review of the history of the U.S. banking system. Banking prior to the Civil War was described first followed by how and when thrift institutions entered the banking system. Legislation passed to govern the banking system and to protect depositors' funds then was covered.

From the beginning of the nation's history, laws have shaped and channeled the activities of banks, savings and loan associations, savings banks, and credit unions. However, a number of these laws have, in fact, been partially responsible for some of the major problems of these institutions in recent years.

Modern depository institutions accept deposits and grant loans. They also provide safekeeping for depositors, transference of payments through checking services, record keeping, and risk selection functions. The principal assets of depository institutions are cash, securities, and loans. Sources of funds include liabilities, primarily deposits and deferred credits, and owners' equity. Traditional distinctions in functions by type of depository institution have become blurred over time and it is now difficult to distinguish among these institutions.

Concentration in banking control takes place primarily in the form of branch banking and through bank holding companies. The banking environment within the financial system has also been influenced greatly in recent years by the growth of international banking and through competition from nonbank financial conglomerates.

KEY TERMS

bank holding company
banking system
branch banks
certificates of deposit
nonbank financial
    conglomerates

prime rate
secured loan
thrift institutions
unsecured loan

DISCUSSION QUESTIONS

1. Describe the composition of depository institutions that make up the banking system.
2. Compare the operations of commercial banks during the nation's colonial period with those of today's modern commercial banks.
3. How vital a role has the banking system played in the development of the U.S. economy? Has its importance decreased or increased with industrialization?

4. Distinguish between commercial banks and thrift institutions.
5. Why was it considered necessary to create the Federal Reserve System when we already had the benefits of the National Banking Act?
6. Comment on the objectives of the Depository Institutions Deregulation and Monetary Control Act of 1980.
7. Why was the Garn-St. Germain Depository Institutions Act thought to be necessary?
8. Describe the principal functions of the four depository institutions that make up the banking system.
9. Why do regulatory authorities insist on certain minimum capital requirements for depository institutions before they may begin operations?
10. What are the sources of capital for depository institutions? Why would an institution wish to increase its capital after operations had begun and its initial capital requirements were met?
11. Bank regulatory authorities recently increased the standard for the ratio of primary capital to total assets. Why was this action taken?
12. Has concentration in banking control in the United States been decreasing or increasing in recent years? Explain the developments in branch banking and in bank holding companies that have been taking place in the United States.
13. Describe the functions assigned to the Resolution Trust Corporation created in 1988.
14. In 1989, the Financial Institutions Reform, Recovery, and Enforcement Act was passed. What are the special features of this legislation?
15. Describe the development and significance of international banking.
16. Comment on the problems faced by the Federal Deposit Insurance Corporation.

PROBLEMS

1. From a recent issue of the *Federal Reserve Bulletin*, identify, on a consolidated basis for all commercial banks,
   a) the dollar amount of the principal sources of funds and
   b) the dollar amount of the principal uses to which the funds were applied.
   For each source and use of funds, compute the percentage represented by each relative to the total sources and uses.
2. As the treasurer of a mid-size industrial manufacturer, your firm's cash balances vary between $300,000 and $1,000,000. During the last three board meetings a board member has asked how you protect this cash while it is being lodged in banks or other temporary facilities. Your problem is to satisfy the board member, obtain some income from the

cash or cash equivalent balances, and have funds available for immediate payout if required. What course of action do you follow?

3. You and three other staff members of the U.S. Office of Comptroller of
    the Currency have been assigned identical projects. You are to review
    the various articles that have been written, the various speeches made,
    and in general the various suggestions that have been offered to
    revamp the structure of the FDIC in order to render it more stable and
    financially able to withstand adverse events. Based on the few sugges-
    tions offered in this chapter and on the basis of your own ideas, what
    is your conclusion?

4. You are the mayor of a community of 12,000 people. You are active in
    virtually all of the civic activities of the town and as such your opin-
    ion is solicited on political, economic, sociological and other factors.
    You have been asked by one of the civic groups to comment on the
    implications for the community of a prospective purchase of the
    largest local commercial bank by an out-of-state bank holding company.
    What is your response?

SELF-TEST QUESTIONS

1. From 1836 until the Civil War, the banking system was dominated by:
    a.   the Second Bank of the United States
    b.   the First Bank of the United States
    c.   savings banks
    d.   state chartered banks
2. The National Banking Act of 1864:
    a.   provided for the creation of a central bank
    b.   provided for the creation of a group of central banks
    c.   made possible the chartering of banks by the federal government
    d.   was repealed because of a host of unrelated amendments
3. Thrift depositories came into existence in the early 1800s primarily to:
    a.   provide a financial basis for home financing
    b.   provide safe depositories for individual savers
    c.   assist consumer finance institutions
    d.   provide high rates of interest income for savers
4. Commercial banks obtain the bulk of their loanable funds from:
    a.   depositors
    b.   the issue of certificates of deposit
    c.   the sale of bank stock
    d.   the sale of subordinated debenture bonds
5. Interstate banks are now:
    a.   permitted on a reciprocal basis by all states
    b.   considered desirable but not yet permitted

    c.   permitted in a majority of states on a regional basis

    d.   not permitted in any state

6. The bank holding company is important primarily:
   a. as a facility for the safekeeping of bank assets
   b. as a means of concentrating bank control
   c. to raise large sums of capital
   d. to implement branch banking
7. Our system of national banks:
   a. was designed to destroy state banking
   b. was an integral part of the Federal Reserve Act
   c. was replaced by Federal Reserve banking
   d. came into existence during the Civil War
8. The Garn-St. Germain Depository Institutions Act:
   a. liberalized money lending and raising practices by S&L's
   b. had little impact on depository practices
   c. was the full title of the National Banking Act
   d. provides the basis for revising the operations of the FDIC
9. The First and Second banks of the United States:
   a. coexisted for a period of 20 years
   b. had very little impact on banking in general
   c. played an important role in the early history of U.S. banking
   d. failed because of poor management

SELF-TEST PROBLEM

The Biz-You Company wants to borrow $70,000 which it plans to repay in one year. One bank quotes a discount loan at 8 percent. Another bank offers the loan at a prime rate of 8.5 percent. Compare the relative effective percentage costs of these two loan alternatives.

SUGGESTED READINGS

Calem, Paul S. "The Proconsumer Argument for Interstate Branching." *Business Review,* Federal Reserve Bank of Philadelphia (May–June 1993): 15–29.

Campbell, Tim S., and William A. Kracaw. *Financial Institutions and Capital Markets.* New York: Harper Collins, 1993. Chapters 4 and 5.

Dewey, D.R. *Financial History of the United States,* 12e. New York: Longmans, Green & Co., 1934.

Frankel, Allen B., and Paul B. Morgan. "Deregulation and Competition in Japanese Banking." *Federal Reserve Bulletin* (August 1992): 579–593.

Hammond, Bray. *Banks and Politics in America from the Revolution to the Civil War.* Princeton, NJ: Princeton University Press, 1957.

Haubrich, Joseph G., Paul Watchel. "Capital Requirements and Shifts in Commercial Bank Portfolios." *Economic Review,* Federal Reserve Bank of Cleveland (Quarter 3 1993): 2–15.

Kaufman, George G., and Larry R. Mote. "Is Banking a Declining Industry?: A Historical Perspective." *Economic Perspectives*, Federal Reserve Bank of Chicago (May/June 1994): 2–21.

Rose, Peter S., and James W. Kolari. *Financial Institutions: Understanding and Managing Financial Services*. Homewood, IL: Irwin, 1995. Chapter 6.

Russel, Steven. "The Government's Role in Deposit Insurance." *Review*, Federal Reserve Bank of St. Louis (January/February 1993): 3–9.

Saunders, Anthony. *Financial Institutions Management: A Modern Perspective*. Burr Ridge, IL: Irwin, 1994. Chap. 1.

Savage, Donald T. "Interstate Banking: A Status Report." *Federal Reserve Bulletin* (December 1993): 1076–1089.

Todd, Walker F. "FDICIA's Emergency Liquidity Provisions." *Economic Review*, Federal Reserve Bank of Cleveland (Quarter 3 1993): 16–23.

ANSWERS TO SELF-TEST QUESTIONS   1. d, 2. c, 3. b, 4. a, 5. c, 6. b, 7. d, 8. a, 9. c

ANSWER TO SELF-TEST PROBLEM

The interest cost on the loan offered at an 8.5 percent prime rate is $5,950 ($70,000 times 0.085) The effective cost is 8.5 percent ($5,950/$70,000). In contrast, the 8 percent discount loan has an effective interest rate of 8.7 percent. First, $5,600 ($70,000 times 0.08) is deducted from the $70,000 loan principal, providing a net loan amount of $64,400 ($70,000 − $5,950). Second, the $5,600 interest divided by the funds available for use of $64,400 is 8.7 percent. Thus the loan offered at a prime rate of 8.5 percent would be preferred.

CHAPTER 4

Federal Reserve System

AFTER STUDYING THIS CHAPTER, YOU SHOULD BE ABLE TO:

- Identify the major financial and banking problems that gave rise to the Federal Reserve System in the United States.
- Describe the general structure of the Federal Reserve System.
- List and discuss the functions of the Federal Reserve System.
- Explain the methods by which the Federal Reserve System carries out the important function of controlling the size of the money supply.
- Describe the ways in which the Reserve Banks accommodate the clearance and collection of checks.

U.S. BANKING PRIOR TO WORLD WAR I

In order to understand the importance of the Federal Reserve Act of 1913 it is important to review the weaknesses of the banking system that gave rise to that Act. Although the National Banking Act had resulted in substantial improvements in banking practices, certain weaknesses persisted. And as the economy expanded, new problems developed. The National Banking Act provided a sound basis for the holding of reserves and the issuance of notes by banks. As we shall see, however, the constraints on note issuance, in the interest of prudent bank management, made it difficult for banks to meet the credit needs of an expanding economy. These matters are discussed below.

WEAKNESSES OF THE BANKING SYSTEM

One of the main weaknesses of the banking system in the late 1800s was the arrangement for holding reserves. A large part of the reserve balances of banks was held as deposits with large city banks, in particular with large New York City banks. Banks outside of the large cities were permitted to keep part of their reserves with their large city bank correspondents. Certain percentages of deposits had to be retained in their own vaults. These were the only alternatives for holding reserve balances. During periods of economic stress, the position of these large city banks was precarious because they had to meet the demand for deposit withdrawals by their own customers as well as by the smaller banks. The frequent inability of the large banks to meet such deposit withdrawal demands resulted in extreme hardship for the smaller banks whose reserves they held.

Another weakness of the banking system under the National Banking Act was the method used to issue bank notes. In an effort to provide the nation with a sound national currency, no provision had been made for the expansion or contraction of national bank notes to reflect variations in business activity. The volume of national bank notes was governed not by the needs of business but rather by the availability and price of government bonds.

The National Banking Act provided that national banks could issue their own notes only against U.S. government bonds the banks held on deposit with the Treasury. Note issues were limited to 90 percent of the par value, as stated on the face of the bond, or the market value of the bonds, whichever was lower. When bonds sold at prices considerably above their par value, the advantage of purchasing bonds as a basis to issue notes was eliminated.

For example, if a $1,000 par value bond were available for purchase at a price of $1,150, the banks would not be inclined to make such a purchase since a maximum of $900 in notes could be issued against the bond, in this case 90 percent of par value. The interest that the bank could earn from the use of the $900 in notes would not be great enough to offset the high price of the bond. When government bonds sold at par or at a discount, on the other hand, the potential earning power of the note issues would be quite attractive and banks would be encouraged to purchase bonds for note issue purposes. The volume of national bank notes, therefore, depended on the government bond market rather than the seasonal or cyclical needs of the nation for currency.

CENTRAL BANKING

The U.S. financial system of the late 1800s appeared to suffer not so much from the shortcomings of the National Banking Act as from the lack of an effective banking structure. Yet a single theme ran through the proposals and counterproposals that preceded the enactment of the Federal Reserve Act: opposition to a strong central banking system. The vast western frontiers and the local independence of the southern areas created distrust of centralized financial control. This distrust deepened by the experience of trust-busting under President Theodore Roosevelt, during the years immediately preceding the Federal Reserve Act. Many of the predatory practices of the large corporate combinations were at that time being made public through legislative commissions and investigations.

The controversy between industrial and financial centers on the one hand and the less developed western and southern states persists to a certain extent to the present time. The senatorial arrangement of two senators from each state is a reflection of this perceived need for adequate representation on the political front. A strong central bank could be counted on, it was assumed at the time, to support restrictive monetary practices at the expense of the credit needs of outlying areas. The financial panic of 1907 illustrates the well justified suspicion of the financial centers of the nation. Trust companies during the early years of this century were comparatively unrestricted by law. Many of these companies branched out into commercial banking and kept inadequate reserves. Inadequacy of reserves made them vulnerable to the first signs of economic downturns. The failure of many of these trust companies resulted in a major financial panic and a growing distrust of centralized financial power.

The United States was one of the last major industrial nations to adopt a permanent system of central banking. However, many financial and political leaders had long recognized the advantages of such a system. These supporters of central banking were given a big boost by the financial panic of 1907. The central banking system adopted by the United States was, in fact, a compromise between the system of independently owned banks in existence in this country and the central banking systems of such countries as Canada, Great Britain, Spain, and Germany. This compromise took the form of a series of central banks, each representing a specific region of the United States. The assumption was that each central bank would be more responsive to the particular financial problems of its region.

central bank
federal government agency that facilitates operation of the financial system and regulates money supply growth

A **central bank** is a Federal government agency that facilitates operation of the financial system and regulates growth of the money supply. In many respects, a central bank resembles a commercial bank with regard to services performed. A central bank lends money to its members; it is required to hold reserves; it is given the responsibility of creating money, generally through bank notes and deposits; and it has stockholders and a board of directors. In contrast with a commercial bank, a central bank is a "banker's bank" that does not generally deal directly with the public nor necessarily operate for profit.

STRUCTURE OF THE FEDERAL RESERVE SYSTEM

The **Federal Reserve System (Fed)** is the central bank in the United States and has responsibility for setting monetary policy and regulating the banking system. Under the authority of the Federal Reserve Act of 1913, 12 Federal Reserve districts were established. Each Federal Reserve district is served by a Federal Reserve Bank, and the activities of the 12 banks are in turn coordinated by a board of governors located in Washington, D.C. The members of the Board of Governors are also members of the Federal Open Market Committee. The Federal Advisory Council provides advice and general information to the Board of Governors. The organizational structure of the Federal Reserve System is shown in Figure 4.1.

Federal Reserve System (Fed)
U.S. central bank that sets monetary policy and regulates banking system

The Fed did not replace the system that existed under the National Banking Act but rather was superimposed upon it. Certain provisions of the National Banking Act, however, were modified to permit greater flexibility of operations.

FEDERAL RESERVE MEMBERSHIP

The Federal Reserve Act provided that all national banks were to become members of the Fed. In addition, state-chartered banks, as well as trust companies, were permitted to join the system if they could show evidence of a satisfactory financial condition. The Federal Reserve Act also required that all member banks purchase capital stock of the Reserve Bank of their district up to a maximum of 6 percent of their paid-in capital and surplus. In practice, however, member banks have had to pay in only 3 percent; the remainder is subject to call at the discretion of the Fed. Member banks are limited to a maximum of 6 percent dividends on the stock of the Reserve Bank that they hold. The Reserve Banks, therefore, are private institutions owned by the many member banks of the Fed.

State-chartered banks and trust companies are permitted to withdraw from membership with the Fed six months after written notice has been submitted to the Reserve Bank of their district. In such cases, the stock originally purchased by the withdrawing member is canceled, and a refund is made for all money paid in.

Approximately 40 percent of the nation's commercial banks are members of the Fed. This appears to be a rather small coverage of banks by the Federal Reserve compared with the 96 percent of all commercial banks

FIGURE 4.1   Organization of the Federal Reserve System

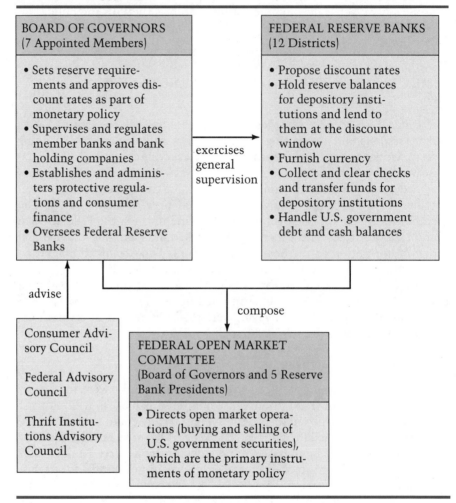

that carry insurance under the provisions of the Federal Deposit Insurance Corporation. These member banks, however, hold approximately 70 percent of the deposits of all commercial banks. Even this figure understates the importance of the Federal Reserve in the nation's financial system. As indicated in Chapter 3, the Monetary Control Act has generally eliminated distinctions between banks that are members of the Fed and other depository institutions by applying comparable reserve and reporting requirements to all these institutions.

FEDERAL RESERVE BANKS

Directors and Officers

Each Reserve Bank has corporate officers and a board of directors. The selection of officers and directors, however, is unlike that of other corporations. Each Reserve Bank has on its board nine directors, who must be residents of the district in which they serve. The directors serve terms of three years, with appointments staggered so that three directors are appointed each year. In order to assure that the various economic elements of the Federal Reserve districts are represented, the nine members of the board of directors are divided into three groups: Class A, Class B, and Class C.

Both Class A and Class B directors are elected by the member banks of the Federal Reserve district. The Class A directors represent member banks of the district, while the Class B directors represent nonbanking interests. These nonbanking interests are commerce, agriculture, and industry. The Class C directors are appointed by the Board of Governors of the Federal Reserve System. These persons may not be stockholders, directors, or employees of existing banks.

The majority of the directors of the Reserve Banks are elected by the member banks of each district. However, the three nonbanking members of each board appointed by the Board of Governors of the Federal Reserve System are in a more strategic position than the other board members. One member appointed by the Board of Governors is designated chairperson of the board of directors and Federal Reserve agent, and a second member is appointed deputy chairperson. The Federal Reserve agent is the Board of Governors' representative at each Reserve Bank. He or she is responsible for maintaining the collateral that backs the Federal Reserve notes issued by each Reserve Bank.

Each Reserve Bank also has a president and first vice-president who are appointed by its board of directors and approved by the Board of Governors. A Reserve Bank may have several additional vice-presidents. The president is responsible for executing policies established by the board of directors and for the general administration of Reserve Bank affairs. All other officers and personnel of the Reserve Bank are subject to the authority of the president.

Federal Reserve Branch Banks

In addition to the 12 Reserve Banks, 25 branch banks have been established. These branch banks are located for the most part in geographical areas not conveniently served by the Reserve Banks themselves. For this reason, the geographically large western Federal Reserve districts have a majority of the Reserve Branch Banks. The San Francisco district has four, the Dallas district has three, and the Atlanta district has five branch banks. The New York Federal Reserve district, on the other hand, has only one branch bank, while the Boston district has no branches. The cities in which Reserve Banks and their branches are located are shown in Figure 4.2.

BOARD OF GOVERNORS

Fed Board of Governors seven-member board of the Federal Reserve that sets monetary policy

The ***Fed Board of Governors*** is composed of seven members and is responsible for setting monetary policy. Each member is appointed for a term of 14 years. The purpose of the 14-year term undoubtedly was to reduce political pressure on the board. Board members can be of any political party, and there is no specific provision concerning the qualifications a member must have. All members are appointed by the President of the United States with the advice and consent of the Senate. One member is designated as the chairperson and another as the vice-chairperson.

FIGURE 4.2   The Federal Reserve System

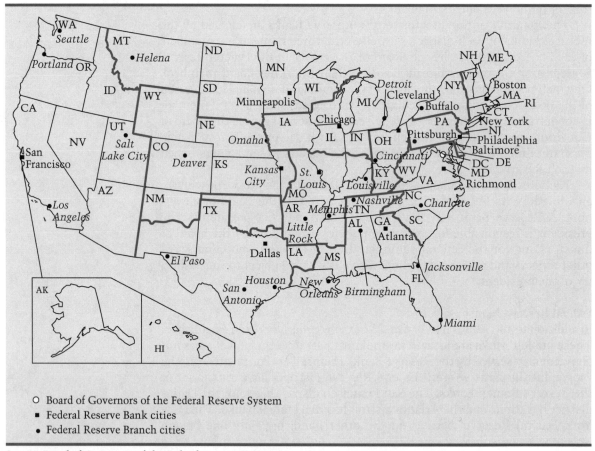

○ Board of Governors of the Federal Reserve System
■ Federal Reserve Bank cities
● Federal Reserve Branch cities

Source: Board of Governors of the Federal Reserve System.

Special authority attaches to the chairperson of any board. The chair of the Board of Governors of the Federal Reserve System is no exception. The holder of that position is generally recognized as the single most powerful influence on monetary policy in the nation. As for any chairperson, the power derives in large measure from the personality, experience, and leadership of the individual.

CHAIRMAN OF THE BOARD

In earlier years, Board presidents Arthur F. Burns and Paul A. Volcker ran one-man shows. In a sense, they had a powerful constituency. Each enjoyed so much prestige that political pressures directed toward them were generally blunted, including presidential efforts to spur aggressive actions against threats of recession. Both Burns and Volcker dominated the Board during their tenures, and the Federal Open Market Committee consistently responded to their leadership.

When Volcker resigned as chairman in June 1987, the financial markets reacted negatively. The U.S. dollar fell relative to other currencies and U.S. government and corporate bond prices fell. Why? In a word, "uncertainty"—uncertainty about the future direction of monetary policy. Volcker was a known inflation fighter. In contrast, the policies of the incoming Fed Chairman, Alan Greenspan, were unknown.

The appointive power of the President and the ability of Congress to alter its structure makes the Board of Governors a dependent political structure. However, it enjoys much independence in its operations by virtue of popular support by the public. The Board of Governors of the Federal Reserve System is, in fact, one of the most powerful monetary organizations in the world. The chairman of the board plays an especially influential role in policy formulation. Because the board attempts to achieve its goals without political considerations, disagreement between the administration in power and the board is common. From time to time pressures from Congress or the President have undoubtedly influenced the board's decisions, but its semi-independence generally prevails.

In addition to setting the nation's monetary policy, the board gives direction and coordination to the activities of the 12 Reserve Banks under its jurisdiction. The board reviews and approves the discount-rate actions of the 12 Reserve Banks. The board is responsible for approving the applications of state-chartered banks applying for membership in the system. It is also responsible for recommending the removal of officers and directors of member banks when they break rules established by the Fed and other regulatory authorities. In addition, the board implements many of the credit control devices that have come into existence in recent decades such as the Truth-in-Lending Act, the Equal Credit Opportunity Act, and the Home Mortgage Disclosure Act.

There is general agreement that in carrying out its various functions the Fed has achieved much respect and confidence on the part of the citizens of the nation. The semi-independence of the system reassures most people that raw politics does not shape policy. From the viewpoint of competition among depository institutions, small firms especially benefit from the backing afforded by their Reserve Banks. The net result has been an improvement of both the stability and growth of the economy.

FEDERAL OPEN MARKET COMMITTEE

As early as 1922, efforts were made to coordinate the timing of purchases and sales of securities by the Federal Reserve Banks in order to achieve desirable national monetary policy objectives. The Federal Open Market Committee (FOMC), with the additional powers granted to it by the Banking Act of 1935, has full control over all open market operations of the Reserve Banks. This committee consists of the seven members of the Board of Governors of the Fed plus five presidents of Reserve Banks.

FUNCTIONS OF THE FEDERAL RESERVE SYSTEM

monetary policy formulated by the Fed to regulate money supply growth

The primary responsibility of the Fed is to formulate **monetary policy** which involves regulating the growth of the supply of money, and therefore regulating its cost and availability. By exercising its influence on the monetary system of the United States, the Fed performs a unique and important function: the promotion of economic stability. It is notable that the system's broad powers to affect economic stabilization and monetary control were not present when the Fed came into existence in 1913. At that time, the system was meant to provide for the contraction and expansion of the money supply as dictated by economic conditions, serve as bankers' banks in times of economic crisis, provide a more effective check clearance system, and establish a more effective regulatory system. Much of these responsibilities initially fell to the 12 Reserve Banks, but as the scope of responsibility for the monetary system was broadened, power was concentrated with the Board of Governors. Today the responsibilities of the Fed may be described as those relating to monetary policy, to supervision and regulation, and to services provided for depository institutions and the government.

DYNAMIC, DEFENSIVE, AND ACCOMMODATIVE FUNCTIONS

Public discussions of Fed operations are almost always directed toward *dynamic actions* that stimulate or repress the level of prices or economic activity. However, we should recognize that this area is but a minor part of the continuous operation of the Federal Reserve System. Far more significant in terms of time and effort are the defensive and accommodative

Alan Greenspan was appointed Fed chairman in June 1987 by Ronald Reagan. He was asked to "fill-the-shoes" of Paul Volcker, who was responsible for guiding Fed policy in bringing down the double-digit inflation of the 1970s. Greenspan's first big test was the stock market crash of October 1987. He responded by immediately pumping liquidity into the banking system. The result was avoidance of monetary contraction and asset devaluation of the kind that followed the stock market crash of 1929. A reversal of policy occurred in mid-1988 when interest rates were raised to fight increasing inflation. A relatively mild recession then occurred during the 1990–91 period. However, inflation has been kept below the 3 percent level since then.

GREENSPAN: IS HE THE BEST FED CHAIRMAN EVER?

How does the business sector view Greenspan's performance? *Fortune* magazine recently surveyed 204 chief executive officers from the 1,000 largest U.S. corporations. An "astounding" 96 percent felt that Greenspan has done a good job and should be reappointed as the Fed chairman. Only time will tell whether this "confidence" will be justified in the future.

Source: Rob Norton, "In Greenspan We Trust," *Fortune* (March 18, 1996), pp. 39–47.

functions. *Defensive activities* are those that contribute to the smooth everyday functioning of the economy. Unexpected developments and shocks are continuously imposing themselves upon the economy; unless these events are countered by appropriate monetary actions, disturbances may develop. Large unexpected shifts of capital out of or into the country and very large financing efforts by big corporations may significantly alter the reserve positions of the banks. Similarly, buyouts and acquisitions of one corporation by another, supported by bank financing, also affect reserve positions. In our competitive market system unexpected developments contribute to the vitality of our economy. Monetary policy, however, has a special responsibility to smoothly absorb these events and avoid many of their traumatic short-term effects. The *accommodative function* of the nation's monetary system is the one with which we are the most familiar. Meeting the credit needs of individuals and institutions, clearing checks, and supporting depositories and other institutions represent accommodative activities.

MONETARY POLICY FUNCTIONS AND INSTRUMENTS

The basic policy instruments of the Fed are setting reserve requirements for depository institutions (banks, for short), lending to banks, and open market operations. By setting reserve requirements, the Fed establishes the maximum amount of deposits the banking system can support with a given level of reserves. The amount of reserves can be affected directly through open market operations, thereby causing a contraction or expansion of deposits by the banking system. Discount or interest rate policy on loans to banks also affects the availability of reserves to banks and influences the way they adjust to changes in their reserve positions. Thus the Fed has a set of tools that together enable it to influence the size of the money supply in working to attain its broader economic objectives.

Reserve Requirements

Banks are required to hold reserves equal to a specified percentage of their deposits. The assets which may be counted as reserves are vault cash and deposits with the Reserve Banks. If a depository institution has reserves in excess of the required amount, it may lend them out. This is how they earn a profit, and it is also the way in which the money supply is expanded. In our system of fractional reserves, control of the volume of checkable deposits depends primarily on reserve management. In Chapter 5 the mechanics of money supply expansion and contraction are explained in detail.

The reserve ratio is essential to the Fed's control. The closer to the required minimum the banking system maintains its reserves, the tighter the control the Fed has over the money creation process through its other instruments. If the banking system has close to the minimum of reserves (that is, if excess reserves are near zero), then a reduction of reserves forces the system to tighten credit in order to reduce deposits. If substantial excess reserves exist, the pressure of reduced reserves is not felt so strongly. When reserves are added to the banking system, depositories may expand their lending but are not forced to do so. However, since depositories earn no interest on reserves, profit maximizing motivates them to lend out excess reserves to the fullest extent consistent with their liquidity requirements. When interest rates are high this motivation is especially strong.

The ability to change reserve requirements is a powerful tool the Fed uses infrequently. For a number of reasons, the Fed prefers to use open market operations to change reserves rather than change reserve requirements. If reserve requirements are changed, the maximum amount of deposits that can be supported by a given level of reserves changes. Total deposits and the money supply can be contracted by holding the amount of reserves constant but raising the reserve requirement. Lowering reserve requirements provides the basis for expansion of money and credit.

It has been argued that changing reserve requirements is too powerful a tool and that its use as a policy instrument would destabilize the banking system. The institutional arrangements through which the banking system adjusts to changing levels of reserves might not respond as efficiently to changing reserve requirements. Another advantage of open market

While we focus on the characteristics, operations, and monetary policy of the Fed, central banks play important roles in all developed economies. Central banks can influence interest rates, inflation rates, and economic growth. However, the success of a central bank seems to depend on its ability to set monetary policy that is relatively independent of government intervention. We know that fighting inflation is a difficult monetary policy task. The task is made even more difficult if governments intervene in an effort to support their fiscal policies. (We address fiscal policy in Chapter 5.)

CENTRAL BANK MONETARY POLICY AROUND THE WORLD

Empirical evidence shows a link between central bank independence from government intervention and inflation and economic growth rates. For example, the central banks of the United States, Switzerland, and Germany (Bundesbank) are viewed as being relatively independent of government influence. These countries have had relatively lower inflation rates and relatively higher economic growth over time. In contrast, the central banks of Spain, New Zealand, and Italy are viewed as being much more closely tied to their countries' fiscal policies. These economies have been characterized by relatively higher inflation rates and relatively lower economic growth rates over time.

What conclusions can we draw? Central bank independence from government intervention has been important in the past when monetary policy has been used to control inflation. Furthermore, central bank independence has not adversely affected economic growth. Evidence suggests that these relationships likely will continue in the future.

Source: J. Bradford De Long and Lawrence H. Summers, "Macroeconomic Policy and Long-Run Growth," *Economic Review*, Federal Reserve Bank of Kansas City (Fourth Quarter 1992): 5–29.

operations is that they can be conducted quietly, while changing reserve requirements requires a public announcement. The Fed feels that some of its actions would be opposed if public attention were directed toward them.

Changing reserve requirements has been used as a policy instrument on occasion. In the late 1930s the nation's banks were in an overly liquid position because of excessive reserves. Banks had large amounts of loanable funds that businesses did not wish, or could not qualify, to borrow because of the continuing depression. The reserves were so huge that the Fed could no longer resolve the situation through its other policy instruments. Therefore it increased reserve requirements substantially in order to absorb excess reserves in the banking system.

Reserve requirements were lowered during World War II in order to assure adequate credit to finance the war effort. But they were raised again in the post-war period to absorb excess reserves. In the 1950s and early 1960s reserve requirements were lowered on several occasions during recessions. In each case, the lowering made available excess reserves to encourage bank lending, ease credit, and stimulate the economy. By using this policy tool, the Fed was publicly announcing its intention to ease credit, in hopes of instilling confidence in the economy.

In the late 1960s and 1970s, reserve requirements were selectively altered to restrain credit because the banking system was experimenting with new ways to get around Fed controls. Banks were using more negotiable certificates of deposit, Eurodollar borrowings, and other sources of reserve funds. This prompted the Fed to impose restraint on the banks by manipulating the reserve requirements on specific liabilities.

The evolution of the banking system eventually led Congress to pass the Depository Institutions Deregulation and Monetary Control Act (DIDMCA) of 1980, which makes significant changes in reserve requirements throughout the financial system. Up to this time the Fed had control over the reserve requirements of its members only. Nonmember banks were subject to reserve requirements established by their own states, and there was considerable variation among states. As checks written on member banks were deposited in nonmember banks, and vice versa, funds moved among banks whose deposits were subject to different reserve requirements. This reduced the Fed's control over the money supply.

The 1980 act applies uniform reserve requirements to all banks with certain types of accounts. For banks that were members of the Fed, these requirements are, in general, lower now than they were prior to the act. At the end of 1994, reserve requirements against transaction account balances were 3 percent on amounts up to $54 million and 10 percent on amounts more than $54 million. In general, transaction accounts include deposits against which the account holder is permitted to make withdrawals for purposes of making payments to third parties or others. Money market deposit accounts (MMDAs) are excluded.

Discount (Interest) Rates on Loans to Depository Institutions

One of the most important Fed policy instruments in the minds of the framers of the 1980 act (the DIDMCA) is the setting of discount (interest) rates on loans to depository institutions so that the amount of currency and loans available correspond to the needs of business. The discount power was given to the Reserve authorities as a basic part of the monetary and credit system because it was felt that it would be effective in regulating the volume of money and loans in the economy.

Loans to depository institutions by the Reserve Banks may take two forms. In one the borrowing institution may receive an *advance,* or loan, secured by its own promissory note together with eligible paper it owns.

In the second, the borrower may *discount,* or sell to the Reserve Bank, its eligible paper. **Eligible paper** includes securities of the U.S. government and federal agencies, promissory notes, mortgages of acceptable quality, and bankers' acceptances.

Stated in somewhat oversimplified terms, discount policy was intended to work in the following fashion. If the Fed wanted to cool an inflationary boom, it would raise the discount rate. An increase in the discount rate would lead to a general increase in interest rates for loans, decreasing the demand for short-term borrowing for additions to inventory and accounts receivable. This in turn would lead to postponing the building of new production facilities and, therefore, to a decreased demand for capital goods. As a consequence, the rate of increase in income would slow down. In time, income would decrease and with it the demand for consumer goods. Holders of inventories financed by borrowed funds would liquidate their stocks in an already weak market. The resulting drop in prices would tend to stimulate the demand for, and reduce the supply of, goods. Thus economic balance would be restored. A reduction in the discount rate was expected to have the opposite effect.

Discount policy is no longer a major instrument of monetary policy and, in fact, is now regarded more as an adjustment or fine-tuning mechanism. As an adjustment mechanism, the discount arrangement does provide some protection to depository institutions in that other aggressive control actions may be temporarily moderated by the ability of banks to borrow. For example, the Fed may take a strong restrictive position through open market operations. Individual banks may counter the pressure by borrowing from their Reserve Banks. The Reserve Banks are willing to tolerate what appears to be an avoidance of their efforts while banks are adjusting to the pressure being exerted. Failure to reduce their level of borrowing can always be countered by additional Fed open market actions. Discount borrowing fluctuates rapidly, but typically is in a range of 1 to 5 percent of total reserves. During the 1990s, excess reserves have generally exceeded borrowed reserves for the banking system as a whole.

Figure 4.3 shows year-end interest rates charged by the Federal Reserve Bank of New York for *adjustment credit* over the 1977–94 period. Adjustment credit takes the form of short-term loans made available to depository institutions that have temporary needs for funds not available through "reasonable" alternative sources. Reserve Banks also can make *seasonal credit* loans and *extended credit* loans which generally carry somewhat higher discount or interest rates. Each Reserve Bank can set its own interest rates on loans to depository institutions in its district. However, very little rate differences have occurred across the Fed's 12 districts in the past.

For comparative purposes, year-end bank prime rates presented in Chapter 3 are also plotted in Figure 4.3. The Fed lending rate and the bank prime rate generally "track" each other over time. Both interest rate series

eligible paper
short-term promissory notes eligible for discounting with Federal Reserve Banks

FIGURE 4.3   Fed Lending Rate versus Bank Prime Rate Changes, 1977–94

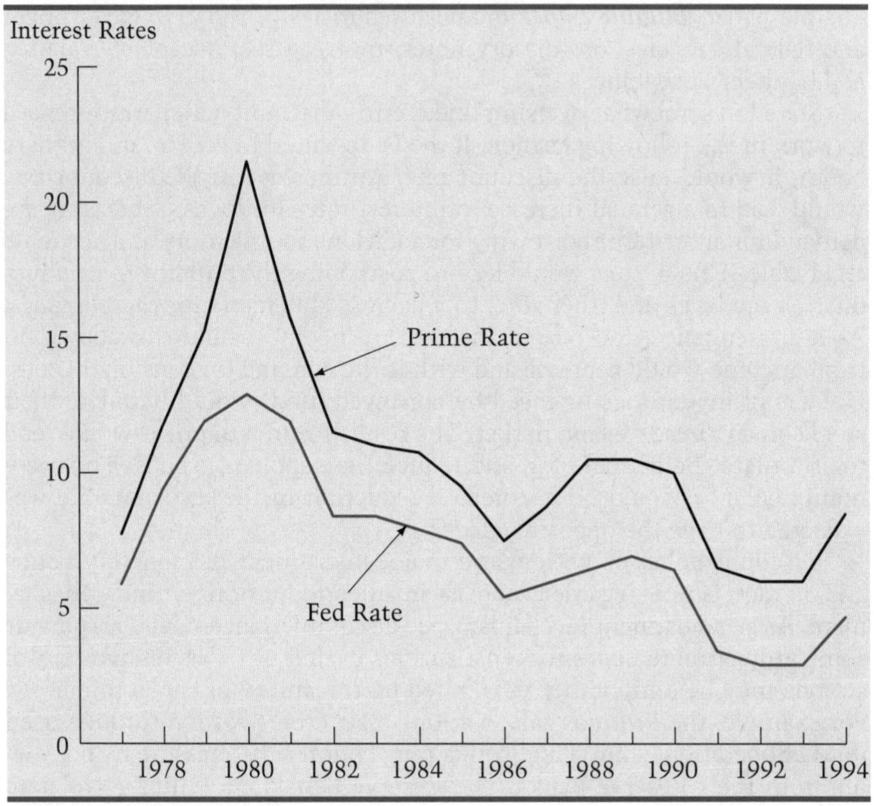

Interest Rates

Source: *Federal Reserve Bulletin,* various issues.

peaked at the end of 1980 and remained high during 1981 when inflation rates were also very high in the United States. The determinants of interest rates will be discussed in detail in Chapter 8. Notice that the Fed lending rate to depository institutions was consistently lower than the bank prime lending rate during the 1977–94 period.

Open Market Operations
The most used instrument of monetary policy is open market operations. **Open market operations** involve the purchase of securities by the Reserve Banks to put additional reserves at the disposal of the banking system or the sale of securities to reduce reserves. The original Federal Reserve Act did not provide for open market operations. In order to maintain stability in the money supply, this policy instrument developed out of the experience of the early post–World War I period.

open market operations *buying and selling of securities by the Federal Reserve to alter the supply of money*

From the beginning of their operations, Reserve Banks bought government securities with funds at their disposal to earn money for meeting expenses and to make a profit in order to pay dividends on the stock held by member banks. All 12 banks usually bought and sold the securities in the New York market. At times their combined sales were so large that they upset that market. Furthermore, the funds used to buy the bonds ended up in New York member banks and enabled them to reduce their borrowing at the Reserve Bank of New York. This made it difficult for the Reserve Bank of New York to maintain effective credit control in its area. As a result, an open market committee was set up to coordinate buying and selling of government bonds. In 1933 the Federal Open Market Committee was established by law. In 1935 its present composition was established: the Federal Reserve Board of Governors plus five of the presidents of the 12 Reserve Banks, who serve on a rotating basis.

Although not provided for in the original organization of the Fed, open market operations have become the most important and effective means of monetary and credit control. These operations can take funds out of the market and thus raise short-term interest rates and help restrain inflationary pressures. Or they can provide for easy money conditions and lowered short-term interest rates. Of course, such monetary ease will not necessarily start business on the recovery road after a recession. When used with discount policy, open market operations are an effective way of restricting credit or making it more easily available.

Open market operations differ from discount operations in that they increase or decrease reserves at the initiative of the Fed, not of individual banking institutions. The process in simplified form works as follows. If the Open Market Committee wants to buy government securities, it contacts dealers to ask for offers and then accepts the best offers that meet its needs. (The Fed restricts its purchases to U.S. government securities, primarily because of their liquidity and safety.) The dealers receive wire transfers of credit for the securities from the Reserve Banks. These credits are deposited with member banks. The member banks, in turn, receive credit for these deposits with their Reserve Banks, thus adding new reserves that form the basis for additional credit expansion.

If the Fed wants to reduce reserves, it sells government securities to the dealers. The dealers pay for them by a wire transfer from a depository to a Reserve Bank. The Reserve Bank then deducts the amount from the reserves of the depository.

Open market operations don't always lead to an immediate change in the volume of deposits. This is especially true when bonds are sold to restrict deposit growth. As bonds are sold by the Reserve Banks, some banks lose reserves and are forced to borrow from their Reserve Bank. Since they are under pressure from the Fed to repay the loan, they use funds from maturing loans to repay the Reserve Bank. Thus, credit can be gradually restricted as a result of the adjustments banks must make to open market operations.

SUPERVISORY AND REGULATORY FUNCTIONS

As the central bank for the nation, the Federal Reserve has a basic responsibility for the financial stability of the economy. This responsibility, shared with other agencies of the government, is directed primarily toward the depository institutions of the nation. A strong and stable depository system is vital to the growth and the stability of the entire economy. Depository supervision is primarily concerned with the safety and soundness of individual firms. It involves oversight to ensure that depository institutions are operated carefully. Depository regulation relates to the issuance of specific rules or regulations that govern the structure and conduct of operations.

Specific Supervisory Responsibilities

On-site examination of depository institutions is one of the System's most important responsibilities. This function is shared with the federal Office of the Comptroller of the Currency (OCC), the Federal Deposit Insurance Corporation, and state regulatory agencies. Although the Federal Reserve is authorized to examine all member banks, in practice it limits itself to state-chartered member banks and all bank holding companies. It cooperates with state examining agencies to avoid overlapping examining authority. The Office of the Comptroller directs its attention to nationally chartered banks and the FDIC supervises insured nonmember commercial banks.

In addition to these three federal banking supervisory agencies, two federal agencies have primary responsibility for supervising and regulating nonbank depository institutions. The National Credit Union Administration (NCUA) has the responsibility for supervising and regulating credit unions and the Office of Thrift Supervision (OTS) has responsibility for all other nonbank depository institutions. The examination of a nonbank depository institution generally entails (1) an appraisal of the soundness of the institution's assets; (2) an evaluation of internal operations, policies, and management; (3) an analysis of key financial factors, such as capital and earnings; (4) a review for compliance with all banking laws and regulations; and (5) an overall determination of the institution's financial condition.

The Federal Reserve conducts on-site inspections of parent bank holding companies and their nonbank subsidiaries. These inspections include a review of nonbank assets and funding activities to ensure compliance with the Bank Holding Company Act.

The Federal Reserve has broad powers to regulate the overseas activities of member banks and bank holding companies. Its aim is to allow U.S. banks to be fully competitive with institutions of host countries in financing U.S. trade and investment overseas. Along with the OCC and the FDIC, the Federal Reserve also has broad oversight authority for the supervision of all federal and state-licensed branches and agencies of foreign banks operating in the United States.

Specific Regulatory Responsibilities

The Federal Reserve has legal responsibility for the administration of the Bank Holding Company Act of 1956, the Bank Merger Act of 1960, and the Change in Bank Control Act of 1978. Under these acts, the Fed approves or denies the acquisitions of banks and other closely related nonbanking activities by bank holding companies. Furthermore, it permits or rejects changes of control and mergers of banks and bank holding companies.

The Federal Reserve has responsibilities for writing rules or enforcing a number of major laws that offer consumers protection in their financial dealings. In 1968 Congress passed the Consumer Credit Protection Act, which requires the clear explanation of consumer credit costs and garnishment procedures—taking wages or property by legal means—and prohibits overly high priced credit transactions. Regulation Z, which was drafted by a Federal Reserve task force, enacts the Truth in Lending section of the act. The purpose of the law and Regulation Z is to make consumers aware of, and able to compare, the costs of alternate forms of credit. Regulation Z applies to consumer finance companies, credit unions, sales finance companies, banks, S&Ls, residential mortgage brokers, credit card issuers, department stores, automobile dealers, hospitals, doctors, dentists, and any other individuals or organizations that extend or arrange credit for consumers.

The law requires a breakdown of the total finance charge and the annual percentage rate of charge. The finance charge includes all loan costs including not only interest or discount but service charges, loan fees, finder fees, insurance premiums, and points (an additional loan charge). Fees for such items as taxes not included in the purchase price, licenses, certificates of title, and the like may be excluded from the finance charge if they are itemized and explained separately. Figure 4.4 lists the Truth in Lending and other consumer protection acts that fall under Fed jurisdiction.

In addition to consumer protection laws, the Federal Reserve, through the Community Reinvestment Act of 1977, encourages depository institutions to help meet the credit needs of their communities for housing and other purposes while maintaining safe and sound operations. This is particularly true in neighborhoods of families with low or moderate income.

SERVICE FUNCTIONS

As the operating arm of the nation's central bank, the Reserve Banks provide a wide range of important services to depository institutions and to the U.S. government. The most important of these services is the payments mechanism, a system whereby billions of dollars are transferred each day.

FIGURE 4.4   Consumer Protection Responsibilities of the Federal Reserve System

- The *Truth in Lending Act* requires disclosure of the finance charge and the annual percentage rate of credit along with certain other costs and terms to permit consumers to compare the prices of credit from different sources. This act also limits liability on lost or stolen credit cards.

- The *Fair Credit Billing Act* sets up a procedure for the prompt correction of errors on a revolving charge account and prevents damage to credit ratings while a dispute is being settled.

- The *Equal Credit Opportunity Act* prohibits discrimination in the granting of credit on the basis of sex, marital status, race, color, religion, national origin, age, or receipt of public assistance.

- The *Fair Credit Reporting Act* sets up a procedure for correcting mistakes on credit records and requires that records be used only for legitimate business purposes.

- The *Consumer Leasing Act* requires disclosure of information to help consumers compare the cost and terms of one lease of consumer goods with another and to compare the cost of leasing versus buying on credit or for cash.

- The *Real Estate Settlement Procedures Act* requires disclosure of information about the services and costs involved at the time of settlement when property is transferred from seller to buyer.

- The *Electronic Fund Transfer Act* provides a basic framework regarding the rights, liabilities, and responsibilities of consumers who use electronic transfer services and of the financial institutions that offer them.

- The *Federal Trade Commission Improvement Act* authorizes the Federal Reserve Board to identify unfair or deceptive acts or practices on the part of banks and to issue regulations to prohibit them.

Source: *The Federal Reserve System Purposes & Functions,* Board of Governors of the Federal Reserve System, Washington, D.C., 1984.

Other services include electronic fund transfers, net settlement facilities, safekeeping and transfer of securities, and serving as fiscal agent for the United States.

The Payments Mechanism
The payments mechanism has many aspects, including providing currency and coin, processing and clearing checks, providing for the settlement of checks, and wire transfers.

   Currency and Coin. Discussion about the nation's trend toward a cashless society notwithstanding, we remain highly dependent on currency and coin. The Federal Reserve is responsible for ensuring that the economy has an adequate supply to meet the public's demand. Currency and coin are put into or retired from circulation by the Reserve Banks, which use depository institutions for this purpose. Virtually all currency in circulation is in the form of Federal Reserve notes. These notes are printed by the Bureau of Engraving and Printing of the U.S. Treasury.

Check Clearance and Collection. One of the Fed's important contributions to the smooth flow of financial interchange is facilitating the clearance and collection of checks of the depository institutions of the nation. Each Reserve Bank serves as a clearinghouse for all depository institutions in its district, provided that they agree to pay the face value on checks forwarded to them for payment.

An example of the check-clearance process through the Reserve Banks will demonstrate the facility with which these clearances are made at the present time. Assume that the owner of a business in Sacramento, California, places an order for merchandise with a distributor in San Francisco. The order is accompanied by a check drawn on the owner's depository in Sacramento. This check is deposited by the distributor with its depository in San Francisco, at which time the distributor receives a corresponding credit to its account with the depository. The distributor's depository will then send the check to the Reserve Bank of its district, also located in San Francisco. The Reserve Bank will in turn forward the check to the depository in Sacramento on which the check was originally drawn. The adjustment of accounts is accomplished at the Reserve Bank through an alternate debit and credit to the account of each depository institution concerned in the transaction. The San Francisco depository, which has honored the check of its customer, will receive an increase in its reserve with the Reserve Bank, while the depository in Sacramento will have its reserve decreased by a corresponding amount. The depository in Sacramento will then reduce the account of the business on which the check was written. Hence, the exchange is made with no transfer of currency.

CHECK CLEARANCE BETWEEN FEDERAL RESERVE DISTRICTS. If an order was also placed by the Sacramento firm with a distributor of goods in Chicago, the check would be subject to an additional step in being cleared through the Fed. The Chicago distributor, like the San Francisco distributor, deposits the check with the depository of its choice and in turn receives an increase in its account. The Chicago depository deposits the check for collection with the Reserve Bank of Chicago, which then forwards the check to the Reserve Bank of San Francisco. The Reserve Bank of San Francisco, of course, then presents the check for payment to the depository on which it was drawn. Thus there are two routes of check clearance: the *intradistrict settlement,* where the transaction takes place entirely within a single Federal Reserve district, and the *interdistrict settlement,* in which there are relationships between banks of two Federal Reserve districts.

As previously described, Reserve Banks are able to minimize the actual flow of funds by increasing or decreasing reserves of the participating depository institutions. In the same way, the Interdistrict Settlement Fund eliminates the flow of funds between the Reserve Banks needed to make interdistrict settlements. The Interdistrict Settlement Fund in Washington, D.C., has a substantial deposit from each of the Reserve Banks. These deposit credits are alternately increased or decreased, depending upon the clearance balance of the day's activities on the part of each Reserve Bank. At a certain hour each day, each Reserve Bank informs the Interdistrict Settlement Fund by direct wire of the amount of checks it received the previous day that were drawn upon depository institutions in other Federal Reserve districts. The deposit of each Reserve Bank with the Interdistrict Settlement Fund is increased or decreased according to the balance of the day's check-clearance activities.

CHECK CLEARANCE THROUGH FEDERAL RESERVE BRANCH BANKS. Branch banks of the Reserve Banks enter into the clearance process in a very important way. If a check is deposited with a depository located closer to a Reserve Branch Bank than to a Reserve Bank, the Branch Bank, in effect, takes the place of the Reserve Bank. The Federal Reserve facilitates the check-clearing services of the Reserve Banks and their branches by maintaining a small group of regional check-processing centers.

CHECK ROUTING. Over one-quarter of the total personnel of the 12 Reserve Banks are engaged in the task of assisting in the check-clearance process by the Fed. Great effort has been exercised to make this task easier, and much timesaving machinery has been introduced into the operation. Fundamental to the clearance process is a machine that has the ability to read a system of symbols and numerals, shown in Figure 4.5. Although these symbols are slightly different from conventional numbers, they are easily read by human eyes as well. Information about the clearance process is printed on the lower part of the check form in magnetic ink that contains iron oxide. Processing machines can read this information directly from checks. The system has been named Magnetic Ink Character Recognition (MICR). In addition to the clearance symbol, depository institutions with compatible electronic accounting equipment include a symbol for each customer's account. This makes it possible to electronically process checks for internal bookkeeping purposes. Banks continue to include the older check routing symbol in the upper right-hand corner of their checks. It is useful for physically sorting checks that are torn or otherwise unsuitable for electronic sorting.

TRANSFER OF CREDIT. The Fed provides for the transfer of hundreds of millions of dollars in depository balances around the country daily. The communication system called Fedwire may be used by depository institutions to transfer funds for their own accounts, to move balances at

FIGURE 4.5   Check Routing Symbols

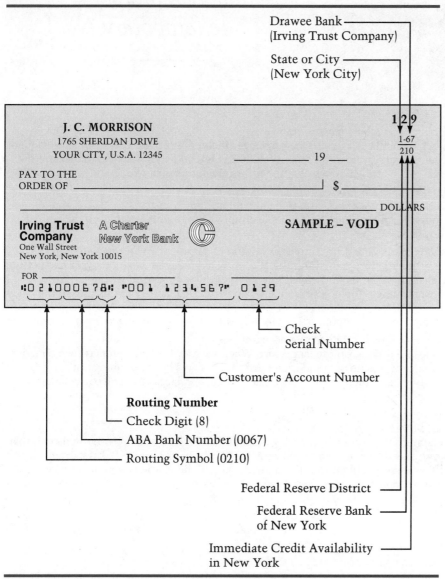

correspondent banks, and to send funds to another institution on behalf of customers.

ELECTRONIC FUNDS TRANSFERS. The tremendous growth in volume of check clearance and the relatively high cost of wire transfers through the Federal Reserve leased system have resulted in efforts to bring computers into the process. While the use of credit cards has taken some pressure off

CHRISTIANNE LEPPERT

Collection Manager
BenchMark Federal
Savings Bank

*"Most people's
financial problems
are temporary."*

Q: *Describe your job responsibilities.*
A: My responsibilities as collection manager include mortgage collections, delinquent accounts, and foreclosures. I am also the REO (Real Estate Owned) manager. I manage all of the real estate we end up with through foreclosures.

Q: *Why do people normally get behind on their payments?*
A: Obviously each person's situation is different, but catastrophic illness and job loss are often involved. And many people simply have trouble organizing their financial priorities.

Q: *When you contact someone who is behind on payments, what is your goal?*
A: I am trying to protect the interests of all parties involved. It's more than just getting the customers to make the past due payment. I want to collect the payment, but I also want to help them get through whatever difficulty they are having so that they can catch up on payments and stay current over the long term. Most people's financial problems are temporary. I try to help them understand that and act accordingly.

Q: *When does foreclosure become necessary?*
A: Foreclosure is the absolute last resort. When we foreclose on a property we take over complete ownership of it and then need to sell it. We have no interest in being in the property management business. Foreclosure just replaces one kind of a problem with another kind of problem. So we only exercise that option when every other available alternative has been exhausted.

Q: *What makes you good at your job?*
A: My communication skills are a big help. I think I take a more positive approach than many collectors. I don't just call and say "Give us our money!" I try to empathize with whatever problem they're having and then offer some potential solutions. It's a proactive approach, and it seems to work pretty well.

Q: *You've been with this bank for nine years. What changes have you seen?*
A: A big change has occurred in the sophistication of our customers. They now have a much better understanding of their options and are prepared and willing to shop around to find the best option available.

Q: *How have you responded to that change?*
A: In order to satisfy these more educated customers, we've added to our product line and bundled products together to try to fill as many of their banking needs as possible. We also provide a bi-weekly mortgage that results in a huge interest savings over the course of the loan.

Q: *How did you get started in banking?*
A: I started as a teller and then transferred to mortgage operations before I became a manager. BenchMark is a small community-oriented bank, so I've had the opportunity to work in many different capacities and departments at one point or another. That variety has helped me understand all sides of the industry.

check-clearance facilities, the problem remains. Credit cards, of course, permit payment for many transactions to be completed with a single check at the end of the billing cycle. Established in the early 1970s, automated clearinghouses (ACHs) have grown into a nationwide clearing and settlement mechanism for electronically originated debits and credits. Examples of such transfers are the direct deposit of payments for wages, pensions, social security, and so on to the payee's account at his or her depository institution. In spite of the speed and convenience of electronic transfers, the growth of this process has not been as great as had been hoped.

The Fed as Government Fiscal Agent

A substantial portion of the employees of the Fed hold jobs that are directly related to its role as **fiscal agent** for the U.S. government. The services include holding the Treasury's checking accounts, assisting in the collection of taxes, transferring money from one region to another, and selling, redeeming, and paying interest on federal securities. The federal government makes most of its payments to the public from funds on deposit at the Reserve Banks. The Fed also acts as fiscal agent for foreign central banks and international organizations such as the International Monetary Fund.

fiscal agent
role of the Fed in collecting taxes, issuing checks, and other activities for the Treasury

Reports, Publications, and Research

The consolidated balance sheet of the Reserve Banks is published weekly and provides an accounting summary of all phases of Federal Reserve Bank operations. This information is valuable for studying business conditions and formulating forecasts of business activity. In addition to the weekly statement, all 12 of the Reserve Banks, as well as the Board of Governors, engage in intensive research in monetary matters. The Board of Governors makes available the *Federal Reserve Bulletin,* which carries articles of current interest to economists and business persons in general and also offers a convenient source of the statistics compiled by the Fed. The *Bulletin* is a convenient secondary source for certain statistical series and data prepared by other government agencies and private organizations such as the F.W. Dodge reports on construction contracts, and the New York Stock Exchange reports on stock prices and sales.

SUMMARY

This chapter began with a description of the development of central banking in the United States. Coverage then focused on the organization and structure of the Federal Reserve System in terms of membership, Federal Reserve Banks, the Board of Governors, and the Federal Open Market Committee.

The Fed performs dynamic, defensive, and accommodative functions. Dynamic activities attempt to influence economic activity by controlling the money supply. Defensive activities attempt to smooth changes in day-to-day economic operations. Accommodative activities provide credit and checking-related services to individuals and institutions.

The basic policy instruments of the Fed include setting reserve requirements, lending to depository institutions at the discount rate, and conducting open market operations involving the purchase and sale of U.S. government securities. Service functions of the Fed include providing currency and coin, clearing and collecting checks, electronic transferring of funds, and publishing research results.

KEY TERMS

central bank	fiscal agent
eligible paper	monetary policy
Fed Board of Governors	open market operations
Federal Reserve System (Fed)	

DISCUSSION QUESTIONS

1. To what extent did the Federal Reserve Act of 1913 supplant bank regulation and operation under the National Banking Act?
2. The Federal Reserve Act of 1913 provided for the establishment of a group of central banks. How do the operations of a central bank differ from those of a commercial bank?
3. Describe the organizational structure of the Federal Reserve System.
4. Banking and large, medium, and small businesses are represented on the board of directors of each Reserve Bank. Explain how this representation is accomplished.
5. What is meant by Reserve Branch Bank? How many such branches exist, and where are most of them located geographically?
6. The Federal Reserve System is under the general direction and control of the Board of Governors of the Federal Reserve System in Washington, D.C. How are members of the Board of Governors appointed? To what extent are they subject to political pressures?
7. Discuss the structure, the functions, and the importance of the Federal Open Market Committee.
8. Reserve Banks have at times been described as bankers' banks due to their lending powers. What is meant by this statement?
9. Explain the usual procedures for examining national banks. How does this process differ from the examination of member banks of the Federal Reserve System holding state charters?
10. Explain the process by which the Federal Reserve Banks provide the economy with currency and coin.

11. Describe how a check drawn on a commercial bank but deposited for collection in another bank in a distant city might be cleared through the facilities of the Federal Reserve System.
12. What is the special role of the Federal Reserve Interdistrict Settlement Fund in the check-clearance process?
13. In what way do the Reserve Banks serve as fiscal agents for the U.S. government?
14. Distinguish among the dynamic, defensive, and accommodative functions of the Fed.

PROBLEMS

1. You are a resident of Seattle, Washington, and maintain a checking account with a bank in that city. You have just written a check on that bank to pay your tuition. Describe the process by which the banking system enables your college to collect the funds from your bank.
2. As the executive of a bank or thrift institution you are faced with an intense seasonal demand for loans. Assuming that your loanable funds are inadequate to take care of the demand, how might your Reserve Bank help you with this problem?
3. The Federal Reserve Board of Governors has decided to "ease" monetary conditions to counter early signs of an economic downturn. Because price inflation had been a burden in recent years, the Board is anxious to avoid any action that the public might interpret as a return to inflationary conditions. How might the Board use its various powers to accomplish the objective of monetary ease without drawing unfavorable publicity to its actions?
4. An economic contraction (recession) is now well under way and the Fed plans to use all facilities at its command to halt the decline. Describe the measures that it may take.
5. You have recently retired and are intent on extensive travel to many of the exotic lands you have only read about. You will not only be receiving a pension check and Social Security check but also dividends and interest from several corporations. You are concerned about the deposit of these checks during your several months of absence and you have asked your banker if there is an arrangement available to solve this problem. What alternative might the banker suggest?

SELF-TEST QUESTIONS

1. The creation of the Federal Reserve System and its central banking arrangement was long in coming compared to other industrialized nations because:

    a.   of the nation's poor communication system in early years
    b.   of the physical size and diversity of the nation
    c.   the existing system worked quite well
    d.   of general opposition to a strong central banking system

2. A central bank serves the nation:
    a.   as a source of consumer credit when it's not otherwise available
    b.   by influencing the cost, availability, and supply of money
    c.   as a secondary source of funds for home financing
    d.   as the strong right arm of the U.S. Treasury

3. Sales and purchases of securities by the Federal Reserve System are carried out by:
    a.   the Federal Open Market Committee
    b.   the Federal Advisory Council
    c.   the U.S. Treasury
    d.   each Reserve Bank for its own account

4. Reserve Banks are responsible for:
    a.   more than 90 percent of all currency in circulation
    b.   insuring bank deposits up to $100,000 for each depositor
    c.   the appointment of members of the Board of Governors of the System
    d.   all bank examinations and supervision

5. The Federal Reserve Board has responsibility for:
    a.   establishing margin requirements on stock market credit
    b.   setting interest rates on consumer credit
    c.   establishing the terms and conditions of real estate credit
    d.   setting interest rates for bank-issued certificates of deposit

6. The capital stock of each Federal Reserve Bank:
    a.   is owned by the Board of Governors of the Fed
    b.   can be issued in an emergency to provide funds for the Fed
    c.   is owned by members of the individual Federal Reserve Banks
    d.   has been reserved for purchase of the U.S. Treasury

7. The Fed spends most of its time and effort on:
    a.   activities described as dynamic
    b.   activities characterized as defensive
    c.   clearing checks for the public
    d.   supervision and examination of member banks

8. An important reason why the Fed carries out its operations through its Open Market Committee is that:
    a.   there is a legal requirement
    b.   it is less costly
    c.   approval by the U.S. Treasury is not required
    d.   public announcement is not required

9. Which one of the following statements is *true* when describing Federal Reserve Banks?
    a.   they are located in each of the 50 states

b.   every Federal Reserve Bank has at least one branch
c.   they have been moved from city to city as the U.S. developed
d.   two Federal Reserve Banks are located in the same state

SELF-TEST PROBLEM

The Federal Reserve identifies districts by number and Reserve Bank city. Identify the district that serves the western part of the United States including Alaska and Hawaii. Also identify the Federal Reserve Branch cities in that district. In addition, if you live in the United States, identify the Federal Reserve district within which your home town is located. Is your home town a Federal Reserve bank city or branch city?

SUGGESTED READINGS

Feinman, Joshua N. "Reserve Requirements: History, Current Practice, and Potential Reform." *Federal Reserve Bulletin* (June 1993): 570–589.

Gardner, Mona J., and Dixie L. Mills. *Managing Financial Institutions: An Asset/Liability Approach.* Fort Worth, TX: The Dryden Press, 1994. Chap. 3.

Kidwell, David S., Richard L. Peterson, and David W. Blackwell. *Financial Institutions, Markets, and Money,* 5e. Fort Worth, TX: The Dryden Press, 1993. Chap. 4.

Maxwell, Charles E. *Financial Markets and Institutions: The Global View.* St. Paul, MN: West Publishing Company, 1994. Chap. 13.

Rose, Peter S. *Money and Capital Markets,* 5e. Homewood, IL: BPI/Irwin, 1994, Chap. 22.

Schwartz, Anna J. "The Misuse of the Fed's Discount Window." *Review,* The Federal Reserve Bank of St. Louis (September/October 1992): 58–69.

Summers, Bruce J. "Clearing and Payment Systems: The Role of the Central Bank." *Federal Reserve Bulletin* (February 1991): 81–91.

Terrell, Henry S. "U.S. Branches and Agencies of Foreign Banks: A New Look." *Federal Reserve Bulletin* (October 1993): 913–928.

Weiner, Stuart E. "The Changing Role of Reserve Requirements in Monetary Policy." *Economic Review,* Federal Reserve Bank of Kansas City (Fourth Quarter 1992): 45–64.

ANSWERS TO SELF-TEST QUESTIONS   1. d, 2. b, 3. a, 4. a, 5. a, 6. c, 7. b, 8. d, 9. d

ANSWER TO SELF-TEST PROBLEM

As shown in Figure 4.2, the San Francisco district serves the western part of the United States (including Alaska and Hawaii). Branch cities in this District are: Los Angeles, Portland, Salt Lake City, and Seattle. Figure 4.2 can be used to determine the Federal Reserve district within which your home town is located, as well as allow you to determine whether your home town is a Federal Reserve bank city or branch city. Additional help may be provided by referring to maps of Federal Reserve System in the back of each issue of the *Federal Reserve Bulletin.*

CHAPTER 5

Economic Objectives, Policy Makers, and the Money Supply

AFTER STUDYING THIS CHAPTER, YOU SHOULD BE ABLE TO:

- Discuss the objectives of national economic policy and the conflicting nature of these objectives.
- Identify the major policy makers and briefly describe their primary responsibilities.
- Identify the policy instruments of the U.S. Treasury and briefly explain how the Treasury manages its activities.
- Describe U.S. Treasury tax policy and debt management responsibilities.
- Discuss how the expansion of the money supply takes place in the U.S. banking system.
- Briefly summarize the factors that affect bank reserves.
- Explain the meaning of the monetary base and money multiplier.
- Explain what is meant by the velocity of money and give reasons why it is important to control the money supply.

The role of the Federal Reserve as administrator of monetary policy was discussed in Chapter 4. However, it is important to recognize that the Fed does not operate in isolation but rather in conjunction with other policy makers (i.e., the President, Congress, and the U.S. Treasury) in attempting to achieve national policy objectives. We will see in this chapter that these policy makers influence the operation of the financial system and the economy through their policies or decisions designed to influence national policy objectives.

The Fed attempts to regulate the supply of money (and the availability of credit) because the size of the total money supply compared to the demands put upon it influences the supply of funds available for investment. The relationship between the money supply and demand in turn affects the level of prices and economic activity in our market economy. Therefore, the process by which the money supply is increased and decreased is a very important factor to the success of the economy.

NATIONAL ECONOMIC POLICY OBJECTIVES

The government's involvement in the economy influences its course and affects the lives of everyone. While people with differing views debate the proper role of government, there is broad agreement that the decisions of policy makers have a significant effect in certain areas. There is also a strong tradition in our system that the objectives be pursued with minimum interference to the economic freedom of individuals. Economic policy actions are directed toward the four general goals of (1) economic growth, (2) high and stable employment levels, (3) price stability, and (4) international financial equilibrium.

ECONOMIC GROWTH

The standard of living of the nation's citizens has increased dramatically over our history as a result of the growth of the economy and its productivity. But growth means more than merely increasing total output. It requires that output increase faster than the population so that the average output per person expands. Growth is a function of two components: an increasing stock of productive resources—the labor force and stock of capital —and improved technology and skills.

The output of goods and services in an economy is referred to as the **gross domestic product (GDP).** The United States began the decade of the 1980s with a double-dip recession or economic downturn in "real" terms (i.e., after price changes have been factored out). A mild economic decline occurred in 1980 followed by a deeper decline that lasted from mid-1981 through most of 1982. GDP then grew in real terms throughout the remainder of the 1980s before a mild downturn occurred beginning in mid-1990 and lasting through the first quarter of 1991. Since then the economy has continued to grow in real terms. Even so, some industries have been particularly hard-hit and have been forced to undergo substantial downsizing and restructuring.

gross domestic product (GDP)
measures the output of goods and services in an economy

HIGH AND STABLE LEVELS OF EMPLOYMENT

Unemployment represents a loss of potential output and imposes costs on the entire economy. The economic and psychological costs are especially hard on the unemployed. While there is some disagreement over what we should consider full employment, it is a stated objective of the government to promote stability of employment and production at levels close to our potential. It seeks to avoid large changes in economic activity, minimizing the hardships that accompany loss of jobs and output.

The U.S. unemployment rate reached double-digit levels during the early 1980s with a peak at about 11 percent near the end of 1982. As the economy began expanding, unemployment levels declined throughout the remainder of the 1980s when the rate fell below 5.5 percent. The recession that began in mid-1990 along with other job dislocations, associated with corporate downsizing and restructuring, resulted in the unemployment rate exceeding 7.5 percent in 1992 before it again began trending downward.

PRICE STABILITY

inflation
occurs when an increase in the price of goods or services is not offset by an increase in quality

In recent decades the importance of stable prices has become well accepted but difficult to achieve. Consistently stable prices help create an environment in which the other economic goals are more easily reached. **Inflation** occurs when a rise or increase in the prices of goods and services is not offset by increases in the quality of those goods and services. Inflation discourages investment by increasing the uncertainty about future returns. Therefore high inflation rates are no longer considered acceptable as a price to pay for high levels of employment.

Inflation was at double-digit levels during the early part of the 1980s and this was reflected in record-high interest rates. However, as the economy turned down in the 1981–82 recession, inflation rates also started down and continued down until inflation fell below the 3 percent level. Inflation remained low throughout the first part of the 1990s.

INTERNATIONAL FINANCIAL EQUILIBRIUM

The increasing importance of international trade and international capital markets has resulted in a new emphasis on worldwide financial affairs. The U.S. economy is so large that the actions taken with respect to our own affairs influence the economies of other nations as well. Economic policy makers therefore must always maintain a world view rather than a narrow nationalistic approach.

Nations that produce and sell (export) more that they buy (import) will have a net capital inflow or surplus, and vice versa. For example, Japan is using its large surplus of exports greater than imports with the United States to make investments there. Nations that continually operate with international trade deficits will become increasingly weaker economically while those with consistent surpluses will become economically stronger. Movement towards international financial equilibrium over time thus is in the best interests of worldwide trade and economic growth.

The decade of the 1980s and the first half of the 1990s shows that the United States has consistently operated with a large negative merchandise trade balance. In recent years, merchandise trade imports have consistently exceeded merchandise trade exports by more than $20 billion annually. While our service exports are larger than our service imports, this favorable balance is swamped by the negative merchandise trade balance. This negative balance remains of great concern to policy makers today.

GOVERNMENT INFLUENCE ON THE ECONOMY

The federal government plays a dual role in the economy. In its traditional role it provides services that cannot be provided as efficiently by the private sector. In this role it acts like a firm, employing resources and producing a product. The magnitude of this role and its influence on economic activity have led to its more modern role: guiding or regulating the economy. The decisions of a number of policy-making entities must be coordinated in order to achieve the desired economic objectives.

A government raises funds to pay for its activities in three ways: levies taxes, borrows, or prints money for its own use. Since this last option has tempted some governments, with disastrous results, Congress delegated the power to create money to the Fed. Our federal government collects taxes to pay for most of its spending, and it borrows, competing for funds in the financial system, to finance its deficits.

To illustrate the complex nature of the government's influence on the economy, consider the many effects of a federal deficit. To finance it, the government competes with other borrowers in the financial system. This absorbs savings, and it may raise interest rates. Private investment may be reduced if it becomes more difficult for firms to borrow the funds needed. On the other hand, a deficit stimulates economic activity. The government is either spending more or collecting less in taxes, or both, leaving more income for consumers to spend. The larger the deficit, the more total spending, or aggregate demand, there will be. In some circumstances this stimulation of the economy generates enough extra income and savings to finance both the deficit and additional investment by firms.

Furthermore, the Fed may buy government securities, financing some of the deficit and providing additional reserves to the banking system, thus increasing the money supply. This process is known as **monetizing the deficit.** The Fed has at past times monetized some of the deficit, especially during World Wars I and II. It does not now do so since that would be counter to current monetary policy. It would also have a significant

*monetizing the deficit
the Fed increases the
money supply by pur-
chasing government
securities*

CAREER OPPORTUNITIES IN FINANCE

Field: Government or Not-for-Profit Organizations

Opportunities:
The federal government is the largest single employer in the United States. In addition, state and local governments also hire thousands of workers across the nation. Not-for-profit organizations, such as hospitals, also employ numerous workers with backgrounds in business and finance. Many job seekers, however, never consider that government and not-for-profit organizations need the same financial services as do businesses. Therefore, jobs that are available in this field often go unnoticed. All federal and state jobs are listed at your local state employment services office. Also, you may contact your state or regional Federal Employment Information Center for more information on federal jobs (your state or federal representative will know how to get in touch with these offices).

Jobs:
A *financial manager* manages cash funds, makes asset acquisition decisions, controls costs, and obtains borrowed funds. A financial manager with either a government or a not-for-profit organization must also stay abreast of current legislation and public and private grant opportunities.

A *financial analyst* assesses the short- and long-term financial performance of a government or not-for-profit organization, while a *financial planner* uses this analysis to develop a financial plan.

Education:
A knowledge of economics and finance is necessary for these jobs, and an understanding of the executive and legislative process is helpful. In addition, a primary way in which government and not-for-profit groups obtain funds is through the acquisition of grants; therefore, strong research and writing skills also are essential.

impact on the financial markets. The competition for funds would make it more difficult for some borrowers to meet their financing needs. The characteristics and maturities of debt sold by the Treasury would determine which sectors are most affected.

The decisions of policy makers enter this process at a number of points. The President and the Council of Economic Advisors formulate a program of **fiscal policy:** the relationship of the Treasury's tax plans to its expenditure plans to influence the economy of the nation. Congress must pass legislation authorizing the Treasury's plans or a variation of it. The

fiscal policy
government influence on economic activity through taxation and expenditure plans

Treasury has responsibility for actually collecting taxes and disbursing funds. The Treasury also is responsible for the huge task of debt management, which includes financing current deficits and refinancing the outstanding debt of the government. As discussed in the previous chapter, the Fed contributes to the attainment of the nation's economic goals by formulating monetary policy. It uses its powers to regulate the growth of the money supply and thus influence interest rates and the availability of loans. Figure 5.1 shows the relationship between policy makers and economic objectives.

The principal responsibilities of these policy makers have not always been the same. When the Fed was established in 1913, most of the power to regulate money and credit was placed in its hands. However, as the public debt grew during World War I, the Great Depression of the 1930s, and World War II, the Treasury became vitally interested in credit conditions. Policies that affect interest rates and the size of the money supply affect the Treasury directly, since it is the largest borrower in the nation. Therefore, the U.S. Treasury took over, and continues to have, primary responsibility for management of the federal debt. In managing the large public debt and various trust funds placed under its jurisdiction, the Treasury has the power to influence the money market materially. The Fed came back into its own in the 1950s and is now the chief architect of monetary policy.

When it is felt that the Fed is not being responsive to the needs of the economy, the President will usually exercise pressure. The President also formulates budgetary and fiscal policy, but Congress must enact legislation to implement these policies. Congress regularly exercises its authority to modify presidential proposals before enacting legislation. In short, there is much overlap of influence among those who make policy decisions. All three types of policies, however, are directed toward achieving the four objectives of economic growth, high employment, price stability, and international financial equilibrium.

FIGURE 5.1   Policy Makers and Economic Policy Objectives

Policy Makers	Types of Policies or Decisions	Economic Objectives
Federal Reserve System		Economic Growth
	Monetary Policy	High Employment
The President		
	Fiscal Policy	Price Stability
Congress		
	Debt Management	International Equilibrium
U.S. Treasury		

It should not be surprising that the policy instruments of the various policy makers at times put them at cross-purposes. A long-standing debate continues over the balance between full employment and price stability. A particular policy that leads toward one may make the other more difficult to achieve, yet each objective has its special supporters. As with all governmental policy, economic objectives are necessarily subject to compromise and tradeoffs.

POLICY INSTRUMENTS OF THE U.S. TREASURY

The Treasury has vast power to affect the supply of money and credit. The very magnitude of Treasury operations, however, dictates that it must play as defensive or neutral a role as possible. The power to regulate the money supply has been placed primarily in the hands of the Fed; close cooperation between the Treasury and the Fed must exist if Treasury operations are not to disrupt the money supply.

Consider the impact on monetary affairs of a massive withdrawal of taxes from the banking system without offsetting actions. The decrease in bank deposits would result in a temporary breakdown of the system's ability to serve the credit needs of the public. Yet, taxes are periodically claimed by the federal government without significant impact on lending institutions. In like manner, borrowing by the government or the refunding of maturing obligations could be traumatic in their effect on money and credit, but such is not the case. In short, the Fed efficiently manages these dynamic aspects of money and credit while the Treasury largely limits its actions to taxing, borrowing, paying bills, and refunding maturing obligations. The Treasury carries out these functions with as little interference with the conduct of monetary affairs as possible. This is no small challenge.

MANAGING THE TREASURY'S CASH BALANCES

Treasury operations involve spending over one trillion dollars a year. It is necessary to maintain a large cash balance, since Treasury receipts and payments do not occur on a regular basis throughout the year. This makes it critical for the Treasury to handle its cash balances in such a way that it will not create undesirable periods of credit ease or tightness. In order to affect bank reserves as little as possible, the Treasury has developed detailed procedures for handling its cash balances.

Treasury Tax and Loan Accounts

The Treasury's primary checkable deposit accounts for day-to-day operations are kept at Reserve Banks. Most cash flows into the Treasury through Treasury Tax and Loan Accounts of banks, S&Ls, and credit unions (referred to as banks, for short). Employers deposit withheld income taxes, Social Security, and railroad retirement taxes in these Treasury Tax and Loan Accounts. They have the option of depositing these government receipts either with Reserve Banks or one of the other banks. Most employers make their payments to the latter.

The Treasury may also make payments of income and eligible profits taxes in Tax and Loan Accounts. Many excise taxes may also be paid either to a Reserve Bank or to a qualified bank with a Tax and Loan Account. The proceeds from a large portion of the sales of new government securities also flow into Tax and Loan Accounts. If the Treasury feels its balances at the Reserve Banks are too large, it can transfer funds to its accounts at the banks.

Treasury Receipts and Outlays

The Treasury tries to handle its cash receipts, outlays, and balances so as to avoid large changes in bank reserves. To do this, the Treasury tries to keep balances in its accounts at the Reserve Banks relatively stable. Almost all Treasury disbursements are made by checks drawn against its deposits at the Reserve Banks. Most Treasury receipts are deposited in Tax and Loan Accounts at the various banks, but some are deposited directly in the Treasury accounts at the Reserve Banks. The Treasury adjusts the withdrawal of funds from its accounts at the banks in such a way as to keep its balances at the Reserve Banks as stable as possible. This means that the funds shifted from banks and the funds deposited directly in Reserve Banks must closely correspond to the volume of Treasury checks that are likely to be presented to the Reserve Banks.

If the Treasury accounts at the Reserve Banks are kept at about the same level, bank reserves are not changed. This is possible only if accurate forecasts are made of the daily receipts and spending from the Treasury account so that funds from the Tax and Loan Accounts may be shifted in the right amounts at the right time. If the forecasts were not worked out with a reasonable degree of success, Treasury operations would cause bank reserves to change a great deal over short periods of time. Despite these precautions, the Treasury's account frequently does fluctuate by as much as several billion dollars from day to day. The Fed closely monitors the Treasury account and takes any changes into consideration in conducting daily open market operations in order to minimize the effect on bank reserves.

POWERS RELATING TO THE FEDERAL BUDGET AND TO SURPLUSES OR DEFICITS

The government may also influence monetary and credit conditions indirectly through taxation and expenditure programs, especially by having a significant cash deficit or surplus. Decisions in the budget-making area rest with Congress and are usually based on the needs of the government and political considerations, without giving much weight to monetary and credit effects. Because of the magnitude of the federal budget, government income and spending may be one of the most important factors in determining credit conditions.

General Economic Effects of Fiscal Policy

Economic activity depends to a large extent on aggregate demand, or total spending in the economy. An increase in aggregate demand will generally cause an increase in production and employment but may also cause prices to rise. If the economy is already close to full employment, increases in aggregate demand will be likely to increase prices more than output. Similarly, decreases in aggregate demand will result in lower employment and reduced prices.

Fiscal policy has a significant effect on aggregate demand and economic activity. Not only is government spending itself a large component of aggregate demand, but any change in government spending has a multiplied effect on aggregate demand. An increase in government spending increases employment and incomes, and thus also increases consumer spending. In a downturn, not only does spending decrease, but tax receipts of all types, including those for Social Security, decrease when fewer people are at work because these taxes are based on payrolls. Changes in taxes also have a direct impact on disposable income and affect aggregate demand through consumer spending.

automatic stabilizers
continuing federal
programs that stabilize
economic activity

Various federal government programs act to stabilize disposable income and, in turn, economic activity in general. Some act on a continuing basis as ***automatic stabilizers.*** Other government fiscal actions are discretionary and depend on specific congressional actions.

One of the automatic stabilizers is the unemployment insurance program, funded in large part by the states. Under this program, payments are made to workers who lose their jobs, thus providing part of their former incomes. Another stabilizer is welfare payments under federal and state aid programs. Both unemployment and welfare benefits are examples of ***transfer payments,*** or income payments for which no current productive service is rendered.

transfer payments
government payments
for which no current
services are given in
return

Another important automatic stabilizer is the pay-as-you-go progressive income tax. Pay-as-you-go refers to the requirement that tax liabilities of individuals and institutions be paid on a continuing basis throughout the year. The progressive nature of our income tax means that as income increases to various levels, the tax rate increases. In other words, as incomes increase, taxes increase at a faster rate. The reverse is also true: at certain stages of decreased income, the tax liability decreases more quickly. The result is generally immediate since, for most wages subject to withholding taxes, tax revenues change almost as soon as incomes change.

These programs are a regular part of our economy. In times of severe economic fluctuations, Congress can help to stabilize disposable income. Income tax rates have been raised to lower disposable income and to restrain inflationary pressures; they have been lowered during recessions to increase disposable income and spending. Government spending can also be increased during recessions to increase disposable income. Likewise, it could be cut during prosperity to reduce disposable income, but for political reasons attempts to do this have not been successful.

When a recession is so severe that built-in stabilizers or formulas are not adequate to promote recovery, there is seldom complete agreement on the course of action to take. A decision to change the level of government spending and/or the tax rates must be made. Increased spending or a comparable tax cut would cost the same number of dollars initially, but the economic effects would not be the same. When income taxes are cut, disposable income is increased almost immediately under our system of tax withholding. This provides additional income for all sectors of the economy and an increase in demand for many types of goods.

Congress may decide to increase government spending. But the effects of increased government spending occur more slowly than those of a tax cut since it takes time to get programs started and put into full operation. The increased income arises first in those sectors of the economy where the money is spent. Thus, the initial effect is on specific areas of the economy rather than on the economy as a whole.

The secondary effects of spending resulting from a tax cut or from increased government spending depend on how and what proportion the recipients spend. To the extent that they spend it on current consumption, aggregate demand is further increased in the short run. The goods on which recipients spend the income determine the sectors of the economy that receive a boost. If they invest the added income and later use it to purchase capital goods, spending is also increased. But in this case there is a time lag and different sectors of the economy are affected. If the money is saved—thus added to idle funds available for investment—there is no secondary effect on spending.

The effects must also be considered if economic activity is to be restrained by a decrease in government spending or by a tax increase. A decrease in spending by the government will cut consumer spending by at least that amount; the secondary effects may cut it further. A tax increase may not cut spending by a like amount since some taxpayers may maintain their level of spending by reducing current saving or by using accrued savings. A tax increase could, however, cut total spending more if it should happen to discourage specific types of spending, such as on home building or on credit purchases of consumer durable goods. This could lead to a spending cut that is substantially greater than the amount of money taken by the higher taxes.

Effects of Tax Policy

The **tax policy** and tax program of the federal government have a direct effect on monetary and credit conditions which may work in several ways.

tax policy
setting the level and structure of taxes to affect the economy

The level of taxes in relation to national income may affect the volume of saving and thus the funds available for investment without credit expansion. The tax structure also determines whether saving is done largely by upper-income groups, middle-income groups, or by all groups. This in turn can affect the amount of funds available for different types of investment. Persons in middle-income groups may be more conservative than those with more wealth. Therefore they tend to favor bonds or mortgages over equity investments. Persons in high tax brackets, on the other hand, tend to invest in securities of state and local governments, because income from these investments is not subject to income taxes. They also may invest for capital gains since taxes on the gains may be deferred until the asset is sold.

Changes in corporate tax rates also may affect the amount of funds available for short-term investment in government bonds and the balances kept in bank accounts. The larger the tax payments, the less a corporation has available for current spending. Also, if tax rates are raised with little advance warning, as sometimes happens, a corporation may be forced to use funds it had been holding for future use. Businesses that are short of funds may be forced to borrow to meet their taxes. In either case, a smaller amount of credit is available for other uses.

Effects of Deficit Financing

The government spending program affects not only the overall economy but also monetary and credit conditions. When the spending rate is faster than the collection of taxes and other funds, **deficit financing** will affect the monetary and banking system. The effect will depend on how the deficit is financed. Budgetary deficits result in government competition for private investment funds. When credit demands are great, there may be a threat of **crowding out** private borrowers from the capital markets. When credit demands are slack, the sale of Treasury obligations puts idle bank reserves to use. When deficit financing is so large that the private sector cannot or will not absorb the Treasury obligations offered, the Fed may purchase a significant portion of the issues.

deficit financing
how a government finances its needs when spending is greater than revenues

crowding out
lack of funds for private borrowing caused by the sale of government obligations to cover large federal deficits

DEBT MANAGEMENT

debt management
various Treasury decisions connected with refunding debt issues

Debt management includes determining the types of refunding to carry out, the types of securities to sell, the interest rate patterns to use, and decision making on callable issues. Since World War II, federal debt management has become an important Treasury function affecting economic conditions in general and money markets in particular. The economy and the money markets are affected in several ways by the large government debt. First, interest must be paid on government securities. This has become one of the major items in the federal budget, estimated at nearly $235 billion for fiscal year 1994. Interest payments do not transfer resources from the private to the public sector, but they do represent a transfer of funds from taxpayers in general to security holders. When the debt is widely held, there is little or no redistribution of income among groups. However, the taxes levied to pay the interest may have a negative effect on the taxpayer incentive and so affect economic activity. This could lead to less risk taking and thus slow down economic growth.

One of the basic objectives of debt management is to handle it in such a way as to help establish an economic climate that encourages orderly growth and stability. In order to avoid inflation in boom periods, large numbers of individuals have been encouraged to save and to buy bonds. During recessions, the Treasury can borrow in ways that are least likely to compete with private demands for funds. For instance, the Treasury can sell short-term securities to attract idle short-term funds, especially idle bank reserves. Thus, there will be no restriction of credit for business and individuals. Credit will be available in larger amounts to the extent that bank purchases of bonds lead to credit expansion.

Another objective of debt management policy is to hold down Treasury interest costs. The influence of Treasury policies may also tend to reduce all interest rates. Lower interest rates tend to stimulate home building, the construction of business plant and equipment, commercial building, and so forth. This objective and the first one may, however, conflict when higher interest rates help to restrain inflationary pressures.

A lesser Treasury objective is to maintain satisfactory conditions in the government securities market through maintaining investor confidence. It also tries to discourage wide price swings and maintain orderly buying and selling.

Among the more technical objectives are issuing securities to fit the needs of various investor groups and obtaining an evenly spaced scheduling of debt maturities to ease debt retirement if funds are available, or refunding when that is necessary. Our heavy dependence on foreign investors to purchase new issues in recent years has added a special dimension to the problem of U.S. debt management. Terms of new issues must now be geared to the special needs of foreign investors, especially the Japanese.

CHANGING THE MONEY SUPPLY

As we saw in Chapter 2, the M1 definition of the money supply consists of currency (including coins), demand deposits, other checkable deposits, and travelers' checks. Currency is in the form of Federal Reserve notes and are backed by gold certificates, Special Drawing Rights (SDRs), eligible paper, or U.S. government and agency securities. SDRs are a form of reserve asset or "paper gold" created by the International Monetary Fund. Their purpose is to provide worldwide monetary liquidity and to support international trade. Eligible paper in the form of business notes and drafts provides little collateral today. Instead, Federal Reserve notes have been increasingly backed by government securities. At the end of September 1995, the backing for $386.3 billion in Federal Reserve notes was $11.1 billion of gold certificates, $10.2 billion of SDRs, and $365.0 billion of U.S. government and agency securities.[1]

Demand deposits and other checkable deposits at commercial banks, S&Ls, savings banks, and credit unions comprise over 70 percent of the M1 money supply and are collectively termed *checkable deposits.* To further simplify discussion of money supply expansion and contraction, we will refer to checkable deposits simply as *deposits* in the *banking system* which includes all of the depository institutions. The word *bank* also is used generically to refer to a depository institution.

The banking system of the United States can change the volume of deposits as the needs for funds by individuals, businesses, and governments change. This ability to alter the size of the money supply is based on the use of a **fractional reserve system.** In our fractional reserve system, banks must hold with the Fed reserves equal to a certain percentage of their deposits. To understand the deposit expansion and contraction process, one must study the operations of banks as units in a banking system and the relationship of bank loans to deposits and to bank reserves.

fractional reserve system
reserves held with the Fed that are equal to a certain percentage of bank deposits

In analyzing deposit expansion, it is helpful to make a distinction between primary deposits and derivative deposits. For example, the deposit of a check drawn on the Fed is a **primary deposit** because it adds new reserves to the bank where deposited and to the banking system. A **derivative deposit** occurs when reserves created from a primary deposit are made available to borrowers through bank loans. Borrowers then deposit the loans so they can write checks against the funds. When a check is written and deposited in another bank, there is no change in total reserves of the banking system. The increase in reserves at the bank where the check is deposited is offset by a decrease in reserves at the bank on which the check is drawn. Banks must keep reserves against both primary and derivative deposits.

primary deposit
deposit that adds new reserves to a bank

derivative deposit
deposit of funds that were borrowed from the reserves of primary deposits

Checkable Deposit Expansion

When reserves were first required by law, the purpose was to assure depositors that banks had the ability to handle withdrawals of cash. This was before the establishment of the Federal Reserve System, which made it possible for a healthy bank to obtain additional funds in time of need. Depositor confidence is now based on deposit insurance and more com-

---

1.   *Federal Reserve Bulletin* (December 1995): A11.

plete and competent bank examinations by governmental agencies. Today, the basic function of reserve requirements is to provide a means for regulating deposit expansion and contraction.

Deposit creation takes place as a result of the operations of the whole system of banks, but it arises out of the independent transactions of individual banks. To explain the process, therefore, we will consider the loan activities of a single bank. First we will focus on the bank itself; then we will examine its relationship to a system of banks. This approach is somewhat artificial since a bank practically never acts independently of the actions of other banks, but it has been adopted to clarify the process. Furthermore, it helps to explain the belief of some bankers that they cannot create deposits since they only loan funds placed on deposit in their banks by their depositors. This analysis shows how a system of banks, in which each bank is carrying on its local activities, can do what an individual banker cannot do.

For illustration, let us assume that a bank receives a primary deposit of $10,000, and that it must keep reserves of 20 percent against deposits. The $10,000 becomes a cash asset to the bank as well as a $10,000 liability since it must stand ready to honor a withdrawal of the money. The bank statement, ignoring all other items, would then show the following:

ASSETS		LIABILITIES	
Reserves	$10,000	Deposits	$10,000

Against this new deposit of $10,000 the bank must keep required reserves of 20 percent, or $2,000. Therefore, it has $8,000 of excess reserves available. Excess reserves are reserves above the level of required reserves.

It may appear that the banker could proceed to make loans for $40,000, since all that is needed is a 20 percent reserve against the resulting checkable deposits. If this were attempted, however, the banker would soon be in difficulty. Since bank loans are usually obtained just before a demand for funds, checks would very likely be written against the deposit accounts almost at once. Many of these checks would be deposited in other banks, and the bank would be faced with a demand for cash as checks were presented for collection. This demand could reach the full $40,000. Since the bank has only $8,000 to meet it, it could not follow such a course and remain in business.

The amount that the banker can safely lend is the $8,000 of excess reserves. If more is lent, the banker runs the risk of not being able to make payments on checks. After an $8,000 loan, the books show:

ASSETS		LIABILITIES	
Reserves	$10,000	Deposits	$18,000
Loans	8,000		

If a check were written for the full amount of the derivative deposit ($8,000) and sent to a bank in another city for deposit, the lending bank would lose all of its excess reserves. This may be seen from its books, which would appear as follows:

ASSETS		LIABILITIES	
Reserves	$2,000	Deposits	$10,000
Loans	8,000		

In practice a bank may be able to loan somewhat more than the $8,000 in this example. This is because banks frequently require customers to keep an average deposit balance of about 15 to 20 percent of the loan. The whole of the additional $1,500 to $2,000 cannot be loaned safely, because an average balance of $1,500 to $2,000 does not prevent the full amount of the loan from being used for a period of time. With an average balance in each derivative deposit account, however, all accounts will not be drawn to zero at the same time. Therefore, some additional funds will be available for loans.

It may be argued that a banker will feel sure that some checks written against the bank will be redeposited in the same bank and that therefore larger sums can be lent. However, because any bank is only one of thousands, the banker cannot usually count on such redepositing of funds. Banks cannot run the risk of being caught short of reserves. Thus, when an individual bank receives a new primary deposit, it cannot lend the full amount of that deposit but only the amount available as excess reserves. From the point of view of an individual bank, therefore, deposit creation appears impossible. Because a part of every new deposit cannot be loaned out due to reserve requirements, the volume of additional loans is less than new primary deposits.

What cannot be done by an individual bank can be done by the banking system. This occurs when many banks are expanding loans and derivative deposits at the same time. To illustrate this point, assume that we have an economy with just two banks, A and B. This example can be realistic if we assume further that Bank A represents one bank in the system and Bank B represents all other banks combined. Bank A, as in our previous example, receives a new primary deposit of $10,000 and is required to keep reserves of 20 percent against deposits. Therefore, its books would appear as follows:

BANK A

ASSETS		LIABILITIES	
Reserves	$10,000	Deposits	$10,000

A loan for $8,000 is made and credited as follows:

BANK A

ASSETS		LIABILITIES	
Reserves	$10,000	Deposits	$18,000
Loans	8,000		

Assume that a check is drawn against this primary deposit almost immediately and deposited in Bank B. The books of the two banks would then show the following:

BANK A

ASSETS		LIABILITIES	
Reserves	$2,000	Deposits	$10,000
Loans	8,000		

BANK B

ASSETS		LIABILITIES	
Reserves	$8,000	Deposits	$8,000

The derivative deposit arising out of a loan from Bank A has now been transferred by check to Bank B where it is received as a primary deposit. Bank B must now set aside 20 percent as required reserves and may lend or reinvest the remainder. Its books after such a loan (equal to its excess reserves) would appear as follows:

BANK B

ASSETS		LIABILITIES	
Reserves	$8,000	Deposits	$14,400
Loans	6,400		

Assume that a check is drawn against the derivative deposit of $6,400 arising out of the loan by Bank B. This reduces its reserves and deposits as follows:

BANK B

ASSETS		LIABILITIES	
Reserves	$1,600	Deposits	$8,000
Loans	6,400		

The check for $6,400 will most likely be deposited in a bank, in our example in Bank A or Bank B itself, since we have assumed that only two banks exist. In the U.S. banking system, it may be deposited in one of the thousands of banks or other depository institutions.

Deposit expansion as when a bank makes a loan can take place in the same way when it buys securities. Assume, as we did in the case of a bank loan, the following situation:

BANK A

ASSETS		LIABILITIES	
Reserves	$10,000	Deposits	$10,000

Securities costing $8,000 are purchased and the proceeds credited to the account of the seller, giving the following situation:

BANK A

ASSETS		LIABILITIES	
Reserves	$10,000	Deposits	$18,000
Investments	8,000		

Assume that a check is drawn against the seller's deposit and is deposited in Bank B. The books of the two banks would then show:

BANK A

ASSETS		LIABILITIES	
Reserves	$2,000	Deposits	$10,000
Investments	8,000		

BANK B

ASSETS		LIABILITIES	
Reserves	$8,000	Deposits	$8,000

As in the case of a loan, the derivative deposit has been transferred to Bank B where it is received as a primary deposit.

At each stage in the process, 20 percent of the new primary deposit becomes required reserves, and 80 percent becomes excess reserves that can be loaned out. In time, the whole of the original $10,000 primary deposit will have become required reserves, and $50,000 of deposits will have been credited to deposit accounts, of which $40,000 will have been loaned out.

Table 5.1 further illustrates the deposit expansion process for a 20 percent reserve ratio. A primary deposit of $1,000 is injected into the banking system, making excess reserves of $800 available for loans and investments. Eventually, $5,000 in checkable deposits will be created.

The multiple expansion in the money supply created by the banking system through its expansion of deposits also can be expressed in formula form as follows:

$$\frac{\text{Increase in excess reserves}}{\text{Reserve ratio}} = \text{Change in checkable deposits}$$

In the example presented in Table 5.1, the maximum expansion in the money supply (checkable deposits component) would be:

money multiplier
the ratio formed by 1 divided by the reserve ratio, which indicates maximum expansion possible in the money supply

$$\frac{\$1,000}{0.20} = \$5,000$$

which is the same as the final stage figure shown for checkable deposit liabilities. The maximum increase in deposits (and money supply) that can result from a given increase in excess reserves is called the **money multiplier.** The money multiplier (*m*) is equal to 1 divided by the reserve

TABLE 5.1 Multiple Expansion of Deposits—20 Percent Reserve Ratio

| | ASSETS | | | | LIABILITIES |
| | RESERVES | | | | |
	TOTAL	REQUIRED	EXCESS	LOANS AND INVESTMENTS	CHECKABLE DEPOSITS
INITIAL RESERVES	$1,000	$ 200	$800	$ -0-	$1,000
Stage 1	1,000	360	640	800	1,800
Stage 2	1,000	488	512	1,440	2,440
Stage 3	1,000	590	410	1,952	2,952
Stage 4	1,000	672	328	2,362	3,362
Stage 5	1,000	738	262	2,690	3,690
Stage 6	1,000	790	210	2,952	3,952
Stage 7	1,000	832	168	3,162	4,162
Stage 8	1,000	866	134	3,330	4,330
Stage 9	1,000	893	107	3,464	4,464
Stage 10	1,000	914	86	3,571	4,571
.	.	.	.	.	.
.	.	.	.	.	.
.	.	.	.	.	.
Final Stage	$1,000	$1,000	$ -0-	$4,000	$5,000

ratio. For our example, $m = 1/0.20 = 5$. In our complex economy, however, there are several factors or leakages that reduce the ability to reach the maximum expansion in the money supply depicted in this simplified example.

OFFSETTING OR LIMITING FACTORS

Deposit creation can go on only to the extent that the activities described actually take place. If for any reason the proceeds of a loan are withdrawn from the banking system, no new deposit arises to continue the process. A new deposit of $10,000 permits loans of $8,000 under a 20 percent required reserve; but if this $8,000 were used in currency transactions without being deposited in a bank, no deposit could be created. The custom of doing business by means of checks makes deposit creation possible.

In the examples above, no allowance was made for currency withdrawal or cash leakage from the system. In actual practice, as the volume of business in the economy increases, some additional cash is withdrawn for hand-to-hand circulation and to meet the needs of business for petty cash.

Money may also be withdrawn from the banking system to meet the demand for payments to foreign countries. Or foreign banks may withdraw some of the money they are holding on deposit in U.S. banks. The U.S.

Treasury may withdraw funds it has on deposit in banks. All of these factors reduce the multiplying capacity of primary deposits.

Furthermore, this process can go on only if excess reserves are actually being loaned by the banks. This means that banks must be willing to lend the full amount of their excess reserves and that acceptable borrowers who have a demand for loans must be available.

The nonbank public's decisions to switch funds between checkable deposits and time or savings deposits also will influence the ability to expand the money supply and credit. This will be explored later in the chapter.

Contraction of Deposits

When the need for funds by business decreases, deposit expansion can work in reverse. Expansion takes place as long as excess reserves exist and the demand for new bank loans exceeds the repayment of old loans. Deposit contraction takes place when old loans are being repaid faster than new loans are being granted, and banks are not immediately investing these excess funds.

Assuming that Bank A has no excess reserves, let us see the effect of a loan being repaid. Before the borrower began to build up deposits to repay the loan, the bank's books showed:

BANK A

ASSETS		LIABILITIES	
Reserves	$2,000	Deposits	$10,000
Loans	8,000		

The borrower of the $8,000 must build up his or her deposit account by $8,000 in order to be able to repay the loan. This is reflected on the books as follows:

BANK A

ASSETS		LIABILITIES	
Reserves	$10,000	Deposits	$18,000
Loans	8,000		

After the $8,000 is repaid, the books show the following:

BANK A

ASSETS		LIABILITIES	
Reserves	$10,000	Deposits	$10,000

If no new loan is made from the $10,000 of reserves, deposit contraction will result. This is true because $8,000 of funds have been taken out of the banking system to build up deposits to repay the loan and are now being held idle by Bank A as excess reserves. Furthermore, taking out $8,000 of reserves from the banking system may be cumulative on the contraction side just as it was during expansion.

FACTORS AFFECTING BANK RESERVES

The extent to which deposit expansion or contraction can and does take place is governed by the level of a bank's excess reserves. This is true for an individual bank and for the banking system as a whole. Therefore, the factors which affect the level of bank reserves are significant in determining the size of the money supply. ***Total reserves*** in the banking system consist of reserve balances and vault cash used to meet reserve requirements. Reserve balances are deposits held at the Reserve Banks by commercial banks and other depository institutions. Vault cash is currency, including coin, held on the premises of these institutions.

    Total reserves can be divided into two parts: The first, ***required reserves,*** is the minimum amount of total reserves that a depository institution must hold. The percentage of deposits that must be held as reserves is called the ***reserve ratio.*** The second part of total reserves is ***excess reserves,*** the amount by which total reserves exceed required reserves. If required reserves are larger than the total reserves of an institution, the difference is called ***deficit reserves.***

    Two kinds of factors affect total reserves: those that affect the currency holdings of the banking system and those that affect deposits at the Fed. Currency flows in response to changes in the demand for it by households and businesses. Reserve balances are affected by a variety of transactions involving the Fed and banks, which may be initiated by the banking system or the Fed, by the Treasury, or by other factors. Although the Fed does not control all of the factors which affect the level of bank reserves, it does have the ability to offset increases and decreases. Thus it has broad control over the total reserves available to the banking system. Figure 5.2 provides a summary of the transactions that affect bank reserves. Discussion of these transactions follow.

total reserves
deposits held in Federal Reserve Banks and cash in depository institutions

required reserves
the minimum amount of total reserves that a depository institution must hold

reserve ratio
the percentage of deposits that must be held as reserves

excess reserves
the amount that total reserves are greater than required reserves

deficit reserves
the amount that required reserves are greater than total reserves

FIGURE 5.2   Transactions Affecting Bank Reserves

NONBANK PUBLIC	FEDERAL RESERVE SYSTEM	UNITED STATES TREASURY
Change in the non-bank public's demand for currency to be held outside the banking system	Change in reserve ratio Open market operations (buying and selling government securities) Change in bank borrowings Change in float Change in foreign deposits held in Reserve Banks Change in other Federal Reserve accounts	Change in Treasury spending out of accounts held at Reserve Banks Change in Treasury cash holdings

HOLIDAY-RELATED
CHANGES IN THE
MONEY SUPPLY

Changes in the components of the money supply typically occur during holiday periods, with the most pronounced change taking place during the Christmas season. These changes are beyond the immediate control of the Fed, which must anticipate and respond to them in order to carry out its money-supply growth targets. Following are the money supply (M1) component figures (not seasonally adjusted) in billions of dollars for the end of 1994 and the beginning of 1995 as reported in the *Federal Reserve Bulletin:*

	NOV. `94	DEC. `94	JAN. `95
Currency	$ 353	$ 358	$ 356
Travelers checks	8	8	8
Demand deposits	391	400	389
Other checkable deposits	403	408	406
M1	$1,155	$1,174	$1,159

Notice the increase in currency outstanding between November and December 1994 and the subsequent slight decline during January 1994. This $5 billion increase in circulating currency prior to the Christmas holidays requires adjustment by the Fed in its effort to control the money supply. As large amounts of cash are withdrawn from depository institutions, deposit contraction might occur unless the Fed moves to offset it by purchasing government securities in the open market.

Also notice the increase in demand deposits ($9 billion) and other checkable deposits ($5 billion) between November and December 1994 and the subsequent decline in early 1995. This also seems to reflect the public's surge in spending during the Christmas holiday season and the payment for many of the purchases in early 1995 by writing checks on demand deposit accounts. The Fed, in its effort to control bank reserves and the money supply, also must take corrective actions to temper the impact of these seasonal swings in currency and checking account balances.

CHANGES IN THE DEMAND FOR CURRENCY

Currency-flows into and out of the banking system affect the level of reserves of the banks receiving the currency for deposit. Let us assume that an individual or a business finds they have excess currency of $100 and deposit it in Bank A. Deposit liabilities and the reserves of Bank A are increased by $100. The bank now has excess reserves of $80, assuming a 20 percent level of required reserves. These reserves can be used by the banking system to create $400 in additional deposits. If the bank does not need the currency but sends it to its Reserve Bank, it will receive a $100 credit to its account. The volume of Federal Reserve notes in circulation is decreased by $100. These transactions may be summarized as follows:

1. Deposits in Bank A are increased by $100 ($20 in required reserves and $80 in excess reserves).
2. Bank A's deposit at its Reserve Bank is increased $100.
3. The amount of Federal Reserve notes is decreased by $100.

The opposite takes place when the public demands additional currency. Let us assume that a customer of Bank A needs additional currency and cashes a check for $100. The deposits of the bank are reduced by $100, and this reduces required reserves by $20. If the bank has no excess reserves, it must take steps to get an additional $80 of reserves either by borrowing from its Reserve Bank, demanding payment for a loan or not renewing one which comes due, or by selling securities. When the check is cashed, the reserves of the bank are also reduced by $100. If the bank has to replenish its supply of currency from its Reserve Bank, its reserve deposits are reduced by $100. These transactions may be summarized thus:

1. Deposits in Bank A are reduced by $100 ($20 in required reserves and $80 in excess reserves).
2. Bank A's deposit at its Reserve Bank is reduced by $100.
3. The amount of Federal Reserve notes in circulation is increased by $100.

FEDERAL RESERVE SYSTEM TRANSACTIONS

Transactions of banks with the Fed and changes in reserve requirements by the Fed also affect either the level of total reserves or the degree to which deposits can be expanded with a given volume of reserves. Such transactions are initiated by the Fed when it buys or sells securities, by a depository institution when it borrows from its Reserve Bank, or by a change in Federal Reserve float. These are examined here in turn, and then the effect of a change in reserve requirements is described. Finally, we will look at Treasury transactions, which can also affect reserves in the banking system.

Open Market Operations

When the Fed, through its open market operations, purchases securities such as government bonds, it adds to bank reserves. The Fed pays for the bonds with a check. The seller deposits the check in an account and receives a deposit account credit. The bank presents the check to the Reserve Bank for payment and receives a credit to its account. When the Fed buys a $1,000 government bond, the check for which is deposited in Bank A, the transactions may be summarized as follows:

1. Bank A's deposit at its Reserve Bank is increased by $1,000. The Reserve Bank has a new asset—a bond worth $1,000.
2. Deposits in Bank A are increased by $1,000 ($200 in required reserves and $800 in excess reserves).

The opposite takes place when the Fed sells securities in the market.

In contrast to the other actions that affect reserves in the banking system, open market operations are entirely conducted by the Fed. For this reason they are the most important policy tool the Fed has to control reserves and the money supply. Open market operations are conducted virtually every business day, both to smooth out ups and downs caused by other transactions, and to implement changes in the money supply called for by the Federal Open Market Committee.

Depository Institution Transactions

When a bank borrows from its Reserve Bank, it is borrowing reserves; so reserves are increased by the amount of the loan. Similarly, when a loan to the Reserve Bank is repaid, reserves are reduced by that amount. The transactions when Bank A borrows $1,000 from its Reserve Bank may be summarized as follows:

1. Bank A's deposit at its Reserve Bank is increased by $1,000. The assets of the Reserve Bank are increased by $1,000 by the note from Bank A.
2. Bank A's excess reserves have been increased by $1,000. It also has a new $1,000 liability—its note to the Reserve Bank.

This process is reversed when a debt to the Reserve Bank is repaid.

Federal Reserve Float

Changes in Federal Reserve float also affect bank reserves. Float arises out of the process of collecting checks handled by Reserve Banks. **Federal Reserve float** is the temporary increase in bank reserves that results when checks are credited to the reserve account of the depositing bank before they are debited from the account of the banks on which they are drawn. Checks drawn on nearby banks are credited almost immediately to the account of the bank in which they were deposited and debited to the account of the bank on which the check was drawn. Under Fed regulations, all checks are credited one or two days later to the account of the bank in which the check was deposited. It may take longer for the check to go through the collection process and be debited to the account of the bank upon which it is drawn. When this happens, bank reserves are increased, and this increase is called *float*. The process by which a $1,000 check drawn on Bank B is deposited in Bank A and credited to its account before it is debited to the account of Bank B may be summarized:

1. Bank A transfers $1,000 from its Cash Items in the Process of Collection to its account at the Reserve Bank. Its reserves are increased by $1,000.

Federal Reserve float
temporary increase in bank reserves from checks credited to one bank's reserves and not yet debited to another's

2. The Reserve Bank takes $1,000 from its Deferred Availability Account and transfers it to Bank A's account.

Thus, total reserves of banks are increased temporarily by $1,000. They are reduced when Bank B's account at its Reserve Bank is reduced by $1,000 a day or two later.

Changes in reserve requirements change the amount of deposit expansion that is possible with a given level of reserves. With a reserve ratio of 20 percent, excess reserves of $800 can be expanded to $4,000 of additional loans and deposits. If the reserve ratio is reduced to 10 percent, it is possible to expand $800 of excess reserves to $8,000 of additional loans and deposits. When the reserve ratio is lowered, additional expansion also takes place because part of the required reserves becomes excess reserves. This process is reversed when the reserve ratio is raised.

Bank reserves are also affected by changes in the level of deposits of foreign central banks and governments at the Reserve Banks. These deposits are maintained with the Reserve Banks at times as part of the monetary reserves of a foreign country and may also be used to settle international balances. A decrease in such foreign deposits with the Reserve Banks increases bank reserves; an increase in them decreases bank reserves.

Treasury Transactions

Bank reserves are also affected by the transactions of the Treasury. They are increased by spending and making payments and decreased when the Treasury increases the size of its accounts at the Reserve Banks. The Treasury makes almost all of its payments out of its accounts at the Reserve Banks, and such spending adds to bank reserves. For example, the recipient of a check from the Treasury deposits it in a bank. The bank sends it to the Reserve Bank for collection and receives a credit to its account. The Reserve Bank debits the account of the Treasury. When a Treasury check for $1,000 is deposited in Bank A and required reserves are 20 percent, the transactions may be summarized as follows:

1. The deposits of Bank A are increased by $1,000, its required reserves by $200, and excess reserves by $800.
2. Bank A's reserves at the Reserve Bank are increased by $1,000.
3. The deposit account of the Treasury at the Reserve Bank is reduced by $1,000.

Treasury funds from tax collections or the sale of bonds are generally deposited in its accounts in banks. When the Treasury has a need for payment funds from its accounts at the Reserve Banks, it transfers funds from commercial banks to its accounts at the Reserve Banks. This process reduces bank reserves. When $1,000 is transferred from the account in Bank A and required reserves are 20 percent, transactions may be summarized as follows:

1. The Treasury deposit in Bank A is reduced by $1,000, required reserves by $200, and excess reserves by $800.
2. The Treasury account at the Reserve Bank is increased by $1,000, and the account of Bank A is reduced by $1,000.

The Treasury is the largest single depositor at the Fed. The volume of transfers between the account of the Treasury and the reserve accounts of banks is large enough to cause significant changes in reserves in the banking system. For this reason, the Fed closely monitors the Treasury's account and often uses open market operations to minimize its effect on bank reserves. This is accomplished by purchasing securities to provide reserves to the banking system when the Treasury's account increases, and selling securities when the account of the Treasury falls to a low level.

The effect on bank reserves is the same for changes in Treasury cash holdings as it is for changes in Treasury accounts at the Reserve Banks. Reserves are increased when the Treasury decreases its cash holdings, and reserves are decreased when it increases such holdings.

THE MONETARY BASE AND THE MONEY MULTIPLIER

Earlier in this chapter we examined the deposit multiplying capacity of the banking system. Recall that, in the situation shown in Table 5.1, excess reserves of $1,000 were introduced into the banking system with a 20 percent reserve ratio, resulting in a deposit expansion of $5,000. This can also be viewed as a money multiplier of 5.

In our complex financial system, the money multiplier is not quite so straightforward. It will be useful to focus on the relationship between the monetary base and the money supply in order to better understand the complexity of the money multiplier. The **monetary base** is defined as banking system reserves plus currency held by the public. More specifically, the monetary base consists of reserve deposits held in Reserve Banks, vault cash or currency held by depository institutions, and currency held by the nonbank public. Thus the monetary base can either be used as cash holdings for the public or as reserves to support bank deposits. The monetary base (*MB*) times the money multiplier (*m*) produces the M1 definition of the money supply. It can be expressed in formula form as:

monetary base
banking system reserves
plus currency held by
the public

$$MB \times m = M1$$

The size and stability of the money multiplier is important because the Fed can control the monetary base, but it cannot directly control the size of the money supply. Changes in the money supply are caused by changes in the monetary base, in the money multiplier, or in both. The Fed can change the size of the monetary base through open market operations or changes in the reserve ratio. The money multiplier is not constant. It can and does fluctuate over time depending on actions taken by the Fed as well as by the nonbank public and the U.S. Treasury.

As of June 1995, the money multiplier was approximately 2.7 as determined by dividing the $1,143.8 billion M1 money stock by the $429.7 billion monetary base.[2]

Taking into account the actions of the nonbank public and the Treasury, the formula for the money multiplier in today's financial system can be expressed as:[3]

$$m = \frac{1 + k}{r(1 + t + g) + k}$$

where

   r is the ratio of reserves to total deposits (checkable, noncheckable time and savings, and government)

   k is the ratio of currency held by the nonbank public to checkable deposits

   t is the ratio of noncheckable deposits to checkable deposits

   g is the ratio of government deposits to checkable deposits.

Let's illustrate how the size of the money multiplier is determined by returning to our previous example of a 20 percent reserve ratio. Recall that in a more simple financial system, the money multiplier would be determined as $1/r$ or $1/0.20$, which equals 5. However, in our complex system we also need to consider leakages into currency held by the nonbank public, noncheckable time and savings deposits, and government deposits. Let's further assume that the reserve ratio applies to total deposits, a k of 20 percent, a t of 10 percent, and a g of 5 percent. The money multiplier then would be estimated as:

$$m = \frac{1 + 0.20}{0.20(1 + 0.10 + 0.05) + 0.20} = \frac{1.20}{0.43} = 2.8$$

Of course, if a change occurred in any of the components, the money multiplier would adjust accordingly as would the size of the money supply.

At this point, we should ask why it is important to regulate and control the supply of money. The money supply (M1) is linked to the gross domestic product (GDP) via the velocity or turnover of money. More specifically, the **velocity of money** measures the rate of circulation of the money supply. It is expressed as the average number of times each dollar is spent on purchases of goods and services and is calculated as nominal GDP (GDP in current dollars) divided by M1. Changes in the growth rates for money

velocity of money
the rate of circulation
of the money supply

2.   *Federal Reserve Bulletin* (October 1995): A13 and A14.
3.   The reader interested in understanding how the money multiplier is derived will find a discussion in most money and banking textbooks.

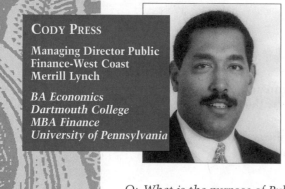

CODY PRESS

**Managing Director Public
Finance-West Coast
Merrill Lynch**

*BA Economics
Dartmouth College
MBA Finance
University of Pennsylvania*

> *"The people who
> use the bridge pay
> for it throughout
> its useful life."*

Q: *What is the purpose of Public Finance?*
A: The short answer is that we help municipalities and other nonprofit entities solve their financing problems.

Q: *Who are these entities?*
A: Basically you can use the rule that anyone who is tax-exempt and needs to raise money could be a client. Municipalities, museums, counties, states, nonprofit hospitals, and so on. In many cases we will be hired to secure financing for a specific project, such as a bridge or a toll road.

Q: *Let's take a simple example. How would a city finance a bridge?*
A: There could be several options, but in many cases we will help the city issue bonds to generate the money necessary to build the bridge. The city borrows the money by selling bonds and repays it over time, quite possibly through a toll or fee for using the bridge. This is generally a better option than raising taxes because it means that the people who use the bridge pay for it throughout its useful life.

Q: *What role do you play in this transaction?*
A: We work with the municipality on two levels. We work with the elected officials on the higher level decisions, helping them understand what their options are for raising the funds they need to implement their plans. Then we work with their staff people on the more technical aspects of the bond issue, how it will be structured and so forth. When the bonds are sold we keep a percentage of the proceeds as our compensation.

Q: *Would you describe your function as sales or management?*
A: It's a combination of both. Several years ago there were 20 people in my group so I spent more time on management then. Now I have eleven people so I spend more time on sales. I spend at least two days a week out of the office meeting mostly with our existing clients.

Q: *Is this a competitive field?*
A: It's very competitive. The size of the market is much smaller now than it was just a few years ago, so we all compete for the available deals.

Q: *What skills do you rely on most?*
A: Common sense and judgment are very important. There are always decisions about where to focus your time and resources, and good judgment is essential in making the right choices. Honesty is an important quality too.

Q: *What are the career options in this field?*
A: That's an interesting issue. Because public finance is so specialized, it's not easy to move to another field. You really have to be very interested in working with government clients for the long haul, because you may not have a lot of other options.

130

supply ($M1_g$) and money velocity ($M1V_g$) affect the growth rate in real economic activity ($RGDP_g$) and the rate of inflation (I_g) and can be expressed in equation form as follows:

$$M1_g + M1V_g = RGDP_g + I_g$$

For example, if the velocity of money remains relatively constant, then a link between money supply and nominal GDP should be observable. Likewise, after nominal GDP is adjusted for inflation, the resulting real GDP growth can be examined relative to M1 growth rates. Changes in money supply have been found to lead to changes in economic activity.

The ability to predict M1 velocity, in addition to money supply changes, is important in making successful monetary policy. Fed M1 growth targets need to take into consideration expected velocity movements in order to achieve the desired effects on real GDP and inflation. It would be naive, however, to believe that regulating and controlling the supply of money and credit is all that is needed to manage our complex economy. We also know that economic activity is affected by government actions concerning government spending, taxation, and the management of our public debt.

SUMMARY

This chapter began with the identification and discussion of the four national policy objectives—real growth in GDP, high levels of employment, stable prices, and a balance in international activities. The Federal Reserve System, the President, Congress, and the U.S. Treasury then were identified as major policy makers. Policy instruments of the Treasury were discussed next in terms of fiscal and debt management policies.

The remainder of the chapter focused on several aspects of the money supply. First, the mechanics of deposit expansion and contraction within the "banking system" were covered. This was followed by a discussion of the factors that affect bank reserves. Finally, the terms *monetary base* and *money multiplier* were defined and the importance of controlling the money supply was discussed.

KEY TERMS

automatic stabilizers	fiscal policy
crowding out	fractional reserve system
debt management	gross domestic product (GDP)
deficit financing	inflation
deficit reserves	monetary base
derivative deposit	monetizing the debt
excess reserves	money multiplier
Federal Reserve float	primary deposit

required reserves   total reserves
reserve ratio   transfer payments
tax policy   velocity of money
tax policy

DISCUSSION QUESTIONS

1. List and describe briefly the economic policy objectives of the nation.
2. Describe the relationship between policy makers, types of policies, and policy objectives.
3. Describe the effects of tax policy on monetary and credit conditions.
4. Federal government deficit financing may have a very great influence on monetary and credit conditions. Explain.
5. Discuss the various objectives of debt management.
6. Explain how Federal Reserve notes are supported or backed in our financial system.
7. Why is the expansion and contraction of deposits by the banking system possible in our financial system?
8. Trace the effect on its accounts of a loan made by a bank that has excess reserves available from new deposits.
9. Explain how deposit expansion takes place in a banking system consisting of two banks.
10. Explain the potential for deposit expansion when required reserves average 10 percent and $2,000 in excess reserves are deposited in the banking system.
11. Trace the effect on bank reserves of a change in the amount of cash held by the public.
12. Describe the effect on bank reserves when the Federal Reserve sells U.S. government securities to a bank.
13. Summarize the factors that can lead to a change in bank reserves.
14. What is the difference between the monetary base and total bank reserves?
15. Briefly describe what is meant by the money multiplier and indicate the factors that affect its magnitude or size.
16. Define the velocity of money and explain why it is important to anticipate changes in money velocity.
17. Why does it seem to be important to regulate and control the supply of money?

PROBLEMS

1. An economic recession has developed and the Federal Reserve Board has taken several actions to retard further declines in economic activ-

ity. The U.S. Treasury now wishes to take steps to assist the Fed in this effort. Describe the actions the Treasury might take.

2. Determine the maximum deposit expansion in a financial system where the reserve ratio is 11 percent, initial excess reserves are $1 million, and there are no currency or other leakages. What would the money multiplier be? What would your answer be if the reserve requirement had been 9 percent?

3. Assume a financial system has a monetary base of $25 million. The reserve ratio is 10 percent and there are no leakages in the system. What is the size of the money multiplier? What will be the system's money supply? How would the money supply change if the reserve ratio is increased to 14 percent?

4. A complex financial system has these relationships: the ratio of reserves to total deposits is 12 percent and the ratio of noncheckable deposits to checkable deposits is 40 percent. In addition, currency held by the nonbank public amounts to 15 percent of checkable deposits. The ratio of government deposits to checkable deposits is 8 percent, and the monetary base is $300 million.
   a. Determine the size of the M1 money multiplier and the size of the money supply.
   b. If the ratio of currency in circulation to checkable deposits were to drop to 13 percent, what would be the impact on the money supply?
   c. What would happen to the money supply if the reserve requirement increased to 14 percent while noncheckable deposits to checkable deposits fell to 35 percent? Assume the other ratios remain as originally stated.

5. Obtain a current issue of the *Federal Reserve Bulletin* and use it to:
   a. Find M1 and the monetary base and then estimate the money multiplier.
   b. Determine the nominal gross national product (GNP in current dollars). Estimate the velocity of money using M1 from the first part and nominal GNP.
   c. Indicate how the money multiplier and the velocity of money have changed between two recent years.

6. Determine the change in checkable deposits and the money multiplier for a simple financial system where the reserve ratio is 0.15, initial excess reserves are $1,000, and there are no other leakages or adjustments in the system.

7. A complex financial system has the following relationships. The ratio of reserves to total deposits is 15 percent, and the ratio of noncheckable deposits to checkable deposits is 40 percent. In addition, currency held by the nonbank public amounts to 20 percent of checkable deposits. The ratio of government deposits to checkable deposits is 8 percent and the initial reserves are $900 million.

    a.   Determine the size of the M1 money supply and the M1 multiplier.

    b.   What will happen to the financial system's M1 money supply and money multiplier if the reserve requirement decreases to 10 percent while the ratio of noncheckable deposits to checkable deposits falls to 30 percent? Assume the other ratios remain as originally stated.

SELF-TEST QUESTIONS

1. U.S. national policy objectives include:
   a. real economic growth
   b. high employment
   c. stable prices
   d. all of the above
2. Government financing of large budgetary deficits:
   a. absorbs savings and decreases interest rates
   b. may temporarily stimulate economic activity
   c. is known as monetizing the deficit
   d. reduces total consumer spending and demand
3. Fiscal policy is *not* administered by which one of the following policy makers?
   a. Federal Reserve System
   b. the President
   c. Congress
   d. U.S. Treasury
4. Debt management is carried out by which one of the following?
   a. Federal Reserve System
   b. the President
   c. Congress
   d. U.S. Treasury
5. U.S. Federal Reserve notes are primarily backed by which one of the following items?
   a. gold certificates
   b. Special Drawing Rights
   c. U.S. government and agency securities
   d. silver coins and bullion
6. Deposits that add new reserves to the bank where they are deposited are called:
   a. primary deposits
   b. derivative deposits
   c. secondary deposits
   d. Special Drawing Rights

7. Total reserves in the banking system consist of:
   a. currency and coin
   b. reserve deposits and secondary deposits
   c. vault cash and derivative deposits
   d. reserve deposits and vault cash
8. Transactions that affect bank reserves can be initiated by the:
   a. nonbank public
   b. Federal Reserve System
   c. U.S. Treasury
   d. all of the above
9. Banking system reserves plus currency held by the nonbank public is referred to as the:
   a. money supply
   b. monetary base
   c. monetary multiplier
   d. monetary requirement

SELF-TEST PROBLEMS

1. Important policy objectives of the federal government include economic growth, high employment, price stability, and international financial equilibrium. The objectives are functions of monetary policy, fiscal policy, and debt management. These policies and objectives are addressed by the Federal Reserve System, the President, the Congress, and the U.S. Treasury. How is the responsibility for each allocated among these areas of government?

2. Determine the maximum deposit expansion in a financial system where the reserve requirement is 12 percent, initial excess reserves are $100,000, and there are no currency or other leakages. What would be the money multiplier? What would your answers be if the reserve requirement were only 8 percent?

SUGGESTED READINGS

Abel, Andrew B. "Can the Government Roll Over Its Debt Forever?" *Business Review*, Federal Reserve Bank of Philadelphia (November–December 1992): 3–18.

Becketti, Sean, and Charles S. Morris. "Does Money Still Forecast Economic Activity?" *Economic Review*, Federal Reserve Bank of Kansas City (Fourth Quarter 1992): 65–77.

Carlson, John B., and Susan M. Byrne. "Recent Behavior of Velocity: Alternative Measures of Money." *Economic Review*, Federal Reserve Bank of Cleveland (Quarter 1 1992): 2–10.

Fabozzi, Frank J., Franco Modigliani, and Michael G. Ferri. *Foundations of Financial Markets and Institutions*. Englewood Cliffs, NJ: Prentice Hall, 1994. Chap. 5.

Kidwell, David S., and Richard L. Peterson. *Financial Institutions, Markets, and Money*, 5e. Fort Worth, TX: The Dryden Press, 1993. Chaps. 4 and 26.

Kretzmer, Peter E. "Monetary vs. Fiscal Policy: New Evidence on an Old Debate." *Economic Review*, Federal Reserve Bank of Kansas City (Second Quarter 1992): 21–30.

Manypenny, Gerald D., and Michael L. Bermudez. "The Federal Reserve Banks as Fiscal Agents and Depositories of the United States." *Federal Reserve Bulletin* (October 1992): 727–737.

Sill, D. Keith. "Managing the Public Debt." *Business Review*, Federal Reserve Bank of Philadelphia (July–August 1994): 3–13.

ANSWERS TO SELF-TEST QUESTIONS 1. d, 2. b, 3. a, 4. d, 5. c, 6. a, 7. d, 8. d, 9. b.

ANSWERS TO SELF-TEST PROBLEMS

1. The President of the United States along with his advisors formulates fiscal policy. Congress enacts legislation to implement fiscal policy (after exercising its authority to modify the policy). The Fed has primary responsibility for monetary policy, while the Treasury handles debt management.

2. Maximum deposit expansion: $100,000/0.12 = $833,333
    Money multiplier: $1/0.12 = 8.333$
    Maximum expansion for an 8% reserve requirement: $100,000/0.08 = $1,250,000
    Money multiplier for an 8% reserve requirement: $1/0.08 = 12.5$

CHAPTER 6

International Trade and Finance

AFTER STUDYING THIS CHAPTER, YOU SHOULD BE ABLE TO:

- Explain the importance of finance to the effective conduct of international commerce and investment.
- Describe how international payments are made.
- Describe the nature of foreign exchange markets.
- Discuss the effect of exchange rates on international trade and explain arbitrage and exchange quotations.
- Explain the role of financial managers of businesses in reducing foreign exchange risks.
- Describe how the banking systems of the world facilitate the financing of sales by exporters and purchases by importers.
- Show how the Export-Import Bank aids in financing international trade.
- Describe the components of the U.S. balance of payments.
- Discuss characteristics of the international financial system.

The productive capacity of the U.S. economy is the result of many factors, including vast natural resources, suitable weather conditions, and a population with the motivation and the ability to profit by these natural advantages. Of equal importance to the nation's productive growth is a form of government that has encouraged individual effort. The government has made a major contribution in this respect by facilitating trade throughout the nation. Thus each geographical area can specialize in the activities associated with its natural resources.

It is difficult to imagine the situation that would exist if each of the 50 states tried to be self-sufficient. Under these circumstances, the northern states would not enjoy citrus fruits. Floridians would not eat beef from Kansas, and houses in Oklahoma could not be built with lumber from the Northwest. Nor could we expect the tobacco-growing states to have modern farm machinery, since the market for large machines in a single state would not warrant production on a scale necessary for economical manufacture.

While these principles of specialization are obvious enough within the United States, it may be less easy to appreciate their application beyond the nation's borders. Yet what is true about specialization of effort within a nation holds true with equal force among nations. Aside from specialization there is now a virtual flood of plant relocations to countries with ample and economical labor supplies. The simplest consumer item may be a product of several areas of the world. As the world of commerce becomes increasingly integrated the requirements for effective international financial arrangements increases in importance.

The United States has developed an efficient operating system of finance to settle claims of indebtedness among parties to domestic transactions. However, there is no world central bank to provide a world monetary unit to accommodate commerce across national boundaries. Historically, forms of currency, such as gold, silver, or other commodities have served as acceptable international monetary units. Standards of value for such monetary units have at times been set by central banks of the leading trading nations but all too often international commerce has suffered from chronic problems with such systems. Although the U.S. dollar has had its share of problems it has for many years served as the acknowledged world money. Its general acceptance throughout the world has placed upon it the responsibility for serving as a medium of exchange and a unit of account for international transactions, a store of value, and as a standard of deferred payment for longer-term borrowing and lending.

Valiant efforts are now being made to form a European Monetary Union (EMU). With the establishment of a European Central Bank a common unit of money may be forthcoming. Such a monetary unit may carry a designation such as European Currency Unit (ECU). Such units of money presumably would be accepted throughout the European trading area and beyond. Such a development would involve giving up the sovereignty of individual European countries with respect to their monetary systems, and much difficulty is being experienced in this respect. In the meantime, the U.S. dollar serves the world in settling international monetary claims.

INTERNATIONAL TRANSACTIONS

The U.S. dollar can be converted easily into other currencies. Therefore, foreign exporters are usually quite willing to accept dollars in payment. In contrast to the United States, importers in many countries must arrange payments in the currency of the exporter's country. The strength of the U.S. dollar makes it popular for the settlement of transactions among other countries as well as between the United States and foreign countries.

PAYMENTS BY INDIVIDUALS

In the United States, those who offer goods and services expect payment in dollars. Likewise, a U.S. citizen who orders leather goods from Mexico, glassware from Italy, or a year's subscription to the *London Times* may at times need to arrange payment in the appropriate foreign currency. When it is necessary or desirable to make a payment in the currency of another country, actual possession of that currency is unnecessary. In the situation of a U.S. resident subscribing to the *London Times,* the following example illustrates how this works.

If the person subscribing to the *Times* needs a claim for 250 pounds, she or he might find a British tourist willing to write a check against a bank in England for that amount. In return, the American would give the tourist the appropriate number of dollars, which the visitor could spend while touring this country. The subscriber would then send the check together with the order to England, where the check would be deposited for collection at the newspaper's bank.

To carry out this transaction with a tourist would be an awkward process, however. It is much more likely that the subscriber would go to a bank and, using dollars, buy a claim against British pounds sterling equivalent to the subscription cost of the paper. This claim is in the form of a bill of exchange, an order by telegraph, or similar instrument. Banks and foreign exchange brokers provide this service for a small fee. Although not all banks have foreign exchange departments, practically all have correspondent relations with banks that do offer the service. Hence, one can buy a foreign money claim at a local bank.

Banks that deal directly in foreign exchange may do so by maintaining monetary deposits in foreign banks, against which they may write drafts for sale to their home customers. In other cases, banks may operate branches in foreign countries, as authorized by the Federal Reserve. There are currently about 1,000 foreign offices of U.S. banks. Likewise, foreign banking corporations have a network of contacts outside their countries. In addition to maintaining correspondent relations with U.S. banks, foreign banks are permitted to operate agencies and to set up subsidiaries in this country. These foreign banking corporations are not subject to any special U.S. restrictions.

DEVELOPMENT OF
INTERNATIONAL
FINANCE

International finance probably began about 5,000 years ago when Babylonian cities rose to importance as centers of trading between the Mediterranean sea and civilizations in the East. Gold was used for transactions and as a store of value probably beginning around 3000 B.C. when the Pharaohs ruled Egypt. Centers of international finance shifted to the Greek city of Athens around 500 B.C. and to the Roman Empire and Rome around 100 B.C.* It appears that whenever international trade developed, financial institutions came into existence and international bankers followed.

Instruments and documents similar to those in use today were designed to control movement of cargo, insure against losses, satisfy government requirements, and transfer funds. Financial centers shifted to the northern European cities during the 1500s, and in more recent years to London, New York, and Tokyo. Today, international trade takes place and international claims are continuously settled around the clock. It is no longer necessary to have a physical center—such as a city—to carry out international finance.

*For a more detailed look at the early development of international finance, see: Robert D. Fraser, *International Banking and Finance*, 6th ed. Washington, D.C.: R&H Publishers, 1984, Chapter 2.

FOREIGN EXCHANGE MARKETS

foreign exchange markets
electronic network that connects the major financial centers of the world

We ordinarily think of a market as a specific place or institution, but this is not always so. **Foreign exchange markets** are in reality electronic communication systems connecting the major financial centers of the world. When an individual or business firm engaged in a foreign transaction deals with a local bank, it is, in effect, dealing with the exchange markets of the world. Transactions throughout the world may be completed in only a few minutes by virtue of the effective communications network serving the various financial institutions, including central banks of every nation.

EXCHANGE RATES

In Chapter 2 we defined an exchange rate as the value of one currency in terms of another. There are two basic methods for quoting the value of one currency relative to another currency. First, is the *direct quotation* method. For example, if we focus on the U.S. dollar relative to the French franc, the direct quotation would be the number of U.S. dollars needed to buy one French franc. The *indirect quotation method* would express the number of French francs required per U.S. dollar.

TABLE 6.1   Selected Foreign Exchange Rates, October 31, 1995

COUNTRY	CURRENCY	U.S. DOLLAR EQUIVALENT	CURRENCY PER U.S. DOLLAR
Australia	Dollar	0.7607	1.3145
Austria	Schilling	0.1010	9.9055
Britain	Pound	1.5805	0.6327
Canada	Dollar	0.7438	1.3445
Denmark	Krone	0.1832	5.4595
France	Franc	0.2049	4.8810
Germany	Mark	0.7107	1.4070
Hong Kong	Dollar	0.1293	7.7313
India	Rupee	0.02924	34.200
Italy	Lira	0.0006289	1590.00
Japan	Yen	0.009809	101.95
Malaysia	Ringgit	0.3935	2.5413
Mexico	Peso	0.1415	7.0650
New Zealand	Dollar	0.6586	1.5183
Saudi Arabia	Riyal	0.2666	3.7505
Singapore	Dollar	0.7072	1.4140
South Africa	Rand	0.2742	3.6470
Sweden	Krona	0.1508	6.6295
Switzerland	Franc	0.8807	1.1354
Taiwan	Dollar	0.0705	26.987
Venezuela	Bolivar	0.005890	169.79

Source: *The Wall Street Journal* (November 1, 1995): c15.

Table 6.1 shows both direct and indirect exchange rates for a variety of foreign currencies relative to the U.S. dollar as of the end of October, 1995. For example, one French franc was worth 0.2049 U.S. dollars or between $0.20 and $0.21 using the direct quotation method. On an indirect basis, it takes 4.8810 French francs to equal one U.S. dollar. One Japanese yen was worth 0.009809 U.S. dollars or about $0.01. This converts to about 102 yen per U.S. dollar. The Italian lira is worth even less per U.S. dollar as indicated by a direct quotation of 0.0006289 or about $0.001 in U.S. dollars. In other words, it takes 1,590 lira to equal one U.S. dollar. It should be apparent if you know the direct (indirect) exchange rate you can easily find the indirect (direct) exchange rate by dividing the direct (indirect) value into the number one. For example, if the French franc is worth U.S. $0.2049, then the number of French francs needed to buy one U.S. dollar is 4.8810 (1/0.2049). Or, converting from an indirect quotation to a direct quotation for the French franc we would have 1/4.8810 which equals 0.2049.

Since the newspaper records the exchange ratio of large unit transfers within the foreign exchange market, an individual buying foreign currency claims would not get exactly the same ratio. The prices for an individual always favor the seller, who makes a margin of profit.

The balance in the foreign account of a U.S. bank is subject to constant drain as the bank sells claims to individuals who import goods or obtain services from other countries. These banks may reestablish a given deposit level in their correspondent banks either through selling dollar claims in the foreign countries concerned or by buying claims from another dealer in the foreign exchange.

The supply and demand relationship involving two currencies is said to be in "balance" or equilibrium at the current or *spot* exchange rate. Demand for a foreign currency derives from the demand for that country's goods, services, and financial assets. For example, U.S. consumers and investors demand a variety of German goods, services, and financial assets most of which must be paid for in German Marks or deutsche Marks (DMs). The supply of DMs comes from German demand for U.S. goods, services, and financial assets. A change in the relative demand for German Marks versus U.S. dollars will cause the spot exchange rate to change. Currency exchange rates also depend on relative inflation rates, relative interest rates, and political and economic risks.

Figure 6.1 illustrates how exchange rates are determined in a foreign exchange market. Graph A depicts a supply and demand relationship between the U.S. dollar and German deutsche Mark (DM). The market, in our example, is in balance when one German Mark is worth $0.60 in terms of U.S. dollars. This price reflects the market-clearing price that equates the demand (D_1) for DMs relative to the supply (S_1) of DMs.

Now, assume Americans increase their demand for German products and services that are priced in deutsche Marks. Americans will need to exchange their dollars for DMs in order to pay for their German product purchases. The consequence is an increase or shift in demand for DMs from D_1 to D_2 as is depicted in Graph B. The supply of DMs reflects German demand for U.S. products and services, and as long as there is no change, S_1 will remain unchanged. As a consequence of this scenario, the increased demand for DMs results in a new higher equilibrium price of $0.61.

A further increased demand for German goods and services could cause the dollar price or value of one deutsche Mark to increase even more. Graph C in Figure 6.1 depicts such an increase as a shift from D_2 to D_3. Again, with no change in the supply of DMs, the new market-clearing price of a DM might be $0.62. Of course, as the DM dollar value increases, the price of German products also increase. At some point, as German products become more costly, U.S. demand for these foreign goods will decline. Graph D depicts this cutback in U.S. demand for DMs as a shift downward from the D_3 level in Graph C to the D_2 level. In a similar fashion, the higher dollar value of the DM in Graph C makes U.S. goods and services less costly to Germans and thus the supply of DMs might increase or shift from S_1 to S_2. The net result could be a new equilibrium exchange rate where the dollar price of a DM is $0.60.

FIGURE 6.1   Exchange Rate Determination in the Foreign Exchange Market

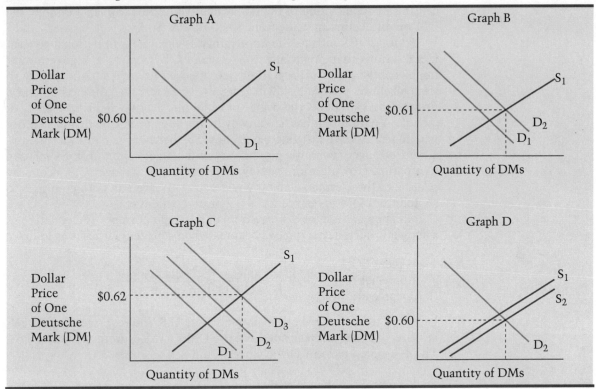

Now let's turn our attention to what happens if changes occur in relative interest rates and inflation rates between two countries. A nation with relatively higher interest rate levels will attract investors who seek out the highest returns on their investment funds much like a nation with a higher relative economic growth rate attracts capital investments. For example, if interest rates in the United States decline relative to those in Germany, investors will switch or move their debt investments denominated in U.S. dollars into DM-denominated debt investments. This increased demand for deutsche Marks relative to U.S. dollars will cause the DM dollar value to increase. Using an equilibrium DM dollar value of $0.60, the DM will rise to, say, $0.63 to reflect the greater demand for DMs relative to dollars.

A nation with a relatively lower inflation rate will have a relatively stronger currency. For example, if inflation becomes lower in the United States relative to Germany, German products of comparable quality will become increasingly more expensive. Americans will find it less expensive to buy American products and so will Germans. The result will be fewer

German imports into the United States and greater U.S. exports to Germany causing an appreciation of the dollar relative to the DM. For example, the DM might decline in value from $0.60 to, say, $0.58.

Political risk reflects the uncertainty associated with national government actions that might affect asset values. For example, a government might confiscate or expropriate assets held by foreigners. A nation with relatively lower political risk will generally have a relatively stronger currency. *Economic risk* reflects the degree of economic growth and the stability of growth. A nation that has a relatively higher economic growth and stability will generally have a stronger currency. Furthermore, a nation with a relatively stronger economic growth rate will attract capital inflows relative to a nation growing more slowly. For example, a stronger U.S. economy relative to the German economy will cause investors in both countries to switch from DM investments to dollar investments.

An appreciation (or depreciation) of a foreign currency (FC) relative to a domestic currency is typically expressed on a percentage basis as follows:

$$\text{Percent FC Appreciation (Depreciation)} = \frac{\text{FC's New Dollar Value} - \text{FC's Old Dollar Value}}{\text{FC's Old Dollar Value}}$$

Let's first turn to the above example where U.S. interest rates decline relative to German interest rates and the DM increases from $0.60 to $0.63. The associated percent DM change would be:

$$\text{Percent DM Change} = \frac{\$0.63 - \$0.60}{\$0.60} = \frac{\$0.03}{\$0.60} = 5.0\%$$

In other words, the DM would have appreciated by 5 percent relative to the dollar.

For our example where the U.S. inflation rate decreases relative to the German inflation rate and the dollar price of the deutsche Mark declines, we have:

$$\text{Percent DM Change} = \frac{\$0.58 - \$0.60}{\$0.60} = \frac{-\$0.02}{\$0.60} = -3.3\%$$

Thus, the deutsche Mark has depreciated by 3.3 percent relative to the U.S. dollar because of the new relatively higher German inflation rate.

The amount of U.S. dollar ($US) appreciation or depreciation also can be easily calculated since the value of one currency is simply the inverse of the other currency. For example, when the dollar price of a DM is $0.60, one $US is worth DM1.667 (i.e., 1/$0.60). Similarly, when the dollar price of a DM rises to $0.63, one $US is worth 1/0.63, or 1.587. When the dollar value of the DM increases, one dollar can be exchanged for fewer deutsche Marks, and vice versa.

An appreciation (or depreciation) of a domestic currency (DC) relative to a foreign currency can be expressed on a percentage basis as follows:

$$\text{Percent DC Change} = \frac{\dfrac{1}{(\text{FC's New Dollar Value})} - \dfrac{1}{(\text{FC's Old Dollar Value})}}{1/(\text{FC's Old Dollar Value})}$$

Using the above data for the relative interest rate example involving the American dollar and the German Mark, we have:

$$\text{Percent \$US Change} = \frac{1/\$0.63 - 1/\$0.60}{1/\$0.60}$$

$$= \frac{\text{DM1.587} - \text{DM1.667}}{\text{DM1.667}} = \frac{-0.08}{1.667} = -4.8\%$$

Thus, the U.S. dollar in this example depreciated by 4.8% relative to the German deutsche Mark. Notice that the $US depreciation is not the exact percentage change as the DM appreciation calculated above. This is because the bases from which the calculations are made are different.

Arbitrage

Arbitrage is the simultaneous, or nearly simultaneous, purchasing of commodities, securities, or bills of exchange in one market and selling them in another where the price is higher. In international exchange, variations in quotations between countries at any time are quickly brought into alignment through the arbitrage activities of international financiers. For example, if the exchange rate in New York was reported at £1 = $1.51 and in London the rate was quoted at £1 = $1.50, alert international arbitrageurs would simultaneously sell claims to British pounds in New York at the rate of $1.51 and have London correspondents sell claims on U.S. dollars in London at the rate of $1.50 for each pound sterling. Such arbitrage would be profitable only when dealing in large sums. If an arbitrageur, under these circumstances, sold a claim on £100 million in New York, $151 million would be received. The corresponding sale of claims on American dollars in London would be at the rate of £100 million for $150 million. Hence, a profit of $1 million would be realized on the transaction. A quotation differential of as little as one-sixteenth of one cent may be sufficient to encourage arbitrage activities.

The ultimate effect of large-scale arbitrage activities on exchange rates is the elimination of the variation between the two markets. The sale of large amounts of claims to American dollars in London would drive the price for pounds sterling up, and in New York the sale of claims to pounds sterling would force the exchange rate down.

arbitrage
buying commodities, securities, or bills of exchange in one market and immediately selling them in another to make a profit from price differences in the two markets

Quotation Variance Among Instruments

If you ask at the local bank about the exchange rate for a foreign currency, you will generally be given a banker's sight draft rate. A *banker's sight draft*, or banker's check as it is commonly called, differs from the common bank check only in that it is drawn by one bank on another bank. When the draft is presented for payment at the foreign bank, the balance of the drawing bank is reduced. Several days or weeks may elapse between the time the check is issued by the bank and the time it is presented for payment at the foreign bank or foreign correspondent bank. During this interval, the foreign balance of the issuing bank is not affected by the transaction.

If requested, the quotation may be based on a cable rate. The bank may cable a certain amount of money to its foreign correspondent or branch to credit the account of a specified individual or business. The cost of a cable order is more than a banker's check because it reduces the balance of the bank's foreign deposit almost immediately. A reduction in deposits reduces the earnings that would otherwise result from the investment of the deposits.

The *banker's time draft* provides a rate that is lower than either the banker's sight draft or cable rate. This instrument, sometimes called long exchange or a long bill, is payable at a specified future date, usually 30 days or some multiple thereof. The quotations on these time drafts are, of course, lower because they reduce the balance of the foreign branch or correspondent only after a specified period of time.

BUSINESS MANAGEMENT OF FOREIGN EXCHANGE

Firms that have foreign sales must be concerned with the stability of the governments and changing values of currency in the countries in which they do business. They must also pay attention to commodity price changes and other uncertainties related to monetary systems.

Large firms usually have special departments that handle international transactions. These firms may engage in foreign exchange speculation as opportunities arise, but risk reduction is their primary goal. Among the possible actions of skilled foreign exchange specialists are hedging, adjusting accounts receivable and payable procedures, cash management, and borrowing and lending activities. Existing or anticipated variations in the value of the foreign currencies guide all of these actions. For example, a seller with a claim for payment within 90 days may anticipate a possible decline in the currency value of his customer's country. The seller can hedge by entering into a futures contract for the delivery of that currency at the existing exchange rate on the day of the contract.[1] By so doing, a loss

1.   We discuss futures contracts in the Appendix to Chapter 11.

in the collection process is offset by a gain in the delivery process 90 days hence. The fee for the futures contract becomes a cost of the transaction.

Large multinational companies enjoy special opportunities for risk reduction and speculation since they can move cash balances from one country to another as monetary conditions warrant. For example, if a decline in the value of a particular currency is expected, cash in the branch in that country may be moved back to the United States. Or, a firm may borrow funds in a foreign market and move them immediately to the United States (or to another country) with the expectation of repaying the loan at a reduced exchange rate. This is speculation rather than a risk-reduction activity. An expected decline in a currency may lead to an attempt to accelerate collection of accounts receivable, with funds transferred quickly to another country. Payments on accounts payable may be delayed in the expectation of a decline in exchange rates. If, on the other hand, a foreign currency is expected to increase in relative value, the preceding actions would be reversed.

New career opportunities have developed with the increasing importance of multinational financial management. Some corporations maintain special departments to study foreign business activities and their prospective profitability; to analyze governmental attitudes, tax rates and duties; and to determine how foreign operations are to be financed. In addition, almost constant attention must be given to day-to-day exchange rate changes to protect bank balances and other investments. International financial management will undoubtedly increase in scope and importance as the markets of the world become increasingly integrated. In the following sections we describe the various instruments of foreign exchange and their special uses.

FINANCING INTERNATIONAL TRADE

One of the substantial financial burdens of any industrial firm is the process of manufacture itself. When a U.S. manufacturer exports goods to distant places such as India or Australia, funds are tied up not only for the period of manufacture but also for a lengthy period of transportation. In order to reduce costs, manufacturers may require the foreign importer to pay for the goods as soon as they are on the way to their destination. In this way, a substantial financial burden is transferred to the importer.

FINANCING BY THE EXPORTER

If the exporter has confidence in foreign customers and is in a financial position to sell to them on open-book account, then sales arrangements should operate very much as in domestic trade, subject, of course, to the complex nature of any international transaction.

Sight and Time Drafts

As an alternative to shipping merchandise on open-account financing, the exporter may use a collection draft. A *draft,* or *bill of exchange,* is an unconditional written order, signed by the party drawing it, requiring the party to whom it is addressed to pay a certain sum of money to order or to bearer. A draft may require immediate payment by the importer upon its presentation—on demand—or it may require only acceptance on the part of the importer, providing for payment at a specified future time. An instrument requiring immediate payment is classified as a *sight draft;* one requiring payment later is a *time draft.* A draft may require remittance, or payment, in the currency of the country of the exporter or of the importer, depending upon the transaction's terms. An example of a sight draft form is shown in Figure 6.2.

Drafts may be either documentary or clean. A *documentary draft* is accompanied by an order bill of lading and other papers such as insurance receipts, certificates of sanitation, and consular invoices. The *order bill of lading* represents the written acceptance of goods for shipment by a transportation company and the terms under which the goods are to be transported to their destination. In addition, the order bill of lading carries title to the merchandise being shipped, and only its holder may claim the merchandise from the transportation company. (See Figure 6.3.) The documentary sight draft is generally referred to as a D/P draft (documentary payments draft), while the documentary time draft is referred to as a D/A draft (documentary acceptance draft).

A *clean draft* is one that is not accompanied by any special documents and is generally used when the exporter has confidence in the importer's ability to meet the draft when presented. Once the merchandise is shipped to the importer, it is delivered by the transportation company regardless of any action taken by the importer concerning the draft.

draft (bill of exchange)
an unconditional order for the payment of money from one person to another

sight draft
draft requiring immediate payment

time draft
draft that is payable at a specified future date

documentary draft
draft that is accompanied by an order bill of lading and other documents

order bill of lading
document given by a transportation company that lists goods to be transported and terms of the shipping agreement

clean draft
a draft that is not accompanied by any special documents

FIGURE 6.2   Sight Draft or Bill of Exchange

$ 2,500.00	New Orleans, Louisiana,	August 15, 19--

At sight - PAY TO THE

ORDER OF   Mervin J. Mansfield

Two thousand five hundred no/100 - - - - - - - DOLLARS

VALUE RECEIVED AND CHARGE TO ACCOUNT OF

TO   Brazilian Import Company

No.   11678 Rio de Janeiro, Brazil

NEW ORLEANS EXPORT COMPANY

Theresa M. Jones

FIGURE 6.3   Order Bill of Lading

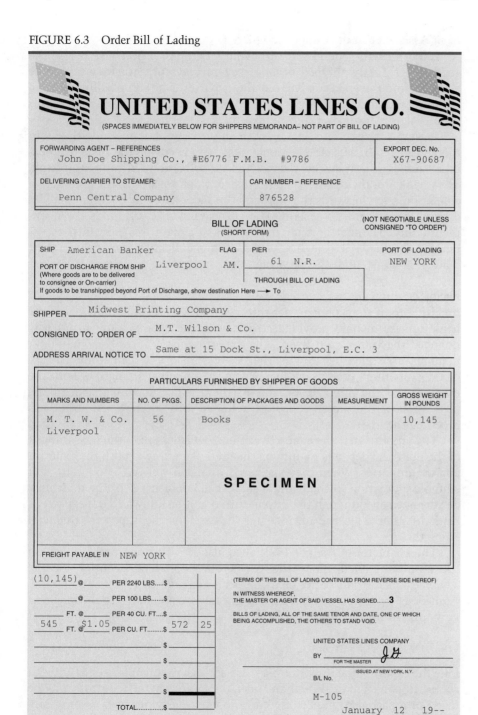

Bank Assistance in the Collection of Drafts

An importer will generally try to avoid paying for a purchase before the goods are actually shipped because several days or perhaps weeks may elapse before the goods arrive. But the exporter is often unwilling to send the draft and documents directly to the importer. Therefore, the exporter usually works through a commercial bank.

A New York exporter dealing with an importer in Portugal with whom there has been little past experience may ship goods on the basis of a documentary draft that has been deposited for collection with the local bank. That bank, following the specific instructions regarding the manner of collection, then forwards the draft and the accompanying documents to its correspondent bank in Lisbon. The correspondent bank holds the documents until payment is made in the case of a sight draft, or until acceptance is obtained if a time draft is used. When collection is made on a sight draft, it is remitted to the exporter.

Financing through the Exporter's Bank

It is important to recognize that throughout the preceding transaction the banking system only provided a service to the exporter and in no way financed the transaction itself. The exporter's bank, however, may offer financing assistance by allowing the exporter to borrow against the security of a documentary draft. Such loans have the financial strength of both the exporter and the importer to support them, since documents for taking possession of the merchandise are released only after the importer has accepted the draft.

The amount that the exporter can borrow is less than the face amount of the draft and depends mainly on the credit standing of both the exporter and the importer. When the exporter is financially strong enough to offer suitable protection to the bank, a substantial percentage of the draft may be advanced even though the importer may not be known to the exporter's bank. In other cases, the advance may be based on the importer's financial strength.

The character of the goods shipped also has an important bearing on the amount loaned, since the goods offer collateral security for the advance. Goods that are not breakable or perishable are better as collateral. And goods for which there is a ready market are preferable to those with a very limited market.

FINANCING BY THE IMPORTER

Like the exporter, the importer may also arrange payment for goods without access to bank credit. When an order is placed, payment in full may be made or a partial payment offered. The partial payment gives some protection to both the exporter and the importer. It protects the exporter against rejection of the goods for no reason. And it gives the importer some bargaining power in the event the merchandise is damaged in shipment or does not meet specifications. When the importer is required to make full payment with an order but wants some protection in the transaction, payment is sent to a bank in the exporter's country. The bank is instructed not to release payment until certain documents are presented to the bank to prove shipment of the goods according to the terms of the transaction. The bank, of course, charges a fee for this service.

Financing through the Importers Bank

In foreign trade, because of language barriers and the difficulty in obtaining credit information about companies in foreign countries, the use of the *banker's acceptance* is common. The banker's acceptance is a draft drawn on and accepted by a bank rather than the importing firm. An example of a banker's acceptance is shown in Figure 6.4. The importer must, of course, make arrangements with the bank in advance. The exporter, too, must know before shipment is made whether or not the bank in question has agreed to accept the draft. This arrangement is facilitated by the use of a **commercial letter of credit.** This is a bank's written statement to an individual or firm guaranteeing acceptance and payment of a draft up to a specified sum if the draft is presented according to the terms of the letter. (See Figure 6.5.)

commercial letter of credit
statement by a bank guaranteeing acceptance and payment of a draft up to a stated amount

Importer Bank Financing—An Example

The issue of a commercial letter of credit and its use in international finance is shown in this example. The owner of a small exclusive shop in Chicago wishes to import expensive perfumes from Paris. Although the

FIGURE 6.4   Banker's Acceptance

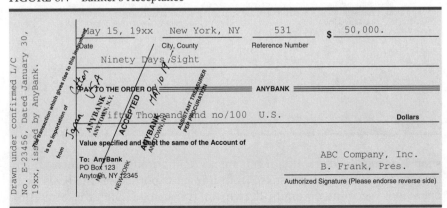

FIGURE 6.5   Irrevocable Commercial Letter of Credit

Irrevocable Commercial Letter Of Credit	AnyBank P.O. Box 123 Anytown, New York 12345	**AnyBank**	Cable Address: AnyBank	Letter Of Credit Division

May 2, 19-- $50,000.

> Drafts drawn hereunder must be marked
> "Drawn under AnyBank Anytown
> L/C Ref.   E-23456   "and indicate the date hereof

ABC Company, Inc.

B. Frank, President

SPECIMEN

Gentlemen:
We hereby authorize you to draw on AnyBank, Anytown

by order of   J. R. Doe & Company, New York, N.Y.

and for account of   J. R. Doe & Company

up to an aggregate amount of   Fifty Thousand Dollars U.S. Currency

available by your drafts at 90 days sight, for full invoice value, in duplicate
accompanied by Commercial Invoice in triplicate . . .
               Consular Invoice in duplicate . . .
               Full set of onboard Bills of Lading to order of AnyBank,
Anytown, marked Notify J. R. Doe & Company, New York,N.Y., and bearing
a separate onboard endorsement signed by the Master and also marked
freight collect at port of destination . . . .

Relating to shipment of Cotton.

. . . Any charges for negotiation of the draft(s) are for your account.
. . . Marine and war risk insurance covered by buyers.

Drafts must be drawn and negotiated not later than   October 2, 19--

The amounts thereof must be endorsed on this Letter Of Credit.
We hereby agree with the drawers, endorsers, and bonafide holders of all drafts drawn under and in compliance
with the terms of this credit, that such drafts will be duly honored upon presentation to the drawee.
This letter of credit is subject to the Uniform Customs and Practice for Documentary Credits (1974 Revision) International Chamber Of Commerce Publication No. 290.

                                              Yours very truly,

                                              D. E. Price

                                              D. E. Price
                                              Vice President
                                              Authorized Signature

shop is well known locally, its financial reputation is not known widely
enough to permit it to purchase from foreign exporters on the basis of an
open-book account or drafts drawn on the firm. Under these circumstances the firm would substitute the bank's credit for its own through the
use of a letter of credit. Upon application by the firm, the bank issues the

letter if it is entirely satisfied that its customer is in a satisfactory financial condition.

The letter of credit is addressed to the French exporter of perfumes. The exporter, upon receipt of the commercial letter of credit, would not be concerned about making the shipment. Although the exporter may not have heard of the Chicago firm, the bank issuing the commercial letter of credit may be known to the exporter or to his bank. (International bank directories provide bank credit information.) The French exporter then ships the perfumes and at the same time draws a draft in the appropriate amount on the bank that issued the letter of credit. The draft and the other papers required by the commercial letter of credit are presented to the exporter's bank. The bank sends the draft and the accompanying documents to its New York correspondent, who forwards them to the importer's bank in Chicago. The importer's bank makes a thorough inspection of the various papers that accompany the draft to make sure that all provisions of the letter of credit have been met. If the bank is satisfied that the terms have been met, the draft is accepted and the appropriate bank officials sign it. The accepted draft, now a banker's acceptance, may be held until maturity by the accepting bank or returned to the exporter on request. If the acceptance is returned to the exporter, it may be held until maturity and sent to the accepting bank for settlement, or it may be sold to other investors. An active market for bankers' acceptances exists in the world's money centers.

After having accepted the draft, the Chicago bank notifies its customer that it has the shipping documents and that arrangements should be made to take them over. As the shop sells the perfume, it builds up its bank account with daily deposits until they are sufficient to retire the acceptance. The bank can then meet its obligation on the acceptance without having advanced its other funds at any time.

In releasing shipping documents to a customer, some banks prefer to establish an agency arrangement between the firm and the bank whereby the bank retains title to the merchandise. The instrument that provides for this is called a ***trust receipt.*** Should the business fail, the bank would not be in the position of an ordinary creditor trying to establish its claim on the business assets. Rather, it could repossess, or take back, the goods and place them with another agent for sale since title had never been transferred to the customer. As the merchandise is sold under a trust receipt arrangement, generally the business must deposit the proceeds with the bank until the total amount of the acceptance is reached.

In summary, the banker's acceptance and the commercial letter of credit involve four principal parties: the importer, the importer's bank, the exporter, and the exporter's bank. Each benefits to a substantial degree through this arrangement. The importer benefits by securing adequate credit. The importer's bank benefits because it receives a fee for issuing the commercial letter of credit and for the other services provided in connection with it. The exporter benefits by being assured that payment will be made

trust receipt
an instrument through which a bank retains title to goods until they are paid for

for the shipment of merchandise. Thus, a sale is made that might otherwise have been rejected because of lack of guaranteed payment. Finally, the exporter's bank benefits if it discounts the acceptance, since it receives a high-grade credit instrument with a definite, short-term maturity. Acceptances held by commercial banks provide a low but certain yield, and they can liquidate them quickly if funds are needed for other purposes.

THE VOLUME AND COST OF BANKERS' ACCEPTANCES

The Board of Governors of the Federal Reserve System authorizes member banks to accept drafts that arise in the course of certain types of international transactions. These include the import and export of goods, the shipment of goods between foreign countries, and the storage of highly marketable staple goods in any foreign country. The maturity of member bank acceptances arising out of such transactions may not exceed six months. This authority to engage in bankers' acceptance financing is intended to encourage banks to participate in financing international trade and to strengthen the U.S. dollar abroad.

Bankers' acceptances are used to finance international transactions on a wide variety of items, including coffee, wool, rubber, cocoa, metals and ores, crude oil, jute, and automobiles. Due to the growth of international trade in general and the increasing competition in foreign markets, bankers' acceptances have become increasingly important. Exporters have had to offer more liberal terms on their sales to compete effectively. The banker's acceptance permits them to do so without undue risk.

The cost of financing an international transaction with the banker's acceptance involves not only the interest cost involved in the exporter's discounting the acceptance but also the commission charge of the importer's accepting bank. From 1961 through 1985 interest costs on bankers' acceptances moved from slightly less than 3 percent to more than 15 percent and back down to below 3 percent in mid-1994. Foreign central banks and commercial banks regard bankers' acceptances as attractive short-term funds commitments. In recent years, more than half of all dollar acceptances have been held by foreign banks, with most of the remainder held by domestic banks. Nonfinancial corporations have played only a small role as investors in acceptances. There are relatively few firms that deal in bankers' acceptances. These dealers arrange nearly simultaneous exchanges of purchases and sales.

OTHER AIDS TO INTERNATIONAL TRADE

THE EXPORT-IMPORT BANK

Export-Import Bank
bank established to aid in financing and facilitating trade between the U.S. and other countries

The **Export-Import Bank** was authorized in 1934 and became an independent agency of the government in 1945. The bank's purpose is to aid in financing and facilitating exports and imports between the United States and other countries. It is the only U.S. agency engaged solely in financing foreign trade.

The Export-Import Bank is a government-owned corporation with capital of $1 billion in nonvoting stock paid in by the U.S. Treasury. It may borrow from the Treasury on a revolving basis and sell short-term discount promissory notes. It pays interest on these loans and dividends on the capital stock. In performing its function, the bank makes long-term loans to private enterprises and governments abroad to finance the purchase of U.S. equipment, goods, and services. The Export-Import Bank also aids substantially in the economic development of foreign countries by giving emergency credits to assist them in maintaining their level of U.S. imports during temporary balance-of-payments difficulties. In addition, the bank finances or guarantees the payment of medium-term commercial export credit extended by exporters and, in partnership with private insurance companies, offers short- and medium-term credit insurance. It lends and guarantees only where repayment is reasonably assured and avoids competition with sources of private capital.

TRAVELER'S LETTER OF CREDIT

A firm's buyer who is traveling abroad may not know in advance from which individuals or firms purchases will be made—for example, an art buyer touring several countries. The buyer could carry U.S. currency, but this involves possible physical loss of the money and a sometimes substantial discount for its conversion into the local currency. A traveler's letter of credit is a convenient and safer method for travelers who need large amounts of foreign currency.

The **traveler's letter of credit** is issued by a bank in one country and addressed to a list of foreign banks. These banks are usually correspondents of the issuing bank and have agreed to purchase sight drafts presented to them by persons with appropriate letters of credit. When a bank issues a letter of credit, it sends a copy of the signature of the person to whom the letter is issued to each of its foreign correspondent banks. When someone presents a draft for payment in foreign currency to one of these correspondent banks, his or her signature is compared with that the bank already has. The bank may also ask the individual for supplementary identification.

traveler's letter of credit issued by a bank to banks in other countries authorizing them to cash checks or purchase drafts presented by the bearer

As with a commercial letter of credit, a maximum total drafts amount is stated in a traveler's letter of credit. In order that an individual with such a letter does not exceed authorized withdrawals, each bank to which the letter is presented enters on it the amount of the draft it has honored.

TRAVELERS CHECKS

Travelers checks, which are offered by banks, express companies, and other agencies in the United States, are generally issued in denominations of

$10, $20, $50, and $100. These checks, generally purchased by an individual before leaving for a foreign country, promise to pay on demand the even amounts indicated on the face of the checks. Each check must be signed by the purchaser twice, once when it is bought and again in the presence of a representative of the business, hotel, or financial institution where it is presented for payment. This allows the person cashing a travelers check to determine whether the signature is authentic.

The use of travelers checks is widespread and offers several advantages to the traveler, including protection in the event of loss and almost certain acceptance when they are presented for payment. Travelers checks are usually sold for their face amount plus a charge of 1 percent. They can now be purchased in the United States in major foreign currency denominations—for example, British pounds. This eliminates a traveler's exposure to changing exchange rates and the extra amount that is often charged (in the form of a less favorable exchange rate than the official rate) when U.S. dollar checks are cashed in a foreign country.

INTERNATIONAL FINANCIAL EQUILIBRIUM

Just as monetary policy plays an important role in the nation's stability, growth, interest rates, and price levels, it also helps keep international financial relationships in balance. Since the dollar is widely held as a medium of international exchange, U.S. monetary policy has especially significant effects on the world economy. No nation is a world unto itself, nor can a nation pursue whatever policies it desires without regard to other nations. Policy makers of all economies must recognize the interdependence of their actions in attempting to maintain international financial equilibrium.

Briefly, the nations of the world attempt to achieve international financial equilibrium by maintaining a balance in their exchange of goods and services. In general, international trade benefits all countries involved. Consumers benefit by getting lower cost goods, since the goods come from the country where they are produced most efficiently. Producers benefit by expanding their markets. Well over one-tenth of the U.S. national income comes from selling goods to foreigners, and a like amount of our needs are met through imports. However, individuals and firms make the decisions to import and export, and problems arise if they are out of balance over a period of time.

NATURE OF THE PROBLEM

Exports are sales to foreigners; they are a source of income to domestic producers. Imports divert spending to foreign producers and therefore represent a loss of potential income to domestic producers. When the two are in balance there is no net effect on total income in the economy. However, an increase in exports over imports tends to expand the economy just as an increase in investment or government spending does. An excess of imports tends to contract the economy.

As in the domestic economy, goods and services are not exchanged directly in international trade; payment flows through monetary or financial transactions. Methods of making payments and financing international trade were discussed earlier. Other short- and long-term lending and investment are conducted across national boundaries on a large scale. In addition, government grants for both military and civilian purposes and private gifts and grants are sources of international financial flows. These flows can have an important impact on domestic economies and may affect monetary policy.

Since producers, consumers, and investors in different countries use different currencies, the international financial system requires a mechanism for establishing the relative values, or exchange rates, among currencies, and for handling their actual exchange. Under the system of *flexible exchange rates* that began in 1973, rates are determined in the actual process of exchange, by supply and demand in the foreign exchange market. This system reduces the impact of international financial transactions on domestic money supplies. Still, changes in exchange rates do affect imports and exports and can thus affect domestic production, incomes, and prices. International financial markets strongly influence domestic interest rates, and vice versa, so that domestic monetary policy still involves international considerations.

In short, domestic economies are linked to each other in a worldwide economic and financial system. The United States has played a leading role in the development and growth of that system. Before we take a closer look at that role, we should examine the accounting system used to keep track of international financial transactions.

flexible exchange rates
a system in which international exchange rates are determined by supply and demand

balance of payments
a summary of all economic transactions between one country and the rest of the world

BALANCE-OF-PAYMENTS ACCOUNTS

The U.S. *balance of payments* involves all of its international transactions, including foreign investment, private and government grants, U.S. military spending overseas, and many other items besides the buying and selling of goods and services. The single most important element of the balance of payments is the *balance of trade,* which is the net balance of exports and imports of goods and services. A more narrow view considers only the import and export of goods and is termed the *merchandise trade balance.* The merchandise trade balance was consistently favorable between the 1950s and the beginning of the 1970s. In recent years, however, imports of goods has exceeded exports. This imbalance has been particularly severe since the latter part of the 1970s.

balance of trade
the net value of a country's exports of goods and services compared to its imports

merchandise trade balance
the net difference between a country's import and export of goods

Figure 6.6 depicts U.S. international transactions over the 1985 through early-1995 period. The merchandise trade balance reached a then record low in 1987 when imports exceeded exports by about $40 billion per quarter. This deficit (imports greater than exports) improved to less than $20 billion per quarter in 1991 before again turning downward to a new low of nearly $50 billion in the second quarter of 1995.

Factors that impact on international trade balances include the exchange value of the U.S. dollar relative to other currencies, relative inflation rates, and economic growth. A relatively stronger U.S. economy means that more will be spent on imports, while the weaker foreign economy means that less will be spent on U.S. exports. A relatively weaker real exchange rate, where the nominal exchange rate is adjusted for inflation differences, makes for a weaker U.S. dollar which lowers the dollar cost of U.S. goods relative to foreign goods.

We can better understand the U.S. balance of payments by examining Table 6.2 which shows an annual merchandise trade balance deficit in excess of $166 billion for 1994. To find the goods and services balance, the

FIGURE 6.6   U.S. International Transactions

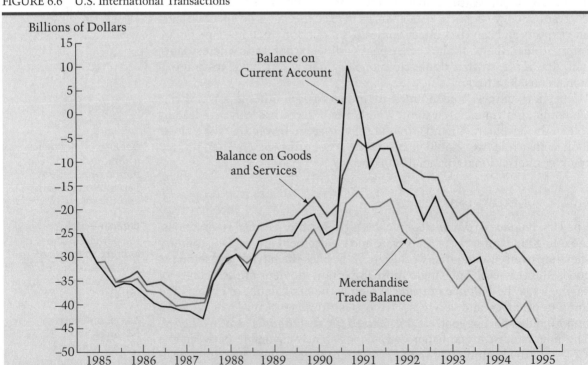

Source: *Economic Indicators*, Council of Economic Advisers (September 1995).

TABLE 6.2   United States Balance of Payments in 1994 (Billions of Dollars)

	INCOME (+)	PAYMENTS (−)	NET
CURRENT ACCOUNT			
Merchandise exports	$502.5		
Merchandise imports		$668.6	
Merchandise trade balance			−166.1
Military transactions, net	2.1		
Investment income, net		9.3	
Other service transactions, net	57.7		
Balance on goods and services			−115.6
Private remittances and other transfers		15.7	
U.S. government pensions and other transfers		4.2	
Government grants		15.8	
Balance on current account			−151.3
CAPITAL ACCOUNT			
Changes in U.S. government assets other than official reserve assets		.3	
Changes in U.S. private assets abroad		130.9	
Changes in foreign official assets in U.S.	39.4		
Changes in foreign private assets in U.S.	252.0		
Changes in U.S. official reserve assets	5.3		
Balance on capital account			165.5
Statistical discrepancy		−14.2	−14.2
Total	$859.0	$859.0	

Source: *Federal Reserve Bulletin* (October 1995): A53.

merchandise trade balance is adjusted for military transactions, foreign investment income, and other service transactions that include tourism, transportation, and banking activities. The 1994 goods and services balance resulted in a deficit of about $116 billion. Next, we find the current account balance by adjusting the goods and services balance for unilateral, or one-way, transfers. These transfers include remittances, pensions, private gifts and grants, and U.S. government grants (excluding military). Thus, the **current account balance** shows the flow of income into and out of the United States during a specified time period. For 1994, the current account balance showed a deficit of about $151 billion. The **capital account balance** includes all foreign private and government investment in the United States netted against U.S. investments in foreign countries.

Deficits or surpluses in the current account must be offset by changes in the capital account. That is, changes in the current account and the capital account must be equal except for statistical discrepancies caused by measurement errors and the inability to keep track of all international

current account balance
the flow of income into and out of the United States during a specified time period

capital account balance
foreign government and private investment in the United States netted against similar U.S. investment in foreign countries

transactions. Thus, in Table 6.2, the balances on current and capital accounts would be equal except for the statistical discrepancy of about $14 billion.

The first item in the capital account section, changes in U.S. government ownership of assets in foreign countries, covers gold, Special Drawing Rights, the reserve position in the International Monetary Fund, and convertible foreign currencies held by the U.S. Treasury and Federal Reserve. The second item, changes in U.S. private ownership of foreign assets, reflects private investments abroad. Both items represent changes that result in outflows of capital.

The third and fourth items reflect foreign ownership changes, both government and private, in investments in the United States. Among those changes are increases in bank deposits, purchases of government and corporate securities, loans, and direct investment in land and buildings. Both of these items give rise to inflows of capital.

From an international monetary management point of view, U.S. government ownership of foreign assets is of special interest. Under the current system of flexible exchange rates, a country's central bank does not have to redeem its currency. However, it may try to control its exchange rate by entering the foreign exchange market to buy or sell that currency, thus adding to demand or supply. Intervention by central banks in the flexible exchange rate system is called a managed or **dirty float.**

dirty float
intervention by central banks to control exchange rates in the foreign exchange market's flexible exchange system

Under a pure flexible system in which central banks do not enter the foreign exchange market at all, there would be no change in the official government ownership of foreign assets. Note, however, that the rest of the accounts would still balance. Any surplus or deficit in current accounts would be balanced by the capital accounts. For example, a trade deficit might be balanced partly by an increase in foreign assets in the United States, including deposits in U.S. banks.

INTERNATIONAL FINANCIAL SYSTEM

For many years after World War II the United States enjoyed a favorable merchandise trade balance. During this period, however, the United States also engaged in massive international aid to countries whose productive facilities were destroyed by the war. The United States also gave great amounts of assistance to developing nations of the world. One of the results of these efforts was the accumulation of foreign claims to U.S. dollars and the loss of a large amount of gold reserves.

Even with loss of gold reserves, the United States had far greater reserves than any other nation. Also, the accumulation of claims against U.S. dollars was long considered desirable. Indeed, one of the most serious difficulties facing international trade in the early post-World War II period was the dollar gap or shortage as the world increasingly relied on the dollar as an international currency. Gold had been the world's international reserve currency and the basic medium of exchange in international commerce. But as the volume of world trade increased over the years, the supply of gold failed to keep pace. Without some form of supplementary international money, the result would have been international deflation.

The U.S. balance of payments problem and the world's need for a growing monetary base to support increasing international liquidity came into sharp focus in the early-1970s. The year-by-year growth in short-term financial claims on the dollar resulting from our continuing unfavorable merchandise trade balance served foreign central banks well. It provided them with a growing base of reserve assets. Since these claims to U.S. dollars could be converted into gold at a fixed rate, the claims were considered to be as good as gold. But just as the world's monetary gold supply was not increasing fast enough to accommodate expanding international trade, eventually the U.S. stock of monetary gold was no longer adequate to support the vast increase in claims against it.

Special Drawing Rights

In January 1968, recognizing that the dollar could no longer serve as a steadily increasing international money, the principal nations of the world agreed to a supplementary world money, ***Special Drawing Rights (SDRs).*** The SDRs, sometimes called paper gold, can be created freely by the International Monetary Fund. The SDRs are assets that the member banks accept from one another up to specified limits. Like gold, they are claims on the world's resources and go to participants in proportion to their International Monetary Fund quotas.

Special Drawing Rights (SDRs) international reserve assets created by the International Monetary Fund that can be drawn upon by member nations

End of the Gold Standard

In 1971, as a result of strong inflation, the U.S. trade balance fell into deficit. Furthermore, higher interest rates in Europe than in the United States created a rush of capital outflows to Europe. As a result, the dollar declined so much that on August 15, 1971, President Nixon stopped the dollar from being converted into gold to protect our declining gold stock.

Flexible International Exchange Rates

Suspension of dollar convertibility in the summer of 1971 was a significant milepost in the worsening U.S. international monetary situation. Equally important was the decision to allow the dollar to float in relation to its exchange rate with other currencies. Under the previous rules of the International Monetary Fund a nation could only alter the established (or pegged) exchange ratio with other currencies with the Fund's approval. The arguments for and against flexible exchange rates had been debated in academic circles for a dozen years. Under flexible exchange rates, some contended, supply and demand would establish appropriate exchange rates between nations, and cost and price structures as well as changing monetary policy would be reflected in the supply-and-demand relationships.

A primary objection to flexible exchange rates is the chance of wide swings in response to changes in supply and demand, with a resulting uncertainty in international trade. After only four months of flexible exchange rates, a group of 10 representatives of central banks in leading industrial nations met at the Smithsonian Institution in Washington in December 1971 to express their concern for monetary stability. Out of this so-called Smithsonian Agreement came a new alignment of fixed exchange rates. Major currencies were officially revalued against the dollar, and the dollar was devalued in terms of gold. However, the Smithsonian Agreement was completely out of use by March 1, 1973, as a result of change of policy. Rather than attempt to establish another realignment of fixed exchange rates, the leading industrial nations decided to again let their currencies float.

Exchange Rate Developments for the U.S. Dollar

The dollar remains the main currency for international commercial and financial transactions. Because of this, both the United States and the rest of the world benefit from a strong and stable U.S. dollar. Its strength and stability depend directly on the ability of the United States to pursue non-inflationary economic policies. In the late 1960s and the 1970s the United States failed to meet this objective. Continuing high inflation led to a dollar crisis in 1978, which, in turn, threatened the stability of international financial markets.

Figure 6.7 shows the strength of the dollar relative to a "basket" of 19 countries who belong to the Organization for Economic Cooperation and

FIGURE 6.7   U.S. Dollar Value Relative to 19 Other Currencies

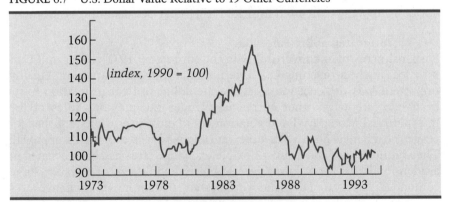

Source: *World Financial Markets,* Morgan Guaranty Trust Company (May/June 1994).

"We always have exchange rates in mind when we set our prices."

KEVIN SANKEY

Account Manager
105° Meridian

BA Psychology
Dartmouth College
MBA Marketing
Northwestern University

Q: *What does 105° Meridian do?*

A: We are a supplier of luggage, sports bags, and travel accessories. We sell some products under our own brand, 105° Meridian, and in some cases we manufacture products to be sold under the label of major retailers. This part of the business is called "private labeling."

Q: *What is your role?*

A: I work mostly on the large private label accounts. On any particular project I may be involved in designing a new product, selecting a manufacturing site, producing samples, selling the final design to the customer, and if we are awarded the contract, the actual production and importing. About half my time is spent on the product development and design side.

Q: *Do you import most of your products?*

A: Yes. Almost everything we sell is produced offshore. Most of our manufacturing takes place in the Far East.

Q: *How do exchange rates affect your business?*

A: Fluctuations in exchange rates can have a huge impact on our profitability. Let me give you an example. We set a firm price with our clients. For instance, on January 1st we may sign a contract with a major retailer to supply a sports bag for $50. We won't deliver product until the middle of the year, but we're committed to that $50 price. So if our manufacturing expense increases because the value of the dollar falls between January and June, our profit shrinks. The margins in this business are tight to begin with, so a 10 percent change in the exchange rate makes a big difference at the bottom line. Of course when the exchange rate moves in favor of the dollar, our profit is greater.

Q: *So how do you deal with these fluctuations?*

A: We always have exchange rates in mind when we set our prices. We try to predict about a year in advance what exchange rates will do. We look not only at the economy of the country where our supplier is located, but also at the stability of the government and other factors. In some cases we have to totally eliminate a country as a possible production site simply because of the instability of its currency or government.

Another variable we consider when selecting a manufacturer is the labor rate. Our products are pretty low tech; a lot of the manufacturing cost is labor. The wages in some countries are extremely low compared to the U.S.—less than a dollar an hour in some cases. But sometimes the lowest labor rate is not the best deal because we can't count on the quality.

Q: *What makes you good at your job?*

A: Because I have experience in many areas of this business, I can see how all the pieces fit together. For instance, I know how a change in design will affect the manufacturing process and costs. Being an expert in just one area is fine, but knowing the entire business helps me make better decisions.

career profiles

163

Development (OECD) over the 1973–early 1994 period. As inflation was brought under control in the early 1980s and economic growth accelerated after the 1981–82 recession, the dollar rose against other major currencies until it reached record highs in 1985. As we discussed earlier, relatively higher economic growth and relatively lower inflation rates leads to a relatively stronger currency. These economic developments, coupled with a favorable political climate, caused the value of the dollar to rise sharply.

However, the renewed strength of the dollar contributed to a worsening of the trade imbalance because import prices were effectively reduced while exported U.S. goods became less cost competitive. Beginning in 1985, U.S. economic growth slowed relative to economic growth in other developed countries. Also, the belief that the U.S. government wanted the dollar to decline on a relative basis so as to reduce the trade deficit contributed to a decline in the desirability to hold dollars. This resulted in a major shift towards holding more foreign assets and fewer U.S. assets. As a consequence, the dollar's value declined by 1987 to levels below those in place when flexible exchange rates were reestablished in 1973. Since 1987 the value of the dollar in international exchange has continued to fluctuate, but within a fairly narrow range compared to the 1980–87 period.

A stronger dollar leads to concern about the deficit in our trade balance but at the same time offers hope of lower inflation. A stronger dollar results in more imports of foreign merchandise since it requires fewer dollars for purchase. Just as a U.S. tourist abroad finds it cheaper to travel when the dollar is strong, importers find prices reduced when their dollars increase in relative strength. When the dollar weakens, inflation may follow, countered by a reduced balance of trade deficit.

SUMMARY

In this chapter we have observed the growing volume and importance of foreign trade. The banking system, along with the arbitrage activities of international financiers, support and facilitate international transactions and activities. Management of foreign exchange is particularly important to multinational corporate financial managers as they attempt to protect their international claims against currency fluctuations.

Foreign exchange markets are electronic communication systems that connect major financial centers throughout the world. Exchange rates are determined by supply and demand relationships, relative interest rate levels, relative rates of inflation, political risk, and economic risk. Alternatives to affect settlement of purchase and sale claims were explored along with the instruments available to exporters and importers for financing their international activities.

Nations of the world try to maintain a balance in their exchange of goods and services, as well as in their payments balances. When international financial equilibrium does not exist, exchange rates usually adjust to reflect these imbalances. Furthermore, when the current account shows a surplus or deficit in the flow of income into and out of the United States, changes in the capital account must offset the current account imbalance. This is accomplished by a change in the relationship between foreign private and government investment in the United States relative to U.S. investment in foreign countries. We concluded the chapter with a discussion of the changes in the value of the U.S. dollar relative to other currencies that took place in recent years.

KEY TERMS

arbitrage	Export-Import Bank
balance of payments	flexible exchange rates
balance of trade	foreign exchange markets
capital account balance	merchandise trade balance
clean draft	order bill of lading
commercial letter of credit	sight draft
current account balance	Special Drawing Rights (SDRs)
dirty float	time draft
documentary draft	traveler's letter of credit
draft (bill of exchange)	trust receipt

DISCUSSION QUESTIONS

1. A smoothly functioning system of international finance makes possible specialization of productive effort by the nations of the world. Why is such specialization of effort desirable?
2. How do commercial banks provide for the financial settlement of international transactions? Describe the arrangements of commercial banks for maintaining deposits in foreign countries.
3. Explain the role of supply and demand as it relates to the establishment of exchange rates between countries.
4. Describe the activities and economic role of the arbitrageur in international finance.
5. Foreign exchange quotations may be given in terms of sight drafts, cable orders, and time drafts. What is the relative cost of these different types of drafts? Why should such cost differences exist?

6. Describe the nature of foreign exchange markets.
7. Why should managers of multinational companies be concerned with foreign relationships?
8. Describe the various ways by which an exporter may finance an international shipment of goods. How may commercial banks assist the exporter in the collection of drafts?
9. How do importers protect themselves against improper delivery of goods when they are required to make payment when placing an order?
10. Describe the process by which an importing firm may substitute the credit of its bank for its own credit in financing international transactions.
11. How may a bank protect itself after having issued a commercial letter of credit on behalf of a customer?
12. Describe the costs involved in connection with financing exports through bankers' acceptances.
13. Describe the ultimate sources of funds for export financing with bankers' acceptances. How are acceptances acquired for investment by these sources?
14. Explain the role played by the Export-Import Bank in international trade. Do you consider this bank to be in competition with private lending institutions?
15. Commercial letters of credit, travelers' letters of credit, and travelers' checks all have an important role in international finance. Distinguish among these three types of instruments.
16. Briefly indicate the problems facing the United States in its attempt to maintain international financial equilibrium.
17. The U.S. international balance of payments position is measured in terms of the current account balance. Describe the current account balance and indicate its major components. Also indicate developments in the current account balance during recent years.
18. Discuss the meaning of the capital account balance and identify its major components.
19. A great deal of concern has been expressed about the lack of international monetary stability in recent years. In connection with this concern, describe some of the developments in terms of gold and flexible exchange rates in relation to the U.S. dollar.
20. Discuss some of the recent foreign exchange developments as they affect the United States and its recent balance of trade deficits.

PROBLEMS

1. Assume that the French franc (FF) has a current dollar ($US) value of $0.18.

    a.   Determine the number of FF that can be purchased with one $US.

    b.   Calculate the percentage change (appreciation or depreciation) in the French franc if it falls to $0.16.

    c.   Calculate the percentage change (appreciation or depreciation) in the U.S. dollar if the FF falls to $0.16.

2. The U.S. dollar ($US) value of the Australian dollar is $0.73 while the U.S. dollar value of the Hong Kong dollar is $0.13.

    a.   Determine the number of Australian dollars that can be purchased with one $US.

    b.   Determine the number of Hong Kong dollars that can be purchased with one $US.

    c.   In $US terms, determine how many Hong Kong dollars can be purchased with one Australian dollar.

3. One U.S. dollar ($US) can currently purchase 1.316 Swiss francs. However, it has been predicted that one $US soon will be exchangeable for 1.450 Swiss francs.

    a.   Calculate the percentage change in the $US if the exchange rate change occurs.

    b.   Determine the dollar value of one Swiss franc at both of the above exchange rates.

    c.   Calculate the percentage change in the dollar value of one Swiss franc based on the above exchange rates.

4. As an exporter of relatively expensive electronic equipment you have a substantial investment in the merchandise that you ship. Your foreign importers are typically small- or medium-size firms without a long history of operations. Although your terms of sales require payment upon receipt of the merchandise, you are concerned about the possible problem of nonpayment and the need to reclaim merchandise that you have shipped. How might the banking system assist and protect you in this situation?

5. As an importer of merchandise you depend upon the sale of the merchandise for funds to make payment. Although customary terms of sale are 90 days for this type of merchandise, you are not well known to foreign suppliers because of your recent entry into business. Furthermore, your suppliers require almost immediate payment to meet their own expenses of operations. How might the banking systems of the exporter and importer accommodate your situation?

6. As a speculator in the financial markets you notice that for the last few minutes German deutsche Marks are being quoted in New York at a price of $0.5849 and in Frankfurt at $0.5851.

    a.   Assuming that you have access to international trading facilities, what action might you take?

    b.   What would be the effect of your actions and those of other speculators on these exchange rates?

7. You manage the cash for a large multinational industrial enterprise. As a result of credit sales on 90-day payment terms you have a large claim against a customer in Madrid. You have heard rumors of the possible devaluation of the Spanish peseta. What actions, if any, can you take to protect your firm against the consequences of a prospective devaluation?

8. Assume, as the loan officer of a commercial bank, one of your customers has asked for a "commercial letter of credit" to enable his firm to import a supply of well known French wines. This customer has a long record of commercial success yet has large outstanding debts to other creditors. In what way might you accommodate the customer and at the same time establish protection for your bank?

9. For the entire year the nation's balance of trade with other nations has been in a substantial deficit position, yet, as always, the overall balance of payments will be in "balance." Describe the various factors that accomplish this overall balance, in spite of the deficit in the balance of trade.

SELF-TEST QUESTIONS

1. Foreign exchange markets may be described as:
   a. specific locations in major industrial cities
   b. major financial centers connected by good communications systems
   c. money markets outside of the United States
   d. facilities of central banks for foreign exchange

2. Quotations of foreign exchange rates in the many cities of the world are identical or nearly so because of:
   a. central bank control
   b. price fixing
   c. clearinghouse activities
   d. arbitrage activities

3. The least costly form of claim in foreign exchange is a:
   a. banker's sight draft
   b. cable order
   c. time draft
   d. bill of exchange

4. A documentary draft is accompanied, among other things, by a(n):
   a. order bill of lading
   b. manifest
   c. trust receipt
   d. letter of credit

5. A banker's acceptance differs from a trade draft in that:
   a. it is drawn on a bank rather than on an importer
   b. it is always accompanied by a bank letter of credit
   c. its acceptance depends entirely on the goodwill of the importer

    d.   There is no difference.
6. Commercial letters of credit are:
    a.   customarily required by importers of their suppliers
    b.   negotiable in the money markets of major cities
    c.   customarily provided by banks to their customers to accommodate their import activities
    d.   ordinarily provided by issuing bank at no charge to customers
7. Travelers' letters of credit are:
    a.   issued by a bank and addressed to a list of banks in other countries
    b.   especially popular with tourists
    c.   convertible into cash at most large banks
    d.   of special value to exporters
8. To protect against loss as a result of adverse currency fluctuations, an export firm may:
    a.   demand cash settlement
    b.   purchase a futures contract as a hedge
    c.   require the customer to make payment in the exporter's currency
    d.   require a government guarantee against currency loss of value
9. Intervention by central banks in the flexible exchange rate system is called:
    a.   clean float
    b.   flexible float
    c.   dirty float
    d.   usage of Special Drawing Rights

SELF-TEST PROBLEMS

1. The U.S. dollar ($US) value of one German deutsche mark (DM) is $0.63.

    a.   Determine the number of DMs that can be purchased with one $US.
    b.   Calculate the percentage change in the DM if the German mark appreciates to $0.65.

2. You are the owner of a business that has offices and production facilities in several foreign countries. Your product is sold in all of these countries, and you maintain bank accounts in the cities in which you have offices. At present you have short-term notes outstanding at most of the banks with which you maintain deposits. This borrowing is to support seasonal production activity. One of the countries in which you have offices is now strongly rumored to be on the point of a devaluation, or lowering, of their currency relative to that of the rest of the world. What actions might this rumor cause you to take?

3. Explain the concept of "balance" as it relates to a nation's balance of payments.

SUGGESTED READINGS

Aguiler, Linda M. "NAFTA: A Review of the Issues." *Economic Perspectives,* Federal Reserve Bank of Chicago (January/February 1993): 12–20.

Eiteman, David K., Arthur I. Stonehill, and Michael H. Moffett. *Multinational Business Finance,* 6e. Reading, MA: Addison-Wesley, 1992. Chaps. 4 and 18.

Evans, Charles L. "Interest Rates and the Dollar." *Economic Perspectives,* Federal Reserve Bank of Chicago (September/October 1994): 11–24.

Kidwell, David S., Richard L. Peterson, and David W. Blackwell. *Financial Institutions, Markets, and Money,* 5e. Fort Worth, TX: The Dryden Press, 1993. Chap. 12.

Pollard, Patricia S. "Trade Between the United States and Eastern Europe." *Review,* The Federal Reserve Bank of St. Louis (July/August 1994): 25–46.

Ross, Stephen A., Randolph W. Westerfield, and Jeffrey F. Jaffe. *Corporate Finance,* 3e. Homewood, IL: Irwin, 1993. Chap. 31.

Schlesinger, Helmut. "On the Way to a New Monetary Union: The European Monetary Union." *Review,* The Federal Reserve Bank of St. Louis (May/June 1994): 3–10.

Shapiro, Alan C. *Foundations of Multinational Financial Management,* 2e. Boston: Allyn & Bacon, 1994. Chaps. 13 and 21.

Van Horne, James C. *Financial Market Rates and Flows,* 4e. Englewood Cliffs, NJ: Prentice-Hall, 1994. Chap. 12.

ANSWERS TO SELF-TEST QUESTIONS 1. b, 2. d, 3. c, 4. a, 5. a, 6. a, 7. a, 8. b, 9. c.

ANSWERS TO SELF-TEST PROBLEMS

1.   a. One U.S. dollar can purchase 1.587 DMs (i.e., 1/$0.63).
     b. Percent DM change = ($0.65 − $0.63)/$0.63 = 0.032 or 3.2%.
2.   You could try to hedge against your financial claims in that country losing value by moving some of the funds in your bank account to another country. In anticipation of moving the funds, you could try to accelerate the collection of your receivables. You might also slow down your payments on liabilities with the expectation of moving funds back into the country after devaluation, receiving more local funds in so doing. Other devices, such as dealing in futures contracts, may also be available to you.
3.   In one sense there is never a precise count that establishes a balance since it is impossible to record all transactions that enter into the schedule. Hence, an item referred to as statistical discrepancy solves that problem nicely. Aside from the practical matter of counting, however, the schedule must always be in balance in a theoretical sense. It's true that we can have deficits in our current account. In other words, our export of goods and services may fall short of our imports, but this must be made up in one or both of the other parts of the schedule. It can be made up by a reduction in our gold reserves or other reserve assets, or we can increase the amount that we owe abroad. Like a three-piece jig-saw puzzle with fixed boundaries, the change in the shape of one piece must result in the change in shape of one or both of the other two pieces.

PART 2

INTRODUCTION

Part 2 focuses on the financial markets and the process of investing funds in them. Money flows into the financial markets from one source: savings, primarily from households and firms' retained earnings. Funds flow into financial institutions such as banks and life insurance companies, which, in turn, invest the funds in various securities. The term "security" means more than just bonds and stocks. Financial securities represent anything that has a debt or equity claim on income or property, such as a car loan, a mortgage, or an equity investment in a small partnership. Financial institutions facilitate the work of the financial markets by directing funds from savers to those individuals, firms, or governments who need funds to finance current operations or growth.

Part 2 introduces many of the important concepts and tools that financial institutions and investors use in the financial markets. For example, no one would want to invest (except perhaps altruistically) $100 now and expect to receive only their $100 back after one year. Because they give up the use of their money for some time, investors expect a return on their investments. Thus we say that money has a "time value." Having one dollar today is of greater value to us than the promise of receiving one dollar sometime in the future.

How much can we expect to receive for our $100 investment? That is the role of the financial markets. As with any other market, the financial markets consider demand and supply forces to determine the "price" of money, namely the interest rate or the expected return on an investment. The amount of interest received on a certificate of deposit or a bond, or the expected return on a common stock investment, all depend upon the workings of the financial markets and the marketplace's evaluation of the investment opportunity.

It is through the investing process that institutions, firms, and individual investors come together. Firms and governments go to the financial markets, seeking investors and institutions to whom they can sell financial securities. Investors and institutions participate in the financial markets seeking profitable

Investments

investments to help meet their goals. For an investor, the goal may be a comfortable retirement or accumulating funds to purchase a car or house. For a financial institution, the higher the returns they earn on prudent investments, the greater will be their profits and the stronger their competitive position. A financial institution that prudently earns higher returns in the financial markets will be able to offer current and potential customers higher interest rates on their deposits than a competitor whose financial market returns are lower.

Part 2 introduces us to the process of investing and tools that can be used to evaluate financial market securities. Chapter 7 begins this section by examining the work of financial markets to direct savings into various investments. Chapter 8 discusses influences that affect the financial market's determination of the price of money, or the interest rate or expected return on an investment. Chapter 9 examines the effect of interest rates more closely by introducing the concept of time value of money. This chapter shows us how we can compare different dollar amounts of cash over time to determine if an investment is attractive or not. Chapter 10 introduces us to bonds and stocks. We review their characteristics and we use the time value concepts from Chapter 9 in a pragmatic manner to see how we can estimate the value of bonds and stocks. We also learn in Chapter 10 how to read and interpret information about bonds and stocks from the financial pages of papers such as *The Wall Street Journal.*

Chapter 11 delves deeper into the workings of the financial markets. It focuses on the process that institutions and firms use to issue securities and the process that investors use when buying or selling securities. Chapter 12 completes our overview of investing in the financial markets by examining the trade-off between risk and expected return: that is, in order to give investors an incentive to invest in higher risk securities, they must have the expectation of higher returns. Chapter 12 introduces us to the tools that investors and financial market participants use to evaluate and to control investment risk.

CHAPTER 7

Savings and Investment Process

AFTER STUDYING THIS CHAPTER, YOU SHOULD BE ABLE TO:

- Identify and briefly describe the major components of the gross domestic product.
- Describe how the balance between exports and imports affects the gross domestic product.
- Discuss the link between gross private domestic investment and gross savings in the United States.
- Briefly describe the historical role of savings in the United States.
- Describe how financial assets and liabilities are created.
- Indicate the scope and magnitude of the federal budget and identify the principal sources of revenues and expenditures.
- Explain the nature of federal government borrowing and describe recent trends in borrowing.
- Identify the major sources of savings in the United States.
- Explain how funds flow from savings into investments.
- Identify and describe the factors that affect savings.

All of a nation's output of goods and services may be consumed, or a portion of them may be saved. Individuals consume by making expenditures on durable and nondurable goods, and services. Governments consume by

174

purchasing goods and services. If all output is not consumed, "savings" can be "invested" to construct residential and nonresidential structures, manufacture producers' durable equipment, and increase business inventories. This process is termed **capital formation** and results in economic growth.

Recall from Chapter 1 that an effective financial system provides the funds needed for capital formation by channeling savings into investment. The savings-investment process in the U.S. financial system begins by first generating savings. These savings may be directly invested by savers, or be accumulated by financial intermediaries which, in turn, lend and invest the savings.

capital formation
process of constructing residential and nonresidential structures, manufacturing producers' durable equipment, and increasing business inventories

GROSS DOMESTIC PRODUCT AND CAPITAL FORMATION

Gross domestic product (GDP) was previously defined as a nation's output of goods and services for a specified period of time. GDP is comprised of both consumption and investment components, as well as the net export of goods and services. More specifically, GDP includes personal consumption expenditures, government purchases of goods and services, gross private domestic investment, and net exports of goods and services. **Personal consumption expenditures (PCE)** indicates expenditures by individuals for durable goods, nondurable goods, and services. Government purchases (GP) includes expenditures for goods and services by both the federal and the state and local governments. **Gross private domestic investment (GPDI)** measures fixed investment in residential and nonresidential structures, producers' durable equipment, and changes in business inventories. The final component of GDP is the net exports (NE) of goods and services (or, exports minus imports).

personal consumption expenditures (PCE)
expenditures by individuals for durable goods, nondurable goods, and services

gross private domestic investment (GPDI)
investment in residential and nonresidential structures, producers' durable equipment, and business inventories

In equation form, we have:

$$GDP = PCE + GP + GPDI + NE$$

Consumption is reflected by the sum of personal consumption expenditures and government purchases of goods and services. Savings used for capital formation produces the gross private domestic investment. In addition, if the exports of goods and services exceed imports, GDP will be higher.

Table 7.1 shows the breakdown in these components for the United States over the 1992–94 period. For 1994, the gross domestic product was over $6.7 trillion. Personal consumption expenditures of nearly $4.6 trillion accounted for about 69 percent of GDP. Adding the nearly $1.2 trillion in government purchases of goods and services (about 17 percent of GDP) to PCE results in total consumption being about 86 percent of GDP. The remainder of GDP, adjusted for the netting out of exports and imports, was available for capital formation in the form of GDPI.

TABLE 7.1   Gross Domestic Product Consumption, Investment and International
Components (in Billions of Dollars)

	1992	1993	1994
Total gross domestic product	$6,038.5	$6,377.9	$6,738.4
Personal consumption expenditures	4,139.9	4,391.8	4,628.4
Durable goods	497.3	537.9	591.5
Nondurable goods	1,300.9	1,350.0	1,394.3
Services	2,341.6	2,503.9	2,642.7
Gross private domestic investment	796.5	891.7	1,032.9
Fixed investment	789.1	876.1	980.7
Nonresidential	565.5	623.7	697.6
Structures	172.6	178.7	182.8
Producer's durable equipment	392.9	445.0	514.8
Residential structures	223.6	252.4	283.0
Change in business inventories	7.3	15.6	52.2
Nonfarm	2.3	21.1	45.9
Net exports of goods and services	–29.6	–63.6	–98.2
Exports	640.5	661.7	718.7
Imports	670.1	725.3	816.9
Government purchases of goods and services	1,131.8	1,158.1	1,175.3
Federal	448.8	443.4	437.3
State and local	683.0	714.6	738.0

Source: *Federal Reserve Bulletin* (June 1994 and October 1995): A51.

IMPLICATIONS OF INTERNATIONAL PAYMENT IMBALANCES

Table 7.1 shows that imports of goods and services exceeded exports by
nearly $98 billion in 1994. While this figure is only about 1.5 percent of
the U.S. GDP, the consequence is a GDP lower than what would have
existed under conditions of an export-import equilibrium. This, in turn,
translates into a lower standard of living in the United States because of
the lower GDP.

The importance of international financial equilibrium was discussed
in Chapter 6. Recall that when completing the accounting transactions for
the U.S. balance of payments, a deficit balance on goods and services in the
"current account" is offset in the "capital account" by a net increase in
foreign government and private ownership of U.S. assets. For example, the
United States has been running a large trade deficit in goods and services
with Japan in recent years. This means that the United States has been
buying more from Japan than Japan has been buying from the United
States. One consequence is that Japan could have been investing more in
the United States by purchasing U.S. assets (both financial and real) rela-

tive to U.S. investments in Japan. However, if the Japanese decide to hold relatively fewer claims on U.S. assets, the exchange rate between the yen and the dollar must change.

Also recall from Chapter 6 that an equilibrium exchange rate between the currencies of two countries is established by the supply and demand for those currencies. A U.S. trade deficit in goods and services with Japan means that the demand for yen by Americans will be greater than the supply of yen by the Japanese. That is, Americans will demand more yen to pay for their purchases of Japanese goods and services relative to the supply of yen reflected in the demand by Japanese for American goods and services. The result will be a stronger yen and a weaker dollar unless offsetting actions occur such as a willingness of the Japanese to invest more in U.S. assets, or government intervention in the foreign exchange markets to support the dollar.

The actual outcome was a collapse in the dollar. For example, in 1990 one U.S. dollar could be exchanged for over 150 yen. However, by late 1995 the exchange rate was about 100 yen per dollar. In other words, the dollar value of one yen had increased from roughly $0.007 (1/150) to $0.01 (1/100). Of course, in a worldwide market economy, at some point the lower dollar should lead to fewer imports of Japanese goods and services (because of their higher cost in terms of dollars) by Americans. At the same time, the Japanese will find American goods and services to be less costly (because of the stronger yen) and American exports to Japan should increase. The net result of a lower dollar could be to reduce the trade deficit with Japan in the future.

Link Between GPDI and Gross Savings

Table 7.2 shows the link between gross private domestic investment and gross savings in the United States. For 1994, gross private savings were estimated to be about $1.1 trillion. Gross savings are comprised of personal savings, undistributed corporate profits, capital consumption allowances, and government surpluses or deficits. Individuals provided over $203 billion in net savings in 1994, which represented about 19 percent of gross private savings. Corporate profits that were not distributed to owners amounted to $135 billion before inventory valuation and capital consumption adjustments. Undistributed corporate profits thus represented about 13 percent of gross private savings. **Capital consumption allowances,** sometimes referred to as depreciation, are estimates of the "using up" of plant and equipment assets for business purposes. These allowances provided about $432 billion in corporate savings and nearly $283 billion in noncorporate savings. Taken together, capital consumption allowances accounted for about 68 percent of gross private savings and represent the primary sources of savings from year to year.

capital consumption allowances
estimates of the "using up," or depreciation of, plant and equipment assets for business purposes

TABLE 7.2   Gross Savings in the United States (in Billions of Dollars)

	1992	1993	1994
Gross saving	**$ 717.8**	**$ 780.9**	**$ 920.6**
Gross private saving	986.9	1,005.2	1,053.5
Personal saving	238.7	189.9	203.1
Undistributed corporate profits*	110.4	124.0	135.1
Corporate inventory valuation adjustment	−5.3	−7.1	−19.5
Capital consumption allowances			
Corporate	396.6	408.8	432.2
Noncorporate	261.3	262.5	283.1
Government surplus or deficit (−)	−269.1	−224.3	−132.9
Federal	−276.3	−226.2	−159.1
State and local	7.2	1.9	26.2
Gross investment	**$ 741.4**	**$ 795.4**	**$ 889.7**
Gross private domestic investment	796.5	891.7	1,032.9
Net foreign investment	−55.1	−96.2	−143.2
Statistical discrepancy	**$ 23.6**	**$ 14.6**	**$ −30.9**

*Before inventory valuation and capital consumption adjustments.

Source: *Federal Reserve Bulletin* (June 1994 and October 1995): A52.

However, gross private savings were reduced by the government deficit of approximately $133 billion in 1994 resulting in a gross savings of about $921 billion. Closer examination shows that the federal deficit was about $159 billion while the state and local governments produced a net surplus of about $26 billion in 1994. We will discuss the implications of large federal budget deficits later in the chapter.

Now, let's complete the link between gross savings and gross private domestic investment. By definition, gross investment must equal gross savings. Thus, any measurement differences are explained in the form of a statistical discrepancy. For 1994, the statistical discrepancy was about −$31 billion in order to get gross savings up to the gross investment of approximately $890 billion. Gross private domestic investment then is found by adding the net foreign investment of approximately $143 billion in 1993 to the gross investment amount. The negative net foreign investment in 1994 is consistent with the above discussion concerning the large U.S. trade deficits in goods and services. In order to bring the current account deficits in balance with the capital account, foreign government and private ownership of U.S. assets must exceed U.S. ownership of foreign assets. The result is a negative net foreign investment by the United States.

HISTORICAL ROLE OF SAVINGS IN THE UNITED STATES

As the size of U.S. businesses expanded, the importance of accumulating and converting large amounts of financial capital to business use increased. The corporate form of organization provided a convenient and flexible legal arrangement for bringing together available financial capital. These advantages of the corporation over sole proprietorship, or private owner-ship, and partnership are described in Chapter 13.

Developments in public transportation were often too costly and spec-ulative for private promoters to undertake. The magnitude of early canal, turnpike, and railroad construction was such that the government under-took much of the financing of these projects. In fact, until the end of the 19th century, governmental units contributed more funding to these efforts than did private interests. Since this government financing was accomplished largely through bond issues rather than current revenues, the ultimate source of funds was the savings of individuals who bought the bonds.

FOREIGN SOURCES OF SAVINGS

Large amounts of the securities sold by both government and private pro-moters were purchased by foreign investors. Foreign capital played a decisive role in the development of the nation's early transportation system.

The huge role that foreign capital played in the economic development of the United States is paralleled by the developing nations of today. These nations now face many of the financial problems that the United States experienced during its early years. Private savings in many of these countries is negligible because almost all current income must be used for immediate consumption. Individual nations and such international organizations as the World Bank supply large amounts of capital to the developing nations of the world to increase their productive capacity.

The flow of development capital not only stimulates economic expan-sion in these countries but it also makes their capital much more efficient. For example, speedier transportation reduces the amount of goods in transit, thus releasing working capital for other purposes. In due time, as internal capital formation increases, it is hoped that the need for foreign capital will be eliminated and that these countries can then enjoy an independent capital formation process.

DOMESTIC SUPPLY OF SAVINGS

As capital formation began increasing at a faster and faster rate after the Civil War, the demand for funds also increased. Wealthy Americans and foreign investors could no longer provide funds at a rapid enough rate. Britain was investing heavily in India because of political commitments, and the other European countries were not large or wealthy enough to continue supplying funds in quantities adequate to sustain our growth. The American family soon took over the function of providing savings for the capital formation process. Per capita income rose to a level where American families could afford luxuries well beyond the subsistence level and could save part of what they had earned. Thus, the United States gradually developed to the stage where it could generate sufficient capital to finance its own expansion. Ultimately the result was a change in our status from a debtor nation to a creditor nation.

CREATION OF FINANCIAL ASSETS AND LIABILITIES

real assets
include ownership of land, buildings, machinery, inventory, commodities, and precious metals

financial assets
claims in the form of obligations or liabilities issued by individuals, businesses, financial intermediaries, and governments

Today the U.S. financial system is viewed as comprising three basic economic units: individuals, business firms (including financial intermediaries), and governments (federal, state, and local). At any point in time, these units are likely to be holders of real and financial assets. *Real assets* include direct ownership of land, buildings, machinery, inventory, commodities, and precious metals. *Financial assets* are claims against (obligations or liabilities of) individuals, businesses, financial intermediaries, and governments who issued them. Examples would be savings accounts held at depository institutions and debt obligations issued by business firms or the federal government.

Economic units are also likely to have certain financial liabilities or obligations. And, to the extent that their holdings of real and financial assets exceed their financial liabilities, these economic units will have net worth or owners' equity positions. These concepts will become clearer as we proceed.

In addition to measuring an economic unit's assets, liabilities, and net worth position as of a specific point in time, we are also interested in how these components change over a time period such as one year. This is because, for any measured time period, some of the basic economic units may be savings surplus units while others may be savings deficit units.

savings
income that is not consumed but held in the form of cash and other financial assets

savings surplus
occurs when current income exceeds investment in real assets

savings deficit
occurs when investment in real assets exceeds current income

Savings occur when all of an economic unit's income is not consumed and are represented by the accumulation of cash and other financial assets. *Savings surplus* occurs when an economic unit, such as individuals taken as a group, has current income that exceeds its direct investment in real assets. These surplus savings are made available to savings deficit units. For example, business firms as a group are often unable to meet all of their plant and equipment investment needs out of undistributed profits or earnings retained in the business, which are profits remaining after taxes and, in the case of corporations, after the cash dividends are paid to stockholders. When expenditures on real assets exceed current income, a *savings deficit* situation exists and it becomes necessary to acquire funds from a savings surplus unit.

Figure 7.1 illustrates how financial assets and liabilities are created when balancing savings surplus and savings deficit units. The process might begin with a group of individuals placing their savings in time deposit accounts at a commercial bank. The bank might, in turn, loan some of these deposits to a savings deficit business firm that wishes to purchase more equipment. This process of channeling savings into investment through the use of a financial institution or intermediary results in the creation of two types of financial assets and two types of financial liabilities. The time deposits represent financial assets to the individuals who save funds. At the same time, these time deposits are financial liabilities to the commercial bank. Likewise, the business loan represents a financial asset to the commercial bank but a financial liability to the borrowing firm. It should be recognized that the total system remains in balance because the increase in time deposits held by the group of individuals results in a corresponding increase in their net worth, and the business loan is used to increase that firm's real assets.

The individuals receive safety of principal, liquidity, and a return on their savings over time. At the other end, the business firm anticipates earning a return on its investment in real assets that is higher than the interest cost on the bank loan. The bank, of course, earns compensation for facilitating the savings and investment process.

At this point we should distinguish between direct securities and debt instruments and those that are indirect. **Direct financing** involves the use of securities such as corporate stocks and bonds that represent specific contracts between the savers and the borrowers themselves. The same

direct financing
involves use of securities that represent specific contracts between the savers and borrowers themselves

FIGURE 7.1   Creation of Financial Assets and Liabilities

INDIVIDUALS	
Real Assets	Financial Liabilities
Financial Assets: Time Deposits	Owners' Equity

COMMERCIAL BANK	
Real Assets	Financial Liabilities: Time Deposits
Financial Assets: Business Loan	Owners' Equity

BUSINESS FIRM	
Real Assets	Financial Liabilities: Business Loan
Financial Assets	Owners' Equity

indirect financing
financing created by
an intermediary that
involves separate instru-
ments with lenders and
borrowers

instrument represents the financial asset of the saver and the claim or lia-bility on the borrower. Direct financial transactions may be handled by brokers or other intermediaries, but the instruments do not represent a claim or obligation of the intermediary. In **indirect financing**, the inter-mediary creates and is a party to separate instruments with the ultimate lenders and the borrowers. In the example above, the business loan and the time deposits are indirect instruments. The business firm owes money to the bank, and the bank owes money to the individuals, but the firm and the individuals have no direct relationship. Indirect instruments could have been avoided in the above example if the individual had supplied funds directly to the business firm by purchasing bonds issued by that firm. This would have resulted in the creation of one type of financial asset—bond securities held by the individuals, and one type of financial liability—bond securities issued by the business firm.

There are reasons, of course, why the individuals might not choose to invest directly in the firm's bonds. If they are small savers, they may be unable to individually purchase a bond. There is also less liquidity and safety of principal in such investments. Thus, financial institutions and intermediaries can play an important role in channeling savings into investments.

Security transactions involving both direct and indirect financing ini-tially occur in primary markets. Many of these securities can be sold by their owners, the original lenders, in secondary markets. Secondary market transactions allow the owners of securities to convert them to cash prior to the time the original borrower has agreed to repay the indebtedness, in order to reclaim their savings for other purposes. Such transactions do not affect the original borrowers except that their debt is now owed to some-one else. However, secondary markets provide liquidity to the original lenders, and this feature is important in attracting savings to certain pri-mary markets. For example, the New York Stock Exchange is a secondary market. Its existence makes it easier for corporations to sell new issues of stock to individuals and other organizations in the primary market.

EXPENDITURES AND RECEIPTS OF THE FEDERAL GOVERNMENT

Table 7.2 indicated that in recent years the federal government has had a savings deficit in excess of $150 billion annually. In essence, the federal government continues to spend much more than it receives in the form of taxes and other revenues. On the one hand, fiscal policy can use a deficit budget to stimulate economic activity. On the other hand, continued large deficits have resulted in a national debt that is about $5 trillion and annual interest payments on the national debt that are becoming more and more significant.

The federal government relies primarily on tax revenues to support its various expenditure programs. In addition, revenues for general expenditures are received for specific services benefiting the persons charged. Examples of these revenues include postal receipts, rental receipts from federal housing projects, and food and housing payments collected from some government employees. The federal government also receives substantial insurance trust revenues from contributions to such programs as Old Age, Survivors, and Disability Insurance. In turn, it makes large disbursements from these revenues. Although these trust fund receipts and expenditures represent a tremendous flow of funds, we are primarily concerned here with the general revenues and expenditures of the federal government. Finally, the federal government relies on borrowing to bridge the gap between revenues and expenditures. In fact, since 1960 the federal government has depended upon borrowed funds to support its program of expenditures in every year except 1969.

Figure 7.2 provides a graphic illustration of revenues and expenditures for fiscal year 1996. The major revenue sources are from individual income taxes and social insurance receipts, which together account for over two-thirds of total receipts. Notice that corporate income taxes account for 10 percent of total receipts and that about 12 percent of the total must be borrowed in order to balance the budget. The primary expenditure is direct benefit payments for individuals, which amount to nearly one-half of total expenditures. For many years national defense expenditures constituted the largest single item in the budget. As a result of the slowdown in defense spending and the growth of general expenditures it is now about 16 percent of the budget. Also of note is that net interest payments now comprise about 16 percent of total expenditures.

In order to better see the actual expenditure picture, refer to Table 7.3, which breaks down federal budget outlays into detailed categories and also accounts for sources of income. Notice that the size of the annual deficits differs between Tables 7.2 and 7.3. This is because the former table is based on calendar years and the latter table provides fiscal year data.

The most important expenditure items are those for the welfare of individuals and include health, Medicare, and Social Security expenditures; as well as income security expenditures. It is interesting to note that one of the smallest items in the budget is general operations of the government itself. This item includes the operations of the judicial system, the executive branch, the Congress, all regulatory agencies, and most departments of government with the exception of the Department of Defense.

Local governments depend heavily on property taxes for their revenues, while state governments depend largely on sales taxes and special taxes such as those on motor fuel, liquor, and tobacco products. In contrast, the federal government relies primarily on income taxes, along with social insurance taxes, for its revenues.

FIGURE 7.2   The Federal Government Dollar, Fiscal Year 1996 Estimates

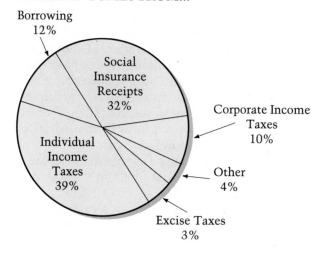

WHERE IT COMES FROM...

Borrowing 12%

Social Insurance Receipts 32%

Corporate Income Taxes 10%

Individual Income Taxes 39%

Other 4%

Excise Taxes 3%

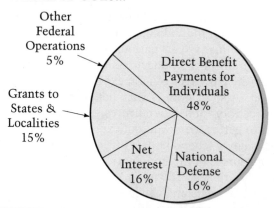

WHERE IT GOES...

Other Federal Operations 5%

Direct Benefit Payments for Individuals 48%

Grants to States & Localities 15%

Net Interest 16%

National Defense 16%

Source: *Budget of the United States Government, Fiscal Year 1996,* U.S. Office of Management and Budget.

The Budget

Until 1968 the form of budget presented annually to Congress did not include the expenditures and receipts of the various federal government trust funds, such as Old Age, Survivors, and Disability Insurance. As such it failed to reflect the full effect of government activity on the economy. Therefore, many economists preferred to use the so-called cash budget to analyze the economy. The cash budget recorded transactions with the public,

TABLE 7.3
Federal Budget Receipts, Outlays, and Total Public Debt (in Billions of Dollars)

	FISCAL YEAR		
	1978	1989	1994
BUDGET RECEIPTS BY SOURCE	$ 399.6	$ 990.8	$1,257.7
Individual income taxes	181.0	445.7	543.1
Corporation income taxes	60.0	103.3	140.4
Social insurance taxes	121.0	359.4	461.5
Excise taxes	18.4	34.4	55.2
Estate and gift taxes	5.3	8.7	15.2
Custom duties	6.6	16.3	20.1
Miscellaneous receipts	6.6	22.9	18.0
All other	0.8	1.5	4.3
BUDGET OUTLAYS BY FUNCTION	$ 458.7	$1,142.8	$1,460.9
National defense	104.5	303.6	281.6
International affairs	7.5	9.6	17.1
General science, space, and technology	4.9	12.9	16.2
Energy	8.0	3.7	5.2
Natural resources and environment	11.0	16.1	21.1
Agriculture	11.4	16.9	15.1
Commerce and housing credit	6.3	27.8	−5.1
Transportation	15.5	27.6	38.1
Community and regional development	11.8	5.8	10.5
Education, training, employment, and social services	26.7	35.7	46.3
Health, Medicare, and Social Security	135.2	365.9	561.4
Income security	61.5	136.8	214.0
Veterans' benefits and services	19.0	30.1	37.6
Administration of justice	3.8	9.4	15.3
General government	12.0	8.9	11.3
Interest	35.4	169.3	203.0
Undistributed offsetting receipts	−15.7	−37.2	−37.8
TOTAL SURPLUS OR DEFICIT(−)	$ −59.2	$ −152.0	$ −203.2
OUTSTANDING DEBT— END OF PERIOD	$ 780.4	$2,886.2	$4,643.7

Sources: U.S. Office of Management and Budget and Treasury Department.

and included such items as trust fund expenditures and receipts. It was concerned primarily with cash transactions between the public and the federal government. But even the cash budget did not include all cash expenditures and receipts. For example, the various enterprises operated by the federal government were reflected on a net earnings or net deficit basis rather than on the basis of total expenditures and receipts.

In October 1967, the President's Commission on Budget Concepts recommended the use of a new unified budget to replace all the older budget concepts. The resulting budget incorporates the best features of several previous budget concepts. All receipts and expenditures are included on a consolidated cash basis. The unified budget covers lending as well as spending, but these two categories are shown separately to facilitate analysis. Lending is included because of the obvious impact it has on the economy. It is separated from spending because it is believed that these two types of outlays differ significantly in their impact on economic activity.

The excess of total expenditures, excluding net lending, over total receipts reflects the deficit in expenditures. The relationship of total outlays to total receipts reflects the total budget surplus or deficit. Political as well as economic considerations enter into structuring the federal budget. The size of the federal deficit is a key political issue. For example, the inclusion of the Old Age, Survivors, and Disability Insurance in the budget as revenue serves to reduce the size of the federal deficit. It is argued by many that these funds should be set aside for their future use as needed. At this time receipts of social insurance taxes far exceed payments but as the population of the nation ages, payments will far exceed revenues. It is estimated that this reversal will exist as early as the year 2020.

Off-Budget Outlays

off-budget outlays
funding for some govern-
ment agencies that is not
included in the federal
budget

The unified budget concept was designed to be comprehensive in coverage. However, since 1973 the funding for some federal agencies has been excluded from budget totals. These are called ***off-budget outlays.*** The existence of off-budget receipts and outlays, which showed a surplus of nearly $90 billion in 1990, prevents the unified budget from completely achieving its objective. Among the off-budget agencies are the U.S. Postal Service, the U.S. Railway Association, the Rural Telephone Bank, and the Federal Financing Bank. The Federal Financing Bank is by far the most important and active of the off-budget agencies, accounting for the bulk of these agencies' outlays.

There is some pressure for the return of these accounts to the basic budget. While some arguments can be made for their continued off-budget status, a stronger case can be made for their inclusion in the basic budget. The existence of off-budget federal agencies adds confusion to the government's financial statements, and it is acknowledged that programs financed outside the unified budget receive less congressional scrutiny than programs contained within the budget. This may explain why the recent growth rate of the off-budget outlays was higher than that for unified budget outlays.

It is nearly impossible to obtain a clear understanding of off-budget outlays without recourse to the basic budget document. While periodic publications of the federal government—such as the *Treasury Bulletin*, *Economic Indicators*, the *Survey of Current Business*, and the *Federal Reserve Bulletin*—provide summary data on off-budget outlays, details are not available. This may add to the increasing concern over lack of control by independent budget analysts.

Debt Financing

As we have observed, the federal government obtains funds for expenditures primarily through tax revenues. When these tax and other general revenues fail to meet expenditures, a **budgetary deficit** is incurred. Until recent years these deficits have been of modest size compared to total government expenditures. However, their cumulative impact has created a vast increase in the total federal debt. Although **federal statutory debt limits** have been set by Congress, it has been necessary to raise the limits at frequent intervals to accommodate the continuing deficits of the federal government.

budgetary deficit occurs when expenditures are greater than revenues

federal statutory debt limits limits on the federal debt set by Congress

A brief review of the growth of budgetary deficits since the beginning of the 1950s will help in understanding the magnitude of the problem. From 1950 until 1961 relatively small surpluses and deficits prevailed, but from 1961 to the present (except for 1969, as indicated earlier) deficits have been increasing dramatically. Figure 7.3 depicts the federal budget deficits since 1982. Deficits were near the $200 billion level during the mid-1980s. Some improvement in reducing annual deficits began in 1987 and continued until 1989. The annual deficits then began growing larger until reaching a high in 1992. However, since 1993 the size of the annual deficits has been declining.

In contrast with some nations, the federal debt of the United States is owned to a large extent by its own citizens and institutions. Indeed, part of our debt is due to our role as a creditor nation from 1918 until 1985. Until World War I the United States depended heavily upon foreign investment, and it was not until 1985 that liabilities to foreign creditors again exceeded claims against foreign creditors. Our return to being a debtor nation has been due in large measure to high domestic interest rates, relative political stability in the world arena, and the development of an extremely unfavorable balance of trade. The nation's excess of imports relative to exports since 1964 has been in excess of $100 billion each year. To the extent that foreign claims resulting from a surplus of imports are invested in federal obligations, foreign ownership of the federal debt increases.

The burden of the national debt is reflected in part in Table 7.4 where it can be seen that the total gross federal debt relative to the gross domestic product increased from just under 39 percent in fiscal 1970 to nearly 71 percent for fiscal 1995. Over the same period, the percentage of gross federal debt held by the public increased from about 29 percent to about 52 percent.

The persistent growth of the federal deficit has met with increasing concern but little meaningful action. In an effort to make progress in reducing

FIGURE 7.3   Federal Budget Deficits Since 1982

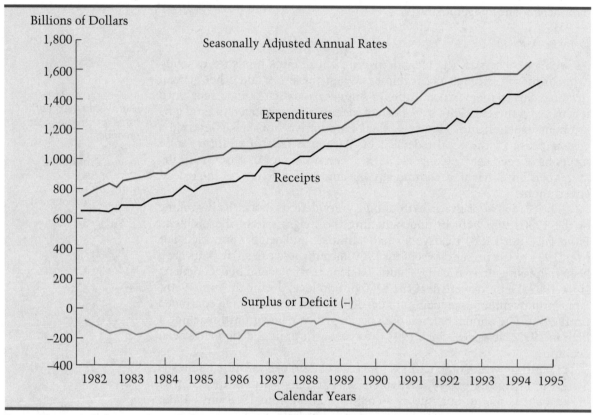

Source: *Economic Indicators,* Council of Economic Advisers (September 1995).

federal spending and the deficit, Congress passed the Balanced Budget and Emergency Deficit Control Act of 1985. This act became commonly referred to as the Gramm-Rudman-Hollings (GRH) Act and was designed to produce a balanced budget by 1991. By an amendment to the GRH act in 1987, the date was changed to 1993. Targets, however, have not been met because of continuing congressional resolutions providing funds for federal activities. By the end of the second week of the 1990 fiscal year, lacking a legislated budget from Congress with a genuine deficit reduction, President Bush ordered a *sequester* as required by the GRH act. A sequester is a legal impounding of property or money to resolve the disputed matter. This sequester would have required an across-the-board cut in expenditures by all functions of the government except for Social Security and Medicare. On the very last day, when these cuts were to have been made, budget negotiators reached a compromise. Thus the sequester

TABLE 7.4
Gross Federal Debt as a Percentage of Gross Domestic Product (GDP)

FISCAL YEAR	GROSS FEDERAL DEBT	
	TOTAL	HELD BY PUBLIC
1970	38.7%	28.7%
1971	38.8	28.8
1972	38.0	28.1
1973	36.6	26.8
1974	34.5	24.5
1975	35.9	26.1
1976	37.3	28.3
1977	36.8	28.6
1978	36.0	28.2
1979	34.1	26.4
1980	34.4	26.8
1981	33.6	26.5
1982	36.4	29.5
1983	41.4	34.1
1984	42.3	35.2
1985	45.8	37.8
1986	50.3	41.2
1987	52.7	42.4
1988	54.1	42.7
1989	55.4	42.3
1990	58.5	44.0
1991	63.4	47.4
1992	67.6	50.6
1993	69.5	51.9
1994	70.0	51.7
1995 (est.)	70.6	51.8

Source: *Economic Report of the President,* 1995.

did not go into effect. The prospect of radical employee cuts in many essential government functions brought immense pressure from the public for a legislated budget. The Omnibus Budget Reconciliation Act of November 1990 represents another effort to reduce future deficits. Further efforts to reduce the budget deficit continue under the Clinton administration and in the Republican-dominated Congress.

Nowhere in the economy is the significance of a smoothly functioning financial system more apparent than in connection with the federal debt. Not only does the financial system accommodate the federal government by financing its frequent budgetary deficits, but it also provides for the smooth transition from old debt issues that mature to the new issues that replace them. The financial markets face a greater challenge in such refunding of government issues than in absorbing net new debt. Just as the nation's industrial development has depended upon an equally efficient development of financial institutions, so too, many of the financial activities of modern government depend upon these same institutions.

It is notable that public borrowing is a relatively modern development. During the Middle Ages, governments were forced to borrow from wealthy merchants and others on an individual basis. Often crown jewels were offered as collateral for such advances. Large public borrowing by governments, as for businesses, became possible only when monetary systems were refined and efficient financial institutions developed that could facilitate the transfer of monetary savings.

It is important here to note that federal debt growth has taken place in an expanding economy, and that the burden of the debt is a function of the interest on the debt relative to the ability of the nation to pay. With interest in the neighborhood of $200 billion a year, the ability to meet these ongoing interest obligations and to simultaneously move to a balanced budget is not trivial.

MAJOR SOURCES OF SAVINGS

voluntary savings
financial assets set aside for future use

contractual savings
savings accumulated on a regular schedule by prior agreement

An important savings sector in the economy is personal savings. **Voluntary savings** are simply financial assets set aside for use in the future. **Contractual savings** include such savings as the accumulation of reserves in insurance and pension funds. Contractual savings are not determined by current decision. They are disciplined by previous commitments which the saver has some incentive to honor.

It is from individuals that most financial intermediaries accumulate capital. Individuals as a group consistently represent a savings surplus unit. Corporations also represent an important source of savings. However, their large demand for investment funds, as is also the case for unincorporated business firms, generally results in a net need for external funds. While financial intermediaries can also save, their primary role in our financial system is to aid the savings-investment process. Our governments on balance have operated as a savings deficit unit in recent years. Thus, the ability to provide adequate funds to meet our investment needs is dependent primarily on the savings of individuals and corporations.

PERSONAL SAVINGS

Table 7.5 shows personal savings during recent years in the United States. The savings rate, which is personal saving as a percent of disposable personal income, has been averaging a comparatively low 4 to 5 percent in recent years. However, the dollar amount of personal savings exceeded $200 billion in 1994.

TABLE 7.5   Personal Savings in the United States (in Billions of Dollars)

	1992	1993	1994
Personal income	$5,144.9	$5,388.3	$5,701.7
Less: taxes and other payments	644.8	681.6	742.1
Disposable personal income	$4,500.2	$4,706.7	$4,959.6
Less: personal outlays	4,261.5	4,516.8	4,756.5
Personal savings	$ 238.7	$ 189.9	$ 203.1
Savings rate (personal savings/ disposable personal income)	5.3%	4.0%	4.1%

Source: *Federal Reserve Bulletin* (June 1994 and October 1995): A52.

Private individuals maintain savings for a number of reasons. They set aside a part of their current income for the acquisition of costly durable consumer goods, such as cars and appliances. Savings are set aside by individuals to meet unforeseeable financial needs. These savings are not set aside for specific future consumption; instead, they represent emergency or rainy-day funds. Individuals may also save for such long-term foreseeable spending as children's college education or for retirement. For short periods of time people may save a portion of current income simply because desirable goods and services are not available for purchase.

There are a number of media in which to maintain savings, ranging in liquidity from cash balances to pension funds. Three factors usually influence a person's choice of medium: liquidity, degree of safety, and return.

Cash Balances

The most liquid form of savings that an individual can maintain is cash. Cash savings are generally in the form of checkable deposits and pocket cash. People maintain this liquidity in order to meet current commitments or to make purchases in the very near future. Cash savings may also be hoarded. These hoards are not held for specific consumption purposes but rather out of distrust of depository institutions or because an individual wants monetary wealth to be close at hand. Hoarded funds are withdrawn from circulation and add nothing to the capital formation process. Checkable deposits and currency declined as a percent of disposable income between the 1950s and 1980s and are currently below the 15 percent level.

Time and Savings Deposits

A wide choice of facilities providing both safety of principal and a reasonable return is available to the individual saver. The combination of easy access to funds and regular earning power resulted in a substantial rate of growth for time and savings deposits during the 1950s and 1960s. More recently, financial assets have been directed towards money market deposit accounts

SAVINGS HABITS OF AMERICANS

Savings by individuals provide a crucial source of funds for investment purposes. Everyone must decide what portions of their disposable personal income to spend or to save. U.S. income tax laws stemming from the Great Depression of the 1930s were designed to encourage spending rather than saving. In order to stimulate economic activity, savings were heavily taxed. As a consequence, the savings rate has been relatively lower in the United States compared with Japan and the industrialized countries of Western Europe.

Following are U.S. personal savings rates, or personal savings as a percent of disposable income, by five-year intervals beginning with 1960.

YEAR	SAVINGS RATES
1960	5.8%
1965	7.0
1970	8.1
1975	9.2
1980	7.1
1985	4.5
1990	4.3

Notice that the savings rate increased from a level less than 6 percent in 1960 to more than 9 percent by 1975. Tax reform in the form of lower personal income tax rates in the mid-1960s and in the 1970s may have contributed to this higher personal savings rate. However, the savings rate declined to less than 5 percent by 1985. Although not shown, the savings rate reached a low of 3.2 percent in 1987 before increasing to 4.3 percent in 1990. Since then, the savings rate increased to a little more than 5 percent in 1992 before again falling to the 4 percent level.

Source: *Federal Reserve Bulletin*, various issues.

(MMDAs) and money market fund shares. These offer limited check-writing privileges and returns based on the investment of money market funds in bank certificates of deposit and corporate commercial paper. Household investments in large time deposits (amounts of $100,000 or more) also grew rapidly during the 1970s and 1980s.

Insurance Reserves and Pension Funds
The contractual savings embodied in insurance reserves and pension funds grew rapidly as a percent of disposable personal income during the 1950s. Growth in this area of financial assets accelerated again during the 1980s. Life insurance and pension fund reserves continue to account for an

increasing portion of total household assets. Individuals may acquire life insurance through private organizations and may belong to private pension plans or funds. Retirement funds are the principal form of individual savings provided by state and local governments. The federal government accumulates reserves for the accounts of individuals through the Old Age and Survivors Insurance Trust Fund, the Disability Insurance Trust Fund, the National Service Life Insurance Fund, and others. These savings of individuals as represented by government-held reserves are invested primarily in the obligations of federal, local, and state governments. As such, they satisfy a part of the demand for funds by governments.

Securities

Because of the wide diversity of securities—corporate stock, corporate bonds, and government securities—individuals can usually find a security that is well suited to their special savings objectives. For persons desiring growth of principal, corporate stocks with the likelihood of growth are available. These stocks usually provide a lower current income to the saver than is available from most other securities. Other savers may place primary emphasis on stability of principal for liquidity purposes. The stocks of public utilities and other recession-resistant companies serve this purpose, as do high-grade corporate and government bonds. There is a wide spectrum of risk, growth potential, and yield in which virtually every saver who chooses securities as a savings medium can find a place for funds consistent with his or her own individual objectives and preferences.

Shares of investment companies add to the importance of common stock as a form of individual savings. These shares have played a large role for the saver with limited funds because they are readily available in small quantities. Investment companies have also instituted convenient procedures for accumulating shares on a regular basis out of current income.

CORPORATE SAVINGS

Table 7.6 shows corporate savings during recent years in the United States. Corporations save by producing profits after taxes and then not paying all of these profits out to investors in the form of dividends. The proportion of after-tax profits retained in the organization is referred to as *undistributed profits*. Notice that corporations retained between about 36 and 40 percent of their after-tax profits in recent years, with a dollar amount of corporate savings of approximately $117 billion in 1994. When the undistributed corporate profits are adjusted for inventory valuation changes and capital consumption adjustments, the result is an adjusted undistributed profits figure comparable to that shown in Table 7.2.

Corporate saving for short-term working capital purposes is by far the most important reason for accumulating financial assets. Seasonal business changes create an uneven demand for corporate operating assets, such as

TABLE 7.6   Corporate Savings in the United States (in Billions of Dollars)

	1992	1993	1994
Profits before taxes	$395.4	$450.0	$524.5
Less: tax liabilities	146.3	174.3	202.5
Profits after taxes	$249.1	$275.7	$322.0
Less: dividends	150.5	169.0	205.2
Undistributed profits	$ 98.6	$106.7	$116.9
Inventory valuation	–5.3	–7.1	–19.5
Capital consumption adjustment	17.1	24.4	37.7
Adjusted undistributed profits	$110.4	$124.0	$135.1
Retention rate (undistributed profits/profits after taxes)	39.6	38.7	36.3

Source: *Federal Reserve Bulletin* (June 1994 and October 1995): A35.

inventories and accounts receivable. And because of these seasonal changes, cash inflow is seldom in just the right amount and at the right time to accommodate the increased levels of operating assets. Quarterly corporate income tax liabilities also impose the necessity of accumulating financial assets. The short-term accumulation of financial assets on the part of business corporations does not add to the level of long-term savings of the economy as a whole. However, these funds do enter the monetary stream and become available to users of short-term borrowed funds. As such, these short-term savings serve to meet a part of the demand for funds of consumers, government, and other businesses. These savings are typically held by a corporation in the form of checkable deposits with commercial banks, short-term obligations of the federal government, commercial paper, and certificates of deposit issued by commercial banks. These financial assets meet the requirements of safety and liquidity.

Corporations also engage in the savings process for purposes of meeting planned spending in the future. Reserves are often set up to provide all or part of the cost of construction, purchase of equipment, or major maintenance and repairs to existing facilities. Savings committed to these purposes are often invested in securities that have longer maturities and higher yields than those held for short-term business purposes. These securities include the debt obligations of both corporations and government and, to a limited extent, corporate stock.

FLOW OF FUNDS FROM SAVINGS INTO INVESTMENTS

Individuals represent the most important source of savings in our financial system. As we have discussed, they may invest their savings directly in bonds, stocks, and real estate mortgages or indirectly by placing their savings with financial intermediaries.

Table 7.7 shows the importance of private financial intermediation as a source of funds supplied to credit markets. Total funds supplied, excluding corporate equities, increased from about $823 billion in 1992 to about $958 billion in 1993 and continued to increase to $1,037 billion in 1994. Approximately 56 percent of these total funds were provided in 1992 through financial intermediation. The ratio of financial intermediation funds to total funds supplied increased to approximately 66 percent in 1993 before declining to about 40 percent in 1994. Thus, the importance of financial intermediation to the savings and investment process remains important but volatile.

Funds supplied by commercial banks increased over the 1992–94 period while thrift institutions went from a negative supplier of funds (i.e., they withdrew funds) to a positive supplier over the same period. In contrast, insurance and pension funds, while large suppliers in 1992 and 1993, contributed substantially less funds in 1994. A similar pattern was exhibited by the other financial intermediaries (finance companies, mortgage companies, mutual funds, Real Estate Investment Trusts, etc.). The reduction in funds provided by the financial sectors in 1994 was offset by increased net lending in the credit markets by the private domestic nonfinancial sectors, particularly households.

Table 7.8 shows how funds were used or raised in the credit markets by borrowing sector and by instrument. Borrowing by the U.S. federal government has been the single largest borrowing sector and accounted for 52 percent of net borrowing in 1992. During 1993, households borrowed $251 billion or about 41 percent of the total borrowing by domestic nonfinancial sectors. This compared with about 42 percent for the U.S. government. In 1994, borrowing by households continued to increase rapidly and represented 59 percent of the net borrowing by domestic nonfinancial sectors.

TABLE 7.7   Net Lending in Credit Markets (in Billions of Dollars)

	1992	1993	1994
Total net lending	$822.9	$958.2	$1,037.0
Funds advanced by private financial intermediaries:			
Commercial banks	94.8	142.2	162.0
Thrift institutions	−59.5	−1.7	35.2
Insurance and pension funds	177.9	204.1	100.6
Other financial intermediaries	243.2	284.8	113.7
Total	$456.4	$629.4	$411.5
Financial intermediation funds as a percent of total net lending	55.5%	65.7%	39.7%

Source: *Federal Reserve Bulletin* (June 1994 and October 1995): A42.

TABLE 7.8   Funds Raised in the Credit Markets (in Billions of Dollars)

	1992	1993	1994
Net borrowing by domestic nonfinancial sectors	$582.4	$606.5	$595.0
By borrowing sector:			
U.S. government	304.0	256.1	155.9
State and local governments	59.4	64.7	−48.2
Households	215.1	251.1	351.5
Farms	1.2	2.0	2.4
Nonfarm noncorporate	−39.4	−19.3	13.5
Corporate	42.1	51.9	119.9
Total	$582.4	$606.5	$595.0
By instrument:			
U.S. government securities	$303.8	$248.3	$155.7
Tax-exempt obligations	65.7	59.4	−34.1
Corporate bonds	67.5	71.3	22.0
Mortgages	120.8	172.2	186.5
Consumer debt	9.3	49.0	117.5
Bank loans	−5.6	4.7	74.0
Other debt	20.9	1.6	73.4
Total	$582.4	$606.5	$595.0
Total nonfinancial corporate equities	$ 27.0	$ 23.0	$−40.9

Source: *Federal Reserve Bulletin* (June 1994 and October 1995): A40–A41.

This has led many to express concern about the heavy indebtedness of households in the United States.

Corporate borrowing ranked fourth in borrowing in 1993 (9 percent of the total) behind borrowing by state and local governments (11 percent of the total). Corporate borrowing continued to increase in 1994 while state and local governments actually were net savers as a group.

Table 7.8 also shows recent borrowing activities by instrument. Mortgage borrowing amounted to about $187 billion in 1994 and comprised about 31 percent of total borrowings. The mortgage category consists largely of home mortgages and to a lesser extent, in order of importance, commercial property mortgages, multifamily residential mortgages, and farm mortgages. Household borrowing is primarily in the form of home mortgages and consumer debt, which was about $118 billion in 1994 or approximately 20 percent of the total net borrowing. In contrast, consumer debt was less than 2 percent of the total borrowings in 1992. Borrowings in the form of bank loans and other debt also increased dramatically over the 1992–94 period.

The largest instrument for raising borrowed funds used to be U.S. government securities, which was about $248 billion in 1993 and comprised about 41 percent of total borrowing. But, borrowing in the form of mortgages surpassed borrowing through U.S. government securities in 1994. Borrowing by issuing corporate bonds was relatively more important in 1992 and 1993 compared with 1994.

The significance of borrowing by the corporate sector, however, is somewhat obscured because corporations use a variety of debt instruments to meet their borrowing needs. For example, corporations issue their own bonds, take out commercial property mortgages, obtain bank loans, and acquire other debt, such as by issuing their own short-term promissory notes. Corporations also raise funds by issuing new shares of stock. Total funds raised from net new nonfinancial corporate equity issues amounted to $23 billion in 1993. However, the efforts by many U.S. firms to repurchase some of their outstanding shares caused a reduction in nonfinancial corporate equities of approximately $41 billion in 1994, as shown at the bottom of Table 7.8.

FACTORS AFFECTING SAVINGS

Among the several factors influencing the total amount of savings that exist in any given time period are: levels of income, economic expectations, cyclical influences, and the life stage of the individual saver or corporation. The precise relationship between savings and consumption is the subject of much debate and continuing study, however, and we limit our observations here to broad generalizations.

LEVELS OF INCOME

For our purposes, savings have been defined as current income minus tax payments and consumption spending. Keeping this definition in mind, let us explore the effect of changes in income on the levels of savings of individuals. As income falls, the individual attempts to maintain his or her present standard of living as long as possible. In so doing, the proportion of his or her consumption spending increases and total savings diminish. As income is further reduced, the individual may be forced to curtail consumption spending, and this results in a lower standard of living. Such reduction is reasonably limited, however, since the basic needs of the individual, or family unit, must be met. Not only will personal savings be eliminated under circumstances of drastic reductions in income, but the individual may also ***dissave,*** that is, spend accumulated savings rather than reduce further consumption spending.

dissave
to liquidate savings for consumption uses

As income increases, the individual will again be in a position to save. However, the saving will not necessarily begin immediately, as the individual may desire to buy the things that he or she could not afford during the low-income period. The amount of this need, notably for durable consumer goods, largely determines the rate of increase in savings during periods of income recovery.

On the whole, income levels are closely associated with levels of employment. Changes in business activity, in turn, influence employment levels. Downturns in the economy during 1970 and 1974–75 resulted in declines in employment levels and correspondingly lowered levels of income. Employment also suffered during the first part of the 1980s when unemployment levels rose to post–World War II highs, in excess of 10 percent.

ECONOMIC EXPECTATIONS

The anticipation of future events has a significant effect on savings. If individuals believe that their incomes will decrease in the near future, they may tend to curtail their current spending in order to establish a reserve for the expected period of low income. A worker anticipating a long and protracted labor dispute may increase current savings as partial protection against the financial impact of a strike.

Expectations of a general increase in price levels may also have a strong influence upon the liquidity that savers want to maintain. The prospect of price increases in consumer durable goods may cause an increase in their sales as individuals try to buy before prices increase. Savings are thus quickly converted to consumer spending. Corporate savings too may be reduced as a result of price increase expectations. In addition to committing funds to plant and office equipment before price increases take place, corporations typically increase their inventory positions. As for the individual, the prospect of an interruption in the supply of inventory because of a labor strike or other cause often results in a rapid stockpiling of raw materials and merchandise. The prospect of price decreases and of large production capacity has the opposite effect—the liquidity and financial assets of a business increase relative to its operating assets.

Unprecedented price increases during the inflationary 1970s led many individuals to develop a "buy it now because it will cost more later" philosophy. This resulted in a classic example of the impact of price increase expectations on the spend-save decisions of individuals. When the economy began recovering during 1975, employment and income levels also began rising. The personal savings rate increased in 1975 before it began declining under the pressure of renewed price inflation during the latter part of the 1970s. As previously noted, the personal savings rate remained low throughout the 1980s.

ECONOMIC CYCLES

While changes in levels of income may be caused mainly by cyclical movements in the economy, they do not represent the complete effect that the cycle has on savings. Cyclical movements affect not only the amounts but also the types of savings.

To illustrate this point, let us observe the effect that changes in economic activity have on the shifting of savings from one type to another, notably between time and savings deposits at commercial banks or thrift institutions. Short-term interest rates usually decrease during a period of economic downturn or recession for such money market instruments as U.S. Treasury bills, commercial paper, and obligations of U.S. government agencies. This was the case during the latter part of 1974 and into 1975. Short-term money market rates also tend to remain relatively low during the early stages of economic recovery or expansion, such as occurred during 1976. However, as the economy continues to expand, short-term interest rates begin to move up rapidly, as occurred during 1977 and 1978. These money market rates usually peak at about the same time that a peak in economic activity occurs. For example, short-term interest rates peaked in early 1980 and in mid-1981 just prior to economic downturns.

Until recently, interest rates paid on time and savings deposits (excluding large negotiable CDs) held at commercial banks and thrift institutions were regulated and thus varied little with economic activity. Financial intermediation took place so long as the interest rates on time and savings deposits exceeded money market rates. However, disintermediation became particularly pronounced during periods when money market interest rates grew higher than interest rate ceilings set on time and saving deposits. Passage of the Depository Institutions Deregulation and Monetary Control Act of 1980 called for the elimination of rate ceilings on time and savings deposits. This act seems to have caused the lessening of cyclical swings between intermediation and disintermediation during the 1980s.

LIFE STAGES OF THE INDIVIDUAL SAVER

The pattern of savings over an individual's life span follows a somewhat predictable pattern when viewed for the total population. An individual saves very little during the youthful years simply because little income is produced. One's income has increased considerably by the time he or she has matured and begun to raise a family. Expenses, however, have also increased during these early family-forming years; one's savings are typically limited to those accruing to life insurance reserves. By the time the individual reaches middle age, two factors come into play that result in increased savings. First, income is typically much higher than at any previous time; second, the expense of raising children has been reduced or eliminated. Thus it is this middle-aged group that saves the most.

At retirement the individual's income is sharply reduced. He or she may now begin the process of dissaving. Pension fund payments along with accumulated savings are drawn upon for current living expenses.

The level of savings of individuals is therefore a function of the age composition of the population as a whole. A population shift to a large proportion of individuals in the productive middle-age years would result in a greater savings potential.

JAMIE BREEN

Marketing
Disciplined Investment
Advisors

BS Radio, TV, and Film
Northwestern
MBA Marketing/Finance
Northwestern

*"For lack of a
more specific title,
I'm the marketing guy."*

Q: *Describe the firm you work for.*
A: I work for Disciplined Investment Advisors which is a small money management firm. We manage (invest) money for corporate pension funds.

Q: *You say it's a small firm. How small?*
A: We manage over a billion dollars for our clients. That's a lot of money, but compared to a Fidelity with several hundred billion, we're definitely at the lower end. In the industry we'd be called a "boutique" firm.

Q: *And what do you do there?*
A: For lack of a more specific title, I'm the marketing guy. It's my job to spread the word about what we do, generate new clients, and keep existing ones.

Q: *So you call on pension fund managers.*
A: Yes, that's part of it. Our clients all have a person or team in charge of managing the pension fund, trying to invest it profitably and safely. So I call on those people. But there's another group of people that I spend even more time with. They are the outside consultants that help the pension managers decide whom to hire.

Q: *What do you do with these consultants?*
A: Basically I try to demonstrate to them that we are a good firm to recommend to their clients. I present them with information about our investment strategy and our performance during previous periods. But more important than the numbers is demonstrating to the consultants that we can help them look good, that we can make a professional presentation to their clients, explain our strategy coherently, and so on.

Q: *So if you impress the consultant, the consultant may recommend you to take over the investing of a company's pension fund.*
A: Part of a company's pension fund. In order to diversify, most funds divide the investment job between a number of companies like ours. Four or five for a smaller fund, up to a hundred or more for a very large corporation.

Q: *Is this a competitive business?*
A: It's very competitive because there's so much money involved. There are probably a thousand money managers that we could conceivably compete against. So even if our results are excellent, say in the top quartile, there are another 250 companies that can say the same thing.

Q: *So how do you differentiate yourself from the crowd?*
A: One of the unique aspects of our company is that it was founded by university professors, true experts in the field of Finance. So part of our message is based on the amount and quality of research that backs up our investment strategy. We provide both the pension fund managers and the consultants with a great deal of research data and information that helps them do their jobs. In return we hope to be selected to manage their money. And the other piece of the puzzle is simply establishing trust and credibility. Like any other sales job.

200

LIFE STAGES OF THE CORPORATION

Just as the financial savings of an individual are governed in part by age, so the financial savings generated by a business firm are a function of its life stage. It is true, of course, that all business firms do not proceed through a fixed life-stage cycle. To the extent, however, that a firm experiences the typical pattern of vigorous early growth and ultimate maturity and decline, its flow of financial savings may experience a predictable pattern.

During the pioneering and early expansion years of a successful business, the volume of physical assets typically increases rapidly. So rapid is this growth, the firm is unable to establish a strong position with respect to its financial assets. Indeed, it is during these years of the corporate life cycle that there is a large need for borrowed capital. At this time the corporation is typically a heavy user of financial assets rather than a provider.

More intensive market penetration and expanding geographic areas of distribution make it possible for the firm to continue its growth. Continuing profitable expansion becomes more difficult, however, as the managerial talent of the firm reaches the limit of its ability to direct and control operations and as competing firms in the industry also grow. The combination of a slow-down in expansion and a continuing large flow of cash generation results in financial savings. As the enterprise matures and ceases to expand, it reaches its peak of savings. Earnings are high, and commitment of funds to increased operating assets is reduced or eliminated.

As the firm begins to decline in the final phase of the life cycle, its ability to create financial savings is reduced. During the early years of the decline of a business, however, it may continue to provide a reasonably high level of financial savings. This is true, notwithstanding lower profits, because of the conversion of physical assets to financial assets through depreciation allowances.

As the final stages of decline are reached, the firm is unable to generate further financial savings and probably perpetuates itself largely on the basis of the sustaining power of its previously accumulated financial assets.

SUMMARY

This chapter focused on how savings are created and how they are converted into investments. The major components of gross domestic product were identified and discussed in terms of consumption, investment, and the net exports balance of goods and services. A discussion followed of how financial assets and liabilities are created.

The three basic economic units were identified as individuals, business firms (including financial intermediaries), and governments. It was shown that the federal government has been a savings deficit unit in recent years with the result being large annual budget deficits and an ever-increasing national debt. Major sources of savings in the U.S. come from individuals and business firms. These savings may be directly invested and accumulated in financial intermediaries and then loaned or invested. The last section discussed factors that affect the level of savings.

KEY TERMS

budgetary deficit	indirect financing
capital consumption allowances	off-budget outlays
capital formation	personal consumption
contractual savings	expenditures (PCE)
direct financing	real assets
dissave	savings
federal statutory debt limits	savings deficit
financial assets	savings surplus
gross private domestic	voluntary savings
investment (GPDI)	

DISCUSSION QUESTIONS

1. Explain what is meant by capital formation.
2. Describe the major components of gross domestic product.
3. Identify the major components of gross savings and describe their relative contributions in recent years.
4. Briefly describe the historical role of savings in the United States.
5. Compare savings surplus and savings deficit units and indicate which economic units are generally one type or the other.
6. Identify the various sources of revenues of the federal government.
7. Comment on the evolution of the "unified federal budget."
8. Why is government lending now included in the federal budget? Why is this lending identified and shown separately in the budget?
9. Describe the nature and significance of off-budget federal outlays.
10. Differentiate between voluntary and contractual savings.
11. Describe and illustrate how financial assets and liabilities are created through the savings-investment process involving financial intermediaries.
12. What types of savings media are available to individuals?
13. How and why do corporations save?
14. Which types of institutions are the major sources of funds through financial intermediation? Indicate the relative importance of these institutions as suppliers of funds.
15. Explain in terms of borrowing sector the relative importance of funds raised in the credit markets.

16. Identify and explain the relative importance of debt instruments used to raise funds in the credit markets.
17. Describe the principal factors that influence the level of savings by individuals.
18. How do economic cycle movements affect the media or types of savings by businesses?
19. Why are the financial savings generated by a business a function of its life cycle?

PROBLEMS

1. The components that comprise a nation's gross domestic product were identified and discussed in the chapter. Assume the following accounts and amounts were reported by a nation last year. Government purchases of goods and services were $5.5 billion; personal consumption expenditures were $40.5 billion; gross private domestic investment amounted to $20 billion; capital consumption allowances were $4 billion; personal savings were estimated at $2 billion; imports of goods and services amounted to $6.5 billion; and the exports of goods and services were $5 billion.
   a. Determine the nation's gross domestic product.
   b. How would your answer change if the dollar amounts of imports and exports are reversed?

2. A nation's gross domestic product is $600 million. Its personal consumption expenditures are $350 million and government purchases of goods and services are $100 million. Net exports of goods and services amount to $50 million.
   a. Determine the nation's gross private domestic investment.
   b. If imports exceed exports by $25 million, how would your answer to Part A change?

3. A nation's gross domestic product is stated in U.S. dollars at $40 million. The dollar value of one unit of the nation's currency (FC) is $0.25.
   a. Determine the value of GDP in FC's.
   b. How would your answer in part a change if the dollar value of one FC increases to $0.30?

4. A country in Southeast Asia states its gross domestic product in terms of yen. Last year its GDP was 50 billion yen when one U.S. dollar could be exchanged into 120 yen.
   a. Determine the country's GDP in terms of U.S. dollars for last year.
   b. Assume the GDP increases to 55 billion yen for this year. However, the dollar value of one yen is now $0.01. Determine the country's GDP in terms of U.S. dollars for this year.
   c. Show how your answer in part b would change if one U.S. dollar could be exchanged for 110 yen.

5. Determine a nation's gross savings based on the following information:

Capital consumption allowances	$150 million
Undistributed corporate profits	40 million
Personal consumption expenditures	450 million
Personal savings	50 million
Corporate inventory valuation adjustment	–5 million
Federal government deficit	–30 million
State and local governments surplus	1 million
Net exports of goods and services	–2 million

6. Obtain a current issue of the *Federal Reserve Bulletin* and determine:
   a. the current personal savings rate in the United States.
   b. the amount of current corporate savings as reflected in the amount of undistributed profits.
7. Obtain a current issue of the *Federal Reserve Bulletin* and determine for the most current year the:
   a. amount of total funds supplied to domestic nonfinancial sectors through financial intermediaries.
   b. relative importance of several financial intermediaries in the financial intermediation process.
   c. relative significance of funds raised in the credit markets by both borrowing sector and by type of instrument.

SELF-TEST QUESTIONS

1. Which of the following is *not* a major component of the U.S. gross national product:
   a. government purchases of goods and services
   b. gross private savings
   c. personal consumption expenditures
   d. net exports of goods and services
2. Which one of the following sources of savings is consistently the largest on an annual basis?
   a. personal savings
   b. undistributed corporate profits
   c. federal, state, and local government surpluses
   d. capital consumption allowances
3. Which one of the following is an example of indirect financing?
   a. corporate bonds
   b. corporate stocks
   c. business bank loan
   d. U.S. government bonds
4. Expenditures of the federal government rank as follows in terms of dollar amount:

    a. national defense, human resources, interest on the national debt
    b. interest on the national debt, human resources, national defense
    c. human resources, national defense, interest on the national debt
    d. human resources, administrative expenses of government operations, national defense

5. With respect to revenues of the federal government:
    a. corporate income taxes are the major source
    b. individual income taxes are about equal to the revenues produced by corporate taxes
    c. individual income taxes produce more than four times the revenues of corporate taxes
    d. over the last decade the revenue-producing magnitude of individual income taxes has been decreasing relative to that of corporate taxes

6. Savings are the accumulation of cash and other financial assets and are generally classified into which of the following two categories?
    a. voluntary and contractual savings
    b. primary and secondary savings
    c. personal and governmental savings
    d. voluntary and corporate savings

7. The personal savings rate is calculated as:
    a. personal savings divided by personal outlays
    b. personal savings divided by disposable personal income
    c. disposable personal income divided by personal outlays
    d. personal income divided by personal outlays

8. In recent years, what has been the average personal savings rate in the United States?
    a. 1–2 percent
    b. 4–5 percent
    c. 7–8 percent
    d. 10–11 percent

9. Which one of the following instruments generates the largest amount of funds annually in the credit markets?
    a. tax-exempt obligations
    b. corporate bonds
    c. mortgages
    d. bank loans

SELF-TEST PROBLEMS

1. Determine a nation's gross domestic product from the following data:
      personal consumption expenditures = $4 billion
      net exports of goods and services = $.1 billion
      gross private domestic investment = $.8 billion

> government purchases of goods and services = \$1 billion
> undistributed corporate profits = \$1 billion

2.   A nation's GDP is \$500 million. Convert its dollar value GDP into foreign currency (FC) units where the dollar value of one FC is \$0.50.

SUGGESTED READINGS

Bernheim, B. Douglas, and John Karl Scholz. "Do Americans Save Too Little?" *Business Review*, Federal Reserve Bank of Philadelphia (September–October 1993): 3–20.

Kidwell, David S., Richard L. Peterson, and David W. Blackwell. *Financial Institutions, Markets, and Money*, 5e. Fort Worth, TX: The Dryden Press, 1993. Chap. 2.

Meyer, Stephen A. "Savings and Demographics: Some International Comparisons." *Business Review*, Federal Reserve Bank of Philadelphia (March–April 1992): 13–23.

Rose, Peter S., and James W. Kolari. *Financial Institutions: Understanding and Managing Financial Services*. Homewood, IL: Irwin, 1995. Chap. 5.

Rose, Peter S. *Money and Capital Markets*, 5e. Homewood, IL: Richard D. Irwin, 1994. Part 1.

Thygerson, Kenneth J. *Financial Markets and Institutions: A Managerial Approach*. New York: Harper Collins, 1993. Chap. 1.

Van Horne, James C. *Financial Market Rates and Flows*, 4e. Englewood Cliffs, NJ: Prentice-Hall, 1994. Chaps 1 and 2.

ANSWERS TO SELF-TEST QUESTIONS   1. b, 2. d, 3. c, 4. c, 5. c, 6. a, 7. b, 8. b, 9. c.

ANSWERS TO SELF-TEST PROBLEMS

1.   The gross domestic product would be determined as:

Personal consumption expenditures:	\$4.0 billion
Gross private domestic investment:	0.8 billion
Government purchases of goods and services:	1.0 billion
Net exports of goods and services:	0.1 billion
Gross domestic product	\$5.9 billion

Note that undistributed corporate profits represent a form of private savings and thus are not a specific item in a nation's gross domestic product.

2.   The value in foreign currency units would be 250 million FCs (i.e., \$500 million times \$0.50).

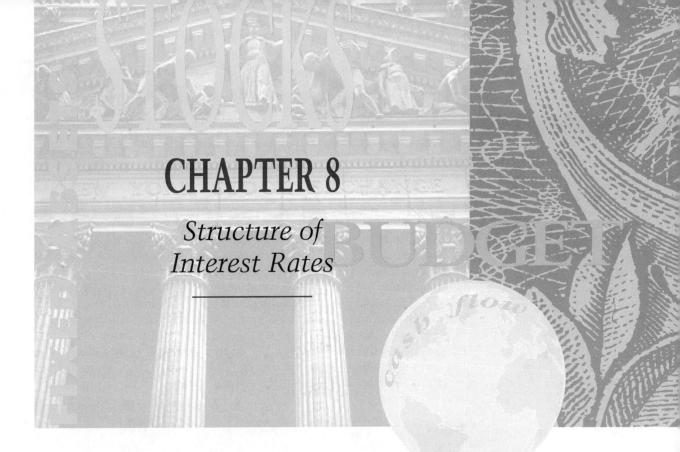

CHAPTER 8

Structure of
Interest Rates

AFTER STUDYING THIS CHAPTER, YOU SHOULD BE ABLE TO:

- Describe how interest rates change in response to shifts in the supply and demand for loanable funds.
- Identify major historical movements in interest rates in the United States.
- Describe what is meant by the loanable funds theory of interest rates.
- Identify the major determinants of market interest rates.
- Describe the types of marketable securities issued by the U.S. Treasury.
- Describe the ownership of Treasury securities and the maturity distribution of the federal debt.
- Explain what is meant by the term or maturity structure of interest rates.
- Identify and briefly describe the three theories used to explain the term structure of interest rates.
- Recount the broad historical price level changes in the U.S. and other economies and discuss their causes.
- Describe the various types of inflation and their causes.
- Discuss the effect of default risk premiums on the level of long-term interest rates.

In a market economy, financial capital is made available to borrowers by lenders. In Chapter 7 we focused on the process of getting funds from savings into investment. Recall that savings may be directly lent or invested, or savings may be accumulated by financial intermediaries who, in turn, supply or lend the savings. Demand for financial capital by borrowers may be met directly from savers, or indirectly from financial intermediaries who have accumulated the savings of others.

In this chapter we focus on the cost or price of borrowed (also called "debt") capital. The basic price that equates the demand for and supply of loanable funds in the financial markets is the **interest rate.** An understanding of interest rates, what causes them to change, and how they relate to changes in the economy is of fundamental importance in the world of finance. We begin with a discussion of the supply and demand for loanable funds and how an equilibrium interest rate is set in the marketplace. Then our attention turns to factors that determine interest rates as of a specific point in time. Next we discuss the term structure of interest rates, showing the relationship between time to maturity and yields. The last section of the chapter focuses on how inflation, the economy, and other factors affect differences between interest rates in capital markets.

interest rate
price that equates the demand for and supply of loanable funds

SUPPLY AND DEMAND FOR LOANABLE FUNDS

Lenders are willing to supply funds to borrowers as long as lenders can earn a satisfactory return (i.e., an amount greater than that which was lent) on their loans. Borrowers will demand funds from lenders as long as borrowers can invest the funds so as to earn a satisfactory return above the cost of their loans. Actually, the supply and demand for loanable funds will take place as long as both lenders and borrowers have the *expectation* of satisfactory returns. Of course, returns received may differ from those expected due to inflation, failure to repay loans, and poor investments. Return experiences will, in turn, impact on future supply and demand relationships for loanable funds.

Figure 8.1 depicts how interest rates are determined in the financial markets. Graph A shows the interest rate (r) that clears the market by bringing the demand (D_1) by borrowers for funds in equilibrium with the supply (S_1) by lenders of funds. For illustrative purposes we have arbitrarily chosen a rate of 7 percent to be the cost or price that makes savings equal to investment (i.e., where the supply and demand curves intersect).

Interest rates may move from an equilibrium level if an unanticipated change or "shock" occurs that will cause the demand for, or supply of, loanable funds to change. For example, an increase in the desire to invest in business assets because of an expanding economy might cause the demand for loanable funds to increase or shift upward (i.e., from D_1 to D_2). The result as depicted in Graph B will be an increase or rise in interest

FIGURE 8.1   Interest Rate Determination in the Financial Markets

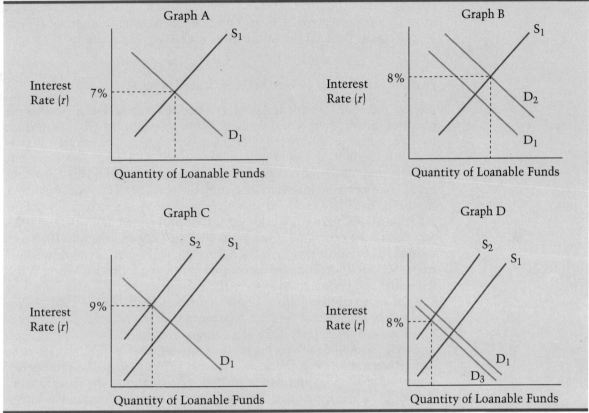

rates to, say, 8 percent, assuming no immediate adjustment in the supply of funds. Of course, as higher interest rates become available to savers, savings may increase which, in turn, could cause the supply of loanable funds to increase. A decline in business activity would be expected to have the opposite impact on interest rates.

Graph C depicts an unanticipated increase in inflation whereby lenders (suppliers) require a higher rate of interest. This is shown by the shift in supply from S_1 to S_2, which for illustrative purposes shows an increase in the interest rate from 7 percent to 9 percent. At this point, we have not taken into consideration the fact that borrowers also may adjust their demand for loanable funds because of likelihood of more costly loans. Graph D depicts the situation that borrowers (users) may cut back on their demand for loanable funds from D_1 to D_3 because of the unanticipated increase in inflation. For example, this would occur if borrowers felt that their higher borrowing costs could not be passed on to their customers and thus the returns on their investments would be adversely affected by the higher inflation rates. Thus, instead of the unanticipated increase in inflation shock causing the interest rate to rise to 9 percent, the new equilibrium rate where supply equals demand (investment) might be only 8 percent.

HISTORICAL CHANGES IN U.S. INTEREST RATE LEVELS

Interest rates for loanable funds have varied throughout our history as the result of shifting supply and demand. Since just after the Civil War, there have been four periods of rising or relatively high long-term interest rates and three periods of low or falling interest rates on long-term loans and investments. The rapid economic expansion after the Civil War caused the first period of rising interest rates from 1864 to 1873. The second period, from 1905 to 1920, was based on both large-scale prewar expansion and the inflation associated with World War I. The third period, from 1927 to 1933, was due to the economic boom from 1927 to 1929 and the unsettled conditions in the securities markets during the early part of the depression, from 1929 to 1933. The rapid economic expansion following World War II led to the last period, from 1946 to the present.

The first period of falling interest rates was from 1873 to 1905. As the public debt was paid off and funds became widely available, the supply of funds grew more rapidly than the demand for them. Prices and interest rates fell, even though the economy was moving forward. The same general factors were at work in the second period, 1920 to 1927. The third period of low interest rates, from 1933 to 1946, resulted from the government's actions in fighting the Great Depression and continued during World War II, when interest rates were pegged, or set.

Beginning in 1966 interest rates entered a period of unusual increases, leading to the highest rates in our history. This increase in rates began as a result of the Vietnam War. It continued in the 1970s because of a policy of on-again, off-again price controls and increased demands for capital arising from ecological concerns and the energy crisis. Furthermore, several periods of poor crops coupled with sharp price increases for crude oil caused worldwide inflation. Interest rates peaked at the beginning of the 1980s, with short-term rates above 20 percent and long-term rates in the high teens. To sum up, double-digit inflation, a somewhat tight monetary policy, and heavy borrowing demand by business contributed to these record levels.

Short-term interest rates generally move up and down with the business cycle. They therefore show many more periods of expansion and contraction. Both long-term and short-term interest rates tend to rise in prosperity periods during which the economy is expanding rapidly. The only major exception was during World War II, when interest rates were pegged. During this period the money supply increased rapidly, laying the base for post-war inflation.

LOANABLE FUNDS THEORY

The ***loanable funds theory*** holds that interest rates are a function of the supply of and demand for loanable funds. This is a flow theory, in that it focuses on the relative supply and demand of loanable funds during a specified period of time. How the supply of and the demand for loanable funds interact determines both the interest rate and the quantity of funds that flows through the financial markets during any period. If the supply of funds increases, holding demand constant, interest rates will tend to fall. Likewise, an increase in the demand for loans will tend to drive up interest rates. This is depicted in Graph B of Figure 8.1.

loanable funds theory states that interest rates are a function of the supply of and demand for loanable funds

Sources of Loanable Funds

There are two basic sources of loanable funds: (1) current savings and (2) the expansion of deposits by depository institutions. The supply of savings comes from all sectors of the economy, and most of it flows through our financial institutions. Individuals may save part of their incomes, either as voluntary savings or through contractual savings programs such as purchasing whole life or endowment insurance policies or repaying installment or mortgage loans. Governmental units and nonprofit institutions sometimes have funds in excess of current expenditures. Corporations may have savings available because they are not paying out all their earnings as dividends. Depreciation allowances that are not being used currently to buy new capital equipment to replace older equipment may also be available for lending.

Pension funds, both governmental and private, provide another source of savings. These funds, which are building up large reserves to meet future commitments, are available for investment.

Some savings are invested as ownership equity in businesses either directly in single proprietorships or partnerships or by buying stock in corporations. This is, however, only a small part of total savings. The bulk of the total savings each year is available as loanable funds. Funds may be loaned directly: for example, when someone lends money to a friend to enable the friend to expand business operations. However, most savings are loaned through financial institutions, one of whose basic functions is the accumulation of savings.

The other basic source of loanable funds is that created by the banking system. Banks and other depository institutions not only channel savings to borrowers, but they also create deposits, which are the most widely used form of money in our economy. This process was discussed in detail in Chapter 5. Net additions to the money supply are a source of loanable funds; during periods when the money supply contracts, the flow of loanable funds drops below the level of current savings.

Loanable funds can be grouped in several ways. They may be divided into short-term funds and long-term funds. We can also group funds by

(1) use, such as business credit, consumer credit, agricultural credit, and government credit, and by (2) the institutions supplying each type.

Factors Affecting the Supply of Loanable Funds

Many factors affect the supply of loanable funds. Both sources of funds have some tendency to increase as interest rates rise. However, this effect is often small compared to other factors that limit or otherwise affect the volume of savings or the ability of the banking system to expand deposits.

Volume of Savings. The major factor that determines the volume of savings, corporate as well as individual, is the level of national income. When income is high, savings are high; when it is low, savings are low. The pattern of income taxes—both the level of the tax and the tax rates in various income brackets—also influences savings volume. Furthermore, the tax treatment of savings itself influences the amount of income saved. For example, the tax deferral (or postponement) of savings placed in individual retirement accounts (IRAs) increases the volume of savings.

The age of the population has an important effect on the volume of savings. As we learned in Chapter 7, little saving is done by young adults, especially those with school-age children. Therefore, an economy with a large share of young couples with children will have less total savings than one with more late middle-aged people.

The volume of savings is also dependent on the factors that affect indirect savings. The more effectively the life insurance industry promotes the sale of whole life and endowment insurance policies, the larger the volume of savings. The greater the demand for private pension funds, which are built up during working years to make payments on retirement, the larger the volume of savings. The effect of interest rates on such savings is often just the opposite of the normal effect of price on supply. As interest rates decrease, more money must be paid for insurance for the same amount of coverage, because a smaller amount of interest will be earned from the reinvestment of premiums and earnings. Inversely, as interest rates rise, less money need be put into reserves to get the same objectives. The same is true of the amount of money that must be put into annuities and pension funds.

When savings result from the use of consumer credit, the effect of interest rates is delayed. For example, assume a car is bought with a three-year auto loan. Savings, in the form of repaying the loan, must go on for three years regardless of changes in interest rates. There may even be an opposite effect in the case of a mortgage because, if interest rates drop substantially, the loan can be refinanced. At the lower interest rate the same dollar payments provide a larger amount for repayment of principal, that is, for saving.

Expansion of Deposits by Depository Institutions. The amount of short-term credit available depends largely on the lending policies of commercial banks and other depository institutions, and on the policies of the Federal Reserve System. Lenders are influenced by such factors as present business conditions and future prospects. But the Federal Reserve has great control over the ability of the banking system to create new deposits, as discussed in Chapter 5.

How much long-term credit of different types is available depends on the policies of the different suppliers of credit. Since depository institutions do not play a major role in this field, the money supply is not expanded directly to meet long-term credit demands. Indirectly, however, their policies and those of the Federal Reserve are very important because, if the banking system expands the money supply to meet short-term needs, a larger proportion of the supply of loanable funds can be used for long-term credit.

Liquidity Attitudes. How lenders see the future has a significant effect on the supply of loanable funds, both long-term and short-term. Lenders may feel that the economic outlook is so uncertain that they are reluctant to lend their money. This liquidity preference can be so strong that large amounts of funds lie idle, as they did during the depression of the 1930s. Lenders may also prefer liquidity because they expect interest rates to go up in the near future, or opportunities for direct investment to be more favorable. Thus, liquidity attitudes may result in keeping some funds idle that would normally be available for lending.

Effect of Interest Rates on the Demand for Loanable Funds

The demand for loanable funds comes from all sectors of the economy. Business borrows to finance current operations and to buy plant and equipment. Farmers borrow to meet short-term and long-term needs. Institutions such as hospitals and schools borrow primarily to finance new buildings and equipment. Individuals finance the purchase of homes with long-term loans and purchase durable goods or cover emergencies with intermediate and short-term loans. Governmental units borrow to finance public buildings, bridge the gap between expenditures and tax receipts, and meet budget deficits.

The factors affecting the demand for loanable funds are different for each type of borrower. We have considered such factors in detail when analyzing the various types of credit. Therefore, this discussion will cover only how interest rates affect the major types of borrowing.

One of the biggest borrowers is the federal government, and Congress generally gives little consideration to interest rates in its spending programs. Minor changes in interest rates do not affect short-term business borrowing. However, historical evidence shows that large increases in short-term interest rates do lead to a decrease in the demand for bank loans and other forms of short-term business borrowing.

Changes in long-term interest rates also affect long-term business borrowing. Most corporations put off long-term borrowing when rates are up, if they expect rates to go down in the near future.

Likewise, minor changes in interest rates have little effect upon consumer borrowing. For short-term installment loans the monthly repayments of principal are so large compared to the interest cost that the total effect on the repayment schedule is small. However, larger interest rate changes have strongly influenced consumer borrowing in the past. This happened in recent years when home mortgage rates reached historically high levels and new housing starts declined sharply.

Roles of the Banking System and the Government

While the effect of interest rates on loanable funds varies, both the supply of and the demand for loanable funds are affected by the actions of the banking system and the government. When depository institutions expand credit by increasing the total volume of short-term loans, the supply of loanable funds increases. When credit contracts, the supply of loanable funds decreases. The actions of the Federal Reserve in setting discount rates, buying securities in the open market, and changing reserve requirements also affect the supply of loanable funds. In fact, all actions that affect the level of banking system reserves and creation of checkable deposits, as described in Chapter 5, affect the supply of loanable funds in the market.

Government borrowing has now become a major influence on demand for funds and will remain so in the foreseeable future. Government surpluses or deficits make funds available in the market or take them out of the market in substantial amounts. Treasury debt management policies also affect the supply-and-demand relationships for short-term, intermediate, and long-term funds.

The financial markets are thus under the influence of the Treasury, and the Federal Reserve strongly influences the supply of funds. The Treasury, through tax policies and other government programs, also has some role on this side of the market. However, the Treasury's major influence is on the demand for funds, as it borrows heavily to finance federal deficits.

International Factors Affecting Interest Rates

Interest rates in the United States are now no longer only influenced by domestic factors. The large trade surplus of Japan, with its accumulation of funds to invest, has had an important influence on the rates the federal government pays in issuing new securities. This international influence adds to the critical need to balance the national budget and avoid the frequency of financing. As production has shifted to many other countries, investment has also shifted. In short, the Treasury and the Federal Reserve must now carefully consider the influence of international movements of funds on domestic interest rates.

DETERMINANTS OF MARKET INTEREST RATES

In addition to supply and demand relationships, interest rates are determined by a number of specific factors. First, the interest rate (r) that we observe in the marketplace is called a **nominal interest rate** because it includes a premium for expected inflation. Second, a nominal interest rate that is not free from the risk of default by the borrower also will have a default risk premium. Thus, in its simplest form, the nominal interest rate can be expressed as:

$$r = RR + IP + DRP \qquad (8\text{-}1)$$

where RR is the real rate of interest, IP is an inflation premium, and DRP is the default risk premium. The **real rate of interest** is the interest rate on a risk-free financial debt instrument when no inflation is expected. The **inflation premium** is the average inflation rate expected over the life of the instrument. The **default risk premium** indicates compensation for the possibility that the borrower will not pay interest and/or repay principal according to the financial instrument's contractual arrangements.

In order to cover both short-term and long-term debt instruments (as well as other securities such as common stocks), two additional premiums are frequently added to the equation for explaining nominal interest rates. This expanded version can be expressed as:

$$r = RR + IP + DRP + MRP + LP \qquad (8\text{-}2)$$

where MRP is the maturity risk premium and LP is the liquidity premium on a financial instrument. The **maturity risk premium** is the added return expected by lenders or investors because of interest rate risk on instruments with longer maturities. **Interest rate risk** reflects the possibility of changes or fluctuations in market values of fixed-rate debt instruments as market interest rates change over time. There is an inverse relationship between debt instrument values or prices and nominal interest rates in the marketplace. For example, if interest rates rise from, say, 7 percent to 8 percent because of a previously unanticipated inflation rate increase, the values of outstanding debt instruments will decline. Furthermore, the longer the remaining life until maturity, the greater the reduction in a fixed-rate debt instrument's value to a given interest rate increase. We will explore these concepts with numerical calculations in Chapter 10.

nominal interest rate
interest rate that is observed in the marketplace

real rate of interest
interest rate on a risk-free debt instrument when no inflation is expected

inflation premium
average inflation rate expected over the life of the security

default risk premium
compensation for the possibility of the borrower's failure to pay interest and/or principal when due

maturity risk premium
compensation expected by investors due to interest rate risk on debt instruments with longer maturities

interest rate risk
possible price fluctuations in fixed-rate debt instruments associated with changes in market interest rates

liquidity premium
compensation for securities that cannot easily be converted to cash without major price discounts

The **liquidity premium** is compensation for those financial debt instruments that cannot be easily converted to cash at prices close to their estimated fair market values. For example, a corporation's low quality bond may be traded very infrequently. As a consequence a bondholder who wishes to sell tomorrow may find it difficult to sell except at a very large discount in price.

We will now discuss these factors that influence the nominal interest rate throughout the remainder of this chapter. We begin with the concept of a risk-free interest rate and discuss why U.S. Treasury securities are used as our best estimate of the risk-free rate. Other sections focus on the term or maturity structure of interest rates, inflation expectations and associated premiums, and default risk and liquidity premium considerations.

RISK-FREE SECURITIES: U.S. TREASURY DEBT OBLIGATIONS

risk-free rate of interest
interest rate on a debt instrument with no default, maturity, or liquidity risks (Treasury securities are the closest example)

By combining the real rate of interest and the inflation premium, we have the **risk-free rate of interest,** which in the United States is represented by U.S. Treasury debt instruments or securities. It is generally believed that even with the large national debt, the U.S. government is not going to renege on its obligations to pay interest and repay principal at maturity on its debt securities. Thus, we view U.S. Treasury securities as being default-risk free. Technically, a truly risk-free financial instrument also has no liquidity risk or maturity risk (as reflected by interest rate risk). Treasury marketable securities are considered to have virtually no liquidity risk and only longer-term Treasury securities have maturity or interest rate risk associated with changes in market-determined interest rates that occur over time.

Economists have estimated that the real rate of interest in the United States and other countries has averaged in the 2 to 4 percent range in recent years. One way of looking at the risk-free rate is to say that this is the minimum rate of interest necessary to get individuals and businesses to save. There must be an incentive to invest or save idle cash holdings. One such incentive is the expectation of some real rate of return above expected inflation levels. For illustrative purposes, let's assume 3 percent is the current expectation for a real rate of return. Let's also assume that the nominal interest rate is currently 7 percent for a one-year Treasury security.

Given these assumptions, we can turn to equation 8.1 to determine the average inflation expectations of holders or investors as follows:

$$7\% = RR + IP + DRP$$
$$7\% = 3\% + IP + 0\%$$
$$IP = 7\% - 3\% = 4\%$$

Thus, investors expect a 4 percent inflation rate over the next year and if they also want a real rate of return of 3 percent, the nominal interest rate must be 7 percent.

Let's now also use the expanded equation to explain nominal interest rates as expressed in equation 8.2. However, since this is a Treasury security there is no liquidity premium and no maturity risk premium if we were planning to hold the security until its maturity at the end of one year. Thus, equation 8.2 would be used as follows to find the average expected inflation rate:

$$7\% = RR + IP + DRP + MRP + LP$$
$$7\% = 3\% + IP + 0\% + 0\% + 0\%$$
$$IP = 7\% - 3\% = 4\%$$

Of course, the answer has not changed and is still 4 percent since there were no additional risk premiums. We will introduce the impact of a maturity risk premium after we discuss the types of marketable securities issued by the Treasury.

MARKETABLE OBLIGATIONS

Marketable government securities, as the term implies, are those that may be purchased and sold through customary market channels. Markets for these obligations are maintained by large commercial banks and securities dealers. In addition, nearly all other securities firms and commercial banks, large or small, will help their customers purchase and sell federal obligations by routing orders to institutions that do maintain markets in them. The investments of institutional investors and large personal investors in federal obligations are centered almost exclusively in the marketable issues. These marketable issues are bills, notes, and bonds, the difference between them being their maturity at time of issue. Although the maturity of an obligation is reduced as it remains in effect, the obligation continues to be called by its original descriptive title. Thus, a 30-year Treasury bond continues to be described in the quotation sheets as a bond throughout its life.

marketable government securities
securities that may be bought and sold through the usual market channels

Treasury Bills

Treasury bills bear the shortest maturities of Federal obligations. They are typically issued for 91 days, with some issues carrying maturities of 182 days. Treasury bills with a maturity of one year are also issued at auction every four weeks. Issues of Treasury bills are offered each week by the Treasury to refund the part of the total volume of bills that matures. In effect, the 91-day Treasury bills mature and are rolled over in 13 weeks. Each week, approximately 1/13 of the total volume of such bills is refunded.

When the flow of cash revenues into the Treasury is too small to meet expenditure requirements, additional bills are issued. During those periods of the year when revenues exceed expenditures, Treasury bills are allowed to mature without being refunded. Treasury bills, therefore, provide the Treasury with a convenient financial mechanism to adjust for the lack of a regular revenue flow into the Treasury. The volume of bills may also be increased or decreased in response to general surpluses or deficits in the federal budget from year to year.

Treasury bills
federal obligations that bear the shortest original maturities

Treasury bills are issued on a discount basis and mature at par. Each week the Treasury bills to be sold are awarded to the highest bidders. Sealed bids are submitted by dealers and other investors. Upon being opened, these bids are arrayed from highest to lowest. Those bidders asking the least discount (offering the highest price) are placed high in the array. The bids are then accepted in the order of their position in the array until all bills are awarded. Bidders seeking a higher discount (offering a lower price) may fail to receive any bills that particular week. Investors interested in purchasing small volumes of Treasury bills ($10,000 to $500,000) may submit their orders on an average competitive price basis. The Treasury deducts these small orders from the total volume of bills to be sold. The remaining bills are allotted on the competitive basis described above. Then these small orders are executed at a discount equal to the average of the successful competitive bids for large orders.

The investor is not limited to purchasing Treasury bills on their original issue. Because Treasury bills are issued weekly a wide range of maturities in the over-the-counter market is available. A look at the Treasury bonds, notes, & bills section of *The Wall Street Journal* shows available maturities from one week to one year. The bid and ask quotations are shown in terms of annual yield equivalents. The prices of the various issues obtained from a dealer would reflect a discount based on these yields. Because of their short maturities and their absence of risk, Treasury bills provide the lowest yield available on taxable domestic obligations.

Although some business corporations and individuals invest in Treasury bills, by far the most important holders of these obligations are the commercial banks of the nation.

Treasury Notes

Treasury notes
federal obligations
issued for maturities
of one to ten years

Treasury notes are issued at specified interest rates usually for maturities of more than one year but not more than ten years. These intermediate-term federal obligations are also held largely by the commercial banks of the nation.

Treasury Bonds

Treasury bonds
obligations of any
maturity but usually
over five years

Treasury bonds may be issued with any maturity but generally have an original maturity in excess of five years. These bonds bear interest at stated rates. Many issues of these bonds are callable, or paid off, by the government several years before their maturity. For example, the 25-year, 8 percent bonds issued in 1976 are described as having a maturity of 1996–2001. This issue may be called for redemption at par as early as 1996 but in no event later than 2001. The longest maturity of Treasury bonds is 30 years. As for the other marketable securities of the government, active markets for their purchase and sale are maintained by dealers.

All marketable obligations of the federal government, with the exception of Treasury bills, are offered to the public through the Federal Reserve

Banks at prices and yields set in advance. Investors place their orders for new issues, and these orders are filled from the available supply of the new issue. If orders are larger than available supply, investors may be allotted only a part of the amount they requested.

Treasury bonds, because of at least initial long-term maturities, are subject to maturity or interest rate risk. Treasury notes with shorter maturities are affected to a lesser extent. For illustrative purposes, let's assume that the nominal interest rate on ten-year Treasury bonds is currently 9 percent. Let's further assume that investors expect the inflation rate will average 4 percent over the next ten years. By applying equation 8.2 we can find the maturity risk premium to be:

$$9\% = RR + IP + DRP + MRP + LP$$
$$9\% = 3\% + 4\% + 0\% + MRP + 0\%$$
$$MRP = 9\% - 3\% - 4\% = 2\%$$

Our interpretation is that the holders or investors require a 2 percent maturity risk premium to compensate them for the possibility of volatility in the price of their Treasury bonds over the next ten years. If market-determined interest rates rise and investors are forced to sell before maturity, the bonds will be sold at a loss. Furthermore, even if these investors hold their bonds to maturity and redeem them with the government at the original purchase price, the investors would have lost the opportunity of the higher interest rates being paid in the marketplace. This is what is meant by interest rate risk. Of course, if market-determined interest rates decline after the bonds are purchased, bond prices will rise above the original purchase price.

DEALER SYSTEM

The **dealer system** for marketable U.S. government securities occupies a central position in the nation's financial markets. The smooth operation of the money markets depends on a closely linked network of dealers and brokers. The market for U.S. government securities centers on the dealers who report activity daily to the Federal Reserve Bank of New York. In recent years there were 44 such dealers, 18 of which were commercial banks and the remaining 26, nonbank dealers. New dealers are added only when they can demonstrate a satisfactory responsibility and volume of activity. The dealers buy and sell securities for their own account, arrange transactions with both their customers and other dealers, and also purchase debt directly from the Treasury for resale to investors. Dealers do not typically charge commissions on their trades. Rather they hope to sell securities at prices above the levels at which they were bought. The dealers' capacity to handle large Treasury financing has expanded enough in recent years to handle the substantial growth in the government securities market. In addition to the dealers' markets, new issues of federal government securities may be purchased directly at the federal reserve banks.

dealer system *depends on a small group of dealers in government securities with an effective marketing network throughout the United States*

TAX STATUS OF FEDERAL OBLIGATIONS

Until March 1941, interest on all obligations of the federal government was exempt from all taxes. The interest on all federal obligations is now subject to ordinary income taxes and tax rates. The Public Debt Act of 1941 terminated the issuance of tax-free federal obligations. Since that time, all issues previously sold to the public have matured or have been called for redemption. Income from the obligations of the federal government is exempt from all state and local taxes. Federal obligations, however, are subject to both federal and state inheritance, estate, or gift taxes.

OWNERSHIP OF PUBLIC DEBT SECURITIES

nonmarketable government securities
issues that cannot be transferred between persons or institutions but must be redeemed with the U.S. government

The U.S. national debt must be financed and refinanced through the issuance of government securities, both marketable and nonmarketable. ***Nonmarketable government securities*** are those that cannot be transferred to other persons or institutions and can be redeemed only by being turned in to the U.S. government. The sheer size of the national debt of approximately $5 trillion makes the financing process a difficult one. In fact, the United States must rely on the willingness of foreign and international investors to hold a substantial portion of the outstanding interest-bearing public debt securities issued to finance the national debt.

Ownership of public debt securities is shown by groups in Table 8.1. Private investors owned 71 percent of the total outstanding federal debt securities in 1989 and about 67 percent in 1994. Of the total owned by private investors, foreign and international investors held about 15 percent of federal debt securities in 1989 and about 14 percent in 1994. While the dollar amount of foreign ownership has been increasing annually, the rate of increase has been less than the amount of increase in public debt securities.

During the last half of the 1980s, the annual increase in foreign ownership was due primarily to the flow of Japanese capital to this country. Japanese investment in real estate and corporate securities has been well publicized. However, as the dollar declined relative to the Japanese yen and other major foreign currencies, investment in U.S. assets became less attractive after interest and other returns were converted back into the foreign currencies.

Some economists contend that a movement towards a balanced federal budget will not only reduce borrowing requirements but will also instill confidence in the financial soundness of the U.S. economy. Continuing large budgetary deficits will not only make the nation increasingly dependent on foreign investment but may also cause those investors to lose confidence and become less willing to support our deficits. Policy makers must, therefore, walk a fine line between the burden and difficulty of achieving fiscal discipline or the possibility of losing foreign investment capital if budgetary discipline is not achieved.

TABLE 8.1   Ownership of Federal Debt Securities

	PERCENT OF TOTAL DEBT	
	1989	**1994**
U.S. Government Agencies, Trust Funds, and Federal Reserve Banks	**29.0**	**33.3**
Total for Private Investors:	**71.0**	**66.7**
Foreign and international investors	15.1	13.9
State and local governments	17.2	10.8
Corporations	3.3	4.9
Individuals	7.6	7.0
Commercial banks	5.8	6.7
Insurance companies	4.4	5.3
Money market funds	.5	1.3
Other miscellaneous groups of investors*	17.1	16.8
Total	**100.0**	**100.0**

*Includes savings and loan associations, credit unions, savings banks, corporate pension trust funds, dealers and brokers, government-sponsored agencies, and non-profit institutions.

Source: *Treasury Bulletin*, various issues.

MATURITY DISTRIBUTION OF MARKETABLE DEBT SECURITIES

Earlier in this section we described the various types of marketable obligations of the federal government. However, the terms *bills*, *notes*, and *bonds* describe the general maturity ranges only at the time of issue. In order to determine the *maturity distribution* of all obligations, therefore, it is necessary to observe the remaining life of each issue regardless of its class. The maturity distribution and average length of marketable interest-bearing federal obligations are shown in Table 8.2. Notice that the average maturity dropped from six years in 1989 to five years and eight months in 1994.

The heavy concentration of debt in the very short maturity range (approximately one-third of the total amount outstanding have maturities of less than one year) poses a special problem for the Treasury. This is a problem for the securities markets as well because the government is constantly selling additional securities to replace those that mature. The heavy concentration of short-term maturities will not be changed by simply issuing a larger number of long-term obligations. Like all institutions that seek funds in the financial markets, the Treasury has to offer securities that will be readily accepted by the investing public. Furthermore, the magnitude of federal financing is such that radical changes in maturity distributions can upset the financial markets and the economy in general. The management of the federal debt has become an especially challenging financial problem, and much time and energy are spent in meeting the

TABLE 8.2   Average Length and Maturity Distribution of Marketable
Interest-Bearing Federal Obligations

MATURITY CLASS	PERCENT OF TOTAL MARKETABLE DEBT	
	1989	1994
Within 1 year	33.0	32.3
1–5 years	35.0	41.5
5–10 years	15.0	10.7
10–20 years	4.9	3.2
20 years and over	12.1	12.3
	100.0	100.0
Average maturity of all marketable issues:	6 years; 0 months	5 years; 8 months

Source: *Treasury Bulletin,* various issues.

challenge. Recall our discussion on the influence of the Treasury's debt management policies on the financial system and on the economy in Chapter 5. Here we are only concerned with describing the maturity distribution of the debt.

If the Treasury refunds maturing issues with new short-term obligations, the average maturity of the total debt is reduced. As time passes, longer-term issues are brought into shorter-dated categories. Net cash borrowing resulting from budgetary deficits must take the form of maturities that are at least as long as the average of the marketable debt if the average maturity is not to be reduced. The average length of the marketable debt reached a low level of two years and five months in late 1975. Since that time, progress has been made in raising the length of maturities by selling long-term obligations.

One of the new debt-management techniques used to extend the average maturity of the marketable debt without disturbing the financial markets is *advance refunding.* This occurs when the Treasury offers the owners of a given issue the opportunity to exchange their holdings well in advance of the holdings' regular maturity for new securities of longer maturity.

In summary, the Treasury is the largest and most active single borrower in the financial markets. The Treasury is continuously in the process of borrowing and refinancing. Its financial actions are tremendous in contrast with all other forms of financing, including that of the largest business corporations. Yet, the financial system of the nation is well adapted to the smooth accommodation of its requirements. Indeed, the very existence of a public debt of this magnitude is predicated upon the existence of a highly refined monetary and credit system.

TERM OR MATURITY STRUCTURE OF INTEREST RATES

The **term structure** of interest rates indicates the relationship between interest rates or yields and the maturity of comparable quality debt instruments. This relationship is typically depicted through the graphic presentation of a **yield curve.** A properly constructed yield curve must first reflect securities of similar default risk. Second, the yield curve must represent a particular point in time, and the interest rates should reflect yields for the remaining time to maturity. That is, the yields should not only include stated interest rates but should also consider that instruments and securities could be selling above or below their redemption values. (We will show the process for calculating yields to maturity in the next chapter on the time value of money.) Third, the yield curve must show yields on a number of securities with differing lengths of time to maturity.

U.S. government securities provide the best basis for constructing yield curves because Treasury securities are considered to be risk free, as we previously noted in terms of default risk. Table 8.3 contains interest rates for Treasury securities at selected dates and for various maturities. In early 1980, the then annual inflation rate was at double-digit levels. As a result, interest rates were very high even though the economy was in a mild recession. Longer-term interest rates were even higher in March 1982 even though the economy was in a deep recession. Apparently, investors still were expecting the high levels of inflation to continue. However, by the latter part of the 1980s interest rates had dropped dramatically because of reduced inflation. As the economy was recovering from a mild recession in 1990, interest rates on one-year Treasury bills were at 6 percent in March 1991 compared with 14 percent in March 1980. Interest rates declined further

term structure
relationship between interest rates or yields and the time to maturity for debt instruments of comparable quality

yield curve
graphic presentation of the term structure of interest rates at a given point in time

TABLE 8.3   Term Structure of Interest Rates for Treasury Securities at Selected Dates

TERM TO MATURITY	MARCH 1980	MARCH 1982	MARCH 1991	SEPT. 1995
6 months	15.0%	12.8%	5.9%	5.3%
1 year	14.0	12.5	6.0	5.3
5 years	13.5	14.0	7.8	6.0
10 years	12.8	13.9	8.1	6.2
20 years	12.5	13.8	NA	6.7
30 years	12.3	13.5	8.3	6.6

Note: NA indicates that interest rates were not available on 20-year Treasury Bonds in March 1991.

Source: *Federal Reserve Bulletin*, various issues.

as the economy began expanding from a mild recession. As of September 1995, after the Fed first pushed up short-term interest rates in an effort to head off possible renewed inflation and then lowered rates in an effort to avoid a recession, interest rates were relatively flat across different maturities.

Figure 8.2 shows yield curves for March 1980 and September 1995 reflecting the plotting of some of the data in Table 8.3. Because of high inflation rates and an economic downturn, the March 1980 yield curve was downward sloping but still at very high interest rate levels. In contrast, the relatively flat September 1995 yield curve occurred when inflation rates and expectations were much lower and the economy was growing moderately in real terms.

RELATIONSHIP BETWEEN YIELD CURVES AND THE ECONOMY

Historical evidence suggests that interest rates generally rise during periods of economic expansion and fall during economic contraction. Therefore the term structure of interest rates as depicted by yield curves shifts upwards or downwards with changes in economic activity. Interest rate levels generally are the lowest at the bottom of a recession and the highest at the top of an expansion period. Furthermore, when the economy is moving out of a recession, the yield curve slopes upward. The curve begins to flatten out during the latter stages of an expansion and typically starts sloping downward when economic activity peaks. As the economy turns downward, interest rates begin falling and the yield curve again goes through a flattening-out phase, to become upward sloping when economic activity again reaches a low point.

FIGURE 8.2   Yield Curves for Treasury Securities at Selected Dates

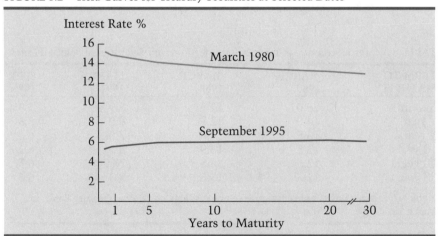

TERM STRUCTURE THEORIES

There are three theories commonly used to explain the term structure of interest rates. The **expectations theory** contends that the shape of a yield curve reflects investor expectations about future inflation rates. If the yield curve is flat, expectations are that the current short-term inflation rate will remain essentially unchanged over time. When the yield curve is downward sloping, investors expect inflation rates to be lower in the future. Recall from Figure 8.2 that the shape of the yield curve in March 1980 was downward sloping. Thus, investors believed that the double-digit inflation rates prevailing in 1980 were expected to decline in the future. In contrast, the relatively flat yield curve in September 1995 suggested that investors expected the relatively low inflation rates in late 1995 to remain at low levels in the future.

expectations theory states that shape of the yield curve indicates investor expectations about future inflation rates

Let's now illustrate different yield curve shapes in terms of equations 8-1 and 8-2. First, recall that the liquidity and the default risk premiums are zero for Treasury securities. Thus, equation 8-2 for Treasury securities becomes equation 8-1 plus a maturity risk premium (MRP). However, the expectations theory in its purest form also assumes the MRP to be zero. Given this assumption, we have reduced equation 8-2 back to equation 8-1 such that the yield curve reflects only the real rate (RR) of interest plus the expectation for an inflation premium (IP) over the life of the security.

Let's assume that the current rates of interest or yields are: one-year Treasury bills = 7 percent, two-year Treasury notes = 8 percent, and ten-year Treasury bonds = 9 percent. And, using a 3 percent real rate of return, we have the following relationships:

MATURITY	k		RR		IP
1–Year	7%	=	3%	+	4%
2–Year	8	=	3	+	5
10–Year	9	=	3	+	6

Thus, the inflation rate is expected to be 4 percent over the next year. However, the inflation rate is expected to average 5 percent per year over the next two years. Or, if inflation is 4 percent the first year then the rate for the second year must be more than 5 percent. Working with simple averages, 5 percent average inflation times two years means that the total inflation will be 10 percent. And, 10 percent less 4 percent means that inflation in the second year must be 6 percent.

For years three through ten, inflation must exceed 6 percent annually in order to average 6 percent over the ten-year period. We can find the simple average by starting with the fact that inflation will be 60 percent (6% times 10 years) over the full ten-year period. And, 60 percent less the 10 percent for the first two years means that cumulative inflation for the last eight years will be 50 percent. Then dividing 50 percent by eight means that inflation will have to average 6.25 percent over years three through ten. In summary, we have:

TIME PERIOD	AVERAGE INFLATION		NUMBER OF YEARS		CUMULATIVE INFLATION
Year 1	4%	×	1	=	4%
Year 2	6	×	1	=	6
Years 3–10	6.25	×	8	=	50
Total Inflation					60%
Total Years					10
Average Inflation (60%/10 years)					6%

These are only simple arithmetic averages. Technically, we have ignored the impact of the compounding of inflation rates over time. The concept of compounding will be covered in the next chapter, which focuses on the time value of money.

liquidity preference theory
states that investors are willing to accept lower interest rates on short-term debt securities which provide greater liquidity and less interest rate risk

The **liquidity preference theory** holds that investors or debt instrument holders prefer to invest short-term so that they have greater liquidity and less maturity or interest rate risk. Lenders also prefer to lend short-term because of the risk of higher inflation rates and greater uncertainty about default risk in the future. Borrowers prefer to borrow long-term so that they have more time to repay loans. The net result is a willingness to accept lower interest rates on short-term loans as a trade-off for greater liquidity and lower interest rate risk.

market segmentation theory
states that interest rates may differ because securities of different maturities are not perfect substitutes for each other

The **market segmentation theory** holds that securities of different maturities are not perfect substitutes for each other. For example, commercial banks concentrate their activities on short-term securities because of their demand and other deposit liabilities. On the other hand, the nature of insurance company and pension fund liabilities allows these firms to concentrate holdings in long-term securities. Thus, supply-and-demand factors in each market segment affect the shape of the yield curve. Thus, in some time periods interest rates on intermediate-term Treasury securities may be higher (or lower) than both short-term and long-term treasuries.

INFLATION PREMIUMS AND PRICE MOVEMENTS

Actions or factors that change the value of the money unit or the supply of money and credit affects the whole economy. The change affects first the supply of loanable funds and interest rates and, later, both the demand for and the supply of goods in general. We have demonstrated that when investors expect higher inflation rates they will require higher nominal interest rates so that a real rate of return will remain after the inflation. Recall from Chapter 5 that we defined inflation as an increase in the price of goods or services that is not offset by an increase in quality.

We can get a clearer understanding of investor expectations about inflation premiums by first reviewing past price movements, then exploring possible types of inflation.

HISTORICAL PRICE MOVEMENTS

Changes in the money supply or in the amount of metal in the money unit have influenced prices since the earliest records of civilization. The money standard in ancient Babylon was in terms of silver and barley. The earliest available price records show that one shekel of silver was equal to 240 measures of grain. At the time of Hammurabi, about 1750 B.C., a shekel in silver was worth between 150 and 180 measures of grain, while in the following century it declined to 90 measures. After Persia conquered Babylonia in 539 B.C., the value of the silver shekel was recorded as between 15 and 40 measures of grain.

The greatest inflationary period in ancient history was probably caused by Alexander the Great, when he captured the large gold hoards of Persia and brought them to Greece. Inflation was high for some years; but 20 years after the death of Alexander, a period of deflation began that lasted over 50 years.

The first recorded cases of deliberate currency debasement (lowering the value) occurred in the Greek city-states. The government would debase currency by calling in all coins and issuing new ones containing less of the precious metals. This must have been a convenient form of inflation, for there are many such cases in the records of Greek city-states.

Ancient Rome

Similar inflation occurred in Roman history. Caesar Augustus brought so much precious metal from Egypt that prices rose and interest rates fell. During the Punic Wars devaluation led to inflation, as the heavy bronze coin was reduced in stages from one pound to one ounce. From the time of Nero, debasements were frequent. The weight of gold coins was gradually reduced, and silver coins had baser metals added to them so that they were finally only 2 percent silver. Few attempts were made to arrest or reverse this process of debasement of coins as the populace adjusted to the process. When Aurelian tried to improve the coinage by adding to its precious metal content, he was resisted so strongly that armed rebellion broke out.

The Middle Ages through Modern Times

During the Middle Ages princes and kings debased the coinage to get more revenue. The rulers of France used this ploy more than others, and records show that profit from debasement was sometimes greater than the total of all other revenues.

An important example of inflation followed the discovery of America. Gold and silver poured into Spain from Mexico and Peru. Since the riches were used to buy goods from other countries, they were distributed over the continent and to England. Prices rose in Spain and in most of Europe, but not in proportion to the increase in gold and silver stocks. This was because trade increased following the discovery of America and because many people hoarded the precious metals.

Paper money was not used generally until the end of the seventeenth century. The first outstanding example of inflation due to the issuing of an excessive amount of paper money was in France. In 1719 the government gave Scottish banker John Law a charter for a bank that could issue paper money. The note circulation of his bank amounted to almost 2,700 million livres (the monetary unit in use at that time in France) against which he had coin of only 21 million livres and bullion of 27 million livres. Prices went up rapidly, but they fell just as fast when Law's bank failed. Afterwards, the money supply was again restricted.

The next outstanding period of inflation was during the time of the American Revolution. For example, in Europe the government of the French Revolution issued paper currency in huge quantities. This currency, called *assignats*, declined to one-half of one percent of its face value.

Spectacular inflation also took place in Germany in 1923, when prices soared to astronomical heights. And, during World War II, runaway inflation took place in China and Hungary, as well as in other countries.

INFLATION IN THE UNITED STATES

Monetary factors have often affected price levels in the United States, especially during major wars.

Revolutionary War

The war that brought this nation into being was financed mainly by inflation. The Second Continental Congress had no real authority to levy taxes and thus found it difficult to raise money. As a result the congress decided to issue notes for $2 million. They issued more and more notes until the total rose to over $240 million, and the individual states issued $200 million more. Since the notes were crudely engraved, counterfeiting was common, adding to the total of circulating currency. Continental currency depreciated in value so rapidly that the expression "not worth a continental" became a part of the American language.

War of 1812

During the War of 1812, the government tried to avoid repeating the inflationary measures of the Revolutionary War. But since the war was not popular in New England, it was impossible to finance it by taxation and borrowing. Paper currency was issued in a somewhat disguised form: bonds of small denomination bearing no interest and having no maturity date. The wholesale price index, based on 100 as the 1910–14 average prices, rose from 131 in 1812 to 182 in 1814. Prices declined to about the pre-war level by 1816 and continued downward as depression hit the economy.

Civil War

The Mexican War (1846–48) did not involve the total economy to any extent and led to no inflationary price movements. The Civil War (1861–65), however, was financed partly by issuing paper money. In the early stages, Congress could not raise enough money by taxes and borrowing to finance all expenditures, and therefore it resorted to inflation by issuing United States Notes with no backing, called *greenbacks*. In all, $450 million was authorized. Even though this was but a fraction of the cost of the war, prices went up substantially. Wholesale prices on a base of 100 increased from 93 in 1860 to 185 in 1865. Attempts to retire the greenbacks at the end of the war led to deflation and depression in 1866. As a result, the law withdrawing greenbacks was repealed.

World War I

Although the government did not print money to finance World War I, it did practice other inflationary policies. About one-third of the cost of the war was raised by taxes and two-thirds by borrowing. The banking system provided much of this credit, which added to the money supply. People were even persuaded to use Liberty bonds as collateral for bank loans to buy other bonds. The wholesale price index rose from 99 in 1914 to 226 in 1920. Then, as credit expansion was finally restricted in 1921, it dropped to 141 in 1922.

World War II and the Postwar Period

The government used fewer inflationary policies to finance World War II. Nevertheless, the banking system still took up large sums of bonds. By the end of the war, the debt of the federal government had increased by $207 billion. Bank holdings of government bonds had increased by almost $60 billion. Prices went up by only about one-third during the war because they were held in check after the first year by price and wage controls. They then rose rapidly when the controls were lifted after the war. In 1948 wholesale prices had risen to 236 from a level of 110 in 1939.

Wholesale prices increased during the Korean War and again during the 1955–57 expansion in economic activity, as the economy recovered from the 1954 recession. Consumer goods prices continued to move upward during practically the entire post-war period, increasing gradually even in those years in which wholesale prices hardly changed.

Recent Decades

Wholesale consumer goods prices again increased substantially when the Vietnam War escalated after mid-1965. Prices continued upward after

American participation in the Vietnam War was reduced in the early-1970s. After American participation in the war ended in 1974, prices rose at the most rapid levels since World War I. Inflation was worldwide in the middle-1970s; its effects were much worse in many other industrial countries than in the United States.

As the 1970s ended, economists realized the full impact of a philosophy based on a high inflation rate. Many economists thought high inflation could keep unemployment down permanently, even though history shows that it does not. The government's efforts to control interest rates by increasing the money supply reinforced people's doubts that such policies would reduce inflation and high interest rates. By October 1979, the Federal Reserve System abandoned this failed approach to interest rate control and adopted a policy of monetary growth control. The result was twofold. First, there was a far greater volatility in interest rates as the Federal Reserve concentrated on monetary factors. Second, during the first three quarters of 1980 some monetary restraint was exercised. This monetary restraint had a depressing effect on production and employment. The Federal Reserve System quickly backed off from this position of restraint, and by the end of 1980 a far greater level of monetary stimulus had driven interest rates to new peaks.

By this time the prime rate had risen to 21.5 percent and three-month Treasury bills had doubled in yield from their midyear lows. These high interest rates had a profound negative effect on such interest-sensitive industries as housing and automobiles. The Fed reversed the rapid growth of money supply throughout 1981 and until late in 1982. Unemployment climbed as the effects of monetary restraint were imposed on the economy, but the back of inflation was broken. By the end of 1982, economic recovery was in place—along with an easing of monetary restraint.

Inflation stayed moderate through the remainder of the 1980s. Figure 8.3 shows inflation in terms of the consumer price index (CPI). After peaking in 1990 above a 6 percent annual rate, the CPI declined to below a 3 percent rate. In early 1994, the Fed moved towards a tighter monetary policy in an effort to keep inflation from rising. More recently, as the economy slowed the Fed began easing monetary policy. Inflation, as indicated by the CPI, continues at approximately a 3 percent annual rate.

TYPES OF INFLATION

Inflation may be associated with a change in costs, a change in the money supply, speculation, and so-called administrative pressures.

Price Changes Initiated by a Change in Costs
The price level can sometimes increase without the original impulse coming from either the money supply or its velocity. If costs rise faster than productivity increases, as when wages go up, businesses with some control

FIGURE 8.3   Consumer Price Index

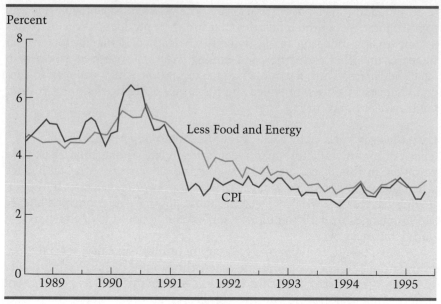

Source: *National Economic Trends*, Federal Reserve Bank of St. Louis.

over prices will try to raise them to cover the higher costs. Such increases are likely to be effective when the demand for goods is strong compared to the supply. The need for more funds to meet production and distribution at higher prices usually causes the money supply and velocity to increase. This type of inflation is called **cost-push inflation.** So this rise in prices comes from the cost side, not from increases in the money supply. Prices may not go up, however, if the monetary authorities restrict credit expansion. In that case only the most efficient businesses will have enough demand to operate profitably. As a result, some resources will be unemployed.

cost-push inflation *occurs when prices are raised to cover rising production costs, such as wages*

Cost-push inflation is different from inflation caused by an increase in the money supply, which is called **demand-pull inflation.** Demand-pull inflation may be defined as an excessive demand for goods and services during periods of economic expansion as a result of large increases in the money supply. In actual practice, both aspects of inflation are likely to occur at the same time, since cost-push can occur only in industries in which labor negotiations are carried out on an industry-wide basis and in which management has the ability to increase prices.

demand-pull inflation *occurs during economic expansions when demand for goods and services is greater than supply*

Demand-pull inflation may also be caused by changes in demand in particular industries. The demand for petroleum, for example, may be greater than demand in general, so that prices rise in this industry before they rise generally. The first raise is likely to be in the basic materials themselves, leading to increased profits in the industries that produce them. Labor will press for wage increases to get its share of the total value of output, and thus labor costs also rise. Price rises in basic industries lead to price increases in the industries that use their products. Wage increases in one major industry are also likely to lead to demands for similar increases in other industries and among the non-organized workers in such industries. Thus, a process is set into motion which can lead to general changes in prices, provided the monetary authorities do not restrict credit so as to prevent it.

Price Changes Initiated by a Change in the Money Supply

The way in which factors that affect prices relate to one another is quite complex. In this discussion we consider the adjustments that take place when the primary change is in the money supply or its velocity. In the following chapter we will consider the more complex relationships arising out of changes in both the money supply and goods side of the equation during business cycles.

An increase in the supply or velocity of money can cause several types of inflation. Inflation may result when the supply of purchasing power increases. In modern times such inflation is often initiated by government deficits financed by creating deposits, and at other times by private demands for funds. If this happens when people and resources are not fully employed, the volume of trade goes up; prices are only slightly affected at first. As unused resources are brought into use, however, prices will go up. When resources such as metals become scarce, their prices rise. As any resource begins to be used up, the expectation of future price rises will itself force prices up, because attempts to buy before such price rises will increase demand above current needs. Since some costs, such as interest costs and wages set by contract, will lag, profits will rise, increasing the demand for capital goods.

Once resources are fully employed, the full effect of the increased money supply will be felt on prices. Prices may rise out of proportion for a time as expectations of higher prices lead to faster spending and so raise the velocity of money. The expansion will continue until trade and prices are in balance at the new levels of the money supply. Velocity will probably drop somewhat from those levels during the period of rising prices, since the desire to buy goods before the price goes up has disappeared.

Even if the supply of money is increased when people and resources are fully employed, prices may not go up proportionately. Higher prices increase profits for a time and so lead to a demand for more capital and labor. Thus, previously unemployed spouses, retired workers, and similar groups begin to enter the labor force. Businesses may use capital more fully by having two or three shifts use the same machines.

Demand-pull inflation traditionally exists during periods of economic expansion when the demand for goods and services exceeds the available supply of such goods and services. A second version of inflation also associated with increases in the money supply occurs because of monetization of the U.S. government debt. Recall from Chapter 5 that the Treasury finances government deficits by selling U.S. government securities to the public, commercial banks, or the Federal Reserve. When the Federal Reserve purchases U.S. government securities, reserves must be created to pay for the purchases. This, in turn, may lead to higher inflation because of an increase in money supply and bank reserves.

Speculation and Administrative Inflation

When an increased money supply causes inflation, it can lead to additional price pressure called **speculative inflation.** Since prices have risen for some time, people believe that they will keep on rising. Inflation becomes self-generating for a time because, instead of higher prices resulting in lower demand, people may buy more to get goods before they go still higher, as happened in the late-1970s. This effect may be confined to certain areas, as it was to land prices in the 1920s Florida land boom or to security prices in the 1928–29 stock market boom. Such a price rise leads to an increase in velocity as speculators try to turn over their funds as rapidly as possible and many others try to buy ahead of needs before there are further price rises.

speculative inflation caused by the expectation that prices will continue to rise, resulting in increased buying to avoid even higher future prices

For three decades, until the early-1980s, price pressures and inflation were continuous despite occasional policies of strict credit restraint. During this long period, in fact, prices continued upward in recession periods, though at a slower rate than in prosperity periods. The need to restrain price rises hampered the Fed's ability to promote growth and fight recessions. Prices and other economic developments during this period led many to feel that the economy had developed a long-run *inflationary bias*. However, the continued low inflation rates of the latter part of the 1980s and the first part of the 1990s may now have curtailed these beliefs somewhat.

Those economists who believe that long-run inflationary bias will continue do so on the basis of the following factors: (1) Prices and wages tend to rise during periods of boom in a competitive economy. This tendency is reinforced by wage contracts that provide escalator clauses to keep wages in line with prices and by wage increases that are sometimes greater than increases in productivity. (2) During recessions, prices tend to remain stable rather than decrease. This is because major unions have long-run contracts calling for annual wage increases no matter what economic conditions are at the time. The tendency of large corporations to rely on nonprice competition (advertising, and style and color changes) and to reduce output rather than cut prices also keeps prices stable. Furthermore, if prices do decline drastically in a field, the government is likely to step in with programs to help take excess supplies off the market. There is little doubt that prices would decline in a severe and prolonged depression. Government takes action to counter resulting unemployment, however, before the economy reaches such a level. Thus we no longer experience the downward price pressure of a depression.

administrative inflation
the tendency of prices,
aided by union-
corporation contracts,
to rise during economic
expansion and to
resist declines during
recessions

The inflation resulting from these factors is called **administrative inflation.** This is to distinguish it from the type of inflation that happens when demand exceeds the available supply of goods, either because demand is increasing faster than supply in the early stages of a recovery period, or because demand from monetary expansion by the banking system or the government exceeds available supply.

Traditional monetary policy is not wholly effective against administrative inflation. If money supplies are restricted enough, prices can be kept in line; but this will lead to long-term unemployment and slow growth. It is also difficult for new firms and small growing firms to get credit since lending policies are likely to be conservative. The government must develop new tools to deal with administrative inflation effectively.

DEFAULT RISK PREMIUMS

Default risk is the risk that a borrower will not pay interest and/or repay the principal on a loan or other debt instrument according to the agreed contractual terms. The consequence may be a lower than expected interest rate or yield, or even a complete loss of the amount originally lent. The premium for default risk will increase as the probability of default increases.

In order to examine default risk premiums for debt securities, it is necessary to hold some of the other risk premiums constant. By referring back to equation 8-2 we can develop a procedure for measuring that portion of a nominal interest rate (r) attributable to default risk. Recall that the nominal interest rate is a function of a real interest rate, an inflation premium, a default risk premium, a maturity risk premium, and a liquidity risk premium.

First, we will constrain our analysis to the long-term capital markets. This is done by considering long-term Treasury bonds and long-term corporate bonds. Thus, by considering only long-term securities, the maturity risk will be the same for all the bonds and can be set at zero for analysis purposes. We have also said that the liquidity premium is zero for Treasury securities because they can be readily sold without requiring a substantial price discount. Corporate securities are less liquid than Treasury securities. However, we can minimize any possible liquidity premiums by considering the bonds of large corporations. This also allows us to set the liquidity premium at zero for analysis purposes.

Now let's assume the real rate is 3 percent, the nominal interest rate is 8 percent for long-term Treasury bonds, and high-quality corporate bonds have a 9 percent nominal interest rate. Using equation 8-2 we have:

$$r = RR + IP + DRP + MRP + LP$$
$$9\% = 3\% + 5\% + DRP + 0\% + 0\%$$
$$DRP = 9\% - 3\% - 5\% - 0\% - 0\% = 1\%$$

Since the 8 percent Treasury bond represents the risk-free rate of interest, subtracting the 3 percent real rate results in a long-term average annual inflation premium of 5 percent. Another way of looking at the default risk premium (assuming zero maturity risk and liquidity premiums) is that it is the difference between the interest rates on the risky (corporate) and risk-free (Treasury) securities. In our example, we have:

$$DRP = 9\% - 8\% = 1\%$$

Thus investors require a 1 percent premium to hold or invest in the corporate bond instead of the Treasury bond.

Another corporate bond with a higher default risk may carry an interest rate of, say, 11 percent. If the other assumptions used above are retained, the *DRP* would be:

$$11\% = 3\% + 5\% + DRP + 0\% + 0\%$$
$$DRP = 11\% - 3\% - 5\% - 0\% - 0\% = 3\%$$

Alternatively, we could find *DRP* as follows:

$$DRP = 11\% - 8\% = 3\%$$

Thus, in order to get investors to invest in these riskier corporate bonds, a default risk premium of 3 percentage points must be offered above the interest rate or yield on Treasury bonds.

Now, let's examine actual default risk premiums. Table 8.4 shows long-term interest rates for Treasury bonds and two corporate bonds with different degrees of default risk. While we will be discussing the characteristics of corporate bonds in Chapter 10, one way that potential default risk is measured is through bond ratings. The highest rating is Aaa and indicates the lowest likelihood of default. Investors in these bonds require

TABLE 8.4   Default Risk Premiums on Corporate Bonds at Selected Dates

	MARCH 1980	MARCH 1982	MARCH 1991	SEPT. 1995
Aaa-Rated Corporate Bonds	13.0%	14.6%	8.9%	7.3%
Less: 20-year Treasury Bonds	12.5	13.8	8.3	6.7
Equals: Default Risk Premium on Aaa Bonds	.5	.8	.6	.6
Baa-Rated Corporate Bonds	14.5%	16.8%	10.1%	7.9%
Less: 20-year Treasury Bonds	12.5	13.8	8.3	6.7
Equals: Default Risk Premium on Baa Bonds	2.0	3.0	1.8	1.2

Note: The yield for the 30-year Treasury bond in March 1991 was used to estimate risk premiums because no yields were available on 20-year bonds.

Source: *Federal Reserve Bulletin,* various issues.

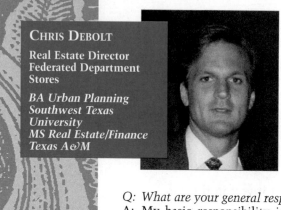

CHRIS DEBOLT

Real Estate Director
Federated Department
Stores

BA Urban Planning
Southwest Texas
University
MS Real Estate/Finance
Texas A&M

"Negotiation is a very big part of my job."

career profiles

Q: *What are your general responsibilities?*

A: My basic responsibility is to negotiate the acquisition and development of new department stores. This includes a very wide range of activities from locating possible sites, to negotiating a favorable financial deal, to working with developers on the construction or remodeling of the property.

Q: *How do you select sites for stores?*

A: There are a number of requirements. First, the demographic profile of the area has to match our target market. If that match exists, we project the sales volume we can expect for that location. Then we look at our costs for either the purchase or lease of the property plus the remodeling or construction costs. If our projected sales are great enough to justify the expense, we'll go ahead with the project. Obviously we are only interested in opening new stores that will add to the profitability of the company.

Q: *How long does this process take?*

A: It may take a month to a year to find a desirable site and complete the financial end of the deal. Then the development (construction) phase may add another 1 to 2 years.

Q: *How do you finance these purchases?*

A: We do not secure financing on a project by project basis, meaning we don't go to a bank and say we need a loan to open a new store in Orlando. Federated has a number of sources of capital. It sells stock. It can issue bonds. And it has access to existing lines of credit with banks. So money for a new store comes from one or more of those general sources, rather than from a loan for that particular project.

Q: *How do interest rate levels affect your work?*

A: Interest rates are very important. When interest rates are higher, Federated's cost of capital goes up. For instance, new bonds issued by Federated would have to pay a higher yield. That means we need to be even more selective in choosing the best possible site and negotiating the best possible deal in times of higher interest rates. Otherwise we won't be able to make the higher rate of return we expect on our investment relative to this higher interest rate risk.

Another important impact involves our developers, the firms which construct or remodel our stores. If their costs go up due to higher interest rates, those costs will inevitably be passed on to us. This is a less obvious effect of higher interest rates, but equally relevant to our bottom line.

Q: *What makes you good at your job?*

A: I have learned to always keep the big picture in mind, but I can still focus my attention on the smallest details and not let go until they are resolved. I also am very proactive. There are inevitably problems of one kind or another that jeopardize the success of our deals. By anticipating those problems, they can be solved much more quickly. I'm also a good negotiator. I know how to be both honest and persuasive at the same time, and how to ensure that the desired result is reached by both parties through compromise. Negotiation is a very big part of my job.

a small default risk premium over Treasury bonds. Baa-rated bonds have higher default risks but still are considered to be of investment quality.

In March 1980, the default risk premium on corporate Aaa bonds over 20-year Treasuries was 0.5 of a percentage point (i.e., 13.0% − 12.5%). The default risk premium of the highest quality corporate bonds over Treasury bonds generally falls in the one-half to three-fourths of a percentage point range. In fact, the default risk premium was about 0.8 of a percentage point in March 1982 when the economy was in a deep recession. The default risk premium on Aaa-rated corporate bonds then was reduced to 0.6 of a percentage point in March 1991 and remained at 0.6 of a percentage point in September 1995.

The default risk premiums on Baa corporate bonds are generally better indicators than those on Aaa bonds of investor pessimism or optimism about economic expectations. More firms fail or suffer financial distress during periods of recession compared with periods of economic expansion. Thus, investors tend to require higher premiums to compensate for default risk when the economy is in a recession or is expected to enter one. Notice that the risk premium on Baa-rated bonds was 2 percentage points in March 1980 (14.5% − 12.5%) and then increased to 3 percentage points in March 1982 when a deep recession existed. The comparable default risk premium was down to 1.8 percentage points in March 1991. By September 1995 the risk premium on Baa corporate bonds was down to 1.2 percentage points. This recent low default risk premium reflects substantial consumer confidence that real growth will continue in the future.

SUMMARY

This chapter began by illustrating how interest rates change given shifts in demand and/or supply curves. The loanable funds theory for explaining interest rates was presented. This was followed by a discussion of the following determinants of market interest rates: real rate of interest, inflation premium, default risk premium, maturity risk premium, and liquidity premium.

Three types of U.S. Treasury securities—bills, notes, and bonds—were identified and described. Then, the term structure of interest rates was defined and depicted through a yield curve graph. Next, the three theories used to explain the term structure—expectations, liquidity preference, and market segmentation—were presented. Major historical price movements were identified and the types of inflation—cost-push, demand-pull, speculative, and administrative—were described. The final topic focused on how default risk premiums are estimated and what causes them to change over time.

KEY TERMS

administrative inflation
cost-push inflation
dealer system
default risk premium
demand-pull inflation
expectations theory
inflation premium
interest rate
interest rate risk
liquidity preference theory
liquidity premium
loanable funds theory
market segmentation theory

marketable government securities
maturity risk premium
nominal interest rate
nonmarketable government
   obligations
real rate of interest
risk-free rate of interest
speculative inflation
term structure
Treasury bills
Treasury bonds
Treasury notes
yield curve

DISCUSSION QUESTIONS

1. Describe how interest rates may adjust to an unanticipated increase in inflation.
2. Identify major periods of rising interest rates in U.S. history and describe some of the underlying reasons for these interest rate movements.
3. Describe how the loanable funds theory is used to explain the level of interest rates.
4. What are the main sources of loanable funds? Indicate and briefly discuss the factors that affect the supply of loanable funds.
5. Indicate the sources of demand for loanable funds and discuss the factors that affect the demand for loanable funds.
6. Identify the factors, in addition to supply and demand relationships, that are the determinants of market interest rates.
7. Identify the types of marketable obligations issued by the Treasury.
8. Explain the mechanics of issuing Treasury bills, indicating how the price of a new issue is determined.
9. Describe the dealer system for marketable U.S. government obligations.
10. Explain the tax status of income from federal obligations.
11. Describe any significant changes in the ownership pattern of federal debt securities.
12. Describe the process of advance refunding of the federal debt.
13. What is meant by the *term structure of interest rates* and how is it expressed?

14. Identify and describe the three basic theories used to explain the *term structure of interest rates.*
15. Describe the process by which inflation took place before modern times.
16. Discuss the early periods of inflation based on the issue of paper money.
17. Discuss the basis for inflation during World Wars I and II.
18. Discuss the causes of the major periods of inflation in American history.
19. Explain the process by which price changes may be initiated by a general change in costs.
20. Explain the process by which a change in the money supply leads to a change in the price level.
21. Discuss the speculative type of inflation.
22. Describe what is meant by a default risk premium and indicate how it can change over time.

PROBLEMS

1. Find the nominal interest rate for a debt security given the following information: real rate = 2%, liquidity premium = 2%, default risk premium = 4%, maturity risk premium = 3%, and the inflation premium = 3%.
2. Find the default risk premium for a debt security given the following information: inflation premium = 3%, maturity risk premium = 2.5%, real rate = 3%, liquidity premium = 0%, and the nominal interest rate is 10%.
3. Assume that the interest rate on a one-year Treasury bill is 6 percent and the rate on a two-year Treasury note is 7 percent.
   a. If the expected real rate of interest is 3 percent, determine the inflation premium on the Treasury bill.
   b. If the maturity risk premium is expected to be zero, determine the inflation premium on the Treasury note.
   c. What is the expected inflation premium for the second year?
4. A Treasury note with a maturity of four years carries a nominal rate of interest of 10 percent. In contrast, an 8-year Treasury bond has a yield of 8 percent.
   a. If inflation is expected to average 7 percent over the first four years, what is the expected real rate of interest?
   b. If the inflation rate is expected to be 5 percent for the first year, calculate the average annual rate of inflation for years two through four.
   c. If the maturity risk premium is expected to be zero between the two Treasury securities, what will be the average annual inflation rate expected over years five through eight?

5. The interest rate on a ten-year Treasury bond is 9.25 percent. A comparable maturity Aaa-rated corporate bond is yielding 10 percent. Another comparable maturity but lower quality corporate bond has a yield of 14 percent which includes a liquidity premium of 1.5 percent.
   a. Determine the default risk premium on the Aaa-rated bond.
   b. Determine the default risk premium on the lower quality corporate bond.

6. A corporate bond has a nominal interest rate of 12 percent. This bond is not very liquid and consequently requires a 2 percent liquidity premium. The bond is of low quality and thus has a default risk premium of 2.5 percent. The bond has a remaining life of 25 years resulting in a maturity risk premium of 1.5 percent.
   a. Estimate the nominal interest rate on a Treasury bond.
   b. What would be the inflation premium on the Treasury bond if investors required a real rate of interest of 2.5 percent?

7. Obtain a current issue of the *Federal Reserve Bulletin* and find interest rates on U.S. Treasury securities and on corporate bonds with different bond ratings.
   a. Prepare a yield curve or term structure of interest rates.
   b. Identify existing default risk premiums between long-term Treasury bonds and corporate bonds.

8. As an economist for a major bank you are asked to explain the present substantial increase in the price level, notwithstanding the fact that neither the money supply nor the velocity of money has increased. How can this occur?

9. As an advisor to the United States Treasury you have been asked to comment on a proposal for easing the burden of interest on the national debt. This proposal calls for the elimination of federal taxes on interest received from Treasury debt obligations. Comment on the proposal.

10. As one of several advisors to the U.S. Secretary of the Treasury, you have been asked to submit a memo in connection with the average maturity of the obligations of the federal government. The basic premise is that the average maturity is far too short. As a result, issues of debt are coming due with great frequency and needing constant reissue. On the other hand, the economy is presently showing signs of weakness. It is considered unwise to issue long-term obligations and absorb investment funds that might otherwise be invested in employment-producing construction and other private sector support. Based on these conditions, what do you recommend as a course of action to the U.S. Secretary of the Treasury?

11. Assume a condition in which the economy is strong, with relatively high employment. For one reason or another the money supply is increasing at a high rate and there is little evidence of money creation slowing down. Assuming the money supply continues to increase, describe the evolving effect on price levels.

SELF-TEST QUESTIONS

1. The loanable funds theory used to explain the level of interest rates holds that interest rates are a function of the:
   a. supply of loanable funds and the demand for money
   b. supply of loanable funds and the demand for loanable funds
   c. supply of money and the demand for loanable funds
   d. supply of money and the demand for money
2. The risk-free interest rate is composed of:
   a. an inflation premium and a default risk premium
   b. a default risk premium and a maturity risk premium
   c. a real rate of interest and a liquidity premium
   d. a real rate of interest and an inflation premium
3. Which one of the following is not a marketable government security?
   a. Treasury stock
   b. Treasury bill
   c. Treasury note
   d. Treasury bond
4. Interest on obligations of the federal government:
   a. is not taxable by state or local governments
   b. is not taxable by the federal government
   c. is taxable by both the federal and state governments
   d. except for Treasury notes is taxable by the federal government
5. The federal debt is owned primarily by:
   a. foreign and international investors
   b. commercial banks
   c. insurance companies
   d. the sum of all private investors
6. The average maturity of the marketable debt of the United States:
   a. is of little importance, unlike that of private corporations
   b. has been decreasing for the last two decades
   c. remains unchanged unless new obligations are issued
   d. decreases day by day unless new obligations are issued to offset such decreases
7. The yield curve or term structure of interest rates is typically downward sloping when:
   a. short-term Treasury interest rates are lower than long-term Treasury interest rates
   b. short-term and long-term Treasury interest rates are the same
   c. long-term Treasury interest rates are lower than short-term Treasury interest rates
   d. long-term Treasury interest rates are higher than short-term Treasury interest rates
8. Price inflation has been characteristic of:
   a. modern industrial society

    b.   our post gold-standard period

    c.   the history of prices since earliest recorded history

    d.   only industrialized societies

9. Inflation caused by an increase in the money supply is called:

    a.   demand-pull inflation

    b.   cost-push inflation

    c.   administrative inflation

    d.   a combination of administrative and speculative inflation

SELF-TEST PROBLEMS

1. Find the nominal interest rate on a bond with a default risk premium of 3 percent, an inflation premium of 4 percent, a real rate of 2.5 percent, and no maturity and liquidity risk premiums.

2. Assume that the nominal interest rates are 6.5 percent on a one-year Treasury bill and 8.5 percent on a 20-year Treasury bond. Investors expect a 3 percent real rate of interest on their investments.

    a.   Determine the expected inflation premium on the Treasury bill.

    b.   If the inflation premium in part a is expected to be the same on the Treasury bond, calculate the maturity risk premium on the bond.

SUGGESTED READINGS

Campbell, Tim S., and William A. Krakaw. *Financial Institutions and Capital Markets.* New York: Harper Collins College Publishers, 1993. Chap. 10.

Kidwell, David S., Richard L. Peterson, and David W. Blackwell. *Financial Institutions, Markets, and Money,* 5e. Fort Worth, TX: The Dryden Press, 1993. Chap. 4.

Kohn, Meir. *Financial Institutions and Markets.* New York: McGraw-Hill, 1994. Chaps. 5 and 7.

Rose, Peter S. *Money and Capital Markets,* 5e. Homewood, IL: Richard D. Irwin, 1994. Part 3.

Russell, Steven. "Understanding the Term Structure of Interest Rates: The Expectations Theory." *Review,* Federal Reserve Bank of St. Louis (July/August 1992): 36–50.

Shen, Pu. "Benefits and Limitations of Inflation Indexed Treasury Bonds." *Economic Review,* Federal Reserve Bank of Kansas City (Third Quarter 1995): 41–56.

Thygerson, Kenneth J. *Financial Markets and Institutions: A Managerial Approach.* New York: Harper Collins, 1993. Chap. 2.

Van Horne, James C. *Financial Market Rates and Flows,* 4e. Englewood Cliffs, NJ: Prentice-Hall, 1994. Chaps. 5 and 7.

ANSWERS TO SELF-TEST QUESTIONS 1. b, 2. d, 3. a, 4. a, 5. d, 6. d, 7. c, 8. c, 9. a

ANSWERS TO SELF-TEST PROBLEMS

1. $r = RR + IP + DRP$
    $r = 2.5\% + 4\% + 3\% = 9.5\%$
2. a. $6.5\% = 3\% + IP$
         $IP = 6.5\% - 3\% = 3.5\%$
    b. $8.5\% = 3\% + 3.5\% + MRP$
         $MRP = 8.5\% - 3\% - 3.5\% = 2\%$

CHAPTER 9

Time Value
of Money

AFTER STUDYING THIS CHAPTER, YOU SHOULD BE ABLE TO:

- Explain what is meant by the time value of money.
- Describe the concept of simple interest.
- Describe the process of compounding.
- Describe discounting to determine present values.
- Find interest rates and time requirements for problems involving compounding or discounting.
- Describe the meaning of an annuity and differentiate between an ordinary annuity and an annuity due.
- Find interest rates and time requirements for problems involving annuities.
- Calculate annual annuity payments.
- Make compounding and discounting calculations using time intervals that are less than one year.
- Describe the difference between the annual percentage rate and the effective annual rate.

In order to understand the pricing and valuation of bonds, stocks, and real asset investments, we must first understand the mathematics of finance known as the *time value of money*. Money has a time value as long as interest can be earned by saving or investing money. For example, money can increase or grow over time if we can invest it and earn a return on our investment. However, if we have to wait to receive our money in the future, it has a lower value to us today since we lose the opportunity of being able to invest it now and earn a return.

time value of money
the mathematics of finance whereby interest is earned over time by saving or investing money

Most individuals have experienced compounding by watching a savings account grow or increase over time when interest is reinvested. Discounting is the opposite of compounding, as we will see following the discussion of basic compounding concepts.

Financial calculators or computer software programs will perform the calculations and procedures discussed in this chapter. However, we first describe the calculation procedures in detail to enhance the understanding of the logic involved in the time value of money concepts. By learning to work the problems the long way with basic calculators and time value of money tables, following the steps given for financial calculators and computer software should make more sense. We encourage students to use all three computational approaches.

SIMPLE INTEREST

Let's begin by discussing how a savings account works. Assume you have $1,000 to save or invest. The $1,000 is the value now or *present value* of your savings which becomes an investment once you deposit or loan the money. The amount of your investment also is referred as the investment's *principal*. A bank offers to accept your savings for one year and agrees to pay to you an 8 percent interest rate for use of your $1,000. This amounts to $80 in interest (0.08 × $1,000). The total payment by the bank at the end of one year is $1,080 ($1,000 principal plus $80 in interest). This $1,080 is referred to as the *future value* or value after one year. In word terms, we have:

Future value = present value + (present value × interest rate)

or,

Future value = present value × (1 + interest rate)

In our example, we have:

$1,080 = $1,000 + ($1,000 × 0.08)

or,

$1,080 = $1,000 × 1.08

simple interest
interest earned only
on the principal of the
initial investment

Let's now assume that your $1,000 investment remains on deposit for two years but the bank pays only **simple interest** which is interest earned only on the investment's principal. In word terms, we have:

Future value =
    present value × [1 + (interest rate) × (number of periods)]

For our example, this becomes:

$1,160 = $1,000 × [1 + (0.08 × 2)]
$1,160 = $1,000 × 1.16

Another bank will pay you a 10 percent interest rate on your money. Thus, you would receive $100 in interest ($1,000 × 0.10) or a return at the end of one year of $1,100 ($1,000 × 1.10) from this second bank. While the $20 difference in return between the two banks ($1,100 versus $1,080) is not great, it has some importance to most of us. For a two-year deposit where simple interest is paid annually, the difference increases to $40. The second bank would return $1,200 ($1,000 × 1.20) to you versus $1,160 from the first bank. If the funds were invested for ten years, we would accumulate $1,000 × [1 + (0.08 × 10)] or $1,800 at the first bank. At the second bank we would have $1,000 × [1 + (0.10 x 10)] or $2,000, a $200 difference. This interest rate differential between the two banks will become even more important when we introduce the concept of compounding.

COMPOUNDING TO DETERMINE FUTURE VALUES

compounding
an arithmetic process
whereby an initial value
increases at a compound
interest rate over time to
reach a future value

compound interest
interest earned on
interest in addition to
interest earned on the
principal or investment

Compounding is an arithmetic process whereby an initial value increases or grows at a compound interest rate over time to reach a value in the future. **Compound interest** involves earning interest on interest in addition to interest on the principal or initial investment. To understand compounding, let's assume that you leave the investment with a bank for more than one year. For example, the first bank referred to above accepts your $1,000 deposit now, adds $80 at the end of one year, retains the $1,080 for the second year and pays you interest at an 8 percent rate. The bank returns your initial deposit plus accumulated interest at the end of the second year. How much will you receive as a future value? In word terms, we have:

Future value = present value × [(1 + interest rate) × (1 + interest rate)]

For our two-year investment example,

$1,166 = $1,000 × (1.08)(1.08)
$1,166 = $1,000 × 1.166

A *time line* also can be used to illustrate this two-year example as follows:

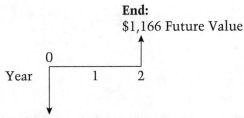

End:
$1,166 Future Value

0

Year   1   2

Begin:
Present Value $1,000 × 1.08 × 1.08

Thus, for a one-year investment, the return would be $1,080 ($1,000 × 1.08) which is the same as the return on a simple interest investment as was previously shown. However, a two-year investment at an 8 percent compound interest rate will return $1,166 compared to $1,160 using an 8 percent simple interest rate.

The compounding concept also can be expressed in equation form as

$$FV_n = PV(1 + r)^n \qquad\qquad (9\text{-}1)$$

where *FV* is the future value, *PV* is the present value, *r* is the interest rate, and *n* is the number of periods in years. For our $1,000 deposit, 8 percent, two-year example, we have

$$
\begin{aligned}
FV_2 &= \$1,000(1 + 0.08)^2 \\
     &= \$1,000(1.116) \\
     &= \$1,166
\end{aligned}
$$

If we extend the time period to ten years, the $1,000 deposit would grow to:

$$
\begin{aligned}
FV_{10} &= \$1,000(1 + 0.08)^{10} \\
        &= \$1,000(2.159) \\
        &= \$2,159
\end{aligned}
$$

Most financial calculators are programmed to readily find future values. Typically, financial calculators will have a present value key (PV), a future value key (FV), a number of time periods key (N), an interest rate key (usually designated %*i*), and a compute key (usually designated as CPT). If you have a financial calculator, you can verify the future value result for the ten-year example.

First, clear any values stored in the calculator's memory. Next, enter 1000 and press the PV key (some financial calculators require that you enter the present value amount as a minus value because it is an investment or outflow). Then, enter 8 and press the %*i* key (most financial calculators are programmed so that you enter whole numbers rather than decimals for the interest rate). Next, enter 10 for the number of time periods (usually years) and press the N key. Finally, press the CPT key followed by the FV key to calculate the future value of 2158.93 which rounds to $2,159. Actually, financial calculators are programmed to calculate answers to 12 significant digits.

Financial Calculator Solution:

Inputs　　　10　　　8　　1000

　　　　　　[N]　　[%i]　　[PV]

Press　　[CPT]　[FV]

Solution　2158.93

Computer software programs also are available for finding future values. In addition, tables have been prepared to simplify the calculation effort if financial calculators or computer programs are not available. Equation 9-1 can be rewritten as:

$$FV_n = PV(FVIF_{r,n}) \tag{9-2}$$

where the $(1 + r)^n$ part of equation 9-1 is replaced by a future value interest factor ($FVIF$) corresponding to a specific interest rate and a specified time period.

Table 9.1 shows $FVIF$ values for a partial range of interest rates and time periods. [Table 1 in the Appendix provides a more comprehensive $FVIF$ table.] Let's use Table 9.1 to find the future value of $1,000 invested at an 8 compound interest rate for a ten-year period. Notice that at the intersection of the 8 percent column and ten years, we find a $FVIF$ of 2.159. Putting this information into equation 9-2 gives:

$$FV_{10} = \$1,000(2.159)$$
$$= \$2,159$$

Further examination of Table 9.1 shows how a $1 investment grows or increases with various combinations of interest rates and time periods. For example, if another bank offers to pay you a 10 percent interest rate compounded annually, notice that the $FVIF$ at the intersection of 10 percent and ten years would be 2.594, making your $1,000 investment worth

TABLE 9.1　Future Value Interest Factor of $1 ($FVIF$)

YEAR	5%	6%	7%	8%	9%	10%
1	1.050	1.060	1.070	1.080	1.090	1.100
2	1.102	1.124	1.145	1.166	1.188	1.210
3	1.158	1.191	1.225	1.260	1.295	1.331
4	1.216	1.262	1.311	1.360	1.412	1.464
5	1.276	1.338	1.403	1.469	1.539	1.611
6	1.340	1.419	1.501	1.587	1.677	1.772
7	1.407	1.504	1.606	1.714	1.828	1.949
8	1.477	1.594	1.718	1.851	1.993	2.144
9	1.551	1.689	1.838	1.999	2.172	2.358
10	1.629	1.791	1.967	2.159	2.367	2.594

$2,594 ($1,000 × 2.594). Now the difference between the 8 percent and 10 percent rates is much more significant at $435 ($2,594 − $2,159) than the $200 difference that occurred with simple compounding over ten years. Thus, we see the advantage of being able to compound at even slightly higher interest rates over a period of years.

The compounding or growth process also can be depicted in graphic form. Figure 9.1 shows graphic relationships among future values, interest rates, and time periods. For example, notice how $1 will grow differently over a ten-year period at 5 percent versus 10 percent interest rates. Of course, if there is no interest being earned, then the initial $1 investment will remain at $1 no matter how long the investment is held. At a 10 percent interest rate, the initial $1 grows to $2.59 (rounded) after ten years. This compares with $1.63 (rounded) after ten years if the interest rate is only 5 percent. Notice that the future value increases at an increasing rate as the interest rate is increased and as the time period is lengthened.

INFLATION OR PURCHASING POWER IMPLICATIONS

The compounding process as just described does not say anything about the purchasing power of the initial $1 investment at some point in the future. As we previously saw, $1 growing at a 10 percent interest rate would be worth $2.59 (rounded) at the end of ten years. With zero inflation, you could purchase $2.59 of the same quality of goods after ten years

FIGURE 9.1   Future Value, Interest Rate, and Time Period Relationships

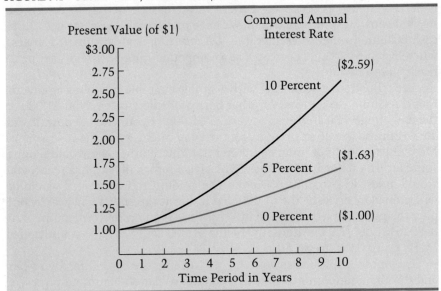

relative to what you could purchase now. However, if the stated or *nominal* interest rate is 10 percent and the inflation rate is 5 percent, then in terms of increased purchasing power, the "net" or differential compounding rate would be 5 percent (10 percent − 5 percent) and $1 would have an inflation-adjusted value of $1.63 after ten years. This translates into an increased purchasing power of $0.63 ($1.63 − $1.00).

Also note that if the compound inflation rate is equal to the compound interest rate, the purchasing power would not change. For example, if in Figure 9.1 both the inflation and interest rates were 5 percent, the purchasing power of $1 would remain the same over time. Thus, to make this concept operational, subtract the expected inflation rate from the stated interest rate and compound the remaining (differential) interest rate to determine the change in purchasing power over a stated time period. For example, if the interest rate is 10 percent and the inflation rate is 3 percent, the savings or investment should be compounded at a differential 7 percent rate. Turning to Table 9.1, $1 invested at a 7 percent interest rate for ten years would grow to $1.967 ($1.97 rounded) in terms of purchasing power. Of course, the actual dollar value would be $2.594 ($2.59 rounded).

DISCOUNTING TO DETERMINE PRESENT VALUES

Most financial management decisions involve present values rather than future values. For example, a financial manager who is considering purchasing an asset wants to know what the asset is worth now rather than at the end of some future time period. The reason that an asset has value is because it will produce a stream of future cash benefits. To determine its value now in time period zero, we have to discount or reduce the future cash benefits to their present value. **Discounting** is an arithmetic process whereby a future value decreases at a compound interest rate over time to reach a present value.

discounting
an arithmetic process
whereby a future value
decreases at a compound
interest rate over time to
reach a present value

Let's illustrate discounting with a simple example involving an investment. Assume that a bank or other borrower offers to pay you $1,000 at the end of one year in return for use of $1,000 of your money now. If you are willing to accept a zero rate of return you might make the investment. Most of us would not jump at an offer like this! Rather, we would require some return on our investment. To receive a return of, say, 8 percent, you would invest less than $1,000 now. The amount to be invested would be determined by dividing the $1,000 that is due at the end of one year by one plus the interest rate of 8 percent. This results in an investment amount of $926 ($1,000/1.08). Alternatively, the $1,000 could have been multiplied by 1/1.08 or 0.926 to get $926.

Let's now assume that you will not receive the $1,000 for two years and the compound interest rate is 8 percent. What dollar amount (present value) would you be willing to invest? In word terms, we have:

Present Value = future value × [1/(1 + interest rate)
                        × 1/(1 + interest rate)]

For our two-year investment example,

$857 = $1,000 × (1/1.08 × 1/1.08)
$857 = $1,000 × (0.926 × 0.926)
$857 = $1,000 × 0.857

A *time line* also can be used to illustrate this two-year example as follows:

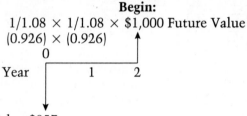

Begin:
1/1.08 × 1/1.08 × $1,000 Future Value
(0.926) × (0.926)
0

Year   1   2

End:
Present Value $857

Thus, for a one-year investment, the present value would be $926 ($1,000 × 1/1.08, or 0.926). A two-year investment would have a present value of only $857 ($1,000 × 0.926 × 0.926).

The discounting concept can be expressed in equation form as:

$$PV = FV_n/(1 + r)^n$$

or,

$$PV = FV_n[1/(1 + r)^n]$$ (9-3)

where the individual terms are the same as those defined for the future-value equation. Notice that the future-value equation has simply been rewritten to solve for the present value. For the $1,000, 8 percent, two-year example, we have:

$$PV = \$1,000[1/(1 + 0.08)^2]$$
$$= \$1,000(1/1.116)$$
$$= \$1,000(0.857)$$
$$= \$857$$

If we extend the time period to ten years, the $1,000 future value would decrease to:

$$PV = \$1,000[1/(1 + 0.08)^{10}]$$
$$= \$1,000(1/2.159)$$
$$= \$1,000(0.463)$$
$$= \$463$$

Most financial calculators are programmed to readily find present values. As previously noted, financial calculators typically have a present value (PV) key, a future value (FV) key, a number of time periods (N) key, an interest rate (%*i*) key, and a compute (CPT) key. If you have a financial calculator, you can verify the present value result for the ten-year example. First, clear the calculator. Then, enter 1000 and press the FV key, enter 8 and press the %*i* key, and enter 10 and press the N key. Finally, press the compute (CPT) key followed by the PV key to calculate the present value of 463.19, which rounds to $463.

Financial Calculator Solution:

Inputs   10   8   1000

            | N | | %*i* | | FV |

Press | CPT | | PV |

Solution 463.19

Computer software programs also are available for finding present values. In addition, tables have been prepared to simplify the calculation effort if financial calculators or computer programs are not available. Equation 9-3 can be rewritten as:

$$PV = FV_n (PVIF_{r,n}) \qquad (9\text{-}4)$$

where the $1/(1 + r)^n$ part of equation 9-3 is replaced by a present value interest factor ($PVIF$) corresponding to a specific interest rate and a specified time period.

Table 9.2 shows $PVIF$ values for a range of interest rates and time periods. [Table 2 in the Appendix provides a more comprehensive $PVIF$ table.] Let's use Table 9.2 to find the present value of $1,000 invested at an 8 percent compound interest rate for a ten-year period. Notice that at the intersection of the 8 percent column and ten years, we find a $PVIF$ of 0.463. Then, putting this information in equation 9-4 gives:

$$PV = \$1{,}000(0.463)$$
$$= \$463$$

TABLE 9.2   Present Value Interest Factor of $1 ($PVIF$)

YEAR	5%	6%	7%	8%	9%	10%
1	.952	.943	.935	.926	.917	.909
2	.907	.890	.873	.857	.842	.826
3	.864	.840	.816	.794	.772	.751
4	.823	.792	.763	.735	.708	.683
5	.784	.747	.713	.681	.650	.621
6	.746	.705	.666	.630	.596	.564
7	.711	.665	.623	.583	.547	.513
8	.677	.627	.582	.540	.502	.467
9	.645	.592	.544	.500	.460	.424
10	.614	.558	.508	.463	.422	.386

Further examination of Table 9.2 shows how a $1 investment decreases with various combinations of interest rates and time periods. For example, if another bank offers to pay interest at a 10 percent compound rate, the *PVIF* at the intersection of 10 percent and ten years would be 0.386 resulting in your $1,000 future value being worth an investment of $386 ($1,000 × 0.386). The difference in required investments needed to accumulate $1,000 at the end of ten years between 8 percent and 10 percent interest rates is $77 ($463 − $386). In essence, the present value of a future value decreases as the interest rate increases for a specified time period.

The discounting process also can be depicted in graphic form. Figure 9.2 shows graphic relationships among present values, interest rates, and time periods. For example, notice how a $1 future value will decrease differently over a ten-year period at 5 percent versus 10 percent interest rates. Of course, at a zero interest rate, the present value remains at $1 and is not affected by time. Of course, if there is no interest being earned, the $1 future value will have a present value of $1 no matter how long the investment is held. At a 5 percent interest rate, the present value of $1 declines to $0.61 (rounded) if an investor has to wait 10 years to receive the $1. This compares with a present value of $1 of only $0.39 (rounded) if the interest rate is 10 percent and the investor must wait ten years to receive $1. Notice that the present value decreases at an increasing rate as the interest rate is increased and as the time period is lengthened.

FIGURE 9.2   Present Value, Interest Rate, and Time Period Relationships

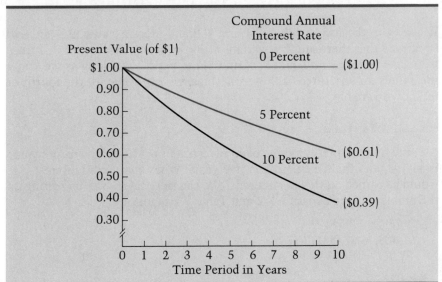

EQUATING PRESENT VALUES AND FUTURE VALUES

Also notice that equations 9.1 and 9.3 are two ways of looking at the same process involving compound interest rates. That is, if we know the future value of an investment, we can find its present value and vice versa. For example, an initial investment of $1,000 will grow to $1,116.40 at the end of two years if the interest rate is 8 percent. Note that in order to reduce the impact of rounding errors, we are carrying our calculations here to four decimal places as follows:

$$
\begin{aligned}
FV_2 &= \$1,000(1 + 0.08)^2 \\
&= \$1,000(1.1664) \\
&= \$1,166.40
\end{aligned}
$$

Now, let's ask what is the present value of a $1,166.40 future value if we must wait two years to receive the future value amount and if the interest rate is 8 percent? The solution would be:

$$
\begin{aligned}
PV &= \$1,166.40[(1/1 + 0.08)^2] \\
&= \$1,166.40(1/1.1664) \\
&= \$1,166.40(0.8573) \\
&= \$1,000
\end{aligned}
$$

Thus, an investor should be indifferent between receiving a $1,000 present value now or a $1,166 future value two years from now if the compound interest rate is 8 percent.

FINDING INTEREST RATES AND TIME REQUIREMENTS

Recall from the future value (9.1 and 9.2) and present value (9.3 and 9.4) equations that there are four variables: PV = present value, FV = future value, r = interest rate, and n = number of periods. As long as we know the values for any three of these variables, we can solve for the fourth or unknown variable.

SOLVING FOR INTEREST RATES

Assume that the present value of an investment is $1,000, the future value is $1,403, and the time period is five years. What compound interest rate would be earned on this investment? We can find the answer by setting up the problem using equation 9.2 and Table 9.1 as follows:

$$
\begin{aligned}
FV_5 &= PV(FVIF_{r,5}) \\
\$1,403 &= \$1,000(FVIF_{r,5}) \\
FVIF_{r,5} &= 1.403
\end{aligned}
$$

Since we know that the number of time periods is five, we can turn to Table 9.1 and read across the year five row until we find *FVIF* of 1.403. Notice that this occurs under the 7 percent column indicating that the interest rate (r) is 7 percent.

We also can work the problem using equation 9.4 and Table 9.2 as follows:

$$PV = FV_5(PVIF_{r,5})$$
$$\$1{,}000 = \$1{,}403(PVIF_{r,5})$$
$$PVIF_{r,5} = 0.713$$

Turning to Table 9.2 we read across the year five row until we find the *PVIF* of 0.713. This occurs under the 7 percent column indicating that the interest rate (r) is 7 percent.

We also can solve this problem using a computer software program or a financial calculator. If a financial calculator is used, enter $PV = 1000$, $FV = 1403$, $N = 5$, and press the compute (CPT) key followed by the %i key to find an r of 7.01 or 7 percent rounded (some calculators may require either the *PV* entry or *FV* entry to be negative).

Financial Calculator Solution:

Inputs	5	1000	1403
	N	PV	FV
Press	CPT	%i	
Solution	7.01		

SOLVING FOR TIME PERIODS

Now let's assume an investment has a present value of $1,000, a future value of $1,403, and an interest rate of 7 percent. What length of time does this investment involve? We can find the answer by using equation 9.2 and Table 9.1 as follows:

$$FV_n = PV(FVIF_{7\%,n})$$
$$\$1{,}403 = \$1{,}000(FVIF_{7\%,n})$$
$$FVIF_{7\%,n} = 1.403$$

Since we know the interest rate is 7 percent, we can turn to Table 9.1 and read down the 7 percent column until we find *FVIF* of 1.403. Notice that this occurs in the year five row indicating that the time period (n) is five years.

We also can work the problem using equation 9.4 and Table 9.2 as follows:

$$PV = FV_n(PVIF_{7\%,n})$$
$$\$1{,}000 = \$1{,}403(PVIF_{7\%,n})$$
$$PVIF_{7\%,n} = .713$$

Turning to Table 9.2 we read down the 7 percent column until we find
PVIF of 0.713. This occurs at the year five row indicating that the time
period (*n*) is five years.

We also can solve this problem using a computer software program or
a financial calculator. If a financial calculator is used, enter *PV* = 1000 (or
−1000), *FV* = 1403, *%i* = 7, and press the compute (CPT) key followed
by the N key to find an *n* 5.01 or 5 years rounded.

Financial Calculator Solution:

Inputs	7	1000	1403
	%i	PV	FV
Press	CPT	N	
Solution	5.01		

RULE OF 72

Investors often ask: "How long will it take for my money to double in
value at a particular interest rate?" We can turn to Table 9.1 to illustrate
the process for answering this question. We pick a particular interest rate
and read down the table until we find an *FVIF* of 2.000. For example, at an
8 percent interest rate, it will take almost exactly 9 years (note the *FVIF* of
1.999) for an investment to double in value. At a 9 percent interest rate,
the investment will double in about 8 years (*FVIF* of 1.993). An investment
will double in a little over 7 years (*FVIF* of 1.949) if the interest rate is 10
percent.

A shortcut method referred to as the "Rule of 72" can be used to
approximate the time required for an investment to double in value. This
method is applied by dividing the interest rate into the number 72 to determine the number of years it will take for an investment to double in value.
For example, if the interest rate is 8 percent, 72 divided by 8 indicates that
the investment will double in value in nine years. Notice that this is the
same conclusion drawn from Table 9.1. Likewise, at an interest rate of 10
percent it will take approximately 7.2 years (72/10) for your investment to
double in value. The reader should be aware that at very low or very high
interest rates, the "Rule of 72" does not approximate the compounding
process as well and thus a larger estimation error occurs in terms of the
time required for an investment to double in value.

FUTURE VALUE OF AN ANNUITY

Our previous discussion has focused on cash payments or receipts that
occurred only as lump sum present and future values. However, many
finance problems involve equal payments or receipts over time which we

refer to as *annuities*. More specifically, an **annuity** is a series of equal payments (receipts) that occur over a number of time periods.

Ordinary Annuity

An **ordinary annuity** exists when the equal payments (receipts) occur at the end of each time period. For example, suppose you want to invest $1,000 per year for three years at an 8 percent interest rate. However, since you will not make your first payment until the end of the first year, this will be an ordinary annuity.

We can also illustrate this problem using a *time line* as follows:

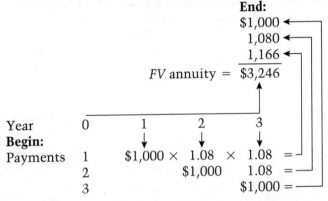

End:
$$\$1,000$$
$$1,080$$
$$1,166$$
$$FV \text{ annuity} = \$3,246$$

Year	0	1	2	3	
Begin:					
Payments 1		$1,000 × 1.08 ×	1.08	=	
2			$1,000 1.08	=	
3				$1,000 =	

Notice that in order to calculate the future value of this ordinary annuity we must add the future values of the first payment ($1,166), the second payment ($1,080), and the third payment ($1,000). This results in a future value of $3,246. To summarize, since the first payment is made at the end of the first year, it is compounded for two years. The second payment is compounded for one year and the third payment earns zero interest since the payment is made at the end of the third year.

We also can find the future value of this annuity by making the following computations:

$$
\begin{aligned}
FV \text{ ordinary annuity} &= \$1,000(1.08)^2 + \$1,000(1.08)^1 + \$1,000(1.08)^0 \\
&= \$1,000(1.166) + \$1,000(1.080) + \$1,000(1.000) \\
&= \$1,000(3.246) \\
&= \$3,246
\end{aligned}
$$

While the computational process was relatively easy for our three-year ordinary annuity example, the required calculations become much more cumbersome as the time period is lengthened. As a result the following equation was derived for finding the future value of an ordinary annuity (*FVA*):

$$FVA_n = PMT[((1 + r)^n - 1)/r] \tag{9-5}$$

where *PMT* is the periodic equal payment, *r* is the compound interest rate, and *n* is the total number of periods. Inserting the data from the above three-year annuity example results in:

$$FVA_3 = \$1,000[((1 + 0.08)^3 - 1)/0.08]$$
$$= \$1,000[(1.2597 - 1)/0.08]$$
$$= \$1,000(3.246)$$
$$= \$3,246$$

Most financial calculators are programmed to readily find future values of annuities. In addition to the previously identified keys, financial calculators also will have a payments (PMT) key for purposes of working problems involving ordinary annuities. If you have a financial calculator, you can verify the result for the three-year ordinary annuity.

First, clear the calculator. Next, enter 1000 (or –1000) and press the PMT key. Then, enter 8 and press the %*i* key, and enter 3 and press the N key. Finally, press the CPT key followed by the FV key to calculate the FVA of 3246.40, which rounds to $3,246. Note that because this problem involves a periodic outflow of $1,000, some financial calculators require that the payment be entered as a negative number in order to solve for a positive FVA.

Financial Calculator Solution:

Inputs	3	8	−1000
	N	%*i*	PMT
Press	CPT	FV	

Solution 3246.40

Computer software programs also are available for finding future values of annuities. In addition, tables have been prepared to simplify the calculation effort if financial calculators or computer programs are not available. Equation 9-5 can be rewritten as:

$$FVA_n = PMT(FVIFA_{r,n}) \tag{9-6}$$

where the $[(1 + r)^n - 1]/r$ part of equation 9-5 is replaced by a future value interest factor of an annuity (*FVIFA*) corresponding to a specific interest rate and a specified time period.

Table 9.3 shows *FVIFA* values for a partial range of interest rates and time periods. (Table 3 in the Appendix provides a more comprehensive *FVIFA* table.) Let's use Table 9.3 to find the future value of an ordinary annuity involving annual payments of $1,000, an 8 percent interest rate, and a three-year time period. Notice that at the intersection of the 8 percent column and 3 years, we find a *FVIFA* of 3.246. Then, putting this information into equation 9-6 gives:

$$FVA_3 = \$1,000(3.246)$$
$$= \$3,246$$

TABLE 9.3   Future Value Interest Factor for a $1 Ordinary Annuity (*FVIFA*)

YEAR	5%	6%	7%	8%	9%	10%
1	1.000	1.000	1.000	1.000	1.000	1.000
2	2.050	2.060	2.070	2.080	2.090	2.100
3	3.152	3.184	3.215	3.246	3.278	3.310
4	4.310	4.375	4.440	4.506	4.573	4.641
5	5.526	5.637	5.751	5.867	5.985	6.105
6	6.802	6.975	7.153	7.336	7.523	7.716
7	8.142	8.394	8.654	8.923	9.200	9.487
8	9.549	9.897	10.260	10.637	11.028	11.436
9	11.027	11.491	11.978	12.488	13.021	13.579
10	12.578	13.181	13.816	14.487	15.193	15.937

Further examination of Table 9.3 shows how a $1 annuity grows or increases with various combinations of interest rates and time periods. For example, if $1,000 is invested at the end of each year (beginning with year one) for ten years at an 8 percent interest rate, the future value of the annuity would be $14,487 ($1,000 × 14.487). And, if the interest rate is 10 percent for ten years, the future value of the annuity would be $15,937 ($1,000 × 15.937). These results demonstrate the benefits of higher interest rates on the future values of annuities.

ANNUITY DUE

In contrast with an ordinary annuity, an **annuity due** exists when the equal periodic payments occur at the beginning of each period. Let's return to our example involving a three-year annuity, $1,000 annual payments, and an 8 percent interest rate. However, the first payment now is made at the beginning of the first year, namely at time zero. This will allow the first $1,000 payment to earn interest for three years, the second payment to earn interest for two years, and the third payment to earn interest for one year.

annuity due exists when the equal payments occur at the beginning of each time period

We can demonstrate the calculation process to find the future value of this annuity due problem as follows:

$$
\begin{aligned}
FV \text{ annuity due} &= \$1,000(1.08)^3 + \$1,000(1.08)^2 + \$1,000(1.08)^1 \\
&= \$1,000(1.260) + \$1,000(1.166) + \$1,000(1.080) \\
&= \$1,000(1.260 + 1.166 + 1.080) \\
&= \$1,000(3.506) \\
&= \$3,506
\end{aligned}
$$

Notice that by making the first payment now the future value of this annuity at the end of three years will be $3,506. This contrasts with a future value of $3,246 if payments are delayed by one year as would be the case with an ordinary annuity.

Equation 9-6 can be easily modified to handle annuity due problems as follows:

$$FVAD_n = PMT(FVIFA_{r,n})(1 + r) \qquad (9\text{-}7)$$

where *FVAD* is the future value of an annuity due and the $(1 + r)$ factor effectively compounds each payment by one more year to reflect the fact that payments start at the beginning of each period. In the above problem, the annual payment is $1,000, the time period is three years, and the interest rate is 8 percent. Using equation 9-7, the future value of this annuity due would be:

$$
\begin{aligned}
FVAD_3 &= \$1,000(FVIFA_{8\%,3})(1 + 0.08) \\
&= \$1,000(3.246)(1.08) \\
&= \$1,000(3.506) \\
&= \$3,506
\end{aligned}
$$

Recall that the *FVIFA* of 3.246 comes from Table 9.3 at the intersection of the 8 percent interest rate column and the year three row.

Annuity due problems also can be solved with computer software programs and financial calculators. In fact, most financial calculators have a DUE key (or a switch) for shifting payments from the end of time periods to the beginning of time periods. If you have a financial calculator, you can verify the future value of an annuity due result for the three-year annuity problem. First, clear the calculator. Next, enter 1000 (or –1000) and press the PMT key. Then enter 8 and press the %*i* key, and enter 3 and press the N key. Finally, instead of pressing the CPT key, press the DUE key followed by the FV key to find the future value of an annuity due of 3506.11 which rounds to $3,506.

Financial Calculator Solution:

Inputs	3	8	–1000
	N	%*i*	PMT
Press	DUE	FV	
Solution	3506.11		

PRESENT VALUE OF AN ANNUITY

Many present-value problems also involve cash flow annuities. Usually these are ordinary annuities. Let's assume that we will receive $1,000 per year beginning one year from now for a period of three years at an 8 percent compound interest rate. How much would you be willing to pay now for this stream of future cash flows? Since we are concerned with the value now this becomes a present value problem.

We can illustrate this problem using a *time line* as follows:

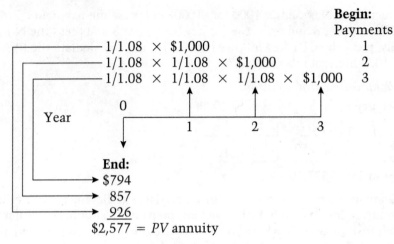

$$PV \text{ ordinary annuity} = \$1,000[1/(1.08)^1] + \$1,000[1/(1.08)^2]$$
$$+ \$1,000[1/(1.08)^3]$$
$$= \$1,000(0.926) + \$1,000(0.857) + \$1,000(0.794)$$
$$= \$1,000(2.577)$$
$$= \$2,577$$

Notice that in order to calculate the present value of this ordinary annuity we must sum the present values of the first payment ($794), the second payment ($857), and the third payment ($926). This results in a present value of $2,577.

We also can find the present value of this annuity by making the following computations:

While the computational process was relatively easy for our three-year ordinary annuity example, the required calculations become much more cumbersome as the time period is lengthened. As a result the following equation was derived for finding the present value of an ordinary annuity (PVA):

$$PVA_n = PMT[[1 - (1/(1 + r)^n)]/r] \tag{9-8}$$

where the various inputs are the same as previously defined. Inserting the data from the above three-year annuity example results in:

$$PVA_3 = \$1,000[[1 - (1/1 + 0.08)^3]/0.08]$$
$$= \$1,000[[1 - (0.7938)]/0.08]$$
$$= \$1,000[0.2062/0.08]$$
$$= \$1,000(2.577)$$
$$= \$2,577$$

Most financial calculators are programmed to readily find present values of annuities. If you have a financial calculator, you can verify the result for the three-year present value of an ordinary annuity problem. First, clear the calculator. Next, enter 1000 (or –1000) and press the payments (PMT) key. Then, enter 8 and press the %*i* key, and enter 3 and press the N key. Finally, press the CPT key followed by the PV key to calculate the PVA of 2577.10, which rounds to $2,577.

Financial Calculator Solution:

Inputs	3	8	1000
	N	%*i*	PMT

Press   CPT   PV

Solution 2577.10

Computer software programs also are available for finding present values of annuities. In addition, tables have been prepared to simplify the calculation effort if financial calculators or computer programs are not available. Equation 9-8 can be rewritten as:

$$PVA_n = PMT(PVIFA_{r,n}) \qquad (9\text{-}9)$$

where the $[1 - (1/(1 + r)^n)]/r$ part of equation 9-8 is replaced by a present value interest factor of an annuity (*PVIFA*) corresponding to a specific interest rate and a specified time period.

Table 9.4 shows *PVIFA* values for a partial range of interest rates and time periods. (Table 4 in the Appendix provides a more comprehensive *PVIFA* table.) Let's use Table 9.4 to find the present value of an ordinary annuity involving annual payments of $1,000, an 8 percent interest rate, and a three-year time period. Notice that at the intersection of the 8 percent interest rate column and three years, we find a *PVIFA* of 2.577. Then, putting this information into equation 9-9 gives:

$$PVA_3 = \$1,000(2.577)$$
$$= \$2,577$$

TABLE 9.4   Present Value Interest Factor for a $1 Ordinary Annuity (*PVIFA*)

YEAR	5%	6%	7%	8%	9%	10%
1	0.952	0.943	0.935	0.926	0.917	0.909
2	1.859	1.833	1.808	1.783	1.759	1.736
3	2.273	2.673	2.624	2.577	2.531	2.487
4	3.546	3.465	3.387	3.312	3.240	3.170
5	4.329	4.212	4.100	3.993	3.890	3.791
6	5.076	4.917	4.767	4.623	4.486	4.355
7	5.786	5.582	5.389	5.206	5.033	4.868
8	6.463	6.210	5.971	5.747	5.535	5.335
9	7.108	6.802	6.515	6.247	5.995	5.759
10	7.722	7.360	7.024	6.710	6.418	6.145

Further examination of Table 9.4 shows how the present value of a $1 annuity decreases with various combinations of interest rates and time periods. For example, if $1,000 is paid at the end of each year (beginning with year one) for ten years at an 8 percent interest rate, the present value of the annuity would be $6,710 ($1,000 × 6.710). And, if the interest rate is 10 percent for ten years, the present value of the annuity would be $6,145 ($1,000 × 6.145). These results demonstrate the costs of higher interest rates on the present values of annuities.

Occasionally there are present value annuity due problems. For example, leasing arrangements often require the person leasing equipment to make the first payment at the time the equipment is delivered. Let's illustrate by assuming that lease payments of $1,000 will be made at the beginning of each year for three years. If the appropriate interest rate is 8 percent, what is the present value of this annuity due leasing problem?

We can demonstrate the calculation process to find the present value of this annuity due problem as follows:

$$
\begin{aligned}
\text{PV annuity due} &= \$1,000[1/(1.08)^0] + \$1,000[1/(1.08)^1] \\
&\quad + \$1,000[1/(1.08)^2] \\
&= \$1,000(1.000) + \$1,000(0.926) + \$1,000(0.857) \\
&= \$1,000(2.783) \\
&= \$2,783
\end{aligned}
$$

Notice that by making the first payment now, the present value of this annuity is $2,783. This contrasts with a present value of $2,577 if payments are delayed by one year as would be the case with an ordinary annuity.

Equation 9-9 can be easily modified to handle annuity due problems as follows:

$$
PVAD_n = PMT(PVIFA_{r,n})(1 + r) \tag{9-10}
$$

where *PVAD* is the present value of an annuity due and the $(1 + r)$ factor effectively compounds each payment by one more year to reflect the fact that payments start at the beginning of each period. In the above problem, the annual payment is $1,000, the time period is three years, and the interest rate is 8 percent. Using equation 9-10, the present value of this annuity due would be:

$$
\begin{aligned}
PVAD_3 &= \$1,000(PVIFA_{8\%,3})(1 + 0.08) \\
&= \$1,000(2.577)(1.08) \\
&= \$1,000(2.783) \\
&= \$2,783
\end{aligned}
$$

Recall that the *PVIFA* of 2.577 comes from Table 9.4 at the intersection of the 8 percent interest rate column and the year three row.

Present value annuity due problems also can be solved with computer software programs and financial calculators. If you have a financial calculator, you can verify the present value of an annuity due result for the above three-year annuity problem. First, clear the calculator. Next, enter 1000 and press the PMT key. Then enter 8 and press the %i key, and 3 and press the N key. Finally, instead of pressing the CPT key, press the DUE key followed by the PV key to find the present value of an annuity due of 2783.26, which rounds to $2,783.

Financial Calculator Solution:

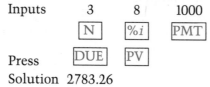

Inputs   3   8   1000
         N   %i   PMT

Press   DUE PV
Solution 2783.26

INTEREST RATES AND TIME REQUIREMENTS FOR ANNUITIES

Earlier in this chapter, we discussed how to find or solve for interest rates or time periods for problems involving a lump sum present value or future value. Recall that we originally worked with four variables: PV = present value, FV = future value, r = interest rate, and n = number of periods. We now add a fifth variable to reflect payments (PMT) involving annuities.

SOLVING FOR INTEREST RATES

Assume that the future value of an ordinary annuity is $5,751, the annual payment is $1,000, and the time period is five years. What is the interest rate for this problem? We can find the answer by setting up the problem using equation 9-6 and Table 9.3 as follows:

$$FVA_5 = PMT(FVIFA_{r,5})$$
$$\$5,751 = \$1,000(FVIFA_{r,5})$$
$$FVIFA_{r,5} = 5.751$$

Since we know that the number of time periods is five, we can turn to Table 9.3 and read across the year five row until we find $FVIFA$ of 5.751. Notice that this occurs under the 7 percent column indicating that the interest rate (r) is 7 percent.

Let's now assume that we know the present value of the above ordinary annuity is $4,100. We could then find the interest rate for the problem using present value annuity tables as follows:

$$PVA_5 = PMT(PVIFA_{r,5})$$
$$\$4,100 = \$1,000(PVIFA_{r,5})$$
$$PVIFA_{r,5} = 4.100$$

There are a number of ways of acquiring a million dollars. Probably the easiest legal way is to inherit it. As for those of us who won't do that, we must save a portion of our disposable personal income and then live long enough to take advantage of compounding interest. For example, if you could invest $10,000 now, the following combinations of annual compound interest rates and time periods would make you a millionaire.

SO YOU WANT TO BECOME A MILLIONAIRE!

INTEREST RATE	AMOUNT OF TIME
5%	94.4 years
10%	48.3 years
15%	33.0 years
20%	25.3 years

Notice that at a 5 percent compound rate it would take more than 94 years to accumulate $1 million. This is probably not acceptable (or possible) for most of us. Even if we could compound our interest at a 20 percent annual rate, it would take a little more than 25 years to become a millionaire.

An alternative approach would be to create an investment annuity of $10,000 per year. The following chart shows the time required to become a millionaire under the assumptions of both an ordinary annuity (where the first investment will be made one year from now), and an annuity due (where the first investment is made now).

	AMOUNT OF TIME	
INTEREST RATE	ORDINARY ANNUITY	ANNUITY DUE
5%	36.7 years	35.9 years
10%	25.2 years	24.3 years
15%	19.8 years	18.9 years
20%	16.7 years	15.8 years

With this approach the time required, particularly at higher interest rates, is more feasible. Compounding at 5 percent would still require making annual investments for about 36 years to accumulate $1 million. At 10 percent, it would take you only 24 to 25 years to attain that goal. Of course the most critical factor, which might be easier said than done, is whether you will be able to come up with $10,000 per year out of your disposable personal income. Good luck!

Turning to Table 9.4 we read across the year five row until we find the *PVIFA* of 4.100. This occurs under the 7 percent column indicating that the interest rate (*r*) is 7 percent.

A computer software program or a financial calculator also could be used to solve this problem if either the *FV* or *PV* of the ordinary annuity is known.

If you have a financial calculator, and you know the future value, enter *FV* = 5751, *PMT* = 1000 (or –1000), and *N* = 5. Press the CPT key followed by the %*i* key to find an *r* of 7 percent. Note: some financial calculators will give an "error" message unless the 1000 PMT is entered as a minus number (outflow) using the +/– key. If the present value of the ordinary annuity is known instead of the future value, the above procedure would be followed except that *PV* = 4100 would be entered instead of the future value amount.

Financial Calculator Solution:

Inputs	5	–1000	5751
	N	PMT	FV
Press	CPT	%*i*	
Solution	7.00		

As we previously saw, tables containing *FVIFA* and *PVIFA* factors are not readily available for annuity due problems. Thus, the use of a computer software program or a financial calculator would be preferable when trying to find the interest rate for an annuity due problem. Let's assume that the future value of an annuity due problem is $6,153, each payment is $1,000, and the time period is five years. What is the interest rate on this problem? If you have a financial calculator, enter: *FV* = 6153, *PMT* = 1000 (or – 1000), and *N* = 5. Press the DUE key and the %*i* key to find an *r* of 7 percent. If the present value of the annuity due is known instead of the future value, the problem could be worked by substituting the *PV* value for the *FV* value.

Financial Calculator Solution:

Inputs	5	–1000	6153
	N	PMT	FV
Press	DUE	%*i*	
Solution	7.00		

SOLVING FOR TIME PERIODS

Let's assume that the future value of an ordinary annuity is $5,751, the annual payment is $1,000, and the interest rate is 7 percent. How long would it take for your $1,000 annual investments to grow to $5,751? We can set up the problem by using equation 9-6 and Table 9.3 as follows:

$$FVA_n = PMT(FVIFA_{7\%,n})$$
$$\$5,751 = \$1,000(FVIFA_{7\%,n})$$
$$FVIFA_{7\%,n} = 5.751$$

Since we know the interest rate is 7 percent, we can turn to Table 9.3 and read down the 7 percent column until we find *FVIFA* of 5.751. Notice that this occurs in the year five row indicating that the *n* time period is five years.

If we knew the present value of the above ordinary annuity was $4,100, we could also work the problem using equation 9-9 and Table 9.4 as follows:

$$PVA_n = PMT(PVIFA_{7\%,n})$$
$$\$4,100 = \$1,000(PVIFA_{7\%,n})$$
$$PVIFA_{7\%,n} = 4.100$$

Turning to Table 9.4 we read down the 7 percent column until we find *PVIFA* of 4.100. This occurs at the year five row indicating that the *n* time period is five years.

We also can solve this problem using a computer software program or a financial calculator. If a financial calculator is used and we know that the future value of the ordinary annuity is $5,751, enter *FV* = 5751, *PMT* = 1000 (or − 1000), *%i* = 7, and press the CPT key followed by the N key to find an *n* of five years. If we knew the present value of the annuity instead of the future value, we could work the problem by substituting the *PV* for the *FV*.

Financial Calculator Solution:

Inputs	7	−1000	5751
	%i	PMT	FV
Press	CPT	N	
Solution	5.00		

We also can solve for the *n* time periods involved in an annuity due problem. However, since neither *FVIFA* nor *PVIFA* tables are readily available for annuity due problems, we would use either a computer software program or a financial calculator.

DETERMINING ANNUAL ANNUITY PAYMENTS

There are many instances for which we would want to determine the periodic equal payment required for an annuity. For example, you may wish to accumulate $10,000 at the end of five years from now by making equal annual payments beginning one year from now. If you can invest at a compound 6 percent interest rate, what will be the amount of each of your annual payments? Since this is a future value of an ordinary annuity problem, we can use equation 9-6 and Table 9.3 as follows:

$$FVA_n = PMT(FVIFA_{r,n})$$
$$\$10{,}000 = PMT(FVIFA_{6\%,5})$$
$$\$10{,}000 = PMT(5.637)$$
$$PMT = \$1{,}774 \text{ (rounded)}$$

The *FVIFA* factor of 5.637 is taken from Table 9.3 at the intersection of the 6 percent column and the year five row.

amortized loan
a loan repaid in equal payments over a specified time period

As another example, we might want to find the equal payment necessary to pay off, or *amortize*, a loan or real estate mortgage. An **amortized loan** is repaid in equal payments over a specified time period. Let's assume that a lender offers you a $20,000, 10 percent interest rate, three-year loan that is to be fully amortized with three annual payments. The first payment will be due one year from the loan date making the loan an ordinary annuity. How much will you have to pay each year?

This is a present-value problem because the $20,000 is the value or amount of the loan now. The annual payment can be found by using equation 9-9 and Table 9.4 as follows:

$$PVA_n = PMT(PVIFA_{10\%,3})$$
$$\$20{,}000 = PMT(2.487)$$
$$PMT = \$8{,}042 \text{ (rounded)}$$

The *PVIFA* factor of 2.487 is taken from Table 9.4 at the intersection of the 10 percent column and the year three row.

loan amortization schedule
a schedule of the breakdown of each payment between interest and principal, as well as the remaining balance after each payment

Table 9.5 illustrates the repayment process with a **loan amortization schedule,** which shows the breakdown of each payment between interest and principal, as well as the remaining balance after each payment. Since the interest rate is 10 percent, the first year you will pay interest of $2,000 ($20,000 × 0.10). Subsequent interest payments are based on the remaining loan balances, which are smaller each year (also referred to as the declining balance). Since $6,042 ($8,042 − $2,000) of the first year's $8,042 payment is used to repay part of the principal, the second year's interest payment will only be $1,396 ($13,958 × 0.10). The third and last payment covers the final year's interest of $731 plus the remaining principal balance.

TABLE 9.5   Sample Loan Amortization Schedule

YEAR	ANNUAL PAYMENT	INTEREST PAYMENT	PRINCIPAL REPAYMENT	LOAN BALANCE
0	–	–	–	$20,000
1	$8,042	$2,000	$6,042	13,958
2	8,042	1,396	6,646	7,312
3	8,042	731	7,311*	0

*Because of rounding, the final principal repayment is off by $1.

This loan amortization process is the same as that used to determine monthly payments on home mortgages. However, because the discounting interval is very short, it would be unwieldy to calculate the monthly payment the long way for a typical 30-year loan. Therefore a financial calculator or computer program is used.

MORE FREQUENT COMPOUNDING OR DISCOUNTING INTERVALS

There are many situations in which compounding or discounting may occur more often than annually. For example, recall from the beginning of this chapter the $1,000 that could be invested at one bank at an 8 percent annual interest rate for two years. Remember that the future value at the end of two years was:

$$FV_2 = \$1,000(1.08)^2$$
$$= \$1,000(1.166)$$
$$= \$1,166$$

Now let's assume that another bank offers the same 8 percent interest rate but with semiannual (twice a year) compounding. We can find the future value of this investment by modifying equation 9-1 as follows:

$$FV_n = PV(1 + r/m)^{n \times m} \qquad (9\text{-}11)$$

where m is the number of compounding periods per year. For our problem, we have:

$$FV_2 = \$1,000(1 + 0.08/2)^{2 \times 2}$$
$$= \$1,000(1.04)^4$$
$$= \$1,000(1.170)$$
$$= \$1,170$$

Thus, by compounding semiannually the future value would increase by $4.

We also can describe the more frequent than annual compounding process operationally as follows. First divide the annual interest rate of 8 percent by the number of times compounding is to take place during the year $(0.08/2 = 0.04)$. We also need to increase the total number of periods to reflect semiannual compounding. To do this, multiply the number of years for the loan times the frequency of compounding within a year (2 years $\times$ 2 = 4 periods).

Earlier in the chapter, we found that a $1,000 investment at an 8 percent interest rate would grow to $2,159 at the end of ten years. However, if semiannual compounding had been available the future value of the $1,000 investment would have been:

$$FV_{20} = \$1,000(1.04)^{20}$$
$$= \$1,000(2.191)$$
$$= \$2,191$$

The 2.191 future-value interest factor (*FVIF*) can also be found in Table 1 in the Appendix. Notice that semiannual compounding will result in $32 more than the $2,159 earned with annual compounding. It follows that more frequent compounding, such as quarterly or monthly, produces even higher earnings.

The process described above also applies to discounting problems when discounting occurs more frequently than annually. The use of financial calculators and computer software is more expedient as the frequency of compounding or discounting within a year increases.

APR VERSUS *EAR*

annual percentage rate (APR)
determined by multiplying the interest rate charged per period by the number of periods in a year

Banks, finance companies, and other lenders are required by law to disclose their borrowing interest rates to their customers. Such a rate is called a *contract or stated rate*, or more frequently, an **annual percentage rate (APR).** The method of calculating the *APR* on a loan is set by law. The *APR* is the interest rate charged per period multiplied by the number of periods in a year:

$$APR = r \times m \tag{9-12}$$

Thus, a car loan that charges interest of 1 percent per month has an *APR* of 12 percent (i.e., 1 percent times 12 months). An unpaid credit card balance that incurs interest charges of 1.5 percent per month has an *APR* of 18 percent (1.5 times 12 months).

effective annual rate (EAR)
measures the true interest rate when compounding occurs more frequently than once a year

However, the *APR* misstates the true interest rate. The **effective annual rate (EAR),** sometimes called the annual effective yield, is the true opportunity cost measure of the interest rate, as it considers the effects of periodic compounding. For example, an unpaid January balance of $100 on a credit card accumulates interest at the rate of 1.5 percent per month. The interest charge is added to the unpaid balance; if left unpaid, February's balance will be $101.50. If the bill remains unpaid through February, the 1.5 percent monthly charge is levied based upon the total unpaid balance of $101.50. In other words, interest is assessed on previous months' unpaid interest charges. Thus, since interest compounds, the *APR* formula will *understate* the true or effective interest cost. This will always be true except in the special case where the number of periods is one per year; that is, in annual compounding situations.

If the periodic interest charge *r* is known, the *EAR* is found by using Equation 9-13:

$$EAR = (1 + r)^m - 1 \tag{9-13}$$

> *"We take a resource,
> the money of our clients,
> and produce a product."*

BRUCE ELIOT

Portfolio Manager
Helix Investment Partners

*BA Economics
Claremont Men's College
MBA Finance
University of Chicago*

career profiles

Q: *Before you took your current position, you worked in the business valuation field. What is that?*

A: There are a number of circumstances when the owner of a business may need to determine the value of his or her firm. For instance, if I was going to sell part of the ownership of my company to someone else, I'd need to know how to price it. Or if I was going to use it as collateral for a loan, I'd need to demonstrate the value to the lender.

Q: *How did you determine a company's value?*

A: There are several methods. Sometimes we would look for similar firms that had been sold recently and use those as comparisons. Or we'd look for similar firms that are publicly traded and look at the value of their stock. In other cases we would look at their present value from a cash flow perspective.

Q: *Describe that process.*

A: It's not unlike the process you would use to determine the value of a stock or bond. We'd look at the discounted value of the projected cash flow for the next five years, and then the terminal value, which is the amount you would expect to sell the business for in five years, again discounted to present value.

Q: *Now you're a Portfolio Manager.*

A: Right. I basically invest other people's money. In a way it's like a manufacturing business. We take a resource, the money of our clients, and produce a product, which is the return on their investment. We manage about $180 million currently.

Q: *How do you decide what to invest in?*

A: Our investment strategy could be described as fairly complex. We look for firms with quite specific capital conditions. We look at their existing debt (bonds) and their existing equity (stock) values. When we see a certain relationship between those values, we see an opportunity to make a positive return. Applying our strategy, we will often end up buying a company's bonds and selling its stock short.

Q: *Why would this strategy work?*

A: In very simple terms, when we see certain stock and bond values, we conclude that there is a misvaluation, that the stock is overpriced relative to the bond, for instance. So if we're right, we're able to take advantage of that misvaluation by buying the underpriced security and shorting the overpriced one. As I said, it's a fairly complex strategy.

Q: *What do you do on a daily basis?*

A: I spend essentially the entire day on the telephone, discussing the value of securities, mostly with brokers. Since the bonds we buy are not traded on an exchange like stocks, I may need to call four or five sources for those bonds to determine the going price. The other piece of my job is to manage the existing portfolio, making day-to-day adjustments based on the changing values of securities. Using the metaphor of a manufacturing business, I adjust the settings on the production line so the products are manufactured correctly.

271

where m is the number of periods per year. If the *APR* is known instead, divide the *APR* by m and use the resulting number for r in Equation 9-13.

As an example of the effective annual rate concept, let's find the true annual interest cost of a credit card that advertises an 18 percent *APR*. Since credit card charges are typically assessed monthly, m, the number of periods per year, is 12. Thus, the monthly interest rate is:

$$r = APR/m = 18\%/12 = 1.5\%$$

From equation 9-13, the *EAR* is:

$$(1 + 0.015)^{12} - 1 = 1.1956 - 1 = 0.1956, \text{ or } 19.56\%$$

The true interest charge on a credit card with an 18 percent APR is really 19.56 percent!

When the annual stated rate stays the same, more frequent interest compounding helps savers earn more interest over the course of a year. For example, is it better to put your money in an account offering (a) 8 percent interest per year, compounded quarterly, or (b) 8 percent interest per year, compounded monthly?

Compounding interest quarterly means that the bank is paying interest four times a year to its depositors. Option (a) involved four periods per year and a periodic interest rate r of 8 percent divided by 4, or 2 percent. Every dollar invested under option (a) will grow to $1.0824 [$1(1 + 0.02)^4]$ after one year's time. Another way of expressing this is that the effective annual rate of 8 percent compounded quarterly is 8.24 percent.

Under option (b), the relevant time period is one month and the periodic interest rate is 8 percent/12 or 0.67 percent. Every dollar invested under option (b) will grow to $1.0830 [$1(1 + 0.0067)^{12}]$. Thus, the effective annual rate of 8 percent compounded monthly is 8.30 percent.

As option (b) gives the depositor more interest over the course of a year, depositors should choose it over option (a). This example illustrates that, for the same *APR* or stated rate, more frequent compounding increases the future value of an investor's funds more quickly.

SUMMARY

This chapter has introduced the reader to the concept of the time value of money which is the basis of many financial applications. We began with an explanation and illustration of simple interest. Then, compounding to determine future values and discounting to determine present values were discussed. We also discussed how to find interest rates and time requirements in problems involving future and present values.

Future value and present value problems involving annuities were described and the calculation process illustrated. How to find interest rates and time requirements for annuities also were covered. We then provided a discussion on how to determine annual annuity payments and a section on how to handle more frequent compounding or discounting intervals. The chapter concluded with a comparison of two interest rate concepts— the annual percentage rate versus the effective annual rate.

KEY TERMS

amortized loan	discounting
annual percentage rate (*APR*)	effective annual rate (*EAR*)
annuity	loan amortization schedule
annuity due	ordinary annuity
compounding	simple interest
compound interest	time value of money

DISCUSSION QUESTIONS

1. Briefly describe what is meant by the time value of money.
2. Explain the meaning of simple interest.
3. Describe the process of compounding and the meaning of compound interest.
4. Briefly describe how inflation or purchasing power impacts on stated or nominal interest rates.
5. What is meant by discounting? Give an illustration.
6. Briefly explain how present values and future values are related.
7. Describe the process for solving for the interest rate in present and future value problems.
8. Describe the process for solving for the time period in present and future value problems.
9. How can the Rule of 72 be used to determine how long it will take for an investment to double in value?
10. What is an annuity? How do ordinary annuities and annuities due differ?
11. Briefly describe how to solve for the interest rate or the time period in annuity problems.
12. Describe the process for determining the size of a constant periodic payment that is necessary to fully amortize a loan.
13. Describe what is meant by compounding or discounting more often than annually.
14. Explain the difference between the annual percentage rate and the effective annual rate.

PROBLEMS

1. Determine the future values if $5,000 is invested in each of the following situations:
   a) 5 percent for ten years,
   b) 7 percent for seven years, and
   c) 9 percent for four years.
2. Assume you are planning to invest $5,000 each year for six years and will earn 10 percent per year. Determine the future value of this annuity if your first $5,000 is invested now. How would your answer change if you waited one year before making the first investment?
3. Determine the present value if $15,000 is to be received at the end of eight years and the discount rate is 9 percent. How would your answer change if you had to wait six years to receive the $15,000?
4. What is the present value of a loan that calls for the payment of $500 per year for six years if the discount rate is 10 percent and the first payment will be made one year from now? How would your answer change if the $500 per year occurred for ten years?
5. Determine the annual payment on a $15,000 loan that is to be amortized over a four-year period and carries a 10 percent interest rate. Also prepare a loan amortization schedule for this loan.
6. Assume a bank loan requires an interest payment of $85 per year and a principal payment of $1,000 at the end of the loan's eight-year life.
   a. How much could this loan be sold for to another bank if loans of similar quality carried an 8.5 percent interest rate? That is, what would be the present value of this loan?
   b. Now, if interest rates on other similar quality loans were 10 percent, what would be the present value of this loan?
   c. Finally, what would be the present value of the loan if the interest rate is 8 percent on similar quality loans?
7. Use a financial calculator or computer software program to answer the following questions:
   a. What would be the future value of $15,555 invested now if it earns interest at 14.5 percent for seven years?
   b. What would be the future value of $19,378 invested now if the money remains deposited for eight years and the annual interest rate is 18 percent?
   c. How would your answer for part b change if interest on your investment is compounded quarterly?
8. Use a financial calculator or computer software program to answer the following questions:
   a. What is the present value of $359,000 that is to be received at the end of 23 years if the discount rate is 11 percent?
   b. How would your answer for part a change if semiannual discounting were used?

   c. How would your answer for part a change if monthly discounting were used?

9. Use a financial calculator or computer software program to answer the following questions:

   a. What would be the future value of $7,455 invested annually for nine years beginning one year from now if the annual interest rate is 19 percent?

   b. What would be the present value of a $9,532 annuity for which the first payment will be made beginning one year from now, payments will last for 27 years, and the annual interest rate is 13 percent?

   c. How would your answer for part b change if quarterly discounting occurred and $2,383 is invested at the end of each quarter?

SELF-TEST QUESTIONS

1. Time value of money problems can be solved by using which of the following methods?
   a. equations and appropriate time value of money tables
   b. a financial calculator
   c. an appropriate computer software program
   d. all of the above

2. Interest earned only on an investment's principal or original amount is referred to as:
   a. simple interest
   b. compound interest
   c. discount interest
   d. annuity interest

3. When solving for the future value of an amount deposited now, which one of the following factors would *not* be an input?
   a. present value amount
   b. 1 plus the interest rate
   c. 1 divided by the sum of 1 plus the interest rate
   d. number of periods to compound over

4. When using a financial calculator to solve for the present value of a single future payment, which of the following calculator keys would not be used?
   a. the N key
   b. the %*i* key
   c. the PV key
   d. the FV key
   e. the PMT key

5. The basic future and present value equations contain four variables. Which one of the following is not included?
   a. present value (PV)

 b. future value (*FV*)
 c. interest rate (*r*)
 d. inflation rate (*I*)
 e. number of periods (*n*)

6. A series of equal payments or receipts that occur at the beginning of each of a number of time periods is referred to as:
 a. an ordinary annuity
 b. a deferred annuity
 c. an annuity due
 d. an extraordinary annuity

7. A loan that is repaid in equal payments over a specified time period is referred to as:
 a. a discounted loan
 b. an amortized loan
 c. a simple interest-free loan
 d. an inflation-indexed loan

8. When compounding more than once a year, the true opportunity cost measure of the interest rate is indicated by the:
 a. annual percentage rate
 b. contract rate
 c. stated rate
 d. effective annual rate

SELF-TEST PROBLEMS

1. Assume you are planning to invest $100 each year for four years and will earn 10 percent per year. Determine the future value of this annuity if your first $100 is invested now. How would your answer change if you waited one year before making the first investment?

2. Assume that you are applying for a $20,000 loan to help finance the remainder of your education. You can borrow the money at a 10 percent interest rate for five years. The loan is an amortized loan and will require equal annual payments. What will be the annual payment on this loan?

SUGGESTED READINGS

Brealey, Richard A., Stewart C. Myers, and Alan J. Marcus. *Fundamentals of Corporate Finance*. New York: McGraw-Hill, 1995. Chap. 3.

Brigham, Eugene E. *Fundamentals of Financial Management*, 7e. Hinsdale, IL: The Dryden Press, 1995. Chap. 6.

Keown, Arthur J., David F. Scott Jr., John D. Martin, and J. William Petty. *Foundations of Finance*. Englewood Cliffs, NJ: Prentice-Hall, 1994. Chap. 5.

Marsh, William H. *Basic Financial Management.* Cincinnati: South-Western College Publishing, 1995. Chap. 2.

Peterson, Pamela P. *Financial Management and Analysis.* New York: McGraw-Hill, 1994. Chap. 5.

Pinches, George E. *Essentials of Financial Management,* 3e. New York: Harper & Collins, 1992. Chap. 3.

Ross, Stephen A., Randolph W. Westerfield, and Bradford D. Jordan. *Fundamentals of Corporate Finance,* 3e. Chicago: Irwin, 1995. Chap. 5.

Shao, Stephen P., and Lawrence P. Shao. *Mathematics for Management and Finance,* 6e. Cincinnati: South-Western College Publishing, 1991. Part 3.

ANSWERS TO SELF-TEST QUESTIONS 1. d, 2. a, 3. c, 4. e, 5. d, 6. c, 7. b, 8. d

ANSWERS TO SELF-TEST PROBLEMS

1. First investment now (annuity due problem):
    $100(4.641 × 1.10) = $100(5.105) = $510.50. First investment at end of 1 year (ordinary annuity problem): $100(4.641) = $464.10

2. $20,000 = *PMT* times 3.791, which is the *PVIFA* factor at 10 percent for five years. $20,000/3.791 = $5,275.65 or $5,276 rounded.

CHAPTER 10

Bonds and Stocks:
Characteristics
and Valuations

AFTER STUDYING THIS CHAPTER, YOU SHOULD BE ABLE TO:

- **Identify the major sources of external long-term financing for corporations.**
- **Describe major characteristics of corporate bonds.**
- **Describe major characteristics of common stock.**
- **Describe major characteristics of preferred stock.**
- **Explain how financial securities are valued.**
- **Explain how bonds are valued.**
- **Explain how preferred stocks are valued.**
- **Calculate rates of return.**

financial assets
claims against the
income or assets of indi-
viduals, businesses, and
governments

In Chapter 7, we described ***financial assets*** as claims against the income or assets of individuals, businesses, and governments. Businesses obtain long-term external financial capital either by borrowing or by obtaining equity funds. Long-term borrowing can be privately negotiated or be obtained by issuing debt obligations called bonds. Equity capital may be obtained by finding new partners with financial capital to invest, or through the public markets by issuing shares. This chapter describes the characteristics of bonds and stocks issued by corporations.

Another important issue for business managers and investors is how bonds and stocks are valued or priced. We will apply the time value of money techniques from Chapter 9 to see how this is done. Finally, we will learn how to calculate rates of return—both holding-period returns and annualized rates of return.

LONG-TERM EXTERNAL FINANCING SOURCES FOR BUSINESSES

Businesses obtain long-term financing from internal funds, which are generated from profits, and external funds, obtained from capital markets. Some firms will have little need for external funds. They may be able to generate sufficient internal funds to satisfy their need for capital, or they may require little investment in fixed assets (for example, firms operating in service industries). Other businesses, such as high technology firms that experience rapid growth, cannot generate enough internal funds for their capital needs and may be forced to seek financing often from the capital markets.

The proportion of internal to external financing varies over the business cycle. During periods of economic expansion, firms usually rely more on external funds. This is because the funds need for investment opportunities outstrip the firms' ability to finance them internally. During periods of economic contraction the reverse is true. As profitable investment opportunities become fewer, the rate of investment is reduced and reliance on external capital markets decreases.

Long-term funds are obtained by issuing corporate bonds and stocks. Table 10.1 shows that the total of new security issues amounted to more than $765 billion in 1993 and $580 billion in 1994. Most of the annual funds raised from security issues come from corporate bond sales. In fact, corporate bonds accounted for approximately 84 percent of total new security issues from 1991 to 1994. Firms issue more bonds than equities for two basic reasons. First, as we will see in Chapter 18, it is cheaper to borrow than to raise equity financing. Second, bonds and other loans have a maturity date, when they expire or come due; at times, new bonds are sold to repay maturing ones. Equity, on the other hand, never matures.

Table 10.1 further shows that corporations annually raise approximately three-fourths of their long-term debt funds by selling their bonds through public issues in the United States. The second important method of raising long-term debt funds is through private sales or placements in the United States. Public security sales are offered for sale to all investors, must be approved by the Securities and Exchange Commission (SEC), and are accompanied by public disclosure of the firm's financial statements and other information. Private placements are sold to specific qualified investors and do not go through SEC scrutiny, nor do they require public disclosure of company information. U.S. firms may also raise funds overseas. Although usually less than 10 percent of the annual bond sales by U.S. cor-

TABLE 10.1   Total New Security Issues (in Billions of Dollars)

	1991		1992		1993		1994	
	Amount	Percent	Amount	Percent	Amount	Percent	Amount	Percent
New Security Issues								
Corporate Bonds	$389.8	83.8%	$471.5	83.1%	$642.5	83.9%	$497.4	85.4%
Corporate Stocks	75.4	16.2	96.1	16.9	123.0	16.1	85.1	14.6
Total	**$465.2**	**100.0%**	**$567.6**	**100.0%**	**$765.5**	**100.0%**	**$582.6**	**100.0%**
Bonds by Type of Offering								
Public, domestic	$286.9	73.6%	$378.1	80.2%	$487.9	75.9%	$365.1	73.4%
Private Placement, domestic	74.9	19.2	65.9	14.0	116.2	18.1	76.1	15.3
Sold Abroad	28.0	7.2	27.6	5.8	38.4	6.0	56.2	11.3
Total	**$389.8**	**100.0%**	**$471.5**	**100.0%**	**$642.5**	**100.0%**	**$497.4**	**100.0%**
Stocks by Type of Offering								
Preferred	$ 17.1	22.7%	$ 21.3	22.2%	$ 20.5	16.6%	$ 12.5	14.7%
Common	48.2	63.9	57.1	59.4	90.6	73.7	47.8	56.2
Private Placement	10.1	13.4	17.6	18.3	11.9	9.7	24.8	29.1
Total	**$ 75.4**	**100.0%**	**$ 96.1**	**100.0%**	**$123.0**	**100.0%**	**$ 85.1**	**100.0%**

Source: *Federal Reserve Bulletin* (March 1996): A34.

porations are made in foreign markets, this percentage is increasing over time. There are three reasons why more and more firms are raising funds outside of the United States. First, if they have overseas plants or factories, it may make financial sense to raise funds in the country in which the plant is built. Second, financing costs such as interest rates are sometimes lower overseas. Third, if securities are issued outside of the United States, the issuer avoids the costly and time-consuming SEC approval process.

Table 10.1 also shows that the predominant type of stock offering is in the form of common stock sold to the public. Over the 1991–94 time frame, common stock issued slightly over 60 percent of all equity sales.

DEBT CAPITAL

Holders of debt capital have certain rights and privileges not enjoyed by the holders of equity capital (common or preferred stock) in a corporation. A debt holder may force the firm to abide by the terms of the debt contract even if the result is reorganization or dissolution of the firm. The periodic interest payments due the holders of debt securities must be paid or else the creditors can force the firm into bankruptcy. In the event of liquidation, claims of debt holders are paid or settled first; claims of equity holders are settled last.

Offsetting the advantages of owning debt is its lower return. The interest payments creditors receive usually are considerably less over a period of years than the returns received by equity holders. Also, as long as the corporation meets its contractual obligations, the creditors have little voice in its management and control, except for those formal agreements and restrictions that are stated in the loan contract.

Long-term corporate debt securities fall into two categories: secured obligations and unsecured obligations. A single firm can have many types of debt contracts outstanding. Although ownership of many shares of stock may be evidenced by a single stock certificate, the bondholder has a separate security for each bond owned. Bonds can be either registered or bearer bonds. Bonds currently issued in the United States are **registered bonds,** in that the bondholders' names are known to the issuer and interest payments are sent directly to the bondholder. **Bearer bonds** have coupons that are literally "clipped" and presented, like a check, to a bank for payment. Thus, the bond issuer does not know who is receiving the interest payments. Bearer bonds are more prevalent outside of the United States. Regulations prevent their issuance in the United States, primarily because unscrupulous investors may evade income taxes on the clipped coupons.

Except for (rarely issued) perpetuities, all debt issues have maturity dates when issuers are obligated to repay principal amounts to bondholders. (These amounts are also called the denomination, **par value,** or **face value;** in the United States par value is usually $1,000 for corporate bonds.) All but zero-coupon issues pay interest, called **coupon payments.** As all bonds represent borrowing-lending agreements, bondholders have the legal status as creditors, not owners, of the firm. As such, they have priority claims on the firm's cash flows and assets. The debt holder's priority claim means that they must receive their interest payments before the firm's owners receive their dividends. In case of bankruptcy, the debt holders must receive the funds owed them before funds are distributed to the firm's owners.

BOND COVENANTS

The **trust indenture** is an extensive document and includes in great detail the various provisions and covenants of the loan arrangement. A **trustee** represents the bondholders to ensure the indenture's provisions are respected by the bond issuer. In essence, the indenture is a contract between the bondholders and the issuing firm. The indenture details the par value of the issue, its maturity date, and coupon rate. A bond indenture may also include **covenants,** which can impose restrictions or extra duties on the firm.

Positive covenants require the issuer to take certain actions. *Negative,* or *restrictive, covenants* restrict or limit the actions the firm can take. The trustee ensures that the issuer observe any bond covenants. If the issuer violates a covenant, the issue is technically in default and the trustee can pursue a legal remedy in court, including immediate repayment of the bond's face value.

registered bonds
the issuer knows the names of the bondholders and the interest payments are sent directly to the bondholder

bearer bonds
have coupons that are literally "clipped" and presented, like a check, to the bank for payment. The bond issuer does not know who is receiving the interest payments

par value (face value)
principal amount that the issuer is obligated to repay at maturity

coupon payments
interest payments paid to the bondholders

trust indenture
contract that lists the various provisions and covenants of the loan arrangement

trustee
individual or organization that represents the bondholders to ensure the indenture's provisions are respected by the bond issuer

covenants
impose additional restrictions or duties on the firm

Examples of positive covenants include stipulations that the firm must maintain a minimum level of net working capital, keep pledged assets in good working order, and send audited financial statements to bondholders. Examples of negative covenants include restrictions on the amount of the firm's debt, its dividend payments, the amount and type of additional covenants it may undertake, and asset sales.

These examples illustrate the purpose of covenants: to protect the bondholders' stake in the firm. Bonds have value, first, because of the firm's ability to pay coupon interest and, second, because of the value of the assets or collateral backing the bonds in case of default. Without proper covenant protection, the value of a bond can decline sharply if a firm's liquidity and assets depreciate or if its debt grows disproportionately to its equity. These provisions affect the bond rating (discussed below) of the issue and the firm's financing costs, since bonds giving greater protection to the investor can be sold with lower coupon rates. The firm must decide if the restrictions and duties in the covenants are worth the access to lower cost funds.

Covenants are important to bondholders. Holders of RJR-Nabisco bonds owned high quality, A-rated bonds prior to the firm's takeover in 1988 by a leveraged buyout. After the buyout, large quantities of new debt were issued; RJR-Nabisco's original bonds were given a lower rating and fell by 17 percent in value. Lawsuits by disgruntled bondholders against the takeover were unfruitful. The courts decided that the bondholders should have sought protection against such increases in the firm's debt load by seeking appropriate covenant language before investing, rather than running to the courts after the fact to correct their mistake. Covenants are the best way for bondholders to protect themselves against dubious management actions or decisions.

BOND RATINGS

bond rating
assesses both the collateral underlying the bonds as well as the ability of the issuer to make timely payments of interest and principal

Most bond issuers purchase **bond ratings** from one or more agencies such as Standard & Poor's (S&P), Moody's, Fitch, and Duff and Phelps. For a one-time fee of about $25,000, the rater examines the credit quality of the firm (e.g., its ability to pay the promised coupon interest), the indenture provisions, covenants, and the expected trends of firm and industry operations. From its analysis and discussions with management, the agency assigns a bond rating, as shown in Table 10.2. which indicates the likelihood of default (nonpayment of coupon or par value, or violation of the bond indenture) on the bond issue.[1] In addition, the rating agency commits to continually reexamine the issue's risk. For example, should the financial position of the firm weaken or improve, S&P may place the issue on its

---

1. For a review of S&P's rating process, see G. Hessol, "Financial Management and Credit Ratings," *Midland Corporate Finance Journal* (Fall 1985): 49–52.

TABLE 10.2 Examples of Bond Rating Categories

MOODY'S	STANDARD & POOR'S	DUFF & PHELPS	
Aaa	AAA	1	Best quality, least credit risk
Aa1	AA+	2	High quality, slightly more risk
Aa2	AA	3	than a top-rated bond
Aa3	AA−	4	
A1	A+	5	Upper-medium grade, possible future
A2	A	6	credit quality difficulties
A3	A−	7	
Baa1	BBB+	8	Medium quality bonds
Baa2	BBB	9	
Baa3	BBB−	10	
Ba1	BB+	11	Speculative issues, greater
Ba2	BB	12	credit risk
Ba3	BB−	13	
B1	B+	14	Very speculative, likelihood of
B2	B		future default
B3	B−		
Caa	CCC		Highly speculative, either in default
Ca	CC		or high likelihood of going into
C	C		default
	D		

Credit Watch list with negative or positive implications. Shortly thereafter, S&P will either downgrade, upgrade, or reaffirm the original rating.

Despite the initial cost and the issuer's concern of a lower-than-expected rating, a bond rating makes it much easier to sell the bonds to the public. The rating acts as a signal to the market that an independent agency has examined the qualities of the issuer and the bond issue and has determined that the credit risk of the bond issue justifies the published rating. An unrated bond issue will likely obtain a cool reception from investors. Investors may have good reason to wonder, "What is the firm trying to hide? If this really was an attractive bond issue, the firm would have had it rated." In addition, certain types of investors, such as pension funds and insurance companies, may face restrictions against purchasing unrated public debt.

A bond's security or collateral provisions (discussed below) affect its credit rating. Bonds with junior or unsecured claims receive lower bond ratings, leading investors to demand higher yields to compensate for the higher risk. Thus bond issues of a single firm can have different bond ratings if their security provisions differ.

In addition to its traditional credit quality ratings, Standard & Poor's has also instituted "r" ratings. An "r" appended to an issue's credit quality rating (such as AAAr or AAr) signifies that the price volatility of the issue is expected to be especially high. Such may be the case when bonds have special provisions that make their prices especially sensitive to interest rate, commodity, or exchange rate trends.

BONDHOLDER SECURITY

collateralized bonds
pledge securities to protect the bondholders against loss in case of default

Collateralized bonds pledge securities to protect bondholders against loss in case of default. An example of collateralized bonds are collateralized mortgage obligations (CMOs) sold by firms and agencies involved in the housing market. The CMO is backed by a pool of mortgages. Other examples of collateralized bonds include bonds backed by credit card receivables issued by banks and bonds backed by car loans issued by the finance subsidiaries of car manufacturers. The issuer pays interest and principal on such a collateralized bond over time as homeowners, credit card users, and car buyers pay off their own loans.

mortgage bonds
backed or secured by specifically pledged property of a firm (real estate, buildings, and other assets classified as real property)

Mortgage bonds, despite their name, are not secured by home mortgages! Rather, they are backed or secured by specifically pledged property of a firm. As a rule, the mortgage applies only to real estate, buildings, and other assets classified as real property. For a corporation that issues bonds to expand its plant facilities, the mortgage usually includes only a lien, or legal claim, on the facilities to be constructed.

equipment trust certificate
gives the bondholder a claim to specific "rolling stock"(movable assets) such as railroad cars or airplanes

When a parcel of real estate has more than one mortgage lien against it, the first mortgage filed for recording at the appropriate government office, generally the county recorder's office, has priority. The bonds outstanding against the mortgage are known as *first mortgage bonds.* The bonds outstanding against all mortgages subsequently recorded are known by the order in which they are filed, such as second or third mortgage bonds. Because first mortgage bonds have priority with respect to asset distribution if the business fails, they generally provide a lower yield to investors than the later liens. An **equipment trust certificate** gives the bondholder a claim to specific "rolling stock" (movable assets) such as railroad cars or airplanes. The serial numbers of the specific items of rolling stock are listed in the bond indenture and the collateral is periodically examined by the trustee to ensure its proper maintenance and repair.

closed-end mortgage bond
does not permit future bond issues to be secured by any of the assets pledged as security to it

open-end mortgage bond
allows the same assets to be used as security in future issues

There are two basic types of mortgage bonds. A **closed-end mortgage bond** does not permit future bond issues to be secured by any of the assets pledged as security under the closed-end issue. Alternatively, an **open-end mortgage bond** is one that allows the same assets to be used as security in future issues. As a rule, open-end mortgages usually stipulate that any additional real property acquired by the company automatically becomes a part of the property secured under the mortgage.

debenture bonds
unsecured obligations that depend on the general credit strength of the corporation for their security

Debenture bonds are unsecured obligations and depend on the general credit strength of the corporation for their security. They represent no specific pledge of property; their holders are classed as general creditors of the corporation equal with the holders of promissory notes and trade creditors. Debenture bonds are used by governmental bodies and by many industrial and utility corporations. The riskiest type of bond is a **subordinated debenture.** As the name implies, the claims of these bondholders are subordinate, or junior, to the claims of debenture holders. Most bonds with low bond ratings, sometimes called *junk bonds,* or *high-yield bonds,* are subordinated debentures.

OTHER BOND FEATURES

A **convertible bond** can be changed or converted, at the investor's option, into a specified number of shares of the issuer's common stock (defined as the bond's **conversion ratio**). The conversion ratio is set initially to make conversion unattractive. If the firm meets with success, however, its stock price will rise and the bond's price will be affected by its **conversion value** (the stock price times the conversion ratio) rather than just its value as a straight bond. For example, suppose a firm has just issued a $1,000 par value convertible bond. Its conversion ratio is 30 and the stock currently sells for $25 a share. The conversion value of the bond is 30 × $25/share or $750. It makes sense to hold onto the bond rather than convert a bond with a purchase price of about $1,000 into stock that is worth only $750. Should the stock's price rise to $40, the bond's conversion value will be 30 × $40/share or $1,200. Now it may be appropriate for an investor to convert his bond into the more valuable shares.

Callable bonds can be redeemed prior to maturity by the firm. Such bonds will be called and redeemed if, for example, a decline in interest rates makes it attractive for the firm to issue lower coupon debt to replace high-coupon debt. A firm with cash from successful marketing efforts or a recent stock issue also may decide to retire its callable debt.

Most indentures state that, if called, callable bonds must be redeemed at their **call prices,** typically par value plus a *call premium* of one year's interest. Thus, to call a 12 percent coupon, $1,000 par value bond, an issuer must pay the bondholder $1,120.

Investors in callable bonds are said to be subject to **call risk.** Despite receiving the call price, investors are usually not pleased when their bonds are called away. As bonds are typically called after a substantial decline in interest rates, the call eliminates their high coupon payments; investors will have to reinvest the proceeds in bonds that offer lower yields.

In order to attract investors, callable bonds must offer higher coupons or yields than noncallable bonds of similar credit quality and maturity. Many indentures specify a **call deferment period** immediately after the bond issue during which the bonds cannot be called.

Putable bonds (sometimes called **retractable bonds**) allow investors to force the issuer to redeem them prior to maturity. Indenture terms differ as to the circumstances when an investor can "put" the bond to the issuer

---

subordinated debenture
claims of these bonds are subordinate or junior to the claims of the debenture holders

convertible bond
can be changed or converted, at the investor's option, into a specified number of shares of the issuer's common stock

conversion ratio
number of shares into which a convertible bond can be converted

conversion value
stock price times the conversion ratio

callable bonds
can be redeemed prior to maturity by the issuing firm

call price
price paid to the investor for redemption prior to maturity, typically par value plus a call premium of one year's interest

call risk
risk of having a bond called away and reinvesting the proceeds at a lower interest rate

call deferment period
specified period of time after the issue during which the bonds cannot be called

putable bonds (retractable bonds)
allow the investor to force the issuer to redeem the bonds prior to maturity

prior to the maturity date and receive its par value. Some bond issues can be put only on certain dates. Some can be put to the issuer in case of a bond rating downgrade. The put option allows the investor to receive the full face value of the bond, plus accrued interest. Since this protection is valuable, investors must pay extra for it. Issuers can lower their debt costs by attaching put provisions to their bond issues.

Extendable notes have their coupons reset every two or three years to reflect the current interest rate environment and any changes in the firm's credit quality. At each reset, the investor may accept the new coupon rate (and thus effectively extend the maturity of the investment) or put the bonds back to the firm.

An indenture may require the firm to retire the bond issue over time through payments to a **sinking fund.** A sinking fund requires the issuer to retire specified portions of the bond issue over time. This provides for an orderly and steady retirement of debt over time. Sinking funds are more common in bonds issued by firms with lower credit ratings. A higher quality issuer may have only a small annual sinking fund obligation due to a perceived ability to repay investor's principal at maturity.

GLOBAL BOND MARKET

Many U.S. corporations have issued Eurodollar bonds. **Eurodollar bonds** are dollar-denominated bonds that are sold outside the United States. Because of this, they escape review by the SEC, somewhat reducing the expense of issuing the bonds. Eurodollar bonds usually have fixed coupons with annual coupon payments. Most mature in five to ten years, so they are not attractive for firms that want to issue long-term debt. Most Eurodollar bonds are debentures. This is not a major concern to investors, as only the largest, financially strongest firms have access to the Eurobond market. Investors *do* care that the bonds are sold in bearer form, because investors can remain anonymous and evade taxes on coupon income. Some researchers believe that this is the main reason that Eurodollar bond interest rates are low relative to U.S. rates.[2]

U.S. firms aren't the only issuers of securities outside their national borders. For example, foreign firms can issue securities in the United States if they follow U.S. security registration procedures. **Yankee bonds** are U.S. dollar-denominated bonds that are issued in the United States by a foreign issuer. Some issuers find the longer maturities of Yankees attractive to meet long-term financing needs. While Eurodollar bonds typically mature in five to ten years, Yankees may have maturities as long as 30 years. Japanese firms often find it necessary to issue bonds outside their national

extendable notes
have their coupons reset every two or three years to reflect the current interest rate environment and any changes in the firm's creditworthiness. The investor can accept the new coupon rate or put the bonds back to the firm

sinking fund
requirement that the firm retire specific portions of the bond issue over time

Eurodollar bonds
dollar denominated bonds sold outside the United States

Yankee bonds
dollar denominated bonds issued in the United States by a foreign issuer

2.   W. Marr and J. Trimble, "The Persistent Borrowing Advantage of Eurodollar Bonds: A Plausible Explanation," *Journal of Applied Corporate Finance* (Summer 1988): 65–70.

borders. Regulations and a requirement for mandatory bank guarantees on publicly traded debt in Japan limit the market for Japanese domestic debt issues to only the largest, blue-chip firms.

Increasingly, the international bond market is ignoring national boundaries. A growing number of debt issues are being sold globally. In 1989, the World Bank was the first issuer of **global bonds;** in 1993, over $15 billion of global bonds were issued. Global bonds usually are denominated in U.S. dollars. As they are marketed globally, their offering sizes typically exceed $1 billion. In addition to the World Bank, issuers include the governments of Finland and Italy and corporations such as Matsushita Electric Industrial Co., Citicorp, First Chicago Corp., and Korea Electric Power Co.

global bonds
generally denominated in U.S. dollars and marketed globally

READING BOND QUOTES

Figure 10.1 shows part of the bond quotation listings from the Monday, September 25, 1995, edition of *The Wall Street Journal.* The exhibit highlights a bond quote for a bond issued by AMR Corporation. This listing refers to trading that occurred on the previous business day, Friday, September 22, 1995.

The AMR bond has a coupon rate of 9 percent, indicated in the quotation as "9s." Like most corporate bonds, the AMR issue has a par value of $1,000, so it pays interest of $90 per year. The bond matures (that is, the principal repayment comes due) in 2016, indicated by "16" in the quotation. The column headed "Close" reports the closing price of the bond, expressed as a percentage of par value. Since its par value is $1,000, the closing price of 106 3/8 gives a value for the bond of $1,063.75.

The current yield of the bond appears in the column headed "Cur Yld." This is calculated as the annual coupon interest divided by the current price. The AMR bond's current yield is $90/$1,063.75 = 8.46 percent, or 8.5 percent (the listings allow only one decimal place). The current yield does not adequately represent the return on a bond investment. The total return on a bond includes coupon income plus any gains or losses due to price changes; we explain this concept of *yield to maturity* later in the chapter.

The "Vol" column represents actual bond trading volume; only five bonds from this AMR issue changed hands on September 22, 1995. The

FIGURE 10.1   Sample Bond Quotation

Bond	Cur Yld	Vol	Close	Net Chg
AMR9s16	8.5	5	106⅜	−1

Source: Reprinted from *The Wall Street Journal* (September 25, 1995): C16. Reprinted by permission of *The Wall Street Journal,* ©1995 Dow Jones & Company, Inc. All Rights Reserved Worldwide.

"Net Chg" column gives the bond's change in price, in percentage points, from the previous day's close. As the price fell 1 point, it must have closed on September 21, 1995 at 107 3/8, or $1,073.75.

CORPORATE EQUITY CAPITAL

corporate equity capital
financial capital sup-
plied by the owners of
a corporation

stock certificate
certificate showing an
ownership claim of a
specific company

Corporate equity capital is the financial capital supplied by the owners of a corporation. This ownership claim is represented by the ***stock certificate,*** as shown in Figure 10.2. The stock certificate shows the type of stock held by the owner, the name of the company, the name of the stock's owner, and the signatures of certain company officers. Stock certificates generally are issued for 100 shares or multiples thereof. The stock certificate also has a space on the reverse for its assignment in the event that it is transferred to another person. As a protection against forgery, all signatures on transferred stock certificates usually are certified by a commercial bank's representative or a stock broker.

When a stockholder sells his or her shares, the assigned stock certificate is forwarded to the company by the broker, and it is destroyed by the secretary of the corporation. A new certificate is issued to the new owner,

FIGURE 10.2   Common Stock Certificates

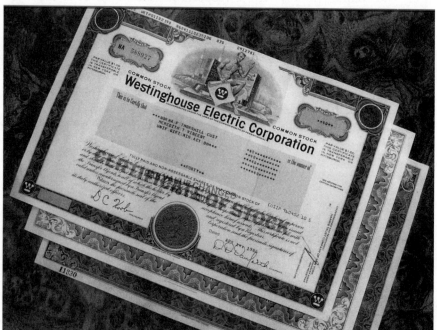

whose name will then be carried on the stock record. For larger corporations an official transfer agent, generally a trust company or a bank, is appointed for this task. The larger corporations may also have an independent stock registrar to supervise the transfer of securities. When an investor sells stock, the stock certificate must be delivered to the stockbroker within three business days (called $T+3$). When stock is purchased, adequate funds must be brought to the broker within three business days.

Stock certificates can be kept in the owner's name and in his or her possession. Many investors find it convenient, however, to keep their stock holdings in **street name.** Stock held in street name is kept in the name of the brokerage house, but the broker's accounting system keeps track of dividends, voting, and so on. Some investors find it convenient to keep shares in street name; there is no need for the investor to safeguard the certificates, and delivery of the certificates within the $T+3$ time frame is automatic.

street name allows stock to be held in the name of the brokerage house

Equity securities of the corporation may be grouped broadly into two classes: common stock and preferred stock. We discuss each below.

COMMON STOCK

Common stock represents ownership shares in a corporation. It is the voting privilege of the common stockholders that governs the selection of the corporation's board of directors. The board of directors, in turn, exercises general control over the firm. In addition to voting for the board, common shareholders may also vote on major issues facing the firm, such as corporate charter changes and mergers.

common stock represents ownership shares in a corporation

The common shareholders have a claim on all business profits that remain after the holders of all other classes of debt and equity securities have received their coupon payments or returns. But the firm may wish to retain some of those profits to reinvest in the firm to finance modernization, expansion, and growth. When so declared by the board of directors, owners of a firm's common stock receive dividend payments. The dividend is typically a cash payment that allows shareholders to receive some income from their investment. To many investors, an attractive characteristic of common stock dividends is their potential to increase over time. As a firm achieves success, its profits should grow and the shareholders can expect to see the dollar amount of their dividends rise. Of course, success and growth are not guaranteed! A firm may experience poor earnings or losses, in which case shareholders bear the risk of smaller dividends or even the elimination of dividend payments until the firm's financial situation improves.

The common stockholders have the lowest standing when a business venture is liquidated or fails. All creditors, bond holders, and preferred stockholders must, as a rule, be paid in full before common stockholders receive proceeds from liquidation. As with dividends, all bankruptcy or liquidation proceeds remaining after prior obligations are settled accrue to the common stockholders. But it is rare when the proceeds of an asset sale from a bankrupt corporation fulfill the claims of creditors and preferred stockholders. Common stockholders generally receive little, if anything, from liquidation proceedings. The common stockholders, therefore, are affected hardest by business failure, just as they enjoy the primary benefits of business success.

par value
stated value of a stock;
accounting and legal
concept bearing no rela-
tionship to a firm's stock
price or book value

The common stock of a corporation may be assigned a ***par value***, or stated value, in the certificate of incorporation. It usually bears little relationship to the current price or book value of the stock. If the corporation sells stock for less than the par value, the owners of the stock may become liable to creditors for the difference between the selling price and the par value if the company fails. Thus the limited liability of the stockholders may be lost.[3]

Common stock may be divided into special groups, generally Class A and Class B, in order to permit the acquisition of additional capital without diluting the control of the business. When a corporation issues two classes of common stock, it will often give voting rights to only one class, generally Class B. Except for voting, owners of Class A stock will usually have most, if not all, of the other rights and privileges of common stockholders. Issuing nonvoting equity securities is opposed by some government agencies, including the Securities and Exchange Commission, because it permits the concentration of ownership control. The New York Stock Exchange refuses to list the common stock of corporations that issue nonvoting classes of common stock. At times, different stock classes are created following an acquisition of one corporation by another. For example, General Motors' Class E shares and Class H shares were issued to help finance GM's acquisition of EDS and Hughes Aircraft, respectively. The dividends on GM's Class E and H shares are related into the earnings of their respective subsidiary.

PREFERRED STOCK

preferred stock
equity security that
has preference, or a
senior claim, to the
firm's earnings and
assets over common
stock

Preferred stock is an equity security that has a preference, or senior claim, to the firm's earnings and assets over common stock. Preferred shareholders must receive their fixed dividend before common shareholders can receive a dividend. In liquidation, the claims of the preferred shareholders are to be satisfied before common shareholders receive any proceeds.

In contrast with common stock, preferred stock generally carries a stated fixed dividend. The dividend is specified as either a percentage of par value or as a fixed number of dollars per year. For example, a preferred

---

3.   This technicality seldom creates any difficulty, however, since most stock is first sold at or above its par value. In addition, legal devices exist to protect against this contingent liability in such instances. Aside from the possibility that stock might be sold at less than its par value, par value has little significance. In fact, most states permit corporations to issue no-par stock which has no contingent liability.

stock may be a 9-percent preferred, meaning that its annual dividend participation is not to exceed 9 percent of its par or stated value. The dividend for no-par preferred stock is stated in terms of a dollar amount, for example, preferred as to dividends in the amount of $9 annually. The holder of preferred stock accepts the limitation on the amount of dividends as a fair exchange for the priority held in the earnings and assets of the company.

Thus, unlike with common stock, the par value of a preferred stock is important: dividends often are expressed as a percentage of par and the par value represents the holder's claim on corporate assets in case of liquidation. Additionally, when shares of preferred stock are first issued, the initial selling price is frequently close to the share's par value.

Because preferred stocks are frequently nonvoting, many corporations issue them as a means of obtaining equity capital without diluting the control of the current stockholders. Unlike debt, the fixed preferred stock dividend is not a tax-deductible expense. A major source of preferred stock issues are regulated public utilities, such as gas and electric companies. For regulated firms, the non-deductibility of dividends is not as much of a concern as for other firms, because the utilities' tax payments affect the rates they are allowed to charge.

For foreign firms to issue preferred stock, they must do so in the United States. The U.S. security markets are the only public financial markets (as of 1995) in which preferred stock can be sold.

Preferred stock may have special features. For example, it may be cumulative or non-cumulative. **Cumulative preferred stock** requires that before dividends on common stock are paid, preferred dividends must be paid not only for the current period but also for all previous periods in which no preferred dividends were paid. It is important to remember that, unlike debt holders, the preferred stockholders cannot force the payment of their dividends. They may have to wait until earnings are adequate to pay dividends. Cumulative preferred stock offers some protection for periods during which dividends are not declared.

Non-cumulative preferred stock, on the other hand, makes no provision for the accumulation of unpaid dividends. The result may be that management may be tempted to declare preferred dividends only when it appears that sufficient earnings are available to pay common stock dividends as well. Practically all modern preferred stock is cumulative.

Callable preferred stock gives the corporation the right to retire the preferred stock at its option. **Convertible preferred stock** has a special provision that makes it possible to convert it to common stock of the corporation, generally at the stockholder's option. This, like many of the special features that preferred stock may have, exists primarily to attract investors to buy securities at times when distribution would otherwise be difficult. Preferred stock that is both cumulative and convertible is a popular financing choice for investors purchasing shares of stock in small firms with high growth potential.

cumulative preferred stock requires that before dividends on common stock are paid, preferred dividends must be paid not only for the current period but also for all previous periods in which preferred dividends were missed

non-cumulative preferred stock makes no provision for the accumulation of past missed dividends

callable preferred stock gives the corporation the right to retire the preferred stock at its option

convertible preferred stock has special provision that makes it possible to convert it to common stock of the corporation, generally at the stockholder's option

The one tax advantage of preferred stock goes to corporate investors who purchase another firm's preferred. When one corporation buys stock of another firm, 70 percent of the dividend income received by the corporation is exempt from taxes. Thus, for every $100 of dividend income, only $30 is taxable to an investing corporation.

READING STOCK QUOTES

Figure 10.3 shows part of the stock quotations from the Monday, September 25, 1995, edition of *The Wall Street Journal.* The exhibit highlights the price quote for AFLAC's stock. The information in the quote reflects trading that occurred on the previous business day, Friday, September 22, 1995. Besides stock prices, the quote gives information about recent trends or volatility in prices, the dividend paid by the company, and its earnings per share.

The first two columns present AFLAC's high and low stock prices for the previous 52 weeks. The wide range (the high price is about 40 percent higher than the low price) is not uncommon. Review for yourself the 52-week ranges of different stocks from a current issue of *The Wall Street Journal.*

The fourth column gives AFLAC's trading symbol, an abbreviation of three letters or less that identifies reports of all transactions in AFLAC stock on the stock market for the day. The fifth column lists the latest 12-month dividend paid by the firm; AFLAC had paid $0.52 per share in dividends to its owners in the previous year.

The sixth column gives the dividend yield of the stock. The dividend yield is calculated as the stock's annual dividend divided by its current price, identified in the column labeled "Close." Since the current price is 41 1/8, the dividend yield is $0.520/$41 1/8, or 1.26 percent; this becomes 1.3 percent as the stock listings allow for only one decimal place. The closing price of 41 1/8 means that the last trade of the day took place at a price of $41 1/8 per share. By convention, share prices are quoted in eighths of a point. One point equals $1, so the minimum movement in price between trades is 1/8 of a point, or $0.125.

The column labeled PE gives the price/earnings ratio of the stock. This value is computed by dividing the firm's latest annual earnings per share into its current stock price. Stock listings report only integer values of P/E

FIGURE 10.3   Selected NYSE Stock Transactions

52 weeks							Yld		Vol			Net
Hi	Lo	Stock	Sym	Div	%	PE	100s	Hi	Lo	Close	chg
44¾	31⅝	AFLAC	AFL	.52	1.3	13	1006	41⅛	40¾	41⅛	...

Source: Reprinted from *The Wall Street Journal* (September 25, 1995): C3. Reprinted by permission of *The Wall Street Journal,* ©1995 Dow Jones & Company, Inc. All Rights Reserved Worldwide.

ratios, so AFLAC's reported P/E ratio of 13 means the actual P/E may range from 12.50 to 13.49.

From the closing price and the P/E ratio given in the stock listings, we can compute an approximation of AFLAC's earnings per share:

Price/EPS = 13 = ($41 1/8)/EPS; EPS = $3.16

The column headed "Vol 100s" tells how many shares of AFLAC stock were traded, in hundreds. On the day of the quote 100,600 shares changed

---

U.S. TREASURY CHANGES ITS DEBT FINANCING STRATEGY

In early 1993, the yield of 7.1 percent on the 30-year Treasury bond was the lowest since the government resumed selling such bonds in the late 1970s. But at the same time, the three-month Treasury bill was yielding only 3 percent. Officials in the U.S. Treasury Department, seeking ways to lower the borrowing costs of the federal debt, decided to reduce sales of long-term bonds in favor of the lower interest T-bills. Officials estimated that borrowing more heavily in the short-term market could save $11.5 billion in interest expense over four years. Although short-term rates are typically lower than long-term interest rates, they are also more volatile and subject to sharper increases and decreases than longer-term rates.

Throughout the early 1990s, but especially in 1992 and 1993, corporations rushed to issue long-term bonds to take advantage of low long-term interest rates. Corporate America was deciding it was more prudent to lock in low long-term financing costs rather than take a chance with lower, but potentially volatile, short-term rates. Usually, the longest maturity for a newly issued bond is 30 years, but the lowest long-term rates in a generation tempted issuers to lock in low long-term financing rates. Low rates also led investors to seek higher yields by seeking longer maturity investments. Boeing, Tennessee Valley Authority, and other firms responded by issuing 50-year bonds. Several firms, including Disney, ABN AMRO Holding NV (a Netherlands bank), BellSouth, Columbia/HCA Healthcare, and Coca-Cola even issued 100-year bonds! Yield-hungry investors quickly bought the higher-coupon issues in the primary market.

The U.S. Treasury's actions were exactly the opposite of the wisdom of Corporate America. Who was right? Only time will tell.

Source: Constance Mitchell and Thomas T. Vogel, Jr., "U.S. Plan to Cut Long-Term Bond Sales May Be Costly if Short-Term Rates Jump," *The Wall Street Journal* (February 18, 1993): C1, C14; David R. Kotok, "Shorten Treasurys' Maturities? How Short-Sighted," *The Wall Street Journal* (April 13, 1993): A13; Anonymous, "Treasury's Borrowing Plan Is Backed by Budget Office," *The Wall Street Journal* (January 27, 1995); Fred Vogelstein, "BellSouth Unit's 100-Year Issue Underscores Belief That Long-Term Rates Have Hit Bottom," *The Wall Street Journal* (November 29, 1995): C20.

hands. The high and low prices during the day were 41 1/8 and 40 3/4, respectively; as mentioned earlier, the closing price was 41 1/8; the closing price in this case was also the high. The final column, "Net Chg," gives the change in price from the previous day's close. The dots (...) indicate that the closing price was unchanged from the previous trading day; this means the closing price on Thursday, September 21, 1995, was also 41 1/8.

Dots (...) will appear in the dividend yield column for some stocks. This indicates that the firms did not pay dividends in the previous 12 months. Lack of a number under the PE column indicates a firm with a negative net income.

This section discussed the basic characteristics of debt and equity securities. The following section applies the Chapter 9 time value of money principles to debt and equity expected cash flows. The process of valuation is important to business managers considering ways to issue securities as well as to investors who must make security buy and sell decisions.

VALUATION PRINCIPLES

All securities are valued on the basis of the cash inflows that they are expected to provide to their owners or investors. We can express this security price in general terms as follows:

$$\text{price} = f(\text{CF}_1, \text{CF}_2, ... \text{CF}_n)$$

where price is a function of the cash flows (CF) expected in the future (i.e., periods one through n). However, since these cash flows occur over time, we also need to apply some of the time value of money concepts learned in Chapter 9. Thus, our general model is restated as:

$$\text{price} = \frac{\text{CF}_1}{(1+r)^1} + \frac{\text{CF}_2}{(1+r)^2} + ... + \frac{\text{CF}_n}{(1+r)^n} \tag{10.1}$$

or,

$$\text{price} = \sum_{t=1}^{n} \frac{\text{CF}_t}{(1+r)^t} \tag{10.1a}$$

that is, value or current price should equal the present value of expected future cash flows. Recall from Chapters 8 and 9 that the r represents the appropriate discount rate or the rate of return required by investors. For securities with no default risk such as Treasury bonds, the r reflects only the time value of money as measured by the risk-free interest rate. For securities with default risk such as the bonds and stocks issued by corporations, the r represents a risk-free rate plus a premium to reflect default risk.

For illustration purposes, let's assume that a security is expected to pay its owner $100 per year for five years. Let's also assume that investors expect a 10 percent annual compound rate of return on this investment. The 10 percent rate is based on a risk-free rate of 6 percent plus a 4 percent default risk premium. Now let's ask: what is the security's current or present value?

The answer can be determined by using present value tables, a financial calculator, or a computer software program. For example, using Table 2 (Present Value of $1) in the book's appendix, we can identify the appropriate present value interest factors (PVIF) at 10 percent as follows:

YEAR	CASH FLOW	×	PVIF @ 10%	=	PRESENT VALUE
1	$100		0.909		$ 90.90
2	100		0.826		82.60
3	100		0.751		75.10
4	100		0.683		68.30
5	100		0.621		62.10
				price =	$379.00

Thus, the current or present value of the security at a 10 percent discount rate should be $379.

Of course, since the security's cash flow reflects a $100 five-year annuity, we could have used Table 4 (Present Value of a $1 Ordinary Annuity) in the book's appendix to determine the security's present value as follows:

price = cash flow annuity × PVIFA @ 10%
     = $100 × 3.791
     = $379.10

where PVIFA refers to the present value interest factor of an annuity. Notice that there is a slight rounding error due to the use of three-digit tables.

The security's present value also can be determined by using a financial calculator as follows. First, clear the calculator's memory. Next, enter 100 (or −100 depending on the calculator) using the annuity or payments (PMT) key. Then, enter 10 and press the %*i* key and enter 5 and press the N key. Finally, press the compute (CPT) key followed by the present value (PV) key to calculate the security's current value of $379.08.

Financial Calculator Solution:

Inputs	5	10	−100
	N	%*i*	PMT

Press   CPT PV
Solution 379.08

Now we are ready to determine the values of bonds and stocks. To do so requires that we understand the differences in cash flow patterns produced by these securities. We first begin with how to value bonds since conceptually the valuation concept is similar to many of the present value examples covered in Chapter 9.

VALUATION OF BONDS

Corporate and government bonds usually provide for periodic payments of interest plus the return of the amount borrowed or par value when the bond matures. Equation 10.1 can be modified to incorporate these bond cash flows.

DETERMINING A BOND'S PRESENT VALUE

The value of a bond with annual coupon payments can be expressed as follows:

price = PV (expected future cash flows)
      = PV (coupon payments) + PV (principal)

$$\text{price} = \frac{C_1}{(1+r_b)^1} + \frac{C_2}{(1+r_b)^2} + \dots + \frac{C_n}{(1+r_b)^n} + \frac{\text{Par}_n}{(1+r_b)^n} \qquad (10.2)$$

$$= \sum_{t=1}^{n} \frac{C_t}{(1+r_b)^t} + \frac{\text{Par}_n}{(1+r_b)^n} \qquad (10.2a)$$

where price is the bond's value now or in period zero, C is the annual dollar amount of interest, Par is the return of the bond's principal amount, and r_b is the rate of return required by investors on this quality or risk-class of bonds, given its bond rating.

In words, to compute a bond's price we first find the present value of the bond's expected coupon payments. Second, we compute the present value of the bond's principal payment. Third, we add these two present values together to find the bond's price.

Most corporate bonds are issued in $1,000 denominations. To illustrate how a corporate bond's value is calculated, let's assume that a bond with $1,000 face value has a stated interest rate of 9 percent and a ten-year life before maturity. Thus an investor will receive $90 ($1,000 × 0.09) at the end of each year in interest and will receive $1,000 at the end of ten years.[4] We determine the bond's present value based on the interest rate required by investors on similar quality bonds. Let's assume investors require a 9 percent rate of return on bonds of similar quality. We then would discount the $90 annuity portion of the bond at the PVIFA at 9 percent for ten years, which is 6.418 (see Table 4 in the book's Appendix). Since the $1,000 principal will be received only at the end of ten years, we use the 0.422 PVIF at 9 percent for ten years from Table 2 in the Appendix.

---

4.   In actual practice, most bonds pay interest semiannually. For example, this bond might pay $45 every six months over the ten years, making a total of 20 payment periods.

Taking these together we have:

90×6.418 = $577.62
$1,000 \times 0.422$ = 422.00
Bond value = $999.62

which rounds to $1,000. Thus the bond is worth $1,000 and will remain so as long as investors receive a 9 percent rate of return.

However, what if investors required a 10 percent return, or yield, on bonds of similar quality? The bond must then fall in price to compensate for the fact that only $90 in annual interest is received by the investor. The appropriate discount factors at 10 percent for ten years from Tables 2 and 4 in the Appendix would be:

90×6.145 = $553.05
$1,000 \times 0.386$ = 386.00
Bond value = $939.05

Thus an investor would be willing to pay only $939 (rounded) for the bond. Although interest remains $90 per year, a new investor would earn a 10 percent return because she or he would pay only $939 now and get back $1,000 at the end of ten years. A bond that sells below par value, such as this one, is said to be selling at a *discount* and is called a **discount bond.** Someone who purchases this discount bond today and holds it to maturity will receive, in addition to the stream of coupon interest payments, a gain of $61, the difference between the bond's price ($939) and its principal repayment ($1,000).

discount bond
bond that is selling below par value

A bond's price will reflect changes in market conditions while it remains outstanding. With its fixed 9 percent coupon rate, this bond will no longer be attractive to investors when alternative investments are yielding 10 percent. The bond's market price will have to fall in order to offer buyers a combined return of 10 percent from the coupon payments and the par value. That is the reason why bond prices change with changes in interest rates.

If investors required less than a 9 percent (e.g., 8 percent) return for bonds of this quality, then the above-described bond would have a value greater than $1,000; if it was selling to yield a return of 8 percent to investors, the bond's price would be $1,066.90, rounded to $1,067 (check this on your own). When a bond's price exceeds its par value, it is selling at a *premium*, and it is called a **premium bond.** The investor who holds the bond until maturity will receive the above-market coupon payments of 9 percent per year, offset by a loss of $67 (the difference between its purchase price and par value). In most cases where the bond sells at a premium, interest rates have fallen after the bond's issue. This bond's 9 percent coupon rate makes it very attractive to investors; buying pressure increases its price until its overall yield matches the stated annual rate of 8 percent.

premium bond
bond that is selling in excess of its par value

CALCULATING THE YIELD TO MATURITY

yield to maturity (YTM)
return on a bond if it is
held to maturity

Many times, rather than compute price, investors want to estimate the return on a bond investment if they hold it until it matures (this is called the **yield to maturity** or **YTM**). Financial calculators and spreadsheet packages such as Lotus, Quattro Pro, or Excel can be used to find exact return. An approximate answer for the yield to maturity can be obtained by using the following formula:

$$\text{Approximate yield to maturity} = \frac{\text{Annual interest} + \dfrac{\text{par} - \text{price}}{\text{No. of years until maturity}}}{\dfrac{\text{par} + \text{price}}{2}} \quad (10.3)$$

The numerator of Equation 10.3 equals the annual coupon interest plus a straight-line amortization of the difference between the current price and par value. It represents an approximation of the annual dollar return the bondholder expects to receive, as over time the bond's value will rise or fall so it equals its par value at maturity. This estimated annual return is divided by the average of the bond's par value and its current price to give us an approximate yield or percentage return if the bond is held until maturity.

From the example above, we know that if the bond can be purchased for $939, it offers investors a 10 percent return. Let's use Equation 10.3 to estimate the approximate yield to maturity if we know the price is $939, annual coupons are $90, and the bond matures in 10 years with a par value of $1,000:

$$\text{Approximate yield to maturity} = \frac{\$90 + \dfrac{\$1000 - \$939}{10}}{\dfrac{\$1000 + \$939}{2}} = \frac{\$90 + \$6.10}{\$969.50}$$

$$= \quad 0.0991 \text{ or } 9.91 \text{ percent.}$$

The approximate answer of 9.91 percent is fairly close to the exact yield to maturity of 10 percent.

Of course, the use of a financial calculator will give us a precise answer for the yield to maturity. We illustrate the calculation process for a ten-year bond paying interest of $90 per year and a $1,000 principal repayment at maturity. First, we assume the bond is currently trading at $1,000. Second, we assume the price to be $939.

Financial Calculator Solution:

$1,000 Current Price:

Inputs	10	1000	90	1000
	N	PV	PMT	FV
Press	CPT	%i		
Solution	9			

A yield to maturity of 9 percent for a bond trading at $1,000 indicates that the current yield of $90/$1,000 or 9 percent is the same as the investors' required rate of return on bonds of comparable quality.

Financial Calculator Solution:

$939 Current Price:

Inputs	10	939	90	1000
	N	PV	PMT	FV

Press   CPT   %i

Solution   9.99

At a current unrounded bond price of $938.55, the yield to maturity would be exactly 10 percent.

SEMI-ANNUAL COUPONS

Thus far, for simplicity, our bond examples have assumed annual coupon payments. In fact, this is how Eurodollar bonds pay interest: one coupon payment per year. In the United States, however, most bonds pay semiannual coupons. That is, one-half of the annual interest is paid every six months.

We know from Chapter 9 that when cash flows occur more frequently than once a year, adjustments must be made to n, the number of periods, and to r, the discount rate. The number of periods n becomes the number of years multiplied by the number of cash flows per year. Usually, a bond's market interest rate or yield to maturity is the same as the effective annual rate we learned about in Chapter 9. To obtain a bond's semiannual interest rate, we will have to use Equation 9.13. To properly discount the semiannual coupons, we must determine the periodic interest rate r that corresponds to the effective annual rate.

Recalling Equation 9.13, we can calculate the effective annual rate as:

$$\text{EAR} = \text{YTM} = (1 + r)^m - 1$$

Rearranging, we can solve for the periodic interest rate r:

$$r = (1 + \text{YTM})^{1/m} - 1$$

If the yield to maturity is given as 10 percent for a bond that makes coupon payments semiannually, the appropriate discount rate is

$(1 + 0.10)^{1/2} - 1 = 0.04881$ or 4.881 percent per period.

Let's illustrate this in an example.

Assuming semiannual coupon payments, let's find the price of our ten-year, 9 percent coupon bond when its yield to maturity is 10 percent. Annual interest payments for this bond are $90, so every six months investors receive interest of $45. The number of periods is 20 (ten years times 2 cash flows per year). Since the yield to maturity is given, the periodic interest rate is

$(1 + 0.10)^{1/2} - 1 = 0.04881$ or 4.881 percent per period

The present value of the coupon annuity is:

$$PV \text{ (Coupon)} = \$45 \times [\text{PVIFA}(4.881 \text{ percent, 20 periods})]$$
$$= \$45 \times 12.589 \text{ (obtained from a calculator)} = \$566.51$$

The present value of the par value is:

$$PV(\text{Par}) = (\$1,000) \times [\text{PVIF}(4.881 \text{ percent, 20 periods})]$$
$$= \$1,000 \times 0.386 = \$386.00$$

Thus, the current market price of the bond should be $566.51 plus $386.00, or $952.51. This is higher than the price of the bond ($939) when coupons were paid annually, because one-half of each year's coupon payments occurs earlier. Since some cash flows arrive sooner, their present value is higher when they are discounted at the same yield to maturity.

It is important to note that the present value of the par value is $386.00 regardless of whether the coupon interest is paid annually or semiannually. When the effective annual rate is 10 percent, $1,000 ten years from now is worth $386.00 in present value terms, regardless of the frequency of the coupon payments.

Given what we know about bonds and our time value of money techniques, the following will be true, if all other influences are kept constant:

- The larger the coupon interest, the higher the bond's price. We've already seen that with a yield to maturity of 9 percent, a ten-year bond that pays annual interest of $90 will have a present value or price of $1,000. A bond which is identical except it has a 10 percent coupon rate will have a price of $100 \times 6.418 + \$1,000 \times 0.422 = \$1,063.80$.
- The more frequent the coupon payments (e.g., semiannually instead of annually), the higher the bond's price, as some cash flows occur sooner in time than they would otherwise. This was illustrated in the semi-annual coupon example above.
- The higher the discount rate or yield to maturity, the lower the price of the bond; the lower the yield to maturity, the higher the bond's price. We have already seen this; when a ten-year bond with a 9 percent coupon paid annually is selling at an 8 percent yield to maturity, its price is $1,067; when it sells at a 9 percent yield to maturity, its price is $1,000. More risky bonds (those with lower bond ratings) will have higher required yields and will sell at lower prices.

RISK IN BOND VALUATION

Basically, investors in domestic bonds face three types of risk: credit risk, interest rate risk, and reinvestment rate risk. Investors in foreign bonds are subject to two additional risks: political risk and exchange rate risk.

Credit Risk

The cash flows to be received by bond market investors are not certain; like individuals, corporate debtors may pay interest payments late or not at all. They may fail to repay principal at maturity. To compensate investors for this **credit risk,** or **default risk,** rates of return on corporate bonds are higher than those on government securities with the same terms to maturity. Government securities are presumed to be free of credit risk. In general, as investors perceive a higher likelihood of default, they demand higher default-risk premiums. Since perceptions of a bond's default risk may change over its term, the bond's yield to maturity may also change, even if all else remains constant. Firms such as Moody's, Standard & Poor's, and Duff and Phelps provide information on the riskiness of individual bond issues through their bond ratings.

credit risk (default risk) the chance of nonpayment or delayed payment of interest or principal

Interest Rate Risk

The general level of interest rates in an economy does not remain fixed, it fluctuates. For example, interest rates will change in response to changes in investors' expectations about future inflation rates. In Figure 10.4 we can see that the "seesaw effect" means that a rise in interest rates renders the fixed coupon interest payments on a bond less attractive, lowering its price. Therefore, bondholders are subject to the risk of capital loss from such interest rate changes should the bonds have to be sold prior to maturity.

A longer term to maturity, all else equal, increases the sensitivity of a bond's price to a given change in interest rates as the discount rate change compounds over a longer time period. Similarly, a lower coupon rate also increases the sensitivity of the bond's price to market interest rate changes. This occurs because lower coupon bonds have most of their cash flow occurring further into the future, when the par value is paid.

Because of **interest rate risk,** investors will demand a larger risk premium for bonds whose price is especially sensitive to market interest rate changes. Hence, we would expect higher yields to maturity for long-term bonds with low coupon rates than for short-term bonds with high coupon rates.

interest rate risk fluctuating interest rates lead to varying asset prices. In the context of bonds, rising (falling) interest rates result in falling (rising) bond prices

FIGURE 10.4
Relationship Between Current Interest Rates and Bond Prices: The Seesaw Effect

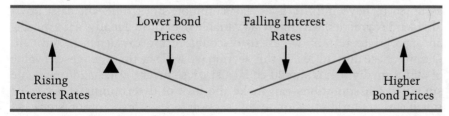

Reinvestment Rate Risk

The return an investor receives from a bond investment equals the bond's yield to maturity only if the coupon payments can be reinvested at a rate equal to the bond's yield to maturity. Recall the form of the interest factor in bond price Equation 10.2: $(1 + r_b)^n$. This assumes that all the cash flows are reinvested at the periodic rate r_b. Should the coupons be reinvested at a lower rate, the investor's actual yield will be less than the bond's yield to maturity. Thus, **reinvestment rate risk,** or **rollover risk,** occurs when fluctuating interest rates cause coupon payments to be reinvested at different interest rates. Another illustration of reinvestment rate risk occurs when maturing bank CDs are rolled over into new CDs. The risk benefits the investor when the new CD rate is higher than the maturing CD rate; it works against the investor when the new CD rate is lower.

Risks of Nondomestic Bonds

Investors in nondomestic securities face a number of risks beyond those of domestic securities. Among these are political risk and exchange rate risk. **Political risk** can affect a bond investor in a number of ways. A foreign government may block currency exchanges, preventing the investor from repatriating coupon income. Social unrest may lead a foreign corporation to default on its bonds. Of course exchange rate changes will cause fluctuations in the values of cash flows in terms of U.S. dollars; this is called **exchange rate risk.**

VALUATION OF STOCKS

The principle for determining an appropriate stock price is the same as that for determining a bond price: find the present value of future expected cash flows. With bonds, this is a relatively straightforward process; the typical corporate bond has a definite life, fixed coupon payments and par value, and a yield to maturity that will be close to that of similarly rated bonds.

IMPORTANCE OF CASH FLOWS FROM DIVIDENDS

Equity offers no such certainty. Common and preferred stocks are generally assumed to have infinite lives. For common stock, relevant cash flows (dividend payments) will likely be variable over time. Finally, determining an appropriate rate at which to discount future dividends is difficult. Despite these difficulties, in this section we will see that the present value of all future dividends should equal a stock's current price, and that some simplifying assumptions can make the task of determining stock value much easier. Our discussion in this section focuses on common stock. As

---

reinvestment rate risk (rollover risk)
fluctuating interest rates cause coupon or interest payments to be reinvested at different interest rates over time

political risk
actions by a sovereign nation to interrupt or change the value of cash flows accruing to foreign investors

exchange rate risk
fluctuating exchange rates lead to varying levels of U.S. dollar-denominated cash flows

we will see, the method for valuing preferred stock is a special case of common stock valuation.

It may seem rather strange to treat the stock price as nothing more than the present value of all future dividends. Who buys stock with no intention of ever selling it, even after retirement? Investors generally buy stock with the intention of selling it at some future time ranging from a few hours to 30 years or longer. Despite the length of any one investor's time horizon, the current price of any dividend-paying common stock should equal the present value of all future dividends:[5]

$$P_0 = \sum_{t=1}^{\infty} \frac{D_t}{(1 + r_s)^t} \qquad (10.4)$$

What if a corporation currently pays no dividends and has no plans to pay dividends in the foreseeable future? The value of this company's stock will not be zero. First, just because the firm has no plans to pay dividends does not mean that it never will. To finance rapid growth, young firms

---

5.   Let the present value, or current market price, of a share of common stock be denoted by P_0. Let $D_1, D_2, \ldots$ be the successive annual dividends and $P_0, P_1, P_2, \ldots$ be the price per share of the stock at the end of each successive year. Suppose that a share of stock is held for one year. At the year's end, after receiving dividend payment D_1, the stockholder could sell the stock for an amount P_1. Then, if future returns are discounted at the required rate of return, r_s, the present value of the investor's cash flows comes to:

$$P_0 = \frac{D_1}{1 + r_s} + \frac{P_1}{1 + r_s}$$

Suppose that someone else purchases the stock at price P_1 at the end of the first year and holds it for one year. The purchase price one year from now should equal:

$$P_1 = \frac{D_2}{1 + r_s} + \frac{P_2}{1 + r_s}$$

Substituting this into the Equation above gives us:

$$P_0 = \frac{D_1}{1 + r_s} + \frac{D_2}{(1 + r_s)^2} + \frac{P_2}{(1 + r_s)^2}$$

Continuing in this way, looking N years into the future, we have:

$$P_0 = \frac{D_1}{1 + r_s} + \frac{D_2}{(1 + r_s)^2} + \cdots + \frac{D_N}{(1 + r_s)^N} + \frac{P_N}{(1 + r_s)^N}$$

If we continue this process indefinitely, the time horizon N becomes infinitely large. In that case, the present value of the price in year N becomes quite small and loses significance compared to the sum of the dividend terms. For all purposes, it can be ignored. Thus, we have the result:

$$P_0 = \sum_{t=1}^{\infty} \frac{D_t}{(1 + r_s)^t}$$

The present value of a share of stock is the sum of all future dividend payments, discounted to the present. It does not depend on the investment horizon of any individual investor.

often retain all their earnings; when they mature, they often begin paying out a portion of earnings as dividends. Second, at the very least, the firm's stock should be worth the per-share liquidation value of its assets.

Estimating all future dividend payments is impractical. Matters can be simplified considerably if we assume that the firm's dividends will remain constant or will grow at a constant rate over time.

VALUING STOCKS WITH CONSTANT DIVIDENDS

If the firm's dividends are expected to remain constant, so that $D_0 = D_1 = D_2 \ldots$, we can treat its stock as a perpetuity. We know that preferred stock dividends are constant over time, so this situation is most applicable for valuing shares of preferred stock. The present value of a perpetuity is the cash flow divided by the discount rate. For stocks with constant dividends, this means Equation 10.4 becomes

$$P_0 = D_0/r_s \tag{10.5}$$

Most preferred stocks are valued using Equation 10.5 since preferred stocks typically pay a constant dollar dividend and do not usually have finite lives or maturities. For example, if the Foo-Yong Corporation's preferred stock currently pays a $2.00 dividend and investors require a 10 percent rate of return on preferred stocks of similar riskiness, the preferred stock's present value is:

$$P_0 = \$2.00/0.10 = \$20.00$$

For a preferred stock with no stated maturity and a constant dividend, changes in price will occur only if the rate of return expected by investors changes.

VALUING STOCKS WITH CONSTANT DIVIDEND GROWTH RATES

Many firms have sales and earnings that increase over time; their dividends may rise, as well. If we assume that a firm's dividends grow at an annual rate of g percent, next year's dividend, D_1, will be $D_0(1+g)$; the dividend in two years' time will be $D_0(1+g)^2$. Generalizing,

$$D_t = D_0 (1 + g)^t$$

Equation 10.4 now can be shown in expanded form as:

$$P_0 = \frac{D_0(1+g)}{(1+r_s)} + \frac{D_1(1+g)^2}{(1+r_s)^2} + \frac{D_0(1+g)^3}{(1+r_s)^3} + \ldots +$$

As long as the dividend growth rate g is less than the discount rate r_s, each future term will be smaller than the preceding term. Although technically there is an infinite number of terms, the present value of dividends received farther and farther into the future become closer and closer to zero. By accepting the fact that the sum of all these terms is finite, Equation 10.4 becomes

$$P_0 = \frac{D_1}{r_s - g} \qquad (10.6)$$

This result is known as the **Gordon Model,** or the **constant dividend growth model.** The model assumes that a dividend is currently being paid and that this dividend will grow or increase at a constant rate over time. Of course, the assumption of constant growth in dividends may not be realistic for a firm that is experiencing a period of high growth (or negative growth, that is, declining revenues). Neither will constant dividend growth be a workable assumption for a firm whose dividends rise and fall over the business cycle.

Gordon Model (constant dividend growth model) a means of estimating common stock prices by assuming constant dividend growth over time

Let's assume that the cash dividend per share for XYZ Company for last year was $1.89 and it is expected to be $2 at the end of this year. This represents a percentage increase of six percent [($2 − $1.89)/$1.89]. If investors expect a 12 percent rate of return, then the estimated current stock value (P_0) would be:

$$P_0 = \frac{\$1.89(1.06)}{0.12 - 0.06} = \frac{\$2.00}{0.06} = \$33.33$$

Thus, if investors believed that the cash dividends would grow at a 6 percent rate indefinitely into the future and expected a 12 percent rate of return, they would pay only $33.33 for the stock.

From this discussion, we can see that there are four major influences on a stock's price. First is the firm's earnings per share and second is the firm's dividend payout ratio; together, they determine a firm's dollar amount of dividends. The third influence is the firm's expected growth rate in dividends, which will itself be affected by a number of firm, industry, and economic influences. Fourth is the shareholders' required return; from Chapter 8, we know this return is itself affected by the real interest rate in the economy, the expected inflation rate, and a risk premium to compensate investors for purchasing risky equities.

RISK IN STOCK VALUATION

Investors in common stocks face a number of risks that bondholders do not. This additional risk leads them to require a higher rate of return on a firm's stock than on its debt securities. For example, in the event of corporate failure, the claims of stockholders have lower priority than those of bondholders. So stockholders face a greater risk of loss than bondholders. Dividends can be variable and omitted, whereas bond cash flows have a legal obligation to be met.

If the general level of interest rates rises, investors will demand a higher required rate of return on stocks to maintain their risk premium differential over debt securities. This will force stock prices downward. Therefore, stockholders risk capital loss from any general upward movement of market interest rates.

Also, future dividends, or dividend growth rates, are not known with certainty at the time stock is purchased. If poor corporate performance or adverse general economic conditions lead investors to lower their expectations about future dividend payments, this will lower the present value of shares of the stock, leaving the stockholder with the risk of capital loss. Stock analysts systematically review economic, industry, and firm conditions in great detail to gain insight into corporate growth prospects and the appropriate level of return that an investor should require of a stock.

CALCULATING RATES OF RETURN

An investment provides two sources of returns: income and price changes. Bonds pay coupon interest (income) and, as we saw earlier in the chapter, fluctuating market interest rates can lead to changing bond prices and capital gains or losses. Stocks may pay dividends (a source of investor income) and rise or fall in value over time, leading to capital gains or losses. Such is the case with other investment vehicles such as real estate or mutual funds.

HOLDING PERIOD RETURNS

The dollar return on a single financial asset held for a specific time, or holding period, is given by:

$$\text{Dollar return} = \text{Income received} + \text{Price change} \qquad (10.7)$$

Suppose during the time Amy held a share of stock, she received dividends of $2 while the stock price rose from a purchase price of $25 to its current level of $30. Should Amy sell the stock today, her dollar return would be:

$$\text{Dollar return} = \text{Income received} + \text{price change}$$
$$= \$2 + (\$30 - \$25)$$
$$\$7 = \$2 + \$5$$

She received $2 in dividends and the value of her investment rose by $5 for a total dollar return of $7. To compare this investment return with others, it is best to measure the dollar return relative to initial price paid for the stock. This percentage return is simply the dollar return divided by the initial price of the stock:

$$\text{Percentage return} = \frac{\text{Dollar return}}{\text{Initial price}} \qquad (10.8)$$

Amy's percentage return was

$$\text{Percentage return} = \frac{\text{Dollar return}}{\text{Initial price}} = \frac{\$7}{\$25} = 0.28$$

or 28 percent.

ANNUALIZED RATES OF RETURN

To compare accurately the returns on one investment with another, they should be measured over equal time periods, such as a year, a month, or a day. By convention, most investors use annual returns as a means by which to compare investments. To **annualize a return** means to state it as the annual return that would result in the observed percentage return. Equation 10.9 gives us a formula for determining annualized returns:

$$\text{Annualized return} = (1 + \text{percentage return})^{1/n} - 1 \qquad (10.9)$$

where n is the number of years an investment was held. For the above one-year example, Amy's annualized return is the same as her percentage return. This can be shown as follows:

$$
\begin{aligned}
\text{Annualized return} &= (1 + 0.28)^{1/1} - 1 \\
&= (1.28)^1 - 1 \\
&= 1.28 - 1 \\
&= 0.28 \text{ or 28 percent}
\end{aligned}
$$

annualize a return
stating the return as the annual return that would result in the observed percentage return

Notice that the superscript fraction 1/1 indicates that Amy's investment was for one year. When investments are held for longer than one year, the fraction becomes less than "one" indicating that the percentage return must be spread over a longer time period. For example, if Amy's investment was purchased two years ago, her annualized return would be:

$$
\begin{aligned}
\text{Annualized return} &= (1 + 0.28)^{1/2} - 1 \\
&= (1.28)^{.5} - 1 \\
&= 1.131 - 1 \\
&= 0.131 \text{ or 13.1 percent}
\end{aligned}
$$

Also notice that the annualized return is not just the 28 percent total return divided by two years or 14 percent which would be a simple average annual return. Rather, the annualized return measured by Equation 10.9 also captures the compounding or discounting effects of holding investments longer than one year.

It should now be apparent that as the investment holding period lengthens the annualized return gets progressively smaller. For example, let's now assume that Amy earned her 28 percent total return over a period of four years. Her annualized return would be calculated as:

$$\text{Annualized return} = (1 + 0.28)^{1/4} - 1$$
$$= (1.28)^{.25} - 1$$
$$= 1.064 - 1$$
$$= 0.064 \text{ or } 6.4 \text{ percent}$$

A financial calculator also can be used to simplify the calculation effort as follows:

Financial Calculator Solution:

> 1-Year Investment:
> Exponent $1/n = 1/1 = 1$
>
> Inputs   1.28 $\boxed{Y^x}$ then 1 $\boxed{=}$ −1 $\boxed{=}$
>
> Solution   0.28

> 2-Year Investment:
> Exponent $1/n = 1/2 = .5$
>
> Inputs   1.28 $\boxed{Y^x}$ then .5 $\boxed{=}$ −1 $\boxed{=}$
>
> Solution   0.131

> 4-Year Investment:
> Exponent $1/n = 1/4 = .25$
>
> Inputs   1.28 $\boxed{Y^x}$ then 0.25 $\boxed{=}$ −1 $\boxed{=}$
>
> Solution   0.064

Annualized returns also can be calculated for investments that are held for less than one year. Let's assume that Amy held her investment for only 9 months while earning a percentage return of 28 percent. What would be Amy's annualized return under this scenario?

$$\text{Annualized return} = (1 + 0.28)^{1/(9/12)} - 1$$
$$= (1.28)^{1/0.75} - 1$$
$$= (1.28)^{1.33} - 1$$
$$= 1.389 - 1$$
$$= 0.389 \text{ or } 38.9 \text{ percent}$$

Because most individual and institutional investors are interested in comparing annualized returns, it is important that you know how to compute percentage returns and how to annualize them.

"Trust is a good motivator to do a good job."

CHRIS GARDNER

Senior VP—Funds
Management
Sterling Bank

BBA Finance
St. Bonaventure University
MBA Finance
Northeastern University

Q: What has been your best job experience?

A: I was very fortunate to work for Sterling Bank, a small bank in New England, several years ago. I was Senior Vice President of Funds Management. I managed the bank's entire investment portfolio. I developed the strategy for how the bank's assets should be invested, and implemented that strategy on a day-to-day basis. The portfolio was more than $600 million by the time I left.

Q: Sounds like a lot of responsibility for a 30-year-old.

A: It was. I was given an unusual amount of responsibility by the president of the bank. He was sort of a mentor to me and provided a lot of support. He gave me advice when I asked for it, but he trusted me, too. Trust is a good motivator to do a good job.

Q: You say you were "managing the bank's investment portfolio." What does that mean in day-to-day terms?

A: I looked each day at the composition of our investment portfolio—how much in stocks, how much in bonds, our exposure to changes in interest rates, and so on. I compared these to our targets, the levels we had set for these various measures. Then I'd make the various buy and sell trades necessary to bring the portfolio in line with our strategy. That meant choosing between the hundreds of securities available at any given time.

Q: How did you make these trades?

A: In general this was done over the phone with Wall Street firms, or in the case of bonds, I often talked with the government agencies which were issuing bonds that matched our requirements. I was in the job long enough to build a good network of contacts, so I eventually knew where I needed to call to find whatever financial instruments we needed for the portfolio.

Q: Did you feel like your efforts had an impact on the results of the bank?

A: I know they did because I looked at the balance sheet every day. The economy was weak at the time, so the bank was not issuing many loans, and was not generating much loan income. The only other way the bank could make money was by investing its deposits in securities. So when I did well the bank's portfolio grew in value and when I made the wrong choice, the value of the portfolio fell.

Q: Sounds like a great job. You're no longer there. What happened?

A: Sterling Bank was bought by Fleet Financial Group, a much larger bank. Fleet needed branches in some areas where we had locations, so we were a good target. Fleet had its own Funds Management staff, of course, so I was not needed there. Only a handful of Sterling employees stayed on with Fleet.

Q: What are you doing now?

A: I'm a stockbroker now. I'm basically taking all of the experience I gained in *buying* securities and applying it now to *selling* securities to investors.

career profiles

309

SUMMARY

One purpose of this chapter has been to examine the characteristics of bonds and stocks. A second major purpose has been to determine security values by applying the time value of money techniques to the cash flows that investors receive from bond and stock investments. The current price of the securities should equal the present value of future expected cash flows. If security prices are already known, these techniques can also be used to estimate investment returns.

Stock and debt offerings are major sources of long-term funds for businesses. Bonds offer investors a fixed income flow and priority in terms of liquidation. Bond covenants, which are found in the indenture, list some of the obligations of the issuer toward the bond holders. Bonds can be secured by corporate assets or be unsecured; unsecured bonds are called debentures. Bond ratings assess both the collateral underlying the bonds as well as the ability of the issuers to make timely payments of interest and principal. Bonds can be sold overseas by U.S. issuers; non-U.S. firms can issue bonds in the United States, as long as SEC requirements are fulfilled.

Most equity offerings are sales of common stock. Preferred stock gives holders preference over common shareholders with respect to dividends and liquidation. But unlike the common shareholders, the (usually) fixed dividend received by preferred shareholders does not allow them to enjoy the benefits of future profit growth. Many investors buy common shares expecting dividends to rise over time.

Investors are interested in measuring the returns on their investments. We saw how to measure holding-period returns and annualized rates of return.

KEY TERMS

annualize a return	convertible bond
bond rating	convertible preferred stock
callable bond	corporate equity capital
callable preferred stock	coupon payments
call deferment periods	covenants
call price	credit risk (default risk)
call risk	cumulative preferred stock
closed-end mortgage bond	debenture bonds
collateralized bonds	discount bond
common stock	equipment trust certificate
conversion ratio	Eurodollar bonds
conversion value	exchange rate risk

extendable notes
face value
financial assets
global bonds
Gordon Model (constant dividend
   growth model)
interest rate risk
mortgage bonds
non-cumulative preferred stock
open-end mortgage bond
par value
political risk
preferred stock
premium bond

putable bonds
registered bonds
reinvestment rate risk
retractable bonds
rollover risk
sinking fund
subordinated debenture
stock certificate
street name
trustee
trust indenture
Yankee bonds
yield to maturity (YTM)

DISCUSSION QUESTIONS

1. Describe the relationship between internal and external financing in meeting the long-term financial needs of a firm.
2. What are the major sources of long-term funds available to business corporations? Indicate their relative importance.
3. Describe what is meant by bond covenants.
4. What are bond ratings?
5. Briefly describe the types of bonds that can be issued to provide bond-holder security.
6. What is meant by the following terms: convertible bonds, callable bonds, putable bonds, and Eurodollar bonds?
7. List the principal features of a stock certificate. How are stock certificates transferred from person to person?
8. Describe some of the characteristics of common stock.
9. List and briefly explain the special features usually associated with preferred stock.
10. Briefly describe how securities are valued.
11. Describe the process for valuing a bond.
12. What is meant by the "yield to maturity" on a bond?
13. Briefly describe the types of risk faced by investors in domestic bonds. Also indicate the additional risks associated with nondomestic bonds.
14. Describe the process for valuing a preferred stock.
15. Describe the process for valuing a common stock when the cash dividend is expected to grow at a constant rate.
16. Discuss why it is important to annualize a return.

PROBLEMS

1. Assume a $1,000 face value bond pays interest of $85 per year and has an eight-year life. If investors are willing to accept a 10 percent rate of return on bonds of similar quality, what is the present value or worth of this bond?

2. a. By how much would the value of the bond in Problem 1 change if investors wanted an 8 percent rate of return?

   b. A bond with the same par value and annual interest as the bond in Problem 1 has 14 years until maturity. If investors will use a 10 percent discount rate to value this bond, by how much should its price differ from the bond in Problem 1?

3. A $1,000 face value bond issued by the Dysane Company currently pays total annual interest of $79 per year and has a 13-year life.

   a. What is the present value, or worth, of this bond if investors are currently willing to accept a 10 percent annual rate of return on bonds of similar quality?

   b. How would your answer in part a. change if interest payments are made semiannually (i.e., $39.50 every six months) by the Dysane Company?

   c. How would your answer in part b. change if, one year from now, investors only required a 6.5 percent annual rate of return on bond investments similar in quality to the Dysane bond?

   d. Suppose the original bond can be purchased for $925. What is the bond's yield to maturity?

4. The Garcia Company's bonds have a face value of $1,000, will mature in 10 years, and carry a coupon rate of 16 percent. Assume interest payments are made annually.

   a. Determine the present value of the bond's cash flows if the required rate of return is 16 percent.

   b. How would your answer change if the required rate of return is 12 percent?

5. The Fridge-Air Company's preferred stock pays a dividend of $4.50 per share annually. If the required rate of return on comparable quality preferred stocks is 14 percent, calculate the value of Fridge-Air's preferred stock.

6. The Lo Company earned $2.60 per share and paid a dividend of $1.30 per share in the year just ended. Earnings and dividends per share are expected to grow at a rate of 5 percent per year in the future. Determine the value of the stock:

   a. if the required rate of return is 12 percent.

   b. if the required rate of return is 15 percent.

   c.   Given your answers to parts a. and b., how are stock prices affected by changes in investor's required rates of return?

7. Willchris Corporation's stock is selling for $95. It has just paid a dividend of $5 a share. The expected growth rate in dividends is 8 percent.

   a.   What is the required rate of return on this stock?

   b.   Using your answer to part a., suppose Willchris announces developments which should lead to dividend increases of 10 percent annually. What will be the new value of Willchris stock?

   c.   Again using your answer to part a., suppose developments occur that leave investors expecting that dividends will not change from their current levels into the foreseeable future. Now what will be the value of Willchris stock?

   d.   From your answers to parts b. and c., how important are investors' expectations of future dividend growth to the current stock price?

8. The common stock of RMW Inc. is selling at $88 a share. It just paid a dividend of $4. Investors expect a return of 15 percent on their investment in RMW Inc. From this information, what is the expected growth rate of future dividends?

9. Lerman Company has preferred stock outstanding. It pays an annual dividend of $10. If its current price is $70, what is the discount rate investors are using to value the stock?

10. Given the information below, compute annualized returns:

Asset	Income	Price Change	Initial Price	Time Period
A	$ 2	$ 6	$29	15 months
B	0	10	40	11 months
C	50	70	30	7 years
D	3	−8	20	24 months

11. Ritter Incorporated just paid a dividend of $2 per share. Its management team has just announced a technological breakthrough that is expected to result in a temporary increase in sales, profits, and common stock dividends. Analysts expect the firm's per-share dividends to be $2.50 next year, $3 in two years, and $3.50 in three years. After that, normal dividend growth of 5 percent is expected to resume. If shareholders expect a 15 percent return on their investment in Ritter, what should the firm's stock price be?

12. Tough times have hit the retail store chain of Brador, Inc. Analysts expect its dividend of $1.00 a share to fall by 50 percent next year and another 50 percent the following year before it returns to its normal growth pattern of 3 percent a year. If investors expect a return of 18 percent on their investment in Brador stock, what should its current stock price be?

13. Interpret the following stock price quote. In addition, what is Sizzler's approximate earnings per share? What was the stock's closing price the previous day?

52 weeks					Yld		Vol				Net
Hi	Lo	Stock	Sym	Div	%	PE	100s	Hi	Lo	Close	chg
7 1/8	5	Sizzlr	SZ	.16	2.7	25	844	6 1/8	5 7/8	6	−1/4

14. Interpret the following bond price quote. In addition, show how the current yield is computed. What was the closing price of this bond yesterday?

	Cur			Net
Bonds	Yld	Vol	Close	Chg
Deere8.95s19	8.0	100	112 1/8	+3 1/8

SELF-TEST QUESTIONS

1. The largest annual supply of external funds for business corporations comes from which one of the following sources?
   a. issuance of privately placed stocks
   b. issuance of bonds
   c. issuance of preferred stocks
   d. issuance of common stocks
2. The terms or covenants of a bond contract are set out in which of the following documents?
   a. debenture
   b. trust indenture
   c. mortgage
   d. negative pledge clause
3. Which of the following is not a rating category used when rating bonds?
   a. AAA
   b. BBB
   c. B
   d. D
   e. F
4. Which of the following bond types would describe unsecured obligations that depend on the general credit strength of the corporation?
   a. collateralized bonds
   b. mortgage bonds
   c. equipment trust certificates
   d. debenture bonds
5. Which of the following bonds can be redeemed prior to maturity by the firm?

a. callable bonds
b. convertible bonds
c. putable bonds
d. retractable bonds

6. A bond's value is the same as its principal amount when the coupon rate is:
    a. the same as the required rate of return
    b. higher than the required rate of return
    c. lower than the required rate of return
    d. lower than the inflation rate

7. Which of the following risks would not be faced by investors in domestic bonds?
    a. credit (or default) risk
    b. interest rate risk
    c. reinvestment rate (or rollover) risk
    d. exchange rate risk

8. Which of the following is not a component of the Gordon (or constant dividend growth rate) model for valuing stocks?
    a. next year's expected dividend
    b. a constant dividend growth rate
    c. next year's expected earnings
    d. a discount rate that reflects the riskiness of the stock

9. To accurately compare the rate of return on one investment with another, they should be:
    a. equal in size or dollar amount
    b. measured over different time periods
    c. measured over equal time periods
    d. held for more than one year

SELF-TEST PROBLEMS

1. Calculate the price of the following bond, assuming that interest payments are made semiannually and future cash flows are discounted at a 10 percent nominal annual rate or APR:

Par value	Coupon rate	Maturity
$1,000	7%	8 yrs.

2. Ana List estimates that Mertz Company's dividend will grow at 5 percent a year into the foreseeable future. Mertz's dividend this year is $1.80 a share. If stock investors require a 15 percent return on stocks with Mertz's level of risk, what should the current price of Mertz stock be?

SUGGESTED READINGS

Brealey, Richard A., Stewart C. Meyers, and Alan J. Marcus. *Fundamentals of Corporate Finance*. New York: McGraw-Hill, 1995. Chaps. 5 and 13.

Brigham, Eugene F. *Fundamentals of Financial Management*, 7e. Hinsdale, IL: The Dryden Press, 1995. Chap. 7.

Dickerson, Bodil, B.J. Campsey, and Eugene F. Brigham. *Introduction to Financial Management*, 4e. Orlando, FL: The Dryden Press, 1995. Chaps. 16 and 17.

Hessol, G. "Financial Management and Credit Ratings." *Midland Corporate Finance Journal*, Fall 1985, pp. 49–52.

Keown, Arthur J., David F. Scott Jr., John D. Martin, and J. William Petty. *Foundations of Finance*. Englewood Cliffs, New Jersey: Prentice-Hall, 1994. Chaps. 6 and 7.

Marr, W., and J. Trimble. "The Persistent Borrowing Advantage of Eurodollar Bonds: A Plausible Explanation." *Journal of Applied Corporate Finance*, Summer 1988, pp. 65–70.

Peterson, Pamela P. *Financial Management and Analysis*, 8e. Homewood, IL: McGraw-Hill, 1994. Chaps. 11 and 12.

Pinches, George E. *Financial Management*, 5e. New York: Harper & Row, 1994. Chap. 3.

Rao, Ramesh K.S. *Financial Management*, 3e. Cincinnati, Ohio: South-Western College Publishing, 1995. Chaps. 13 and 14.

ANSWERS TO SELF-TEST QUESTIONS   1. b, 2. b, 3. e, 4. d, 5. a, 6. a, 7. d, 8. c, 9. c

ANSWERS TO SELF-TEST PROBLEMS

1. Since coupons are paid semiannually, the number of periods is 8 years x 2 or 16. The nominal rate or APR of 10 percent means the periodic interest rate is 10%/2 or 5%. Every six months investors will receive an interest payment of $[(0.07 \times 1,000)/2]$ or $35. The bond's price will equal the present value of the coupon annuity plus the present value of the par value:

$$\text{price} = \$35 \left[\frac{1 - \left| \frac{1}{1.05} \right|^{16}}{0.05} \right] + \$1,000 \left| \frac{1}{1.05} \right|^{16}$$

price = $35 (10.8377) + $1000 (0.45811) = $837.43.

The bond should sell for $837.43 in the market.

2. Since dividends are assumed to grow at a constant rate of 5% annually, we can use the constant dividend growth model. The current dividend is $1.80; the required return is 15 percent; and the growth rate is 5 percent. Our estimate of Mertz's stock price will be:

$$P_0 = \frac{D_1}{r_s - g} = \frac{(\$1.80)(1.05)}{0.15 - 0.05} = \frac{\$1.89}{0.10} = \$18.90$$

According to this data, Mertz's stock price should be $18.90.

CHAPTER 11

Securities Markets

AFTER STUDYING THIS CHAPTER, YOU SHOULD BE ABLE TO:

- Describe the processes and institutions used by businesses to distribute new securities to the investing public.
- Outline the recent difficulties and changes in structure of the investment banking industry.
- Describe how securities are traded among investors.
- Identify the regulatory mechanisms by which the securities exchanges and the over-the-counter markets are controlled.
- Explain influences that affect broker commissions.

This chapter examines the processes by which the borrowers and lenders of long-term capital are brought together in the primary and secondary markets. Specifically, we describe the activities of investment bankers concerning the origination, distribution, and sale of long-term corporate securities. We discuss the activities of the over-the-counter market and securities exchanges, showing how they facilitate trading between investors.

PRIMARY SECURITIES MARKETS

primary market
original issue market
in which securities are
initially sold

secondary market
market in which securi-
ties are traded among
investors

flotation
initial sale of newly
issued debt or equity
securities

initial public
offering (IPO)
initial sale of equity
to the public

investment bankers
(underwriters)
assist corporations by
raising money through
the marketing of corpo-
rate securities to the
securities markets

public offering
sale of securities to
the investing public

private placement
sale of securities to a
small group of private
investors

due diligence
detailed study of
a corporation

Recall from Chapter 1 that newly created securities are sold in the **primary market** while existing securities are traded in the **secondary market.** The initial sale of newly issued debt or equity securities is called a **flotation;** the initial sale of equity to the public is called an **initial public offering (IPO).** To raise money, corporations usually use the services of firms, called **investment bankers,** or **underwriters,** whose main activity is marketing securities and dealing with the securities markets. Investment bankers act as intermediaries between corporations and the general public when corporations want to raise capital.

PRIMARY MARKET FUNCTIONS OF INVESTMENT BANKERS

Although the specific activities of investment bankers differ depending upon their size and financial resources, the functions of investment bankers include originating, underwriting, and selling newly issued securities.

Originating

Most of the larger investment banking firms engage in originating securities. As an originator, the investment bank seeks to identify firms that may benefit from a **public offering,** or a sale of securities to the investing public, or a **private placement,** which is a sale of securities to a small group of private investors. The public offering process is regulated by the Securities and Exchange Commission (SEC). The private placement process has fewer regulations, but the securities can only be sold to investors who meet certain SEC-regulated guidelines for wealth and investment knowledge. Most of this section will focus on the role of an investment bank in a public offering.

Once the investment bank identifies a firm that may want to sell securities, the investment bank attempts to sell itself to the issuer as the best investment bank to handle the offering.[1] Once an agreement is reached, the investment bank makes a detailed study (called **due diligence**) of the corporation. The investment bank uses this information in order to determine the best means of raising the needed funds. The investment banker will recommend the types, terms, and offering price of securities that should be sold.[2] He or she also aids the corporation in preparing the registration and informational materials required by the Securities and Exchange Commission. One important and carefully regulated piece of

1.   For an example of one firm's process of selecting an investment banker, see Orin C. Smith, "Wanted: The Right Investment Banker," *Financial Executive* (November/December 1994): 14–18. Mr. Smith describes his firm's experience of "going public" when he was chief financial officer of Starbucks Coffee Company.
2.   Chapter 18, Capital Structure and the Cost of Capital, will detail some of the items a firm and its investment bank will consider before deciding the type of securities to be sold.

information is the **prospectus,** which details the issuer's finances and must be provided to each buyer of the security.

Another piece of advice the investment bank gives firms who want to have an initial public offering is when to go public. At times, the investing public is particularly interested in firms operating in certain industries or that develop certain technologies. Firms that go public in "hot" IPO markets are likely to receive better prices for their shares than if they go public in a "cold" market.

Underwriting

Investment bankers not only help to sell securities to the investing public. They also sometimes assume the risk arising from the possibility that such securities may not be purchased by investors. This occurs when the investment banker enters into an **underwriting agreement** with the issuing corporation. As shown in Figure 11.1, with an underwriting agreement, securities are purchased at a predetermined or "firm commitment" price by the underwriters, who then sell them to investors at the **offer price.** The difference between the offer price and the price paid by the investment bank is called a **spread.** The spread is revenue to the investment bank, which is used to cover its expenses and to provide a profit from its underwriting activities.

The issuer has virtually no price risk in a firm commitment offering once the offer price is set. The issuer receives the proceeds from the sale immediately, which it can then spend on the purposes outlined in the prospectus. The investment bank carries, or underwrites, the risk of fluctuating stock prices. Should the market's perception of the issuer change or an economic event (such as an unexpected attempt by the Fed to increase interest rates) result in a stock market decline, the investment bank carries the risk of loss, or at least the possibility of a smaller spread than expected.

Another means of offering securities is called best-effort selling. Under a **best-effort agreement,** investment bankers try to sell the securities of the issuing corporation, but they assume no risk for a possible failure of the flotation. The investment bankers are paid a fee or commission for those securities they sell. The best-effort agreement is typically used when the

---

prospectus
highly regulated document which details the issuer's operations and finances and must be provided to each buyer of a newly issued security

underwriting agreement
contract in which the investment banker agrees to buy securities at a predetermined price and then resell them to the investors

offer price
price at which the security is sold to the investors

spread
difference between the offer price and the price paid by the investment bank

best-effort agreement
agreement by the investment banker to sell securities of the issuing corporation; assumes no risk for the possible failure of the flotation

---

FIGURE 11.1   Diagram of a Firm Commitment Underwriting

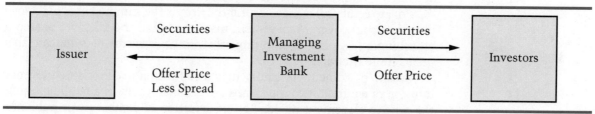

investment bankers anticipate that there may be some difficulty in selling the securities and they are unwilling to assume the underwriting risk. From the perspective of investors, an investment bank putting its money at risk with a firm commitment underwriting agreement would be preferable. Investors should view a best efforts offering with some concern. If the investment banker is not willing to support the firm's security sale, why should other investors?

Firms that are already public and wish to raise additional funds have several choices. They can sell additional securities by using the underwriting process, as discussed above. They can also choose to use shelf registration, sell securities to a private party, have a rights offering, or seek competitive bids. We discuss each of these below.

Shelf Registration. In 1983, the SEC passed Rule 415, which allows firms to register security issues (both debt and equity) and then "put them on the shelf" for sale any time over the succeeding two years. Once registered, the securities can be offered for sale by submitting a short statement to the SEC whenever the firm needs the funds or market conditions are attractive. The **shelf registration** process saves issuers both time and money. There is no cost or penalty for registering shelf securities and then not issuing them. Filing fees are relatively low, and the firm can take some securities from the shelf and sell them immediately through one underwriter and then sell more later with another underwriter. This technique allows the issuer to determine which investment bank offers the best service.

shelf registration allows firms to register security issues (both debt and equity) with the SEC, and have them available to sell for two years

Not every firm can use shelf registration. Firms must meet several size, credit quality, and ethics requirements:

1. The market value of the firm's common stock must be at least $150 million.
2. It must have made no defaults on its debt in the previous three years.
3. The firm's debt must be investment grade (rated BBB or better).
4. The firm must not have been found guilty of violating the Securities Exchange Act of 1934 in the previous three years.

Sell Securities to a Private Party. A publicly held firm can choose to sell securities in a private placement. To keep current shareholders from suspecting any "sweetheart deals," privately placed equity is typically sold at a slight premium to the stock's current market price.

Private equity sales may occur if the firm is the rumored or actual target of a hostile takeover. Management may try to stall the takeover or stop it by selling a large block of voting stock to an investor or syndicate that seems more friendly.

Private placements of equity may also fulfill a need for an emergency infusion of equity. Since the shares are not being sold in a public offering, the private placement avoids SEC registration and subsequent publicity.

The private sale must follow other SEC regulations, however. The firm must disclose the sale after it occurs, and the private investors must meet SEC requirements as "accredited investors." Basically, accredited investors are those who are considered knowledgeable enough or sufficiently strong enough financially to invest without the protection provided by the SEC's registration process. Accredited investors can include wealthy individuals with investment experience as well as financial institutions, such as insurance companies and pension funds.

Rights Offerings. Under the charters of some corporations, if additional shares of common stock, or any security that may be converted to common stock, are to be issued, the securities must be offered for sale first to the existing common stockholders. That is, the existing shareholders have **pre-emptive rights** to purchase newly issued securities. The purpose of this regulation is to permit existing stockholders to maintain their proportional share of ownership. Although once popular in the United States, rights offerings among public corporations became infrequent during the 1980s and 1990s, although they are still used among privately held firms. On the other hand, rights offerings remain popular among public firms in Europe.

pre-emptive rights
right of existing shareholders to purchase any newly issued shares

Competitive Bidding. State, local, and federal government bond issues, as well as those of governmental agencies, usually require competitive bidding by investment bankers before awarding underwriting agreements. This is also the case for debt and equity securities issued by some public utilities. Occasionally, large, financially strong firms will announce that they are seeking competitive bids on a new security offering. Under these circumstances, there may be little initial negotiation between the investment houses and the issuer. In these cases, the issuer decides upon the size of issue and the type of security that it wishes to sell. Then it invites the investment banking houses to offer bids for handling the securities. The investment banking group offering the highest price for the securities, while also providing information showing it will be able to carry through a successful flotation, will usually be awarded the contract.

A great deal of disagreement has existed about the relative advantages and disadvantages of competitive bidding by investment banking houses. Investment bankers strongly contend that the continuing advice they give is essential to an economical and efficient distribution of an issuer's primary market securities. Others contend that competitive bidding enables corporations to sell their securities at higher prices than would otherwise be the case.

Selling

Table 11.1 shows the dollar amount of both debt and equity raised in the United States with the underwriting assistance of various investment bank-

TABLE 11.1   Top U.S. Underwriters of Debt and Equity (1995)

MANAGER	AMOUNT (IN BILLIONS)	MARKET SHARE
Merrill Lynch	$122.3	17.9%
Lehman Brothers	70.3	9.9
Goldman Sachs	68.5	9.7
Morgan Stanley	68.5	9.7
Salomon Brothers	68.1	9.6
CS First Boston	64.6	9.1
J. P. Morgan	40.2	5.7
Bear Stearns	25.4	3.6
Donaldson Lufkin	22.2	3.1
Smith Barney	20.7	2.9
TOP 10	$575.8	81.2%
Industry Total	$709.3	100.0%

Source: Reprinted from *The Wall Street Journal* (January 2, 1996): R38. Reprinted by permission of *The Wall Street Journal*, ©1996 Dow Jones & Company, Inc. All Rights Reserved Worldwide.

ing houses. To assist the underwriting and best efforts process, the majority of large investment banking houses maintain retail outlets throughout the nation. Retail selling is selling to individual investors. There are also many independent retail brokerage outlets not large or financially strong enough to engage in major originating and underwriting functions. These independents may be able to assist the major investment banks in selling new issues. Like the underwriters, they depend upon the resale of securities at a price above their cost to cover expenses and provide profit from operations. A few of the large investment banking houses do not sell to individuals. Rather, they confine their activities entirely to originating, underwriting, and selling securities to institutional investors. Institutional investors are large investors such as insurance companies, pension funds, investment companies, and other large financial institutions.

tombstones
announcements of
securities offerings

Regulatory authorities permit announcements of security offerings to be placed in newspapers and other publications. These announcements, called **tombstones,** are very restricted in wording and must not seem to be soliciting sales. An announcement, published in December, 1995, is shown in Figure 11.2. Note that this tombstone is careful to point out that "This announcement is under no circumstances to be construed as an offer to sell or as a solicitation of an offer to buy any of these securities." The word "tombstone" apparently derives from the small amount of information it provides and the large amount of white space it features. The underwriters are shown on the bottom of the announcement.

The investment bank or banks chosen to originate and handle a flotation are called the lead bankers. In the issue shown in Figure 11.2 the two firms

FIGURE 11.2 A Security Offering Announcement or Tombstone

This announcement is under no circumstances to be construed as an offer to sell or as a solicitation of an offer to buy any of these securities. The offering is made only by the Prospectus.

New Issue December 5, 1995

10,350,000 Shares

Boston Chicken, Inc.

Common Stock

Price $34.50 Per Share

Copies of the Prospectus may be obtained from any State or jurisdiction in which this announcement is circulated from only such of the undersigned or other dealers or brokers as may lawfully offer these securities in such State or jurisdiction.

Merrill Lynch & Co.		**Alex. Brown & Sons** Incorporated
Dean Witter Reynolds Inc.	A.G. Edwards & Sons, Inc.	Goldman, Sachs & Co.
Montgomery Securities	Morgan Stanley & Co. Incorporated	Oppenheimer & Co., Inc.
Piper Jaffray Inc.	Prudential Securities Incorporated	Schroder Wertheim & Co.
Smith Barney Inc.		Nesbitt Burns Securities Inc.
Arnhold and S. Bleichroeder, Inc.	J. C. Bradford & Co.	Equitable Securities Corporation
EVEREN Securities, Inc.	Hanifen, Imhoff Inc.	Interstate/Johnson Lane Corporation
Janney Montgomery Scott Inc.	Edward D. Jones & Co.	Ladenburg, Thalmann & Co. Inc.
Legg Mason Wood Walker Incorporated	Principal Financial Securities, Inc.	Pryor, McClendon, Counts & Co., Inc.
Rauscher Pierce Refsnes, Inc.	Wessels, Arnold & Henderson, L.L.C.	Wheat First Butcher Singer

syndicate
*group of several invest-
ment banking firms that
participate in underwrit-
ing and distributing a
security issue*

of Merrill Lynch & Co. and Alex. Brown & Sons are the lead bankers. These lead bankers formed a **syndicate** of several investment banking firms to participate in the underwriting and distribution of the issue. Syndicate members are listed under the lead bankers in the tombstone ad. For very large issues, two or three hundred firms may be part of the syndicate.

The period after a new issue is initially sold to the public is called the **aftermarket.** This period may vary from a few hours to several weeks. During this period the members of the syndicate may not sell the securities for less than the offering price. Investors who decide to sell their newly purchased securities may depress the market price temporarily, so the syndicate steps in to buy back the securities in order to prevent a larger price drop. This is called **market stabilization.** Although the Securities Exchange Act of 1934 prohibits manipulation of this sort by all others, underwriters are permitted to buy shares if the market price falls below the offering price. If market stabilization is allowed for a particular issue, it must be stipulated in the prospectus. If part of an issue remains unsold after a period of time, for example 30 days, members may leave the syndicate and sell their securities at whatever price the market will allow. The lead underwriter decides when the syndicate is to break up, freeing members to sell at the prevailing market price.

As an example of underwriting risk, at times the lead banker is left holding many more shares of an offering than they would like. Even such well known and respected investment banks as Merrill Lynch, Goldman Sachs, and Morgan Stanley are sometimes left with substantial amounts of stock.[3] Merrill Lynch and its investment funds once owned over one-half of outstanding shares of First USA Inc., a credit card company, more than three months after its initial public offering.

aftermarket
*period of time during
which members of the
syndicate may not sell
the securities for less
than the initial offering
price*

market stabilization
*intervention of the syn-
dicate to repurchase
securities in order to
maintain their price
at the offer price*

Cost of Going Public

One of the drawbacks of going public is its cost. The issuing firm faces direct, out-of-pocket costs for accountants' and lawyers' fees, printing expenses, and filing fees.

In addition, the firm faces two additional costs, which together represent the difference between the market value of the firm's shares in the aftermarket and the actual proceeds the firm receives from the underwriters. The first of these costs is the spread, as discussed earlier. The second cost, **underpricing,** represents the difference between the aftermarket stock price and the offering price. Underpricing represents money left on the table, or money the firm could have received had the offer price better approximated the aftermarket value of the stock. For example, suppose a firm raises $15 million by selling 1 million shares at an offer price of $15.

underpricing
*represents the difference
between the aftermarket
stock price and the offering price*

3.   Alexandra Peers and Craig Torres, "Underwriters Hold Huge Stakes in IPOs," *The Wall Street Journal* (August 12, 1992): C1.

By the close of trading on the first day, the firm's stock price is $20. The firm's market value rose $(20 - 15) \times 1$ million shares or $5 million. Had the securities originally been offered at $20, the firm might have received an additional $5 million for the stock. To view this another way, if the offer price had been $20, the firm could have raised $15 million by selling only 750,000 shares.

Together, these three costs—direct costs, the spread, and underpricing—are the **flotation costs** of an IPO. The flotation costs of an issue depend upon a number of factors, including the size of the offering, the issuing firm's earnings, its industry, and the condition of the stock market. The flotation costs, relative to the amount raised, are usually lower for a firm commitment offering than a best efforts offering. Best efforts offerings have higher costs for two reasons. First, it is typically higher-risk firms that utilize best efforts offerings, so the banker charges higher fees to compensate for his extra efforts. Second, on average, best efforts offerings raise smaller

flotation costs
comprised of direct costs, the spread, and underpricing

Market forces and investor demand for a new issue are hard to estimate. But on a typical day in 1992, Thomas Davis, head of stock capital markets at Merrill Lynch & Co., is trying to do just that. He is coordinating a $148 million stock offering for Countrywide Credit Industries Inc., a mortgage banking company. In coordinating the new issue, Merrill salespeople work the phones, talking to investors in an attempt to "build a book" or gain commitments from potential buyers of the issue before the initial public offering occurs. As managing or lead investment banker, Merrill "runs" the books; that is, Merrill decides how many shares will be allotted to its clients and how many will be to be sold to each syndicate member.

A BEHIND-THE-SCENES LOOK AT A PUBLIC OFFERING

Soon it is evident the deal is "oversubscribed." There are many buyers but not enough shares in the offering to satisfy them. After phoning David Loeb, Countrywide's chairman, Merrill and Countrywide agree to increase the offering from 3 million shares to 3.3 million. At the $43.25 offering price, this will raise an additional $13 million.

The next day Merrill brings out Countrywide's new shares; the stock closes at $43.50. Less than two weeks later, Countrywide's price has fallen $10.75, due to reasons Merrill ambiguously calls "market factors." Merrill Lynch and Countrywide did not have a longer-term market stabilization agreement. Countrywide received the price it expected, but some investors were no doubt not very happy.

Source: M. Siconolfi and W. Power, "Underwriting Boom Puts Tortoises Ahead of Wall Street's Hares," *The Wall Street Journal* (March 26, 1992): A1, A4.

**A VERY
HOT IPO**

The year 1995 featured Netscape Communications' initial public offering. Netscape produces software for Internet servers and World Wide Web browsers. Its original plans were to sell 3.5 million shares at $14. Heavy investor interest led to an IPO of 5 million shares at $28. Still, investors weren't satisfied—there were sufficient orders for 100 million shares. With such heavy demand, there was only one way for the stock price to go: up! The first post-IPO trade occurred at a price of $71. That means Netscape was underpriced by ($71 − $28)/$28 or over 150 percent! With a total of 38.1 million shares held by public investors and company insiders, the first post-IPO trading price of $71 gave Netscape a market value of $2.7 billion—not bad for a 16-month-old company with only $16.6 million in revenues during the first half of 1995! Investor excitement continued to grow. By early December 1995 the stock price had hit over $170 a share, giving it a market value of nearly $6.5 billion. Its P/E ratio was an astronomical 538 times estimated 1996 earnings per share.

Sources: M. Baker and J. Rigdon, "Netscape's IPO Gets an Explosive Welcome," *The Wall Street Journal* (August 9, 1995): C1, C7; M. Baker, "Market Goes Crazy—Really, Just Crazy—Over a Tech Stock," *The Wall Street Journal* (August 10, 1995): A1, A4.

amounts of money (so the fixed costs of preparing the offering are spread over fewer shares sold). One study found that firm commitment flotation costs averaged over 20 percent of IPO gross proceeds; best efforts flotation costs averaged over 30 percent of gross proceeds. Underpricing was the highest single cost of going public for either a firm commitment or best efforts offering, averaging about 15 percent for firm commitment IPOs.

Studies have shown that underpricing varies over time and with IPO volume. In addition, IPO volume is cyclical: periods of frantic IPO activity alternate with periods when few firms go public. There is a close relationship between IPO volume and underpricing. Periods of "hot IPO markets" have heavy IPO volume with large underpricing; periods of low IPO volume or "cold IPO markets" show less underpricing.

IPO underpricing is not just a U.S. phenomenon. Studies have shown that underpricing occurs on IPOs in a number of different countries' stock markets.

Other Functions of Investment Banking Firms

Investment banking firms engage in many activities beyond their primary function of distributing long-term security instruments. For example, they have traditionally dominated the commercial paper market. Commercial paper is an important source of short-term financing for business that we will discuss in Chapter 16. Through buying and selling commercial paper, investment bankers assist with the short-term cash flow needs of many businesses. Four investment banking firms dominate commercial paper activities. They are Goldman, Sachs & Co.; Merrill Lynch & Co.; CS First Boston Corporation; and Lehman Brothers.

In recent years merger and acquisition activities (M & A) have increased in importance for many investment banking firms. Firms with strong M & A departments compete intensely for the highly profitable activity of corporate mergers or acquisitions. It is reported that, for a few investment bankers, profits from M & A activity have exceeded those from all other activities. Investment banking firms act on behalf of corporate clients in identifying firms that may be suitable for merger. Very large fees are charged for this service.

Other activities of investment bankers include the management of pension and endowment funds for businesses, colleges, churches, hospitals, and other institutions. In many cases, officers of investment banking firms are on the boards of directors of major corporations. In this capacity they are able to offer financial advice and participate in the financial planning of the firm. Investment bankers also provide financial counseling on a fee basis.

Not all investment bankers engage in every one of these activities. The size of the firm largely dictates the various services it provides. Some firms, known as boutiques, specialize in only a few activities, such as mergers or underwriting IPOs for high-technology firms.

Investment Banking Regulation

Federal regulation of investment banking is administered primarily under the provisions of the Securities Act of 1933. The chief purposes of the act are: (1) to provide full, fair, and accurate disclosure of the character of newly issued securities offered for sale, and (2) to prevent fraud in the sale of such securities. The first purpose is achieved by requiring that the issuer file a registration statement with the Securities and Exchange Commission and deliver a prospectus to potential investors. The SEC, however, does not pass judgment on the investment merit of any securities. It is illegal for a seller of securities to represent the SEC's approval of a registration statement as a recommendation of investment quality. The philosophy behind the Securities Act of 1933 is that the most effective regulatory device is the requirement that complete and accurate information be disclosed for securities on which investment decisions may be made. Although the SEC does not guarantee the accuracy of any statement made by an issuer of securities in a registration statement or prospectus, legal action may be taken against officers and other representatives of the issuing company for any false or incorrect statements. Full disclosure is, therefore, instrumental in accomplishing the second purpose, that of fraud prevention.

The Securities Exchange Act of 1934 established the Securities and Exchange Commission (SEC) and gave it authority over the securities markets. All brokers and dealers doing business in the organized markets must register with the SEC. A *broker* assists the trading process by buying or selling securities in the market for an investor. A *dealer* satisfies investors' trades by buying and selling securities from his own inventory. In addition, attempts to manipulate securities prices were declared illegal.

In addition to federal regulation of investment banking, most states have **blue-sky laws** to protect investors from fraudulent security offerings. Blue-sky laws apparently get their name from the efforts of some unscrupulous operators who, if not restricted, would promise to sell investors pieces of the blue sky. Because state laws differ in their specific regulations, the federal government is the primary regulator of investment banking. The most common violation of state blue-sky laws is that of misrepresenting the financial condition and asset position of companies.

The Glass-Steagall Act of 1933 ended the ability of commercial banks to act as underwriters of newly issued securities. There were many commercial bank failures during the Great Depression, and there was thought to be evidence at the time that some of the failures resulted from the underwriting activities and poor equity investment of banks.

Until the late 1980s, commercial banks were permitted to underwrite only federal government obligations and general obligation bonds of state and local governments. Financial regulatory controls have now been strengthened to the point where banks may soon be able to again engage in full underwriting activities. Since 1987, commercial banks have been permitted to underwrite new issues of commercial paper and securities backed by mortgages. In 1989, banks were authorized to underwrite corporate bonds, and there is the prospect of this being extended to corporate stock. The easing of restrictions is not complete because these underwriting activities can be carried out only by subsidiaries of the banks and must not exceed 10 percent of the subsidiary's total business. These subsidiaries are wholly owned by, and responsible to, parent banks.

Another move into investment banking was made by commercial banks in 1990. J. P. Morgan & Co., a commercial bank, instituted a computer-based system for the distribution of corporate bonds. This system, named CapitalLink, allows issuers of bonds to bypass Wall Street underwriters and reduce distribution costs. The SEC has approved the device and, as might be expected, there has been strong resistance from investment bankers.

Commercial banks are understandably anxious to see the Glass-Steagall Act repealed. They want to expand into new markets and participate in profitable underwriting activities. They argue that participation in investment banking will help them become larger organizations with stronger capital bases. If domestic commercial banks are to compete inter-

broker
one who assists in the trading process by buying or selling securities in the market for an investor

dealer
satisfies the investor's trades by buying and selling securities from its own inventory

blue-sky laws
Protect the investor from fraudulent security offerings.

nationally, they must have such powers. Large European banks have long combined banking and securities businesses under one roof.

SECONDARY SECURITIES MARKETS

It is safe to say that were it not for secondary securities markets for trading between investors there would be no primary market for the initial sale of securities. Selling securities to investors would be difficult if investors had no easy way to profit from their holdings or no way to sell them for cash. The secondary markets provide liquidity to investors who wish to sell securities. They allow investors to shift their assets into different securities and different markets. Secondary markets provide pricing information, thus providing a means for evaluating a firm's management and for management to determine how its actions are being interpreted by investors. The secondary market for securities has two components: organized security exchanges and the over-the-counter (OTC) market, a network of independent dealers and agents.

A firm that fares poorly is penalized by pressure placed on the firm's management by its stockholders as market prices of its securities fall. In addition, when such a firm seeks new capital, it will have to provide a higher expected return to investors. The position of a firm's management becomes increasingly vulnerable as business deteriorates. Ultimately management may be replaced by the firm's directors, or the firm may be a target of a takeover attempt.

ORGANIZED SECURITY EXCHANGES

An organized securities exchange is a location with a trading floor where all of the trading takes place under rules created by the exchange. Organized exchanges in the United States include the New York Stock Exchange (NYSE) and the American Stock Exchange (AMEX), as well as several regional exchanges such as the Boston, Midwest, Cincinnati, Philadelphia, and Pacific Stock Exchanges. Only the New York Stock Exchange and American Stock Exchange, both located in New York City, may be considered truly national in scope. The New York Stock Exchange accounts for approximately 75 percent of the dollar volume of securities trading on all exchanges. The smaller regional exchanges accommodate trading of the securities of regional and smaller firms, as well as some stocks that are also listed on the NYSE. Such stocks are said to be *dual-listed*.

The organized stock exchanges use the latest in electronic communications. The present methods of transmitting information within cities and

**CAREER
OPPORTUNITIES
IN FINANCE**

Field: Securities Market

Opportunities:
Individuals and institutions invest in stocks and bonds to finance assets and to create wealth. Many times, as with large corporations, these investments for any given day may be in the millions of dollars. Most investors, however, have neither the time nor the resources to properly plan these investments. Instead, investors turn to securities specialists to plan and execute investment decisions. Jobs like these require that individuals have the ability to make sound decision quickly under heavy pressure. For those who excel, though, the opportunities are limitless. Brokerage firms, bank trust departments, and insurance companies typically hire professionals in this field.

Jobs:
Account Executive
Securities Analyst

Responsibilities:
An *account executive*, or securities broker, sells stocks and bonds to individual and institutional customers, as well as manages client funds consistent with client risk-taking objectives. In addition, an account executive must actively pursue new clients and learn about new investment possibilities. Securities firms typically hire account executives to fill entry-level positions.

A *securities analyst* includes being a securities analyst or a securities trader for brokerage firms. A securities analyst must evaluate the value of stocks and bonds and present this information to, or act on this information for, investors.

Education:
A strong background in finance, economics, and marketing is necessary for these jobs. In addition, these jobs require the ability to communicate and negotiate effectively.

between cities is in sharp contrast to the devices used before the introduction of the telegraph in 1844. Quotations were conveyed between New York and Philadelphia through signal flags in the daytime and light signals at night from high point to high point across New Jersey. Although cumbersome compared with modern methods, quotations were often transmitted in this manner in as short a time as ten minutes.

Because of its relative importance and because in most respects its operations are typical of those of the other exchanges, the New York Stock

Exchange, sometimes called the "Big Board," will provide the basis for the following description of exchange organization and activities.

STRUCTURE OF THE NEW YORK STOCK EXCHANGE

Like all the stock exchanges in the nation, the objective of the New York Stock Exchange is to provide a convenient meeting place where buyers and sellers of securities or their representatives may conduct business. In addition, the New York Stock Exchange provides facilities for the settlement of transactions, establishes rules for the trading processes and the activities of its members, provides publicity for the transactions, and establishes standards for the corporations whose securities are traded on the exchange.

The New York Stock Exchange is a voluntary association of 1,366 members. As might be expected, membership seats carry a great value. In order to purchase a seat it is necessary to negotiate with other exchange members who may be willing to sell their membership. Since members' earnings are related to trading activity, seat prices typically rise and fall along with trading volume. On April 20, 1987, during a period of high trading volume, a seat on the New York Stock Exchange sold for a record high price of $1,150,000. The cost of security trading seats since 1980 has generally been within the range of $300,000 to $700,000.

There are four basic types of members: commission brokers, floor brokers, registered traders, and specialists. The largest group of members on the New York Stock Exchange is the commission brokers. The key function of **commission brokers** is to act as agents to execute customers' orders for securities purchases and sales. In return the broker receives a commission for the service. **Floor brokers** are independent brokers who handle the commission brokers' overflow. When trading volume is particularly heavy, commission brokers will ask a floor broker to help them in handling their orders. **Registered traders** buy and sell stocks for their own account. Since they do their own trading, they do not pay any commissions.

Specialists, or assigned dealers, have the responsibility of making a market in an assigned security. Each stock is assigned to a specialist, who has a trading post on the exchange floor. All trades in a specialist's assigned stock need to take place at the specialist's post. As a **market maker,** the specialist maintains an inventory of the security in question and stands ready to buy or sell to maintain a fair and orderly market. That means they must be ready to purchase shares of their assigned stock when there are many sellers and they must be willing to sell shares when traders want to buy. Exchange regulations require the specialist to maintain an orderly market, meaning that trading prices should not change by more than 1/8 of a point from transaction to transaction (a point is equal to $1, so 1/8 of a point is 12 1/2 cents). The specialist maintains bid-and-asked prices for the security, and the margin between the two prices represents the spe-

commission brokers
act as agents to execute customers' orders for securities purchases and sales

floor brokers
independent brokers who handle the commission brokers' overflow

registered traders
buy and sell stocks for their own account

specialists
assigned dealers who have the responsibility of making a market in an assigned security

market maker
one who facilitates market transactions by selling (buying) when other investors wish to buy (sell)

*cialist's gross profit. The **bid price** is that price the buyer is willing to pay for the securities (thus it represents the investors' selling price). The **ask price** is the price at which the owner is willing to sell securities (thus, it represents the investors' purchase price). If the current bid price from brokers is 50 and the current ask price is 51, the specialist may enter a bid of 50 1/2 or 50 3/4 or a lower ask price in order to lower the spread and maintain market order.

bid price
price that the buyer is willing to pay for the security

ask price
price for which the owner is willing to sell the security

Listing Securities

All securities must be listed before they may be traded on the New York Stock Exchange. To qualify for listing its security, a corporation must meet certain requirements regarding profitability, total value of outstanding stock, and number of shareholders. The corporation also pays a fee for the privilege of being listed. The acceptance of the security by the exchange for listing on the Big Board does not constitute endorsement of its quality. The common stocks of more than 1,700 corporations are listed on the New York Stock Exchange.

The American Stock Exchange and all of the regional exchanges permit unlisted trading privileges as well as listed trading privileges. The distinction between these two lies primarily in the method by which the security is placed on the exchange for trading. For unlisted securities, the exchange itself (instead of the issuing corporation) recommends the securities for trading privileges. Unlisted trading privileges must be approved by the SEC. The securities of approximately 1,000 corporations carry unlisted trading privileges on the nation's stock exchanges.

Security Transactions

Investors can place a number of different types of orders. In order to trade, they need to contact a stock brokerage firm where they can set up an account. The investor can then specify the type of order to be placed as well as the number of shares to be traded in specific firms. Securities orders to buy and sell can be market, limit, or stop-loss orders.

Market Order. An order for immediate purchase or sale at the best possible price is a **market order.** The brokerage firm that receives an order to trade shares of stock listed on the New York Stock Exchange at the best price possible transmits the order to its New York office, where the order is transmitted to its commission broker on the floor of the exchange.

market order
open order of an immediate purchase or sale at the best possible price

limit order
maximum buying price (limit buy) or the minimum selling price (limit sell) specified by the investor

Limit Order. In a **limit order,** the maximum buying price (limit buy) or the minimum selling price (limit sell) is specified by the investor. For example, if a commission broker has a limit buy order at 50 from an investor and other brokers have ask prices higher than 50, the order could not be filled at that moment. The broker will wait until a price of 50 or less becomes available. Usually any limit order that is not quite close to the current market price is turned over to the specialist, who places it in his or her **central limit order book.** The specialist will make the trade for the commission broker when the price comes within the limit. Of course, if the price of the stock progresses upward rather than downward, the order will not be completed. Limit orders may be placed to expire at the end of one day, one week, one month, or on a good-until-canceled basis.

central limit order book
limit "book" in which the specialist keeps unexecuted limit orders

Stop-Loss Order. A **stop-loss order** is an order to sell stock at the market price when the price of the stock falls to a specified level. The stockholder may protect gains or limit losses due to a fall in the price of the stock by placing a stop-loss order at a price a few points below the current market price. For example, an investor paying $50 for shares of stock may place a stop-loss order at a price of $45. If the price does fall to $45, the commission broker sells the shares for as high a price as possible. This order does not guarantee a price of $45 to the seller, since by the time the stock is actually sold, a rapidly declining stock price may have fallen to well below $45. On the other hand, if the stock price does not reach the specified price, the order will not be executed.

stop-loss order
order to sell stock at the market price when the price of the stock falls to a specified level

These orders can be used to protect profits. If the stock increases in price after its purchase, the investor can cancel the old stop-loss order and issue a new one, at a higher price.

Short Sale. A **short sale** is sale of securities that the seller does not own. An investor will want to short a stock if she feels the price will decline in the future. Shares of the stock are borrowed by the broker and sold in the stock market. In the event that a price decline does occur, the short seller covers the resulting short position by buying enough stock to repay the lender. If any dividends are paid during the time the stock is shorted, the short seller must pay the dividends owed on the borrowed shares.

short sale
sale of securities that the seller does not own

As an example, suppose Amy thinks AT&T's stock price will fall in the future because of intense competition in the telecommunications industry. She contacts her broker, for example, Merrill Lynch, and gives instructions to sell 100 shares of AT&T short. The broker in turn arranges to borrow the necessary stock, probably from another Merrill Lynch investor who has their stock in **street name,** meaning they keep their stock certificates at the brokerage firm rather than taking personal possession of them. Having sold the borrowed stock, the brokerage house keeps the proceeds of the sale as collateral. In our example, if the securities were sold at 68, the proceeds from the 100 shares, $6,800, would be kept by Merrill Lynch in Amy's account.

street name
an investor's securities are kept in the name of the brokerage house to facilitate record keeping, settlement, safety against loss or theft, and so on

Let's say the stock drops to a price of 58 and Amy wants to cover her short position. She tells her broker to buy 100 shares, which costs her $5,800. The newly purchased shares are returned by Merrill Lynch to the account from which they were borrowed. Amy sold $6,800 worth of stock and purchased $5,800 worth of stock after it fell in price; the difference, $1,000, is Amy's profit, ignoring brokerage commissions. The person from whose account the shares were borrowed will never know that they were borrowed; Merrill Lynch's internal record keeping will keep track of all such transactions.

If the price of AT&T stock rises, the short seller must still cover her short position at the end of some stated time period. If the price rises to $75 a share and the position is closed, Amy will pay $7,500 to purchase 100 shares to cover her position. Amy will suffer a loss of $6,800 − $7,500 or $700 from her short sale.

Because short sales have an important effect on the market for securities, the SEC regulates them closely. Heavy short sale trades can place undue pressure on a firm's stock price. Among the restrictions on short sales is one relating to selling only on an uptick. This means that a short sale can take place only when the last change in the market price of the stock from transaction-to-transaction was an increase. For example, if the most recent transaction prices were: 67 7/8, 67 7/8, 68, 68, 68, the short sale would be allowed as the last price change was an increase. A short sale would not be allowed if the most recent transactions prices were, for example, 68 1/8, 68 1/8, 68 or 68 1/8, 68, 68, since the most recent price change was a decrease.

In addition, both Federal Reserve System and New York Stock Exchange regulations require the short seller to maintain a margin or deposit of at least 50 percent of the price of the stock with the broker. Loans of stock are callable on 24 hours notice.

buying on margin
investor borrows money and invests it along with his own funds in securities

margin
minimum percentage of the purchase price that must represent the investor's equity or unborrowed funds

Buying on Margin. **Buying on margin** means the investor borrows money and invests it along with his own funds in securities. The securities so purchased become collateral for the loan. The **margin** is the minimum percentage of the purchase price that the investor must pay in cash. In other words, margin is the ratio of the investor's equity (own money) to the market value of the security. In order to buy on margin, the investor must have a margin account with the brokerage firm, which in turn arranges the necessary financing with banks.

Margin trading is risky; it magnifies the profits as well as the losses from investment positions. For example, suppose an investor borrows $20,000 and combines it with $30,000 of his own money to purchase $50,000 worth of stocks. His initial margin is 60 percent ($30,000 of his own money divided by the $50,000 value of the securities). Should the market value of his stock rise 10 percent to $55,000, the value of his equity rises to $35,000:

Market value of securities:	$55,000
less: borrowed funds	$20,000
Value of investor's position:	$35,000

This increase in value to $35,000 represents a gain of 16.7 percent ($5,000/$30,000). A 10 percent rise in the stock's value increased the value of the investor's position by 16.7 percent because of the use of margin.

Margin also magnifies losses. If the value of the securities falls by 10 percent to $45,000, the value of the investor's equity would fall to $25,000:

Market value of securities: $45,000
less: borrowed funds $20,000
Value of investor's position: $25,000

This loss in value to $25,000 represents a loss of 16.7 percent. A 10 percent fall in the stock's value decreased the value of the investor's position by 16.7 percent because of the use of margin.

Should the value of the securities used as collateral in a margin trade begin to decline, the investor may receive a ***margin call*** from the brokerage firm. The investor will face a choice of either closing out the position or investing additional cash to increase the position's equity or margin. If the market price of the pledged securities continues to decline and the investor fails to provide the new margin amount, the brokerage house will sell the securities. Under current Federal Reserve regulations, investors must have an ***initial margin*** of at least 50 percent when entering into a margined trade. The minimum ***maintenance margin*** to which the position can fall is 25 percent before the broker will have to close out the position. Depending upon the individual investor's creditworthiness, a brokerage firm can impose more stringent margin requirements.

The combination of falling prices, margin calls, and sales of securities can develop into a downward spiral for securities prices. This kind of spiral played an important role in the stock market crash of 1929. At that time there was no regulatory restraint on margin sales and, in fact, margins of only 10 percent were common.

Record Keeping. When a trade takes place, the information is sent to a central computer system which, in turn, sends the information to display screens across the nation. A section of the securities report and an explanation of the symbols are shown in Figure 11.3. This consolidated report includes all transactions on the New York Stock Exchange as well as those on the Midwest Stock Exchange, Pacific Coast Exchange, Boston Exchange, Cincinnati Exchange, and Philadelphia Exchange.

margin call
investor faces the option of either closing the position or investing additional cash to increase the position's equity or margin

initial margin
initial equity percentage

maintenance margin
minimum margin to which an investment may fall before a margin call will be placed

FIGURE 11.3   Section of Securities Transaction Report

DI	HLT	GM	LIL	PE
$23\frac{3}{8}$	$49\frac{1}{2}$	$46\frac{1}{4}$	$2s28\frac{1}{8}$	$1000s32$

Explanation: Dresser Industries Incorporated, 100 shares sold at 23 3/8; Hilton Hotels, 100 shares sold at 49 1/2; General Motors, 100 shares sold at 46 1/4; Long Island Lighting, 200 shares sold at 28 1/8; Philadelphia Electric Company, 1,000 shares sold at 32.

round lot
sale or purchase of
100 shares

odd lot
sale or purchase of
less than 100 shares

Abbreviations of the securities appear on the upper line of the screen. Immediately below the last letter of the abbreviation are the number of shares and the price. When the sale is for a **round lot** of 100 shares (amounts less than 100 shares are called **odd lots**), only the price is shown.[4] For multiples of 100 shares from 200 through 900, the first digit of the sales figure is followed by an "s." The size of the trade is shown for sales of 1,000 shares and over. The letters "ss" are used to separate the volume from the price for stocks traded in units of 10 rather than 100. Errors and corrections are written out.

The details of the purchase transaction also are sent to the central office of the exchange and then to the brokerage office where the order was originally placed. Trade information is also sent to the registrar of the company whose shares were traded. The company needs this information so new certificates can be issued in either the name of the investor or the brokerage firm (if the shares are to be kept in street name). Likewise, records will be updated so dividends, annual reports, and shareholder voting material can be sent to the proper person.

A security is bought in *street name* when the brokerage house buys the security in its own name on behalf of the investor. The advantage of this is that the investor may sell the securities by simply phoning the broker without the necessity of signing and delivering the certificates. New regulations imposed in 1995 require stock trades to be settled in three days. Before this regulation settlement did not have to take place until five days after the trade. This "T plus 3" requirement means funds to purchase shares or stock certificates of shares that were sold must be presented to the stock broker within the three days of the stock trade. This shorter settlement time should make street name accounts more appealing to investors.

program trading
technique for trading
stocks as a group rather
than individually,
defined as a minimum
of at least 15 different
stocks with a minimum
value of $1 million

Program Trading. Around 1975 stocks began to be traded not only individually, but also in packages or programs. **Program trading** is a technique for trading stocks as a group rather than individually; it is defined as the trading for a group of at least 15 different stocks with a value of at least $1 million. At first program trades were simply trades of any portfolio of stocks held by an equity manager who wanted to change the portfolio's composition for any number of reasons. Today the portfolios traded in package form are often made up of the stocks included in a stock index, such as the Standard & Poor's 500. In 1995, 11.3 percent of all NYSE trading volume were program trades; in 1994 the percentage was 11.6 percent and in 1993 it was 11.9 percent. The most active program traders in 1995 were Morgan Stanley, Nomura Securities, CS First Boston, and Salomon Brothers.

---

4.   For a few high-priced stocks listed on the New York Stock Exchange, the round lot is ten shares.

A wide range of portfolio trading strategies are now described as program trading. The best-known form of program trading is known as *index arbitrage*, when traders buy and sell stocks with offsetting trades in futures and options in order to lock in profits from price differences between these different markets.[5] In 1995, about 30 percent of program trading was because of index arbitrage; in 1994, 39 percent of all program trading was because of index arbitrage. Program trades use computers to keep track of prices in the different markets and to give an execution signal when appropriate. At the moment the signal is given, the orders for the stocks are sent directly to the NYSE trading floor for execution by the proper specialist. The use of computers allows trades to be accomplished more quickly. This can cause problems if price movements trigger simultaneous sales orders by a number of large program traders. A serious plunge in market prices may occur. As a result efforts have been made to control some aspects of program trading by limiting its use on days when the Dow Jones Industrial Average rises or falls more than 50 points in a day.

OVER-THE-COUNTER MARKET

In addition to the organized exchanges, the other major secondary market from securities trading is the over-the-counter market or OTC. Although it trades more than twice as many issues as the NYSE, the OTC is comprised mainly of stocks of smaller firms. The total market value of the shares listed on the NYSE was almost $6 trillion at the end of 1995. The OTC's major trading mechanism, the NASDAQ system, listed shares with a total market value of "only" $1.15 trillion. The OTC is not comprised totally of small firms. Companies such as Intel, Microsoft, Novell, and Apple Computer are listed on it.

There are several differences between the organized exchanges and the OTC market. Organized exchanges have a central trading location or floor, such as the NYSE trading floor on Wall Street in New York City. The OTC is a telecommunications network linking brokers and dealers that trade OTC stocks. The organized exchanges have specialists that make markets and control trading in listed stocks; the OTC has no specialists. Instead, OTC dealers buy from and sell for their own account to the public, other dealers, and commission brokers. In a sense, they operate in the manner of any merchant. They have an inventory, comprised of the securities in which they specialize, which they hope to sell at a price high enough above their purchase price to make a profit. The OTC markets argue that theirs is a competitive system, with multiple dealers making a market in a company's stock.

To trade in an OTC stock, an investor contacts his broker, who then checks a computer listing dealers for that particular stock. After determin-

---

5.   Futures and options are discussed in this chapter's appendix.

ing which dealer has the highest bid price or lowest ask price, the broker contacts the dealer to confirm the price and to execute the transaction.

The OTC market is regulated by the Maloney Act of 1938. This act amended the Securities Exchange Act of 1934 to extend SEC control to the OTC market. The law created the legal basis for OTC brokers and dealers to form national self-regulating trade associations. This was one instance where business itself requested government regulation. It stemmed from the fact that honest dealers in the investment field had little protection against bad publicity resulting from the unscrupulous practices of a few OTC dealers. Under this provision one association, the National Association of Security Dealers, *NASD,* has been formed. All rules adopted by NASD must be reported to the SEC. The SEC has the authority to take away any powers of the NASD.

The NASD has established a lengthy set of rules and regulations intended to ensure fair practices and responsibility on the part of the association's members. Any broker or dealer engaged in OTC activities is eligible to become a member of the NASD as long as it can prove a record of responsible operation and the broker or dealer is willing to accept the NASD code of ethics.

THIRD AND FOURTH SECURITY MARKETS

It should not be surprising that an activity as broad as the security market would give rise to special arrangements. Despite their names, the third and fourth market are two additional types of secondary markets that have evolved over time.

third market
market for large blocks of listed stocks that operates outside the confines of the organized exchanges

The **third market** is a market for large blocks of listed shares that operates outside the confines of the organized exchanges. In the third market, blocks of stock (units of 10,000 shares) are traded OTC. The participants in the third market are large institutions (such as mutual funds, insurance companies, and pension funds) that often need to trade large blocks of shares. Brokers assist the institutions in the third market by bringing buyers and sellers together and, in return, receive a fee.

fourth market
large institutional investors arrange the purchase and sale of securities among themselves without the benefit of broker or dealer

The **fourth market** is even further removed from the world of organized securities trading. Under this arrangement certain large institutional investors arrange purchases and sales of securities among themselves without the benefit of a broker or dealer. They subscribe to an electronic network in which offers to buy or sell are made known to other subscribers. The offers are made by code, and institutions wishing to accept a buy or sell offer know the identity of the other party only upon acceptance of the offer. A fee is paid to the network provider when the trade is completed. Those who support fourth market trading argue that transfers are often quicker and more economical, but the confidentiality is also an important feature to many firms.

A WORD ON COMMISSIONS

It costs money to trade securities. About the only market participants that don't pay commissions are the exchange specialists and registered traders on the NYSE and dealers in OTC stocks.

Stock commissions vary from brokerage firm to brokerage firm. Some brokerage firms, called "full-service" brokerages, not only assist your trades but also have research staffs that analyze firms and make recommendations on which stocks to buy or sell. Their analysts write research reports which are available to the firm's brokerage customers. Examples of full-service brokerages include Merrill Lynch, Paine Webber, A.G. Edwards, and Dean Witter.

"Discount" brokerages are for investors who just want someone to do their stock transactions. Discounters are used by investors who do not desire or need the extra services of a full-service broker. The stereotypical discount investor makes his or her own investment decisions and wishes to trade at the lowest possible costs. Examples of discount brokerages include Brown and Company, Charles Schwab, Muriel Siebert, and Olde Discount.

Commissions on security trades depend upon several additional factors. Commissions generally are lower on more liquid securities (more actively traded securities or securities with a popular secondary market). Commissions generally are higher, as a proportion of the market value of the securities purchased, for smaller trades that involve fewer shares or lower-priced shares. Many brokerages charge a minimum commission which may make small trades relatively costly. They also charge a transaction fee to cover their costs of processing the trade. Others assess fees if your account is inactive for a year; in other words, even if you don't trade, you still pay the broker some fees. As with so many other things in life, a wise investor will shop around for the brokerage firm and broker that best meets his or her particular needs.

SECURITY MARKET INDEXES

If one listens to the radio, watches television, or reads the newspaper, the words "Dow Jones Industrial Average" or "Standard & Poor's 500 Stock Index" will be encountered daily. The 30 stocks that are part of the Dow Jones Industrial Average are listed in Table 11.2. You are probably familiar with most of their names.

Market indexes are useful for keeping track of trends in an overall market (such as the NYSE index, which tracks all stocks listed in the NYSE) or a sector (the S&P 400 industrials summarizes the movements in 400 stocks of industrial firms) or specific industries (such as Dow Jones' various industry indexes). Market indexes exist for many different countries' securities markets, including a variety of both stock and bond market indexes.

TABLE 11.2   Stocks in the Dow Jones Industrial Average (as of January 1996)

AT&T	Allied Signal	Alcoa
American Express	Bethlehem Steel	Boeing
Caterpillar	Chevron	Coca-Cola
Disney	DuPont	Eastman Kodak
Exxon	General Electric	General Motors
Goodyear	IBM	International Paper
McDonalds	Merck	3M
J.P. Morgan	Philip Morris	Procter and Gamble
Sears	Texaco	Union Carbide
United Technologies	Westinghouse	Woolworth

Source: Reprinted from *The Wall Street Journal* (January 4, 1996): C3.

There are many ways in which an index can be constructed; the previous paragraph shows how indexes can cover different security market segments. Indexes also can be computed in different ways. For example, the Dow Jones Industrial Average of 30 large "blue chip" stocks is based upon a sum of their prices; it is an example of a price-weighted index. The S&P 500 stock index is computed in part by summing the market values—the stock price times the number of shares outstanding—of the 500 component stocks; it is an example of a value-weighted index. Still other indexes are based upon other computational schemes.

The 500 stocks comprising the S&P 500 are not the largest 500 firms or the 500 stocks with the largest market values. The stocks in the index are selected by a 19-member committee of Standard & Poor's Corporation. The committee tries to have each industry represented in the S&P 500 index in proportion to its presence among all publicly traded stocks. Most of the changes that occur in the S&P 500 index occur because of firms' mergers, acquisitions, or bankruptcies. Because it is an index based upon market values, large market value firms, or "large capitalization" stocks as they are called, are the main influences on the index's movements over time. The 60 largest capitalization stocks in the S&P 500 account for over half of the market value of the index.[6]

FOREIGN SECURITIES

The growth in the market value of foreign securities has occurred because of general economic expansion, deregulation of exchange rates, and liberalization of regulations of equity markets. The integration of the world's

6.   Robert McGough, "It's Strange! It's Pricy! It's a Winner!," *The Wall Street Journal* (January 5, 1996): R4.

markets is emphasized by the fact that many securities are listed on several markets. The London Stock Exchange, for example, has over 500 foreign listings of which about 200 are U.S. firms. The major U.S. stock markets, the NYSE, AMEX, and NASDAQ, trade about 500 foreign stocks. Foreign stocks can be traded in the United States if they are registered with the Securities and Exchange Commission.

Investors and professional money managers have found it increasingly important to diversify their investments among the world's markets. Such diversification makes possible a broader search for investment values and can reduce the risk in investment portfolios.[7]

Investment in foreign shares by U.S. investors may be facilitated through the use of ***American depository receipts*** or ***ADRs*** for short. These ADRs are traded on our exchanges and are as negotiable as other securities. They are created when a broker purchases shares of a foreign company's stock in its local stock market. The shares are then delivered to a U.S. bank's local custodian bank in the foreign country. The bank then issues depository receipts. There is not necessarily a one-to-one relationship between shares and depository receipts; one depository receipt may represent five, ten, or more shares of the foreign company's stock. ADRs allow U.S. investors to invest in foreign firms without the problems of settling overseas trades or having to personally exchange currencies. ADRs are traded in dollars, and dividends are paid in dollars as well. A ***global depository receipt (GDR)*** is similar to an ADR, but it is listed on the London Stock Exchange. U.S. investors can buy GDRs through a broker in the United States.

American depository receipt (ADR)
receipt which represents foreign shares to U.S. investors

global depository receipt (GDR)
listed on the London Stock Exchange; facilitates trading in foreign shares

INSIDE INFORMATION AND THE LAW

Some persons who deal in securities and have access to non-public or private information about mergers, new security offerings, or earnings announcements may be tempted to trade to take advantage of this information. Taking advantage of one's privileged access to information can lead to large profits from timely purchases or sales (or short sales) of securities. In the United States taking advantage of private "inside" information is thought to be unfair to other investors. These factors, combined with the ease with which inside information can be used, explain why insider trading is not allowed under provisions of the Securities Exchange Act of 1934.

The most obvious opportunity for insider trading is that for personnel of a corporation who, by virtue of their duties, have knowledge of developments that are destined to have an impact on the price of the corporation's stock. But "insiders" are not limited to corporate personnel. Investment

7.   The topic of diversification and its effect on the risk of an investment portfolio is discussed in Chapter 12.

bankers, by virtue of their relationship with such corporations, may be aware of corporate difficulties, major officer changes, or merger possibilities. They, too, must take great care to avoid using such information illegally. Even blue-collar workers at printing firms that print prospectuses or merger offers have been found guilty of trading on private information based upon what they have read from their presses.

Because the insider-trading law is not very clear, it is often difficult to tell when it is illegal to turn a tip into a profit. For example, a stock analyst may discover, through routine interviews with corporate officers, information destined to have an impact on the price of the company's stock. Such information conveyed to the analyst's clients may be, and has been considered to be, insider trading. The almost frantic efforts of large firms to control insider trading is understandable in light of the damage that can occur to their reputations. It is understandable, too, that the SEC has resorted to very strong efforts to resolve the question that continues to exist with respect to a meaningful and fair definition of insider information. After all, it is the investing public without access to this information that pays the price for insider information abuses.

CHANGES IN THE STRUCTURE OF THE STOCK MARKET

In an effort to increase the technological and informational efficiency of the stock market, the SEC has actively promoted major changes in the structure of stock market activities and institutions. Many of the changes proposed have met with resistance from existing interests, especially the NYSE, which fears the effect such changes will have on their particular role in market activities. The NYSE's fears stem from the possible loss of trading on the exchange. However, many of the SEC's recommendations have been adopted and many more will be instituted in due time.

One important change relates to electronic technology. Since the technology is now at hand to link organized exchanges and OTC markets electronically, the SEC would like to see the stock market take the form of one giant trading floor, all at the command of the broker. The broker would be able to tell which market has the best quote on each stock by punching buttons on the quotation machine. Bid and asked prices on covered stocks would be available in all markets. Opponents offer strong arguments against the plan. They claim that not only will many existing market institutions be destroyed, but that in the long run costs for the investor may be higher than under present market arrangements.

Highly automated securities exchanges now exist in the major money-center cities of the world, permitting trading on a global basis. Because of varying time zones, trading is now possible 24 hours a day.

In mid-1990 the New York Stock Exchange announced that, for the first time in its 200-year history, it would permit trading at night. The

"I pay $130,000 a year for the privilege of making trades."

JOHN MURPHY

Independent Floor Broker
New York Stock Exchange

BA History/Business
St. Bonaventure
University

Q: *What does an Independent Floor Broker do?*
A: I buy and sell stocks on the floor of the New York Stock Exchange. The "independent" means I'm not an employee of any of the big brokerage houses. I'm self-employed.

Q: *For whom are you making trades?*
A: I have a few of my own clients and I make trades for them, but the vast majority of my business is overflow for larger brokers. When Merrill Lynch, for instance, has so many customer orders that its own floor traders can't get them all executed in a timely fashion, I am given a portion of the orders to execute for them. Then Merrill pays me a commission for the work I've done.

Q: *Describe what happens on a trade.*
A: Let's say Merrill has a customer that wants to buy 2,000 shares of company X stock at $20 per share or less. Merrill would give me a piece of paper with those instructions. I would then go to the specific area of the floor where company X is traded. I would ask the specialist in company X stock what price people are willing to sell that stock for. If he has a seller at $20 per share or less, he executes the trade.

Q: *What actually happens when it is executed?*
A: The specialist records Merrill as the buyer and whoever the seller is, the number of shares, and the price. And that's pretty much it. I would then go on to the next order. Now if my order is for a larger volume of shares, say 200,000 shares, I may need to stay there for a while executing a bunch of smaller trades. It might take 50 separate trades to come up with 200,000 shares. And I want to make these buys at the lowest possible cost. If I can save an eighth of a point on each share, that's a savings of $25,000.

Q: *Do you only trade certain stocks?*
A: No, I move all over the floor during the course of the day. I might trade 25 to 30 different issues on a given day. And that may involve several hundred individual orders.

Q: *Sometimes we see the Chicago Board of Trade on television, with traders yelling out bids and making hand signals to each other. Is the NYSE like that?*
A: Not really. On the NYSE, all trades take place through the specialist. In fact, many trades, especially smaller ones, are completed via computer instead of by a trader on the floor. The specialist matches up buy and sell orders from brokerages on his computer screen. It's not as wild as the Board of Trade, but it still can get pretty hectic. Recently the trading volume on the exchange has been quite high which means everyone on the floor has lots of trades to execute as quickly as possible. If prices are moving up or down quickly, the urgency is even greater.

Q: *Do you own a seat on the exchange?*
A: No. There is a finite number of seats, or memberships, on the exchange. To make trades there you need to either buy a seat, which costs more than a million dollars now, or lease one, which is what I do. I pay $130,000 a year for the privilege of making trades.

career profiles

343

American Stock Exchange, the Chicago Board Options Exchange, and the Cincinnati Stock Exchange have started a computerized, nighttime trading market for stocks and stock options. These plans are part of an effort to regain trading volume that has been lost to foreign markets, particularly London and Tokyo, as the world moves toward global, around-the-clock trading.

SUMMARY

The accumulation of funds by business establishments to finance plant, equipment, and working capital is a necessary process of an industrial society. In this chapter we described the role of the investment banking industry in facilitating this process. The accumulation of funds is supported by the existence of a secondary market for securities. The constant buying and selling of securities not only provides the investor with the confidence that his or her investment is liquid and can be converted easily to cash but it also provides information to the firm's managers. Businesses that prosper are rewarded by securities that enjoy price increases. The secondary market is made up principally of the organized securities exchanges and the over-the-counter markets. Investment in foreign securities also were described.

Trading on the basis of inside or private information is illegal in U.S. markets, although such trading is accepted as the norm in some overseas securities markets. In the U.S., ethical norms are such that society frowns upon those who, by virtue of their position or access to information, take advantage of their shareholders for personal gain.

KEY TERMS

aftermarket
American depository receipt (ADR)
ask price
best-effort agreement
bid price
blue-sky laws
broker
buying on margin
central limit order book
commission brokers
dealer
due diligence
floor brokers
flotation
flotation costs
fourth market

global depository receipt (GDR)
initial margin
initial public offering (IPO)
investment bankers
limit order
maintenance margin
margin
margin call
market maker
market order
market stabilization
odd lot
offer price
pre-emptive rights
primary market
private placement

program trading	spread
prospectus	stop-loss order
public offering	street name
registered traders	syndicate
round lot	third market
secondary market	tombstones
shelf registration	underpricing
short sale	underwriters
specialists	underwriting agreement

DISCUSSION QUESTIONS

1. Why do corporations employ investment bankers?
2. Identify the primary market functions of investment bankers.
3. Discuss how investment bankers assume risk in the process of marketing securities of corporations. How do investment bankers try to minimize these risks?
4. Briefly describe the process of competitive bidding and discuss the relative advantages and disadvantages.
5. Explain what is meant by market stabilization.
6. Identify the costs associated with going public.
7. Briefly describe how investment banking is regulated.
8. Describe the inroads into investment banking being made by commercial banks.
9. What are some of the characteristics of an organized securities exchange?
10. Describe the four basic types of members of the New York Stock Exchange.
11. Why is there a difference between bid and ask prices at some point in time for a specific security?
12. Describe the differences among the following three types of orders: market, limit, and stop loss.
13. What is meant by a short sale?
14. Describe the meaning of buying on margin.
15. What is meant by program trading?
16. Describe several differences between the organized exchanges and the over-the-counter (OTC) market.
17. How do the third and fourth markets differ from other secondary markets?
18. What are some factors that influence the commission on a stock trade with a broker?
19. Give some examples of market indexes. Why are there so many different indexes?
20. What are American Depository Receipts (ADRs)?
21. Why is it illegal to trade on insider information?

PROBLEMS

1. You are the president and chief executive officer of a family-owned manufacturing firm with assets of $45 million. The company articles of incorporation and state laws place no restrictions on the sale of stock to outsiders.

    An unexpected opportunity to expand arises that will require an additional investment of $14 million. A commitment must be made quickly if this opportunity is to be taken. Existing stockholders are not in a position to provide the additional investment. You wish to maintain family control of the firm regardless of which form of financing you might undertake. As a first step, you decide to contact an investment banking firm.

    a. What considerations might be important in the selection of an investment banking firm?

    b. A member of your board has asked if you have considered competitive bids for the distribution of your securities compared with a negotiated contract with a particular firm. What factors are involved in this decision?

    c. Assuming that you have decided upon a negotiated contract, what are the first questions that you would ask of the firm chosen to represent you?

    d. As the investment banker, what would be your first actions before offering advice?

    e. Assuming the investment banking firm is willing to distribute your securities, describe the alternative plans that might be included in a contract with the banking firm.

    f. How does the investment banking firm establish a selling strategy?

    g. How might the investment banking firm protect itself against a drop in the price of the security during the selling process?

    h. What follow-up services will be provided by the banking firm following a successful distribution of the securities?

    i. Three years later as an individual investor you decide to add to your own holding of the security, but only at a price that you consider appropriate. What form of order might you place with your broker?

2. In late 1992 you purchased the common stock of a company that has reported significant earnings increases in nearly every quarter since your purchase. The price of the stock increased from $12 a share at the time of the purchase to a current level of $45. Notwithstanding the success of the company, competitors are gaining much strength. Further, your analysis indicates that the stock may be overpriced based on your projection of future earnings growth. Your analysis, however, was the same one year ago and the earnings have continued to increase. Actions that you might take range from an outright sale of the stock (and the payments of capital gains tax) to a straight holding

action. You reflect on these choices as well as other actions that could be taken. Describe the various actions that you might take and their implications.

3. You purchased shares of Broussard Company using 50 percent margin; you invested a total of $20,000 (buying 1,000 shares of a price of $20 per share) by using $10,000 of your own funds and borrowing $10,000. Determine your percentage profit or loss under the following situations (ignore borrowing costs, dividends, and taxes):

   a. the stock price rises to $23 a share
   b. the stock price rises to $30 a share
   c. the stock price falls to $16 a share
   d. the stock price falls to $10 a share

4. Currently the price of Mattco stock is $30 a share. What is your percentage profit or loss under the following situations (ignore dividends and taxes)

   a. you purchase the stock and it rises to $33 a share
   b. you sell the stock short and it rises to $35 a share
   c. you purchase the stock and it falls to $25 a share
   d. you sell the stock short and it falls to $20 a share

5. The four stocks below are part of an index. Using the information below:

   a. Compute a price-weighted index by adding their prices at time t and time $t+1$. What is the percentage change in the index?
   b. Compute a value-weighted index by adding their market values at time t and time $t+1$. What is the percentage change in the index?
   c. Why is there a difference between your answers to parts a. and b.?

STOCK	# OF SHARES OUTSTANDING	PRICE AT TIME t	PRICE AT TIME $t+1$
Eeny	100	10	15
Meeny	50	20	22
Miney	50	30	28
Moe	20	40	42

SELF-TEST QUESTIONS

1. Existing securities are traded:
   a. in the primary market
   b. in the secondary market
   c. only on organized exchanges
   d. only over-the-counter

2. Which one of the following is not a primary market function of investment bankers?
   a. originating

     b.   underwriting

     c.   selling

     d.   making loans

3. An agreement whereby an investment banker tries to sell securities of an issuing corporation but assumes no risk if the flotation is unsuccessful is called a:

     a.   due diligence agreement

     b.   best-effort agreement

     c.   firm commitment price agreement

     d.   shelf registration agreement

4. Which one of the following is not a cost to the issuing firm of going public with an initial stock offering?

     a.   direct costs (legal fees, accounting fees, etc.)

     b.   underwriter's spread

     c.   overpricing

     d.   underpricing

5. The regulation of new security sales by individual states is referred to as:

     a.   the registration process

     b.   a truth-in-securities requirement

     c.   the rating of security quality

     d.   blue-sky laws

6. Commercial banks were for many years prohibited from full-fledged investment banking by the:

     a.   Glass-Steagall Act

     b.   Garn-St. Germain Depository Institutions Act

     c.   Securities Act of 1933

     d.   National Association of Securities Dealers

7. Which one of the following is not a basic type of member of the New York Stock Exchange?

     a.   commission brokers

     b.   floor brokers

     c.   registered traders

     d.   specialists

     e.   security regulators

8. An order for immediate purchase or sale at the best possible price is called a:

     a.   market order

     b.   limit order

     c.   stop loss order

     d.   margin order

9. A market whereby large institutional investors arrange purchases and sales of securities among themselves without the benefit of a broker or dealer is referred to as the:

     a.   primary market

     b.   secondary market

c.   third market
d.   fourth market

SELF-TEST PROBLEM

You are the fortunate owner of a listed common stock that has increased substantially in recent months. Although you are concerned about the ability of the stock to hold its price, you hesitate to sell because of the possibility of further increases in its market price. Describe the process by which you may be able to achieve some protection against a price decline while at the same time remaining in a position to benefit from further increases in the price of the stock.

SUGGESTED READINGS

Brooks, Donald E., and Robert H. Hertz. *Guide to Financial Instruments.* New York, NY: Coopers and Lybrand, 1994.

Campbell, Tim S., and William A. Kracaw. *Financial Institutions and Capital Markets.* New York: Harper-Collins College Publishers, 1993. Chap. 3.

Eaker, Mark R., Frank J. Fabozzi, and Dwight Grant. *International Corporate Finance.* Fort Worth, TX: The Dryden Press, 1996. Chap. 12.

Fabozzi, Frank J., Franco Modigliani, and Michael G. Ferri. *Foundations of Financial Markets and Institutions.* Englewood Cliffs, NJ: Prentice Hall, 1994. Chaps. 14 and 15.

Kidwell, David S., Richard L. Peterson, and David W. Blackwell. *Financial Institutions, Markets, and Money,* 5e. Hinsdale, IL: The Dryden Press, 1993. Chap. 9.

Kohn, Meir. *Financial Institutions and Markets.* New York: McGraw-Hill, 1994. Chap. 12.

Reilly, Frank K., and Edgar A. Norton, *Investments,* 4e. Fort Worth, Texas: The Dryden Press, 1995.

Shapiro, Alan C. *Foundations of Multinational Financial Management,* 2e. Boston: Allyn & Bacon, 1994. Chap. 21.

Smith, Orin. C. "Wanted: The Right Investment Banker." *Financial Executive* (November/ December 1994): 14–18.

ANSWERS TO SELF-TEST QUESTIONS   1. b, 2. d, 3. b, 4. c, 5. d, 6. a, 7. e, 8. a, 9. d

ANSWER TO SELF-TEST PROBLEM

You may attempt to limit your loss from a decline in the market price of your stock by instructing your broker to use a stop-loss order. By setting a trigger price for the sale of your stock somewhat below the current market price, your broker has your authority to sell the stock without further contact with you once the stock falls to that price or below. It should be recognized, however, that this does not provide a guaranteed sale price since the stock may be falling so quickly that by the time your broker places your order the price may be far below your stop-loss point. Notwithstanding, your broker will sell the stock at the best price available once the trigger point has been breached. It should be also recognized that if you set the stop-loss price too close to the present market price, a minor decline in the price of the stock may initiate its sale after which the price of the stock may climb to greater heights (probably to your considerable distress).

APPENDIX 11A

Introduction to Futures and Options

In addition to stocks and bonds, the financial system has developed other investment vehicles to meet the needs of various market participants. A type of instrument that is gaining widespread use among institutional investors and corporate financial managers is derivative securities. A **derivative security** has its value determined by, or derived from, the value of another investment vehicle. They go by a variety of names, such as forwards, futures, options, and swaps. In this appendix we will focus on two types of derivatives, futures and options.

derivative security
value determined by
the value of another
investment vehicle

WHY DO DERIVATIVES EXIST?

Most assets that you are probably familiar with, such as stocks, bonds, gold, or real estate, are traded in the cash or **spot market.** The stock exchanges and the primary and secondary markets we examined earlier in the text are examples of spot markets. Trades occur in these markets, and cash, along with ownership of the asset, is transferred from buyer to seller.

spot market
cash market for trading
stocks, bonds, or other
assets

At times, however, it may be advantageous to enter into a transaction now with the promise that the exchange of asset and money will take place at a future time. Such an exchange allows a transaction price to be determined today for a trade that will not occur until a mutually agreed upon future date. Such is the case with a futures contract. As an example, in June a wheat farmer may desire to lock in the price at which he can sell his harvest in September. That way, his profits will not be affected by price swings in the wheat spot market between now and harvest.

For others, it may be desirable to enter into an agreement that allows for a future cash transaction, but only if the contract buyer finds it in his best interest to do so. A derivative security called an option contract allows the purchaser to ultimately decide whether or not to execute the trade in the future. For example, a real estate developer may purchase an option for $10,000 to buy property at a fixed price of $500,000 sometime in the next year. Should the value of the property rise above $500,000 in the coming year, he will most likely choose to execute the option and purchase the land for $500,000. Or a wheat farmer may enter into an option contract to sell his harvest at a predetermined price, say, $5.00 a bushel. Should the spot market wheat price at harvest be $4.50/bushel, he will execute his option and receive the predetermined price of $5.00 a bushel. Should the spot wheat price be higher, say $6.00, he will choose to sell his wheat at the higher spot price and let the option contract expire. Similar option contracts exist for financial assets such as individual stocks, stock indexes, interest rates, and currencies.

Thus, over time, derivatives such as futures and options have evolved to fulfill desirable economic purposes. They help shift risk from those who don't like risk to those who are willing to bear it. They assist in bringing additional information into the market. And their trading mechanisms have evolved so that it may be less costly, in terms of both commissions and required investment, to invest in derivatives than in the cash market.

The prudent use of derivatives to **hedge,** or reduce risk, is similar to the concept of insurance. For example, auto insurance is used as a hedge against the large dollar expenses that could arise from a car accident. We pay an up-front price or premium to buy a certain level of protection for a limited amount of time. This is comparable to the concept of hedging with derivatives; hedging with derivatives can protect the investor from large adverse price fluctuations in the value of an asset.

hedge
reduce risk

The growth in the volume of outstanding derivatives increased five-fold for the five-year period 1986–1991, and by the end of that period had reached nearly $10 trillion on a worldwide basis. By the end of 1995, some estimates have placed the amount of derivatives contracts at over $40 trillion.[8]

Speculation, or investing in derivatives in the anticipation of a favorable change in the cash market price, is a very risky investment strategy. Speculators are not hedging an underlying investment. They hope for a price

---

8.   Nicholas Bray, "OTC Derivatives Trading Globally Put at $41 Trillion," *The Wall Street Journal* (December 19, 1995): C17.

move that will bring them profits. The complexity of some derivatives have resulted in some investors undertaking risks that they were not (so they say!) aware of. In recent years, firms such as Barings PLC, Gibson Greetings, Metallgesellschaft, Procter and Gamble, and several municipalities and colleges have suffered large losses and even bankruptcy because of inappropriate speculation in the derivatives markets. In the following pages we describe several basic derivative securities.

FUTURES CONTRACTS

futures contract obligates the owner to purchase the underlying asset at a specified price on a specified day

exercise price (strike price) price at which an underlying asset can be traded

A **futures contract** obligates the owner to purchase the underlying asset at a specified price (the **exercise price** or **strike price**) on a specified day. Exchange-traded futures contracts are traded on major futures exchanges. Exchange-traded futures contracts are standardized as to terms and conditions, such as quality and quantity of the underlying asset and expiration dates (for example, corn delivered under a futures contract must meet certain moisture content standards, among others). This standardization allows futures to be bought and sold, just as common stocks are bought and sold in secondary markets. Someone purchasing (selling) a futures contract can negate their obligation by selling (purchasing) the identical type of contract. This is called a reversing trade.

Today, futures contracts are traded not only on agricultural goods and precious metals, but they are also traded on oil, stock indexes, interest rates, and currencies. Some exchanges on which futures contracts are traded are listed in Table 11.1A.

initial margin required deposit of funds for those who are purchasers and sellers of futures, usually 3 to 6% of the contract

A risk of entering a contract such as a futures contract is the creditworthiness of the entity on the other side of the transaction. Fortunately, exchange-traded futures have little credit or default risk. Purchasers and sellers of futures are required to deposit funds, or **initial margin,** in a margin account with the exchange's clearing corporation or clearinghouse. The

TABLE 11.1A   Selected U.S. Futures Exchanges

Chicago Board of Trade (CBOT). The Board of Trade handles futures contracts for agricultural commodities such as corn, wheat, and soybeans. It is also a leading marketplace for trading in financial futures contracts, especially those involving Treasury securities.

Chicago Mercantile Exchange (CME). "The Merc" handles trading in stock index, interest rate, and foreign currency futures.

Commodity Exchange (COMEX). Metals futures contracts are traded on the Comex.

Coffee, Sugar, and Cocoa Exchange (CSCE). As its name implies, it handles trading in coffee, sugar, and cocoa contracts.

initial margin requirement is usually 3 to 6 percent of the price of the contract. Funds are added to or subtracted from the margin account daily, reflecting that day's price changes in the futures contract. At the end of each trading day, a special exchange committee determines an approximate closing price, called the **settlement price.** Thus, futures are cash-settled every day through this process, known as "marking to the market." As in the case with common stocks, should an investor's margin account become too low, the maintenance margin limit will be reached. The investor must place additional funds in the margin account or have his position closed.

settlement price determined by a special committee that determines the approximate closing price

Thus, rather than buying or selling futures from a specific investor, the futures exchange becomes the counterparty to all transactions. Should an investor default, the exchange covers any losses rather than a specific investor. But the daily settling of accounts through marking to the market and maintenance margin requirements helps to prevent an investor's losses from growing indefinitely until contract maturity.

Figure 11.1A presents an example of the futures quotation page from *The Wall Street Journal.* Suppose you were considering buying a futures contract on the S&P 500 stock market index. The listing shows that the contract trades at the Chicago Mercantile Exchange and each contract has a value equal to $500 times the value of the S&P 500 stock index. The value of the contract traded on the Merc will, over time, closely follow the variations in the actual value of the S&P 500 index in the cash or spot market.

FIGURE 11.1A   Listing of the S&P 500 Futures Contract

S&P 500 INDEX (CME) $500 times index

	Open	High	Low	Settle	Chg	High	Low	Open Interest
Dec	585.95	587.00	583.30	586.60	+ 1.70	592.60	474.50	183,171
Mr96	589.40	591.40	588.20	591.30	+ 1.65	597.15	511.00	7,329
June	594.00	596.60	592.90	596.15	+ 1.80	601.90	554.25	1,707

Est vol 71,130; vol Wd 51,181; open int 192,232, 692.
Indx prelim High 582.63; Low 579.58; Close 582.63 + 1.16

S&P MIDCAP 400 (CME) $500 times index

| Dec | 210.50 | 212.90 | 210.15 | 212.85 | + 2.35 | 221.75 | 174.45 | 11,965 |

Est vol 675; vol Wd 810; open int 12,007, −24.
The index: High 211.10; Low 209.32; Close 211.06 + 1.41

NIKKEI 225 STOCK AVERAGE (CME)-$5 times index

| Dec | 18310. | 18350. | 18160. | 18210. | − .0055 | 20315 | 14485 | 31,059 |
| Ju96 | ... | ... | | 18335. | − .0055 | 18925. | 14655. | 259 |

Est vol 970; vol Wd 521; open int 31,360, +161.
The index: High 18100.64; Low 18220.41; Close 18220.41 + 75.33

Source: Reprinted from *The Wall Street Journal* (October 6, 1995): C12. Reprinted by permission of *The Wall Street Journal,* ©1995 Dow Jones & Company, Inc. All Rights Reserved Worldwide.

The December 1995 contract opened at 585.95 per contract (thus having a total contract value of 585.95 × $500 or $292,975), had a high of 587.00, and a low of 583.30. The settlement price, which is roughly the closing price, is the price at which contracts are marked-to-market and it was 586.60. The settlement price was up by 1.70 from the previous day. During the preceding lifetime of the December 1995 contract, its high was 592.60 and its low was 474.50. The open interest, which is the number of contracts currently outstanding, is 183,171.

OPTIONS

option
financial contract that gives the owner the option or choice of buying or selling a particular good at a specified price on or before a specified expiration date

An ***option*** is a financial contract that gives the owner the option or choice of buying or selling a particular good at a specified price (called the *strike price* or *exercise price*) on or before a specified time or expiration date. Most of us are familiar with option arrangements of one sort or another. In some ways a sports or theater ticket is an option. We can exercise it by attending the event at the appropriate time and place, or we can choose not to attend and let the ticket expire worthless. As another example of an option, the owner of real estate may be paid a certain amount of money in return for a contract to purchase property within a certain time period at a specified price. If the option holder does not exercise the purchase privilege according to the terms of the contract, the option expires.

call option
contract for the purchase of a security within a specified time period and at a specified price

A contract for the purchase of securities is a ***call option.*** A ***put option*** is a contract for the sale of securities within a specific time period and at a specified price. Similar to futures trading, exchange-traded options are standardized in terms of expiration dates, exercise prices, and the quantity and quality of the underlying asset upon which the contract is based. Thus, exchange-traded options are liquid. A secondary market exists for trading in them. Today, options are traded on individual stocks, bonds, currencies, metal, and a wide variety of financial indexes. While the Chicago Board Options Exchange remains the main market, the New York, American, Pacific, and Philadelphia exchanges also deal in option contracts.

put option
contract for the sale of securities within a specified time period and at a specified price

Traditionally, most individual investors were limited to put and call option purchases. Through the organized exchanges the individual investor can now sell or create the options. The seller of option contracts is called the ***option writer.***

option writer
seller of option contracts

The price paid for the option itself is called the ***option premium.*** It is what a call buyer must pay for the right to acquire the asset at a given price at some time in the future and what a put buyer must pay for the right to sell the asset at a given price at some time in the future. The seller or writer of the option receives the premium when they sell the option contract.

option premium
price paid for the option itself

Figure 11.2A presents an example of the option quotation page from the *The Wall Street Journal.* Suppose you were considering buying a call

FIGURE 11.2A   Stock Option Quotations

Option/Strike		Exp.	–Call–		–Put–	
			Vol.	Last	Vol.	Last
ADC Tel	40	Nov	130	$2\frac{3}{4}$	...	...
$39\frac{15}{16}$	50	Oct	50	$\frac{1}{4}$	...	...
AK Sti	25	Mar	100	6	...	...
...	35	Mar	100	$1\frac{1}{8}$	...	...
A M R	75	Nov	56	$1\frac{1}{8}$	...	...
A S A	$42\frac{1}{2}$	Oct	420	3/8	...	...
$41\frac{5}{8}$	45	Oct	315	$\frac{1}{16}$	...	...
AT&T	45	Jan	69	$19\frac{3}{4}$	...	...
$63\frac{7}{8}$	50	Jan	106	$14\frac{7}{8}$	6	$\frac{1}{8}$
$63\frac{7}{8}$	55	Jan	45	$9\frac{1}{2}$	18	$\frac{3}{16}$
$63\frac{7}{8}$	55	Apr	44	$10\frac{1}{2}$	...	...
$63\frac{7}{8}$	60	Nov	106	$4\frac{5}{8}$	90	$\frac{3}{8}$
$63\frac{7}{8}$	60	Jan	160	$5\frac{1}{4}$	128	$\frac{3}{4}$
$63\frac{7}{8}$	65	Oct	104	$\frac{11}{16}$	25	$1\frac{1}{2}$
$63\frac{7}{8}$	65	Nov	307	$1\frac{1}{4}$	...	...
$63\frac{7}{8}$	65	Jan	204	$2\frac{1}{8}$	10	$2\frac{5}{8}$
$63\frac{7}{8}$	70	Oct	200	$\frac{1}{16}$	...	...
$63\frac{7}{8}$	70	Jan	61	$\frac{3}{4}$	...	...
$63\frac{7}{8}$	70	Apr	120	$1\frac{11}{16}$	...	...
Abbt L	40	Oct	125	$3\frac{3}{4}$	...	...
$43\frac{7}{8}$	40	Nov	85	$4\frac{1}{8}$	50	$5\frac{3}{16}$
$43\frac{7}{8}$	45	Oct	182	$\frac{3}{8}$	20	$1\frac{15}{16}$
$43\frac{7}{8}$	45	Nov	123	$1\frac{1}{16}$	...	...
$43\frac{7}{8}$	45	Feb	70	$2\frac{1}{8}$	...	...
Aclaim	15	Jan	50	7	...	...
$22\frac{3}{4}$	$17\frac{1}{2}$	Oct	48	$5\frac{1}{8}$	28	$\frac{3}{16}$
$22\frac{3}{4}$	20	Oct	136	$2\frac{7}{8}$	220	$\frac{5}{8}$
$22\frac{3}{4}$	20	Nov	...	...	115	1
$22\frac{3}{4}$	20	Jan	34	$4\frac{3}{4}$	100	$2\frac{7}{16}$
$22\frac{3}{4}$	$22\frac{1}{2}$	Oct	42	$1\frac{1}{4}$	105	$2\frac{1}{4}$
$22\frac{3}{4}$	$22\frac{1}{2}$	Nov	337	$2\frac{5}{8}$	40	$2\frac{13}{16}$
$22\frac{3}{4}$	25	Oct	271	$\frac{7}{16}$	45	$4\frac{1}{4}$
$22\frac{3}{4}$	25	Jan	124	$2\frac{3}{8}$	53	$5\frac{1}{4}$

Source: *The Wall Street Journal* (October 6, 1995): C16. Reprinted by permission of *The Wall Street Journal*, ©1995 Dow Jones & Company, Inc. All Rights Reserved Worldwide.

on AT&T. Under AT&T's name is the prior day's closing price on AT&T stock: 63 7/8. Next to AT&T's name, in the second and third column, you'll find a number of expiration months and exercise (or strike) prices on popular AT&T options contracts. The fourth and fifth column give the day's trading volume and the last price for a call option trade; the sixth and seventh column present the trading volume and last price for a put option trade. If "..." appears under the call or put columns, it indicates that option contract did not trade that day. If you had done the last trade on the AT&T January 50 call, the price would have been 14 7/8 or $14.875 per option. Because each contract is for 100 calls, the total cost of buying the call option would have been $1,487.50.

OPTION PAYOFF DIAGRAMS

Futures carry an obligation to execute the contract (unless offset by another contract so the investor's net position is zero). An option contract is just that—it gives the owner the option to purchase (call option) or sell (put option) an asset. Thus, if exercising the option will cause the owner to lose wealth, the option can expire unexercised and have a value of zero. Whereas losses on futures can grow as a result of adverse moves in the value of the underlying asset, the owner of an option contract may be able to limit losses by merely choosing not to exercise the contract.

How valuable is a call option? Suppose AT&T's January 50 option is about to expire and the price of AT&T's stock is 63 7/8. If the call option's price were $10, investors could buy the option for $10 and immediately choose to exercise it, since they could buy the stock by paying only $50 a share. They will then sell these shares on the NYSE at AT&T's market price of $63 7/8 and receive a profit of $3 7/8 (they paid a total of $10 (option) plus $50 (exercise price) or $60; selling the stock for $63 7/8 results in a $3 7/8 profit). This is an example of an ***arbitrage*** operation in which mispricing between two different markets leads to risk-free opportunities to profit. Other investors would also want to take advantage of this opportunity. The buying pressure in the options market and selling pressure in the stock market by arbitragers would cause the option and/or stock prices to change and eliminate the risk-free profit opportunity. Thus, if the AT&T January 50 call option were about to expire, its price would have to be 13 7/8 to eliminate arbitrage opportunities. With a price of 13 7/8, investors would be indifferent between buying the stock for 63 7/8 or buying the call for 13 7/8 and exercising it (total cost, 13 7/8 + 50 = 63 7/8).

On the other hand, suppose the January 65 call option for AT&T was also about to expire. With the price of AT&T stock at 63 7/8, an investor that pays any price for the option is making a mistake; why pay for an option to purchase the stock at $65 a share when the stock can be purchased now for only $63 7/8 a share? The value of the about-to-expire January 65 call option would be zero.

To summarize: just before it expires, the intrinsic value of a call option will either be the asset's value minus the strike or exercise price (if the asset's value exceeds the strike price) or zero (if the asset's value is less than the strike price). For the January 50 call option, the option's price would be 63 7/8 − 50 or 13 7/8; otherwise arbitrage would occur. In the

arbitrage
operation that takes place if there is a mispricing between two different markets for the same asset that leads to a risk-free profit

case of the January 65 option, the option's value would be zero. If we let V equal the market value of the underlying asset (say, the AT&T stock price) and X denote the option's exercise price, the value of an option just prior to expiration will be the maximum of $V - X$ or 0; this can be written Max $[0, V - X]$. Panel A in Figure 11.3A illustrates a payoff diagram for a call option.

The payoff diagram for the seller or writer of the call option is shown in panel B of Figure 11.3A; it is the opposite of the payoff to the option buyer. For the option writer, increases in the asset's price value above the exercise price are harmful, since the call option allows the buyer to purchase the higher-priced asset at the lower exercise price. In the case of the January 50 call option, the writer may be forced to sell AT&T stock for only $50 a share when its market value is $63 7/8 per share. As the stock's value climbs, the call writer faces a larger loss.

FIGURE 11.3A   Payoff Diagrams for Call and Put Options

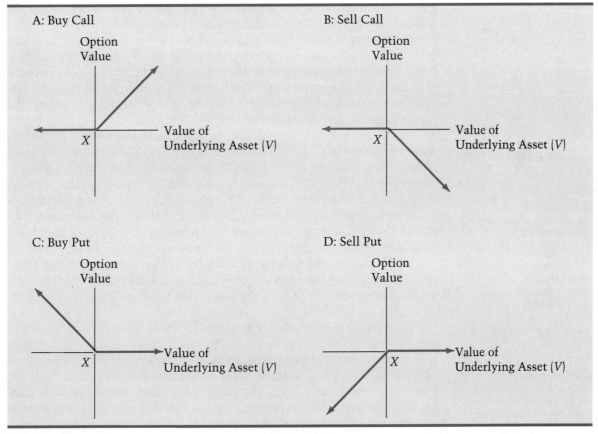

Payoff diagrams for put option buyers and writers are shown in panels C and D in Figure 11.3A. The put option allows the owner to sell the underlying asset at the exercise price, so the put option becomes more valuable to the buyer as the value of the asset falls below the exercise price.

Let's look at the AT&T January 65 put option. As in the case of the call option, arbitrage will ensure that this put option's price will be at least $1 1/8. For example, should the put's price be $0.50, arbitragers will buy the put for $0.50 and buy the stock for $63 7/8; they will then immediately exercise the put, forcing the put writer to purchase their stock at the exercise price of $65. The arbitragers will gain a risk-free profit of $0.625 on every share (they paid $0.50 (put option) + $63 7/8 (stock's market value) or $64 3/8; selling the stock by exercising the put gains them $65, for a profit of $65 − $64 3/8 = 5/8, which is $0.625). Thus, if the put option is about to expire, its price should be $65 − 63 7/8 or 1 1/8 to prevent arbitrage.

If the January 60 put option was about to expire, the value of the put option would be worthless. No one would want to buy a put option that gives them to right to sell AT&T at $60 a share when they can sell the stock on the NYSE for the current market price of 63 7/8.

This example shows the intrinsic value of the put option at expiration is the maximum of $X − V$ or zero, or Max $[0, X − V]$. As the asset's value falls below the exercise price X, the value of the put option rises in correspondence with the fall of the asset's value, as seen in panel C.

The situation is reversed for the writer or seller of the put option. The payoff diagram for the writer of the put is shown in panel D of Figure 11.3A. As the asset's value falls below the exercise price, the put writer will be forced to purchase the asset for more than its current market value and suffer a loss. For example, with the January 65 put option, the put writer may have to purchase the stock at the $65 exercise price, thereby paying $1 1/8 more than the stock's current market price of $63 7/8.

at-the-money
an option's exercise price equals the current market price of the underlying asset

in-the-money
option has a positive intrinsic value; for a call (put) option, the underlying asset price exceeds (is below) the strike price

out-of-the-money
option has a zero intrinsic value; for a call (put) option, the underlying asset price is below (exceeds) the strike price

Here's some more option terminology: an option is **at-the-money** if its exercise price just happens to equal the current market price of the underlying asset. An **in-the-money** option has a positive intrinsic value; that is, for a call (put) option, the underlying asset price exceeds (is below) the strike price, X. An **out-of-the-money** option has a zero intrinsic value; that is, for a call (put) option, the underlying asset price is below (exceeds) the strike price, X.

Thus far, to keep the analysis at a basic level, we have only reviewed the intrinsic value of options. In reality, the option's value will equal its intrinsic value only at expiration. At all other times, the option's premium or price will exceed its intrinsic value. A major reason for this is *time*. The longer the time to expiration, the greater the chance of the option becoming in-the-money (if it was originally at- or out-of-the-money) or to become even more in-the-money than it originally was. Another important influence on the option premium is the variability in the price of the underlying asset. The greater the asset's variability over time, the greater the chance of the option going in-the-money and increasing in value. Therefore, high volatility in the price of the underlying asset *increases* the option premium for both puts and calls.

SUMMARY

From recent headlines to investment seminars, derivatives are an investment vehicle that will become more and more prevalent. This appendix has reviewed two types of derivatives, futures and options. A futures contract represents an obligation to buy or sell the underlying asset at a specified price by a certain date. An options contract is similar, except the owner has the option not to exercise the contract. Futures contracts can be used to "lock in" prices now for a transaction that will not occur until sometime later. They can be used to reduce the risk of price fluctuations. For example, the risk of changing prices in a long asset position can be countered by a short position in an appropriate futures contract. The increases in the value of one position will offset the decreases in the value of the other. Options are useful for hedging positions as well. Some option positions, such as buying a call option, have the added benefit of maintaining profit potential should the value of the underlying asset rise while limiting the dollar losses should the underlying asset's value fall.

KEY TERMS

arbitrage	in-the-money
at-the-money	option
call option	option premium
derivative security	option writer
exercise price (strike price)	out-of-the-money
futures contract	put option
hedge	settlement price
initial margin	spot market

DISCUSSION QUESTIONS

1. Briefly describe what is meant by a derivative security.
2. What is a futures contract?
3. What is an option contract?
4. Indicate the difference between a call option and a put option.

PROBLEMS

1. Determine the intrinsic values of the following call options when the stock is selling at $32 just prior to expiration of the options.
    a. $25 call price
    b. $30 call price
    c. $35 call price

2. Determine the intrinsic values of the following put options when the stock is selling at $63 just prior to expiration of the options.
    a. $55 put price
    b. $65 put price
    c. $75 put price

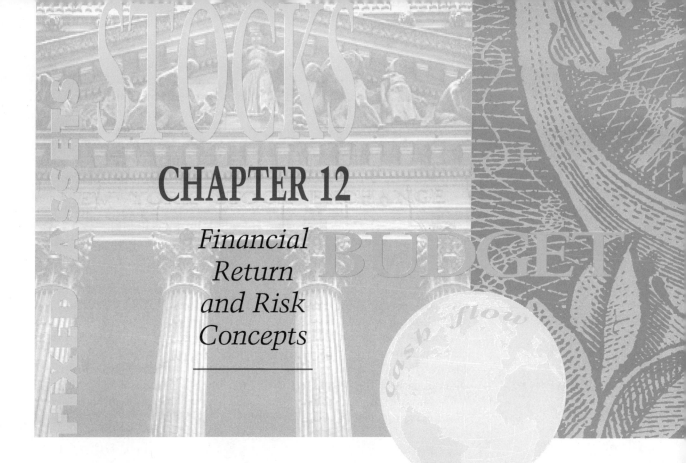

CHAPTER 12

Financial Return and Risk Concepts

AFTER STUDYING THIS CHAPTER, YOU SHOULD BE ABLE TO:

- Describe the difference between historical and expected rates of return.
- Know how to compute arithmetic averages, variances, and standard deviations using return data for a single financial asset.
- Know the historical rates of return and risk for different securities.
- Explain the three forms of market efficiency.
- Explain how to calculate the expected return on a portfolio of securities.
- Understand how and why the combining of securities into portfolios reduces the overall or portfolio risk.
- Explain the difference between systematic and unsystematic risk.
- Explain the meaning of "beta" coefficients and describe how they are calculated.
- Describe the capital asset pricing model (CAPM) and discuss how it is used.

Investors place their funds in stocks, bonds, and other investments to try to attain their financial goals. But stock and bond market values rise and fall over time, based on what happens to interest rates, economic expectations, and other factors. Since no one can predict the future, the returns earned on investments are, for the most part, not known. Some may look backward and see how different investments performed in the past and predict that future returns will be similar. Others do sophisticated economic and financial analyses in order to estimate future returns.

Chapter 8 has already introduced us to the fact that interest rates depend upon the supply and demand of funds, expected inflation, and risk factors such as default risk and maturity risk. Expected investment returns are based on forecasts of nominal risk-free interest rates and risk premiums. Chapter 9 used these interest rates or expected returns as discount rates or compounding rates in order to find present or future values. In Chapter 10, we reviewed the characteristics of stocks and bonds and applied time value of money concepts to value them. The final focus in the chapter was on how to calculate rates of return.

In this chapter we will first learn how risk is measured relative to the average return for a single investment. We also review historical data showing the risk-return relationship. We will see that higher risk investments must compensate investors over time with higher returns. Our emphasis then shifts to a discussion of the efficient markets hypothesis and its implications for investors. This leads to a discussion of the use and advantages of portfolio diversification. We conclude the chapter with a discussion of systematic versus unsystematic risk, the beta coefficient as a measure of relative risk, and the capital asset pricing model.

HISTORICAL RETURN AND RISK FOR A SINGLE FINANCIAL ASSET[1]

Figure 12.1 shows the annual returns over time for stocks A and B. Stock A has fairly stable returns, whereas Stock B shows more fluctuation. The risk of an asset will be reflected in the variability of its returns. For comparison, an analyst may want to determine the level of return and the variability in returns for these two stocks to see whether investors in the higher-risk stock earned a higher return over time.

ARITHMETIC AVERAGE ANNUAL RATES OF RETURN

If historical, or ex-post, data on a stock's returns are known, the analyst can easily compute historical average return and risk measures. If R_t represents the stock's return for period t, the *arithmetic average return*, $\overline{R}$, over n periods is given by:

---

1.   For simplicity, we will use stocks in our discussion here. The concepts are applicable to any asset.

FIGURE 12.1   Returns for Two Stocks Over Time

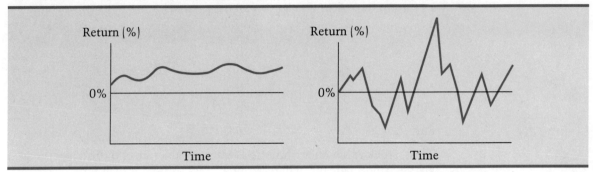

$$\overline{R} = \frac{\displaystyle\sum_{t=1}^{n} R_t}{n} \tag{12.1}$$

For example, let's assume that Padric earned a 6 percent rate of return on his investment in stock A during the first year he held the stock. He bought a share of stock at $50 at the beginning of the year, earned a $1 cash dividend during the year, and sold the stock for $52 at the end of the year. Recall that we calculate the rate of return as the dollar return divided by the initial investment. The dollar return is $1 in dividends plus the price change (ending − initial) of $2 (i.e., $52 − $50) for a total of $3. The percentage return then is calculated as:

$$\frac{\text{Percentage}}{\text{Return}} = \frac{\$1 + (\$52 - \$50)}{\$50} = \frac{\$1 + \$2}{\$50} = \frac{\$3}{\$50} = 0.06$$

$$= 6 \text{ percent}$$

Since the holding period is one year, this means that his annual rate of return was also 6 percent.

Suppose Padric earned a 12 percent return during the second year of his investment. The arithmetic average annual rate of return over the two-year period would be:

$$\overline{R} = \frac{0.06 + 0.12}{2} = \frac{0.18}{2} = 0.09 = 9 \text{ percent}$$

Now let's assume that Padric actually held stock A over the past six years. Furthermore, Serinca owned stock B over the same six-year period. Following is a list of annual rates of returns over the past six years for stocks A and B:

YEAR	STOCK A	STOCK B
1	6%	20%
2	12	30
3	8	10
4	−2	−10
5	18	50
6	6	20
Sum	48	120
Sum/6 = $\overline{R}$	8%	20%

Thus, stock A has an arithmetic average annual rate of return over the past six years of 8 percent, whereas the average annual return for stock B over the same six-year period was 20 percent. If we are willing to ignore risk as reflected in the variability of returns, an investment in stock B would be preferred. However, all investors do not have the same tolerance for uncertainty or risk associated with possibly wide swings in stock B's returns. Let's now see how we might quantify this variability in past returns.

VARIANCE AS A MEASURE OF RISK

The historical risk of a stock can be measured by the variability of its returns in relation to this average. Some quantitative measures of this variability are the variance, standard deviation, or coefficient of variation. All these measures use ***deviations*** of periodic returns from the average return, that is, $R_t - \overline{R}$, where $\overline{R}$ denotes the average arithmetic return over some time frame. Note that the sum of the deviations, $\Sigma (R_t - \overline{R})$, is always zero.

deviations
computed as a periodic return minus the average return

variance
derived by summing the squared deviations and dividing by n − 1

The ***variance***, σ^2, from a sample of data, is computed by summing the squared deviations and dividing by $n - 1$:[2]

$$\sigma^2 = \frac{\displaystyle\sum_{t=1}^{n} (R_t - \overline{R})^2}{n - 1} \tag{12.2}$$

Stated in words, first find the average annual return, $\overline{R}$, over the time period being analyzed. Second, subtract the average return from the individual annual returns. Third, square each individual difference. Fourth, sum the squared differences and then divide this sum by the number of observation minus 1 to get the variance.

We now can find the historical variance in returns for stocks A and B over the past six years as shown in Table 12.1. The results indicate an estimated variance of 44.8 for stock A and 400 for stock B.

---

2.   The reader may recall from a prior course in statistics that when a sample is drawn from a population, dividing by $n - 1$ observations instead of n observations provides a more accurate estimate of the variance and standard deviation characteristics of the population.

TABLE 12.1
Finding the Variances and Standard Deviations for the Returns on Stocks A and B

| | STOCK A | | | STOCK B | |
| | RETURN DIFFERENCE FROM | RETURN DIFFERENCE | RETURN DIFFERENCE FROM | RETURN DIFFERENCE |
YEAR	THE AVERAGE	SQUARED	THE AVERAGE	SQUARED
1	$6\% - 8\% = -2\%$	$(-2\%)^2 = 4$	$20\% - 20\% = 0\%$	$(0\%)^2 = 0$
2	$12 - 8 = 4$	$(4)^2 = 16$	$30 - 20 = 10$	$(10)^2 = 100$
3	$8 - 8 = 0$	$(0)^2 = 0$	$10 - 20 = -10$	$(-10)^2 = 100$
4	$-2 - 8 = -10$	$(-10)^2 = 100$	$-10 - 20 = -30$	$(-30)^2 = 900$
5	$18 - 8 = 10$	$(10)^2 = 100$	$50 - 20 = 30$	$(30)^2 = 900$
6	$6 - 8 = -2$	$(2)^2 = 4$	$20 - 20 = 0$	$(0)^2 = 0$
Sum		$224\%^2$		$2,000\%^2$
Sum/$(6 - 1)$		$44.8\%^2$		$400\%^2$

STANDARD DEVIATION AS A MEASURE OF RISK

Squaring the deviations can make variance difficult to interpret. What do units like percent squared or dollars squared tell an investor about a stock's risk? Because of this difficulty, analysts often prefer to use the ***standard deviation,*** σ, which is simply the square root of the variance:

$$\sigma = \sqrt{\sigma^2} \tag{12.3}$$

standard deviation
square root of the variance

The standard deviation formula gives units of measurement that match those of the return data.

Taking the square root of the variance of 44.8 for stock A gives a standard deviation of 6.7 percent. This compares to a standard deviation of 20.0 percent (i.e., the square root of 400) for stock B. Thus, stock B has both a relatively higher average return (20 percent versus 8 percent) and standard deviation (20.0 percent versus 6.7 percent) when compared to stock A. Of course, these results indicate only what has happened in the past and are based on only six years of data.

The square root also can be found using a financial calculator with a square root key as follows:

Financial Calculator Solution:

Stock A: Stock B:
Input   44.8   Input   400
         $\boxed{\sqrt{x}}$ $\boxed{\sqrt{x}}$

Solution 6.69   Solution 20.0

The standard deviation also can be given a statistical interpretation to help give the investor an intuitive feel for the possible range of returns that can occur. As shown in Figure 12.2, *if* the underlying distribution of returns is continuous and approximately normal (that is, bell-shaped), then we expect 68 percent of actual periodic returns to fall within one standard deviation of the mean, that is $\overline{R} \pm 1\sigma$. About 95 percent of observed returns will fall within two standard deviations of the average: $\overline{R} \pm 2\sigma$. Actual returns should fall within three standard deviations of the mean, $\overline{R} \pm 3\sigma$, about 99 percent of the time. Thus, if the mean and standard deviation are known, a rough range for expected returns over time can be estimated.

For stocks A and B, if we believe that the annual returns over a long period of time were approximately normally distributed and our six years of observations were a reasonable representation of returns over the long run, Table 12.2 shows the range of possible outcomes along with approximate probabilities of occurrence. In words, we can say that 95 percent of the time the annual return on stock A will fall between −5.4 percent and +21.4 percent with an expected average return of 8 percent. For stock B, the annual return will fall within the range of −20.0 percent and +60.0 percent 95 percent of the time and the expected average return will be 20 percent.

One problem with using the standard deviation as a measure of risk is that we cannot tell which stock is riskier by looking at the standard deviation alone. For example, stock A's returns have a standard deviation of 6.7 percent per year while stock B has a standard deviation of 20 percent a year. Stock B clearly has a higher standard deviation, but it also had a higher average return of 20 percent versus 8 percent for stock A. Which stock is the riskier?

The coefficient of variation allows us to make comparisons because it controls for the size of the average. The ***coefficient of variation (CV)*** is a measure of risk per unit of return. The coefficient of variation is computed as

coefficient of variation measures the risk per unit of return

$$CV = \sigma/\overline{R} \qquad\qquad (12.4)$$

A higher coefficient of variation indicates more risk per unit of return. A lower coefficient of variation indicates less risk per unit of return. Stock

FIGURE 12.2   Normal Distribution

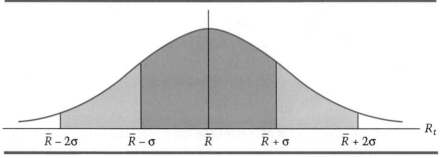

$\overline{R} - 2\sigma$ $\overline{R} - \sigma$ $\overline{R}$ $\overline{R} + \sigma$ $\overline{R} + 2\sigma$ R_t

TABLE 12.2   Distribution of Returns for Stocks A and B

| STOCK | PERCENT OF RETURNS | RETURN ESTIMATES | | |
		DOWNSIDE	AVERAGE	UPSIDE
A	68%	1.3%	8%	14.7%
	95	−5.4	8	21.4
	99	−12.1	8	28.1
B	68	0	20	40
	95	−20	20	60
	99	−40	20	80

A has a coefficient of variation of $\sigma/\overline{R}$ of 6.7/8 or 0.84, or 0.84 units of risk for every unit of return. Stock B has a coefficient of variation of 20/20 or 1.00 units of risk per unit of return. Based upon the coefficient of variation, Stock B is the riskier of these two stocks.

EXPECTED MEASURES OF RETURN AND RISK

The use of historical data to look backward is valuable for examining returns and performance over time. But today's investment and business decisions must be made by looking forward, not backward. Future returns will depend upon our decisions today and upon future events. We need to develop a way to estimate expected, or ***ex-ante***, measures of return and risk.

ex-ante
expected or forecasted

A popular method to forecast future returns is to develop scenarios of future *states of nature.* A state of nature includes a set of economic trends and business conditions. The investor cannot control or predict what future states of nature will occur. One set of scenarios could be the following:

1. *Boom economy:* The domestic economy will grow at an above average pace; inflation will increase slowly; interest rate trends will be slightly upward. Company sales will be assisted by a healthy export environment.
2. *Normal conditions:* The domestic economy will grow at a pace close to its long-run average. Inflation rates and interest rates will be relatively stable. No major disruptions in our export markets are expected.
3. *Recession:* The domestic economy will grow slowly, or maybe contract. Inflation will peak and start to decline; short-term interest rates will fall. Slow export markets will lead to lower levels of foreign sales.

Each of the above three scenarios is a state of nature. The states of nature can be complicated or simple, few or many; but as a whole, they should include all reasonable (and maybe a few unreasonable) possible future environments. The above three scenarios assumed inflation, interest rate, and a firm's exports will follow the trends in the overall domestic economy. This, of course, does not have to be the case. A more complex set of states of nature may include separate scenarios for the domestic economy, inflation, interest rates, exports, and any other variables deemed important by the investment analyst.

Once the possible states of nature are projected, the analyst must assign a probability, or a chance of occurrence, to each one. For the above three scenarios, suppose the first scenario of a growing economy has a probability (p_1) of 0.30; the second scenario of normal conditions has a probability (p_2) of 0.40; the third recession scenario has a probability (p_3) of 0.30. In reality, these probabilities are developed from a combination of the analyst's experience or, "gut feel," economic and industry forecasts, monetary policy, and a review of what has happened in the past under similar conditions. There is no nice formula that can be used to determine probabilities for each state of nature. The only rules are that each state of nature needs a non-negative probability assigned to it, and that the probabilities of all the states of nature must sum to 1.00.

The analyst must also forecast the stock's return for the year under each state of nature. If the above three states of nature are being used, analysts may forecast a 20 percent return under good economic conditions, 10 percent in normal times, and −5 percent in a recession.

The expected return can now be found, using Equation 12.5:

$$\textit{Expected return } E(R) \; = \; \sum_{i=1}^{n} \; p_i \, R_i \qquad\qquad (12.5)$$

where p_i = probability of the ith scenario
R_i = the forecasted return in the ith scenario.

The expected return $E(R)$ is a weighted average of the different state of nature returns, where the weights are the probabilities of each state of nature occurring. Using the above probabilities and forecasted returns, the expected return using Equation 12.5 is:

$E(R) = (0.3)(20) + (0.4)(10) + (0.3)(-5) = 8.5$ percent.

This number, or any other so calculated, represents the average return if the state of nature scenarios could be replicated many times under identical conditions. In any one year, of course, the outcome will be either "boom" (and a return of 20 percent), "normal" (10 percent return) or "recession" (return of −5 percent). If the cycle could be repeated many times, the average return would be 8.5 percent. Thus, the expected return *does not* refer to the expected outcome of a particular situation. It only refers to the long-run average outcome that would occur if the situation could be replicated many, many times. But this concept does provide analysts with an intuitive measure of central tendency. It also allows us to develop measures of possible return variability, or risk.[3]

Just as for historical data, measures of dispersion or variance can be computed once the average or expected value is found. The variance, σ^2, is found by using Equation 12.6:

$$\sigma^2 = \sum_{i=1}^{n} p_i[R_i - E(R)]^2 \tag{12.6}$$

As with historical or ex-post measures, the standard deviation is simply the square root of the variance. The coefficient of variation is the standard deviation divided by the expected return. As with ex-post or historical data, the coefficient of variation is easily interpreted; it represents the risk per unit of expected return.

Let's compute the variance, standard deviation, and coefficient of variation for the stock return using the three scenarios developed above. The stock return forecast was 20 percent in an economic boom (30 percent probability), 10 percent in a normal economy (40 percent probability), and −5 percent in a recession (30 percent probability). The expected return was computed to be 8.5 percent. Using Equation 12.6, the variance of the forecast is:

$$\sigma^2 = (0.3)(20 - 8.5)^2 + (0.4)(10 - 8.5)^2 + (0.3)(-5 - 8.5)^2$$
$$= \quad 39.675 \quad + \quad 0.90 \quad + \quad 54.675$$
$$= 95.25 \text{ percent squared.}$$

The standard deviation will be the square root of this number, or 9.76 percent. The coefficient of variation is the standard deviation divided by the expected return, or $9.76/8.5 = 1.15$.

HISTORICAL RETURNS AND RISK OF DIFFERENT ASSETS

In Chapter 10 we learned the value of an asset is the present value of the expected cash flows that arise from owning the asset. To compute a present value, we need to know the size and timing of expected future cash flows from an asset. We also must know the appropriate discount rate, or

3. The process of computing expected returns from scenarios is not easy to practically apply. Thus, some analysts prefer to estimate expected returns from historical return data and forecasts of future conditions, much the same way returns were estimated in Chapter 8 by adding various asset risk premiums such as a default risk or a liquidity risk premium to the expected nominal interest rate. For example, an investor may believe a stock investment in AT&T deserves a risk premium of 5 percent over the nominal interest rate. If Treasury bills are currently offering a return of 6 percent, the expected return on an investment in AT&T stock would be 6 percent plus 5 percent or 11 percent. When using this method, however, it becomes difficult to estimate measures of future risk.

the required rate of return at which to discount expected cash flows back to the present. Chapter 8 identified three components of required rate of return: the real risk-free rate of return, inflation expectations, and a risk premium.

The first two components are the same for all investments. Their combined effect is approximated by the yield on a short-term Treasury bill. Required returns differ as a result of different risk premiums. Thus, finance professionals say that *risk drives return*. A low-risk investment will have a lower required return than a high-risk investment. High-risk investments will have to offer investors higher expected returns in order to convince (typically) risk-averse people to place their savings at risk. Thus, longer-term Treasury bonds will have to offer investors higher expected returns than Treasury bills. Common stock, by virtue of its equity claim and low priority on company cash flows and assets, will have to offer investors a still larger expected return to compensate for its risk.

Evidence that high returns go hand-in-hand with high risk is seen in Table 12.3, which reports the average annual returns and standard deviations for different types of investments. The return distributions for small-company common stocks and all common stocks have large standard deviations, indicating much more risk than the bond investments. Clearly, however, investors who undertake such risk earn high rewards over the long haul, since stock returns reward investors more than conservative bond investments.

Investors in small company stocks (the smallest 20 percent of those listed on the New York Stock Exchange) had an average annual return of 17.6 percent, but at a high level of risk; the standard deviation of the returns was nearly 35 percent. Recalling our interpretation of a standard deviation, that means about two-thirds of the time the annual return from investing in small stocks fell between -17 percent and $+53$ percent (roughly 18 percent plus and minus 35 percent).

TABLE 12.3   Historical Returns and Standard Deviations of Returns from Different Assets, 1926–94

ASSET	AVERAGE ANNUAL RETURN	STANDARD DEVIATION
Small company stocks	17.6%	34.8%
Large company stocks	12.3	20.5
Long-term corporate bonds	5.9	8.4
Long-term government bonds	5.4	8.7
U.S. Treasury bills	3.7	3.3
Inflation rate	3.2	4.6

Source: *Stocks, Bonds, Bills, and Inflation 1994 Yearbook*™, Ibbotson Associates, Inc. Chicago (annually updates work by Roger G. Ibbotson and Rex A. Sinquefeld).

Large company stocks, as measured by the Standard & Poor's stock market index of 500 stocks, return an average 12.3 percent to investors with an annual standard deviation of 20.5 percent. Large company equities are less risky than those of small firms, so as expected we see a lower average return. The return and risk measures for long-term government bonds show that less risk does result in less return. Treasury bills' average annual return is the lowest in the table, as is the standard deviation of their returns over time.

The seeming curiosity of long-term corporate bonds having higher returns and a lower standard deviation than long-term government bonds can be explained by digging deeper into how these measures were constructed. Historically, the government's "long-term" bond issues have had longer terms to maturity than corporate bond issues. From Chapter 10 we know longer time-to-maturity issues have greater interest rate risk, so it is not surprising that the standard deviation of the government's long-term bonds is greater than those of the corporates. The higher average return on the corporate bonds is expected, since we know they have greater credit risk than Treasury securities.

Although future returns and risk cannot be predicted precisely from past measures, the data in Table 12.3 does present information that investors find useful when considering the relative risks and rewards of different investment strategies. It is important to note that risk is a real factor for investors to consider. Just because large company stocks have an arithmetic average return of 12.3 percent does not mean we necessarily should expect the stock market to rise by that amount each year. As the standard deviation of the annual returns indicates, 12.3 percent is the average return over a long time frame, during which there were substantial deviations—both positive and negative—from the average.

EFFICIENT CAPITAL MARKETS

Prices on securities change over the course of time. Sometimes identifiable news can cause assets' prices to change. Unexpected good news may cause investors to view an asset as less risky or to expect increases in future cash flows. Either reaction leads to an increase in an asset's price. Unexpected bad news can cause an opposite reaction: the asset may be viewed as more risky or its future cash flows may be expected to fall. Either reaction results in a falling asset price.

If a market adjusts prices quickly after the arrival of important news surprises, it is said to be an ***efficient market.*** If the market for IBM stock is efficient, we should see a quick price change shortly after any announcement of an unexpected event that affects sales, earnings, or new products, or after an unexpected announcement by a major competitor. A quick

efficient market
market in which prices adjust quickly after the arrival of new information and the price change reflects the economic value of the information

movement in the price of a stock such as IBM should take no longer than several minutes. After this price adjustment, future price changes should appear to be random. That is, the initial price reaction to the news should fully reflect the effects of the news.

In an efficient market, only unexpected news or surprises should cause prices to move markedly up or down. Expected events should have no impact on asset prices, since investors' expectations would already be reflected in their trading patterns and the asset's price. For example, if investors *expected* IBM to announce that earnings for the past year rose 10 percent, IBM's stock price should be at a level commensurate with that expectation. If IBM does indeed announce a 10 percent earnings increase, no significant price change should occur, as IBM's stock price already reflected that information. If, however, IBM announced an earnings increase of 20 percent (a good news surprise) or an earnings decline of 5 percent (a bad news surprise), the market would quickly adjust IBM's price in reaction to the unexpected news.

Every time IBM's stock price changes in reaction to new information, it should show no continuing tendency to rise or fall after the price adjustment. Figure 12.3 illustrates this. After new information hits the market and the price adjusts, no steady trend in either direction should persist.

Any consistent trend in the same direction as the price change would be evidence of an *inefficient market* that does not quickly and correctly process new information to properly determine asset prices. Likewise, evidence of price corrections or reversals after the immediate reaction to news implies an inefficient market that overreacts to news.

In an efficient market, it is difficult to consistently find stocks whose prices do not fairly reflect the present values of future expected cash flows.

FIGURE 12.3   Price Reactions in Efficient and Inefficient Markets*

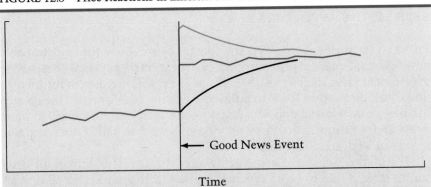

*Examples of price reactions in an efficient market (———) and inefficient markets following good news about a company. An inefficient market with an over-reaction is indicated by (———); an inefficient market with an under-reaction is indicated by (———).

Prices will change when the arrival of new information indicates that an upward or downward revision in this present value is appropriate.

This means that in an efficient market, investors cannot consistently earn above-average profits (after controlling for risk differences among assets) from trades made after new information arrives at the market. The price adjustment occurs so rapidly that no buy or sell order placed after the announcement can, in the long run, result in risk-adjusted returns above the market's average return. An order to buy after the arrival of good news may result in large profits, but such a gain will occur only by chance, as will comparable losses. Stock price trends always return to their random ways after initially adjusting to the new information.

Efficient markets result from interactions among many market participants, all analyzing available information in pursuit of advantage. Also, the information flows they analyze must be random, both in timing and content (in an efficient market, no one can consistently predict tomorrow's news). The profit motive leads investors to try to buy low and sell high on the basis of new information and their interpretation of it. Hordes of investors analyzing all available information about the economy and individual firms quickly identify incorrectly priced stocks. Resulting trading pushes those stocks to their correct levels. This causes prices in an efficient market to move in a ***random walk,*** meaning that they appear to fluctuate randomly over time, driven by the random arrival of new information.[4]

Different assumptions about how much information is reflected in prices give rise to different types of market efficiency. A market in which prices reflect *all* knowledge, including past and current publicly known and private information, is a ***strong-form efficient market.*** In such an efficient market, even corporate officers and other insiders cannot earn above-average, risk-adjusted profits from buying and selling stock. Even their detailed, exclusive information is already reflected in current stock prices. Few markets can ever pass the test of strong-form efficiency, and insiders can profit from information not known by others. As discussed in the previous chapter, that is a reason why U.S. laws prohibit insider trading, or trading based on important, nonpublic information.

In a ***semi-strong form efficient market,*** all public information, both past and current, is reflected in asset prices. The U.S. stock market appears to be a fairly good example of a semi-strong form efficient market. News about the economy or individual companies appears to produce quick stock price changes without subsequent trends or price reversals.

random walk
prices appear to fluctuate randomly over time, driven by the random arrival of new information

strong-form efficient market
market in which prices reflect all public and private knowledge, including past and current information

semi-strong form efficient market
market in which all public information, both current and past, is reflected in asset prices

---

4.   The insightful reader may be wondering how prices can demonstrate a random walk when evidence presented earlier shows common stocks increasing in value by 12 percent per year on average. Such a return seems to imply an upward trend, not random deviations. Market efficiency does not eliminate long-run upward and downward trends in the economy; it simply means investors cannot consistently predict which stocks will outperform or underperform the market averages on a risk-adjusted basis.

Field: Personal Financial Planning

Opportunities: Personal financial planning involves preparing for emergencies and protecting against catastrophes such as premature death and the loss of real assets. Personal financial planning also involves planning for the accumulation of wealth during an individual's working career in order to provide an adequate standard of living after retirement. Job opportunities include the fields of insurance (life, health, and property) and investments (money management, individual bonds and stocks, and mutual funds).

Jobs:
Financial Planner
Financial Advisor

Responsibilities:

A *financial planner* helps individuals develop personal financial plans that include establishing current and future financial goals and assists individuals in setting up steps for carrying out the goals. Financial goals are set for cash reserves, insurance protection, and investing or saving to accumulate wealth over an individual's working lifetime.

A *financial advisor* focuses on maintaining and increasing the investment wealth of individuals. Investment advice is given in reference to the existing stage in the individual's "life cycle," as well as in terms of the individual's attitude toward investment risk. Advice is given on the target mix among cash reserves, bonds, and stocks. Specific investment recommendations also may be provided.

Education:
A bachelor's degree usually is a prerequisite. Additional education and training often is needed in the insurance and securities areas. Certification programs must be completed in order to sell securities. A Certified Financial Planner designation also is available.

---

weak-form efficient market market in which prices reflect all past information

chartists (technicians) study graphs of past price movements, volume, etc., to try to predict future prices

A ***weak-form efficient market*** is a market in which prices reflect all past information, such as information in last year's annual report, previous earnings announcements, and other past news. Some investors, called **chartists**, or **technicians**, examine graphs of past price movements, number of shares bought and sold, and other figures to try to predict future price movements. A weak-form efficient market implies that such investors are wasting their time; they cannot earn above-average, risk-adjusted profits by projecting past trends in market variables.

Market efficiency has several important practical implications. First, for investors, efficient markets make it difficult to invest to consistently "beat the market" by earning average returns after taking risk differences into account. Thus, over time, more and more individual and institutional investors have chosen to "index," that is, to invest in stocks which comprise the market indexes (such as the Standard & Poor's 500 or Merrill Lynch's corporate bond index) rather than try to choose specific stocks or bonds. Investors try to match the market's performance by placing funds in securities in the same proportion as their weight in the chosen index.[5]

Second, for corporate financial managers, stock price reactions to a firm's announcements of dividend changes, mergers, and strategies will present a fair view of how the marketplace feels about management's actions. Announcements followed by stock price declines indicate that the market believes the decision will hurt future cash flows or increase the riskiness of the firm. Announcements followed by stock price increases indicate that investors feel future cash flows will rise or risk will fall. By watching the market, managers can see how investors perceive their actions.

Now that we have discussed how difficult it is to earn rates of return higher than risk-adjusted "market" returns, what is an investor to do? First, an investor can establish the amount of financial risk she or he is willing to accept and then find investments that have demonstrated comparable levels of risk. Second, the investor can diversify away that portion of total risk which is said to be "unsystematic," or separate from movements in the economy and the overall market. In the next section, we discuss the financial risk reduction benefits of portfolio diversification, which allows investors to reduce their exposure to unsystematic risk.

PORTFOLIO RETURNS AND RISK

Let's return to our earlier discussion of stocks A and B. Recall that Padric received an arithmetic average rate of return of 8 percent on stock A with a standard deviation of 6.7 percent over the past six years. Serinca's average return and risk achieved by investing in stock B over the same six-year period was 20 percent and 20 percent, respectively. Mary also is considering investing in common stocks but believes that stock B is too risky and that stock A is too conservative. She could search for another stock that would have return-risk characteristics in between stocks A and B, or she could invest a portion of her investment funds in stock A and stock B. This latter choice would be an example of building or forming a portfolio. A ***portfolio*** is any combination of financial assets or investments.

portfolio
*any combination
of financial assets
or investments*

5.   In practice, it is difficult for index funds to exactly match the performance of the chosen index because of the index funds' need to reinvest dividend or coupon income over time, as well as their need to handle cash coming in from new investors and to sell shares from investors who want to take their money out of the index fund.

EXPECTED RETURN ON A PORTFOLIO

The expected rate of return on a portfolio, $E(R_p)$, is simply the weighted average of the expected returns, $E(R_i)$, of the individual assets in the portfolio:

$$E(R_p) = \sum_{i=1}^{n} w_i E(R_i) \tag{12.7}$$

where w_i is the weight of the ith asset, or the proportion of the portfolio invested in that asset. The sum of these weights must equal 1.0.

While we know that historical returns and risk are not guaranteed to repeat themselves in the future, many investors, analysts, and investment managers believe that historical return-risk information is useful in estimating likely future return-risk performance. Let's assume that Mary is willing to invest 50 percent of her investment funds in stock A and 50 percent in stock B. Table 12.4 shows the outcome if she had diversified in this manner over the past six-year period. Notice that Mary's arithmetic return would have been 14 percent, which is halfway between the average return for stock A's 8 percent and stock B's 20 percent. This occurs because an equal amount was invested in each stock.

Figure 12.4 illustrates the annual portfolio returns that would have occurred over the past six years if Mary had invested an equal amount in both stocks A and B. Also notice that by forming a portfolio the variability of the portfolio's returns falls in between the variability of returns for stocks A and B. We will explore this concept next.

However, before we move on, let's now assume that these past returns are expected to occur again in the future. We can use Equation 12.7 to arrive at the same expected portfolio return, assuming equal investments in stocks A and B, of 14 percent, as we found in Table 12.4. Here we work directly with the average annual returns of 8 percent for stock A and 20

TABLE 12.4   Portfolio Return Calculations: Based on 50% Investment in Stock A and 50% in Stock B

	STOCK A				STOCK B									WEIGHTED
YEAR	INVESTMENT PERCENTAGE	×	RETURN	+	INVESTMENT PERCENTAGE	×	RETURN	=	A	+	B	=		RETURN
1	0.50	×	6%	+	0.50	×	20%	=	3%	+	10%	=		13%
2	0.50	×	12	+	0.50	×	30	=	6	+	15	=		21
3	0.50	×	8	+	0.50	×	10	=	4	+	5	=		9
4	0.50	×	−2	+	0.50	×	−10	=	−1	+	−5	=		−6
5	0.50	×	18	+	0.50	×	50	=	9	+	25	=		34
6	0.50	×	6	+	0.50	×	20	=	3	+	10	=		13
					Sum of Weighted Returns									84%
					Portfolio Average Return: Sum/6									14%

FIGURE 12.4   Portfolio Returns When Investments Are Equally Weighted in Stocks A and B

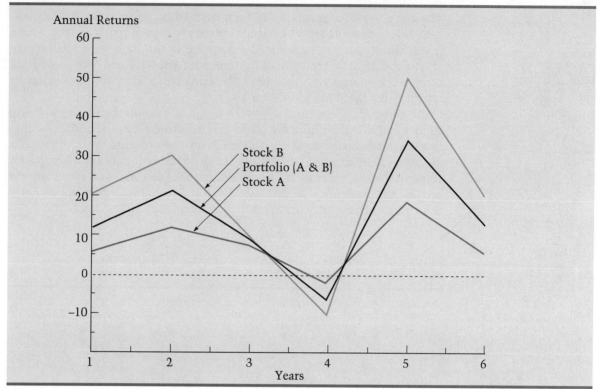

percent for stock B. Again, assuming these are average expected returns, we have:

$$E(R_p) = 0.50(8\%) + 0.50(20\%) = 4\% + 10\% = 14\%$$

Now, let's assume that Ramon is willing to accept a little more variability in his portfolio returns relative to Mary as a trade-off for a higher expected return. Consequently, Ramon has decided to invest 25 percent of his investment funds in stock A and 75 percent in stock B. His expected average annual return on his portfolio would be:

$$E(R_p) = 0.25(8\%) + 0.75(20\%) = 2\% + 15\% = 17\%$$

Of course, this higher expected return will coincide with wider swings or variations in expected annual returns relative to Mary's portfolio. We could recalculate portfolio returns using the procedure shown in Table 12.4 and also prepare a revised Figure 12.4 to show this relationship between expected return and risk.

VARIANCE AND STANDARD DEVIATION OF RETURN ON A PORTFOLIO

The total risk of a portfolio can be measured by its variance or the standard deviation of its returns. Extending the concept of portfolio return, one might think that the variance of a portfolio is simply a weighted average of asset variances. Unfortunately, this first guess is not correct and we cannot use an equation like 12.7. To see why, look at the time series of returns illustrated in Figure 12.5.

Suppose that the firm shown in graph A manufactures snow skiing equipment. It is clear from the graph that its returns are not constant; skiing is a seasonal business. The graph for Firm B represents the returns on a swimsuit manufacturer. Its returns are also seasonal, but they are opposite those of the ski equipment firm. In winter, skis sell well and swimsuits do not; in the summer, the opposite is true. From the variability of their returns over time, the two firms appear to be risky investments.

FIGURE 12.5   Benefits of Diversification: Combining Two Risky Assets May Lead to Lower Portfolio Risk

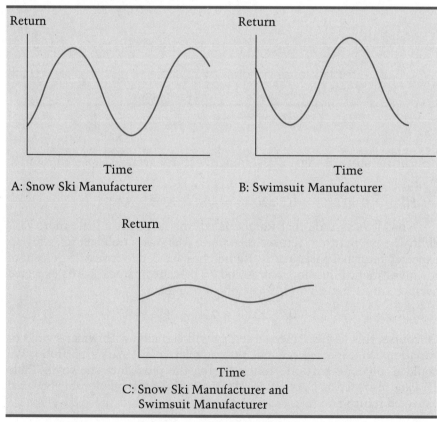

Suppose however, that either through merger or through investors buying shares of both, the two firms are combined in a portfolio. The portfolio's combined return in graph C in Figure 12.5 shows very little risk; the returns over time appear to be fairly stable. Why do the portfolio returns vary so much less than either firm alone?

Lower portfolio variability arises from the benefits of diversification. **Diversification** occurs when we invest in several different assets rather than just a single one. The benefits of diversification are greatest, as we see in Figure 12.5, when asset returns have **negative correlations,** that is, they tend to move in opposite directions.

A further look at Figure 12.4, which illustrated the returns for an equally weighted portfolio of stocks A and B, shows the impact of diversification even when the returns on two stocks move in the same direction over time. Stocks A and B are said to have a **positive correlation** because their returns move together over time. Even so, the portfolio is less risky than stock B because of the lower variability in annual returns over time.

Although the calculation of this measure is beyond the scope of this text,[6] **correlation** is a statistical concept that relates movements in one set of returns to movements in another set over time. Part of many investors' strategy is to have investments in their portfolio which are not highly positively correlated with each other. The less positive or the more negative the correlation, the greater the risk reduction benefits from diversifying into different assets.

diversification
occurs when we invest in several different assets rather than just a single one

negative correlation
two time series tend to move in opposite directions

positive correlation
two time series tend to move in conjunction with each other

correlation
statistical concept that relates movements in one set of returns to movements in another set over time

PORTFOLIO RISK AND THE NUMBER OF INVESTMENTS IN THE PORTFOLIO

What happens to portfolio risk as more and more assets are added to a portfolio? Adding a second asset to a one-asset portfolio may reduce portfolio risk. Will portfolio risk continue to decline if we continue to diversify the portfolio by adding a third, a tenth, or a fiftieth asset to the portfolio?

The answer is no. The greatest reductions in portfolio risk come from combining assets with negative correlations. As each new asset reduces the variability of a portfolio's returns, it becomes more difficult to find still more assets that have low correlations with the portfolio because all assets share a common environment. In U.S. markets, most assets' returns react in some way to the business cycle. Once a portfolio includes a certain number of assets, the pervasive effects of national economic and financial market trends reduce the likelihood that further diversification can offer significant benefits.

We may look beyond our national borders and include non-U.S. assets in the portfolio to gain some additional reduction in portfolio risk since

6.   The development and calculation of correlations for portfolios can be found in most investments textbooks. See, for example, Frank K. Reilly and Edgar A. Norton, *Investments*, 4th edition, 1995, Chapter 6.

the world's economies and financial markets do not move in lockstep. Even though the global product and financial markets are becoming more and more integrated, remaining differences suggest that a well diversified global asset portfolio will have a lower total risk than a well diversified portfolio of U.S. assets. Even with a choice of global assets, however, diversification benefits are limited. The world's economies do not move in lockstep, but neither do they have large negative correlations. Eventually the benefits of further diversification will disappear.

U.S. stock market data confirm this expected pattern.[7] By constructing a number of sample portfolios, with one stock, two stocks, three stocks, and so on, researchers have found that average portfolio risk declines as additional securities are added to the portfolio, as shown in Figure 12.6. After a portfolio includes 20 to 30 stocks, the risk reduction effect of adding more stocks is nil. The total risk of a well diversified portfolio of U.S. stocks appears to be about one-half the risk of the average one-stock portfolio. In other words, constructing a well diversified portfolio of about 20 stocks can reduce overall portfolio risk by one-half!

Further reductions in portfolio risk are documented when international securities are included in the analysis. It appears that only about 15 international stocks are needed to exhaust the risk-reducing benefits of diversification. The total risk of a well diversified international portfolio of stocks is about one-third of the risk of an average one-stock portfolio; that is, up to two-thirds of portfolio risk can be eliminated in a well diversified international portfolio!

SYSTEMATIC AND UNSYSTEMATIC RISK

Figure 12.6 shows that two types of risk affect both individual assets and portfolios of assets: risk that can be diversified away, and risk that cannot be diversified away.

Figure 12.7 resembles Figure 12.6 with labels for these types of risks. The risk that is diversified away as assets are added to a portfolio is the firm- and industry-specific risk, or the "microeconomic" risk. This is known as **unsystematic risk.**

unsystematic risk
risk that can be
diversified away

Information that has negative implications for one firm may contain good news for another firm.[8] In a well diversified portfolio of firms from different industries, the effects of good news for one firm may effectively cancel out bad news for another firm. The overall impact of such news on the portfolio's returns should approach zero. In this way, diversification

---

7.   J. Evans and S. H. Archer, "Diversification and the Reduction of Dispersion: An Empirical Analysis," *Journal of Finance* (December 1968): 761–67.

8.   For example, news of rising oil prices may be bad news for airlines, but good news for oil companies. The announcement of the resignation of a well respected CEO may be bad for the company, but good for competing firms. One firm's announcement of its intentions to build a technologically advanced plant may mean bad news for its competitors.

FIGURE 12.6   Risk and Portfolio Diversification

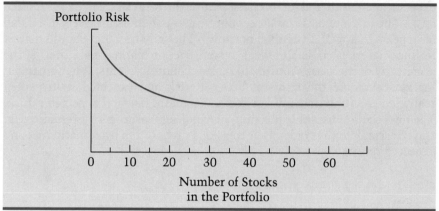

can effectively eliminate unsystematic risk. A well diversified portfolio can reduce the effects on portfolio returns of firm- or industry-specific events, such as strikes, technological advances, and entry and exit of competitors, to zero.

Diversification cannot eliminate risk that is inherent in the macro-economy. This risk is called **systematic risk,** or **market risk.** General financial market trends affect most companies in similar ways. Macroeconomic events such as changes in GDP, war, major political events, rising optimism or pessimism among investors, tax increases or cuts, or a stronger or weaker dollar have broad effects on product and financial markets. Even a well diversified portfolio cannot escape these effects.

systematic risk (market risk)
risk that cannot be eliminated through diversification

FIGURE 12.7   Systematic and Unsystematic Risk

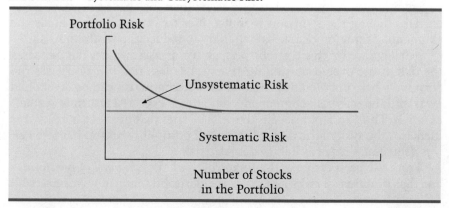

Thus, the total risk of an asset should not affect the market's return expectations for that asset, because part of the total risk can be diversified away. The unsystematic, microeconomic component of an asset's total risk disappears in a well diversified portfolio. The only risk that should matter to financial markets is an asset's systematic, or market, risk; that is, the sensitivity of the asset's returns to macroeconomic events. When financial markets evaluate the trade-off between risk and expected return, they really focus on the trade-off between systematic risk and expected return. The next section uses this insight to develop a measure for systematic risk, and to formalize the trade-off or relationship between systematic risk and expected return.

CAPITAL ASSET PRICING MODEL

We've just seen how investors, either on their own or by investing in vehicles such as mutual funds, can diversify their investments. We've seen how it is the level of each investment's systematic risk that determines its expected return. Regardless of their total risk (or standard deviation of returns), assets with higher levels of systematic risk should have higher expected returns; assets with lower levels of systematic risk should have lower levels of expected returns. From this perspective, we see that it is not an asset's total risk that is important. What *is* important is how the asset affects the risk of the overall portfolio.

For example, from historical data researchers have found that, by itself, gold is a risky investment. It offers no income stream and its price fluctuates, sometimes with high volatility. But in combination with common stocks, an investment in gold can reduce a portfolio's total risk. The reason is that common stocks usually perform poorly when investors fear inflation, whereas gold prices rise when higher inflation is expected. Including gold to a stock portfolio can have a *negative* effect on risk; that is, it can make the portfolio *less* risky.

Similarly, in isolation, the ski and swimsuit manufacturers from Figure 12.5 may appear risky, but relative to each other, they have a negative effect on risk. Adding the swimsuit manufacturer to a portfolio that holds the ski manufacturer (or vice versa) will help to reduce the portfolio's risk.

When viewed from a portfolio perspective, an asset is risky if it *increases* the risk of the overall portfolio. An asset has less risk if it *decreases* the portfolio's risk. But we know that all unsystematic risk can be diversified away and the only risk component that affects expected return is systematic risk. Thus, to rephrase the above, it is true that an asset is risky if it *increases* the *systematic* risk of the overall portfolio. An asset has less risk if it *decreases* the portfolio's *systematic* risk.

market portfolio
portfolio that contains
all risky assets

From the perspective of the financial markets, the **market portfolio**—one that contains all risky assets—is the portfolio that truly eliminates all

Most people do not have the time and expertise needed to manage an asset portfolio. For many, acquiring the investment capital is difficult, too. Fortunately, such "small" investors, as they are called, have a way to obtain professional investment management and portfolio diversification. They can invest using investment companies.

An *investment company* is a corporation that invests the pooled funds of savers. Many investment companies purchase the stocks and bonds of corporations. Others specialize in holding short-term commercial paper, bank CDs, and U.S. Treasury bills and are known as money market mutual funds. The funds of many investors are pooled for the primary purpose of obtaining expert management and wide diversity in security investments. Both the number and the size of investment companies have increased rapidly in recent years.

DIVERSIFICATION FOR THE SMALL INVESTOR

Classification of Investment Companies

Investment companies come in two types: closed-end funds and mutual, or open-ended, funds, which are much more popular. Both types have the common objective of achieving intelligent diversification, or variety of investments, for the pooled funds of individuals.

Closed-end funds

Ordinarily, money is initially raised to invest by selling stock or ownership shares in a *closed-end fund.* Owners of closed-end fund shares may sell their shares just as they would with any corporate security, that is, by selling them to other investors. The shares of closed-end funds are traded either on an organized securities exchange or in the over-the-counter market.

Mutual funds

A *mutual fund* can invest in equity and debt securities, and it uses dividends and interest from these securities to pay dividends to shareholders. In contrast with closed-end funds, mutual funds continually sell shares to willing investors. Shareholders may sell their shares back to the mutual fund at any time. The purchase and selling price of mutual fund shares is related to the fund's net asset value. A fund's net asset value is the per-share market value of the securities that the fund owns. Some large and well known mutual fund companies are Fidelity, Vanguard, T. Rowe Price, and Scudder.

Securities and Exchange Commission data indicate that more than 7,000 mutual funds hold assets in the form of corporate and government securities in excess of $1 trillion—a popular method of investing indeed!

unsystematic risk. The only risk contained in the market portfolio is systematic risk. That means as the value of the market portfolio fluctuates over time, the pure effect of systematic risk is seen.[9]

Since the market portfolio contains all risky assets, some assets that are especially sensitive to changes in macroeconomic variables such as interest rates or GDP will have higher exposures to systematic risk than the overall market portfolio. Some assets' returns will be less sensitive to these influences and will have less systematic risk. One way we can measure an asset's systematic risk is by comparing its fluctuations in value over time to those of the market portfolio. Those assets whose returns rise and fall in line with the overall market will have the same systematic risk exposure as the market portfolio (see Figure 12.8a). Assets whose returns are more volatile (they typically rise higher and fall lower) than those of the market portfolio have systematic risk exposures that exceed those of the market portfolio (Figure 12.8b). Assets whose returns are less volatile (their returns don't rise as high or fall as low as the market portfolio) have less systematic risk exposure than the market portfolio (Figure 12.8c).

Remember that from a portfolio perspective, an asset's risk is measured by how it affects the risk of the overall portfolio. Assets with higher systematic risk will tend to increase the systematic risk (and the expected return) of the portfolios in which they appear. Assets with low levels of systematic risk will tend to lower the systematic risk (and the expected return) of the portfolios in which they appear.

Capital Asset Pricing Model (CAPM)
states that expected return on an asset depends on its level of systematic risk

These insights are the basis for the ***Capital Asset Pricing Model (CAPM).*** The Capital Asset Pricing Model states that the expected return on an asset depends upon its level of systematic risk. The asset's systematic risk is measured relative to that of the market portfolio. In other words, the relative risk of an asset is that asset's contribution to the risk of a well diversified portfolio.

beta
measure of an asset's systematic risk

Under the CAPM, ***beta (β)*** is the measure of an asset's systematic risk. Beta is a measure of *relative risk.* Beta measures the volatility or variability of an asset's returns *relative* to the market portfolio. For example, if an asset's returns are half as volatile as those of the market portfolio, its beta will be 0.5. That means that if the market portfolio changes in value by 10 percent, on average the asset's value changes by 0.5 as much, or 5 percent. If an asset's beta equals 1.4, then the asset's returns are 40 percent more volatile than the market. When the market changes in value by 10 percent, the asset's value changes, on average, by 1.4 times 10 percent, or 14 percent. With this definition of beta, the beta of the market portfolio, β_{MKT}, is 1.0. By definition, the market is exactly as volatile as itself!

9.   It is only in the case of the market portfolio that the standard deviation (or variance) of returns shows the effect of systematic risk; for all other less-than-perfectly-diversified portfolios, the portfolio's variance measures a combination of systematic and unsystematic risk influences.

FIGURE 12.8 Comparing Asset Returns Over Time with Those of the Market Portfolio

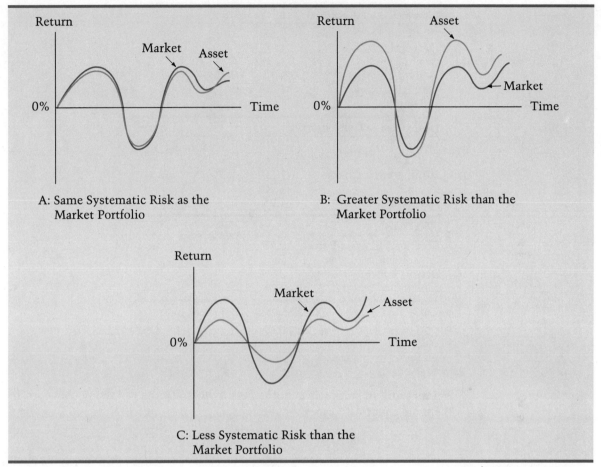

A: Same Systematic Risk as the
Market Portfolio

B: Greater Systematic Risk than the
Market Portfolio

C: Less Systematic Risk than the
Market Portfolio

Assets that are more volatile than the market, or equivalently, those that have greater systematic risk than the market, have betas greater than 1.0. Whatever the market return is, these assets' average returns are larger in *absolute value*. Assets that are less volatile than the market, that is, those that have less systematic risk, have betas less than 1.0. These assets' returns, on average, are less in absolute value than those of the market. Table 12.5 lists the historic betas for some stocks.

ESTIMATING BETA

We can estimate beta for a stock or portfolio of stocks relative to the overall stock market using simple linear regression analysis. The reader might recall the following equation from an earlier course in statistics. However,

TABLE 12.5   Example of Stock Betas

INDUSTRIAL FIRMS	BETA
AT&T	0.85
Coca-Cola	1.00
Disney	1.10
General Electric	1.10
General Motors	1.10
McDonald's	1.00
TRANSPORTATION FIRMS	
AMR	1.30
Alaska Air	1.20
Burlington Northern	1.20
Conrail	1.30
Federal Express	1.25
UTILITIES	
American Electric Power	0.75
Consolidated Edison	0.75
Detroit Edison	0.70
Panhandle Eastern	1.05

Source: *Value Line Investment Survey,* various issues.

prior work in statistics is not necessary to grasp the following concepts. In simple equation form we have:

$$R_i = a + \beta R_{MKT} + e \tag{12.8}$$

where a is the alpha or intercept term, β is the beta or slope coefficient which shows the size of the impact that market returns (R_{MKT}) have on stock returns (R_i), and e is an error term reflecting the fact that changes in market returns are not likely to fully explain changes in stock returns.

There are computer software programs and sophisticated financial calculators that can perform the necessary calculations and find the beta coefficient with little effort. In addition, we can estimate beta the "long way" by using relatively simple calculations that can be done by hand or by using a simple calculator. We will demonstrate the long way of estimating beta so that the reader can develop a better understanding of the underlying process.

Let's begin by assuming that the annual returns over the past six years on the market and stock B (which we discussed earlier in the chapter) were as follows:

YEAR	THE MARKET	STOCK B
1	10%	20%
2	16	30
3	9	10
4	−4	−10
5	28	50
6	13	20

We now want to measure the systematic riskiness of stock B relative to the market. Let's first plot these returns on the graph in Figure 12.9. The market's returns are plotted along the x (horizontal) axis since we are interested in examining how stock B's returns move with or respond to the market's returns. Stock B's annual returns are plotted along the y (vertical) axis. Notice that there is a positive (upward sloping) relationship between the returns on the market and stock B's returns. We also have inserted a line across the scatter plot of annual returns. In addition to having a positive relationship, the steepness of the slope of the line reflects how much stock B's returns respond to a change in the market's returns. Thus, the beta coefficient is the slope of this line and indicates the sensitivity of stock B's returns to the market's returns.

Now let's actually calculate the slope or beta of the relationship between the returns on the market and returns on stock B. The calculations used to estimate beta are shown in Table 12.6. A beta of 1.90 indicates that stock B is riskier than the market. More specifically, we can say that based on six years of past data that on average a 1 percent increase (decrease) in the annual return on the market was accompanied by a 1.90 percentage increase (decrease) in stock B's annual returns. Thus, stock B is

FIGURE 12.9   Plots of the Returns for Stock B and the Market

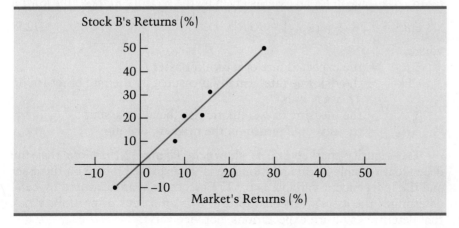

TABLE 12.6   How to Calculate a Beta Coefficient or Measure of Systematic Risk

YEAR	ANNUAL RATES OF RETURN THE MARKET x-AXIS	STOCK B y-AXIS	THE MARKET'S RETURNS SQUARED x^2	STOCK B'S RETURNS SQUARED y^2	PRODUCT OF THE RETURNS $x \times y$
1	0.10	0.20	0.0100	0.0400	0.0200
2	0.16	0.30	0.0256	0.0900	0.0480
3	0.09	0.10	0.0081	0.0100	0.0090
4	−0.04	−0.10	0.0016	0.0100	0.0040
5	0.28	0.50	0.0784	0.2500	0.1400
6	0.13	0.20	0.0169	0.0400	0.0260
	$\Sigma x = 0.72$	$\Sigma y = 1.20$	$\Sigma x^2 = 0.1406$	$\Sigma y^2 = 0.4400$	$\Sigma xy = 0.2470$

Estimating beta where $n = 6$ is the number of years or observations:

$$b = \frac{n\Sigma xy - (\Sigma x)(\Sigma y)}{n\Sigma x^2 - (\Sigma x)^2} = \frac{(6)(0.2470) - (0.72)(1.20)}{(6)(0.1406) - (0.72)(0.72)}$$

$$= \frac{1.4820 - 0.8640}{0.8436 - 0.5184} = \frac{0.6180}{0.3252} = 1.90$$

said to be nearly twice as risky as the market. It is important to note that our estimate was based on only six observations. Normally, betas are estimated using many more data points.

SECURITY MARKET LINE

Once an asset's beta is estimated it can be used to form the basis of return predictions. Another basic aspect of the CAPM is that the expected return/risk tradeoff for an asset is given by the *security market line (SML)*:

$$E(R_i) = RFR + [E(R_{MKT}) - RFR]\beta_i \tag{12.9}$$

where:

$E(R_i)$ = the expected rate of return for asset i

RFR = the risk-free rate, usually measured by the rate of return on Treasury bills

β_i = the measure of systematic risk (beta) for asset i

$E(R_{MKT})$ = the expected return on the market portfolio

The security market line is shown in Figure 12.10. Note that the dependent variable in this relationship is the expected return on the asset and the independent variable is β_i. The asset's risk, as measured by beta, determines the asset's expected return. It is an asset's or portfolio's risk that determines return expectations, not vice versa.

FIGURE 12.10   Security Market Line

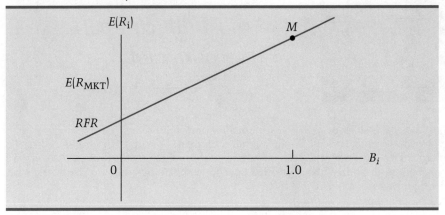

The security market line shows that the reward for taking on systematic risk is the market risk premium, $E(R_{MKT}) - RFR$, which is the slope of the SML. An asset's risk premium, or extra expected return, equals $[E(R_{MKT}) - RFR]\beta_i$.

To illustrate the use of the SML, let's find the expected return on AT&T stock if the market is expected to rise 8 percent. We'll assume the Treasury bill rate is 4.0 percent. We'll need to use Equation 12.9, the Security Market Line, to estimate AT&T's expected return under these conditions. We'll also need to use AT&T's beta listed in Table 12.5. Using its recent beta of 0.85, should the market rise 8 percent, AT&T's expected return is:

$E(R_{AT\&T})$ = 0.04 + [0.08−0.04] × 0.85 − 0.074, or 7.4 percent.

If, for example, the market portfolio is expected to fall by 15 percent, AT&T's expected return will be:

$E(R_{AT\&T})$ = 0.04 + [−0.15−0.04] × 0.85 = −0.122, or −12.2%.

The beta of a portfolio of assets can be estimated at least two ways. First, portfolio returns can be regressed on market returns using Equation 12.8. Second, the beta of a portfolio can be estimated by computing the weighted average of its component's betas:

$$\text{Beta}_p = \sum_{i=1}^{n} w_i \text{beta}_i \qquad (12.10)$$

where w_i is the weight of the ith asset in the portfolio. Unlike the portfolio variance risk measure, the systematic risk of a portfolio does equal the weighted average of its component's systematic risk.

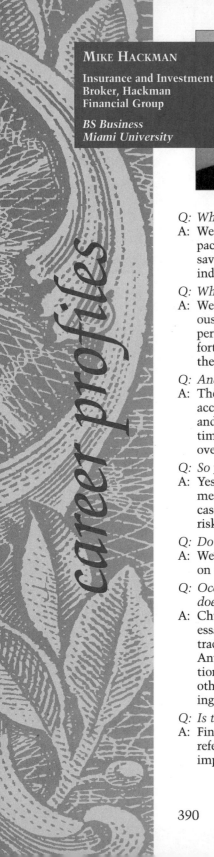

MIKE HACKMAN

Insurance and Investment Broker, Hackman Financial Group

BS Business
Miami University

> ## "Finding new clients is by far the most difficult part of my job."

Q: *What does an Insurance and Investment Broker do?*

A: We provide several services. We help small companies set up their employee benefit packages. Depending on the company, this could include medical insurance, 401(K) savings plans, disability plans, or other special benefit programs. We also work with individual investors.

Q: *What do you do for individuals?*

A: We help them identify and meet their financial goals. I know that sounds sort of obvious, but everything we do revolves around the client's goals. Investments which are perfect for financing a child's college education may be terrible for funding a comfortable retirement. So we spend a lot of time discussing with the client exactly what they wish to accomplish.

Q: *And once you understand their goals . . .*

A: Then we look for the appropriate investment vehicles to meet those goals. We have access to the entire investment spectrum—life insurance, mutual funds, annuities, and everything else. There are so many options that most individuals do not have the time or information necessary to evaluate even a small percentage of them. There are over 7,600 mutual funds alone.

Q: *So you simplify their choices.*

A: Yes. We spend lots of time and energy looking at the performance of various investment options. Then we make suggestions which match the client's goals. In most cases, we'll suggest a diversified portfolio. Diversification helps reduce downward risk in bad years and provide good performance in up years.

Q: *Do you execute the trades for your clients?*

A: We work with a broker/dealer in Florida. They execute trades for our customers based on our instructions. For that service they keep a portion of the commission.

Q: *Occasionally we see the term "churning" in reports about unscrupulous brokers. What does it mean?*

A: Churning is when a broker suggests an investment strategy where there is an unnecessary amount of buying and selling of securities. And the purpose of the frequent trades is not to benefit the client but to generate high commissions for the broker. Anyone serious about making a living in this business learns quickly that it is a relationship business. If you lose the trust of your clients by churning an account or some other bad move, they won't be clients for very long. And if you can't keep your existing clients that means you need to keep finding new ones.

Q: *Is that difficult?*

A: Finding new clients is by far the most difficult part of my job. I work strictly on the referrals and introductions of my clients and other people I meet. That's why it's so important for me to provide sound and ethical advice.

Beta has several practical uses in finance. It is used to determine investors' required rate of return on an investment. Beta also is used to develop estimates of shareholders' required returns on their investments. And as we have seen in here, beta is a valuable measure of the systematic risk of an asset.

SUMMARY

Financial risk and return concepts are among the most mathematical and confusing to the first-time finance student, but they are vital to understanding financial markets, institutions, and management. Much of modern investment analysis, portfolio management, and corporate finance is based upon the topics reviewed in this chapter. At least two individuals—Harry Markowitz (for recognizing the importance of correlation) and William Sharpe (for the CAPM)—have won Nobel Prizes for their groundbreaking work in this area.

Historical returns are computed from past income cash flows and price changes. From annualized returns we can determine the average return on an asset over time as well as measures of risk (variance, standard deviation, and the coefficient of variation). Looking toward the future, scenario analysis is a widely used tool for estimating expected return and risk.

When assets are combined into portfolios, diversification effects may mitigate the effects of each individual asset's risk. When some assets' returns are poor, others may be performing well. Adding assets to a portfolio may help reduce portfolio risk. But after a certain point, all unsystematic risk has been diversified away and only systematic risk remains. Systematic risk, or beta, is the major determinant of returns for individual assets. The security market line graphically shows this expected return and systematic risk relationship.

KEY TERMS

beta
Capital Asset Pricing
  Model (CAPM)
chartists
coefficient of variation (*CV*)
correlation
deviations
diversification
efficient market
ex-ante
market portfolio
negative correlation

portfolio
positive correlation
random walk
semi-strong form efficient market
standard deviation
strong-form efficient market
systematic risk (market risk)
technician
unsystematic risk
variance
weak-form efficient market

DISCUSSION QUESTIONS

1. Explain how a percentage return is calculated and describe the calculation of an arithmetic average return.
2. Describe how the variance and standard deviation are calculated and indicate how they are used as measures of risk.
3. What is meant by the coefficient of variation? How is it used as a measure of risk?
4. Describe the meaning of a "state of nature" and explain how this concept is used to provide expected measures of return and risk.
5. Explain the historical relationships between return and risk for common stocks versus corporate bonds.
6. Explain what is meant by "market efficiency." What are the characteristics of an efficient market?
7. What are the differences among the weak, semi-strong, and strong forms of the efficient market hypothesis?
8. Define what is meant by a portfolio and describe how the expected return on a portfolio is computed.
9. Explain the terms diversification and correlation in the context of forming portfolios.
10. Describe what happens to portfolio risk as more and more assets are added to a portfolio. Are there advantages to international diversification?
11. How does systematic risk differ from unsystematic risk?
12. What is meant by the Capital Asset Pricing Model? Describe how it relates to expected return and risk.
13. Define the concept of "beta" and describe what it measures.
14. Briefly describe how beta can be calculated for an individual stock.
15. What is meant by the security market line? Describe how it is used.

PROBLEMS

1. From the information below, compute the average annual return, the variance, standard deviation, and coefficient of variation for each asset.

ASSET	ANNUAL RETURNS
A	5%, 10%, 15%, 4%
B	−6%, 20%, 2%, −5%, 10%
C	12%, 15%, 17%
D	10%, −10%, 20%, −15%, 8%, −7%

2. Using the Treasury bill return in Table 12.3 as an approximation to the nominal risk-free rate, what is the risk premium from investing in each of the other asset classes listed in Table 12.3?

3. Given her evaluation of current economic conditions, Ima Nutt believes there is a 20 percent probability of recession, a 50 percent chance of continued steady growth, and a 30 percent probability of inflationary growth. For each possibility, Ima has developed an interest rate forecast for long-term Treasury bond interest rates:

ECONOMIC FORECAST:	INTEREST RATE FORECAST:
Recession	6 percent
Constant growth	9 percent
Inflation	14 percent

   a. What is the expected interest rate under Ima's forecast?
   b. What is the variance and standard deviation of Ima's interest rate forecast?
   c. What is the coefficient of variation of Ima's interest rate forecast?
   d. If the current long-term Treasury bond interest rate is 8 percent, should Ima consider purchasing a Treasury bond? Why or why not?

4. Scenario analysis has many practical applications in addition to being used to forecast security returns. In this problem, scenario analysis is used to forecast an exchange rate. Jim Danday's forecast for the deutsch Mark/dollar exchange rate depends upon what the U.S. Federal Reserve and German central bankers do to their country's money supply. Jim is considering the following scenarios and exchange rate forecasts:

CENTRAL BANK BEHAVIOR	JIM'S PROBABILITY OF THE BANK'S BEHAVIOR	JIM'S EXCHANGE RATE FORECAST
Germany increases MS growth; U.S. does not	.20	1.55 DM/$
Germany, U.S. maintain constant MS growth	.30	1.45 DM/$
U.S. increases MS growth; Germany does not	.35	1.35 DM/$
U.S., Germany increase MS growth	.15	1.50 DM/$

   a. What is Jim's expected exchange rate forecast?
   b. What is the variance of Jim's exchange rate forecast?
   c. What is the coefficient of variation of Jim's exchange rate forecast?

5. Using the data in Table 12.3, calculate and interpret the coefficient of variation for each asset class.

6. Stock market forecasters are predicting that the stock market will rise a modest 5 percent next year. Given the beta of each stock below, what is the expected change in each stock's value?

FIRM	BETA
BCD	1.25
NOP	0.70
WXY	1.10
ZYX	1.00

7. Suppose the estimated security market line is:
   $E(R_i) = 4.0 + 7(\beta_i)$
   a. What is the current Treasury bill rate?
   b. What is the current market risk premium?
   c. What is the current expected market return?
   d. Explain what beta (β) measures.

8. Financial researchers at Smith Sharon, an investment bank, estimate the current security market line as:
   $E(R_i) = 4.5 + 6.8(\beta_i)$
   a. Explain what happens to expected return as beta increases from 1.0 to 2.0.
   b. Suppose an asset has a beta of -1.0. What is the expected return on this asset? Would anyone want to invest in it? Why or why not?

9. You've collected data on the betas of various mutual funds. Each fund and its beta is listed below:

MUTUAL FUND	BETA
Weak Fund	0.23
Fido Fund	0.77
Vanwatch	1.05
Temper	1.33

   a. Estimate the beta of your fund holdings if you held equal proportions of each of the above funds.
   b. Estimate the beta of your fund holdings if you had 20 percent of your investments in the Weak fund, 40 percent in Fido, 15 percent in Vanwatch, and the remainder in Temper.

10. Using your answers to parts a. and b. in problem 9, estimate your portfolio's expected return if the security market line is estimated as:
    $E(R_i) = 5.2 + 8.4(\beta_i)$

SELF-TEST QUESTIONS

1. Which of the following is a measure of risk per unit of return?
   a. arithmetic average

   b.   variance

   c.   standard deviation

   d.   coefficient of variation

2. Which one of the following assets has historically had the highest average annual return?

   a.   large company stocks

   b.   long-term corporate bonds

   c.   long-term government bonds

   d.   U.S. Treasury bills

3. Which one of the following assets has historically had the largest standard deviation of annual returns?

   a.   large company stocks

   b.   long-term corporate bonds

   c.   long-term government bonds

   d.   U.S. Treasury bills

4. Which one of the following is not considered to be a generally recognized type of market efficiency?

   a.   strong-form

   b.   semi-strong form

   c.   weak-form

   d.   insider-information form

5. A statistical concept that relates movements in one set of returns to movements in another set over time is called:

   a.   variance

   b.   standard deviation

   c.   coefficient of variation

   d.   correlation

6. The total risk of a well-diversified portfolio of U.S. stocks appears to be about what proportion of the risk of an average one-stock portfolio?

   a.   one-third

   b.   one-half

   c.   two-thirds

   d.   three-fourths

7. The total risk of a well-diversified international portfolio of stocks appears to be about what proportion of the risk of an average one-stock portfolio?

   a.   one-third

   b.   one-half

   c.   two-thirds

   d.   three-fourths

8. Portfolio risk is comprised of:

   a.   systematic and market risk

   b.   unsystematic and microeconomic risk

   c.   systematic and unsystematic risk

   d.   systematic and macroeconomic risk

9. Which of the following is not a component of the security market line equation?
   a. risk-free rate
   b. expected return on the market
   c. an asset's systematic risk
   d. an asset's unsystematic risk

SELF-TEST PROBLEMS

1. Suppose a firm introduces a new product. If the economy starts to grow quickly (probability = 0.30), shareholders expect the price of their shares to rise by 20 percent. If normal economic conditions occur (probability = 0.40) when the product is introduced, the firm's shareholder return will be 10 percent. If a recession occurs during the introduction of the product (probability = 0.30), shareholder wealth will decline by 15 percent. What is the expected return facing the firm's shareholders? What is the variance, standard deviation, and coefficient of variation of their return forecasts?

2. How does investing in the stock described in Problem 1 compare to investing in Treasury bills? Assume under the boom scenario that T-bills will return 6 percent; under the normal scenario, the T-bill yield will be 4.5 percent; in a recession, the T-bill return will be 3.5 percent.

SUGGESTED READINGS

Brealey, Richard A., Stewart C. Myers, and Alan J. Marcus. *Fundamentals of Corporate Finance.* New York: McGraw-Hill, Inc., 1995. Chap. 9.

Dickerson, Bodil, B.J. Campsey, and Eugene F. Brigham. *Introduction to Financial Management,* 4e. Orlando, FL: The Dryden Press, 1995. Chap. 12.

Evans, J., and S.H. Archer. "Diversification and the Reduction of Dispersion: An Empirical Analysis." *Journal of Finance,* December, 1968, pp. 761–67.

Harrington, Diana R. *Corporate Financial Analysis,* 4e. Homewood, IL: Richard D. Irwin, 1993. Chap. 6.

Peterson, Pamela P. *Financial Management and Analysis.* New York, NY: McGraw-Hill, 1994. Chap. 7.

Reilly, Frank K., and Edgar A. Norton. *Investments,* 4e. Fort Worth, TX: The Dryden Press, 1995. Chap. 6.

Ross, Stephen A., Randolph W. Westerfield, and Bradford D. Jordan. *Fundamentals of Corporate Finance.* Homewood, IL: Richard D. Irwin, 1995. Chaps. 10 and 11.

Weston, J. Fred, Scott Besley, and Eugene F. Brigham. *Essentials of Managerial Finance,* 11e. Fort Worth, TX: The Dryden Press, 1996. Chap. 5.

ANSWERS TO SELF-TEST QUESTIONS   1. d, 2. a, 3. a, 4. d, 5. d, 6. b, 7. a, 8. c, 9. d

ANSWERS TO SELF-TEST PROBLEMS

1. The expected return $[E(R)]$ to the shareholders is found by using Equation 12.5:

    $$E(R) = 0.3(20\%) + 0.4(10\%) + 0.3(-15\%) = 5.5\%.$$

    Thus, if these scenarios could be rerun many times, the long-run expected return to the shareholder would be 5.5%. In any one year, however, the shareholders' return will be either 20 percent, 10 percent, or −15 percent, depending upon whether a boom, normal conditions, or recession occurs.

    The shareholders' forecasted variance of returns is computed using the ex-ante formula, Equation 12.6:

    $$\sigma^2 = 0.3(20\% - 5.5\%)^2 + 0.4(10\% - 5.5\%)^2 + 0.3(-15\% - 5.5\%)^2$$
    $$= 63.075\%^2 + 8.1\%^2 + 126.075\%^2$$
    $$= 197.25\%^2$$

    The standard deviation is the square root of the variance, $\sqrt{197.25\%^2}$, or 14.04 percent. The coefficient of variation, CV, is the ratio of the standard deviation to the expected value:

    $$CV = 14.04\%/5.5\% = 2.55$$

    Shareholders are exposed to 2.55 units of risk for every 1 unit of expected return.

2. We need to compare measures of expected return and risk. The expected return and risk from holding the stock were computed in the previous example. Now let's find the expected return and risk for the T-bill. Its expected return is:

    $$(0.3)(6\%) + (0.4)(4.5\%) + (0.3)(3.5\%) = 4.65\%.$$

    The variance of the T-bill's expected return is:

    $$0.3(6\% - 4.65\%)^2 + 0.4(4.5\% - 4.65\%)^2 + 0.3(3.5\% - 4.65\%)^2 = 0.9525\%^2$$

    The standard deviation, σ, is $\sqrt{0.9525\%^2}$, or 0.976%. This gives the T-bill a coefficient of variation of

    $$CV = \sigma/E(R) = 0.976\%/4.65\%$$

    which equals 0.21. The Treasury bill has an expected return of 4.65 percent and exposes its holder to 0.21 units of risk for every one unit of return. The shareholders in the previous example have an expected return of 5.5 percent and are exposed to 2.55 units of risk for every one unit of return. The stock has a higher expected return to go along with its higher risk. But some investors may feel the T-bill is a more prudent investment choice as it has an expected return just 0.85 percent less than the stock but has less than one-tenth the risk.

PART 3

INTRODUCTION

Part 3 deals with the applications of finance within a business firm. The practice of financial management requires businesspeople to work with financial institutions in the context of the financial market. If Wal-Mart needs a short-term loan to help finance inventory for the Christmas selling season, it can go to a bank for the loan. But the interest rate that Wal-Mart pays will be affected by the current level of interest rates in the economy, which is determined by a variety of economic conditions. If Wal-Mart needs to raise many millions of dollars to finance new expansion and construction, it can work with another type of financial institution, an investment bank, which will help Wal-Mart sell bonds or shares of common stock to raise the needed funds. The interest rate on the bonds and the price of the stock is determined by the conditions of the financial markets.

Institutions and investors pay close attention to a firm's financial management policies. Market participants glean information from a firm's financial statements, namely its balance sheet, income statement, and statement of cash flows. Changes in a firm's financial condition inform investors of a firm's strengthening or weakening position against its competitors. Investors and lending institutions may express concern if a firm's financing policy changes so that it begins to use much more debt financing than it has in the past.

A firm's managers use information that they obtain from the financial markets and institutions. They will keep their eyes on the firm's stock price. Changes in the stock price may reflect investor happiness or dissatisfaction with the company and its management's decisions. Managers will use interest rate and stock price information from the financial markets to evaluate the firm's own investments in its lines of business. The level of short-term interest rates, the level of long-

Business Finance

term interest rates, and stock prices will influence management's decisions about how to raise funds to finance the firm's activities.

Chapter 13 introduces the various ways a business can be organized and the financial implications of each organizational form. We discuss the financial goal of maximizing shareholder wealth as well as the three basic accounting statements: the balance sheet, income statement, and statement of cash flows. Chapter 14 continues the discussion of financial statements by showing how the information contained in them can be used to evaluate a firm's strengths and weaknesses. We review how managers use financial statement relationships to estimate the firm's future asset and financing needs.

Any firm will have short-term investment and financing needs as well as long-term investment and financing needs. Chapter 15 discusses strategies and methods for managing a firm's short-term assets such as cash, accounts receivable, and inventory. We show how a cash budget can be used to estimate a firm's future short-term financing needs. Chapter 16 reviews various sources of short-term financing for businesses, including bank loans, trade credit, and many other non-bank financing sources.

In Chapter 17 the focus changes to managing a firm's long-term assets. We introduce capital budgeting, which is a financial technique of deciding which assets a firm should invest in. Chapter 18 concludes Part 3 with a discussion of factors that influence firms' long-term financing choices. We bring the financial markets front and center in our discussion of how a firm uses financial information to determine its financing costs and how the financing costs affect its capital budgeting choices.

CHAPTER 13

Business Organization and Financial Data

AFTER STUDYING THIS CHAPTER, YOU SHOULD BE ABLE TO:

- Describe the three major forms of business organization.
- Identify the goal and functions of financial management.
- Describe the agency relationships in a business organization and their implications for financial management.
- Provide a brief description of the income statement.
- Provide a brief description of the balance sheet.
- Provide a brief description of the statement of cash flows.
- Describe the basis for federal income taxation of individuals and corporations.
- Describe the concept of depreciation and its impact on taxable income.

All businesses require money to run their operations. Money is needed to provide plants and equipment and to support current operations. Some firms require very little capital, and the industries in which these firms operate have a vast number of competitors. Any field of activity that requires little financial capital is open to a host of people who want to establish their own business. At the other extreme, there are businesses that require huge amounts of financial capital to operate even on a minimum scale. The cement and steel industries, for example, because of their capital requirements, have only a few large firms dominating these markets.

We begin this chapter with a brief discussion of some of the factors to consider when deciding to start a business. One of the decisions that has to be made is how the business will be organized. We discuss issues relating to a firm's goals and problems that can arise if a firm's owners are not the same people as the firm's managers.

The remainder of the chapter focuses on the financial data provided by business firms. Those firms organized as corporations must provide a summary of their financial performance in an annual report to their shareholders. Included in annual reports are three basic financial statements— the income statement, the balance sheet, and the statement of cash flows —that businesses need to prepare. Even individually owned, or closely held firms, need to prepare financial statements for tax purposes. We then discuss taxation and depreciation concepts that practicing business managers must understand if they are to be successful in managing their businesses.

STARTING A BUSINESS

In our market economy, individuals have the freedom to establish any legal business they choose. However, they must have adequate financial capital of their own or be able to arrange the necessary financing. The success of a business in raising funds for operations depends upon the extent that profits can be produced from operations. This means that a person starting a business must possess either the necessary financial capital to support initial operations until there is a profit, or must show unusual potential for making profits. Typically, the would-be owner must have the funds, since the potential for profit is seldom great enough to attract financial supporters.

STRATEGIC PLAN WITH A VISION OR MISSION

A business should begin with a vision or mission statement that is consistent with the planned overall strategy. The vision or mission should indicate what the firm wants to produce, distribute, and sell, or indicate what services it wants to provide. Comments on quality objectives and customer and owner focus also are typically found in vision and mission statements. Some statements are idealistic in their views.

Both small and large companies formulate strategic plans with visions and missions. Let's take a look at some of these statements. For example, Celestial Seasonings, Inc., which is the largest herbal tea company in the United States, declares in its "belief statement":

Our products must be superior in quality, of good value, beautifully artistic, and philosophically inspiring.

Ben & Jerry's Ice Cream Company has the following detailed statement of mission:

Ben & Jerry's is dedicated to the creation and demonstration of a new corporate concept of linked prosperity. Our mission consists of three interrelated parts:

Product Mission—*To make, distribute, and sell the finest quality, all-natural ice cream and related products in a wide variety of innovative flavors made from Vermont dairy products.*

Social Mission—*To operate the company in a way that actively recognizes the central role that business plays in the structure of society by initiating innovative ways to improve the quality of life of a broad community— local, national, and international.*

Economic Mission—*To operate the company on a sound financial basis of profitable growth, increasing value for our shareholders, and creating career opportunities and financial rewards for our employees.*

Norwest Corporation, a nationwide diversified financial services company providing banking, insurance, investments, and other financial services, has the following vision as stated in its 1993 annual report:

We want to be recognized as the premier financial services company in the markets we serve and be regarded as one of America's great companies.

In its 1994 annual report, Norwest follows with a "best practices" focus:

Norwest employees have embarked on a company-wide search for "Best Practices." That's finding the single best way to do something and adopting it wherever it applies.

Merck & Company, Inc., which is the world's largest pharmaceutical company, states in its 1993 annual report that:

Our mission is: to provide society with superior products and services— innovations and solutions that satisfy customer needs and improve the quality of life; to provide employees with challenging work and advancement opportunities; and to provide shareholders with a superior rate of return.

As a result of hiring a new chief executive officer (CEO) and the subsequent conducting of a thorough internal review, Merck established the following goals in its 1994 annual report:

First, we established an overriding goal that Merck will remain a top-tier growth company. . . . Second, to achieve this financial objective, we are strengthening our focus on Merck's core business as a research-based ethical pharmaceutical company in human and animal health.

International Business Machines Corporation (IBM) went through major restructuring during the early 1990s. Louis Gerstner, Jr., became Chairman of the Board and Chief Executive Officer in April, 1993. He made the following statement in IBM's 1993 annual report:

I caused quite a flap in the press in July (1993) when, at a press conference, I said, "The last thing IBM needs right now is a vision." A lot of the reports forgot the words "right now" and clucked about where IBM was headed without a vision.

The fact is, no company is going to succeed without a clear set of . . . strategies grounded in a clear understanding of what's happening in the marketplace. Some call it mission. Some call it vision. I call it strategy.

The 1994 IBM annual report followed up with the following mission statement:

We are IBM. We have two fundamental missions. First, we strive to lead in the creation, development and manufacture of the industry's most advanced information technologies. . . . Second, we translate these advanced technologies into value for our customers world-wide . . . .

BUSINESS AND FINANCIAL GOALS

Businesses must support their visions and missions with business and financial goals or plans—sometimes referred to as operating plans. For example, in its mission statement Merck indicated a financial goal was to provide its shareholders with a superior rate of return. Norwest in its 1993 annual report to shareholders states that its customer and financial goals come from its vision statement. For example, Norwest wants three-fourths of its customers to view the company as their first choice when considering the purchase of a new financial product. Norwest also has a goal of providing a return on equity in excess of 17 percent to its shareholders.

A guiding force behind top management's decisions should be the mission statement. Managers should regularly refer back to the firm's mission statement to ensure their actions are aligned with those of the overall firm. At the same time, the mission statement should not be carved in stone; it should be periodically reviewed to ensure it is up-to-date and reflects market needs in a dynamic, global economy. On the other hand, a business cannot chase every idea developed by its managers. Businesses need to stick to what they do best, or in the parlance of management, strategic goals should be related to the firm's core competencies.[1]

---

1.   C.K. Prahalad and G. Hamel, "The Core Competence of the Corporation," *Harvard Business Review* (May-June 1990): 79–91.

Attracting and acquiring financing is necessary in order to obtain the factors of production necessary to conduct business operations. Allocation of these factors is largely automatic under the market system. Resources flow smoothly to those businesses that, through their past operations and the promise of profitable future operations, are able to pay for them. Investors, as providers of debt and equity capital, expect a return on their investment. As we saw in Chapter 12, actual returns usually differ from expected returns. This is the risk faced by investors. But the investor or the financial intermediary who assumes an unusually large risk does so with the full expectation that, if things go well with the firm, the rewards for the investment will be very great. Where the possible risk is very small, the potential reward is small. As explained in Chapter 12, there is a trade-off between expected return and risk. Investment funds flow both to risky firms and very safe firms, invested according to the intermediary's or the investors' risk preferences.

GOAL OF A FIRM

mission statement
statement of a firm's rea-
son for being; sometimes
called a vision statement

Although a firm may have a ***mission statement*** espousing goals of quality, customer service, offering quality products at fair prices, and so on, such qualitative statements are really only a means to an end. The firm's managers need a definite benchmark against which to evaluate alternatives. The goal of any firm should be a financial one, namely the maximization of the owners' (or the common shareholders') wealth.

Creditors have a fixed claim that usually doesn't change with variations in the value of the firm's assets over time. As we learned in Chapter 10, shareholders have a residual or junior claim on the firm's assets. Therefore variations in a firm's value will be mainly reflected in the fluctuating value of the owners' or shareholders' wealth in the firm. Managers will want to select strategies that are expected to increase shareholders' wealth. Alternatives that harm shareholders' wealth should be rejected.[2]

This view is consistent with the process of attracting and acquiring capital and investing it to earn rates of return in excess of the investors' expected returns. If a firm is able to do this, the excess return will accrue to the firm's owners, the shareholders.

MEASURING SHAREHOLDER WEALTH

Shareholder wealth is measurable and observable daily in the financial sections of newspapers (at least for firms whose common stock is publicly

2.   Some mandatory projects, such as the need to retrofit factories due to regulation changes, may be costly and harm shareholder wealth. In this case, if several alternatives exist, the project that hurts shareholder wealth the least should be chosen.

traded). Shareholder wealth is nothing more than the market value of a firm's common stock. This market value of the shareholders' claim on a firm is equal to:

$$\begin{matrix} \text{Shareholder} \\ \text{Wealth} \end{matrix} = \begin{matrix} \text{Common stock} \\ \text{price} \end{matrix} \times \begin{matrix} \text{Number of common} \\ \text{shares outstanding} \end{matrix}$$

This relationship allows analysts to keep track of changes in shareholder wealth on a regular basis to see which firms are most successful at returning value to shareholders. As long as the number of common stock shares outstanding does not change appreciably, the market's perception of the firm and its management's actions appears in the firm's stock price.

For shareholder wealth maximization to be a realistic goal, the financial markets need to provide reasonably accurate information about the value of a firm. The stock market is sometimes criticized in the popular press as being shortsighted and unpredictable. Can it really determine a fair value for the firm? The evidence on efficient markets from Chapter 12 suggests that it can. Many studies show that the market is oriented toward the long-run health and well-being of firms.[3] The weight of evidence favors the idea that the market generally does price stocks fairly.

Focusing on shareholder value does not mean other aspects of good management are ignored. Smart managers make decisions to service customers in a cost-efficient manner. They treat and pay employees fairly. Otherwise, unmotivated and unhappy employees become unproductive employees who increase costs and prevent the firm from satisfying its goals. By focusing on firm value, managers work to maintain satisfactory relationships with financing sources so funds will be available to finance future growth needs. Focusing on shareholder wealth is the best means of helping the long-term survival of the firm in a dynamic, global economy.

Shareholder wealth as a measure of firm performance is objective, forward-looking, and incorporates all influences on the firm and its stakeholders. No other measure of firm performance is so inclusive and practical as a means for evaluating a firm's strategies.

A measure to identify successful firms that is growing in popularity is **market value added (MVA).** MVA measures the value created by the firm's managers. It equals the market value of the firm's liabilities and equity minus the amount of money investors paid to the firm (the book value) when these securities were first issued. That is, market value added (MVA) equals:

market value added (MVA)
measures the value created by the firm's managers

$$\begin{matrix} \text{Market value} \\ \text{of stock} \end{matrix} + \begin{matrix} \text{Market value} \\ \text{of debt} \end{matrix} - \begin{matrix} \text{Book value} \\ \text{of stock} \end{matrix} - \begin{matrix} \text{Book value} \\ \text{of debt} \end{matrix}$$

3. See the table in Alfred Rappaport, "CFOs and Strategists: Forging a Common Framework," *Harvard Business Review* (May-June 1992): 87.

Usually, a firm's market value of debt closely approximates its book value, so a close estimate of MVA is the market value of equity less the book value of equity. Stern Stewart & Company, a financial consulting firm, regularly reports firms' MVAs. Table 13.1 reports firms on the top and bottom of Stern Stewart & Co.'s MVA rankings as of the end of 1994. Among large corporations, Coca-Cola had the largest MVA. Its managers had increased the value of investors' original claims by $60.8 billion. The firm that had destroyed the most value was General Motors. The combined market value of its debt and equity was $17.8 billion less than what bond and stock investors had put into the company.

LINKING STRATEGY AND FINANCIAL PLANS

A firm's managers will want to pay close attention to movements in a company's stock price over time. These movements inform managers how financial market participants view the risk and potential return from investing in the firm. If investors perceive the risk is too great relative to expected returns, they will sell the firm's stock and reinvest their money elsewhere.

TABLE 13.1   Ranking Firms by Market Value Added: The Top Ten Firms and Bottom Ten Firms in the Stern Stewart Performance 1000

RANK	COMPANY	MARKET VALUE ADDED ($ BILLIONS)
1	Coca-Cola	$ 60.8
2	General Electric	52.1
3	Wal-Mart	35.0
4	Merck	31.5
5	Microsoft	29.9
6	Procter & Gamble	27.8
7	Philip Morris	27.3
8	Johnson & Johnson	24.7
9	AT&T	22.5
10	Motorola	21.0
991	Occidental Petroleum	−2.3
992	Federated Department Stores	−2.6
993	Kmart	−2.6
994	Westinghouse Electric	−2.8
995	Chrysler	−3.2
996	Digital Equipment	−4.7
997	IBM	−8.9
998	RJR Nabisco Holdings	−11.8
999	Ford Motor	−13.8
1,000	General Motors	−17.8

Source: Anne B. Fisher, "Creating Stockholder Wealth," *Fortune* (December 11, 1995): 105–16.

Critics frequently argue that emphasizing shareholder wealth may lead managers to focus on quick fixes to problems, even resorting to unethical behavior in an effort to maintain firm value. Some managers, unfortunately, do make decisions to ignore product quality or safety, worker safety, the well-being of communities, or use deceitful selling practices. As long as these practices are not discovered or publicized, they may help keep shareholder value higher than it should be. But let's take a closer look at this accusation.

WHAT ABOUT ETHICS?

Unethical managers will make improper decisions regardless of the performance measure, so using shareholder value as a performance measure probably will not affect such abusive practices. By inflating firm revenues, keeping costs artificially low, or diverting scarce resources from needed to less productive uses, unethical practices would improve virtually any performance measure, be it sales, costs, or market share. Thus to blame ethical lapses on financial measures of firm performance is inappropriate.

But, in point of fact, focusing on firm value may help to keep management's eyes on the longer-term consequences of its actions. Firms engaged in unethical or careless behavior run the danger of having this behavior exposed. Such revelations can harm the firm's reputation and shareholder value for extended periods as customers and employees feel their trust has been violated. Some evidence from a recent study suggests that firms with a social conscience may gain more financially in the marketplace.

Source: Justin Martin, "Good Citizenship Is Good Business," *Fortune* (March 21, 1994), pp. 15–16.

To provide a link between a firm's strategy and its financial plans, managers can first review the firm's performance in the financial markets and determine why the firm performed better or worse than its competitors in the eyes of investors. Managers can then take this information and examine the firm's internal operations. They need to examine financial measures to see how the firm has been generating cash, where this cash is being invested in the firm (new products, subsidiaries, etc.), and the return earned on these investments. Managers can then determine where poor returns are being earned and they can take corrective steps. Managers will want to evaluate the firm's operations and proposed new projects with an eye toward the firm's stock price. Projects that will add to shareholder wealth should be chosen for implementation. Projects that are expected to reduce shareholder wealth should be cast aside.

Executing a firm's financial strategy entails more than just looking at numbers on a computer spreadsheet. It includes making necessary adjustments to the firm's use of debt, equity, and dividend policy in order to create more value to shareholders. It includes seeking new markets or customers for the firm's products; controlling costs or prudently raising prices; and efficiently using the firm's assets. Additionally, to publicize its plans for creating value, management will want to communicate key components of its plan to shareholders and the financial markets. Other activities include using accounting principles and the tax code to minimize the firm's taxes; increasing the efficiency of the firm's cash management; and managing the firm's risk exposures. Many of these topics will be discussed in upcoming chapters.

CRITERION FOR NON-PUBLIC FIRMS

An obvious question to ask is which criterion to employ for organizations that have no observable market prices; for example, a small closely held company or a nonprofit organization. The answer lies in the factors that cause any productive asset to have value. From our Chapter 9 discussion on the time value of money, we know assets have value because of the size, timing, and risk of their cash flows. Management needs to balance the risks, timing, and sizes of the cash flows of the organization to maximize what the decision maker believes would be the market value of owner's equity if it were traded in the financial markets.

Owner-managers of small firms face a different situation, however. Since they own their firms, they seek to maximize their own wealth, but this wealth may defy clear expression in dollar terms. Nonmonetary benefits may be personally important to the owner-manager, such as maintaining control of the firm, keeping the business in the family, or having adequate leisure time. From a purely monetary perspective, owner-managers may not be maximizing the financial wealth of the firm, but as the owners they have to answer only to themselves as long as they make timely payments to their creditors and employees. Their decisions will attempt to maximize their total personal wealth, which includes both monetary and nonmonetary components.

Next, we examine various ways of organizing a business entity in the United States and review some of the financial implications of each organizational form.

FORMS OF BUSINESS ORGANIZATION IN THE UNITED STATES

Three major forms of business ownership are used in the United States: proprietorship, partnership, and corporation. Proprietorships are the most widely used form although they are generally the smallest organizations in terms of assets. About 70 percent of U.S. firms are proprietorships, about 10 percent are partnerships, and the remaining 20 percent are corporations. The choice of a legal form of organization for a business is a strategic matter from many points of view. Managerial lines of authority and control, legal responsibility, and the allocation of income and risk are all directly related to the form the organization takes. In this chapter we look at the relationship between the legal form of organization and its sources and methods of financing and its allocation of risk.

PROPRIETORSHIP

The **proprietorship,** sometimes called a sole proprietorship, is a business venture that is owned by a single individual who personally receives all profits and assumes all responsibility for the debts and losses of the business. Proprietorships far outnumber all other forms of business organization in the United States. However, the economic power of these firms, as measured by number of employees and size of payrolls, is far less than that of the nation's corporations.

proprietorship
business venture that is owned by a single individual who personally receives all profits and assumes all responsibility for the debts and losses of the business

The financial capital of proprietorships is many times limited to the savings of the owner and funds that may be borrowed from friends, relatives, and banks. The investment made by the owner is called **equity capital** or owner's equity. As the business grows and larger investments in capital are required, the owner may reach the point where additional funds cannot be borrowed without an increase in owner's equity. Lenders will generally insist on an increase in the owner's equity because that equity provides a margin of safety for the lender.

equity capital
investment made by the owner into the company

This point is where the proprietorship form of organization displays its basic weakness. In many cases, the owner's original investment exhausts his or her personal resources and often those of friends and relatives. Unless profits from the venture are great enough to meet the increased equity needs, the firm is prevented from achieving its maximum growth. At this stage it may be necessary to adopt a form of organization more appropriate for capital-raising purposes.

Another weakness of proprietorship is that the owner's liability for debts of the firm is unlimited. Creditors may take not only the assets of the business to settle claims but also the personal assets of the proprietor. Thus the proprietor may find his or her home and personal property under claim if the assets of the business are not sufficient to meet the demands of creditors. The unlimited liability of the owner is, therefore, a serious disadvantage of the proprietorship.

On the positive side, a proprietorship business is easily started with minimal expense and generally has fewer government regulations to comply with compared to a corporation. Profits from a proprietorship are taxed at personal or individual rates rather than at corporate income tax rates.

Furthermore, it is relatively easy to convert a business that was established as a proprietorship into a corporation when the need to finance growth warrants such a move.

PARTNERSHIP

partnership
form of business organi-
zation when two or more
people own a business
operated for profit

A ***partnership*** form of business organization exists when two or more persons own a business operated for profit. Although the partnership resembles the proprietorship to some degree, there are important differences.

Undoubtedly, one of the major reasons for the popularity of the partnership arrangement is that it allows individuals to pool their resources of money, property, equipment, knowledge, and business skills without the complications that often accompany incorporation. A partnership form may exist from the beginning of a business operation. In other cases, a firm that began as a proprietorship may reach the point where additional growth is impossible without increased equity capital. Bringing in new equity investors by converting to a partnership arrangement is one method of increasing the equity capital of a firm.

The number of partners that may be taken into a business venture is theoretically unlimited. However, the managerial difficulties and conflicts arising with many partners limit their number to a practical size. Thus the partnership, like the proprietorship, eventually suffers from a lack of large amounts of equity capital. While it is unusual to find more than a few partners in an industrial or commercial firm, some public accounting firms have dozens and even hundreds of partners.

Like the proprietor, the members of a partnership team risk their personal assets as well as their investments in the business venture. In addition, if one of the partners negotiates a contract that results in substantial loss, each partner suffers a portion of the loss, based on a previously determined agreement on distribution of profits and losses. The other partners may, however, sue the offending partner if there is any violation of the articles of co-partnership.

More serious, perhaps, is a partner's liability for the actions of the business. In legal terms each partner is both jointly and severally liable for the partnership's debts. Under partnership law, each partner has unlimited liability for all the debts of the firm. This permits creditors to claim assets from one or more of the partners if the remaining partners are unable to cover their share of the loss.

limited partnership
has at least one general
partner who has unlim-
ited liability; the liability
of the limited partners
is limited to their
investment

limited partners
face limited liability;
their personal assets
cannot be touched to
settle the firm's debt

These liability risks describe a *general* partnership. A ***limited partnership*** addresses the liability concern by identifying at least one general partner who has unlimited liability. The remaining ***limited partners*** face liability limited to their investments in the firm—their personal assets cannot be attached to settle the firm's debts. They are also limited in that they cannot participate in the operations of the firm. Operating decisions may be made only by the general partners.

CORPORATION

A *corporation* is a legal entity created under state law in the United States with an unending life and limited financial liability to its owners. In the case of Dartmouth College versus Woodward in 1819, Chief Justice of the Supreme Court John Marshall described the status of the corporation as follows:

A corporation is an artificial being, invisible, intangible, and existing only in contemplation of law. Being the mere creature of law, it possesses only those properties which the charter of its creation confers upon it, either expressly, or as incidental to its very existence. . . . Among the most important are immortality and individuality—properties by which a perpetual succession of persons are considered as the same and may act as a single individual.

In essence, the law has created an artificial being that has the rights, duties, and powers of a person. The definition includes the concept of many people united into one body that does not change its identity with changes in ownership. Advantages of being organized as a corporation include: the ability to attract outside capital, limited financial liability for the owners, and the ease to which ownership can be transferred from investor to investor.

A corporation that has existed only a short time, like most new ventures, usually finds it difficult to attract investment funds from outsiders. The corporate form of organization does not by itself assure a flow of investment funds into the business. Rather, it removes several of the barriers to the flow of capital that exist in other forms of business organization. But it is only after a corporation has become well established and offers attractive returns for investors that these special features of the corporate form become significant. One of the important reasons corporations can accumulate large sums of capital is that they are allowed to sell capital stock. The stock may be offered to existing stockholders or to new investors in amounts suited to their purposes. As we discussed in Chapter 11, a firm can go public by registering its shares with the Securities and Exchange Commission and then selling them to the investing public. A corporation that has not gone through this process is a privately held corporation.

One of the advantages for corporate stockholders is the limitation on liability. Ordinarily, creditors and other claimants may look only to the assets of the corporation for satisfaction of their claims. They cannot take the personal assets of the owners (stockholders). This advantage is particularly appealing to the owner of a business who has built up considerable personal wealth and has other business interests. The limitation on liability may also make it possible for promoters of new ventures to attract wealthy investors who would otherwise be unwilling to risk claims against their personal property.

On the other hand, the corporate form of organization may not always protect stockholders from personal risk beyond their investment when a

corporation
legal entity created under state law with unending life that offers limited financial liability to its owners

business is relatively new or in a weak financial condition. Creditors may simply require that one or more of the stockholders add their signatures to the obligation of the corporation, making them personally liable for the obligation. After a corporation has established a good credit reputation, however, creditors and suppliers seldom insist on personal guarantees on the part of the stockholders.

Another important advantage of the corporation is the ease with which ownership may be transferred. Corporate stock may be transferred freely from one person to another. The purchaser of the stock then has all the rights and privileges formerly held by the seller. The corporation is not a party to the transfer of ownership and has no power to interfere with the sale or purchase of its stock. In contrast, there must be unanimous approval of the members of a partnership before a new partner can be brought into the business.

However, just like proprietorships and partnerships, the corporate form of organization has its drawbacks. First, setting up a corporation is more time consuming and costly because of legal requirements. Individuals who wish to incorporate must hire a lawyer to prepare both a charter and a set of bylaws. The **charter** provides a corporate name, indicates the intended business activities, provides the names and addresses of directors, and indicates how the firm will be capitalized with stock. A corporation is chartered in a specific state by filing the charter with the secretary of that state. The **bylaws** are the rules established to govern the corporation and include how the firm will be managed, how directors will be elected, and indicate the rights of stockholders. After beginning operation, the corporation must file financial and tax statements with state and federal government agencies.

A second drawback of the corporate form of organization relates to the fact that corporate earnings distributed as shareholder dividends are subject to double taxation. That is, corporate earnings are taxed once at the appropriate corporate income tax rate. Then, if the corporation pays out a portion of its after-tax earnings in the form of dividends, the stockholders must pay personal income taxes on this income.

Two special forms of corporate organization in the United States allow dividends to escape double taxation. A **subchapter S corporation** (named for the section of the tax code that discusses this organization) must have fewer than 35 shareholders, none of which is another corporation. Income from a subchapter S corporation flows untaxed to the shareholders. Thus, it is taxed only once, as personal income of the shareholders.

A **limited liability company (LLC)** organizational form has been authorized by the laws of more than 35 states as of the end of 1994. Similar to a subchapter S corporation, it offers owners limited liability, and its income is taxed only once as personal income of the shareholder. Unlike a subchapter S corporation, an LLC can have an unlimited number of

---

charter
provides the corporate name, indicates the intended business activities, provides names and addresses of directors, and indicates how a firm will be capitalized with stock

bylaws
rules established to govern the corporation; they deal with how the firm will be managed and the rights of the stockholder

subchapter S corporation
has fewer than 35 shareholders, none of which is another corporation. Its income is taxed only once, as personal income of the shareholders

limited liability company (LLC)
organizational form whose owners have limited liability; the firm can have an unlimited number of shareholders; income is taxed only once as personal income of the shareholders

shareholders, including other corporations. The LLC can sell shares without completing the costly and time-consuming process of registering them with the Securities and Exchange Commission (SEC), which is a requirement for standard corporations that sell their securities to the public. The LLC structure has drawbacks in that, should an owner leave, all others must formally agree to continue the firm. Also, all of the LLC's owners must take active roles in managing the company. To protect partners from unlimited liability, some large accounting firms, formerly set up as partnerships, have become LLCs. Some examples include Coopers & Lybrand, Ernst & Young, and Price Waterhouse.[4]

Many countries' laws recognize the corporate form of organization. U.S. corporations may use the suffixes Inc. or Corp. to designate themselves. British corporations use the suffix PLC, which stands for *public limited company*; limited refers to shareholders' liability in the firm. The suffix AG following the names of firms in Germany, Austria, Switzerland, or Liechtenstein is an abbreviation for *Aktiengesellschaft*, which means corporation.

It is up to the firm's owners to weigh the pros and cons and determine which organizational form suits the needs of their firm best. Each has its own implications for taxation, control by the owners, ability to trade ownership positions, limitations on liability, firm life, and raising capital.

CORPORATE GOVERNANCE

In many firms, someone other than the owners makes business decisions. Professional managers run public corporations in the place of the shareholders. In other words, there is a separation of ownership and control. This arrangement may result in a special kind of ethics problem if managers make decisions to benefit themselves rather than to benefit shareholders.

PRINCIPAL-AGENT PROBLEM

The **principals,** or owners of the firm, hire managers (the **agents**) to run the firm. The agents should run the firm with the best interests of the principals in mind. However, ethical lapses, self-interest, or the principals' lack of trust in the agent can lead to conflicts of interest and suspicions between the two parties. This problem in corporate governance is called the **principal-agent problem.**

principals
owners of the firm

agents
hired by the principals
to run the firm

principal-agent problem
conflict of interest
between the principals
and agents

---

4. Bart Ziegler, "Top Accountants to Shield Partners from Lawsuits," *The Wall Street Journal* (July 29, 1994): A4; John R. Emshwiller, "New Kind of Company Attracts Many—Some Legal, Some Not," *The Wall Street Journal* (November 8, 1993): B1; Jeffery A. Tannenbaum, "Partnership, Corporation Aren't Only Ways to Start Out," *The Wall Street Journal* (May 14, 1991): B2.

The shareholders of a firm elect a board of directors. In theory, the board is to oversee managers and to ensure that they are working in the best interests of the shareholders. Often, however, in practice the board has a closer relationship with management than with the shareholders. For example, it is not unusual for top management to sit on the firm's board of directors, and the firm's top managers often nominate candidates for board seats. The board of Archer-Daniels-Midland, a grain processor, in 1995 included the firm's CEO and three of his relatives. These relationships can obscure loyalties and make the board a toothless watchdog for shareholders' interests.

Managers, acting as agents, may seek their own self-interest by increasing their salaries, the size of their staffs, or their perquisites. Better known as "perks," they include club memberships, use of company planes or luxurious company cars, gardening expenses, and low- or no-interest loans. Firms may also do business with other businesses in which the CEO has an ownership stake, blurring the distinction between doing what is best for shareholders and doing favors for the top officer.[5]

Management, in conjunction with the board, may seek to fend off take-overs that would allow shareholders to sell their shares at a price above the current market price, or they may try to pre-empt such merger or acquisition attempts by seeking changes in the corporate charter that would make such take-overs difficult to pursue. Examples of such delaying tactics or **poison pills** include provisions that require super-majorities (for example, two-thirds) of existing shareholders to approve any take-over, provisions to allow the board to authorize and issue large quantities of stock in the event of a take-over attempt, or provisions to make expensive payouts to existing managers in the face of any successful buyout. Although managers may state that such actions are being taken with shareholders' best interests at heart, a possible consequence of their actions is to preserve their own jobs and income in the face of a take-over.

Because of these behaviors, the principal-agent problem imposes **agency costs** on shareholders. Agency costs are the tangible and intangible expenses borne by shareholders because of actual or potential self-serving actions of managers. Agency costs include explicit, out-of-pocket expenses. Examples of these costs include: the costs of auditing financial statements to verify their accuracy; purchasing liability insurance for board members and top managers; monitoring managers' actions by the board or by independent consultants.

Implicit agency costs do not have a direct expense associated with them, but they harm shareholders anyway. Implicit agency costs include restrictions placed against managerial actions (e.g., requiring shareholder votes

poison pills
provisions in a corporate charter that make a corporate take-over more unattractive

agency costs
tangible and intangible expenses borne by shareholders because of the actual or potential self-serving actions of managers

5. Anonymous, "In a Cost-Cutting Era, Many CEOs Enjoy Imperial Perks," *The Wall Street Journal* (March 7, 1995): B1, B10.

for some major decisions) and covenants or restrictions placed on the firm by a lender.[6]

The end result of the principal-agent problem is a reduction in firm value. Investors will not pay as much for the firm's stock because they realize that the principal-agent problem and its attendant costs lower the firm's value. Agency costs will decline, and firm value will rise, as principals' trust and confidence in their agents rises. We will discuss some ways of reducing agency costs in the next section.

Agency problems decline in owner-controlled firms. When principals manage the firm, there is no conflict with agents! Consequently, firms will be managed to better maximize the wealth of the owner.

REDUCING AGENCY PROBLEMS

Two basic approaches can be used to reduce the consequences of managers making self-serving decisions. First, managers' incentives can be aligned to more closely match those of shareholders. A frequently used method for doing this is to offer managers **stock options.** The options allow managers to purchase, at a future time, a stated number of the firm's shares at a specific price. If the firm's stock price rises, the value of the shares, and therefore the managers' wealth, also rises. Decisions that detract from the best interest of shareholders will affect management by making the stock options less valuable.[7] More and more firms are basing compensation of their top managers on the firms' stock prices.[8] Stock-based compensation plans and incentives are also gaining popularity in non-U.S. firms.[9]

stock options
allow managers to purchase a stated number of the firm's shares at a specified price

A second tool that can be used to control self-serving managers is to have closer oversight to make them more accountable. Some firms are increasing the number of independent directors (i.e., individuals who are not part of the firm's management) on their boards. Such independent directors may be more inclined to carefully analyze management's strategies and proposals and their effects on shareholder value. In addition, major institutional investors, such as pension funds and mutual funds, are becoming more vocal investors. Some are taking active roles in overseeing the performance of companies in which they hold stock by requesting

6.   Such covenants are placed on the firm to protect the lender's position and to ensure that available cash flow will be directed to repay the loan.
7.   Business periodicals and the press usually publicize the largest CEO salaries for the previous year. Such salaries can reach $20, $30, $50 million or more. The news reports fail to recognize much of this CEO income comes from exercising stock options. A CEO can make a lot of money on stock options if he or she performs the job well and raises the stock price.
8.   Joann S. Lublin, "Study Finds Pay of More CEOs Is Stock-Based," *The Wall Street Journal* (November 12, 1993): B1, B3.
9.   David P. Hamilton, "Some Pay of Sony Directors Is Linked to Performance," *The Wall Street Journal* (August 11, 1995): A4; Greg Steinmetz, "German Banks Note the Value of Bonuses," *The Wall Street Journal* (May 9, 1995): A17.

meetings with management, criticizing management actions, and suggesting shareholder votes on issues of importance to the firm. As with managerial incentives, this trend is gaining popularity outside the United States as well.[10]

THE ANNUAL REPORT

An important component of manager-owner communication is the firm's financial statements. Firms organized as proprietorships or partnerships are not required to prepare financial reports or statements except for tax purposes. Of course, it is important for proprietors and partners to gather financial data so as to be able to evaluate their financial performance over time. Requests for bank loans will need to be accompanied by recent financial statements, too.

In contrast, companies organized as corporations are required to prepare financial reports annually for the benefit of their shareholders. Public corporations also are required to file annual reports with the U.S. Securities and Exchange Commission.

annual report
contains descriptive information and numerical records on the operating and financial performance during the past year

An ***annual report*** contains descriptive information on operating and financial performance during the past year, a discussion of current and future business opportunities, and financial statements that provide a numerical record of financial performance. Usually financial highlights are provided on the first page or two followed by a letter to the stockholders by the firm's Chairman of the Board and Chief Executive Officer (CEO). The CEO summarizes the financial results for the year and identifies the firm's strengths such as employee talents and the size of its customer base. After the CEO's letter, most companies describe their current business areas, future opportunities, and financial goals, such as a target return on equity or earnings growth rate.

Three important financial statements are provided in the annual report. These are: the statement of income (sometimes called the statement of operations), the balance sheet (sometimes called the statement of financial position), and the statement of cash flows. Detailed notes to these financial statements also are provided by management. Annual reports also typically provide a five- or ten- year summary of selected financial data for the firm.

generally accepted accounting principles (GAAP)
set of guidelines as to the form and manner in which accounting information should be presented

ACCOUNTING PRINCIPLES

Among the inputs used to construct the financial statements are ***generally accepted accounting principles (GAAP)***, which are formulated by the

---

10.   "Whose Company Is It, Anyway?" *The Economist* (November 25, 1995): 59.

Financial Accounting Standards Board (FASB). FASB recognizes it would be improper for all companies to use identical and restrictive accounting principles. Some flexibility and choice is needed as industries and firms within industries differ in their operating environments. On the negative side, this flexibility can result in firms which, at first glance, appear healthier than they really are. It is the task of the financial analyst to dig deep into the available financial information to separate those firms which appear attractive from those which really are in good financial shape.

Fortunately, FASB requires that financial statements include footnotes. These footnotes inform analysts of which accounting principles were used by the firm.

Much of accounting practice is based upon the accrual concept. Under accrual accounting, revenues and their associated expenses are recognized when a sale occurs, regardless of when cash revenues or expenses really occur. Let's use the example of a set of living room furniture that is sold in June. The sofa was finished being crafted the previous November; the coffee table was finished in March; other pieces were also finished in recent months. Although the manufacturer's raw materials suppliers and the workers that made the furniture were paid a long time ago—last year, in the case of the sofa—the expenses will not appear on the firm's accounting books until the set is sold in June. At that time, the selling price of the living room set and its associated expenses are recorded using accrual accounting principles.

From the financial manager's perspective, cash is what matters most. He had to pay the firm's suppliers last year and the workers over the last several months. He also knows, because the customer will pay for her purchase under the monthly installment plan, that although revenue is recognized in June, the actual cash from the sale will come in over several months; the customer will not be finished paying for the furniture until the following year. The cash flows, or the cash expenses and cash revenues, occur over the space of many months and three calendar years. Yet, under accrual accounting, the accounting revenues and expenses appear to have all occurred this year, in the month of June.

As this example illustrates, an analyst may have to "dig deeper" to obtain a true picture of the items featured in the firm's financial statements. In the following sections, we review the firm's major financial statements and their components.

INCOME STATEMENT

The **income statement** reports the revenues generated and expenses incurred by a firm over an accounting period such as a quarter or year. The accrual concept is used to construct the income statement. Table 13.2 presents income statements for the Global Manufacturing Corporation for 1994

income statement reports the revenues generated and expenses incurred by the firm over an accounting period

TABLE 13.2   Income Statements for Global Manufacturing, Inc.

YEARS ENDED DECEMBER 31	1995	1994
Net revenues or sales	$700,000	$600,000
Cost of goods sold	450,000	375,000
Gross profit	250,000	225,000
Operating expenses:		
General and administrative	95,000	95,000
Selling and marketing	56,000	50,000
Depreciation	25,000	20,000
Operating income	74,000	60,000
Interest	14,000	10,000
Income before taxes	60,000	$ 50,000
Income taxes (40%)	24,000	20,000
Net income	$ 36,000	$ 30,000
Number of shares outstanding	50,000	50,000
Earnings per share	$0.72	$0.60

and 1995. In 1995, Global had net revenues of $700,000 compared with $600,000 for 1994, which reflects an increase of 16.7 percent. After deducting production costs and other expenses incurred in running the business, Global's net income was $30,000 in 1994 and $36,000 in 1995, which is a 20 percent increase.

Let's now look at some of the major income statement accounts in greater detail. The starting point of the income statement reflects the revenues or sales generated from the operations of the business. Quite often gross revenues are larger than net revenues. This is due to sales returns and allowances that may occur over the time period reflected in the income statement. Sometimes when customers make early payment on their bills, cash discounts are given by the firm. Also, if customers buy in very large quantities, trade discounts may be given. Thus discounts will reduce gross revenues.

The costs of producing or manufacturing the products sold to earn revenues are grouped under cost of goods sold. These expenses reflect costs directly involved in production, such as raw materials, labor, and overhead, and thus vary with the level of production output.

Selling, general, and marketing expenses tend to be stable or fixed in nature and cover requirements such as record keeping and preparing financial and accounting statements. These expenses also reflect the costs associated with selling the firm's products. This includes salaries and/or commissions generated by the sales force as well as promotional and advertising expenditures.

Depreciation is an estimate of the reduction in the economic value of the firm's plant and equipment caused by manufacturing the firm's products. It is for the time period covered by the income statement. This one-time-period depreciation is accumulated over time, and the accumulated depreciation appears in the balance sheet. No cash outflow is associated with depreciation, so depreciation is considered to be a noncash expense.

Operating income is a firm's income before interest and income taxes and is sometimes referred to as earnings before interest and taxes (EBIT).

Interest expense is subtracted from operating income. When a portion of a firm's assets are financed with liabilities, interest charges usually result. This is true for bank loans and long-term corporate bonds. Operating income less interest expense gives the firm's pre-tax earnings or earnings before taxes.

Businesses are required to pay federal income taxes on any profits. Most states also tax business profits. Taxable earnings or profit is defined as income remaining after all other expenses have been deducted from revenues except income taxes. Effective income tax rates can vary substantially depending on whether the firm is organized as a proprietorship, partnership, or corporation.

The net income or profits remaining after income taxes are paid reflects the earnings available to the owners of the business. This income may be retained in the business to reduce existing liabilities, increase current assets, and/or acquire additional fixed assets. On the other hand, some or all of the income may be distributed to the owners of the business.

Because of accrual accounting, it is important to note that a firm's net income over some period is not necessarily the same as its cash flow. The amount of cash flowing into the firm can be higher or lower than the net income figure.

For a corporation, it is also common to show a firm's net income on a per share basis. This is referred to as the earnings per share (EPS) and is calculated by dividing the net income by the number of shares of common stock that are outstanding. For Global Manufacturing, EPS increased from $0.60 in 1994 to $0.72 in 1995. This is a 20 percent increase just like the increase in net income because the same number of shares were outstanding in 1994 and 1995.

In some instances, corporations have both preferred and common stockholders. Dividends are paid to these "preferred" stockholders out of net income; the remaining earnings are called income available to common stockholders. For example, if Global had paid $2,000 in preferred stock dividends in 1994, the remaining earnings available for common stockholders would have been $28,000 and EPS to common stockholders would have been $0.56 ($28,000/50,000 shares).

Corporations frequently pay cash dividends to their common stockholders. The percentage of net income or earnings paid out as dividends is referred to as the dividend payout ratio. For example, assume that Global

Manufacturing has a policy of paying out one-half or 50 percent of its net income in the form of cash dividends to its common stockholders. In 1995, $18,000 would be paid in dividends out of a net income of $36,000, which would result in a dividend payout ratio of 50 percent ($18,000/$36,000). The remaining $18,000 would be retained in the business. On a per share basis, the dividends per share (DPS) in 1995 would be $0.36 ($18,000/50,000 shares).

THE BALANCE SHEET

balance sheet
statement of a company's financial position as of a particular date

assets
financial and physical items owned by a business

liabilities
creditors' claims on a firm

equity
funds supplied by the owners that represent their residual claim on the firm

The **balance sheet** is a statement of a company's financial position as of a particular date, usually at the end of a quarter or year. Whereas the income statement reflects the firm's operations over a period of time, the balance sheet is a snapshot at a point in time. It reveals two broad categories of information: (1) the **assets**, financial and physical items, owned by a business; and (2) the claims of creditors and owners in the business assets. The creditors' claims, which are the financial obligations of the business, are referred to as **liabilities.** The company's **equity** is the funds supplied by the owners and represents their residual claim on the firm.

In addition to providing a snapshot of a firm's financial condition, the balance sheet also reveals much of the inner workings of the company's financial structure. The various types of assets indicate at once the results of recent business operations and the capacity for future operations. The creditors' claims and the owners' equity in the assets reveal the sources from which these assets have been derived. The term "balance sheet" itself indicates a relationship of equality between the assets of the business and the sources of funds used to obtain them that may be expressed as follows:

Assets = Liabilities + Owners' equity

The balance sheet for the Global Manufacturing Corporation shown in Table 13.3 reveals this equality of assets and the financial interests in the assets. Total assets were $400,000 in 1994 and $500,000 in 1995, representing a 25 percent increase.

Total liabilities increased from $200,000 to $282,000, which is a 41 percent increase. Owner's equity, which for Global Manufacturing is stockholders' equity, provided the balancing figure with $200,000 in 1994 and $218,000 in 1995. This was an increase of 9 percent.

Assets that are most liquid are typically listed first. By liquidity we are referring to the time it usually takes to convert the assets into cash. Two broad groups—current assets and fixed assets—are identified on the balance sheet.

current assets
cash and all other assets that are expected to be converted into cash within one year

working capital
assets needed to carry out the normal operations of the business

The **current assets** of a business include cash and other assets that are expected to be converted into cash within one year. Current assets thus represent the **working capital** needed to carry out the normal operations

TABLE 13.3 Balance Sheets for Global Manufacturing, Inc.

	DECEMBER 31	
	1995	1994
ASSETS		
Cash and marketable securities	$ 25,000	$ 20,000
Accounts receivable	100,000	80,000
Inventories	125,000	100,000
Total current assets	250,000	200,000
Gross plant and equipment	300,000	225,000
Less: accumulated depreciation	− 100,000	− 75,000
Net plant and equipment	200,000	150,000
Land	50,000	50,000
Total fixed assets	250,000	200,000
Total assets	$500,000	$400,000
LIABILITIES AND EQUITY		
Accounts payable	$ 78,000	$ 65,000
Notes payable	34,000	10,000
Accrued liabilities	30,000	25,000
Total current liabilities	142,000	100,000
Long-term debt	140,000	100,000
Total liabilities	$282,000	$200,000
Common stock ($1 par, 50,000 shares)	$50,000	$ 50,000
Paid-in capital	100,000	100,000
Retained earnings	68,000	50,000
Total stockholders' equity	218,000	200,000
Total liabilities and equity	$500,000	$400,000

of the business. The principal current assets of a business are typically its cash and marketable securities, accounts receivable, and inventories.

Cash and marketable securities include cash on hand and cash on deposit with banks; marketable securities, such as commercial paper issued by other firms; and U.S. government securities in the form of Treasury bills, notes, and bonds.

Accounts receivable generally arise from the sale of products, merchandise, or services on credit. The buyer's debts to the business are generally paid according to the credit terms of the sale. Some firms also have notes receivable. A note receivable is a written promise by a debtor of the business to pay a specified sum of money on or before a stated date. Notes receivable may come into existence in several ways. For example, overdue accounts receivable may be converted to notes receivable at the insistence of the seller or upon special request by the buyer. Notes receivable may also occur as a result of short-term loans made by the business to its employees or to other persons or businesses.

The materials and products that a manufacturing firm has on hand are shown as inventories on the balance sheet. Generally, a manufacturing firm categorizes its inventories in terms of raw materials, goods in the process of manufacture, and finished goods. Sometimes the balance sheet will reveal the amount of inventory in each of these categories.

Fixed assets are the physical facilities used in the production, storage, display, and distribution of the products of a firm. These assets normally provide many years of service. The principal fixed assets are plant and equipment and land.

In a manufacturing firm, a large investment in plant and equipment is usually required. As products are manufactured, some of the economic value of this plant and equipment lessens. This is called **depreciation** and accountants reflect this using up of real assets by charging off depreciation against the original cost of plant and equipment. Thus the net plant and equipment at any point in time is supposed to reflect their remaining useful lives. The net is calculated by subtracting the amount of depreciation that has accumulated over time from the gross plant and equipment.

depreciation
devaluing a physical asset over the period of its expected life

Some firms own the land or real property on which their buildings or manufacturing plants are constructed. Other firms may own other land for expansion or investment purposes. The original cost of land owned is reflected on the firm's balance sheet. Under the tax code it is not allowed to be depreciated.

Liabilities are the debts of a business. They come into existence through direct borrowing, purchases of goods and services on credit, and the accrual of obligations such as wages and income taxes. Liabilities are classified as current and long-term.

The current liabilities of a business may be defined as those obligations that must be paid within one year. They include accounts payable, notes payable, and accrued liabilities that are to be met out of current funds and operations. Although the cash on hand plus marketable securities of the Global Manufacturing Company is only $25,000 compared with current liabilities of $125,000, it is expected that normal business operations will convert receivables and inventory into cash in time to meet current liabilities as they become due.

Accounts payable are debts that arise primarily from the purchase of goods on credit terms. Accounts payable arising from the purchase of inventory on credit terms represent trade credit financing as opposed to direct short-term borrowing from banks and other lenders. An account payable shown on one firm's balance sheet appears as an account receivable on the balance sheet of the firm from which goods were purchased.

A note payable is a written promise to pay a specified amount of money to a creditor on or before a certain date. The most common occurrence of a note payable takes place when a business borrows money from a bank on a short-term basis for the purchase of materials or for other current operating requirements.

Current liabilities that reflect amounts owed but not yet due as of the date of the balance sheet are called accrued liabilities or accruals. The most common form of accruals are wages payable and taxes payable. These accounts exist because wages are typically paid weekly, bi-weekly, or monthly and income taxes are paid quarterly.

Business debts with maturities greater than one year are long-term liabilities. As we reviewed in Chapter 11, one of the common methods used by businesses for obtaining a long-term loan is to offer a mortgage to a lender as collateral for a corporate bond. In the event that the borrowing business fails to meet the obligations of the loan contract, the mortgage may be foreclosed. That is, the property may be seized through appropriate legal channels and sold in order to satisfy the indebtedness.

All businesses have owners' equity in one form or another. Owners' equity is the investment of the owners or owner in the business. It initially results from a cash outlay for the purchase of assets to operate the business. In some cases, the owners of a business may place their own assets, such as machinery, real estate, or equipment with the firm, for its operation. In addition to contributing cash or property, owners' equity may also be increased by allowing profits to remain with the business. On the balance sheet, the amount of owners' equity is always represented by the difference between total assets and total liabilities of the business. It reflects the owners' claims on the assets of the business as opposed to the creditors' claims.

In the case of a corporation, the owners' equity is usually broken down into three different accounts as we show for the Global Manufacturing Corporation in Table 13.3. The common stock account reflects the number of outstanding shares of common stock carried at a stated or par value. It is worth noting that the par value is an arbitrary value and thus is not related to a firm's stock price or market value. For example, Global Manufacturing has previously issued 50,000 shares of common stock with a par value of $1. Thus, a $50,000 amount is shown on Global's balance sheet. In the past, the firm's stock had actually been sold for an average price of $3 per share. We know this because the second equity account, the paid-in capital account (or surplus account) is $100,000. If we divide this amount by 50,000 shares, the average selling price above the $1 par value is $2 per share. The sum of the par value per share and the average price above the par value produces the average selling price of $3 per share.

The third account is called the retained earnings account, and it shows the accumulated undistributed earnings (i.e., earnings *not* paid out as dividends) within the corporation over time. These retained earnings do not represent cash. They have been invested in the firm's current and/or fixed assets. Together these three accounts comprise the corporation's common stockholders' or owners' equity.

STATEMENT OF CASH FLOWS

In addition to the income statement and balance sheet, corporate annual reports also try to measure changes in cash flows. All three of the previously described financial statements are prepared using an accrual accounting system whereby items are recorded as incurred but not necessarily when cash is received or disbursed. For example, a sale of $100 is recorded as a sale this year even though the cash is not expected to be collected until next year.

statement of cash flows provides a summary of the cash inflows (sources) and cash out-flows (uses) during a specified accounting period

A ***statement of cash flows*** provides a summary of the cash inflows (sources) and cash outflows (uses) during a specified accounting period. The statement consists of three sections: operating activities, investing activities, and financing activities. The primary approach for constructing a statement of cash flows begins with the net income from the income statement as a cash inflow. We then add back any noncash deductions such as depreciation, which was deducted only to reduce taxable income. The other "cash flow" adjustments are made by examining the differences in the accounts from two consecutive balance sheets. More specifically, cash flows are determined as follows:

Sources
1. Amount of net income plus amount of depreciation
2. Decrease in an asset account
3. Increase in a liability account
4. Increase in an equity account

Uses
1. Increase in an asset account
2. Decrease in a liability account
3. Decrease in an equity account
4. Amount of cash dividends

Changes in the cash account are not included in the above. Rather, in the statement of cash flows, all of the firm's sources and uses of cash are added together. Their sum equals the change in the firm's cash account. If the statement of cash flows is constructed correctly, the sum of the items should equal the difference in the cash account between the two balance sheets used to generate it.

For example, the purchase of raw materials or an increase in the amount of finished goods held requires additional cash. Thus it is a use and is therefore subtracted in the statement of cash flows. In contrast, collections of accounts receivable frees up cash; thus it is a source, and is added in the statement of cash flows. Borrowing money from a bank or receiving an added investment from a partner or stockholder represents a source of cash. In contrast, paying off a bank loan is a use of cash.

Table 13.4 shows the statement of cash flows for the Global Manufacturing Company based on the 1995 income statement and the balance sheets as of year-end 1994 and 1995. Notice that cash flows are grouped on the basis of operating activities, investing activities, and financing activities. Sources of funds from operations begin with net income of $36,000 plus depreciation of $25,000 to reflect the fact that depreciation is a noncash charge against the firm's revenues. Global Manufacturing also generated additional sources of cash from operations by increasing its accounts payable by $13,000 and its accrued liabilities by $5,000. Uses of cash from operations were in the form of a $20,000 increase in accounts receivable and a $25,000 increase in inventories. The overall result was a net cash inflow from operations during 1995 of $34,000. The cash flows from operations is an important figure for businesses. It may be negative for growing firms, but generally a firm cannot exist long if it continually creates net cash outflows from its operations.

Table 13.4 shows that Global invested $75,000 in plant & equipment in 1995. This investing activity also represented the largest single use of cash. The net cash flow from financing activities amounted to $46,000 during 1995. This net figure reflects an increase (source) in notes payable of $24,000, an increase (source) in long-term debt of $40,000, and the payment of cash dividends amounting to $18,000.

The overall result of operating, investing, and financing activities during 1995 was a $5,000 increase in the cash and marketable securities account. This is further verified by the fact that the year-end 1994 cash and marketable securities of $20,000 increased by $5,000 to $25,000 by year-end 1995.

TABLE 13.4   Statement of Cash Flows for Global Manufacturing, Inc.

Cash Flows from Operating Activities		
Net income	$36,000	
Depreciation	25,000	
Increase in Accounts Payable	13,000	
Increase in Accrued Liabilities	5,000	
Increase in Accounts Receivable	(20,000)	
Increase in Inventories	(25,000)	
Net cash provided by operating activities		$34,000
Cash Flows from Investing Activities		
Increase in Plant and Equipment	($75,000)	
Net cash used in investing activities		($75,000)
Cash Flows from Financing Activities		
Increase in Notes Payable	$24,000	
Increase in Long-term Debt	40,000	
Dividend payment	(18,000)	
Net cash provided by financing activities		$46,000
Net increase in Cash and Marketable Securities		$ 5,000

FEDERAL INCOME TAXATION

In addition to financing and risk factors, income tax liabilities also may differ for each form of business organization selected. Income from partnerships and proprietorships is combined with other personal income for tax purposes. Below we show the 1995 rate schedules for: (a) a married couple filing jointly; and (b) for a single person.

FILING STATUS	TAXABLE INCOME	MARGINAL TAX RATE
Married Filing Jointly	$0–39,000	15.0%
	39,001–94,250	28.0
	94,251–143,600	31.0
	143,601–256,500	36.0
	over 256,500	39.6
Single	$0–23,350	15.0
	23,351–56,550	28.0
	56,551–117,950	31.0
	117,951–256,500	36.0
	over 256,500	39.6

progressive
based on the concept that the higher the income the larger the percentage of income that should be paid in taxes

A cursory observation shows that personal income tax rates are **progressive** because the higher the income, the larger the percentage of income that must be paid in taxes. For example, let's assume that the taxable income from a proprietorship is $50,000 and that the owner does not have any additional income. If the owner is married and filing a joint return, and the spouse has no reportable income, the income will be taxed as follows:

$$0.15 \times \$39,000 = \$5,850$$
$$0.28 \times \underline{11,000} = \underline{3,080}$$
$$\$50,000 \$8,930$$

marginal tax rate
rate paid on the last dollar of income

average tax rate
determined by dividing the taxes paid by the taxable income

The **marginal tax rate** is the rate paid on the last dollar of income. In our example it is 28.0 percent and applies to that portion of the taxable income above $39,000. The **average tax rate** is determined by dividing the tax amount of $8,930 by the $50,000 in taxable income and amounts to 17.9 percent.

A proprietor with $50,000 in taxable income who is single would pay the following taxes:

$$0.15 \times \$23,350 = \$3,502.50$$
$$0.28 \times \underline{26,650} = \underline{7,462.00}$$
$$\$50,000 = \$10,964.50$$

While the single taxpayer also would have a 28.0 percent marginal tax rate, the average tax rate will be higher because the income tax liability would be $10,964.50 versus the $8,930 owed by the proprietor who is married and filing a joint return. This occurs because the majority of the $50,000 in taxable income for the single taxpayer is taxed at the higher 28.0 percent rate. In fact, the single taxpayer has an average tax rate of 21.9 percent ($10,964.50/$50,000).

Personal taxable income as examined above is considered to be *ordinary taxable income*. Gains or losses on capital assets such as real estate, bonds, and stocks are taxed differently if held for more than one year. For example, the maximum tax on long-term **capital gains** is 28.0 percent, which provides a tax advantage to individuals who have large amounts of ordinary taxable income.

capital gains
gains or losses on capital assets held for more than one year

Corporations, in contrast with proprietorships and partnerships, are taxed as separate entities. In 1995, the corporate tax rates on their taxable income was:

TAXABLE INCOME	TAX RATE
$0 – 50,000	15%
50,001 – 75,000	25
75,000 – 100,000	34
100,001 – 335,000	39
335,001 – 10 million	34
10 million – 15 million	35
15 million – 18,333,333	38
over 18,333,333	35

The 39 percent tax rate for income between $100,000 and $335,000 is designed to recapture the benefits of the 15.0 percent and 25 percent rates. A similar recapture occurs for taxable income between $15 million and $18.3 million. Because of this, the average and marginal tax rates are both 35 percent for corporate incomes over $18,333,333.

A corporation with taxable income of $50,000 pays $7,500 (a 15 percent marginal and average rate), compared with $8,930 for a proprietor who is married and filing a joint return or $10,964.50 for a proprietor who is single. However, income distributed from after-tax corporate profits to owners is taxed again in the form of personal ordinary income. Thus, deciding whether there would be an income tax advantage associated with being taxed as a corporation rather than a proprietorship or partnership is a complex undertaking.

A corporation with taxable income of $200,000 would have the following tax obligation:

$$
\begin{aligned}
0.15 \times \$\ 50,000 &= \$\ 7,500 \\
0.25 \times\quad 25,000 &=\quad 6,250 \\
0.34 \times\quad 25,000 &=\quad 8,500 \\
0.39 \times\quad \underline{100,000} &=\quad \underline{39,000} \\
\$200,000 &= \$61,250
\end{aligned}
$$

The marginal tax rate would be 39 percent and the average tax rate would be 30.6 percent ($61,250/$200,000).

Small businesses can sometimes qualify as S corporations under the Internal Revenue Code. These organizations receive the limited liability of a corporation but are taxed as proprietorships or partnerships. A corporation pays taxes on its taxable income. Then, if cash from profits is distributed as dividends to stockholders, the stockholders must pay personal income taxes. Thus, double taxation is avoided by the S corporation because the business is taxed as a proprietorship or partnership. Whether or not this taxation option is selected depends upon the level of the owner's personal tax bracket.

Businesses also have the opportunity of carrying operating losses backward for 3 years and forward for 15 years to offset taxable income. A new business corporation that loses, for example, $50,000 the first year can only offset taxable income earned in future years. However, initial losses by a new proprietorship or partnership can be first carried back against personal income taxes paid by owners, permitting them tax refunds. This can be helpful for a new business that has limited funds.

DEPRECIATION BASICS

Depreciation write-offs are particularly important to businesses because depreciation is deductible from income before taxes and thus reduces the firm's income tax liability. The following example illustrates the impact of deducting versus not deducting $20,000 in depreciation before computing income taxes liabilities.

	WITH DEPRECIATION	WITHOUT DEPRECIATION
Income before depreciation and income taxes	$100,000	$100,000
Less: Depreciation	20,000	0
Income before taxes	80,000	100,000
Less: Income taxes (@ 30%)	24,000	30,000
Net income	$ 56,000	$ 70,000

depreciation tax shield
tax reduction due to noncash depreciation expense. It equals the depreciation expense multiplied by the tax rate

The depreciation deduction shields income from taxes. Notice that income before taxes is lower when depreciation is deducted, so the amount of income taxes paid is lower as well. This is an example of the **depreciation tax shield.** With depreciation, taxes are reduced by $6,000. The depreciation tax shield is equal to the tax rate multiplied by the depreciation expense. In this case, it is $0.30 \times \$20,000$ or $6,000.

The Tax Reform Act of 1986 modified the ACRS to make the depreciation schedules less attractive. Examples of current modified accelerated cost recovery system (MACRS) guidelines are as follows:

RECOVERY YEAR	PERCENTAGE DEPRECIATION ALLOWED BY CLASS OF ASSET LIFE	
	3-YEAR	5-YEAR
1	33.00%	20.00%
2	45.00	32.00
3	15.00	19.20
4	7.00	11.52
5		11.52
6		. 5.76

Notice that equipment in the 3-year class has depreciation taken over a four-year period. Likewise automobiles, computers, and some manufacturing tools which qualify in the 5-year class life are actually depreciated over six years. Industrial equipment and buildings must be depreciated over even longer time periods.

For example, let's assume that a business purchases a computer system for $10,000. The amount which could be written off or depreciated each year would be as follows:

YEAR	PURCHASE PRICE		DEPRECIATION PERCENTAGE		DEPRECIATION AMOUNT
1	$10,000	×	0.2000	=	$ 2,000
2	10,000	×	0.3200	=	3,200
3	10,000	×	0.1920	=	1,920
4	10,000	×	0.1152	=	1,152
5	10,000	×	0.1152	=	1,152
6	10,000	×	0.0576	=	576
				Total	$10,000

Thus, the computer system would be fully depreciated by the end of six years. Of course, the computer system may have an economic or useful life that is either less than or more than its depreciable life.

FINANCE IN THE ORGANIZATION CHART

In all but the smallest of firms, a top manager with the title *chief financial officer (CFO)* or *vice president of finance* usually reports to the president. Managers of two areas usually report to the CFO: the firm's *treasurer* and its *controller,* as shown in Figure 13.1. The firm's treasurer oversees the traditional functions of financial analysis: capital budgeting, short-term and long-term financing decisions, and current asset management. The controller traditionally manages accounting, cost analysis, and tax planning.

A firm's strategy for business success is plotted by its top officers and, in the case of a corporation, its board of directors. Often, this strategy will be reflected in the composition of the firm's balance sheet, as seen in

chief financial officer (CFO)
responsible for the controller and the treasury functions of a firm

treasurer
oversees the traditional functions of financial analysis

controller
manages accounting, cost analysis, and tax planning

FIGURE 13.1   Position of Finance in a Typical Organization Chart

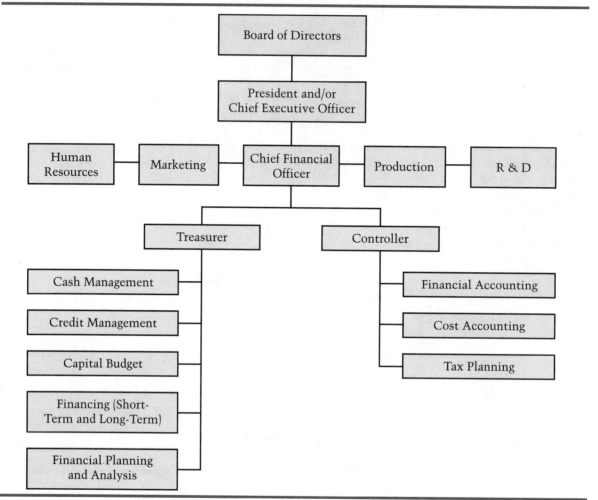

Figure 13.2 on page 432. Those involved in planning the firm's strategy follow the structure provided by the balance sheet in answering several basic questions:

1. The *capital budgeting* question: What fixed or long-term assets should the firm purchase to produce its product?
2. The *capital structure* question: How should the firm finance these purchases?
3. The *operations* or *net working capital* question: How should the firm manage inventory, collect payments from customers, pay suppliers, and manage its cash account?

"A bean-counter personality wouldn't last long here."

WENDY WILSON

Audit Senior Manager
Ernst & Young, LLP

BS Accounting
University of Richmond
Certified Public
Accountant

Q: *What's the difference between public accounting and private accounting?*

A: We are *public* accountants, meaning we provide accounting services to other companies. *Private* accounting refers to the internal accounting departments you would find in large companies.

Q: *What services do you provide for your clients?*

A: Our company provides three main categories of service—audit, tax, and consulting. I'm in the Audit division. We review the financial statements that our clients compile and certify that they are based on generally accepted accounting principles, and that they are free of what we call material misstatements.

Q: *So you evaluate the financial statements and the methods used to develop them. If you find they are in order, then what?*

A: We would then put in writing what we found, that the financial statements were audited and appear to fairly represent the financial standing of the company. The client can then use our opinion to demonstrate the validity of their financial statements to their stockholders, or to a bank when seeking a loan.

Q: *Do you physically review all of the financial records of your clients?*

A: The smaller the client the more likely we are to look at its individual transactions to see if they were reported correctly. With large clients we look more for the proper systems and controls. But we could never look at *all* of the records of any client. That would be extremely time-consuming and expensive.

Q: *What's the toughest part of the job?*

A: Because almost every company's fiscal year ends on December 31, we have an extremely busy season from January to March. We work very long hours in that stretch. sixty hours a week, at least. On the other hand, once the busy season ends we have a liberal vacation policy and excellent benefits. So you pay your dues during the winter, and the rest of the year isn't so bad.

Q: *What do you enjoy most about your job?*

A: I work with a lot of excellent people, both clients and co-workers. I manage several projects at a time and work with different people and issues on each, so there's lots of variety.

Q: *What does the term "Big Six" refer to?*

A: There are six large public accounting firms that dominate the industry. These six companies work with almost every large company in the country in one capacity or another. From an employee's standpoint, the Big Six firms provide an excellent setting to learn the business of accounting.

Q: *There are some stereotypes about accountants. Any comments?*

A: The image of accountants as bean-counters hunched over their adding machines is not accurate at all. We work with such a broad range of clients that we have to have good people skills. A bean-counter personality wouldn't last long here.

career profiles

FIGURE 13.2   Balance Sheet

Operating Decisions	Current Assets	Current Liabilities	Operating Decisions
Capital Budgeting Decisions	Fixed Assets	Long-Term Debt	Capital Structure Decisions
		Equity	

The following chapters will delve into these topics to show you the data that financial managers need, how they analyze it, and how they use the shareholder wealth maximization goals to make decisions.

SUMMARY

Finance provides the basic tools managers can use when seeking to maximize the wealth of the owners. By maintaining the firm's vision or mission when setting operating goals, managers should evaluate strategies in the context of seeking to increase shareholder wealth. Separation of firm ownership and control leads to the principal-agent problem. Agents (managers) may act in their own self-interest rather than in the owners' interest. There are several means of reducing the effects of the agency problem, including linking the compensation of managers to the firm's stock price performance and increasing information about managers' decisions to the firm's owners.

A firm can be organized in one of three basic ways: as a proprietorship, a partnership, or a corporation. Each has implications for capital raising ability, ease of transferring ownership, and taxation.

A basic introduction to finance should also review the firm's accounting statements. The balance sheet indicates the firm's assets and how they were financed by various liabilities and equity as of a point in time. The income statement shows the level of the firm's revenues and expenses over a specific period of time. The statement of cash flows indicates the influences affecting the firm's cash account over time. We reviewed the impact of taxes on income and the effect of depreciation on both income and taxes.

In the following chapter we will use the various accounts listed on the balance sheet and income statement to illustrate some of the duties of a financial analyst. We'll see how to study a firm's financial position and how the financial statements can be used when planning for the future.

KEY TERMS

agency costs
agents
annual report
assets
average tax rate
balance sheet
bylaws
capital gains
charter
chief financial officer (CFO)
controller
corporation
current assets
depreciation
depreciation tax shield
equity
equity capital
generally accepted accounting
    principles (GAAP)

income statement
liabilities
limited liability company (LLC)
limited partners
limited partnership
marginal tax rate
market value added (MVA)
mission statement
partnership
poison pills
principal-agent problem
principals
progressive
proprietorship
statement of cash flows
stock options
subchapter S corporation
treasurer
working capital

DISCUSSION QUESTIONS

1. It has often been said that a business should begin with a vision or mission statement. Explain what this means.
2. How do the financial markets accommodate the needs of both risky firms and very safe firms?
3. Describe the financial goal espoused by business firms.
4. Briefly explain how shareholder wealth is measured.
5. How are financial strategy and financial plans linked together?
6. Identify and briefly describe the three major forms of business ownership used in the United States.
7. What are the differences in owner liability in proprietorships and partnerships versus corporations?
8. Briefly describe the differences between a subchapter S corporation and a limited liability company.
9. What is meant by the principal-agent problem in the context of corporate governance?
10. Explain the two basic approaches used to reduce the agency problem where managers may try to make self-serving decisions.
11. What types of information are included in an annual report?

12. General accounting practice is based upon the accrual concept. Explain what this means and briefly describe how this compares with the financial manager's focus on cash.
13. What is the purpose of the income statement? Also briefly identify and describe the major types of expenses that are shown on the typical income statement.
14. What is the purpose of the balance sheet? Briefly identify and describe the major types of assets and the claims of creditors and owners shown on the typical balance sheet.
15. Describe the three different accounts that comprise the owners' equity section on a typical corporate balance sheet.
16. What is a statement of cash flows? What are the three standard sections contained in a statement of cash flows?
17. Why is it said that the personal income tax rate in the United States is progressive?
18. Corporate tax rates vary with the amount of taxable income. What currently is the range (lowest and highest) of corporate tax rates in the United States?
19. What is meant by the statement that depreciation provides a tax shield? Explain how this works.
20. Briefly describe the financial responsibilities undertaken by a firm's treasurer. What are the responsibilities of a firm's controller?

PROBLEMS

1. Determine the marginal and average tax rates under the tax law for corporations with the following amounts of taxable income: (a) $60,000, (b) $150,000, and (c) $500,000.
2. What would the tax obligation be for a corporation with pre-tax earnings of: (a) $60,000, (b) $150,000, (c) $500,000? What would be the personal tax obligation of a person filing her taxes under the "single" filing status?
3. Use your knowledge of balance sheets to fill in the missing amounts:

Cash	$10,000	Accounts	
Accounts		payable	$12,000
Receivable	100,000	Notes	
Inventory	_____	payable	50,000
Total current assets	220,000	Total current liabilities	_____
Gross plant and equipment	500,000	Long-term debt	_____
Less: accumulated depreciation	_____	Total Liabilities	190,000

Net plant and		Common stock	
equipment	375,000	($1 par, 100,000	
Total Assets	_____	shares)	_____
		Paid-in capital	_____
		Retained earnings	150,000
		Total Stockholders'	
		Equity	_____
		Total Liabilities and	
		Equity	_____

4. Use your knowledge of balance sheets to fill in the missing amounts:

Cash	$50,000	Accounts payable	$12,000
Accounts		Notes payable	50,000
Receivable	80,000	Total current	
Inventory	100,000	liabilities	_____
Total Current Assets	_____		
		Long-term debt	_____
Gross plant and		Total Liabilities	_____
equipment	_____		
Less: accumulated		Common stock	
depreciation	130,000	($1 par, 100,000	
Net plant and		shares)	_____
equipment	600,000	Paid-in capital	250,000
Total Assets	_____	Retained earnings	200,000
		Total Stockholders'	
		Equity	_____
		Total Liabilities and	
		Equity	$830,000

5. Use your knowledge of income statements to fill in the missing items:

Sales	_____
Cost of goods sold	$ 575,000
Gross profit	1,600,000
General and administrative	
expense	200,000
Selling and marketing	
expense	_____
Depreciation	50,000
Operating income	_____
Interest	100,000
Income before taxes	_____
Income taxes (30%)	_____
Net Income	$700,000

6. Use the following information to construct an income statement:

   Interest: $25,000
   Sales: $950,000
   Income tax rate: 25%
   Selling and marketing expenses: $160,000
   General and administrative expenses: $200,000
   Gross profit: $550,000
   Depreciation: $30,000
   Cost of goods sold: $400,000

7. Find the annual depreciation expenses for the following items:
   a. Original cost is $35,000 for an asset in the 3-year class.
   b. Original cost is $70,000 for an asset in the 5-year class.

SELF-TEST QUESTIONS

1. The goal of a business should be:
   a. maximization of the owners' wealth
   b. maximization of accounting profit
   c. maximization of sales
   d. maximization of assets
2. Which of the following is not considered to be one of the three major forms of business ownership in the United States?
   a. proprietorship
   b. partnership
   c. public limited company
   d. corporation
3. Under which one of the following business organizations do the owners have unlimited liability for all debts of the firm?
   a. partnership
   b. limited partnership
   c. corporation
   d. subchapter S corporation
4. The corporate form of organization is recognized in many countries. Which one of the following does not designate a corporation?
   a. Inc.
   b. PLC
   c. AG
   d. SEC
5. For corporations, the principal-agent relationship usually refers to the relationship between:
   a. buyers-sellers
   b. owners-managers
   c. managers-customers

    d. owners-bankers

6. Which one of the following alternatives is commonly used to reduce agency problems as they relate to corporate control?
   a. stock options
   b. higher salaries
   c. larger perquisites ("perks")
   d. less restrictive accountability requirements

7. Generally accepted accounting principles are formulated by the:
   a. Securities and Exchange Commission
   b. Financial Accounting Standards Board
   c. Federal Trade Commission
   d. General Accounting Office

8. Which one of the following financial statements conveys a relationship of equality between assets and liabilities plus owners' equity?
   a. income statement
   b. statement of cash flows
   c. balance sheet
   d. statement of retained earnings

9. Under current tax laws, the lowest marginal tax rate for both individuals and corporations is:
   a. 5 percent
   b. 15 percent
   c. 25 percent
   d. 35 percent

SELF-TEST PROBLEMS

1. The Beagle Manufacturing Company had the following operating results for the last year: net sales were $1 million; the cost of goods sold was one-half of net sales; operating expenses (general, administrative, and marketing) were $200,000; depreciation was $50,000; and interest was $50,000.
   a. Calculate Beagle's net income if the average tax rate was 40%.
   b. Determine the firm's earnings per share (EPS) assuming 100,000 shares are outstanding.
   c. If Beagle's stock price is currently $12 per share, determine the market value of the shareholders' wealth.

2. Assume a corporation earns $75,000 in net income.
   a. Determine the firm's income tax liability.
   b. Calculate the firm's average income tax rate.

3. Assume that a corporation purchases a new piece of equipment for $90,000. The equipment qualifies for a 3-year class life for depreciation purposes.

a. What is the dollar amount of depreciation that can be taken in the first year?
b. Determine the depreciation for the remaining years.

SUGGESTED READINGS

Harrington, Diana R. *Corporate Financial Analysis,* 4e. Homewood, IL: Richard D. Irwin, 1989. Chap. 1.

Helfert, Erich A. *Techniques of Financial Analysis,* 8e. Homewood, IL: Richard D. Irwin, 1994. Chap. 1.

Higgins, Robert C. *Analysis for Financial Management,* 3e. Homewood, IL: Richard D. Irwin, 1992. Chap. 1.

Marsh, William H. *Basic Financial Management.* Cincinnati, Ohio: South-Western College Publishing, 1995. Chap. 1.

Prahalad, C.K., and G. Hamel. "The Core Competence of the Corporation." *Harvard Business Review,* May-June 1990, pp. 79–91.

Rappaport, Alfred. "CFOs and Strategists: Forging a Common Framework." *Harvard Business Review,* May-June 1992, pp. 84–91.

ANSWERS TO SELF-TEST QUESTIONS 1. a, 2. c, 3. a, 4. d, 5. b, 6. a, 7. b, 8. c, 9. b

ANSWERS TO SELF-TEST PROBLEMS

1. a.
Net sales	$1,000,000
Cost of goods sold	− 500,000
Operating expenses	− 200,000
Depreciation	− 50,000
EBIT	$250,000
Interest	− 50,000
Income before taxes	$ 200,000
Income taxes (40%)	− 80,000
Net income	$ 120,000

   b. $120,000/100,000 shares = $1.20 EPS
   c. $12 times 100,000 shares = $1,200,000

2. a. .15 × $50,000 = $ 7,500
       .25 × $25,000 =   6,250
              $75,000 $13,750
    b. $13,750/$75,000 = 18.33 percent average tax rate

3. a. $90,000 times .33 = $29,700
    b. $90,000 times .45 = $40,500
       $90,000 times .15 = $13,500
       $90,000 times .07 = $ 6,300
                             $60,300
       This $60,300 plus the $29,700 for year 1 = $90,000

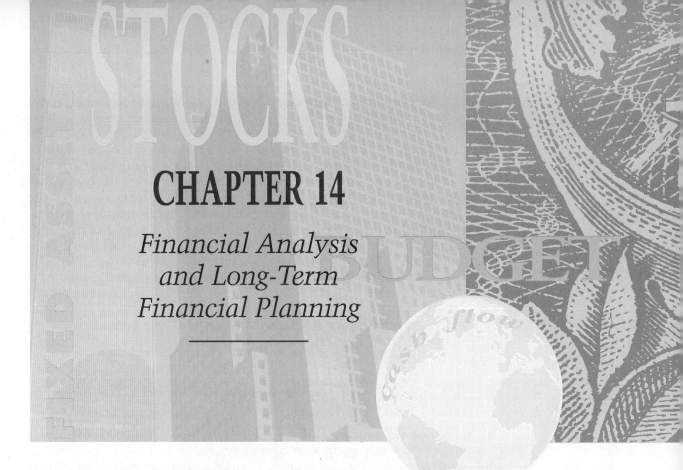

CHAPTER 14

Financial Analysis and Long-Term Financial Planning

AFTER STUDYING THIS CHAPTER, YOU SHOULD BE ABLE TO:

- Describe what is meant by financial statement analysis.
- Describe the five basic types of financial ratios.
- Indicate what is meant by Du Pont analysis and indicate its major components.
- Explain the importance of the quality of financial statements.
- Describe the link between asset investment requirements and sales growth.
- Describe how internally generated financing occurs.
- Describe how additional external financing requirements are determined.
- Describe the cost-volume-profit analysis concept.

Successful financial analysis and planning require an understanding of both a firm's external and internal environments. Prior chapters have discussed important external influences affecting firms such as fluctuations in inflation, interest rates, exchange rates, and government policy. The firm's internal environment includes items that can be affected by management, such as organizational structure, worker motivation and productivity, cost control, and the firm's plant and operations.

There are, of course, a number of interrelationships between a firm's external and internal environment. Firm sales will be affected by the state of the economy, management's ability to handle growth, and the quality and marketing of the firm's product. Pricing decisions are influenced by the state of the economy, actions by competitors, and the firm's production costs.

The joint impact of the external and internal environment on a firm is best reflected in the firm's financial statements. These statements provide measures of the success or failure of the firm's strategies and policies, quantified in financial terms. Such information is valuable to the firm's managers, as well as to stock and bond analysts, bank loan officers, and competitors. The information found on the financial statements is invaluable for analyzing a firm's past as well as for planning for its future.

This chapter addresses how to analyze a firm's financial statements to identify a firm's strengths and weaknesses. We also discuss using financial statement information for financial planning and forecasting purposes, including estimating future asset needs and capital requirements.

FINANCIAL STATEMENT ANALYSIS

The financial statements discussed in Chapter 13 were designed to report a firm's financial position at a point in time as well as the results of its operations over a period of time. The real usefulness of these statements comes from the help they provide in predicting the firm's future earnings and dividends along with the risks associated with these variables.

Financial statement analysis can affect nonfinance operations of a firm. For example, a salesperson could lose a new customer and a sales commission should a check of the customer's financial statements lead to the conclusion that the customer is a bad credit risk. An analysis that indicates excessive levels of inventories could lead to a change in the firm's pricing and marketing strategies and it could affect the firm's production plan, even leading to worker layoffs.

A firm's management reviews its financial statements to determine if progress is being made toward company goals. Internal documents based on this analysis inform division managers of the status of their divisions and product lines and how these results compare to the year's plan.

Many individuals and organizations analyze firms' financial statements. A firm that seeks credit, either from a supplier firm or a bank, typically must submit financial statements for examination. Potential purchasers of a firm's bonds will analyze financial statements in order to gauge the firm's ability to make timely payments of interest and principal. Potential shareholders should examine financial statements as they are an excellent source of firm information. Present shareholders will want to examine financial statements to monitor firm performance.

RATIO ANALYSIS OF BALANCE SHEET AND INCOME STATEMENT

In this section we discuss **ratio analysis** as another means by which to gain insight regarding a firm's strengths and weaknesses. Ratios are constructed by dividing various financial statement numbers into one another. The ratios can then be examined to more easily determine trends and reasons for changes in the financial statement quantities. Ratios are valuable tools, as they standardize balance sheet and income statement numbers. Thus differences in firm size will not affect the analysis. A firm with $1 billion in sales can be easily compared to a firm with $200 million in sales.

Three basic categories of ratio analysis are used. First, financial ratios can be used in **trend** or **time series analysis** to evaluate a firm's performance over time. Second, ratios are used in **cross-sectional analysis,** in which different firms are compared at the same point in time. Third, **industry comparative analysis** is used to compare a firm's ratios against average ratios for other companies in the firm's industry. This allows the analyst to evaluate the firm's financial performance relative to industry norms.

The firm's financial statements are the best information source for time series or cross sectional analysis. These materials appear in annual reports as well as 10-Q and 10-K filings with the Securities and Exchange Commission.

ratio analysis
financial technique that involves dividing various financial statement numbers into one another

trend or time series analysis
used to evaluate a firm's performance over time

cross-sectional analysis
different firms are compared at the same point in time

industry comparative analysis
compares a firm's ratios against average ratios for other companies in the industry

Comparing a firm's ratios to average industry ratios requires extreme caution. Some sources of industry data report the average for each ratio; others report the median; others report the interquartile range for each ratio (that is, the range for the middle 50 percent of ratio values reported by firms in the industry).

Other difficulties can arise as well. First, by their nature, industry ratios are narrowly focused on a specific industry, but the operations of large firms such as AT&T, Exxon, and IBM often cross many industry boundaries.

Second, accounting standards often differ among firms in an industry. This can create confusion, particularly when some firms in the industry adopt new accounting standards (set forth by FASB, the Financial Accounting Standards Board) before others. Adopting standards early can affect a firm's ratios by making them appear unusually high or low as compared to the industry average.

Third, care must be taken when comparing different types of firms in the same industry. In one industry there may be both very large and small firms; both multinational and domestic firms; firms that operate nationally; and those that focus only on limited geographic markets.

THE USE OF INDUSTRY AVERAGE RATIOS

Data for industry average financial ratios are published by a number of organizations, such as Dun & Bradstreet, Robert Morris Associates, Financial Dynamics, Standard & Poor's, and the Federal Trade Commission. These information sources are readily available at most libraries.

How an analyst interprets a ratio depends on for whom the analyst works. Whether a ratio appears favorable or unfavorable depends on the perspective of the user. For example, a short-term creditor such as a bank loan officer wants most to see a high degree of liquidity. This analyst is somewhat less concerned with a firm's profitability. An equity holder would rather see less liquidity and more profitability. Therefore the analyst must keep in mind the perspective of the user in evaluating and interpreting the information contained in financial ratios.

There are many categories of financial ratios. The following categories are the most basic.

TYPES OF FINANCIAL RATIOS

Many types of ratios can be calculated from financial statement data or stock market information. However, it is common practice to group ratios into five basic categories:

1. Liquidity ratios
2. Asset management ratios
3. Capital structure ratios
4. Profitability ratios
5. Market value ratios

The first four categories are based on information taken from a firm's income statements and balance sheets. The fifth category relates stock market information to financial statement items. We will use the financial statements for the Global Manufacturing Corporation that were introduced in Chapter 13 to illustrate how financial statement analysis is conducted. Table 14.1 and 14.2 contain the balance sheets and income statements for 1993, 1994, and 1995 for the Global Manufacturing Corporation. For comparative purposes, for each ratio group we present graphs of Global's ratios as well as the average ratios for its industry over the 1993–95 time period.

LIQUIDITY RATIOS AND ANALYSIS

The less liquid the firm, the greater the risk of insolvency or default. Because debt obligations are paid with cash, the firm's cash flows ultimately determine solvency.

liquidity ratios
indicate the ability of the firm to meet short-term obligations as they come due

However, it is also possible to estimate the firm's liquidity position by examining specific balance sheet items. ***Liquidity ratios*** indicate the ability to meet short-term obligations to creditors as they mature or come due. This

TABLE 14.1 Balance Sheets for Global Manufacturing, Inc.

	DECEMBER 31		
	1995	1994	1993
ASSETS			
Cash and marketable securities	$ 25,000	$ 20,000	$ 16,000
Accounts receivable	100,000	80,000	56,000
Inventories	125,000	100,000	80,000
Total current assets	250,000	200,000	152,000
Gross plant and equipment	300,000	225,000	200,000
Less: accumulated depreciation	− 100,000	− 75,000	− 50,000
Net plant and equipment	200,000	150,000	150,000
Land	50,000	50,000	50,000
Total fixed assets	250,000	200,000	200,000
Total assets	$500,000	$400,000	$352,000
LIABILITIES AND EQUITY			
Accounts payable	$ 78,000	$ 65,000	$ 58,000
Notes payable	34,000	10,000	10,000
Accrued liabilities	30,000	25,000	25,000
Total current liabilities	142,000	100,000	93,000
Long-term debt	140,000	100,000	71,000
Total liabilities	$282,000	$200,000	$164,000
Common stock ($1 par, 50,000 shares)	$ 50,000	$ 50,000	$ 50,000
Paid-in capital	100,000	100,000	100,000
Retained earnings	68,000	50,000	38,000
Total stockholders' equity	218,000	200,000	188,000
Total liabilities and equity	$500,000	$400,000	$352,000

form of liquidity analysis focuses on the relationship between current assets and current liabilities, and the rapidity with which receivables and inventory turn into cash during normal business operations. This means that the immediate source of cash funds for paying bills must be cash on hand, proceeds from the sale of marketable securities, or the collection of accounts receivable. Additional liquidity also comes from inventory that can be sold and thus converted into cash either directly through cash sales or indirectly through credit sales (accounts receivable).

The dollar amount of a firm's **net working capital,** or its current assets minus current liabilities, is sometimes used as a measure of liquidity. But two popular ratios are also used to gauge a firm's liquidity position. The *current ratio* is a measure of a company's ability to pay off its short-term debt as it comes due. The current ratio is computed by dividing the current

net working capital
dollar amount of a firm's current assets minus current liabilities

TABLE 14.2   Income Statements for Global Manufacturing, Inc.

YEARS ENDED DECEMBER 31	1995	1994	1993
Net revenues or sales	$700,000	$600,000	$540,000
Cost of goods sold	450,000	375,000	338,000
Gross profit	250,000	225,000	202,000
Operating expenses:			
General and administrative	95,000	95,000	95,000
Selling and marketing	56,000	50,000	45,000
Depreciation	25,000	20,000	15,000
Operating income	74,000	60,000	47,000
Interest	14,000	10,000	7,000
Income before taxes	60,000	50,000	40,000
Income taxes (40%)	24,000	20,000	16,000
Net income	$ 36,000	$ 30,000	$ 24,000
Number of shares outstanding	50,000	50,000	50,000
Earnings per share	$0.72	$0.60	$0.48

assets by the current liabilities. Both assets and liabilities with maturities of one year or less are considered to be current for financial statement purposes.

A low current ratio (low relative to, say, industry norms) may indicate a company may face difficulty in paying its bills. A high value for the current ratio, however, does not necessarily imply greater liquidity. It may suggest that funds are not being efficiently employed within the firm. Excessive amounts of inventory, accounts receivable, or idle cash balances could contribute to a high current ratio.

We can now calculate the current ratio for 1994 and 1995 as follows:

CURRENT RATIO:	1995		1994	
$\dfrac{\text{Current Assets}}{\text{Current Liabilities}}$ =	$\dfrac{\$250,000}{\$142,000}$	= 1.8 times	$\dfrac{\$200,000}{\$100,000}$	= 2.0 times

Notice that while all the current asset accounts increased between 1994 and 1995, current liabilities had to increase at a faster rate in order for the current ratio to decline.

The *quick ratio,* or *acid test ratio,* is computed by dividing the sum of cash, marketable securities, and accounts receivable by the current liabilities. This comparison eliminates inventories from consideration since inventories are the least liquid of the major current asset categories because they must first be converted to sales.

In general, a ratio of 1.0 indicates a reasonably liquid position in that an immediate liquidation of marketable securities at their current values and the collection of all accounts receivable, plus cash on hand, would be adequate to cover the firm's current liabilities. However, as this ratio declines, the firm must rely increasingly on converting inventories to sales in order to meet current liabilities as they come due. Global's quick ratios for 1994 and 1995 are:

QUICK RATIO:	1995		1994	
$\dfrac{\text{Current Assets} - \text{Inventory}}{\text{Current Liabilities}} =$	$\dfrac{\$125,000}{\$142,000}$	$= 0.9 \text{ times}$	$\dfrac{\$100,000}{\$100,000}$	$= 1.0 \text{ times}$

According to the financial statement data, Global's quick ratio has declined to below 1.0 in 1995. This occurred because current liabilities increased at a faster rate than did the current assets excluding inventories.

When assessing the firm's liquidity position, financial managers also are interested in how trade credit from suppliers, which we call accounts payable, is being used and paid for. This analysis requires taking data from a firm's income statement in addition to the balance sheet. The *average payment period* is computed by dividing the year end accounts payable amount by the firm's average cost of goods sold per day. We calculate the average daily cost of goods sold by dividing the income statement's cost of goods sold amount by 365 days in a year.

AVERAGE PAYMENT PERIOD:

$$\frac{\text{Accounts Payable}}{\text{Cost of Goods Sold}/365} = \frac{\text{Accounts Payable}}{\text{Cost of Goods Sold per Day}}$$

1995			1994		
$\dfrac{\$78,000}{\$450,000/365}$	$= \dfrac{\$78,000}{\$1,233}$	$= 63.3 \text{ days}$	$\dfrac{\$65,000}{\$375,000/365}$	$= \dfrac{\$65,000}{\$1,027}$	$= 63.3 \text{ days}$

On average, it takes Global a little over two months to pay its suppliers.

Figures 14.1a–c illustrate the trend of Global Manufacturing's liquidity ratios in comparison to their industry averages. The industry's liquidity ratios generally rose over the 1993–95 period. Global's current and quick ratios were usually below the industry averages. In particular, in 1993 and 1994 Global's current ratio and quick ratio were fairly close to those of the industry, but in 1995 the industry's ratios rose while Global's fell. This would be a warning sign to an analyst, pinpointing that further research is needed to determine why this occurred and what corrective action, if any, may be needed.

Global's average payment period has remained constant, about 63 days, during this period. This is more than twice as long as the industry average, indicating that Global benefits from longer trade credit financing relative to the "average" firm in the industry. Although this may be a good sign, Global's analysts should be aware of what the impact on the firm would be should Global's suppliers demand prompt payment. There may even be an ethics question here, especially if Global's suppliers request payment in, say, 30 days while Global does not pay its bills until after 63 days. Global's credit may one day be cut off if it does not pay its bills in a

FIGURE 14.1   Liquidity Ratios for Global Manufacturing, Inc.

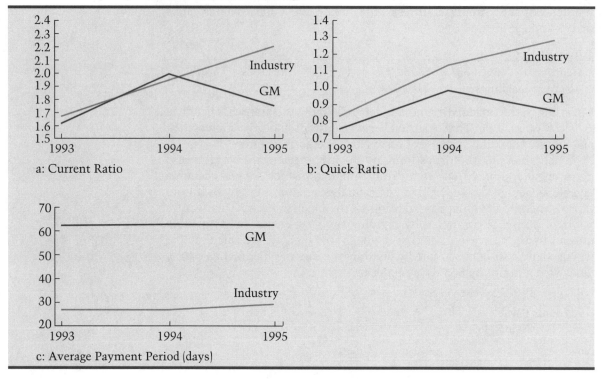

a: Current Ratio

b: Quick Ratio

c: Average Payment Period (days)

more timely manner; then it will be forced to purchase supplies and raw material with immediate cash.

ASSET MANAGEMENT RATIOS AND ANALYSIS

asset management ratios indicate extent to which assets are used to support sales

Asset management ratios indicate the extent to which assets are turned over, or used to support sales. These are also sometimes referred to as *activity* or *utilization ratios* and each ratio in this category relates financial performance on the income statement with items on the balance sheet. Thus, we will be using information for Global Manufacturing from Tables 14.1 and 14.2.

The *total assets turnover ratio* is computed by dividing net sales by the firm's total assets. It indicates how efficiently the firm is utilizing its total assets to produce revenues or sales. It is a measure of the dollars of sales generated by one dollar of the firm's assets. Generally, the more efficiently assets are used, the higher a firm's profits. The size of the ratio is significantly influenced by characteristics of the industry within which the firm operates. Capital intensive electric utilities might have asset turnover ratios as low as 0.33, indicating that they require $3 of investment in assets in order to produce $1 in revenues. In contrast, retail food chains with asset turnovers as high as 10 would require a $0.10 investment in assets to produce $1 in sales. A typical manufacturing firm has an asset turnover of about 1.5. Global's 1995 and 1994 total assets turnover ratios are calculated as follows:

TOTAL ASSETS TURNOVER:	1995		1994	
$\dfrac{\text{Net Sales}}{\text{Total Assets}}$ =	$\dfrac{\$700,000}{\$500,000}$ =	1.4 times	$\dfrac{\$600,000}{\$400,000}$ =	1.5 times

Asset utilization declined slightly between 1994 and 1995 indicating that the investment in assets increased more rapidly than the increase in sales. Although slight, Global's financial manager would want to know why this difference occurred in 1995. This could be accomplished, at least in part, by examining some of the individual asset accounts, particularly fixed assets, accounts receivable, and inventories, in greater detail.

The *fixed assets turnover ratio* is computed by dividing net sales by the firm's fixed assets and indicates the extent to which long-term assets are being used to produce sales. Similar to the interpretation given to the total asset turnover, the fixed assets turnover represents the dollars of sales generated by each dollar of fixed assets. Investment in plant and equipment is usually quite expensive. Consequently unused or idle capacity is very costly and often represents a major factor for a firm exhibiting poor operating performance. On the other hand, a high (compared to competitors or the industry average) fixed assets turnover ratio is not necessarily a favorable sign; it may come about because of efficient use of assets (good) or it may come about because of the firm's use of technologically obsolete equipment which has small book values because of the effects of accumulated depreciation (poor). An astute analyst will do research to determine which is the case for the firm under analysis.

FIXED ASSETS TURNOVER:	1995		1994	
$\dfrac{\text{Net Sales}}{\text{Fixed Assets}}$ =	$\dfrac{\$700,000}{\$250,000}$ =	2.8 times	$\dfrac{\$600,000}{\$200,000}$ =	3.0 times

Global's fixed assets turnover declined from 3.0 to 2.8, indicating that fixed assets increased more rapidly than sales and thus account for at least part of the decline in the assets turnover ratio. In percentage terms, fixed assets increased 25 percent [i.e., ($250,000 − $200,000)/$200,000] compared to 16.7 percent for sales [i.e., ($700,000 − $600,000)/$600,000].

The *average collection period* is calculated as the year-end accounts receivable divided by the average net sales per day and thus indicates the average number of days that sales are outstanding. In other words, it reports the number of days it takes, on average, to collect credit sales made to the firm's customers. The average collection period measures the days of financing that a firm extends to its customers.[1] Because of this, a shorter average collection period is usually preferred to a longer one. Another measure which can be used to provide this same information is the receivables turnover. The *receivables turnover* is computed by dividing annual sales, preferably credit sales, by the year-end accounts receivable. If the receivables turnover is six, this means that, on the average, the average collection period is about two months (12 months divided by the turnover ratio of 6). If the turnover is four times the firm has an average collection period of about three months (12 months divided by the turnover ratio of four). Global's average collection periods for 1994 and 1995 were:

AVERAGE COLLECTION PERIOD:

$$\frac{\text{Accounts Receivable}}{\text{Net Sales}/365} = \frac{\text{Accounts Receivable}}{\text{Net Sales per Day}}$$

1995			1994		
$\dfrac{\$100,000}{\$700,000/365}$	$=$	$\dfrac{\$100,000}{\$1,918} = 52.1 \text{ days}$	$\dfrac{\$80,000}{\$600,000/365}$	$=$	$\dfrac{\$80,000}{\$1,644} = 48.7 \text{ days}$

Global's average collection period has increased from approximately 49 days to 52 days and suggests a possible receivables management problem. In essence, Global financed its customers for an additional three days, on average, in 1995 compared to 1994.

As with other ratios, the average collection period may be too high or low. An unusually low number of days required to collect sales for a particular line of business may indicate an unnecessarily tight internal credit policy that could result in lost sales. The firm may be selecting only the best customers, or may be insisting on unusually strict payment terms. On the other hand, a very high average collection period may indicate that the firm may have too lax a policy concerning customer quality and/or credit payment terms. Thus, in trying to decide on a proper credit policy, it is important to monitor trends over time as well as compare the firm's average collection period relative to industry norms. We will explore credit policies in greater detail in Chapter 15.

The *inventory turnover ratio* is computed by dividing the cost of goods sold by the year-end inventory.[2] Here we are seeking to determine how efficiently the amount of inventory is being managed so that on the one hand the firm does not have to finance excess inventory and on the other

1.   In some ways the average collection period is the "mirror image" of the average payment period, which is the average number of days the firm's suppliers extend credit to the firm. Global is in a positive situation, as it collects from its customers faster (on average in 52.1 days in 1995) than it pays its suppliers (on average 63.3 days in 1995).
2.   Cost of goods sold often is used to compute this ratio instead of sales in order to remove the impact of profit margins on inventory turnover. Profit margins can vary over time, thus making it more difficult to interpret the relationship between volume and inventory.

hand adequate inventory supplies exist in order to avoid costly stock-outs. Stated differently, the inventory turnover ratio indicates whether the inventory is out-of-line in relation to the volume of sales when compared against industry norms or when tracked over time for a specific firm.

INVENTORY TURNOVER:	1995		1994	
$\dfrac{\text{Cost of Goods Sold}}{\text{Inventory}}$	$= \dfrac{\$450,000}{\$125,000}$	$= 3.6$ times	$\dfrac{\$375,000}{\$100,000}$	$= 3.75$ times

Global's annual inventory turnover declined slightly from 3.75 times in 1994 to 3.6 times in 1995.

Inventory management requires a delicate balance between having too low an inventory turnover, which increases the likelihood of holding obsolete inventory, and too high an inventory turnover, which could lead to stock-outs and lost sales. These concepts will be discussed in greater detail in Chapter 15.

When a firm is growing rapidly (or even shrinking rapidly), the use of year-end data might distort the comparison of ratios over time. To avoid such possible distortions, we can use the average inventory (beginning plus ending balances divided by two) to calculate inventory turnovers for comparison purposes.[3] Likewise, average data for other balance sheet accounts should be used when rapid growth or contraction is taking place for a specific firm.

Figures 14.2a–d illustrate Global's asset management ratios in comparison to the industry average between 1993 and 1995. While the industry's asset management ratios remained generally constant or rose, Global's corresponding ratios fell. Global's total asset, fixed asset, and inventory turnovers were all well below industry norms, indicating the strong possibility of inefficient asset use. The average collection period also indicates problems. Although both Global's and the industry's collection periods rose, Global's remained higher than the industry average, indicating slow collections from their customers.

FINANCIAL LEVERAGE RATIOS AND ANALYSIS

Financial leverage ratios indicate the extent to which borrowed or debt funds are used to finance assets, as well as the ability of the firm to meet its debt payment obligations.

The *total debt to total assets* ratio is computed by dividing the total debt or total liabilities of the business by the total assets. This ratio shows the portion of the total assets financed by all creditors and debtors. We obtain the relevant balance sheet information for Global Manufacturing from Table 14.1.

financial leverage ratios indicate the extent to which borrowed funds are used to finance assets, as well as the ability of a firm to meet its debt payment obligations

---

3.   For firms with highly seasonal sales, the average of the inventory balance from the firm's quarterly balance sheets (which are distributed to shareholders of public firms) also can be used.

FIGURE 14.2   Asset Management Ratios for Global Manufacturing, Inc.

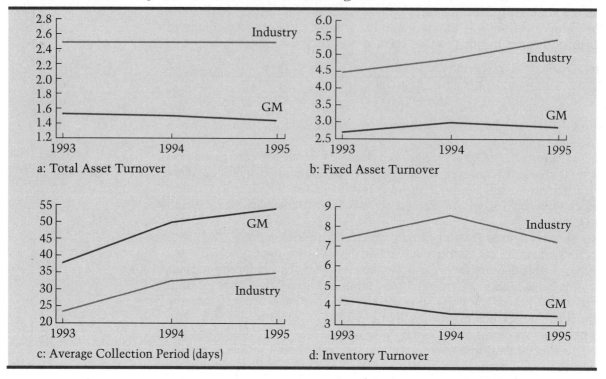

a: Total Asset Turnover

b: Fixed Asset Turnover

c: Average Collection Period (days)

d: Inventory Turnover

TOTAL DEBT TO TOTAL ASSETS:

	1995	1994
$\dfrac{\text{Total Debt}}{\text{Total Assets}} = $	$\dfrac{\$282{,}000}{\$500{,}000} = 0.564 = 56.4\%$	$\dfrac{\$200{,}000}{\$400{,}000} = 0.500 = 50.0\%$

Global's total debt ratio increased substantially during 1995. This was attributable to a 42 percent increase in current liabilities [i.e., ($142,000 − $100,000)/$100,000] and a 40 percent increase in long-term debt [i.e., ($140,000 − $100,000)/$100,000]. Thus, from a financial standpoint the firm has been made more risky at least in the short run. The financial manager needs to monitor this increased leverage development more closely. For example, Global may wish to issue common stock in the near future when the firm needs additional funds so as to lower the debt ratio.

A total debt to asset ratio that is relatively too high tells the financial manager that the opportunities for securing additional borrowed funds are limited. Additional debt funds may be more costly in terms of the rate of interest that will have to be paid. Lenders will want higher expected returns to compensate for their risk of lending to a firm that has a high proportion of debt to assets. It is also possible to have too low a ratio of total debt to total assets. This can be quite costly to the firm.[4] Since interest expenses are deductible for income tax purposes, the government in effect pays a portion of the debt financing costs. Furthermore, as we will see in Chapter 18, a firm's debt costs are lower than the effective costs of equity.

Sometimes a debt ratio is calculated which shows the total debt in relation to the dollars the owners have put in the firm. This is referred to as the *total debt to equity ratio.* Global's ratio for 1995 was 1.3 times ($282,000/$218,000) versus 1.0 times ($200,000/$200,000) in 1994. The interpretation remains the same as we formulated above. That is, Global substantially increased its relative use of debt in 1995 over 1994. In the way of a useful note, notice that a total debt to total assets ratio of 50 percent corresponds to a total debt to equity ratio of 1.0 times as occurred in 1994 for the Global Manufacturing Corporation.

The *equity multiplier ratio,* which provides still another way of looking at the firm's debt burden, is calculated by dividing total assets by the firm's total equity.

EQUITY MULTIPLIER:	1995		1994	
$\dfrac{\text{Total Assets}}{\text{Total Equity}}$ =	$\dfrac{\$500,000}{\$218,000}$	= 2.3 times	$\dfrac{\$400,000}{\$200,000}$	= 2.0 times

Global's equity multiplier increased from 2.0 times in 1994 to 2.3 times in 1995. A rising equity multiplier implies a *greater* use of debt by the firm. At first glance, the ratio appears to have little to do with leverage; it is simply total assets divided by stockholders' equity. But recall the accounting identity: Assets = Liabilities + Equity; more assets relative to equity suggests greater use of debt. Thus, larger values of the equity multiplier imply a greater use of leverage by the firm. This can also be seen by rewriting the equity multiplier using the accounting identity:

$$\frac{\text{Total assets}}{\text{Equity}} = \frac{\text{Liabilities + Equity}}{\text{Equity}} = \frac{\text{Liabilities}}{\text{Equity}} + 1$$

This is simply one plus the debt to equity ratio. Clearly, more reliance on debt results in a larger equity multiplier. While the equity multiplier does not add to the information derived from the other debt ratios, it is useful when financial analysis is conducted using certain financial models, as we will explain later in the chapter.

In addition to calculating debt ratios, the financial manager should be interested in the firm's ability to meet or service its interest and principal repayment obligations on the borrowed funds. This is accomplished through the calculation of interest coverage and fixed charge coverage

---

4.   A low debt ratio can arise from the continued profitability of a firm and its additions to retained earnings. These additions to retained earnings will increase the level of equity relative to debt unless the firm issues additional debt.

ratios. These ratios make use of information directly from the income statement or from footnotes to a firm's financial statements.

The *interest coverage,* or *times-interest-earned ratio,* is calculated by dividing the firm's operating income or earnings before interest and taxes (EBIT) by the annual interest expense:

INTEREST COVERAGE:	1995	1994
$\dfrac{\text{Earnings Before Interest \& Taxes}}{\text{Interest Expense}}$	$= \dfrac{\$74,000}{\$14,000} = 5.3 \text{ times}$	$\dfrac{\$60,000}{\$10,000} = 6.0 \text{ times}$

Global's interest coverage has dropped from six times in 1994 to slightly more than five times in 1995. The interest coverage figure indicates the extent to which the operating income or EBIT level could decline before the ability to pay interest obligations would be impeded. While the financial manager should be concerned about this trend, Global's operating income could drop to one-fifth (in general, to one divided by the interest coverage) of its current level and interest payments still could be met.

sinking fund payments
periodic bond principal repayments to a trustee

In addition to interest payments, there may be other fixed charges such as rental or lease payments and periodic bond principal repayments which are typically referred to as **sinking fund payments.** The *fixed charge coverage* ratio indicates the ability of a firm to meet its contractual obligations for interest, leases, and debt principal repayments out of its operating income.

Rental or lease payments are deductible on the income statement prior to the payment of income taxes just as is the case with interest expenses. In contrast, a sinking fund payment is a repayment of debt and thus is *not* a deductible expense for income tax purposes. However, to be consistent with the other data, we must adjust the sinking fund payment to a before-tax basis. We do this by dividing the after-tax amount by one minus the effective tax rate.

While footnotes to Global's balance sheets are not provided in Table 14.1, for calculation purposes, let's assume that lease payments were $10,000 annually for both 1994 and 1995 and that the sinking fund obligation was $6,000 in 1994 and $9,000 in 1995. This allows us to calculate fixed charge coverage for Global. First, the numerator in the ratio must reflect earnings before interest, lease payments, and taxes, which we determine by adding the lease payment amount to the operating income or EBIT amount. Second, the denominator needs to show all relevant expenses on a before-tax basis.

FIXED CHARGE COVERAGE:

$$\frac{\text{Earnings Before Interest, Lease Payments, \& Taxes}}{\text{Interest} + \text{Lease Payments} + [(\text{Sinking Fund Payment})/(1 - \text{Tax Rate})]}$$

1995

$$\frac{\$74,000 + \$10,000}{\$14,000 + \$10,000 + (\$9,000/0.60)} = \frac{\$84,000}{\$39,000} = 2.2 \text{ times}$$

$$\underset{\text{1994}}{\frac{\$60,000 + \$10,000}{\$10,000 + \$10,000 + (\$6,000/0.60)}} = \frac{\$70,000}{\$30,000} = 2.3 \text{ times}$$

Global's fixed charge coverage ratio declined slightly between 1994 and 1995 due to the increase in interest payment obligations and an increase in debt principal repayment commitments. The firm could suffer more than a 50 percent decline in operating income and still be able to meet its annual fixed charges in the form of interest, sinking fund, and lease payments.

The graphs of Global's financial leverage ratios in Figures 14.3a–c show a rising debt to assets ratio and a rising equity multiplier ratio. Each is higher than the industry average, but that should not be cause for alarm. The interest coverage graph is more worrisome. Between 1993 and 1995 the industry interest coverage ratio rose dramatically, indicating a larger cushion between EBIT and interest expense. Global's interest coverage ratio actually declined, indicating a narrowing cushion. This indicates Global's interest expense rose relative to its level of operating income during this time frame. This also points out the difference between the balance sheet financial leverage ratios (such as the debt to assets ratio) and the

FIGURE 14.3   Financial Leverage Ratios for Global Manufacturing, Inc.

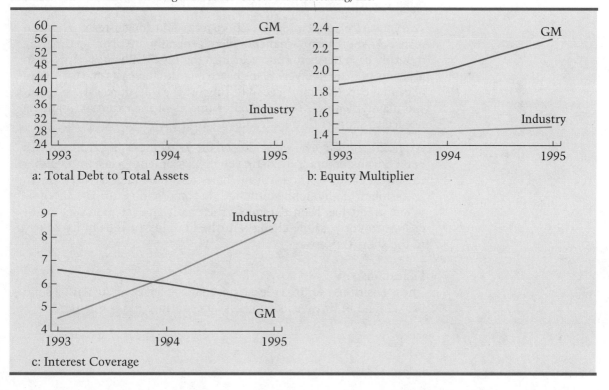

a: Total Debt to Total Assets

b: Equity Multiplier

c: Interest Coverage

CAREER OPPORTUNITIES IN FINANCE

Field: Business Financial Planning

Opportunities:
A business may be small, with a relatively small budget and a straightforward market, or large, with budget well over a billion dollars and a multinational market. In either case, analysts and planners play an important and necessary role in preserving the financial well-being of their firm. These jobs, therefore, are challenging, often unpredictable, and exciting. The risks are often high, but so are the rewards.

Jobs:
Financial Analyst
Financial Planner
Credit Analyst

Responsibilities:
A *financial analyst* calculates a firm's past and ongoing financial performance relative to other firms in the same industry and/or a firm's own performance over time. Once this information is gathered, a financial analyst evaluates the results and presents these findings to other departments of the firm.

A *financial* planner prepares short-term and longer-term financial plans. A short-term financial plan generally involves estimating monthly cash needs for one year into the future. Business firms also typically prepare five-year plans based on sales forecasts and estimates of capital expenditures needed to support the sales forecasts. A financial planner would make annual estimates of the external financing needed to support these sales targets over each five-year plan.

A *credit analyst* evaluates the credit-worthiness of both a firm's potential customers and existing credit customers. Decisions whether to extend credit in the form of short-term financing is based on an assessment of the applicant's liquidity and ability to pay. In cases where credit has been extended, the credit analyst monitors credit customers for possible changes in the liquidity or the ability to pay in the short-run.

Education:
These positions require at least a bachelor's degree along with a solid background in finance, economics, accounting, and computers.

income or cash flow based ones (such as interest coverage). Debt levels may appear stable or even declining according to the balance sheet ratios, but it is cash that pays the interest. Interest coverage is an important ratio for determining a firm's creditworthiness.

PROFITABILITY RATIOS AND ANALYSIS

Profitability ratios indicate the firm's ability to generate returns on its sales, assets, and equity. Two basic profit margin ratios are important to the financial manager. The *operating profit margin* is calculated as the firm's earnings before interest and taxes divided by net sales. This ratio indicates the firm's ability to control operating expenses relative to sales. Table 14.2 contains income statement information for the Global Manufacturing Corporation and provides the necessary information for determining the operating profit margin.

profitability ratios indicate the firm's ability to generate returns on its sales, assets, and equity

OPERATING PROFIT MARGIN: 1995   1994

$$\frac{\text{Earnings Before Interest \& Taxes}}{\text{Net Sales}} = \frac{\$74{,}000}{\$700{,}000} = 0.106 \qquad \frac{\$60{,}000}{\$600{,}000} = 0.100$$

$$= 10.6\% \qquad\qquad = 10.0\%$$

These results indicate that Global was able to improve its operating profitability from 1994 to 1995. Whether it was because of higher selling prices or lower costs, operating profit (EBIT) rose about 23 percent on a sales increase of about 17 percent.

The *net profit margin*, a widely used measure of firm profitability, is calculated as the firm's net income after taxes divided by net sales. In addition to considering operating expenses, this ratio also indicates the ability to earn a return after meeting interest and tax obligations. Global's net profit margin shows a slight improvement in 1995 over 1994:

NET PROFIT MARGIN: 1995   1994

$$\frac{\text{Net Income}}{\text{Net Sales}} = \frac{\$36{,}000}{\$700{,}000} = 0.051 \qquad \frac{\$30{,}000}{\$600{,}000} = 0.050$$

$$= 5.1\% \qquad\qquad = 5.0\%$$

Three basic rate of return measures on assets and equity are important to the financial manager. The *operating return on assets* is computed as the earnings before interest and taxes divided by total assets. Notice that this ratio focuses on the firm's operating performance and ignores how the firm is financed and taxed. Relevant data for Global Manufacturing must be taken from both Tables 14.1 and 14.2.

OPERATING RETURN ON ASSETS: 1995   1994

$$\frac{\text{Earnings Before Interest \& Taxes}}{\text{Total Assets}} = \frac{\$74{,}000}{\$500{,}000} = 0.148 \qquad \frac{\$60{,}000}{\$400{,}000} = 0.150$$

$$= 14.8\% \qquad\qquad = 15.0\%$$

Global's operating return on assets declined slightly as its assets increased by 25 percent (from \$400,000 to \$500,000) while operating profits rose only about 23 percent.

The net return on total assets, commonly referred to as the *return on total assets*, is measured as the firm's net income divided by total assets. Here we measure the return on investment in assets after a firm has covered its operating expenses, interest costs, and tax obligations. Global's return on total assets fell in 1995, as the growth in net income could not keep up with the growth in assets:

RETURN ON TOTAL ASSETS: 1995   1994

$$\frac{\text{Net Income}}{\text{Total Assets}} = \frac{\$36,000}{\$500,000} = 0.072 \qquad \frac{\$30,000}{\$400,000} = 0.075$$

$$= 7.2\% \qquad\qquad = 7.5\%$$

A final profitability ratio is the *return on equity*. It measures the return that shareholders earned on their equity invested in the firm. The return on equity is measured as the firm's net income divided by stockholders' equity. This ratio reflects the fact that a portion of a firm's total assets are financed with borrowed funds. Global's return on equity rose in 1995:

RETURN ON EQUITY: 1995   1994

$$\frac{\text{Net Income}}{\text{Common Equity}} = \frac{\$36,000}{\$218,000} = 0.165 \qquad \frac{\$30,000}{\$200,000} = 0.150$$

$$= 16.5\% \qquad\qquad = 15.0\%$$

Figures 14.4a–e indicate that industry profitability ratios rose during 1993–95 while some of Global's ratios fell in 1995. Although there are a few exceptions, Global's profitability was generally below that of the industry during this time frame. In 1995 all of Global's ratios were less than the industry's. As of 1995 the industry is more cost efficient (as seen in its higher operating and net profit margins) and generates more profit from its asset and equity base (as seen in the operating return on assets, return on total assets, and return on equity) than Global Manufacturing.

MARKET VALUE RATIOS AND ANALYSIS

market value ratios indicate the value of a firm in the market place relative to financial statement values

The **market value ratios** indicate the willingness of investors to value a firm in the marketplace relative to financial statement values. A firm's profitability, risk, quality of management, and many other factors are reflected in its stock and security prices by the efficient financial markets. Financial statements are historical in nature; the financial markets are forward looking.[5] We know that stock prices seem to reflect much of the known information about a company and are fairly good indicators of a company's true value. Hence, market value ratios indicate the market's assessment of the value of the firm's securities.

5.   Recall from Chapter 10 that stock prices are in part based upon investors' *expectations* of *future* dividend growth.

FIGURE 14.4   Profitability Ratios for Global Manufacturing, Inc.

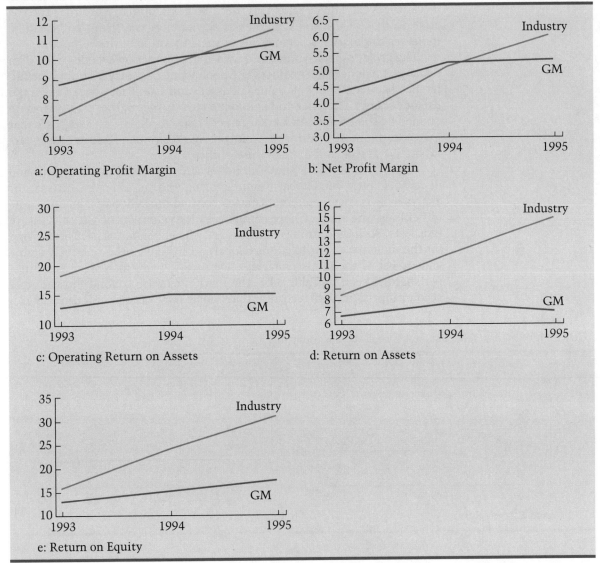

a: Operating Profit Margin

b: Net Profit Margin

c: Operating Return on Assets

d: Return on Assets

e: Return on Equity

The *price/earnings,* or *P/E, ratio,* is simply the market price of the firm's common stock divided by its annual earnings per share. Sometimes called the *earnings multiple,* the P/E ratio shows how much investors are willing to pay for each dollar of the firm's earnings per share. Earnings per share comes from the income statement, so it is sensitive to the many factors that affect net income. Though earnings per share cannot reflect the value of patents or assets, the quality of the firm's management, or its risk, stock prices can and do reflect all these factors. Comparing a firm's P/E relative to that of the stock market as a whole, or the firm's competitors, indicates the market's perceptions of the true value of the company.

The *price-to-book-value ratio* measures the market's value of the firm relative to balance sheet equity. The book value of equity is simply the difference between the book values of assets and liabilities appearing on the balance sheet.[6] The price-to-book-value ratio is the market price per share divided by the book value of equity per share. A higher ratio suggests that investors are more optimistic about the market value of a firm's assets, its intangible assets, and its managers' abilities.

Figures 14.5a and b show us levels and trends in the P/E ratio and price/book ratio for Global Manufacturing and its industry. Just as our analysis of financial statement ratios pointed out, Global is having some difficulties; the market is pessimistic in its valuation of Global's future prospects. Both the earnings multiple and price/book ratios have been rising for the industry as a whole. But Global's ratios have been relatively stable and are below the industry average. Despite Global's increases in earnings per share as seen in Table 14.1, the market can see beyond those simple accounting numbers to recognize that Global may face difficult times ahead.

FIGURE 14.5   Market Value Ratio for Global Manufacturing, Inc.

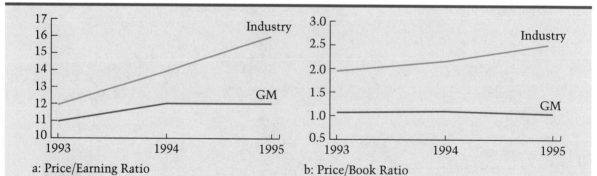

a: Price/Earning Ratio   b: Price/Book Ratio

SUMMARY OF RATIO ANALYSIS FOR GLOBAL MANUFACTURING

Let's review and summarize what we've learned about Global Manufacturing by computing its ratios and comparing them to the industry averages. The liquidity ratios show recent declines in liquidity while

6.   Typically it is equal to stockholders' equity.

industry liquidity is rising (current ratio, quick ratio) and a very slow payment period when compared to the industry. Global may face a severe cash shortage if its suppliers demand quicker payments. Should Global need to raise money quickly, it may not be able to issue debt, as Global's debt ratios are higher than the industry averages (debt to assets, equity multiplier) and its interest coverage is declining while the industry's is rising.

Part of Global's difficulties can be traced to poor cost control (lower than average operating profit margin and operating return on assets) and poor asset management (the asset turnover ratios are below the industry average). The receivables collection period is much longer than average as well. The combination of poor cost control and inefficient asset management has led to poor profitability compared to industry average trends (net profit margin, return on total assets, return on equity). The stock market has recognized these difficulties, and Global's market value ratios (price/earnings, market/book) are lagging behind those of the industry.

DU PONT METHOD OF RATIO ANALYSIS

How does a supermarket generate profits? In general, supermarkets have very low profit margins. Goods are sold for pennies above cost. Profits are generated by rapid turnover. The shelves are restocked daily with new items to take the place of items that were purchased. Thus, supermarkets generally have high asset turnover ratios. Jewelry stores generate their profits differently. They typically have very high profit margins but with low

Financial managers and analysts often talk about the quality of a firm's earnings or the quality of its balance sheet. This has nothing to do with the size of a firm's earnings or assets or who audited the financial statements. Quality financial statements are those that accurately reflect the firm's true economic condition. In other words, various accounting rules were not used to inflate its earnings or assets to make the firm look stronger than it really is. Thus, for a quality income statement, the firm's sales revenues are likely to be repeated in the future. Earnings are not affected by one-time charges. A quality balance sheet will represent inventory that is marketable, not out-of-fashion or technologically obsolete. It will represent limited debt, indicating the firm could easily borrow money should the need arise. The firm's assets will have market values that exceed their accounting book values; in other words, the firm's assets will not be inflated by intangible assets such as "goodwill" or "patents."

THE QUALITY FACTOR

turnover. Jewelry items may sit on the shelf for months at a time until they are sold.

This indicates there are two basic methods by which a firm can generate a return on its assets. It can offer low prices (and low profit margins) seeking high sales volumes like the supermarket, or it can sell its goods at high prices and rely mainly on high profit margins to generate returns on low sales like a jewelry store.

The return on total assets ratio can be used to examine this relationship and to determine how a given firm generates profits. The return on assets can be broken into two components. It equals the product of the profit margin and total asset turnover ratio:

Return on total assets = Profit margin $\times$ Total asset turnover

$$\frac{\text{Net income}}{\text{Assets}} = \frac{\text{Net income}}{\text{Sales}} \times \frac{\text{Sales}}{\text{Total assets}}$$

A supermarket's profit margin may be 1 percent, but its total asset turnover may be 10. This would give it a return on total assets of 1 percent $\times$ 10 or 10 percent. A jewelry store may have a 25 percent profit margin and have a very low asset turnover of 0.40, also giving it a return on total assets of 10 percent (25 percent $\times$ 0.40). Year-to-year variations in a firm's return on total assets can be explained by changes in its profit margin, total asset turnover, or both.

Like the return on total assets, return on equity can be broken down into component parts to tell us why the level of return changes from year to year or why two firms' returns on equity differ. The return on equity is identical to return on total assets multiplied by the equity multiplier:

$$\frac{\text{Net income}}{\text{Equity}} = \frac{\text{Net income}}{\text{Total assets}} \times \frac{\text{Total assets}}{\text{Equity}}$$

We just saw how the return on total assets is itself comprised of two other ratios, so return on equity can be expanded to:

Return on equity = Profit margin $\times$ Asset turnover $\times$ Equity multiplier

$$\frac{\text{Net income}}{\text{Equity}} = \frac{\text{Net income}}{\text{Sales}} \times \frac{\text{Sales}}{\text{Total assets}} \times \frac{\text{Total assets}}{\text{Equity}}$$

Thus, a firm's return on equity may differ from one year to the next, or from a competitor's, as a result of differences in profit margin, asset turnover, or leverage. Unlike the other measures of profitability, return on equity directly reflects a firm's use of leverage, or debt. If a firm uses relatively more liabilities to finance assets, the equity multiplier will rise, and, holding other factors constant, the firm's return on equity will increase. This leveraging of a firm's return on equity does not imply greater operating efficiency, only a greater use of debt financing.

This technique of breaking return on total assets and return on equity into their component parts is called **Du Pont analysis,** named after the company that popularized it. Figure 14.6 illustrates how Du Pont analysis can break return on equity and return on total assets into different com-

Du Pont analysis
technique of breaking down return on total assets and return on equity into their component parts

FIGURE 14.6   The Du Pont System of Financial Analysis

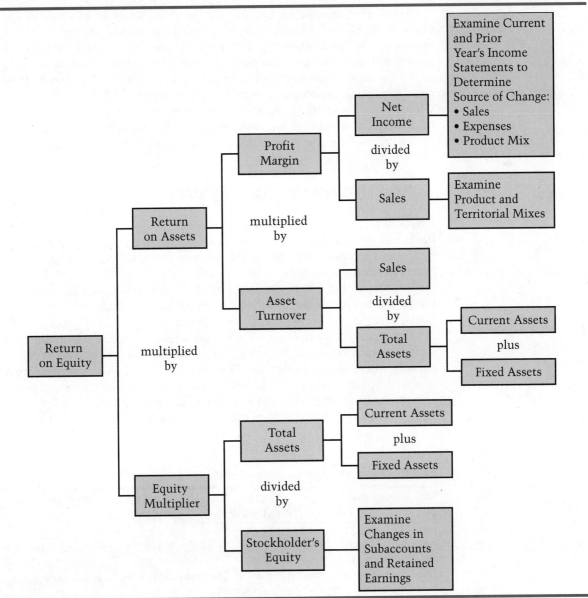

ponents (profit margin, total asset turnover, and equity multiplier) and how these components can, in turn, be broken into their constituent parts for analysis. Thus an indication that a firm's return on equity has increased as a result of higher turnover can lead to study of the turnover ratio, using data from several years, to determine if the increase has resulted from higher sales volume, better management of assets, or some combination of the two.

Table 14.3 illustrates the use of Du Pont analysis to explain the changes in Global Manufacturing's return on equity during 1993–95. Between 1993 and 1994, the main reason for the increase in Global's return on equity was an increase in the net profit margin and an increase in the use of debt (as seen in the larger equity multiplier). Between 1994 and 1995, profit margin and total asset turnover were fairly constant, so Global's return on equity rose primarily as a result of increased leverage, or debt usage. Managers and analysts generally prefer to see increases in the return on equity arising from increased profitability or increased asset efficiency.

LONG-TERM FINANCIAL PLANNING

Financial ratios and financial statement relationships can be used to analyze firms and their competitors, as we have just seen. But they have a second important practical use: managers can use them to assist in the firm's financial planning process.

In order to plan, it is necessary to look forward. We all have perfect hindsight, but foresight is what determines the success of a business. Long-range plans covering several years must be prepared to project growth in sales, assets, and employees. First, a sales forecast needs to be made that includes expected developments in the economy and that reflects possible competitive pressures from other businesses. The sales forecast then must be supported by plans for an adequate investment in assets. For example, a manufacturing firm may need to invest in plant and equipment to produce an inventory that will fill forecasted sales orders. After determining the

TABLE 14.3   Du Pont Analysis of Global Manufacturing, Inc.

YEAR	$\dfrac{\text{NET INCOME}}{\text{SALES}}$	$\times$	$\dfrac{\text{SALES}}{\text{TOTAL ASSETS}}$	$\times$	$\dfrac{\text{TOTAL ASSETS}}{\text{EQUITY}}$	$=$	$\dfrac{\text{NET INCOME}^{*}}{\text{EQUITY}}$
1993	4.4		1.53		1.87		12.8
1994	5.0		1.50		2.00		15.0
1995	5.1		1.40		2.29		16.5

*Return on equity is as reported in the text. The product of the three components may not equal this number exactly because of rounding.

size of the necessary investment, plans must be made for estimating the amount of financing needed and how to acquire it. Adequate investment in human resources must be planned for as well.

In addition to long-range financial plans or budgets, the financial manager is concerned with near-term cash inflows and outflows associated with the business. Cash flows are often monitored on a daily basis for large firms while small firms may make only monthly cash budgets.

Financial analysis using ratios goes hand in hand with successful financial planning. An established firm should conduct a financial ratio analysis of past performance to aid in developing realistic future plans. The new firm should analyze the performance characteristics of other firms in the same industry before making plans.

In the remainder of this chapter, we focus on long-term financial planning techniques. The first, the percentage of sales technique, will illustrate how a sales forecast and knowledge of the firm's balance sheet and income statement can be used to estimate the firm's long-term asset and financing needs. The second, cost-volume-profit analysis, reviews a method a firm can use to determine the profitability of different sales levels and how many product units it needs to sell in order to turn a profit.

PERCENTAGE OF SALES TECHNIQUE

Financial planning begins with a sales forecast for one or more years. These sales forecasts are the basis for written financial plans referred to as **budgets.** For established firms, sales forecasts are usually based on historical sales data that are used in statistical analyses to project into the future. Adjustments may be made to reflect possible changes in sales growth due to expected economic conditions, new products, and so forth. For example, a firm's sales may have been growing at a 10 percent average annual rate in the past. However, if a recession is anticipated, management might forecast only a 5 percent growth rate for the next year or two. In contrast, a booming economic climate might be associated with a 15 percent annual growth rate. New firms without sales histories have to rely on information from the experiences of other firms in their industry. Accurate sales forecasting is an essential element of successful financial management.

budgets
financial plans utilized in sales forecasts

Asset Investment Requirements

Once the sales forecast has been made, plans must be made to acquire the assets necessary to support the new sales level. The relationship of assets and sales is shown in the total assets turnover ratio, which, as we learned above, equals sales divided by total assets.

Recall from earlier in this chapter that Global Manufacturing had an assets turnover ratio of 1.4 based on 1995 sales of $700,000 and total assets of $500,000. By taking the inverse of this ratio, total assets divided by net sales, we can express assets as a percent of sales, which would be 71.4 percent

($500,000/$700,000). This number can be used to help forecast future asset needs. For example, a 10 percent forecasted increase of $70,000 in net sales ($700,000 × 10%) would result in an anticipated new asset investment of about $50,000 ($70,000 × 71.4%).

Table 14.4 shows each major balance sheet item expressed as a percent of sales for 1995 for Global. Notice that the sum total for all the assets is 71.4 percent as calculated above. After forecasting sales, we can use the percentages in Table 14.4 to determine changes in various balance sheet accounts. This is the percent-of-sales method for forecasting asset investment requirements. Actual asset investment required to support a specific sales increase may be altered if either of two developments occur: if the asset turnover ratio changes or certain fixed assets do not have to be increased.

First, if Global could slightly improve its asset turnover ratio to 1.5 times, then assets would be only 66.7 (that is, 1/1.5) percent of sales. This would mean that a $70,000 increase in sales would require an asset investment of about $70,000 × 0.667 or $46,700, or roughly $3,300 less than the earlier calculation.

Second, fixed assets such as land or buildings might not have to be increased each year along with an increase in sales. The deciding factor

TABLE 14.4   Percent-of-Sales Balance Sheets for Global Manufacturing, Inc. (1995)

	DOLLAR AMOUNT	PERCENT OF SALES ($700,000)
ASSETS		
Cash and marketable securities	$ 25,000	3.6%
Accounts receivable	100,000	14.3
Inventories	125,000	17.8
Total current assets	250,000	35.7
Net plant and equipment	200,000	28.6
Land	50,000	7.1
Total fixed assets	250,000	35.7
Total assets	$500,000	71.4
LIABILITIES AND EQUITY		
Accounts payable	$ 78,000	11.1%
Notes payable	34,000	4.9
Accrued liabilities	30,000	4.3
Total current liabilities	142,000	20.3
Long-term debt	140,000	20.0
Total liabilities	282,000	40.3
Total stockholders' equity	218,000	31.1
Total liabilities and equity	$500,000	71.4

usually is whether the firm currently has excess production capacity. For example, according to Table 14.4, if only current assets are expected to increase with sales next year, then the asset investment requirements would be about $25,000 ($70,000 × 35.7%).

Internally Generated Financing

Internally generated funds for financing new asset investments come from profits. Let's assume that for Global Manufacturing the $50,000 asset investment scenario will be what is needed next year. We are now ready to plan how these assets will be financed from anticipated profits or external sources. Recall from Table 14.2 that during 1995 Global earned $36,000 in net income on sales of $700,000 for a profit margin of 5.14 percent. If net sales are expected to rise by 10 percent next year to $770,000, and the profit margin is expected to hold, then profits would be projected at about $39,600 ($770,000 × 5.14%). Let's further assume that management plans to pay out about one half of these profits, or $19,800, as dividends to the owners of the company. This would leave only $19,800 ($39,600 − $19,800) in internally generated funds to finance the $50,000 in assets. The remaining $30,200 in assets would have to be financed with external funds. These can be either short-term debt, long-term debt, or equity funds. Let's consider how the financial manager might plan the mix of short-term and long-term funds from external sources.

External Financing Requirements

Global Manufacturing can expect that a portion of its asset financing requirements will be met by almost automatic increases in certain current liability accounts such as accounts payable and accrued liabilities. To meet planned sales increases, more credit purchases of materials will be necessary to produce the products to make sales. Increases also would be expected in accrued wages and taxes. These automatic liability accounts reduce the need for other external financing since they allow the firm to acquire additional inputs without an immediate cash outlay. As they usually rise and fall along with sales, these current liability accounts provide a spontaneous or automatic source of financing.

Table 14.4 shows that accounts payable plus accrued liabilities were about 15.4 percent of sales in 1995 for Global. Based on a 10 percent expected increase in sales, accounts payable and accrued liabilities would be expected to rise and provide about $10,800 ($70,000 × 15.4%) in spontaneous short-term funds. This would leave an external financing need for Global of about $19,400 ($30,200 minus $10,800) in order to cover the asset investment requirements. Management might choose to borrow the amount from a commercial bank, issue long-term debt, or request more equity funds from the owners.

To summarize briefly, the amount of new external funds needed to finance asset additions can be calculated as follows:

1. Forecast the dollar amount of expected sales increase.
2. Determine the dollar amount of new asset investments necessary to support the sales increase.
3. Subtract the expected amount of retained profits from the planned asset investments.
4. Subtract the amount of spontaneous increases expected in accounts payable and accrued liabilities from the planned asset investments.
5. The remaining dollar amount of asset investments determines the external financing needs (EFN).

COST-VOLUME-PROFIT ANALYSIS

cost-volume-profit analysis
used by managers for financial planning to estimate the firm's operating profits at different levels of unit sales

break-even analysis
used to estimate how many units of product must be sold in order for the firm to break even or have a zero profit

Cost-volume-profit analysis represents another tool used by managers for financial planning purposes. It can be used to estimate the firm's operating profits at different levels of unit sales. A variation, called **break-even analysis,** can be used to estimate how many units of product must be sold in order for the firm to "break even" or have a zero profit.

As an example of cost-volume-profit analysis, let's assume that a firm is considering developing, manufacturing, and selling a basic accounting system software product at $100 per copy. The variable costs—raw materials (such as diskettes and packaging) and direct labor—are estimated at $20 per unit. Fixed costs—renting production facilities, equipment, and various administrative overhead expenses—are expected to be $40,000 annually. Management is interested in knowing what level of operating profit will occur if unit sales are 1,000 per year.

From the format of an income statement (for example, Table 14.2), we know that sales revenues minus various costs gives us operating profit or earnings before interest and taxes (EBIT). Sales can be expressed as unit price multiplied by quantity sold, or $(P)(Q)$. The costs can be expressed by variable costs and fixed costs. The variable cost per unit (VC) times the quantity sold (Q) gives us total variable cost: $(VC)(Q)$. Total fixed costs, FC, are constant; they are called "fixed" because they do not change with increases or decreases in output. Thus, we can find operating income as follows:

$$EBIT = Sales - Variable\ costs - Fixed\ costs$$

or in terms of our symbols, this becomes:

$$EBIT = (P)(Q) - (VC)(Q) - FC \tag{14.1}$$

For our software product example, we have:

$$
\begin{aligned}
EBIT &= \$100(1,000) - \$20(1,000) - \$40,000 \\
&= \$100,000 - \$20,000 - \$40,000 \\
&= \$100,000 - \$60,000 \\
&= \$40,000
\end{aligned}
$$

If sales reach 1,000 units per year, the firm expects an operating profit of $40,000.

Management also may want to know how many units of the software product will have to be sold in order to break even. That is, what volume needs to be reached so that the amount of total revenues equals total costs (variable costs plus fixed costs). At this point, operating income or EBIT is zero. The break-even point in units can be calculated by setting Equation 14.1 equal to zero:

$$\text{EBIT} = (P)(Q) - (VC)(Q) - FC = 0$$

The quantity of unit sales that solves this equation is the break-even quantity; we'll call this Q_{BE}. Solving this equation for the break-even quantity, we have:

$$Q_{BE} = \frac{FC}{(P - VC)} \qquad (14.2)$$

Using data from the software example, we have:

$$Q_{BE} = \frac{\$40,000}{(\$100 - \$20)} = \frac{\$40,000}{\$80} = 500 \text{ units}$$

The firm must sell 500 units of its accounting system in order to break even. This can be confirmed by substituting the relevant information in Equation 14.1 as follows:

$$
\begin{aligned}
\text{EBIT} &= \$100(500) - \$20(500) - \$40,000 \\
&= \$50,000 - \$10,000 - \$40,000 \\
&= \$50,000 - \$50,000 \\
&= 0
\end{aligned}
$$

The break-even point in units, depicted graphically in Figure 14.7, occurs when total revenues equal total costs. The break-even point in sales dollars is equal to the selling price per unit times the break-even point in units. In our example, we have $100 times 500 units or $50,000.

The denominator of Equation 14.2, $(P - VC)$, is called the **contribution margin**. It represents the contribution of each unit sold that goes toward paying the annual fixed costs. In our example, for every unit sold at a price of $100, $20 of the revenue covers the variable costs; the remainder, ($100 − $20) or $80, is the contribution toward paying the fixed costs. Since fixed costs are $40,000, the firm must sell $40,000/$80 units or 500 units before the fixed costs are covered.

contribution margin *contribution of each unit sold that goes toward paying fixed costs*

DEGREE OF OPERATING LEVERAGE

The variability of sales or revenues over time indicates a basic operating business risk which must be considered when developing financial plans. In addition, changes in the amount of income shown on the income state-

FIGURE 14.7   Cost-Volume-Profit Relationships

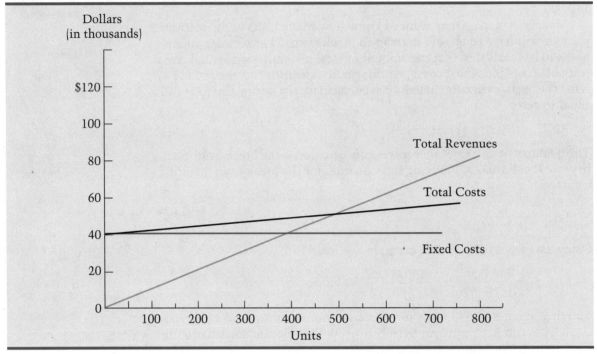

ment are affected by both changes in sales and the use of fixed versus variable costs. The following portion of an income statement illustrates this point.

Net sales	$700,000
Less: variable costs (60% of sales)	420,000
Less: fixed costs	200,000
Earnings before interest and taxes	$ 80,000

Let's examine the impact of both a 10 percent decrease and a 10 percent increase in next year's sales on the firm's operating income or earnings before interest and taxes (EBIT). The revised partial income statement would appear as follows:

	PERCENT CHANGE IN SALES	
	−10%	+10%
Net sales	$630,000	$770,000
Less: variable costs (60% of sales)	378,000	462,000
Less: fixed costs	200,000	200,000
Earnings before interest and taxes	$ 52,000	$108,000
Percent change in operating income (EBIT)	−35%	+35%

> *"I need to be able to understand the financial issues and terminology as well as actually writing the appropriate code."*

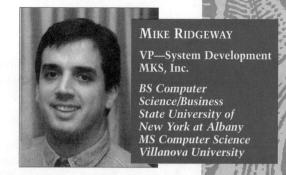

MIKE RIDGEWAY

VP—System Development
MKS, Inc.

BS Computer Science/Business State University of New York at Albany MS Computer Science Villanova University

Q: *Describe the firm you work for.*
A: MKS, Inc. provides a computer package that automates the purchasing, warehousing, accounting and other functions of companies with sales of ten to one hundred million dollars.

Q: *What is your role there?*
A: I basically become the MIS department of our clients. Most of the companies we work with are not large enough or technically sophisticated enough to have their own programers on staff. So they purchase our standard package. Then I get involved. I help them make the transition from their previous operation to the mini or mainframe that our package runs on. I write additional code to handle the specific needs of their business.

Q: *So you've learned a lot about the industries your clients are in.*
A: That's right. Every company has its own vocabulary and operating procedures which their system needs to incorporate. I've worked a lot with a book distributor and a gun company recently. By the time I develop all of the customized functions they need, I have a very thorough knowledge of their business.

Q: *How has your financial knowledge helped in your job?*
A: The package includes many financial and accounting functions. The Accounts Receivable Manager would use the system to track how long it takes clients to pay. At a higher level the General Manager would use the system to evaluate which products are producing the best return. So when they ask for custom reports or modifications to the system, I need to be able to understand the financial issues and terminology as well as actually writing the appropriate code.

Q: *What skills do you use most in your job?*
A: Working under pressure is very important. In many cases I'll get a call from one of my clients who needs a new report or a code change right away, meaning minutes not hours. I need to do several things at once: calm down the customer, understand the request, and solve the problem quickly. Responding to these urgent requests would be impossible if I didn't know the package so thoroughly. Most people probably think of programers as working alone most of the time, but I probably spend at least four hours a day on the phone with clients.

Q: *Your company is fairly small. How does that affect your work?*
A: There are pluses and minuses. We have about fifteen people which is plenty to produce an excellent system, but not enough to go through some of the more formal steps that a larger company might. We're more likely to start programming from a one-page description of the situation. That's where our knowledge of their business and financial concepts become so important. Another result of working in a smaller company is that I have to be available at all hours, especially during the implementation of a new system. We do whatever it takes to get it done.

career profiles

469

degree of operating leverage
measures the sensitivity of operating income to changes in the level of output

A 10 percent change in sales becomes magnified or leveraged into a 35 percent change in operating income! The **degree of operating leverage** measures the sensitivity of operating income to changes in the level of output:

DOL = % change in EBIT/% change in unit sales[7]

If net sales increase by 10 percent next year, from $700,000 to $770,000, and operating income rises from $80,000 to $108,000, a $28,000 or 35 percent increase results ($28,000/$80,000 = 35%). Thus, a 35 percent change in operating income divided by a 10 percent change in net sales produces a 3.5 magnification or leverage effect. DOL also works in reverse and provides negative leverage when net sales decline. A 10 percent decline in sales volume becomes a 35 percent decline in operating income.

This effect is solely due to the level of fixed costs. Suppose that the firm had fixed costs of $250,000. With sales of $700,000, variable costs of $420,000, and fixed costs of $250,000, EBIT will be $30,000. The effect of this higher level of fixed costs on EBIT is seen below:

	PERCENT CHANGE IN SALES	
	−10%	+10%
Net sales	$630,000	$770,000
Less: variable costs (60% of sales)	378,000	462,000
Less: fixed costs	250,000	250,000
Earnings before interest and taxes	$ 2,000	$ 58,000
Percent change in operating income (EBIT)	−93.3%	+93.3%

A 10 percent change in sales becomes magnified or leveraged into a 93.3 percent change in operating income! With $250,000 in fixed costs, the degree of operating leverage is now 93.3%/10% or 9.33.

The magnification or leverage effect is solely due to the level of fixed costs. Higher levels of fixed costs result in higher levels of operating leverage and operating incomes that are more sensitive to sales volume. Sophisticated financial planning models take into consideration the impact of operating leverage when projecting the next year's net income.

SUMMARY

Financial statements, introduced in Chapter 13, are useful only if managers and financial analysts know how to use them. The focus of this chapter has been on the practical application of financial statements for analysis

7.   A simplified formula for DOL is:
$$DOL = \frac{Q(P - VC)}{Q(P - VC) - FC}$$

and financial forecasting. The information in financial statements can be examined by using various financial ratios. The ratios control for size differences between firms or for firm growth over time. By examining one firm's ratios over time, or in conjunction with an industry average, managers and analysts can pinpoint areas of strength and weakness in both their firm and in their competitors.

Liquidity ratios are useful in determining the ability of a firm to pay its short-term obligations. Asset management ratios measure how efficiently the firm's assets are used. Financial leverage ratios provide information on the firm's use of debt to finance its assets. Profitability ratios measure the ability of a firm to earn a return on its sales, assets, and equity. Analysts and managers also use market-based ratios to see how the financial marketplace evaluates the firm and its peers.

Changes in a ratio over time are caused by relative changes in the ratio's numerator and denominator and their components. Financial analysis does not stop with the calculation of a ratio. Changes in ratios over time or difference in ratios between firms should be explained. Du Pont analysis is one such tool for examining return on equity. Changes in the return on equity occur because of changes in the profit margin, total asset turnover, financial leverage, or some combination of these.

Financial planning uses the financial statement relationships to estimate future asset and financing needs. The percent-of-sale methods use the relationship between balance sheet accounts and sales to estimate future asset needs. Combining a sales forecast, profit margin, and dividend policy, managers can estimate the increase in retained earnings that will provide internally generated financing. The difference between the forecasted increase in assets and the internally generated financing (such as additions to retained earnings and spontaneous current liability growth) equals the external financing the firm needs to plan to raise. Other tools, such as cost-volume-profit analysis, break-even analysis, and operating leverage can also be used to forecast future profits and to analyze the financial structure of a firm.

KEY TERMS

asset management ratios
break-even analysis
budgets
contribution margin
cost-volume-profit analysis
cross-sectional analysis
degree of operating leverage
Du Pont analysis
equity multiplier ratio

financial leverage ratios
industry comparative analysis
liquidity ratios
market value ratios
net working capital
profitability ratios
ratio analysis
sinking fund payments
trend or time series analysis

DISCUSSION QUESTIONS

1. List some reasons why financial statement analysis is conducted. Identify some of the participants that analyze firms' financial statements.
2. What is ratio analysis? Also briefly describe the three basic categories or ways that ratio analysis is used.
3. Identify the types of ratios that are used to analyze a firm's financial performance based on its income statements and balance sheets. Which type or category of ratios relates stock market information to financial statement items?
4. What do liquidity ratios indicate? Identify some basic liquidity ratios.
5. What do asset management ratios indicate? Identify some basic asset management ratios.
6. What do financial leverage ratios indicate? Identify some measures of financial leverage.
7. What do profitability ratios indicate? Identify some measures of profitability.
8. What do market value ratios indicate? Identify some market value ratios.
9. Describe the Du Pont method or system of ratio analysis. What are the two major components of the system? How is the system related to both the balance sheet and the income statement?
10. How is the process of financial planning used to estimate asset investment requirements?
11. Explain how internally generated funds are used to reduce the need for external financing to fund asset investments.
12. Explain how financial planning is used to determine a firm's external financing requirements.
13. What is cost-volume-profit analysis? How can it be used by a firm?
14. What is the purpose of knowing the break-even point?
15. What will happen to the break-even point if the contribution margin rises (falls)?
16. What does a firm's degree of operating leverage (DOL) indicate? Describe what would happen to the DOL if all costs are fixed (variable).

PROBLEMS

1. The Robinson Company has the following current assets and current liabilities for these two years:

	1994	1995
Cash and marketable securities	$ 50,000	$ 50,000
Accounts receivable	300,000	350,000
Inventories	350,000	500,000
Total current assets	$700,000	$900,000

Accounts payable	$200,000	$250,000
Bank loan	0	150,000
Accruals	150,000	200,000
Total current liabilities	$350,000	$600,000

   a. Compare the current ratios between the two years.

   b. Compare the acid-test ratios between 1994 and 1995. Comment on your findings.

2. The Robinson Company had a cost of goods sold of $1,000,000 in 1994 and $1,200,000 in 1995.

   a. Calculate the inventory turnover for each year. Comment on your findings.

   b. What would have been the amount of inventories in 1995 if the 1994 turnover ratio had been maintained?

3. The Dayco Manufacturing Company had the following financial statement results for last year. Net sales were $1.2 million with net income of $90,000. Total assets at year-end amounted to $900,000.

   a. Calculate Dayco's asset turnover ratio and its profit margin.

   b. Show how the two ratios in part a. can be used to determine Dayco's rate of return on assets.

   c. Dayco operates in the same industry as Global Manufacturing, whose industry ratios are:

     Return on assets: 15%

     Asset turnover: 2.5 times

     Profit margin: 6%

     Compare Dayco's performance against the industry averages.

4. Next year Global Manufacturing expects its sales to reach $900,000 with an investment in total assets of $600,000. Net income of $70,000 is anticipated.

   a. Use the Du Pont system to compare Global's anticipated performance in 1996 against its 1995 and 1994 results. Comment on your findings.

   b. How would Global compare with the industry if the industry ratios (see Problem 3) remain the same as they were in 1995?

5. Following are selected financial data in thousands of dollars for the Hunter Corporation.

	1995	1994
Current assets	$ 500	$ 400
Fixed assets, net	700	600
Total assets	$1,200	$1,000
Current liabilities	$ 300	$ 200
Long-term debt	200	200
Common equity	700	600
Total liabilities and equity	$1,200	$1,000

Net sales	$1,500	$1,200
Total expenses	−1,390	−1,100
Net income	$ 110	$ 100

a. Calculate Hunter's rate of return on total assets in 1994 and in 1995. Did the ratio improve or worsen?

b. Diagram the expanded Du Pont system for Hunter for 1995. Insert the appropriate dollar amounts wherever possible.

c. Use the Du Pont system to calculate the return on assets for the two years, and determine why they changed.

6. Following are financial statements for the Genatron Manufacturing Corporation for 1994 and 1995.

a. Apply Du Pont analysis to both the 1994 and 1995 financial statements' data.

b. Explain how financial performance differed between 1994 and 1995.

GENATRON MANUFACTURING CORPORATION

BALANCE SHEET	1995	1994
ASSETS		
Cash	$ 40,000	$ 50,000
Accts. receivable	260,000	200,000
Inventory	500,000	450,000
Total current assets	800,000	700,000
Fixed assets, net	400,000	300,000
Total assets	$1,200,000	$1,000,000
LIABILITIES AND EQUITY		
Accts. payable	$ 170,000	$ 130,000
Bank loan, 10%	90,000	90,000
Accruals	70,000	50,000
Total current liabilities	330,000	270,000
Long-term debt, 12%	400,000	300,000
Common stock, $10 par	300,000	300,000
Capital surplus	50,000	50,000
Retained earnings	120,000	80,000
Total liabilities & equity	$1,200,000	$1,000,000

INCOME STATEMENT	1995	1994
Net sales	$1,500,000	$1,300,000
Cost of goods sold	900,000	780,000
Gross profit	600,000	520,000
Expenses: general & administrative	150,000	150,000
Marketing	150,000	130,000
Depreciation	53,000	40,000

Interest	57,000	45,000
Earnings before taxes	190,000	155,000
Income taxes	76,000	62,000
Net income	$ 114,000	$ 93,000

7. This problem uses the financial statements for the Genatron Manufacturing Corporation for the years 1994 and 1995 from problem 6.
   a. Calculate Genatron's dollar amount of net working capital in each
      year.
   b. Calculate the current ratio and the acid-test ratio in each year.
   c. Calculate the average collection period and the inventory turnover
      ratio in each year.
   d. What changes in the management of Genatron's current assets
      seem to have occurred between the two years?

8. Genatron Manufacturing expects its sales to increase by 10 percent in
   1996. Estimate the firm's external financing needs by using the percent-
   of-sales method for the 1995 data. Assume that no excess capacity
   exists and that one-half of the 1996 net income will be retained in the
   business.

9. Genatron wants to estimate what will happen to its income before
   interest and taxes if its net sales change from the 1995 level of
   $1,500,000. Refer to Genatron's 1995 income statement, shown in
   Problem 6, where the income before interest and taxes is $247,000.
   Assume that the cost of goods sold are variable expenses and that the
   other operating expenses are fixed.
   a. Calculate the expected amount of income before interest and taxes
      for both a 10 percent decrease and a 10 percent increase in net sales
      for next year.
   b. Determine the percentage change in income before interest and
      taxes given your calculations in part a., and determine the degree
      of operating leverage.

10. Using the information in Tables 14.1 and 14.2, compute the financial
    ratios we discussed in this chapter for Global Manufacturing using the
    1993 data.

11. Below are the consolidated financial statements for Global Manu-
    facturing's industry. Use Du Pont Analysis on the industry financial
    statements to determine why industry return on equity changed from
    year to year.

Balance Sheets for INDUSTRY:

	December 31		
	1995	1994	1993
ASSETS			
Cash and marketable securities	$ 30,000	$ 25,000	$ 20,000
Accounts receivable	110,000	90,000	60,000

Inventories	100,000	80,000	80,000
Total current assets	240,000	195,000	160,000
Gross plant and equipment	250,000	220,000	200,000
Less: accumulated depreciation	−100,000	−65,000	−50,000
Net plant and equipment	150,000	155,000	150,000
Land	50,000	50,000	50,000
Total fixed assets	200,000	205,000	200,000
Total assets	$ 440,000	$400,000	$360,000
LIABILITIES AND EQUITY			
Accounts payable	$ 58,000	$ 50,000	$ 45,000
Notes payable	50,000	50,000	50,000
Accrued liabilities	0	0	0
Total current liabilities	108,000	100,000	95,000
Long-term debt	32,000	20,000	15,000
Total liabilities	$ 140,000	$120,000	$110,000
Total stockholders' equity	300,000	280,000	250,000
Total liabilities and equity	$ 440,000	$400,000	$360,000

Income Statements for INDUSTRY:

Years Ended December 31	1995	1994	1993
Net revenues or sales	$1,100,000	$1,000,000	$900,000
Cost of goods sold	700,000	650,000	600,000
Gross profit	$ 400,000	$ 350,000	$300,000
Operating expenses:			
General and administrative	143,000	135,000	130,000
Selling and marketing	88,000	80,000	70,000
Depreciation	44,000	40,000	36,000
Operating income	125,000	95,000	64,000
Interest	15,000	15,000	14,000
Income before taxes	110,000	80,000	50,000
Income taxes (40%)	44,000	32,000	20,000
Net income	$ 66,000	$ 48,000	$ 30,000

12. Using the discussion from the text and your answer to problem 11, compare the reasons for the changes in return on equity for Global Manufacturing and its industry.

13. Associated Containers Company is planning to manufacture and sell plastic pencil holders. Direct labor and raw materials will be $2.28 per unit. Fixed costs are $15,300 and the expected selling price is $3.49 per unit.

   a. Determine the break-even point (where operating profit is zero) in units and dollars.

   b. How much profit or loss before interest and taxes will there be if 10,825 units are sold?

   c. What will the selling price per unit have to be if 13,650 units are sold in order to break even?

   d. How much will variable costs per unit have to be in order to break even if only 9,500 units are expected to be sold and the selling price is $3.49?

14. This problem uses the two years of financial statements data provided in Problem 6 for the Genatron Manufacturing Corporation.

   a. Calculate and compare each current assets account as a percentage of total assets for that year.

   b. Calculate and compare each current liabilities account as a percentage of total liabilities and equities for that year.

   c. Calculate the current ratio and the acid-test ratio for each year. Describe the changes in liquidity, if any, that occurred between the two years.

15. The Jackman Company had sales of $1,000,000 and net income of $50,000 last year. Sales are expected to increase by 20 percent next year. Selected year-end balance sheet items were:

Current assets	$400,000
Fixed assets	500,000
Total assets	$900,000
Current liabilities	$200,000
Long-term debt	200,000
Owners' equity	500,000
Total liabilities and equity	$900,000

   a. Express each balance sheet item as a percent of this year's sales.

   b. Estimate the new asset investment requirement for next year, assuming no excess production capacity.

   c. Estimate the amount of internally generated funds for next year, assuming all profits will be retained in the firm.

   d. If all current liabilities are expected to change spontaneously with sales, what will be their dollar increase next year?

   e. Estimate Jackman's external financing requirements for next year.

16. The Kenergy Company is planning to manufacture and sell electronic alarm clocks. Raw materials for each clock will be $3 and direct labor per clock will amount to $6. Fixed administrative overhead costs will amount to $24,000. The clocks are expected to sell for $15 each.

   a. Find the break-even point in units. What is the sales break-even point?

b. How much profit or loss will occur if 5,000 clocks are sold? What if only 3,000 clocks are sold?

SELF-TEST QUESTIONS

1. Ratios used to compare different firms at the same point in time belong to a category of analysis called:
   a. time series analysis
   b. cross-sectional analysis
   c. industry comparative analysis
   d. just-in-time analysis
2. Which one of the following types of financial ratios does not get all of its information from a firm's income statements and balance sheets?
   a. liquidity ratios
   b. asset management ratios
   c. capital structure ratios
   d. profitability ratios
   e. market value ratios
3. Which one of the following types of ratios indicates the ability to meet short-term obligations to creditors as they come due?
   a. liquidity ratios
   b. asset management ratios
   c. capital structure ratios
   d. profitability ratios
   e. market value ratios
4. Which one of the following ratios indicates the average number of days that sales are outstanding?
   a. average payment period
   b. average collection period
   c. quick ratio
   d. interest coverage
5. Rental or lease payments are included in which one of the following ratios?
   a. interest coverage
   b. times-interest-earned
   c. fixed charge coverage
   d. equity multiplier
6. Which one of the following is not a basic component of the Du Pont method of ratio analysis?
   a. profit margin
   b. total asset turnover
   c. equity multiplier
   d. liquidity margin

7. Which one of the following is not a basic element or component of the percentage of sales approach to long-term financial planning?
   a. asset investment requirements
   b. internally generated financing
   c. spontaneous increases in current liabilities
   d. automatic increases in cash inflows

8. Cost-volume-profit analysis can be used to estimate the firm's operating profits at different levels of:
   a. dollar sales
   b. unit sales
   c. dollar fixed costs
   d. unit variable costs

9. The degree of operating leverage (DOL) can be measured by the percent change in operating income (or EBIT) divided by:
   a. percent change in fixed costs
   b. percent change in variable costs
   c. percent change in unit sales
   d. percent change in total costs

SELF-TEST PROBLEMS

1. A balance sheet and income statement is given below for Harris Enterprises.

Harris Enterprises
Balance Sheet, 1995
(millions of dollars)

Cash	$ 2	Accounts payable	$ 5
Receivables	6	Notes payable	4
Inventory	3	Long-term bonds	8
Fixed assets	10	Stockholders' equity	4
Total assets	$21	Total liabilities and equity	$21

Harris Enterprises
Income Statement, 1995
(millions of dollars)

Sales	$50
Cost of goods sold	25
Depreciation	10
Earnings before interest and taxes	15
Taxes	5
Net income	$10

Compute the
a. current ratio
b. total debt-to-assets ratio
c. inventory turnover ratio
d. return on equity, using the Du Pont relationship

2. The Eagle Manufacturing Company had the following financial statement results for last year. Net sales were $1 million with net income of $70,000. Total assets at year end amounted to $800,000.

    a.   Calculate Eagle's asset turnover ratio and its profit margin.

    b.   Show how the two ratios in part a. can be used to determine Eagle's rate of return on assets.

    c.   Eagle operates in the same industry as Global Manufacturing, for which the industry ratios are:

         Return on assets: 15%

         Asset turnover: 2.5 times

         Net profit margin: 6.0%

Compare Eagle's performance against the industry averages.

SUGGESTED READINGS

Brealey, Richard A., Stewart C. Myers, and Alan J. Marcus. *Fundamentals of Corporate Finance.* New York: McGraw-Hill, 1995. Chaps. 17 and 18.

Brigham, Eugene F. *Fundamentals of Financial Management,* 7e. Hinsdale, IL: The Dryden Press, 1995. Chaps. 3 and 17.

Harrington, Diana R. *Corporate Financial Analysis,* 4e. Homewood, IL: Richard D. Irwin, 1993. Chaps. 1 and 2.

Kaen, Fred R. *Corporate Finance.* Cambridge, MA: Blackwell Publishers, 1995. Chaps. 17 and 18.

Keown, Arthur J., David F. Scott Jr., John D. Martin, and J. William Petty. *Foundations of Finance,* 1e. Englewood Cliffs, New Jersey: Prentice-Hall Inc., 1994. Chaps. 3 and 4.

Marsh, William H. *Basic Financial Management.* Cincinnati, Ohio: South-Western College Publishing, 1995. Chaps. 4 and 5.

Pinches, George E. *Financial Management,* 5e. New York: Harper & Row, 1994. Chaps. 24 and 25.

Ross, Stephen A., Randolph W. Westerfield, Bradford D. Jordan. *Fundamentals of Corporate Finance,* 3e. Homewood, IL: Richard D. Irwin Inc., 1995. Chaps. 3 and 4.

ANSWERS TO SELF-TEST QUESTIONS   1. b, 2. e, 3. a, 4. b, 5. c, 6. d, 7. d, 8. b, 9. c

ANSWERS TO SELF-TEST PROBLEMS

1.   a.   The current ratio is current assets divided by current liabilities. Current assets total $11 and current liabilities are $9. The current ratio is $11/$9, or 1.22.

b.   This ratio is total liabilities divided by total assets. Total liabilities include both current liabilities and long-term debt; this equals $9 + $8 or $17. Thus, the total debt-to-assets ratio is $17/$21 = 0.8095 or 80.95%. Nearly 81 percent of Harris' assets are financed by debt.

c.   Inventory turnover equals the cost of goods sold divided by inventory. This is $25/$3 = 8.33.

d.   The Du Pont relationship states that ROE equals:

profit margin (net income/sales) × total asset turnover (sales/total assets) × equity multiplier (total assets/equity).

Obtaining this data from the above statements, we have:

profit margin × total asset turnover × equity multiplier = ($10/$50) × ($50/$21) × ($21/$4) = 0.20 × 2.381 × 5.25 = 2.50 or 250%.

Of course, this is the same result we would have computed had we taken net income and divided it by stockholder's equity:

return on equity = net income/equity = $10/$4 = 2.5 or 250%

2.   a.   The total asset turnover is net sales divided by total assets, or $1,000,000/$800,000 or 1.25. The profit margin is net income ($70,000) divided by net sales ($1,000,000) or 7 percent.

b.   The return on total assets is net income ($70,000) divided by total assets ($800,000) or 8.75 percent. This is the same as the profit margin multiplied by the total asset turnover ratio: 7 percent × 1.25 = 8.75 percent.

c.   Eagle's profit margin of 7 percent is slightly above the industry average. Its total asset turnover of 1.25 is less than the industry average, and its return on total assets of 8.75 is also less than the industry average of 15. Since Eagle's profit margin is similar to the industry profit margin, the reason why Eagle's return on total assets is below the industry average is because its total asset turnover is below the industry average.

CHAPTER 15

Managing Working Capital

AFTER STUDYING THIS CHAPTER, YOU SHOULD BE ABLE TO:

- Explain what is meant by a firm's operating cycle and its cash conversion cycle.
- Describe the impact of the operating cycle on the size of investment in accounts receivable and inventories.
- Explain how seasonal and cyclical trends affect the operating cycle, cash conversion cycle, and investments in current assets.
- Explain how a cash budget is developed and how a treasurer will use it.
- Describe the motives underlying the management of cash and marketable securities.
- Briefly explain what is involved in accounts receivable management and indicate how it is carried out.
- Describe inventory management from the standpoint of the financial manager.

A firm can invest in both working capital and fixed capital. Working capital is a firm's current assets and consists of cash, marketable securities, accounts receivable, and inventories. Fixed capital is a firm's fixed assets, which includes plant, equipment, and property. In this chapter we focus on managing a firm's working capital. The financial manager must decide how much to invest in working capital or current assets and how to finance these current assets.

How important are working capital issues? In a word, very. Firms that cannot obtain needed short-term financing are candidates for bankruptcy. Supplies and raw materials are converted to inventory. When sold, inventory may become an account receivable and ultimately cash. Unexpected increases in inventory or receivables can harm a firm's best-laid long-term plans. As with any other asset, increases in current assets must be financed with either liabilities or equity. If poor planning causes a mismatch between assets and financing sources, or between cash inflows and cash outflows, bankruptcy is a real possibility.

Current assets typically comprise from one-third to one-half of a firm's total assets. They are affected by the firm's day-to-day marketing, production, and human resources issues. A survey of financial managers found they spend nearly 70 percent of their time dealing with financial planning, budgeting, and working capital issues.[1]

The first part of this chapter describes how a firm's operating cycle affects the amount of working capital it carries. Next we review how to prepare and use a cash budget. Our final emphasis is on methods used to manage cash and marketable securities, accounts receivable, and inventories.

OPERATING AND CASH CONVERSION CYCLES

Two important concepts in managing short-term finances are the operating cycle and cash conversion cycle.

OPERATING CYCLE

The **operating cycle** measures the time it takes between ordering materials and collecting cash from receivables. Figure 15.1 graphically depicts the operating cycle for a manufacturing firm. Raw materials are purchased and products are manufactured from them to become finished goods. Effort then is made to sell the finished goods. If the goods are sold on credit, then the receivables must be collected. A service firm would have a similar cycle except for the manufacturing stage. That is, finished goods would be purchased, consumed in the process of providing a service, and receivables collected. Of course, the operating cycles of both service and manufacturing firms would be shortened if sales are made for cash and not on credit.

Figure 15.2 depicts a time line reflecting the operating cycle for a manufacturing firm. The cycle begins with an order being placed for raw materials. The inventory period involves producing or processing the materials into

operating cycle
time between ordering materials and collecting cash from receivables

1. Lawrence J. Gitman and Charles E. Maxwell, "Financial Activities of Major U.S. Firms: Survey and Analysis of *Fortune*'s 1000," *Financial Management* (Winter 1985): 57–65.

FIGURE 15.1   The Operating Cycle

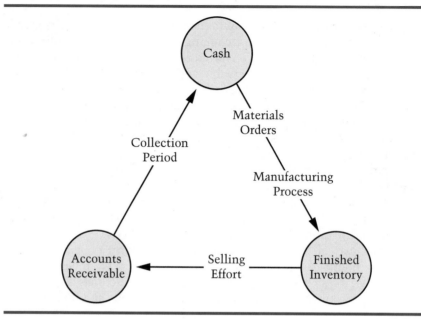

final products or finished goods and ends when the finished goods are sold. If the finished goods are sold on credit, the second major period of interest is the accounts receivable period. It covers the time from when the goods are sold until the receivables are collected in the form of cash. The inventory period and the accounts receivable period together constitute the firms's operating cycle.

CASH CONVERSION CYCLE

In many instances the initial purchase of raw materials or finished goods for resale is on credit. Thus, suppliers can provide financing in the form of accounts payable. The accounts payable period covers the period between when the order for raw materials is placed and when the resulting payable is paid. The accounts payable period is subtracted from the length of the operating cycle to get the ***cash conversion cycle.***

cash conversion cycle time between a firm's paying its suppliers for inventory and collecting cash from customers on a sale of the finished product

    The cash conversion cycle measures a firm's financing gap in terms of *time.* In other words, it is the time between when the firm pays its suppliers and when it collects money from its customers. It is the time between when materials are ordered and receivables are collected less the time over which payables are outstanding. Of course, if no credit is extended by suppliers then the operating cycle and the cash conversion cycle would be the same. The cash conversion cycle is shown in Figure 15.2.

FIGURE 15.2   Time Lines for the Operating and Cash Conversion Cycles

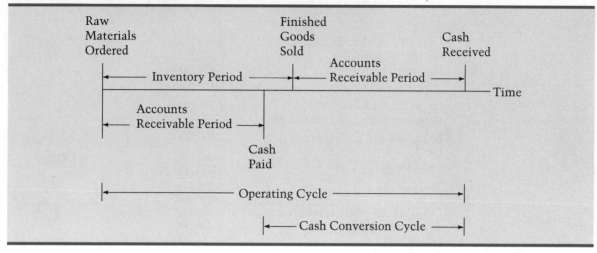

Increases in the cash conversion cycle mean the firm must finance itself for a longer period of time. This will increase the firm's short-term financing needs and financing costs. Financial managers will want to monitor the cash conversion cycle and take action should it begin to lengthen. Shorter cash conversion cycles mean the firm will reduce its short-term financing needs and financing costs.

Two items determine the length of the operating cycle: inventory period and accounts receivable period. Three items affect the cash conversion cycle: inventory period, accounts receivable period, and accounts payable period.

DETERMINING THE LENGTH OF THE OPERATING CYCLE AND CASH CONVERSION CYCLE

We can estimate the length of a firm's operating and cash conversion cycles using information from a firm's income statement and balance sheet. All that needs to be done is to calculate three ratios that will tell us the firm's inventory, accounts receivable, and accounts payable periods. Tables 15.1 and 15.2 contain balance sheets and income statements, respectively, for the Global Manufacturing Corporation.

Inventory Period

First, we would like to know how many days items were in inventory during 1995; that is, the time between when an order for raw materials was placed and when the finished goods were sold. To determine the length of this period, we can use the inventory turnover ratio (cost of goods sold divided

TABLE 15.1   Balance Sheet for Global Manufacturing, Inc.

	DECEMBER 31, 1995
ASSETS	
Cash and marketable securities	$ 25,000
Accounts receivable	100,000
Inventories	125,000
Total current assets	250,000
Gross plant and equipment	300,000
Less: accumulated depreciation	− 100,000
Net plant and equipment	200,000
Land	50,000
Total fixed assets	250,000
Total assets	$500,000
LIABILITIES AND EQUITY	
Accounts payable	$ 78,000
Notes payable	34,000
Accrued liabilities	30,000
Total current liabilities	142,000
Long-term debt	140,000
Total liabilities	$282,000
Common stock ($1 par, 50,000 shares)	50,000
Paid-in capital	100,000
Retained earnings	68,000
Total stockholders' equity	218,000
Total liabilities and equity	$500,000

by inventories) from Chapter 14. As we saw in the last chapter, the inventory turnover for Global Manufacturing is 3.6 times ($450,000/$125,000). That is, Global turns over or transforms its inventory into finished products and sells them 3.6 times a year. To determine the inventory conversion period, we divide the 365 days in a year by this inventory turnover ratio (365/3.6) to get 101 days.

As an alternative calculation, we can divide the 1995 year-end inventories amount by the 1995 cost of goods sold (COGS) per day. In ratio form, we have:

$$\frac{\text{Inventory}}{\text{Conversion Period}} = \frac{\text{Inventory}}{\text{Costs of Goods Sold}/365} = \frac{\text{Inventory}}{\text{COGS per day}}$$

$$= \frac{\$125,000}{\$450,000/365} = \frac{\$125,000}{\$1,233} = 101 \text{ Days}$$

TABLE 15.2   Income Statement for Global Manufacturing, Inc.

YEAR ENDED DECEMBER 31	1995
Net revenues or sales	$700,000
Cost of goods sold	450,000
Gross profit	250,000
Operating expenses:	
General and administrative	95,000
Selling and marketing	56,000
Depreciation	25,000
Operating income	74,000
Interest	14,000
Income before taxes	60,000
Income taxes (40%)	24,000
Net income	$ 36,000
Number of shares outstanding	50,000
Earnings per share	$0.72

By either method, it took on average about 101 days in 1995 for Global to complete the inventory conversion period.

Accounts Receivable Period
The second step is to determine the average collection period in 1995 for Global. We saw this ratio in Chapter 14. It measures the average time between when a product is sold on credit and cash is received from the buyer. It is calculated as follows:

$$\text{Average Collection Period} = \frac{\text{Accounts Receivable}}{\text{Net Sales}/365}$$

$$= \frac{\$100,000}{\$700,000/365} = \frac{\$100,000}{\$1,918} = 52 \text{ Days}$$

The $100,000 for accounts receivable is taken from the balance sheet in Table 15.1 and the $700,000 in net sales comes from the income statement in Table 15.2. It took Global 52 days on average during 1995 from the time finished goods were sold on credit to when the resulting receivables were actually collected.

The operating cycle is determined as follows:

Operating Cycle = Inventory Conversion Period + Average Collection Period

Global's average 1995 operating cycle was 101 days to process and sell its inventory plus 52 days to collect its receivables for a total of 153 days.

Average Payment Period

The *average payment period* represents the time it takes Global to pay its suppliers. We were first introduced to this ratio in Chapter 14. The average payment period is calculated by dividing a firm's accounts payable by its cost of goods sold per day. Using the information from Table 15.1 and Table 15.2, the average payment period is calculated as follows.

$$\text{Average Payment Period} = \frac{\text{Accounts Payable}}{\text{Cost of Goods Sold}/365}$$

$$= \frac{\$78,000}{\$450,000/365} = \frac{\$78,000}{\$1,233} = 63 \text{ Days}$$

Thus, Global was able to get on average about 63 days of credit from its suppliers in 1995.

The cash conversion cycle is the operating cycle less the average payment period:

Cash Conversion Cycle = Operating Cycle − Average Payment Period

For Global, we start with an operating cycle of 153 days and subtract the average payment period of 63 days to arrive at a cash conversion cycle of 90 days for 1995. The average time between when Global paid for materials and when it received payment from its customers after their final sale was 90 days. Managing the cash conversion cycle is a major task of a firm's financial manager. The shorter the cash conversion cycle, the smaller will be the firm's investment in inventory and receivables, and consequently the less will be its financing needs.

WORKING CAPITAL REQUIREMENTS

Let's take a closer look at how the length of the operating cycle affects the amount of funds invested in accounts receivable and inventories. Using Global's 1995 sales of $700,000, average sales per day were $1,918 ($700,000/365). We also know that in 1995 it took Global an average of 52 days to collect its accounts receivable. We can use this information to find Global's average investment in accounts receivable. We multiply the net sales per day of $1,918 times the average collection period:

Receivables Investment Amount = Net Sales Per Day
                            × Average Collection Period

Receivables Investment Amount = $1,918 × 52 Days
                            = $100,000 (rounded)

This should be no surprise to us since we previously used Global's $100,000 accounts receivable balance to determine the average collection period. However, let's now ask: What will the investment be next year in accounts receivable if sales increase by 10 percent to $770,000 and the average collection period remains at 52 days? Intuitively, if there is a constant relationship between sales and receivables, a 10 percent increase in sales should lead to a 10 percent increase in receivables. An estimate of the new receivables balance would be $100,000 (1995 level) plus 10 percent for a total of $110,000.

We can also find the new accounts receivable balance by finding the new sales per day and then multiplying it by the collection period. Dividing $770,000 by 365 we get $2,110 sales per day; multiplying it by 52 days gives us:

$$\text{Receivables Investment Amount} = \$2,110 \times 52 \text{ Days}$$
$$= \$110,000 \text{ (rounded)}$$

In this case, our initial estimate of $110,000 was correct, because the collection period remained the same. Global's investment in accounts receivable will have to increase by $10,000 (i.e., $110,000 − $100,000) in order to support a sales increase of $70,000 (i.e., $770,000 − $700,000) as long as the average collection period remains at 52 days.

What will happen if the relationship between sales and accounts receivable does not remain constant? For example, as sales rise or fall over time the accounts receivable period may change. If the economy goes into a recession, the accounts receivable period may rise as customers take longer to pay their bills. Or focusing the firm's marketing efforts on better credit quality customers may allow the firm to increase sales and reduce its receivables balance if more customers pay early. Now we should ask: What will be the necessary investment in accounts receivable if sales increase to $770,000 but Global is able to decrease its average collection period to 50 days? We find the answer to be:

$$\text{Receivables Investment Amount} = \$2,110 \times 50 \text{ Days}$$
$$= \$106,000 \text{ (rounded)}$$

Thus, a two-day reduction in the average collection period would mean that the amount of increased investment required in accounts receivable to support a 10 percent increase in sales would be only $6,000 ($106,000 − $100,000).

A similar analysis can be conducted in terms of inventories. The 1995 cost of goods sold was $450,000 for the year or $1,233 on a per day basis ($450,000/365). We know that in 1995 it took Global on average 101 days between when a raw materials order was placed and when the finished goods were sold. By multiplying the average cost of goods per day times the inventory conversion period, we can determine the investment required in inventories:

Inventories Investment Amount = Average Cost of Goods Sold Per Day
                                                                × Inventory Conversion Period

For Global in 1995, we have:

$$\text{Inventories Investment Amount} = \$1,233 \times 101 \text{ Days}$$
$$= \$125,000 \text{ (rounded)}$$

This, of course, is the same amount shown for the inventories account in Table 15.1 for Global Manufacturing, Inc.

It should be clear that this required investment will change if either the cost of goods sold changes, the inventory conversion period changes, or both. For example, let's assume that the firm's cost of goods sold increases by 10 percent to $495,000 due to an increase next year in the firm's sales. This would be a new cost of goods sold per day of $1,356 ($495,000/365). If the inventory conversion period remains at 101 days, the new investment in inventories should be about 10 percent higher, too:

$$\text{Inventories Investment Amount} = \$1,356 \times 101 \text{ Days}$$
$$= \$137,000 \text{ (rounded)}$$

which is an increase of $12,000 ($137,000 − $125,000) or about 10 percent.

Of course, if Global could find a way to lower its inventory conversion period to, say, 90 days, the net impact on the investment in inventories of a 10 percent sales rise would be:

$$\text{Inventories Investment Amount} = \$1,356 \times 90 \text{ Days}$$
$$= \$122,000 \text{ (rounded)}$$

Thus, even though sales and cost of goods sold increases in 1996, a decline in the inventory conversion period to 90 days would actually result in a decline in the investment in inventories by $3,000 ($125,000 − $122,000). Global may be able to achieve a reduction of its inventory conversion period through a more efficient management of inventories. Some strategies for doing this are discussed in the last section of this chapter.

The size of the accounts payable account is also affected by two basic factors—the level of the firm's cost of goods sold and the average payment period. Table 15.2 indicates that the cost of goods sold for Global Manufacturing was $450,000 in 1995. On a per day basis the cost of goods sold was $1,233 ($450,000/365). We also previously calculated the 1995 average payment period at 63 days. Given this information, we can determine the required amount of accounts payable as follows:

$$\text{Accounts Payable} = \text{Cost of Goods Sold Per Day}$$
$$\times \text{ Average Payment Period}$$

For Global in 1995, we have:

$$\text{Accounts Payable} = \$1,233 \times 63 \text{ days}$$
$$= \$78,000 \text{ (rounded)}$$

This amount, of course, is the same as the accounts payable amount shown in Table 15.1 for Global Manufacturing at the end of 1995.

Of course, as a firm's cost of goods sold increases its credit purchases and thus its accounts payable also should increase. For example, if Global's cost of goods sold increases by 10 percent to $495,000 next year, we expect accounts payable, currently $78,000, to rise by 10 percent as well, if the payment period does not change. A cost of goods sold of $495,000 gives a daily average cost of goods sold of $495,000/365 days or $1,356. If the average payment period remains at 63 days, the projected amount in the accounts payable account is:

$$\text{Accounts Payable} = \$1,356 \times 63 \text{ Days}$$
$$= \$85,000 \text{ (rounded)}$$

which represents approximately a 10 percent increase in payables.

It now should be recognized that while an increase in sales and cost of goods sold should result in an increase in the investment in accounts receivable and inventories, these increases will be partially offset by an increase in accounts payable, other things being equal. If the accounts payable period rises to 70 days, the new accounts payable balance will be:

$$\text{Accounts Payable} = \$1,356 \times 70 \text{ days} = \$94,920$$

Our estimates of the effects on receivables, inventory, and payables are shown in summary form in Table 15.3 under the assumption that *no changes* occur in the operating and cash conversion cycles.

Thus, while investment in accounts receivable and inventories would be expected to increase by $23,000 from $225,000 to $248,000, the expected increase in accounts payable of $7,000 from $78,000 to $85,000 causes the net impact to be only a $16,000 increase in needed financing. The financial

TABLE 15.3   Effect of 10 Percent Increase in Sales and Cost of Goods Sold on Receivables, Inventory, and Payables*

ACCOUNT	1995 RESULTS FOR GLOBAL	10% INCREASE IN SALES & COST OF GOODS SOLD
Investment:		
Accounts Receivable	$100,000	$110,000
Inventories	125,000	138,000
Total	$225,000	$248,000
Financing:		
Accounts Payable	$ 78,000	$ 85,000
Net Investment:		
Investment − Financing	$147,000	$163,000

*Assumption: Average Collection Period = 52 days; Inventory Period = 101 days; Average Payment Period = 63 days

manager will have to plan ahead to obtain the necessary funds to support this expected increase in net working capital. She can obtain funds from short-term financing sources, which are discussed in Chapter 16, or she may decide it is appropriate to tap long-term sources such as stocks and bonds.

Table 15.4 summarizes our estimates of receivables, inventory, and payables if sales and cost of goods sold rise by 10 percent and changes occur in the operating and cash conversion cycles. Specifically, Table 15.4 shows the effects of an average collection period of 50 days, inventory period of 90 days, and a payables period of 70 days.

The effect of these minor changes in cash conversion cycle components is remarkable. The firm's net investment in these working capital accounts will fall to $133,080, nearly $14,000 less than the current situation, or nearly $30,000 less than the scenario in Table 15.3.

In a later section, we discuss another important topic: the management of working capital assets. From our discussion, it should be clear that more efficient management of working capital assets and faster cash collection will lessen the firm's needs for financing. Small working capital account balances mean less debt and external equity financing needs to be obtained, saving the firm extra financing expenses. Activities that decrease the cash conversion cycle will reduce the firm's need to obtain financing.

CASH BUDGETS

We have seen how financial ratios can be used to estimate the firm's total financing needs over the course of a year. As we learned in Chapter 14, expected sales growth may require the firm to acquire additional assets, both current and fixed, to support higher sales levels. By combining the

TABLE 15.4   Effect of 10 Percent Increase in Sales and Cost of Goods Sold on Receivables, Inventory, and Payables*

ACCOUNT	1995 RESULTS FOR GLOBAL	10% INCREASE IN SALES & COST OF GOODS SOLD
Investment:		
Accounts Receivable	$100,000	$106,000
Inventories	125,000	122,000
Total	$225,000	$228,000
Financing:		
Accounts Payable	$ 78,000	$ 94,920
Net Investment:		
Investment − Financing	$147,000	$133,080

*Assumption: Average Collection Period = 50 days; Inventory Period = 90 days; Average Payment Period = 70 days

Corporate fads may come and go, but one that is sure to stay is the attempt by corporations to reduce their net working capital by reducing their current asset account balances. Some firms have a goal of operating with zero working capital. Although they may not attain it, merely striving for this goal creates opportunities to discover efficiencies, improve production processes and customer relations, and free up cash. At a time when firms need cash to invest in overseas facilities and markets, to invest in new technology, and to service debt, the uncovering of cash by reducing working capital is similar to finding a treasure chest.

AIMING FOR ZERO NET WORKING CAPITAL

The average *Fortune* 500 firm has 20 cents of working capital for every $1 of sales—a grand total of about $500 *billion* for all the firms on the list. A small increase in working capital efficiency can have a significant impact on cash flow. Savings from the efforts of individual firms are impressive: Campbell's Soup reduced working capital by $80 million; American Standard has reduced it by $200 million; Quaker Oats also reduced working capital by $200 million. General Electric estimates that increasing inventory turnover by one turn a year will generate $1 billion in freed-up cash.

Cutting working capital generates cash and can increase company earnings. Financing costs should decline as less financing is needed to support large receivables and inventory balances. Costs of warehousing and handling inventory will fall as inventory levels are pared. Slimmed-down current asset balances will lead to reductions in firm's total assets. The result of cost savings and smaller asset bases will mean higher returns on assets and, in all likelihood, increases in shareholder wealth.

Source: Based on Shawn Tully, "Raiding a Company's Hidden Cash," *Fortune* (August 22, 1994), pp. 82–87.

sales forecast and the firm's total asset turnover ratio, we can estimate the amount of assets needed to support the sales forecast. The projected increase in assets less the estimated increase in current liabilities and retained earnings will give the financial analyst an estimate of the firm's needs for external financing.

The previous section illustrated a quick means of estimating working capital financing needs by comparing expected changes in current assets and current liabilities. The estimated change in current assets minus the expected change in current liabilities measures the change in working capital. This growth (or decline) in working capital must be financed, either via short-term financing or long-term financing such as debt or equity.

Such methods are appropriate as a first approximation toward estimating a firm's yearly financing needs. But a firm needs more precise information than this. Over the course of a year, large bills may need to be paid before subsequent cash inflows occur. Dividend checks will be mailed to shareholders, workers and suppliers will need to be paid, interest on debt and perhaps even the principal that was borrowed will have to be repaid. During any one week or month the firm's need for cash may far exceed the above annual estimates. A firm's treasurer will need to closely track and forecast daily and weekly cash inflows and outflows to ensure that cash is available to pay necessary expenses. Should the firm's cash balance become dangerously low, the treasurer will need to make plans to acquire the needed funds by either borrowing money or selling marketable securities. A **cash budget** is a tool the treasurer uses to forecast future cash flows and estimate future short-term borrowing needs.

A budget is simply a financial forecast of spending, income, or both. A cash budget details the periodic cash inflows and cash outflows of a firm over some time frame. Small- and medium-size firms may prepare monthly cash budgets, whereas larger firms will forecast cash flows weekly or daily. If cash surpluses are forecast, the treasurer can plan how the firm's excess cash can be invested to earn interest.[2] If a cash deficit is forecast, the treasurer can plan how to best raise the necessary funds.

To construct a cash budget, three sets of information are needed: the firm's minimum desired cash balance, estimated cash inflows, and estimated cash outflows. We discuss each of these below.

cash budget

tool the treasurer uses to forecast future cash flows and estimate future short-term borrowing needs

Minimum Desired Cash Balance

Most firms have a minimum desired cash balance. Some cash will be needed to pay the month's bills, but extra cash also may be desired because the forecasts of cash inflows and outflows will not be perfect. To protect against lower than expected cash inflows (or higher than expected cash outflows), a *cash buffer* is needed. The size of the cash buffer depends upon several influences, including the firm's ability to easily acquire financing on short notice, the predictability of cash inflows and outflows, and management's preferences.

Cash Inflows

The estimates of cash inflows are driven by two main factors: the sales forecast and customer payment patterns. Over any period, the main sources of cash inflows for the firm will be cash sales and collections of receivables.

---

2.   Unlike personal checking accounts, business checking accounts earn no interest. Thus, the treasurer will want to invest any cash over and above the firm's immediate needs in order to earn a return on the excess funds.

If we know the proportion of cash sales and the percentage of customers that pay their bills every month we can use sales forecasts to estimate future cash inflows.

Sales forecasts will be affected by seasonal patterns. Obviously, monthly sales figures will differ for swimsuit makers and snow blower manufacturers. Managers can determine seasonal patterns by merely plotting monthly or quarterly sales figures, as in Figure 15.3.

For example, Table 15.5 presents Global Manufacturing's actual November and December 1995 sales, and forecasted sales for January, February, March, and April 1996. From Figure 15.3, Global knows that its sales volume is highly seasonal, with a large proportion of sales occurring in the last few months of the year. All of Global's sales are credit sales and become accounts receivable. From reviewing past payment patterns, Global knows that receivables representing 50 percent of a month's sales are paid one month after purchase while the remaining 50 percent are paid two months later. Thus, for January–April, each month's cash inflows have two sources: cash comes into the firm equal to 50 percent of the sales volume from the previous month and cash comes into the firm equal to 50 percent of the sales volume from two months prior. Thus, for January, cash inflows reflect 50 percent of December's sales (50 percent of December's sales equals $50,000) plus 50 percent of November's sales (50 percent of November's sales equals $40,000), for a total expected inflow of $90,000.

CASH OUTFLOWS

Every month Global will have bills to pay and these cash outflows need to appear in the cash budget. Suppliers of raw materials must be paid, as well as the firm's payroll. Rental or lease payments, utility bills, and so forth

FIGURE 15.3   Sales Data, 1993–95, Global Manufacturing, Inc.

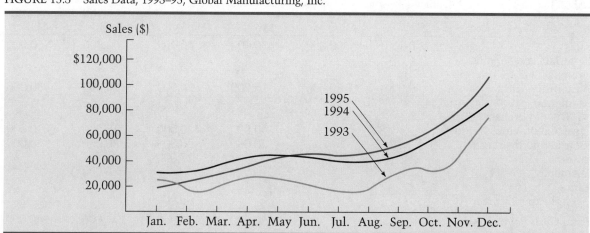

TABLE 15.5   Monthly Cash Inflows, Global Manufacturing, Inc.

	NOV.	DEC.	JAN.	FEB.	MAR.	APR.
Sales	$80,000	$100,000	$30,000	$40,000	$50,000	$60,000
Collections:						
(50% of sales of the previous month)		40,000	50,000	15,000	20,000	25,000
(50% of sales of the second previous month)			40,000	50,000	15,000	20,000
Total Cash Receipts			$90,000	$65,000	$35,000	$45,000

are other examples of regular outflows that should be listed in the budget. Interest on borrowing may be due at specific times, as will dividends and tax payments. Any anticipated purchases of plant and equipment also must be listed in the budget. Production, over the course of the year, can be seasonal, rising and falling along with the sales forecast, or level, producing a constant amount of product every month. Here we assume Global uses seasonal production. Later, we will see the effect of a level production schedule on Global's cash budget.

Table 15.6 shows Global's expected cash disbursements. Raw materials and supplies equal to 50 percent of each month's sales are purchased each month. Global pays its suppliers two months after the goods are purchased. Each month's estimated salary and overhead expenses are $20,000. Interest payments of $7,000 are due in February, and a quarterly dividend, expected to be $6,000, is to be paid in March. Quarterly taxes of $3,000 also need to be paid in March. In anticipation of growing sales, Global is planning to purchase $50,000 worth of capital equipment in February.

TABLE 15.6   Monthly Cash Outflows, Seasonal Production, Global Manufacturing, Inc.

	NOV.	DEC.	JAN.	FEB.	MAR.	APR.
Sales	$80,000	$100,000	$30,000	$ 40,000	$50,000	$60,000
Materials and supplies purchases (50% of monthly sales)	40,000	50,000	15,000	20,000	25,000	30,000
Payments:						
(100% of purchases of the second previous month)			40,000	50,000	15,000	20,000
Salaries and overhead			20,000	20,000	20,000	20,000
Interest				7,000		
Dividends					6,000	
Taxes					3,000	
Capital expenditures				50,000		
Total Cash Payments			$60,000	$127,000	$44,000	$40,000

CONSTRUCTING THE CASH BUDGET

After listing all the expected cash inflows and cash outflows for each month, we can estimate the monthly net cash flow. As shown in Table 15.7, this is simply the difference between Global's cash receipts and cash payments from Tables 15.5 and 15.6.

From Table 15.7 we see that January will be a month with a large positive net cash flow, but that February and March are expected to have larger cash outflows than cash inflows. April is expected to have more cash coming into the firm than going from it. To help Global determine its short-term financing needs, we need to put together a fully developed cash budget that indicates Global's minimum desired cash balance as well as its monthly loan (or loan repayment) needs. We'll assume Global's minimum desired cash balance is $25,000, which is the amount of cash it currently has on hand according to its 1995 balance sheet (Table 15.1). Should the cash position in any month fall below $25,000, Global's treasurer will need to borrow sufficient funds so that the cash balance is restored to the $25,000 level. Table 15.8 illustrates Global's monthly cash budget.

From Table 15.7, we see that January's net cash flow is $30,000; adding this to Global's beginning of January cash balance of $25,000 gives Global a cumulative cash balance of $55,000. Global's treasurer may want to make plans to invest some of this excess cash in marketable securities in order to earn extra interest income.

The end-of-January cash balance becomes the beginning-of-February cash balance. Adding the $55,000 cash balance to February's net cash flow of −$62,000 means that Global is forecasted to spend $7,000 more in cash

TABLE 15.7   Net Monthly Cash Flows, Seasonal Production, Global Manufacturing, Inc.

	JAN.	FEB.	MAR.	APR.
Total Cash Receipts	$90,000	$65,000	$35,000	$45,000
less: Total Cash Payments	60,000	127,000	44,000	40,000
Net Cash Flow	$30,000	($62,000)	($ 9,000)	$ 5,000

TABLE 15.8   Monthly Cash Budget, Seasonal Production, Global Manufacturing, Inc.

	JAN.	FEB.	MAR.	APR.
Net cash flow	$30,000	($62,000)	($ 9,000)	$ 5,000
Beginning cash balance	$25,000	$55,000	$25,000	$25,000
Cumulative cash balance	$55,000	($ 7,000)	$16,000	$30,000
Monthly loan (or repayment)	0	$32,000	$ 9,000	($ 5,000)
Cumulative loan balance	0	$32,000	$41,000	$36,000
Ending Cash Balance	$55,000	$25,000	$25,000	$25,000

than it is expected to have available. To meet the expected payments and to raise the cash balance to its minimum desired level of $25,000, Global's treasurer will need to borrow $7,000 + $25,000 or $32,000 during the month of February. After so doing, the ending cash balance of February will be $25,000.

When March's net cash flow of − $9,000 is added to March's beginning cash balance of $25,000, Global's available cash will be $16,000. To maintain the minimum desired cash balance of $25,000, Global should plan to borrow $9,000. When this is added to the already outstanding loans from February, Global's total loan balance at the end of March will be $32,000 + $9,000 or $41,000. The ending cash balance in March will be $25,000.

April's positive net cash flow, when added to the beginning cash balance, will give Global a positive cash balance of $30,000. This exceeds Global's minimum desired cash balance of $25,000, so in all likelihood the excess cash of $5,000 will be used to repay some of Global's recently acquired debt. By so doing, Global's cumulative loan balance will fall to $36,000.

This example illustrates the usefulness of cash budgeting. Forecasted sales are used to estimate future cash inflows and outflows based upon expected payment patterns. The treasurer can plan ahead to invest excess cash or to borrow needed funds. In addition to its value as a planning tool, the cash budget will be a necessary component of any short-term loan request from a bank. The bank will not only want to see when and how much the firm may need to borrow, but also when the firm will be able to repay the loan.

SEASONAL VERSUS LEVEL PRODUCTION

This above example assumes that Global uses seasonal production to meet its seasonal sales forecast. Raw materials purchases will rise or fall in anticipation of higher or lower sales. Such a strategy can help minimize the effect of seasonal sales on inventory. Goods are manufactured shortly before they are sold. But seasonal production can lead to other problems, such as idle plant and laid-off workers during slow sales months and production bottlenecks during busy times. Consequently, for better production efficiency, some firms with seasonal sales use a level production plan. Under a level production plan, the same amount of raw materials are purchased and the same amount of finished product is manufactured every month. Inventory builds up in anticipation of the higher seasonal sales while cash and accounts receivable are quite low. When the selling season begins, inventories fall and receivables rise. After a time, inventories are nearly exhausted and the firm is collecting cash from its customers. The changing composition of current assets for a firm with a seasonal sales pattern is illustrated in Figure 15.4.

Now let's see how Global's cash budget will be affected if it switches to a level production plan. Table 15.5, the schedule of cash inflows, will

FIGURE 15.4   Changing Composition of Current Assets with Seasonal Sales

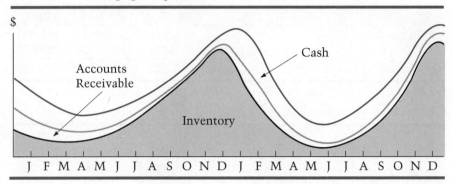

not be affected. But Table 15.6 will be changed to reflect a level pattern of materials purchases. We will assume that the amount of materials and supplies over the course of a year is one-half of estimated sales. If forecasted sales are $700,000, this means Global purchases $350,000 of materials over the course of a year, or approximately $29,200 each month. Table 15.9 shows the revised cash outflow schedule assuming purchases—and subsequent payments—of a constant $29,200 each month.

With these new cash payments, Table 15.10 shows the monthly net cash flows and Table 15.11 shows the new cash budget. In January, the level production plan leads to a higher cash balance than under the seasonal plan. But sustained production levels during Global's slow sales months lead to monthly cash deficits in February, March, and April. Under

TABLE 15.9   Monthly Cash Outflows, Level Production

	NOV.	DEC.	JAN.	FEB.	MAR.	APR.
Sales	$80,000	$100,000	$30,000	$ 40,000	$50,000	$60,000
Materials and supplies purchases (50% of average monthly sales)	29,200	29,200	29,200	29,200	29,200	29,200
Payments: (100% of purchases of the second previous month)			29,200	29,200	29,200	29,200
Salaries and overhead			20,000	20,000	20,000	20,000
Interest				7,000		
Dividends					6,000	
Taxes					3,000	
Capital Expenditures				50,000		
Total Cash Payments			$49,200	$106,200	$58,200	$49,200

TABLE 15.10   Net Monthly Cash Flows, Level Production

	JAN.	FEB.	MAR.	APR.
Total Cash Receipts	$90,000	$65,000	$35,000	$45,000
less: Total Cash Payments	49,200	106,200	58,200	49,200
Net Cash Flow	$40,800	($41,200)	($23,200)	($ 4,200)

TABLE 15.11   Monthly Cash Budget, Level Production

	JAN.	FEB.	MAR.	APR.
Net Cash Flow	$40,800	($41,200)	($23,200)	($ 4,200)
Beginning Cash Balance	25,000	65,800	25,000	25,000
Cumulative Cash Balance	65,800	24,600	1,800	20,800
Monthly Loan (or Repayment)	0	400	23,200	4,200
Cumulative Loan Balance	0	400	23,600	27,800
Ending Cash Balance	$65,800	$25,000	$25,000	$25,000

seasonal production, net cash flow returned to positive in April and some loans could be repaid. With level production, the cumulative loan balance continues to grow through April.

The projections on the cash budget will reflect the firm's marketing efforts as well as its credit policies, how it manages its receivables, and how it decides to manage its production and inventories. In general, firms with larger receivables balances and easier credit terms will have slower cash receipt inflows, but this must be balanced against the competitive impact of tightening up its receivables management policies. Firms with larger inventories will face large accounts payable balances and larger cash payments than firms operating on leaner inventories and tighter production schedules. Thus, how a firm manages its working capital accounts will be a concern to the company's treasurer. We examine these topics in the next section.

MANAGEMENT OF CURRENT ASSETS

Management of current assets involves the administration of cash and marketable securities, accounts receivable, and inventories. On the one hand, the financial manager should strive to minimize the investment in current assets because of the cost of financing them. On the other hand, adequate cash and marketable securities are necessary for liquidity purposes, acceptable credit terms are necessary to maintain sales, and appropriate inventory levels must be kept to avoid running out of stock and losing sales. Successful management thus requires a continual balancing of the costs and benefits associated with investment in current assets.

CASH AND MARKETABLE SECURITIES MANAGEMENT

Business firms should strive to minimize their cash holdings. Some cash is necessary to carry on day-to-day operations. This is the **transactions motive** or demand for holding cash. If cash inflows and outflows could be projected with virtual certainty, the transactions demand for cash could theoretically be reduced to zero. Most businesses prepare cash flow forecasts or budgets, trying to predict the amount of cash holdings they will need. However, most firms are forced to hold some cash because of cash flow uncertainties and because minimum cash balances often are required on loans from commercial banks.

transactions motive demand for cash needed to conduct day-to-day operations

Marketable securities are held primarily to meet **precautionary motives.** These are demands for funds that may be caused by unpredictable events, such as delays in production or in the collection of receivables. Marketable securities can be sold to satisfy such liquidity problems. In the event of strong seasonal sales patterns, marketable securities also can be used to reduce wide fluctuations in short-term financing requirements.

precautionary motives holding funds to meet unexpected demands

Marketable securities may also be held for **speculative motives.** In certain instances a firm might be able to take advantage of unusual cash discounts or price bargains on materials if it can pay quickly with cash. Marketable securities are easily converted into cash for such purposes.

speculative motives holding funds to take advantage of unusual cash discounts for needed materials

For an investment to qualify as a marketable security it must be highly liquid; that is, it must be readily convertible to cash without a large loss of value. Generally this requires that it have a short maturity and that an active secondary market exists so that it can be sold prior to maturity if necessary. The security must also be of high quality, with little chance that the borrower will default. U.S. Treasury bills offer the highest quality, liquidity, and marketability. Other investments that serve well as marketable securities include negotiable certificates of deposit (CDs) and commercial paper, both of which offer higher rates but are more risky and less liquid than Treasury bills. Business firms also can hold excess funds in money market accounts, or they can purchase bankers' acceptances or short-term notes of U.S. government agencies. We discuss the characteristics of several financial instruments used as marketable securities below.

U.S. Treasury Bills

Treasury bills are sold at a discount through competitive bidding in a weekly auction. These bills are offered in all parts of the country, but sell mostly in New York City. Treasury bills also are actively traded in secondary money markets, again mostly in New York.

Figure 15.5 shows the levels and volatility—or tendency to change rapidly—of three-month Treasury bill yields in recent years. Notice that they were over 8 percent in early 1989 and dropped steadily to about 3 percent during 1992–94. It rose to about 6 percent in early 1995 before dropping again. U.S. Treasury bills are considered to be essentially risk-free in that

FIGURE 15.5   Selected Money Market Rates

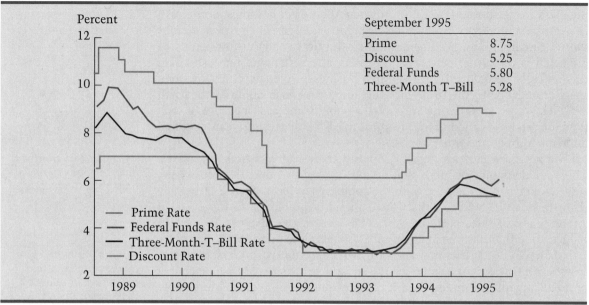

Source: Federal Reserve Bank of St. Louis.

there is virtually no risk of default. Consequently, interest rates are, as we would expect, higher for other money market instruments of similar maturity at the same point in time.

Federal Funds

As a result of normal operations some commercial banks and other depository institutions find they have reserves that are temporarily greater than their required reserves. These temporary excess reserves, federal funds as they are called when loaned, are lent on a day-to-day basis to other depository institutions that are temporarily short of reserves.

The lending for a one-day period is generally done by an electronic funds transfer and can be illustrated with an example involving two commercial banks. The deal may be made by one or more telephone calls from the bank wanting to borrow funds, or it may be arranged through a federal funds broker. Funds are electronically transferred from the lending bank's reserve account to the borrowing bank's reserve account at the Federal Reserve Bank. Repayment of the loan plus interest occurs the next day. Many of these transactions are between New York City banks, but banks in other cities also enter the New York money market, usually as lenders.

The most common trading unit for federal funds is $1 million, but this is often exceeded. Trades may at times be made for $25,000 or multiples thereof; they are almost never made for less. The number of banks trading federal funds has increased substantially in recent years and the volume of funds traded has gone up significantly. Other depository institutions are just beginning to participate.

Federal funds rates usually parallel U.S. Treasury bill rates, as is shown in Figure 15.5. Notice that the federal funds rate has remained above the three-month Treasury bill rate in recent years. Normally the spread or difference between the two rates is narrow. During periods of tight money and credit, however, federal funds can be bid up to very high levels. Banks and other depository institutions choose, within limits, between borrowing at the discount rate from the Federal Reserve and borrowing federal funds to meet reserve requirements. If they could be freely substituted for each other, the discount rate set in accordance with monetary policy objectives would set an upper limit for the federal funds rate, since banks would borrow at the lower of the two rates. In practice, however, banks prefer to borrow federal funds, even at the high rates that occur when money is tight, rather than borrow too frequently from the Federal Reserve, which discourages continued use of this alternative.

Commercial Paper

Commercial paper is the short-term, unsecured notes of well-known business firms such as IBM or General Electric. Both major finance companies and nonfinancial corporations have sold commercial paper through dealers or commercial paper houses for many years. More recently many issuers, particularly finance companies, have begun to issue or sell their own commercial paper.

Interest rates on commercial paper tend to closely follow Treasury bill rates over time. Of course, because of somewhat greater default risk, commercial paper rates for similar maturities are higher than Treasury bill rates at any point in time. Since commercial paper rates are typically below bank prime rates, they are a valuable short-term financing source for high quality business firms.

Negotiable Certificates of Deposit

A major new development in the money market in the 1960s was the greatly increased use of negotiable certificates of deposit, or CDs. A certificate of deposit is in essence a receipt issued by a bank in exchange for a deposit of funds. The bank agrees to pay the amount deposited plus interest to the bearer of the receipt on the date specified on the certificate. Many banks had issued such certificates as early as the turn of the century, but before 1960 they were rarely issued in negotiable form. Negotiable CDs can be traded in the secondary market before maturity.

Within a short time after CDs were issued in substantial amounts, a government securities dealer decided to trade in outstanding negotiable certificates of deposit. This beginning of a secondary market was followed by trading by other security dealers so that by 1969 virtually all of the nonbank dealers and many of the bank dealers in U.S. government securities bought, sold, and maintained an inventory in CDs.

The volume of negotiable CDs (usually issued in denominations of $100,000 or more) has increased dramatically in recent years. Interest rates on these CDs usually parallel rates on other money market instruments, such as commercial paper and bankers' acceptances, and are above the less risky Treasury bill rates.

Bankers' Acceptances

The origination and use of bankers' acceptances were discussed in Chapter 6. As we know, this form of business paper primarily finances exports and imports and, since it is the unconditional obligation of the accepting bank, generally has a high quality rating. Yields on bankers' acceptances closely follow yields on commercial paper.

In the mid-1970s, the volume of bankers' acceptances increased greatly because they were used in domestic transactions. Most of this activity involved goods in storage or transit within the United States.

Eurodollars

Eurodollars are deposits placed in foreign banks that remain denominated in U.S. dollars. A demand deposit in a U.S. bank becomes a Eurodollar when the holder of such a deposit transfers it to a foreign bank or an overseas branch of an American bank. After the transfer, the foreign bank holds a claim against the U.S. bank, while the original deposit holder (usually a business firm) now holds a Eurodollar deposit. It is called a Eurodollar deposit because it is still denominated in U.S. dollars rather than being denominated in the currency of the country in which the foreign bank operates.

In recent years, and especially since 1966, large commercial banks have raised money by borrowing from the Eurodollar market through their overseas branches. Overseas branches of U.S. banks and banks outside the United States get funds in the Eurodollar market by accepting dollars in interest-bearing time deposit accounts. These dollar deposits are lent anywhere in the world, usually on a short-term basis. Banks generally transfer funds by telephone or electronically, lending large sums without collateral between banks. Banks that handle Eurodollars are located in Europe, with London as the center, and in other financial centers throughout the world, including such places as Singapore and the Bahamas.

Eurodollar deposit liabilities have arisen because the dollar is widely used as an international currency and because foreigners are holding more dollars due to ongoing U.S. balance-of-payment problems. Eurodollars are supplied by national and international corporations, banks, insurance companies, wealthy individuals, and some foreign governments and agencies. Eurodollar loan recipients also are a diverse group, but commercial banks, multinational corporations, and national corporations are heavy users.

There are several major reasons why U.S. banks have entered the Eurodollar market by means of their overseas branches: to finance business activity abroad, to switch Eurodollars into other currencies, and to lend to other Eurodollar banks. The most important reason, and the one that has received the most publicity in the United States, is for banking offices in the United States to borrow Eurodollars from their overseas branches. In this way they get funds at lower costs and during periods of tight money.

ACCOUNTS RECEIVABLE MANAGEMENT

The management of receivables involves conducting credit analysis, setting credit terms, and carrying out collection efforts. Taken together, these decision areas determine the level of investment in accounts receivable. The selling of goods on credit is generally driven by industry norms and competitive pressures. The time it takes to collect accounts receivable depends on industry norms in terms of credit terms, as well as the firm's policies for setting credit standards and carrying out collection efforts.

Credit Analysis

Credit analysis involves appraising the creditworthiness or quality of a potential customer. It answers the question, should credit be granted? The decision is made on the basis of the applicant's character, capacity, capital, collateral, and conditions—the five C's of credit analysis. *Character* is the ethical quality of the applicant upon which one can base a judgment about his or her willingness to pay bills and is best judged by reviewing his past credit history for long overdue or unpaid obligations. *Capacity* is the ability to pay bills and often involves an examination of liquidity ratios. *Capital* indicates the adequacy of owners' equity relative to existing liabilities as the underlying support for creditworthiness. *Collateral* reflects whether assets are available to provide security for the potential credit. *Conditions* refer to the current economic climate and state of the business cycle. They are an important consideration in assessing whether the applicant can meet credit obligations.

Once a firm has established its credit quality standards, credit analysis is used to determine whether an applicant is granted credit, is rejected, or falls into a marginal category. Whether or not credit should be extended to marginal applicants depends on such factors as the prevailing economic conditions and the extent to which the selling firm has excess production capacity. During periods of economic downturn and excess capacity, a firm may need to sell to lower quality applicants who may be slow paying but are not likely to default.

Credit-Reporting Agencies

Several sources of credit information are available to aid a firm in deciding whether or not to extend credit. *Credit bureaus* exist to obtain credit information about business firms and individuals. They are nonprofit institutions, established and supported by the businesses they serve.

character
ethical quality upon which one can base a judgment about a customer's willingness to pay bills

capacity
ability to pay bills

capital
adequacy of owners' equity relative to existing liabilities

collateral
whether assets are available to provide security for the potential credit

conditions
current economic climate and state of the business cycle

credit bureaus
source of credit information about business firms and individuals

WHAT'S THE
SCORE?

When many customers want to apply for credit, in-depth credit analysis focusing on the 5 C's is not practical. Companies that offer credit cards use a sophisticated statistical tool called credit scoring. Credit scoring takes information about thousands of customers and, through computer number-crunching, develops a formula that tries to predict who is a good credit risk (someone who will likely pay their bill in a timely manner) and who is a poor credit risk. Credit scoring models use quantitative items such as a person's income, past mortgage or credit card payment history, marital status, homeowner/renter status, and current debts to make this determination.

But such models will make errors. One person applied for a credit card and was rejected despite having a clean credit record. He earns $123,100 in salary at age 41 in a job with excellent security. The person was Lawrence B. Lindsey, who at the time was on the Board of Governors of the Federal Reserve System. A man who helps set interest rate and bank policy was rejected because the computer models could not handle the qualitative data that explained why his credit report appeared as it did. Ironically, in a speech in 1994, Mr. Lindsey predicted the following about credit scoring: "We will obtain the fairness of the machine, but lose the judgment, talents and sense of justice that only humans can bring to decision making."

Source: David Wessel, "A Man Who Governs Credit Is Denied a Toys 'R' Us Card," *The Wall Street Journal* (December 14, 1995): B1.

The local mercantile, or business, credit bureau provides a central record for credit information on firms in the community. Bureau members submit lists of their customers to the bureau. The bureau determines the credit standing of these customers by contacting other bureau members who have extended credit to them. Thus, a member firm need only contact its credit bureau for information on prospective customers rather than deal with many individual firms.

The exchange of mercantile credit information from bureau to bureau is accomplished through the National Credit Interchange System. Credit bureau reports are factual rather than analytical, and it is up to each credit analyst to interpret the facts.

Local retail credit bureaus have been established to consolidate and distribute credit information on individuals in the community. These organizations are generally owned and operated by participating members on a nonprofit basis. A central organization known as the Associated

Credit Bureaus of America enables local retail credit bureaus in the United States to transmit credit information from bureau to bureau.

U.S. businesses selling to foreign customers encounter all the problems involved in a domestic sale, such as credit checking, plus several others. Among these are increased distance, language differences, complicated shipping and government regulations, differences in legal systems, and political instability. To help exporters with these problems, the National Association of Credit Management established the Foreign Credit Interchange Bureau. Just as local credit bureaus increase their information on business credit risks by pooling credit and collection experience, so the members of the Foreign Credit Interchange Bureau have established a central file of information covering several decades of credit experience. The Bureau is located in New York to serve the numerous export and financial organizations there that do business overseas.

Some private firms also operate as credit-reporting agencies. The best known is Dun & Bradstreet, which has been in operation for well over a century and provides credit information on businesses of all kinds. The information that is assembled and evaluated is brought into the company through many channels. The company employs full- and part-time employees for direct investigation, communicates directly with business establishments by mail to supplement information files, and obtains the financial statements of companies being evaluated. All information filed with public authorities and financial and trade papers is carefully gathered and analyzed to produce a credit analysis. The basic service supplied to the manufacturers, wholesalers, banks, and insurance companies who subscribe to Dun & Bradstreet is rendered in two ways: through written reports on individual businesses and through a reference book.

A Dun & Bradstreet report is typically divided into five sections: (1) rating and summary, (2) trade payments, (3) financial information, (4) operation and location, and (5) history. In addition, they publish a composite reference book of ratings on thousands of manufacturers, wholesalers, retailers, and other businesses six times per year.

Credit Terms and Collection Efforts

Credit extended on purchases to a firm's customers is called ***trade credit*** and will be discussed more fully in Chapter 16. This credit appears as accounts payable on the balance sheet of the customer, and as receivables to the seller. The seller sets the terms of the credit. For example, the firm might require full payment in 60 days, expressed as net 60. If all customers pay promptly in 60 days, this would result in a receivables turnover of 365/60 or about six times a year.[3] Thus, annual net sales of $720,000 would

trade credit
credit extended on purchases to a firm's customers

---

3.   The turnover of current asset accounts such as receivables and inventories, like total assets turnover, is an asset utilization ratio. A higher ratio implies better usage of assets.

require an average receivables investment of about $120,000. A change in credit terms or in the enforcement of the terms through the collection effort will alter the average investment in receivables. The imposition of net 50-day terms would lead to an increase in the receivables turnover to 7.3 (365/50) times and the average investment in receivables would decline to about $100,000 ($720,000/7.3). If it costs, say, 15 percent to finance assets, then the $20,000 reduction in receivables would result in a savings of $3,000 ($20,000 × 15%).

We are assuming that a reduction in the credit period and in the receivables portion of the short-term operating cycle will not cause lost sales. The financial manager must be very careful not to impose credit terms that will lower sales and cause lost profits which would more than offset any financing cost savings.

The collection effort involves administering past due accounts. Techniques include sending letters, making telephone calls, and even making personal visits for very large customers with past due bills. If the customer continues to fail to pay a bill, then the account may be turned over to a commercial collection firm. If this fails, the last resort is to take legal action.

A lax collection policy may result in the average collection period for receivables being substantially longer than the credit period stated in the terms. As we have seen earlier, the average collection period is the accounts receivables divided by the net sales divided by 365. For example, a firm might sell on credit terms of net 60 days and have net sales of $720,000 and an accounts receivable balance of $150,000. For this firm, the average collection period is:

$$\frac{\text{Accounts receivable}}{\text{Net sales}/365} = \frac{\$150,000}{\$720,000/365} = \frac{\$150,000}{\$1,973} = 76 \text{ days}$$

This shows that the accounts receivable are outstanding an average of 76 days instead of the 60-day credit period. Increasing credit standards or improving the collection effort might reduce the average collection period to 60 days and the accounts receivable balance to $120,000.

Lowering a firm's credit standards or customer credit quality will cause the average collection period to lengthen—poorer quality customers are generally slower payers. Thus the financial manager must balance the advantages of increased sales from more customers against the cost of financing higher receivable investments and increased collection costs.

For example, suppose a firm is considering lowering its credit standards to increase sales. They estimate sales will rise by $100,000. Additional bad debt expense from poor credit risks is expected to be 5 percent, leaving a net increase of $95,000. With a profit margin of 10 percent, the incremental benefit of lowering standards is $9,500.

The costs of lowering credit standards will be the cost of financing higher receivables and inventory balances. If sales rise $100,000, the firm expects its average receivables balance will rise by $14,000 and its average inventory balance will rise by $18,000, for an increase of $32,000 in current assets. If the cost of financing these assets is 15 percent, the cost of the looser credit policy is $32,000 × 0.15 or $4,800. The incremental benefit of $9,500 is larger than the incremental cost, $4,800, so the firm should go ahead with its plan.

INVENTORY MANAGEMENT

Inventory administration is primarily a production management function. The length of the production process and the production manager's willingness to accept delays will influence the amount invested in raw materials and work-in-process. The amount of finished goods on hand may vary depending on the firm's willingness to accept stock-outs and lost sales.

Costs of owning raw materials, such as financing, storage, and insurance, need to be balanced against the costs of ordering the materials. Production managers attempt to balance these costs by determining the optimal number of units to order that will minimize inventory costs of total raw materials.

Let's assume that a firm's cost of goods sold is $600,000 and it has inventories on hand of $100,000. Recall that the inventory turnover is computed as follows:

$$\frac{\text{Cost of goods sold}}{\text{Inventories}} = \frac{\$600,000}{\$100,000} = 6 \text{ times}$$

If the firm is able to increase its inventory turnover to, say, eight times, then the investment in inventories could be reduced to $75,000 ($600,000/8) and some financing costs would be saved. However, if a tight inventory policy is imposed, lost sales due to stock-outs could result in lost profits that more than offset financing cost savings. Thus the financial manager must balance possible savings against potential added costs when managing investments in inventories.

The just-in-time inventory control system is gaining increased acceptance by firms that are trying to reduce the amount of inventories they must carry. Under this system, substantial coordination is required between the manufacturer and its suppliers so that materials needed in the manufacturing process are delivered just in time to avoid halts in production. For example, automobile manufacturers who used to keep a two-week supply of certain parts now place orders on a daily basis and expect daily shipment and delivery.

career profiles

> "Managing people is probably the hardest and most rewarding part of the job."

Q: Is it correct to describe your work as private accounting?

A: Yes. I am the Controller at Fath Management which is a real estate management company. I manage the in-house accounting department there.

Q: What does your job entail?

A: Our department basically handles all of the money that passes in and out of the company which includes the thousands of rent checks we receive each month from our tenants and all of the expenditures necessary to operate our properties. We also produce a variety of monthly reports which show how each property is performing relative to its budget and to the previous year. These reports help us make decisions about upgrading properties and adjusting rents, among other things. I'm also involved in the creation of next year's budget for each property which we put together in the last quarter of the year.

Q: Where does the title Controller come from?

A: Part of it relates to financial controls. I design and implement the appropriate financial controls and approvals throughout the company so that cash coming in and going out is handled correctly. These are basically checks and balances to protect Fath's interests.

Q: Do you have the same kind of busy season at the end of the year that public accountants do?

A: It is a busy time of year for us. During the winter we assemble our year-end financial statements and the figures needed for our tax returns. We spend a lot of time on taxes. Each of our forty properties has its own tax return, so there's a lot of data to pull together and organize. We have to file returns in the four different states where we own properties, so we have one of the Big Six firms handle the actual return preparation, but we still have to assemble all the required information.

Q: You previously worked for one of the Big Six firms. How would you compare that to your current experience at Fath?

A: The Big Six was an excellent preparation for what I do now. You receive so much training and experience, it's almost like getting another degree. The biggest difference I've found since joining Fath is the size of the organization. Our company has a small management team and we're expected to do a lot. I interact with the owner of the firm all the time. There's more latitude to make decisions and take the initiative, but also the accountability that goes along with that.

Q: Do you manage a staff?

A: Yes. The accounting manager, systems administrator, and seven accounting clerks are in my department. I spend a lot of my time doing the traditional managerial tasks—reviewing, training, motivating, disciplining. Managing people is probably the hardest and most rewarding part of the job. I have a great group and that makes my life a lot easier.

SUMMARY

It is cash, not earnings, that keeps a firm in business. Company treasurers are therefore mainly interested watching a firm's cash flows and forecasting future cash flows to ensure adequate cash is available to pay the firm's obligations when they are due. This chapter discussed several aspects of working capital management that will be of practical concern to those watching the firm's cash flow. A firm's operating cycle measures the time it takes from when raw materials are ordered, processed in finished goods, sold, and cash is collected from their sale. The cash conversion cycle is similar to the operating cycle except that it measures the time between when the firm pays for its materials purchases and when cash is collected from their sale. Firms with faster inventory turnovers, faster receivables turnovers, and slower average payment periods will have shorter cash conversion cycles. The longer this cycle is, the greater the firm's financing needs and accompanying financing costs. The cycle and its components will be affected by seasonal sales patterns and business cycles.

A cash budget provides a treasurer some detail on expected cash inflows and outflows. Specifically, it shows the amounts and the source of expected cash inflows and outflows. By using the cash budget, the treasurer can plan how to best invest cash surpluses and borrow to cover cash deficits. Investing excess cash in marketable securities is a process in which the treasurer tries to balance the need for safety and liquidity of the invested funds with the desire to earn returns on the investment. Popular marketable securities investments include Treasury bills, negotiable CDs, commercial paper, and Eurodollar deposits.

Marketing concerns are a major determinant of accounts receivable policies. Production and purchasing issues may dominate the inventory decision. Nonetheless, financial managers need to be part of these strategic discussions and aware of the factors that affect these decisions. More and more firms have realized that significant amounts of cash are tied up in working capital. Attempts to reduce receivables and inventories can free up cash, lead to more efficient operations, and increase firm profitability and shareholder wealth.

KEY TERMS

capacity	credit bureau
capital	operating cycle
cash budget	precautionary motive
cash conversion cycle	speculative motive
character	trade credit
collateral	transactions motive
conditions	

DISCUSSION QUESTIONS

1. What is meant by working capital?
2. Briefly describe a manufacturing firm's operating cycle.
3. Explain how the cash conversion cycle differs from the operating cycle.
4. Describe how the length of the cash conversion cycle is determined.
5. Explain how the length of the operating cycle affects the amount of funds invested in accounts receivable and inventories.
6. What affects the amount of financing provided by accounts payable as viewed in terms of the cash conversion cycle?
7. What is a cash budget? How does the treasurer use forecasts of cash surpluses and cash deficits?
8. Three sets of information are needed to construct a cash budget. Explain what they are.
9. Why might firms want to maintain minimum desired cash balances?
10. What are the sources of cash inflows to a firm over any time frame?
11. What are the sources of cash outflows from a firm over any time frame?
12. How does the choice of level or seasonal production affect a firm's cash over the course of a year?
13. Describe what happens to a firm's current asset accounts if the firm has seasonal sales and they use a) level production, or b) seasonal production.
14. Describe the three motives or reasons for holding cash.
15. What characteristics should an investment have to qualify as an acceptable marketable security?
16. Identify and briefly describe several financial instruments that are used as marketable securities.
17. What is credit analysis? Identify the five C's of credit analysis.
18. Describe various credit-reporting agencies that provide information on business credit applicants.
19. How do credit terms and collection efforts affect the investment in accounts receivable?
20. How is the financial manager involved in the management of inventories?

PROBLEMS

1. Pretty Lady Cosmetic Products has an average production process time of 40 days. Finished goods are kept on hand for an average of 15 days before they are sold. Accounts receivable are outstanding an average of 35 days, and the firm receives 40 days of credit on its purchases from suppliers.
    a. Estimate the average length of the firm's short-term operating cycle. How often would the cycle turn over in a year?

b. Assume net sales of $1,200,000 and cost of goods sold of $900,000. Determine the average investment in accounts receivable, inventories, and accounts payable. What would be the net financing need considering only these three accounts?

2. The Robinson Company has the following current assets and current liabilities for these two years:

	1994	1995
Cash and marketable securities	$ 50,000	$ 50,000
Accounts receivable	300,000	350,000
Inventories	350,000	500,000
Total current assets	$700,000	$900,000
Accounts payable	$200,000	$250,000
Bank loan	0	150,000
Accruals	150,000	200,000
Total current liabilities	$350,000	$600,000

If sales in 1994 were $1.2 million and sales in 1995 were $1.3 million, and cost of goods sold were 70 percent of sales, how long were Robinson's operating cycles and cash conversion cycles in 1994 and 1995? What caused them to change during this time?

3. The Robinson Company from Problem 2 had net sales of $1,200,000 in 1994 and $1,300,000 in 1995.
    a. Determine the receivables turnover in each year.
    b. Calculate the average collection period for each year.
    c. Based on the receivables turnover for 1994, estimate the investment in receivables if net sales were $1,300,000 in 1995. How much of a change in the 1995 receivables occurred?

4. ˙ Suppose the Robinson Company had a cost of goods sold of $1,000,000 in 1994 and $1,200,000 in 1995.
    a. Calculate the inventory turnover for each year. Comment on your findings.
    b. What would have been the amount of inventories in 1995 if the 1994 turnover ratio had been maintained?

5. Following are financial statements for the Genatron Manufacturing Corporation for the years 1994 and 1995:

SELECTED BALANCE SHEET INFORMATION

	1994	1995
Cash	$ 50,000	$ 40,000
Accounts receivable	200,000	260,000
Inventory	450,000	500,000
Total current assets	$700,000	$800,000
Bank loan, 10%	$ 90,000	$ 90,000
Accounts payable	130,000	170,000

Accruals	50,000	70,000
Total current liabilities	$270,000	$330,000
Long-term debt, 12%	300,000	400,000

SELECTED INCOME STATEMENT INFORMATION

	1994	1995
Net sales	$1,300,000	$1,500,000
Cost of goods sold	780,000	900,000
Gross profit	$ 520,000	$ 600,000
Net income	$ 93,000	$ 114,000

Calculate Genatron's operating cycle and cash conversion cycle for 1994 and 1995. Why did they change between 1994 and 1995?

6. Genatron Manufacturing expects its sales to increase by 10 percent in 1996. Estimate the firm's investment in accounts receivable, inventory, and accounts payable in 1996.

7. Suppose Global Manufacturing is planning to change is credit policies next year. It anticipates that 10 percent of each month's sales will be for cash; two-thirds of each month's receivables will be collected in the following month, and one-third will be collected two months following their sale. Assuming the Global's sales forecast in Table 15.5 remains the same and the expected cash outflows in Table 15.6 remain the same, determine Global's revised cash budget.

8. Global's suppliers are upset that Global takes two months to pay their accounts payable; they demand that in the following year Global pay its bills within 30 days, or one month of the purchase.
   a. Using this new information, update Global's cash outflow forecast shown in Table 15.6.
   b. Using the cash inflows given in Table 15.5, construct a revised cash budget for Global.

9. Of its monthly sales, The Kingsman Company historically has had 25 percent cash sales with the remainder paid within one month. Each month's purchases are equal to 75 percent of the next month's sales forecast; suppliers are paid one month after the purchase. Salary expenses are $50,000 a month, except in January when bonuses equal to 1 percent of the previous year's sales are paid out. Interest on a bond issue of $10,000 is due in March. Overhead and utilities are expected to be $25,000 monthly. Dividends of $45,000 are to be paid in March. Kingsman's 1994 sales totaled $2 million; December sales were $200,000. Kingsman's estimated sales for January are $100,000; February, $200,000; March, $250,000, and April, $300,000.
   a. What are Kingsman's expected monthly cash inflows during January through April?
   b. What are Kingsman's expected monthly cash outflows during January through April?

c. Determine Kingman's monthly cash budget for January through April. Assume a minimum desired cash balance of $40,000 and an ending December cash balance of $50,000.

10. Redo problem number 9, using the following monthly sales estimates:

January	$300,000
February	$250,000
March	$200,000
April	$100,000

11. Pa Bell, Inc., wants to increase its credit standards. They expect sales will fall by $50,000 and bad debt expense will fall by 10 percent of this amount. The firm has a 15 percent profit margin on its sales. The tougher credit standards will lower the firm's average receivables balance by $10,000 and the average inventory balance by $8,000. The cost of financing current assets is estimated to be 12 percent. Should Pa Bell adopt the tighter credit standards? Why or why not?

SELF-TEST QUESTIONS

1. Which one of the following asset accounts is not a part of a firm's working capital?
    a. cash and marketable securities
    b. accounts receivable
    c. inventories
    d. fixed assets

2. A survey of financial managers found they spend nearly what percent of their time dealing with financial planning, budgeting, and working capital issues?
    a. 10 percent
    b. 30 percent
    c. 50 percent
    d. 70 percent

3. The time it takes between when materials are ordered and cash is collected from receivables is referred to as the:
    a. operating cycle
    b. cash conversion cycle
    c. assets turnover cycle
    d. sales or revenues cycle

4. If a firm purchases materials on credit and thus has accounts payable, its cash conversion cycle will be:
    a. longer than its operating cycle
    b. the same length as its operating cycle
    c. shorter than its operating cycle
    d. the same length as its sales turnover cycle

5. Business firms hold cash and marketable securities for which of the following reasons or motives?
   a. transactions, precautionary, and goodwill motives
   b. precautionary, speculative, and goodwill motives
   c. transactions, precautionary, and speculative motives
   d. precautionary, goodwill, and transactions motives
6. Which of the following marketable securities is sold at a discount through competitive bidding in a weekly auction?
   a. U.S. Treasury bills
   b. federal funds
   c. commercial paper
   d. negotiable certificates of deposit
7. Deposits placed in foreign banks that remain denominated in U.S. dollars are called:
   a. bankers' acceptances
   b. Eurodollars
   c. federal funds
   d. commercial paper
8. Which one of the following is not considered to be one of the five C's of credit analysis?
   a. character
   b. capacity
   c. capital
   d. collateral
   e. caution
9. Which one of the following is a private firm that operates as a credit-reporting agency?
   a. National Credit Interchange Bureau
   b. Foreign Credit Interchange Bureau
   c. Dun & Bradstreet
   d. Merrill-Lynch

SELF-TEST PROBLEM

The Deuter Steel Products company has an average production process time of 30 days. Finished goods are kept on hand for an average of 15 days before they are sold. Accounts receivable are outstanding on average for 30 days and Deuter receives 40 days of credit on its purchases from suppliers.
a. Estimate the average length of Deuter's operating and cash conversion cycles.
b. Assume that Deuter has net sales of $1,200,000 and a cost of goods sold of $1,000,000. Determine the average investment in accounts receivable, inventories, and accounts payable. What would be the net financing need considering only these three accounts?

SUGGESTED READINGS

Dickerson, Bodil, B.J. Campsey, and Eugene F. Brigham. *Introduction to Financial Management*, 4e. Orlando, FL: The Dryden Press, 1995. Chaps. 8, 9, and 10.

Gitman, Lawrence J., and Charles E. Maxwell. "Financial Activities of Major U.S. Firms: Survey and Analysis of Fortune's 1000." *Financial Management*, Winter 1985, pp. 57–65.

Harrington, Diana R., and Brent D. Wilson. *Corporate Financial Analysis*, 4e. Homewood, IL: Richard D. Irwin, 1993. Chap. 3.

Keown, Arthur J., David F. Scott Jr., John D. Martin, and J. William Petty. *Foundations of Finance*. Englewood Cliffs, N.J.: Prentice-Hall Inc., 1994. Chaps. 14 and 15.

Klier, Thomas H. "The Impact of Lean Manufacturing on Sourcing Relationships." *Economic Perspectives*, Federal Reserve Bank of Chicago (July/August 1994): 8–18.

Pinches, George E. *Financial Management*, 5e. New York: Harper & Row, 1994. Chaps. 19, 20, and 21.

Peterson, Pamela P. *Financial Management and Analysis*. New York, NY: McGraw-Hill Inc., 1994. Chap. 15.

Rao, Ramesh K.S. *Financial Management*, 3e. Cincinnati, Ohio: South-Western College Publishing, 1995. Chaps. 21 and 22.

ANSWERS TO SELF-TEST QUESTIONS   1. d, 2. d, 3. a, 4. c, 5. c, 6. a, 7. b, 8. e, 9. c

ANSWERS TO SELF-TEST PROBLEM

a.

Inventory period	45 days (30 + 15)
Accounts receivable period	30 days
Operating cycle	75 days
Accounts payable period	−40 days
Cash conversion cycle	35 days

b. Inventory turnover = 365/45 = 8.1 times
Cost of goods sold = $1,000,000
Average inventory investment = $1,000,000/8.1 = $123,457

Accounts receivable turnover = 365/30 = 12.2 times
Net sales = $1,200,000
Average accounts receivable investment = $1,200,000/12.2 = $98,361

Accounts payable turnover = 365/40 = 9.1 times
Cost of goods sold = $1,000,000
Average accounts payable financing = $1,000,000/9.1 = $109,890

Net financing needs:	
Inventory investment	$123,457
Accounts receivable investment	98,361
	221,818
Less accounts payable financing	−109,890
	$111,928

CHAPTER 16

Short-Term Business Financing

AFTER STUDYING THIS CHAPTER, YOU SHOULD BE ABLE TO:

- Identify and describe strategies for financing working capital.
- Identify and briefly explain the factors that affect short-term financing requirements.
- Identify the types of unsecured loans made by commercial banks to business borrowers.
- Describe the use of accounts receivable, inventory, and other sources of security for bank loans.
- Explain the characteristics, terms, and costs of trade credit.
- Explain the role of commercial finance companies in providing short-term business financing.
- Briefly describe how factors function as a source of short-term business financing.
- Describe how the Small Business Administration aids businesses in meeting short-term borrowing needs.
- Describe how and why commercial paper is used as a source of short-term financing by large corporations.

Many times companies use long-term financing sources, such as the stocks and bonds we discussed in Chapter 10, to acquire fixed assets. But the firm's current assets need to be financed as well. Sometimes firms use mainly short-term financing sources to finance current assets, sometimes they rely mainly on long-term sources, and at times they use both.

In this chapter we'll review several strategies for financing current assets. As we shall see, management must make an important strategic decision when deciding on the relative amounts of short-term and long-term financing that the firm uses to finance its assets. The choices a firm makes affect its financing costs, its liquidity, and even the chance of eventual bankruptcy. The chapter closes with a review of various short-term financing sources that firms can access. The tremendous resources of the nation's banking system make commercial banks the largest provider of short-term loan funds for businesses. Short-term funds also come in the form of trade credit extended between businesses. Other important sources of short-term funds are commercial finance companies, factors, the Small Business Administration, and commercial paper.

STRATEGIES FOR FINANCING WORKING CAPITAL

Working capital includes a firm's current assets, which consist of cash and marketable securities in addition to accounts receivable and inventories. Current liabilities generally consist of accounts payable (trade credit), notes payable (bank loans), and accrued liabilities. Net working capital is defined as current assets less current liabilities. When net working capital is positive, it represents the portion of current assets that is financed through long-term financing, as seen in Figure 16.1. Figure 16.1 shows the basic structure of a balance sheet with general account categories. Assets are either current or fixed; financing sources are either current liabilities, long-term debt, or equity. In Figure 16.1 we see that part of current assets are financed by current liabilities, but that current assets are also partially financed by the firm's long-term financing mix of long-term debt and equity. If net working capital is negative (current liabilities are greater than current assets), it represents the portion of fixed assets that are financed by current liabilities, as seen in Figure 16.2.

Figure 16.3 shows how assets may fluctuate over time for a growing firm.[1] We have depicted a pattern of rising and falling asset values within each time interval or year because of seasonal sales patterns. As we saw in Chapter 15, seasonal sales variations will have important implications for a firm's current assets. Inventories must be increased to meet seasonal demand, and receivables will go up (and inventories fall) as sales increase. The need for funds will fall as accounts receivable are collected. Thus sea-

---

1.   Whether the sales or asset trend is rising, falling, or stable over time does not affect our conclusions. We merely use a rising asset trend since many firms do enjoy growth over time.

FIGURE 16.1   Balance Sheet with Positive Net Working Capital

Current Assets Net Working Capital > 0	Current Liabilities
	Long-Term Debt
Fixed Assets	Equity

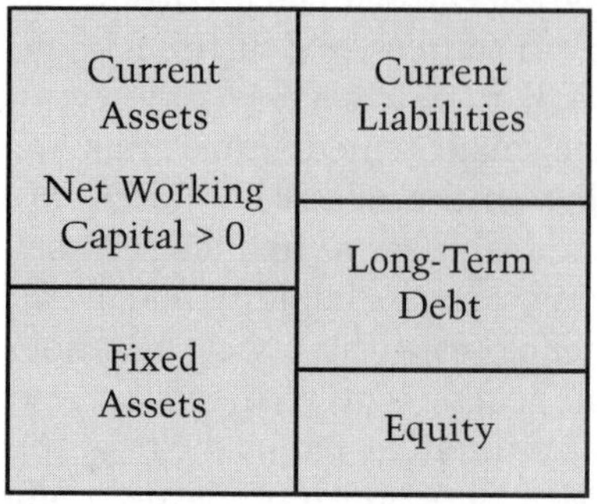

FIGURE 16.2   Balance Sheet with Negative Net Working Capital

Current Assets	Current Liabilities
	Net Working Capital < 0
Fixed Assets	Long-Term Debt
	Equity

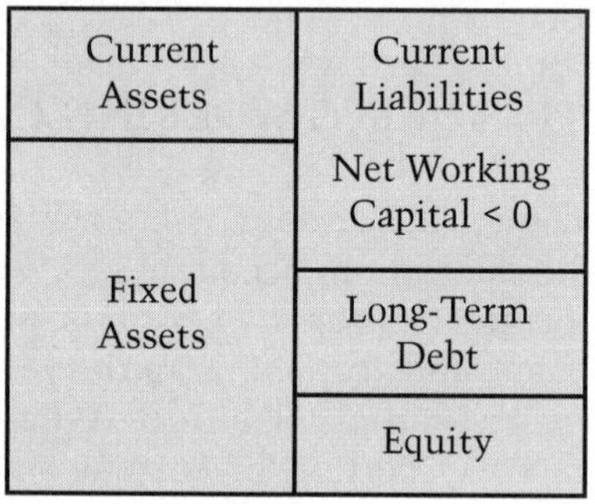

FIGURE 16.3   Asset Trends for a Growing Firm

Assets ($)

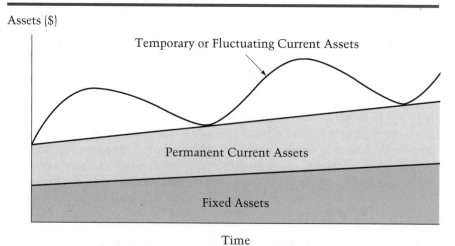

Temporary or Fluctuating Current Assets

Permanent Current Assets

Fixed Assets

Time

sonal variation in sales requires only temporary additional investments in current assets such as inventory and accounts receivable.

This level of current assets actually has two components: permanent current assets and temporary or fluctuating current assets. Temporary current assets rise and fall because of the seasonal sales fluctuations mentioned above. The permanent current assets reflect the minimum investment level in cash, accounts receivable, and inventories needed to support sales.[2] While individual accounts are collected and inventory items sold, they are replaced by others, so the dollar values of the accounts will maintain some minimum level or possibly grow over time as sales rise.

There are several strategies a firm can use to finance its fixed assets, permanent current assets, and temporary current assets. They are illustrated in Figure 16.4.

Panel A of Figure 16.4 shows a balanced approach for financing a firm's assets. Notice that all of the fixed assets and the permanent current assets are financed with long-term debt and equity provided by the firm's owners. The temporary current assets are financed by short-term liabilities. The balanced approach also is referred to as the ***maturity matching approach*** because the financial manager attempts to match the maturities of the assets by financing with comparable maturities. Fixed assets and the level of permanent current assets have long maturities, so they should be financed with long-term financing sources. Temporary current assets are short-lived, so they should be financed with short-term financing. An example would be using a bank loan to finance inventory buildup in anticipation of heavy seasonal sales. After the inventory is sold and cash is received, the loan is repaid. With maturity matching the amount of current assets is greater than that of current liabilities, so net working capital will be positive, as in Figure 16.1. Consequently, firms using maturity matching will have current ratios greater than 1.0.

Panels B and C of Figure 16.4 show two other possible financing strategies. They are deviations from maturity matching. One uses relatively more short-term financing, the other uses relatively more long-term financing than the maturity matching strategy.

Panel B in Figure 16.4 depicts an aggressive approach to the financing of a firm's current assets in that *all* current assets, both temporary and permanent, are financed with short-term financing. Only fixed assets are financed with long-term debt and equity funds. Such an approach could result in liquidity problems should sales decline in the future. Since all current assets are financed with current liabilities, the current ratio would be equal to 1.0 under this aggressive scenario. An even more aggressive approach would be for the firm to rely on short-term funds to finance all the current assets as well as some of the fixed assets. In such a case, the structure

maturity matching approach
financing strategy that attempts to match the maturities of assets with the maturities of the liabilities with which they are financed

2.   For example, recall our Chapter 15 cash budget discussion concerning the firm's minimum desired cash balance; this can be considered a component of the permanent current assets.

FIGURE 16.4   Financing Strategies

Assets ($)

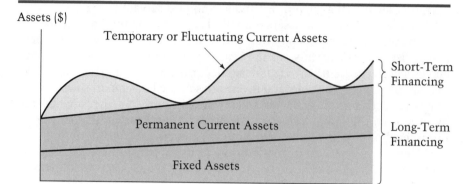

Panel A: Maturity Matching

Assets ($)

Panel B: Aggressive Financing

Assets ($)

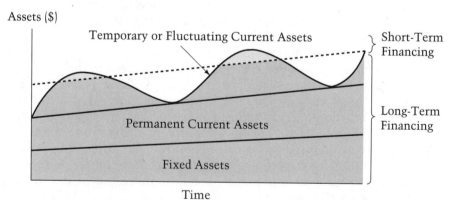

Panel C: Conservative Financing

of the firm's balance sheet would resemble Figure 16.2. Its net working capital would be negative and its current ratio would be less than 1.0.

Panel C in Figure 16.4 depicts a very conservative approach to the financing of a firm's assets. In this case, except for automatic or "spontaneous" financing provided by accounts payable and accrued liabilities, all the financing is done through long-term debt and equity funds. At times the firm will have excess liquidity, when available funds exceed necessary current asset levels. During these periods the firm will have large cash balances and will probably seek to invest the excess cash in marketable securities. As the amount of current assets is much greater than that of current liabilities, net working capital will be positive and the current ratio will comfortably exceed 1.0.

Like many other aspects of finance, the decision as to how much short-term financing the firm should use relative to long-term financing has risk/return implications. Recalling our discussion about the yield curve in Chapter 8, we know that short-term securities generally have lower yields than long-term securities. From the borrower's perspective, that means the cost of paying short-term financing charges (short-term interest rates) will be less than the cost of paying long-term financing charges (long-term interest rates and equity holders' required rates of return).[3] Compared to a conservative plan that relies more on long-term financing, an aggressive financing plan using relatively more short-term financing will generally have lower financing costs and will, all else being equal, be more profitable. As it comes due, short-term debt is replaced by new short-term debt. This replacement is called rolling over the debt. But with the expectation of higher return comes higher risk. Short-term interest rates are more volatile than long-term rates and in periods of tight money or in periods of inflation jitters short-term rates can rise quickly, sharply increasing the cost of using short-term money. Sources of short-term credit also may disappear. In such a credit crunch, banks may not have enough funds to lend to satisfy demand and investors may not be willing to purchase the firm's short-term debt. A conservative financing plan has a higher financing cost, but with lower risk of not being able to borrow when short-term funds are needed.

Caldor Corporation, a discount retailer, was using an aggressive financing approach in the early 1990s. Because of this strategy, it filed for bankruptcy in September 1995 despite earning profits.[4] Caldor chose to finance a major expansion and remodeling project with its working capital. Caldor's working capital fell precipitously—from over $60 million in early 1994 to

---

3.   We discussed security holders' rates of return in Chapters 10 and 12. We will more closely examine the cost of financing a firm with long-term debt and equity in Chapter 18.
4.   As we reviewed in Chapter 13, this is another example that net income and cash flow are *not* the same concept.

1995 was the year of a credit crunch in Germany. Mid-size firms that employ between 20 and 500 workers, the so-called *Mittelstand*, were filing for bankruptcy in record numbers—28,000 in all. Banks, hurt by bad loans during a recent recession, were hesitant to lend and take chances. This was quite a change from past bank and borrower relationships in Germany. In the past, German banks would provide much assistance to such firms. But that formerly paternalistic relationship has turned sour. *Mittelstand* firms had, on the whole, become too reliant on rolling over bank debt. A poll of *Mittelstand* companies showed over half needing capital and over a third stating that banks were being too restrictive.

Source: Matt Marshall, "Timid Lending Hits Germany's Exporters," *The Wall Street Journal* (November 21, 1995): A12.

under $10 million in early 1995, when it should have been flush with cash following the Christmas selling season. Caldor's short-term creditors encouraged it to borrow long-term funds or issue stock to move to a maturity matching or less aggressive financing plan, but Caldor refused. Subsequently, alarmed at Caldor's decreasing liquidity, banks grew hesitant to lend and factors—firms that guaranteed Caldor's payments to its suppliers[5]—grew nervous. Lower than expected sales during the 1994 Christmas season and early 1995 hurt Caldor's cash position even more. When GE Capital Corporation refused Caldor's request for a $30 million loan, suppliers and factors delayed inventory shipments and demanded that Caldor pay its bills faster. Finally, factors told Caldor's suppliers that they would no longer guarantee payment of the money Caldor owed to them, in effect shutting off Caldor's credit and inventory shipments. This was the immediate reason for Caldor's September 1995 bankruptcy filing. But it was Caldor's choice of an aggressive financing plan, relying on short-term funds to finance growing fixed assets, that was the ultimate cause of the failure.[6]

FACTORS AFFECTING SHORT-TERM FINANCING

Whether the firm uses an aggressive approach, a conservative approach, or maturity matching depends upon an evaluation of many factors affecting

5.   Factors are an important source of financing for many firms, especially those in the retail trade. We'll discuss them in more detail later in this chapter.
6.   Laura Bird, "Caldor Files for Bankruptcy Protection in Face of Weak Sales, Jittery Suppliers," *The Wall Street Journal* (September 19, 1995): A3; Roger Lowenstein, "Lenders' Stampede Tramples Caldor," *The Wall Street Journal* (October 26, 1995): C1.

the business. The company's operating characteristics will affect a firm's financing strategy. Other factors having an impact include cost, flexibility, the ease of future financing, and other qualitative influences.

OPERATING CHARACTERISTICS

The nature of the demand for funds depends in part on the industry in which a business operates and on the characteristics of the business itself. It is influenced by such factors as seasonal variations in sales and on the growth of the company. The need for funds also depends upon fluctuations of the business cycle.

Industry and Company Factors

Some industries, such as utilities and oil refineries, have larger proportions of fixed assets to current assets. Others, such as service industries, have larger proportions of current assets to fixed assets. Within each industry, some firms will choose different operating structures with different levels of operating leverage.

The composition of the asset structure, or current assets versus fixed assets, of an industry and of a firm within that industry is a significant factor in determining the relative proportions of their long-term and short-term financing. An industry which has a need for large amounts of fixed capital can do more long-term financing than one which has a relatively small investment in fixed assets.

While manufacturing companies often require substantial investments in fixed assets for manufacturing purposes, they also have significant investments in inventories and receivables. Manufacturers generally have a more equal balance between current and fixed assets than electric utility and telephone companies and so will use relatively more short-term financing than utilities. The same is true for large retail stores. They often lease their quarters and hold substantial assets in the form of inventories and receivables. They are characterized by relatively high current assets to fixed assets ratios and so will have a greater tendency than utilities to use short-term debt.

The size and age of a company and stage in its financial life cycle may also influence management's short-term/long-term financing mix decisions. A new company's only source of funds may be the owner and possibly his or her friends. Some long-term funds may be raised by mortgaging real estate and buying equipment on installment, and some current borrowing may be possible to meet seasonal needs. As a business grows it has more access to short-term capital from finance companies and banks. Further along, its growth and good record of profitability may enable a business to arrange longer-term financing with banks or other financial agencies such as insurance companies. At this stage in its financial development, it may also expand its group of owners as well by issuing stock to people other than the owner and a few friends.

The growth prospects of a company also have an effect on financing decisions. If a company is growing faster than the rate at which it can generate funds from internal sources, it must give careful consideration to a plan for long-term financing. Even if it can finance its needs in the current situation from short-term sources, it may not be wise to do so. Sound financial planning calls for raising long-term funds at appropriate times.

Seasonal Variation

Our earlier discussion of Figure 16.3 pointed out that seasonal variations in sales affect the demand for current assets. Inventories are built up to meet seasonal needs, and receivables rise as sales increase. The peak of receivables will come after the peak in sales, the intervening time depending on the credit terms and payment practices of customers. Accounts payable will also increase as inventories are purchased. The difference between the increase in current assets and accounts payable should be financed by

FAILING FROM SUCCESS

Yes, too much of a good thing can hurt you. Harvey Harris had a great idea—selling personalized calendars. His firm, Grandmother Calendar, failed because his marketing success was too much for his firm's production capabilities and finances.

Grandmother Calendar offered customers a truly personalized calendar. Customers could send in monthly photos or drawings for each of twelve months. Grandmother would scan them into a computer, put in special dates chosen by the customer, and send it back—all for $20. Mail-order firms and large retailers offered the kits, and sales exploded to multiples of Harris' sales expectations. Money required for operations was used instead to expand capacity. Still, only 200 of the complicated personalized calendars a day could be processed and orders were coming in at a rate of 1,000 a day. Overuse led to equipment failures and quality control problems. Many customers paid for their calendar orders by credit card, but Grandmother did not receive money from the credit card companies until the calendar was shipped to the customer. Before long, workers' paychecks began to bounce and soon thereafter Grandmother ceased operations, leaving many customers unhappy and angry.

Says Mr. Harris: "I made mistakes and did not track receivables, payables, and funding. I should have made, well, better decisions." Good words for all businesses to remember!

Source: Louise Lee, "A Company Failing from Too Much Success," *The Wall Street Journal* (March 17, 1995): B1.

short-term borrowing. That is because the need for funds will disappear as inventories are sold and accounts receivable are collected. When a need for additional funds is financed by a short-term loan, such a loan is said to be self-liquidating since funds are made available to repay it as inventories and receivables are reduced.

Sales Trend

A firm's sales trend affects the financing mix. As sales grow, fixed assets and current assets also must grow to support the sales growth, as depicted in Figure 16.3. This need for funds is ongoing unless the upward trend of sales is reversed.

If asset growth is initially financed by short-term borrowing, the outstanding borrowings will continue to rise as sales rise. The amount of debt may rise year by year as the growth trend continues upward. After a while the current ratio will drop to such a level that no financing institution will provide additional funds. The only alternative then is long-term financing.

As we will learn later in this chapter, short-term financing can be increased over time in relatively small increments, if needed, by applying for loans and negotiating with borrowers, as seen in Panel A of Figure 16.5. Long-term external financing, however, is "lumpy." Because of the time and cost of floating a bond or stock issue or negotiating a long-term loan or private placement, long-term securities are usually only issued in large quantities, as seen in Panel B of Figure 16.5.

Cyclical Variations

The need for current funds increases when there is an upswing in the business cycle or the sales cycle of an industry. Since the cycle is not regular in timing or degree, it is hard to predict exactly how much, or for how long, added funds will be needed. The need should be estimated for a year ahead in the budget and checked quarterly. When the sales volume of business decreases, the need for funds to finance accounts receivable and inventory will decrease as well. It is possible, however, that for a time during the downturn the need for financing will increase temporarily. This will occur if the cash conversion cycle lengthens as receivables are collected more slowly and inventories move more slowly and drop in value.

If cyclical needs for funds are met by current borrowing, the loan may not be self-liquidating in a year. There are hazards in financing these needs on a short-term basis. The lending institution may demand payment of all or part of the loan as business turns down. Funds may be needed more than ever at this stage of the cycle, and the need may last until receivables can be collected and inventory can be reduced. Firms in cyclical industries should use a more conservative approach that makes use of long-term financing. Major U.S automobile firms, in a highly cyclical business, have been preparing for the next recession. Ford Motor Company went through

FIGURE 16.5   Patterns of Short-Term and Long-Term Financing Needs Over Time for a Growing Firm

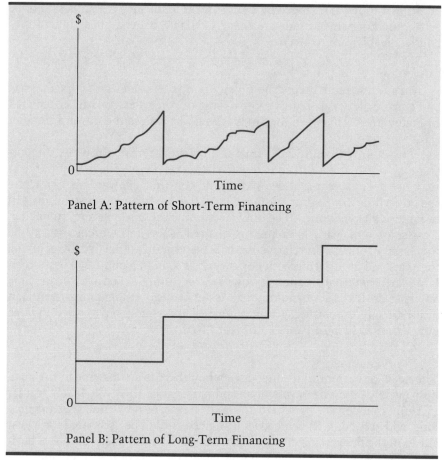

Panel A: Pattern of Short-Term Financing

Panel B: Pattern of Long-Term Financing

$10 billion in cash during the 1990–91 recession. At the end of 1995 Ford had $14 billion in cash and short-term marketable securities as a cushion for the next recession. It wasn't alone: General Motors had $11 billion, Chrysler, $7.6 billion.[7]

OTHER INFLUENCES IN SHORT-TERM FINANCING

There are other advantages to using short-term borrowing rather than other forms of financing. Short-term borrowing has more flexibility than

7.   Thomas T. Vogel, Jr., "Merger Wave Won't Create Debt Swamp," *The Wall Street Journal* (August 2, 1995): A2, A8.

long-term financing, since a business can borrow only those sums needed currently and pay them off if the need for financing diminishes. Long-term financing cannot be retired so easily and it may include a prepayment penalty, as is the case with the call premium for callable bonds. If an enterprise finances its growing current asset requirements entirely through long-term financing during a period of general business expansion, it may be burdened with excess funds and financing costs during a subsequent period of general business contraction. Using short-term financing along with long-term financing creates a financial flexibility that is not possible with long-term financing alone.

Short-term financing has advantages that result from continuing relationships with a bank or other financial institution. The firm that depends almost entirely upon long-term financing for its needs will not enjoy the close relationship with its bank that it might otherwise. A record of frequent borrowing and prompt repayment to a bank is an extremely important factor in sound financial management. A bank will make every effort to accommodate regular business customers who do this. The enterprise that has not established this type of working relationship with its bank will scarcely be in a position to seek special loans when it has emergency needs. The credit experience of a business with short-term financing may be the only basis on which its potential long-term lenders will be able to judge it. Hence, the business that intends to seek long-term loans may wish to establish a good credit reputation based on its short-term financing.

Offsetting these advantages of short-term financing is the need for frequent renewals. Even though short-term credit is usually easy to obtain, time and effort must be spent on it at frequent intervals due to the short duration of these loans. And when sales revenues decline, a great deal of negotiation may be required to receive needed credit.

Frequent maturities also create an added element of risk. The bank or finance company can call the loan whenever it is due. The bank may not want to roll over a loan. Borrowing costs also may rise if short-term interest rates increase. A company in a temporary slump due to the business cycle or some internal problem could possibly work out its problems in time with adequate financing. If the company had acquired funds on a long-term basis, it might have a better chance of resolving its problems. On the other hand, if it relies heavily on short-term financing, its loans may be reduced or not renewed, which may make it nearly impossible to recover and might even lead to liquidation.

Now that we have an understanding of short-term/long-term financing strategies and factors that affect the relative use of short-term financing, we will now turn our attention toward various sources of short-term financing. Short-term financing sources include bank loans, trade credit or accounts payable, commercial paper, and other sources.

COMMERCIAL BANK LENDING OPERATIONS

prime rate
interest rate the bank charges its most credit-worthy customers

Although in recent years many banks have required a pledge of specific assets, the unsecured loan still remains the primary type of loan arrangement. The stated rate on such loans is based upon the bank's **prime rate,** or the interest rate a bank charges its most creditworthy customers. Interest rates on loans typically are stated in terms of the prime rate plus a risk differential, such as prime + 2 percent. Loan papers will call this prime plus 2 or simply P + 2. Higher risk borrowers will have higher differentials to compensate the bank for lending to riskier customers.

BANK LINES OF CREDIT

line of credit
loan limit the bank establishes for each of its business customers

A business and a bank often have an agreement regarding the amount of credit that the business will have at its disposal. The loan limit that the bank establishes for each of its business customers is called a **line of credit.** Lines of credit cost the business only the normal interest for the period during which money is actually borrowed. Under this arrangement, the business does not wait until money is needed to negotiate the loan. Rather, it files the necessary financial statements and other evidences of financial condition with the bank prior to the need for credit. The banker is interested in how well the business has fared in the past and in its probable future. This is because the line of credit generally is extended for a year at a time. The banker may require that other debts of the business be subordinated to, or come after, the claim of the bank. Banks also usually require their business customers to "clean up" their lines of credit for a specified period of time each year—that is, to have no outstanding borrowing against the credit line, usually for a minimum of two weeks. This ensures that the credit line is being used for short-term financing purposes rather than for long-term needs.

Continued access to a line of credit may be subject to the approval of the bank, if there are major changes in the operation of a business. A major shift or change in management personnel or in the manufacture or sale of particular products can influence greatly the future success of a company. Hence, the bank, having contributed substantially to the financial resources of the business, is necessarily interested in these activities. The bank may also seek information on the business through organized credit bureaus, through contact with other businesses having dealings with the firm, and through other banks.

In the event that the business needs more money than was anticipated at the time the line of credit was set up, it may request the bank to increase the limit on its line of credit. It must be prepared, however, to offer very sound evidence of the need for additional funds and the ability of the business to repay the increased loan from business operations. A request for an increased line of credit frequently occurs when a business is growing and needs more capital to make its growth possible. Banks, following the principle of maturity matching discussed above, generally insist that expansion be financed with long-term funds. But they may assist growth by temporarily providing a part of the increased needs. The business that is unable to obtain additional unsecured credit from its bank may seek a loan secured with collateral from the bank or other lenders. These other forms of borrowing are discussed later in this chapter.

Although the practice is diminishing, some banks require a ***compensating balance*** of from 10 to 20 percent of unsecured loans outstanding to be kept on deposit by the business. The most frequently cited justification for this requirement is that because banks cannot lend without deposits, bank borrowers should be required to be depositors also. But compensating balances are also a means of increasing the effective cost of borrowing by increasing the amount on which interest is computed.

compensating balance *requirement that 10 to 20 percent of a loan be kept on deposit at the bank*

COMPUTING INTEREST RATES

Chapter 9, The Time Value of Money, illustrated how to use time value of money concepts to calculate interest rates. The same concepts can be used to calculate the true cost of borrowing funds from a bank. If, for example, Global Manufacturing can borrow $10,000 for 6 months at 8 percent APR, the six-month interest cost will be $8\%/2 \times \$10,000$ or $400. Global will repay the $10,000 principal and $400 in interest after six months. As we learned in Chapter 9, the true or effective interest rate on this loan is

$$\text{EAR} = (1 + \text{APR}/m)^m - 1 \qquad (16.1)$$

or $(1 + 0.08/2)^2 - 1 = 0.0816$ or 8.16 percent.

At times banks will discount a loan. A ***discounted loan*** is one in which the borrower receives the principal less the interest at the time the loan is made. At maturity, the principal is repaid. Discounting has the effect of reducing the available funds received by the borrower while raising the effective interest rate. If Global's loan is discounted, Global will receive $9,600 ($10,000 less $400) and will repay $10,000, in essence paying $400 interest on the $9,600 funds received. This is a periodic rate of $400/$9,600 or 4.17 percent.[8] The effective annual rate is $(1 + 0.0417)^2 - 1$ or 8.51 percent, an increase of 0.35 percentage points when compared to the undiscounted loan.

discounted loan *borrower receives the principal less the interest at the time the loan is made; the principal is repaid at maturity*

When a loan is discounted, a firm has to borrow more money than the amount it really needs. To counteract the effect of discounting, to acquire $10,000 in usable funds they will have to borrow $10,000/(1 − 0.04) or

---

8.   This periodic rate can also be computed using our Chapter 9 concepts. We know that:

   $$FV = PV (1 + r)^n$$

Since *FV* equals $10,000 (the amount to be repaid), *PV* equals $9,600 (the usable funds received after discounting) and *n* is 1 for our six-month time frame, we have

   $$\$10,000 = \$9,600 (1 + r)^1$$

Solving for *r*, we see the periodic interest rate is 4.17 percent.

$10,416.67. When a loan of $10,416.67 is discounted at a six-month rate of 4 percent, the net proceeds to Global will be $10,000 (that is, $10,416.67 − (0.04)(10,416.67) = $10,000). In general, in order to receive the desired usable funds, the loan request must equal:

$$\text{Loan Request} = \text{Desired Usable Funds}/(1 - \text{discount}). \qquad (16.2)$$

A loan with a compensating balance is similar to a discounted loan as far as its effect on the effective interest rate and usable funds is concerned. Compensating balances are equivalent to discounting when the firm currently has no money on deposit at the bank. The firm's loan request should be large enough so that after funds are placed in the compensating balance it will have the usable funds it desires. For compensating balance loans, Equation 16.2 becomes:

$$\text{Loan Request} = \frac{\text{Desired Usable Funds}}{(1 - \text{compensating balance requirement})} \qquad (16.3)$$

which is identical to Equation 16.2, except the discount percent is replaced by the compensating balance percentage.

REVOLVING CREDIT AGREEMENTS

The officers of a business may feel rather certain that an agreed-upon line of credit will provide the necessary capital requirements for the coming year. But the bank is not obligated to continue to offer the credit line if the firm's financial condition worsens. Line of credit agreements usually allow the bank to reduce or withdraw its extension of credit to the firm.

The well established business with an excellent credit rating may be able to obtain a revolving credit agreement. A ***revolving credit agreement*** is a commitment in the form of a standby agreement for a guaranteed line of credit. Unlike a line of credit, a revolving credit agreement is a legal obligation of the bank to provide funds up to the agreed-upon borrowing limit during the time the agreement is in effect. In addition to paying interest on borrowed funds for the period of the loan, the business must pay a commission or fee to the bank based on the unused portion of the credit line, or the money it has "on call" during the agreement period. This fee is usually between 0.25 and 0.50 percent of the unused amount of the line.

To compute the effective cost of a revolving agreement, the joint effect of interest on borrowed funds and the commitment fee on the unborrowed portion of the agreement must be considered. Suppose Global has a one-year $1 million revolving credit agreement with a local bank. The annual interest rate on the agreement is 9 percent with a commitment fee of 0.40 percent on the unborrowed portion. Global expects to have average outstanding borrowings against the revolver of $300,000. Over the year, the interest cost on the average amount borrowed is 0.09 × $300,000 or $27,000. The commitment fee on the average unborrowed portion is 0.0040 × $700,000 or $2,800. With total interest and fees of $29,800 ($27,000 +

revolving credit agreement
legal obligation of the bank to provide up to the agreed-upon borrowing limit

$2,800) on average borrowings of $300,000, the expected annual cost of the revolver is $29,800/$300,000 or 9.93 percent.

ACCOUNTS RECEIVABLE FINANCING

The business that does not qualify for an unsecured bank loan or that has emergency needs for funds in excess of its line of credit may offer a **pledge** of accounts receivable as security. When banks use accounts receivable as security, they make the same sort of credit investigation as they do for unsecured loans. Particular attention is given to the collection experience of the business on its receivables and to certain characteristics of its accounts receivable.

pledge
obtain a short-term loan by using accounts receivable as collateral

The bank may spot-check the receivables of the firm and may in some cases analyze each account to determine how quickly the firm's customers make payments. It is also important for the bank to know something about these customers. Their ability to pay their debts will strongly influence how well the business applying for the loan will be able to collect payment.

In addition, the bank studies the type and quality of goods that are sold. If the merchandise is inferior, there may be objections from the customers and hence slower payment of bills or sales returns. Accounts receivable are of little value as security for a loan if large quantities of merchandise are returned and the amount of accounts receivable is reduced accordingly.

The Bank Management Commission of the American Bankers Association recommends that a loan based on the security of accounts receivable should generally be no more than 80 percent of the gross receivables. Furthermore, it recommends that this amount be reduced by any discounts allowed to customers for quick payment and by the normal percentage of merchandise returns. If there is reason to believe that many of the loan applicant's customers are not suitable risks, or if adequate credit ratings are not available, the bank will lend a lower percentage of the face value of the receivables.

Under the accounts receivable loan arrangement, there is, in addition to the basic interest charge, a fee to cover the extra work that is needed for such a loan. The bank must periodically check the books of the business in order to see that it is, in fact, living up to the terms of the agreement. At the time the loan is made, individual accounts on the ledger of the business are designated clearly as having been pledged for the bank loan. Only those accounts suitable for collateral purposes for the bank are designated. When these accounts are paid in full or become unsatisfactory, they are replaced by other accounts.

In addition to designating pledged accounts in the ledger of the borrowing firm, the bank also requires a schedule of the accounts and a copy of all shipping invoices involved. The business also must execute an assignment, or legal transfer, of these accounts to the bank. A sample copy of a promissory note for this type of loan is shown in Figure 16.6.

FIGURE 16.6   Promissory Note

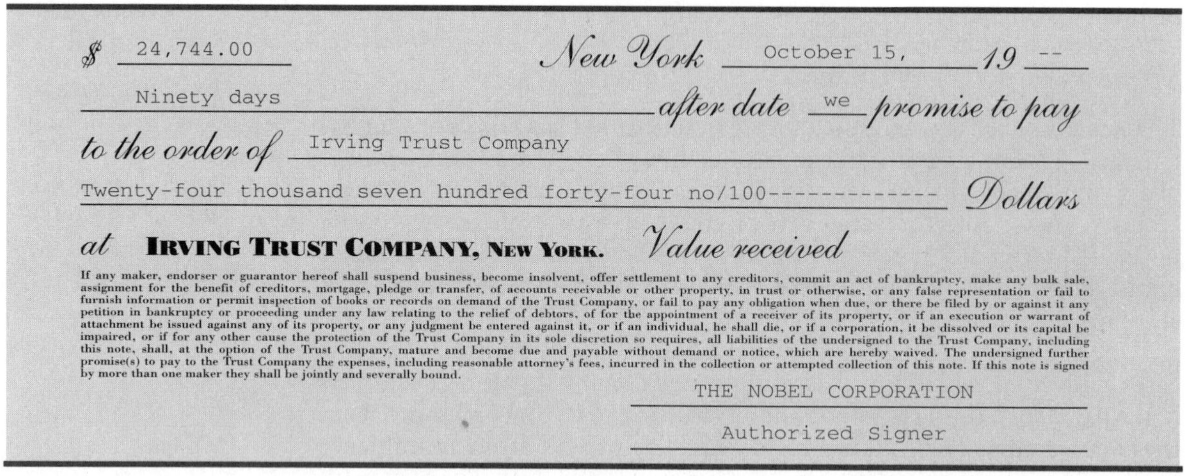

As customers pay their bill on the accounts that have been assigned for the loan, they must be turned over to the bank separately from other funds. The bank also reserves the right to make a direct audit of the business' books from time to time and to have an outside accounting firm examine the books periodically. Checking the accounts in this routine manner leaves customers of the business unaware that their accounts have been pledged as collateral for a loan.

Businesses that use their receivables as collateral for bank loans often prefer to keep this knowledge from their customers. It could be seen as an indication of weakness on the part of the business. Although businesses using this form of loan arrangement frequently are in a financially weak condition, this is not always the case. Some financially sound firms use accounts receivable financing because they feel it has advantages for them over other loan arrangements. Manufacturing companies appear to be the largest users of accounts receivable financing. In particular, this is true of manufacturers of food products, textiles, leather products, furniture, paper, iron, steel, and machinery.

INVENTORY LOANS

A business may use its inventory as collateral for a loan in much the same manner that it may borrow on its receivables. The bank evaluates the physical condition of the firm's inventory and the inventory's general composition. Staple items that are in constant demand serve well as collateral for a loan. Style and fashion items such as designer clothes are not as acceptable as collateral except for brief periods of time. Firms that use inventory as collateral usually do so because they are not in a position to obtain further funds on an unsecured basis.

The bank may protect itself when lending to a business by having a **blanket inventory lien,** or a claim against inventory when individual items are indistinguishable, as may be the case with grain or clothing items. In other cases, when goods can be clearly identified, a **trust receipt** may be used. Money is borrowed against specific items in inventory. This method of financing is used by car dealerships and appliance stores, where inventory items financed by trust receipts can be identified by serial number. Under a trust receipt arrangement, the bank retains ownership of the goods until they are actually sold in the regular course of business. Audits are simply a matter of checking serial numbers of inventory items to determine if items held against a trust receipt have been sold.

In some cases when inventory is used as collateral, the bank may insist that the inventory be placed in a bonded and licensed warehouse. The receipt issued by the warehouse is then turned over to the bank, which holds it until the loan is repaid. A sample copy of a **warehouse receipt** for stored merchandise is shown in Figure 16.7.

It is frequently inconvenient for a business to deliver large bulky items of inventory to a warehouse for storage. This problem is solved by using field warehouses. A field warehousing enterprise has the power to establish a **field warehouse** on the grounds of the borrowing business establishment. Field warehouses differ from the typical public warehouse in that (1) they serve a single customer—that customer on whose property the field warehouse is established, and (2) they exist only until the loan is repaid.

In setting up a field warehouse, the warehouse operator usually must first obtain a lease on that portion of the property which is to be used for warehousing purposes. Then he or she must establish fences, barriers, walks, and other postings to indicate clear possession of the property. This is done to avoid accidental or deliberate removal of stored items during the general course of business operations. A guard may be posted in order to check on the safety of the warehoused goods, or a room may be sealed and the seal inspected periodically to make sure the company is honoring its agreement.

There also must be a complete statement of the commodities or items that are to be warehoused, and agreements must be made about the maintenance of the property, proper fire precautions, insurance, and other necessary physical requirements. Under certain circumstances, the warehouse operator is authorized to release a certain quantity of goods by the day, week, or month to make possible a rotation of merchandise. Under this arrangement, physical inventories must be taken from time to time.

Field warehouses are in operation throughout the United States but are concentrated in the central and Pacific coast regions. Canned goods, miscellaneous groceries, lumber, timber, and building supplies fill about two-fifths of all field warehouses in this country. Those banks that make loans involving commodities will generally accept field warehouse receipts as collateral.

Inventory loans are somewhat more expensive than unsecured loans to business borrowers. The higher cost is due in part to the cost of warehousing

---

blanket inventory lien
claim against a customer's inventory when the individual items are indistinguishable

trust receipt
lien against specific identifiable items in inventory

warehouse receipt
inventory is placed in a bonded warehouse for safekeeping; items are removed as they are paid for

field warehouse
enterprise establishes a warehouse on the grounds of the borrowing business establishment

FIGURE 16.7 Warehouse Receipt

LAWRENCE SYSTEMS, INC.

ORIGINAL WAREHOUSE RECEIPT NOT INSURED

NON-NEGOTIABLE

RECEIVED FROM: Wood Lumber and Moulding Company
FOR STORAGE IN Any Town, Any State
LOCATED AT (STREET) 111 A Street

SUBJECT TO ALL THE TERMS AND CONDITIONS CONTAINED HEREIN AND ON THE REVERSE SIDE HEREOF FOR THE ACCOUNT OF AND TO BE DELIVERED WITHOUT SURRENDER OF THE WAREHOUSE RECEIPT UPON WRITTEN INSTRUCTION OF

FILL IN First National Bank of Any Town
WAREHOUSE RECEIPT HOLDER

RCPT. TYPE	REG. CODE	WAREHOUSE NO.	HOLDER NO.	DATE	RECEIPT NO.	Depositor's Declared Values for which the Warehouseman Assumes No Responsibility
S1-5	02	1218A	S154	11-12-83	51734	

ITEM	CODE NO.	NO. OF UNITS	SAID TO BE OR CONTAIN	UNIT VALUES	EXTENSION (DJM)
	0001	1,151	M. bd. ft. logs pine	105.00	120,855.00
	0002	958	M. bd. ft. logs white fir	80.00	76,640.00
	0003	1,523	M. bd. ft. logs Douglas fir	105.00	159,915.00
	0004	621	M. bd. ft. logs cedar	65.00	40,365.00
		-----			----------
		4,253			397,775,00

CAUTION: LAWRENCE SYSTEMS, INC., WILL NOT BE RESPONSIBLE FOR THE QUANTITIES SHOWN HEREON UNLESS TOTAL NUMBER OF UNITS IS TYPED BELOW.

TOTAL ➤ Four million, two hundred fifty-three thousand board feet

Stored under field warehousing arrangement. Subject to lien for storage, handling and other charges as per contract and lease with the industry served. A general lien is claimed for charges and expenses in regard to other goods deposited by the same depositor. Transfers of merchandise not complete unless made on the books of the warehouse company.

*By agreement goods of same kind or grade may be commingled and where authorized by law unlike units shall be deemed fungible and treated as equivalents.

LAWRENCE SYSTEMS INC.

BY ➤ ______________________
BONDED WAREHOUSE MANAGER
(Do not accept this warehouse receipt if any corrections or changes appear hereon.)

operations, and also because the borrower's credit rating may be low. Bank interest rates for warehouse loans ordinarily are somewhat higher than for unsecured loans.[9] In addition, a warehouse fee of 1 to 2 percent of the loan, depending upon size and other factors, must be paid.

Loans Secured by Stocks and Bonds

Stocks and bonds often are used as collateral for short-term loans. These securities are welcomed as collateral primarily because of their marketability and their value. If the securities are highly marketable, and if their value is high enough to cover the amount of the loan requested even

9. Inventory loans, like receivable loans, are also made by commercial finance companies. Their interest rates usually are higher than those charged by banks.

if the stock's price goes down somewhat, a banker will not hesitate to extend a loan. Securities listed on one of the national exchanges are preferred because frequent price quotations are available. Banks usually will loan from 60 to 70 percent of the market value of listed stocks, and from 70 to 80 percent of the market value of high-grade bonds.

Only assignable stocks and bonds are eligible for this type of collateral financing, with the exception of nonassignable U.S. savings bonds. When assignable securities are placed with a bank, a stock or bond power is executed that authorizes the bank to sell or otherwise dispose of the securities should it become necessary to do so to protect the loan (see Figure 16.8).

FIGURE 16.8   Irrevocable Stock or Bond Power

IRREVOCABLE STOCK OR BOND POWER

FOR VALUE RECEIVED, the undersigned does (do) hereby sell, assign and transfer to

The Third National Bank of St. Louis, Missouri

53-0822721

(SOCIAL SECURITY OR TAXPAYER IDENTIFYING NO.)

IF STOCK, COMPLETE THIS PORTION

100 shares of the Common stock of Black River Timber Company

represented by Certificate(s) No(s). 143001 inclusive,

standing in the name of the undersigned on the books of said Company.

IF BONDS, COMPLETE THIS PORTION

_____ bonds of _____

in the principal amount of $_____, No(s). _____ inclusive,

standing in the name of the undersigned on the books of said company.

The undersigned does (do) hereby irrevocably constitute and appoint _____

my attorney to transfer the said stock or bond(s), as the case may be,

on the books of said Company, with full power of substitution in the premises.

Dated June 17, 19--

Penelope H. Plack

IMPORTANT — READ CAREFULLY
The signature(s) to this Power must correspond with the name(s) as written upon the face of the certificate(s) or bond(s) in every particular without alteration or enlargement or any change whatever. Signature guarantees should be made by a member or member organization of the New York Stock Exchange, members of other Exchanges having signatures on file with transfer agent or by a commercial bank or trust company having its principal office or correspondent in the City of New York.

(PERSON(S) EXECUTING THIS POWER SIGN(S) HERE)

SIGNATURE GUARANTEED

OTHER FORMS OF SECURITY FOR BANK LOANS

Security for short-term bank loans also may include such things as the cash surrender value of life insurance policies, guarantee of a loan by a party other than the borrower, notes, and acceptances.

Life Insurance Loans
Small businesses frequently find it possible to obtain needed short-term bank loans by pledging the cash surrender value, or the amount they will receive upon cancellation, of the owner's life insurance policies. The policies must be assignable, and many insurance companies insist that their own assignment forms be used for such purposes. Because of the safety afforded the bank by the cash surrender values, these loans usually carry a lower interest rate than loans on other types of business collateral. Another reason for the favorable rates is that the borrower could borrow directly from the insurance company. Even so, bank interest rates have been higher in recent years than those of insurance companies to their policyholders. As a result, there has been an increase in the number of these loans made by insurance companies.

Comaker Loans
Many small businesses find it necessary to provide the bank with a guarantor in the form of a cosigner to their notes. It is expected that the cosigner has a credit rating at least as satisfactory as, and usually far better than, the firm requesting the loan.

Acceptances

acceptance
receivable from the sale of merchandise on the basis of a draft or bill of exchange drawn against the buyer or the buyer's bank

Another type of receivable instrument that arises out of the sale of merchandise and which may be sold to a bank is the acceptance. An ***acceptance*** is a receivable from the sale of merchandise on the basis of a draft or bill of exchange drawn against the buyer or the buyer's bank. The accepted draft or bill of exchange is returned to the seller of the merchandise where it may be held until the date payment is due. During this period, the business may discount such acceptances with its bank. Again the seller is contingently liable for these discounted acceptances. The use of the banker's acceptance is discussed in detail in Chapter 6 in connection with an international shipment of goods.

TRADE CREDIT

The most important single form of short-term business financing is the credit extended by one business organization to another. Accounts receivable together with longer-term notes receivable—taken by manufacturers, wholesalers, jobbers, and other businesses that sell products or services to businesses—are known as trade credit.

Estimates claim more than 80 percent of all retail establishments rent their places of business under lease arrangements. Many manufacturing corporations also find it to their advantage to rent their plant facilities. One type of lease arrangement that acts as a substitute for raising long-term financing entails the construction of special facilities for the use of a particular company. For example, Safeway Stores, a grocery store chain, encourages local real estate groups and others with the necessary capital to construct buildings to their specifications. After construction, buildings are leased to Safeway for a number of years in accordance with a predetermined agreement. The company benefits from new retail facilities without having to make an outlay of cash or to increase corporate indebtedness.

LEASES AS LONG-TERM AND SHORT-TERM FINANCING SOURCES

Leasing also can be used to supplement a firm's shorter-term financial needs and may at times replace bank loans as a financing source. Trucks and cars used by firms can be leased, thus providing transportation and shipping needs for several years without having to commit to a purchase. Virtually any piece of equipment, from copiers to computers to forklifts, can be leased on a short-term or long-term basis. Leasing is many times an attractive alternative to purchasing assets.

The establishment of trade credit is the least formal of all forms of financing. It involves only an order for goods or services by one business and the delivery of goods or performance of service by the selling business. The purchasing business receives an invoice stating the terms of the transaction and the time period within which payment is to be made. The purchaser adds the liability to accounts payable. The seller adds the claim to accounts receivable. In some situations, the seller may insist upon written evidence of liability on the part of the purchaser. Such written evidence is usually in the form of a note that is payable by the purchaser and is considered as a note receivable by the seller. Before a business organization delivers goods or performs a service for another business, it must determine the ability and willingness of the purchaser to pay for the order.[10] The responsibility of such credit analysis in most businesses belongs to the credit manager.

TERMS FOR TRADE CREDIT

Sales may be made on terms such as cash, E.O.M. (end of month), M.O.M. (middle of month), or R.O.G. (receipt of goods). Or such terms as 2/10, net 30 may be offered, which means the purchaser may deduct 2 percent from the purchase price if payment is made within 10 days of shipment; if not paid

---

10. We discussed the process of credit evaluation in Chapter 15.

within 10 days, the net amount is due within 30 days. Such **trade discounts** to purchasers for early payment are common and are designed to provide incentive for prompt payment of bills. Occasionally, sellers offer only net terms such as net 30 or net 60.

A cash sale, contrary to its implication, usually involves credit. This is because the purchaser is often permitted a certain number of days within which to make payment. For example, a sale of merchandise in which the purchaser is permitted up to ten days to pay may be considered a cash transaction, but credit is outstanding to the purchaser for that period of time. Even for the firm that purchases products entirely on a cash basis, the volume of accounts payable outstanding on its books at any one time may be large.

COST OF TRADE CREDIT

When trade credit terms do not provide a discount for early payment of obligations, there is no cost to the buyer for such financing. Even when discounts are available, it may *seem* that there is no cost for trade credit since failing to take the early payment discount simply requires the purchaser to pay the net price. There is a cost involved, however, when a discount is not taken. For example, with terms of 2/10, net 30, the cost is the loss of the 2 percent discount that could have been taken if payment were made within the ten-day period.

In order to compare the cost of trade credit and bank credit, the cost of the trade credit must be reduced to an annual interest rate basis. For example, if the terms of sale are 2/10, net 30, the cost of trade credit is the loss of the 2 percent discount that the purchaser fails to take if she or he extends the payment period from ten days up to 30 days. The lost 2 percent is the cost of trade credit for those 20 days. If we also consider that it is the discounted price (invoice price minus the percentage discount) that is being financed, the approximate effective cost (EC) is:

$$\text{EC} = \frac{\% \text{ Discount}}{100\% - \% \text{ Discount}} \times \frac{365 \text{ days}}{\text{Credit period} - \text{Discount days}} \qquad (16.4)$$

For our 2/10, net 30 example,

$$\text{EC} = \frac{2\%}{100\% - 2\%} \times \frac{365}{30 - 10} = 2.04\% \times 18.25 = 37.2\%$$

This shows that the cost of trade credit typically is far in excess of bank rates. Thus it is usually worthwhile to borrow funds to take advantage of cash discounts on trade credit. Failure to take advantage of the trade discount is the same as borrowing from the vendor at the calculated, or effective cost, rate of interest.

The cost of trade credit in most lines of business activity is high when discounts are missed. However, it should not be assumed that high cost necessarily makes trade credit an undesirable source of short-term financing. It can be, in fact, the most important form of financing for small and growing businesses that are unable to qualify for short-term credit through customary financial channels.

The firm in a weak financial condition will find trade credit more readily available than bank credit. The bank stands to gain only the interest on the loan if repayment is made, but it will lose the entire sum loaned if the borrower's obligation is not met. The manufacturer or merchant, on the other hand, has a profit margin on the goods sold. If the purchaser fails to meet the obligation, the seller loses at most the cost of the goods delivered to the purchaser.

COMMERCIAL FINANCE COMPANIES

Shortly after the turn of the century, the first commercial finance company in the United States was chartered. Since that time, the number of these institutions has increased to more than five hundred. Some of these organizations are small, offering limited financial services to their customers, while others have vast resources and engage in broadly diversified programs of business lending.

A ***commercial finance company*** is an organization without a bank charter that advances funds to businesses by (1) discounting accounts receivable, (2) making loans secured by chattel mortgages on machinery or liens on inventory, or (3) financing deferred-payment sales of commercial and industrial equipment. These companies also are known as commercial credit companies, commercial receivables companies, and discount companies.

commercial finance company
organization without a bank charter that advances funds to businesses

Commercial finance companies—such as C.I.T. Financial Corporation, Commercial Credit Company, and Walter E. Heller International offer many of the same services as commercial banks for accounts-receivable financing and inventory financing. Accounts-receivable financing was, in fact, originated by commercial finance companies and only later was it adopted by commercial banks.

Commercial finance companies grew to their present number because they were completely free to experiment with new and highly specialized types of credit arrangements. Also, state laws concerning lending on the basis of accounts receivable were generally more favorable to these non-banking organizations. A third factor is that they were able to charge high enough rates to make a profitable return on high-risk loans. Frequently these rates were far above rates bankers were permitted to charge.

Commercial finance company loans outstanding on accounts receivable total several billions of dollars. These companies also provide a vast amount of credit for businesses by financing commercial vehicles, industrial and farm equipment, and other types of business credit. The Board of Governors of the Federal Reserve System estimates the total volume of business credit outstanding by the commercial finance companies to be more than $200 billion.

The equity position of commercial finance companies is considerably greater than that of banks. However, these organizations do not operate on equity capital alone. Additional long-term capital is acquired by selling debenture, or unsecured, bonds. In addition, commercial banks lend a large volume of money at wholesale rates to commercial finance companies, which in turn lend it to business borrowers at retail rates. Nonbank financial intermediaries, as well as commercial and industrial firms, often find it advantageous to invest their temporary surplus funds in the commercial paper of commercial finance companies. These sources of short-term funds permit the commercial finance companies to meet their peak loan demands without having too much long-term debt, only part of which would be used during slack lending periods.

When viewing the high average cost of 15 to 20 percent for commercial finance company loans, the question may arise as to why a borrower would under any circumstances use these companies. As a matter of fact, a business that has ample current assets and is in a highly liquid position may be well advised to rely on other sources of short-term financing. During periods when business is most brisk and growth possibilities most favorable, the need for additional short-term funds becomes unusually pressing just as it is when customers are slow in paying their bills and the company needs cash.

A business will typically first request an increase in its bank line of credit. Failing this, an additional loan from a bank may be secured by pledging either inventory or receivables as collateral. However, not all banks actively engage in this type of financial arrangement. Thus it may be necessary to deal with a commercial finance company. Commercial finance companies are able to operate through a system of branches on a regional or national basis, unhampered by restrictions on bank branch operations. Therefore, they can acquire the volume of business necessary to cover overhead and provide the needed diversification of risks for high-risk financing. Several bank holding companies have purchased or established commercial finance companies to take advantage of their special operating characteristics.

factor
engages in accounts-receivable financing for business; purchases accounts outright and assumes all credit risks

maturity factoring
firm selling its accounts receivable is paid on the normal collection date or net due date of the account

advance factoring
factor pays the firm for its receivables before the account due date

FACTORS

The **factor,** like the commercial finance company, engages in accounts-receivable financing for businesses. In contrast to the commercial finance companies, however, the factor purchases the accounts outright and assumes all credit risks. Under **maturity factoring,** the firm selling its accounts receivable is paid on the normal collection date or net due date of the account. Under **advance factoring,** the factor pays the firm for its receivables before the account due date. Under a factoring arrangement, customers whose accounts are sold are notified that their bills are payable to the factor. The task of collecting on the accounts is thus shifted from the seller of the accounts to the factor.

Despite the long history of these companies, their growth has taken place largely within the last 30 years. Factoring originated in the textile industry. Because most of the selling and credit-reporting agencies in the textile field are located in New York City, most of the nation's factors can be found there. In addition to serving the textile industry, factors also have proved useful in such fields as furniture, shoes, bottle making, paper, toys, and furs. Some factors include CIT Group Holdings, Republic Factors, and Heller Financial, as well as units of Bank of New York and NationsBank.

To use a factor, a contract is drawn establishing the duties and obligations of the seller and the factor. This contract includes the conditions under which accounts may be sold to the factor, the responsibility for the payment of these accounts, the collection procedures to be followed, and the method of reporting balances due. The contract also provides that the accounts so established be assigned to the factor and that invoices for sales to these customers, together with the original shipping documents, be delivered daily to the factor. All sales must be approved by the factor before goods are delivered. Sales are subject to rejection if the credit rating of the customer does not meet the factor's standards. Daily reports must be given to the factor on all credits, allowances, and returns of merchandise. The contract also stipulates the charges for the factoring service.

The credit analysis department is the heart of the factoring organization since it must conserve the factor's assets and also be in constant contact with its clients. Members of the factor's credit department not only must be extremely prompt and accurate in their credit analyses but also, because they work closely with the firm's clients, must retain the goodwill of the companies that use its services.

The charge for factoring has two components. First, interest is charged on the money advanced. Second, a factoring commission or service charge is figured as a percentage of the face amount of the receivables. This charge typically ranges from 3/4 of 1 percent to 1 1/2 percent of the face amount of the accounts financed. The commission charge is determined after considering such things as the volume of the client's sales, the general credit status of the accounts being factored, and the average size of individual accounts.

As further financial protection, the factor reserves from 5 to 15 percent of the total amount of receivables factored to make adjustments, such as for merchandise that is returned to the seller. This portion of the receivables is returned to the seller if it is not needed for adjustment purposes.

Like the commercial finance companies, factors obtain their operating funds through a combination of equity capital, long-term borrowing, short-term borrowing, and profits from operations.

Although a factor's services may be used by a firm that is unable to secure financing through customary channels, financially strong companies may at times use these services to good advantage. In fact, factors are of greatest benefit to companies enjoying very great success with respect to sales and growth. We have noted that during such periods companies experience extreme shortages of working capital. The sale of receivables without recourse (that is, sellers do not have to repay any funds received from the factor in the case of a bad debt) has the effect of substituting cash for accounts receivable. This may make even greater growth and profitability possible in the long run.

Some firms factor their receivables for other reasons. First, the cost of doing business through credit sales is definite and can be figured in advance because the factor assumes all risks of collection. This is, in effect, a form of credit insurance. Second, factoring eliminates expenses, including bookkeeping costs, the maintenance of a credit department, and the expenses of collecting delinquent accounts. A further advantage, but of a less tangible nature, is that factoring frees the management of a business from concern with financial matters and permits it to concentrate on production and distribution.

In recent years, factoring has become increasingly important in supporting export sales. The firm that is unfamiliar with the problems of financing international shipments of goods is relieved of such details by factoring foreign receivables.

Although factoring services are regarded highly by some businesses, others offer objections to their use. The two reasons cited most frequently are the cost and the implication of financial weakness. The cost of factoring is unquestionably higher than the cost of borrowing from a bank on the basis of an unsecured loan. However, it is difficult to conclude that the net cost is higher. The elimination of overhead costs that would otherwise be necessary plus the reality that management need not concern itself with financial matters may completely offset the additional cost involved in factoring.

With respect to the implication of financial weakness, many borrowers prefer to avoid the factoring plan in favor of the nonnotification plan available through pledging receivables. In this way they avoid having their customers make direct payments to the factor. Outside the textile field, where factoring has long played an important role, businesses often make every effort to avoid letting their customers know that their accounts are being used to secure financing because of the implication of financial weakness.

SMALL BUSINESS ADMINISTRATION

The Small Business Administration (SBA) was established by the federal government to provide financial assistance to small firms that are unable

RETAILING,
FACTORS, AND
BANKRUPTCY

Few industries are affected by factors as much as retailing. Factors guarantee payment to suppliers of many large retail firms. With such guarantees, suppliers ship goods to the retailers, confident that they will get paid. Should factors refuse to guarantee payments to suppliers because the factors believe a retailer to be on shaky financial ground, a retailing firm can find itself with no merchandise to sell. Thus, predictions about poor finances can become a self-fulfilling prophecy.

Bank runs are caused by depositors wanting to get their money back before the bank fails. Many times the liquidity crisis caused by depositors' actions precipitates a failure. Like bank depositors in the 1930s, once one factor hesitates to stand behind a retailer's credit, they all turn their backs on the retailer since no one factor wants to be left alone supporting a financially troubled firm.

Factors act as an early warning signal of a retailer's real or imagined financial deterioration. In June 1995 Bradlees, a discount retailer, filed for Chapter 11 bankruptcy protection after factors refused to guarantee Bradlees' receivables to its suppliers. A few months later, in September 1995, Caldor, another discount retailer, filed for bankruptcy protection for the same reason: the factors would not support it.

When factors refuse to accept a retailer's credit, the retailer's suppliers face a decision: whether to continue shipping and taking the risk of nonpayment by the financially troubled retailer or to stop shipping and possibly lose a client. With 1990s bankruptcy filings of Federated Department Stores, Allied Stores, Macy's, Jamesway, Bradlees and Caldor, it appears the suppliers are choosing to listen to the factors.

Sources: Joseph Pereira, "Bradlees Seeks Bankruptcy Protection, But Denies It Is Facing Liquidity Crisis," *The Wall Street Journal* (June 26, 1995): A10; Susan Pulliam and Laura Bird, "Concern Rises About Retailer Caldor's Ability To Deal With Cutthroat Rivalry; Stock Sinks," *The Wall Street Journal* (August 24, 1995): C2; Laura Bird, "Caldor Files for Bankruptcy Protection In Face of Weak Sales, Jittery Suppliers," *The Wall Street Journal* (September 19, 1995): A3; Roger Lowenstein, "Lenders' Stampede Tramples Caldor," *The Wall Street Journal* (October 26, 1995): C1.

to obtain loans through private channels on reasonable terms. Created in 1953, the SBA provides a wide variety of services in addition to loans through its more than 100 field offices.

The reason businesses use SBA loans is explained by the stated objectives of the SBA: to enable deserving small businesses to obtain financial assistance otherwise not available through private channels on reasonable terms. When the SBA was established, it was recognized that the economic development of the nation depended in large part upon the freedom of new business ventures to enter into active operation. Yet the increased concentration of investable funds with large institutional investors, such as life insurance companies, investment companies, and others, made it increasingly difficult for new and small business ventures to attract investment capital.

If a firm is able to obtain financing elsewhere, its loan application to the SBA is rejected. An applicant for a loan must prove that funds needed are not available from any bank, that no other private lending sources are available, that issuing securities is not practicable, that financing cannot be arranged through the disposal of business assets, and that the personal credit of the owners cannot be used. These loans may not be used for paying existing creditors or for speculative purposes.

The SBA assists in financing small enterprises in three ways: it may make direct loans to businesses; it may participate jointly with private banks in extending loans to businesses; or it may agree to guarantee a bank loan. The SBA can make direct loans of up to $150,000. When participating with banks in making loans, the SBA's share may not exceed $150,000. In guaranteeing loans, the SBA may extend its guarantee to 90 percent of a bank loan or $750,000, whichever is less.

In addition to the business-lending activities described above, the SBA has been vested with the responsibility for several related financial activities. These include loans to development companies, disaster loans, lease guarantees, surety bond support, minority enterprise programs, procurement assistance, and support for investment companies that service small businesses.

SBA working capital loans are limited to seven years, while regular business loans have a maximum maturity of 25 years. The SBA sets the interest rates on its direct loans and on its share-of-participation loans. It also sets a maximum allowable rate which banks can charge on guaranteed loans. These rates are adjusted periodically by the SBA to reflect changes in market conditions.

COMMERCIAL PAPER

commercial paper
short-term promissory note sold by high-credit-quality U.S. corporations; notes are backed solely by the credit quality of the issuer

Large U.S. corporations of high credit quality can issue or sell ***commercial paper,*** which is a short-term promissory note. These notes are backed solely by the credit quality of the issuer. Commercial paper may be sold directly by the issuer to financial institutions or other investors. Alternatively, it can be sold to commercial paper houses or dealers who purchase the promissory notes to resell them to individuals or businesses. A fee based on the amount of notes purchased, charged to the issuer of the notes, provides the basic income of commercial paper dealers.

A firm that wishes to obtain funds from a commercial paper house must have an unquestioned reputation for sound operation. First the commercial paper house makes a thorough investigation of the firm's financial position. If it appears that the notes of the firm can be sold with little difficulty, an agreement is made for the outright sale of a block of the firm's promissory notes to the commercial paper house. They, in turn, will resell these notes as quickly as possible to banks, managers of pension funds, business corporations that have surplus funds, or other investors. The notes are usually prepared in denominations of $100,000 or more with maturities ranging from a few days to 270 days.[11] The size of the notes and the maturities, however, can be adjusted to suit individual investor requirements.

Commercial paper is sold on a discount basis. A commercial paper house will pay the borrower the face amount of the notes minus the interest charge and a fee that may be as low as 1/8 of 1 percent. The interest charge is determined by the general level of prevailing rates in the money market and the strength of the borrowing company. When these notes are resold to banks and other lenders, only the prevailing interest charge is deducted from the face value of the notes. Hence, the commercial paper house receives the fee as compensation for the negotiation.

Global Manufacturing wants to issue $100,000 of commercial paper that will mature in nine months (270 days). The placement fee is 0.30 percent and the interest charge will be 7.5 percent over the nine-month period. To compute Global's effective financing cost we must determine the net proceeds or usable funds that Global will obtain from the sale as well as the total interest charges they will pay.

The net proceeds will be the $100,000 raised minus the interest less the placement fee. This is computed below:

$$\text{Net proceeds} = \$100,000 - (0.075)(\$100,000) - (0.0030)(\$100,000)$$
$$= \$100,000 - \$7,500 - \$300$$
$$= \$92,200$$

The interest charge is (0.075)($100,000) or $7,500 and the placement fee is $300 for total expenses of $7,800. The nine-month financing cost for the commercial paper issue is:

$$\text{9-month cost} = \$7,800/\$92,200 = 0.0846 \text{ or } 8.46 \text{ percent.}$$

The annualized cost of the commercial paper issue will be

$$(1 + 0.0846)^{12/9} - 1 = 11.44 \text{ percent.}$$

The most important reason for directly issuing commercial paper or using commercial paper dealers is that the cost of borrowing is generally

---

11. Commercial paper has a maximum maturity of 270 days as SEC regulations require that securities with maturities exceeding 270 days must go through the costly and time-consuming SEC registration process.

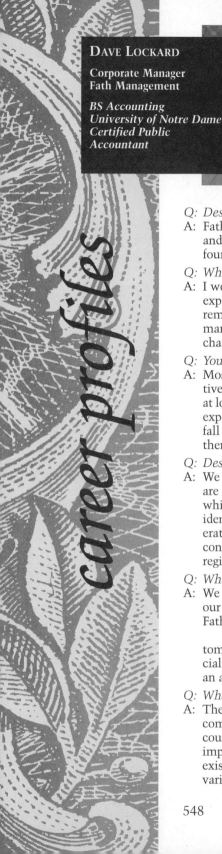

DAVE LOCKARD

Corporate Manager
Fath Management

*BS Accounting
University of Notre Dame
Certified Public
Accountant*

*"I wear lots
of hats."*

Q: *Describe the firm you work for.*
A: Fath Management is a privately owned real estate management company. We own and operate about forty properties, almost all apartment buildings or complexes, in four states. In all we have about 7,000 residential units.

Q: *What is your role there?*
A: I wear lots of hats. I set the operating budgets for our properties, approve significant expenditures, oversee hiring and firing, negotiate contracts for services like waste removal, manage our insurance needs, set company policies and salary guidelines, manage our banking relationships, and evaluate properties that we may want to purchase, among other things.

Q: *You "manage banking relationships." What does that involve?*
A: Most of our properties are purchased via bank loans. Because interest rates are relatively low right now we are continually looking for opportunities to refinance our loans at lower rates. That's basically a cost-justification issue—can we save enough in interest expense to compensate for the refinancing fees we would face? Every time there's a fall in interest rates it opens up the possibility of refinancing more of our loans. And then there are new loans when we buy new properties, of course.

Q: *Describe the acquisition process.*
A: We are not acquiring as many new properties now as we did several years ago, but we are always open to that possibility. I've developed a computer spreadsheet model which we use to assess the financial potential of a property. We use this model to identify the properties that fit best with our strategy and have the potential to generate the rate of return we need. Then we take a closer look at those properties, their condition, the neighborhoods. If we decide to purchase a property, we go to a local or regional bank and negotiate a loan.

Q: *What information do you provide the bank to secure the financing?*
A: We would provide information about the specific property—the projected cash flow, our plans for renovation or improvement, and so on—as well as information about Fath's overall financial position, our operating results, and credit history.

There's another side to our interaction with banks, too. Banks compete for customers just like any other business. In many cases banks will come to us offering special deals on certain types of loans, which may encourage us to take a closer look at an acquisition we might not have pursued otherwise.

Q: *What skills do you use most in your job?*
A: The ability to understand and resolve problems is essential in this job. A lot of issues come up that you could never foresee and you need to be able to determine the right course of action and implement it right away. You have to be able to consider the impact of your actions so that you don't create new problems when you solve an existing one. These problems make the job difficult, but interesting too. I like the variety of issues that I get involved in.

less than regular bank rates.[12] Also, the need for compensating bank balances that increase interest costs on short-term bank loans is avoided. Loan restrictions on the amount that can be borrowed from a single bank also may favor the issuance of commercial paper by large corporations.

Industrial firms and other nonbank lenders often purchase commercial paper as a more profitable alternative than Treasury bills for investing excess cash. In recent years, commercial paper has provided a yield above that of short-term government securities. Although commercial banks were historically the main purchasers of commercial paper, it is now actively held by industrial corporations, money market mutual funds, and other lenders.

Similar to bonds, commercial paper is rated. The rating is important to the issuer, as the higher the rating the lower the interest expense.

Many top-rated U.S. commercial paper issuers can also issue paper overseas. The European commercial paper (Euro CP) market offers advantages to commercial paper issuers just as the Eurodollar bond market offers advantages over the U.S. bond market. There is no SEC regulation of the Euro CP market, so commercial paper maturities are generally a little longer and interest costs are less. In addition, Euro CP is only available to the "cream" of the commercial paper issuers, so no ratings are needed. Investors already know who the safest issuers are. So not having to pay for a rating also makes the Euro CP market attractive to those firms that are able to use it.

SUMMARY

Working capital, it has been said, is the grease that keeps the wheels turning in a company. Inventories are needed to meet customer demands for the firm's products. When they are sold, accounts receivable are created which will one day be converted into cash. This cash is used to pay suppliers, workers, creditors, taxes, and shareholder dividends. A firm without working capital is a firm unlikely to remain in business.

There are two classes of working capital: permanent, or the minimum necessary for smooth company operations, and temporary, which occurs because of seasonal or cyclical fluctuations in sales demand. A company financing strategy that uses long-term sources to finance its working capital is a conservative strategy that reduces profits but increases liquidity. An aggressive strategy that uses more short-term financing has less liquidity but may increase company profits. Several influences affect managers' decisions as to how the firm should be financed, including the characteristics of the firm's industry, its asset base, seasonality, sales cycles, and sales trends.

---

12.   The reason for the lower rates is that only the largest, most financially stable firms can issue commercial paper. And unlike banks, which service a geographic region, commercial paper is sold by dealers to investors worldwide, so international short-term rates help determine commercial paper rates rather than bank loan committees.

Firms face many possible sources of short-term financing, from bank loans (including lines of credit and revolving credit), commercial paper, trade credit, and others. Care should be taken by the treasurer to evaluate the cost of each financing source by calculating its effective annual cost, by incorporating all interest charges and fees into the analysis, and by comparing the principal of the loan with the actual usable funds received. Asset-backed financing, such as pledging, factoring receivables, or using inventory as collateral are usually higher-cost financing sources, primarily because smaller, less creditworthy firms rely upon them for financing.

KEY TERMS

acceptance	line of credit
advance factoring	maturity factoring
blanket inventory lien	maturity matching approach
commercial finance company	pledge
commercial paper	prime rate
compensating balance	revolving credit agreement
discounted loan	trade discounts
factor	trust receipt
field warehouse	warehouse receipt

DISCUSSION QUESTIONS

1. What is meant by net working capital? Briefly describe the financing implications when net working capital is positive.
2. What is meant by "permanent" current assets? How do "temporary" current assets differ from permanent current assets?
3. Explain the strategies businesses can use to finance their assets with short-term and long-term funds.
4. What influences affect the nature of the demand for short-term versus long-term funds?
5. Explain how a conservative approach to financing a firm's assets is a low risk/low expected return strategy whereas an aggressive approach to financing is a high risk/high expected return strategy.
6. Prepare a list of advantages and disadvantages of short-term bank borrowing relative to other short-term financing sources.
7. What is meant by an unsecured loan? Are these loans an important form of bank lending?
8. Explain what a bank line of credit is.
9. Explain how discounting and compensating balances affect the effective cost of bank financing.

10. Describe the revolving credit agreement and compare it with the bank line of credit.
11. When might a business seek accounts receivable financing?
12. What safeguards may a bank establish to protect itself when it lends on the basis of a customer's receivables pledged as collateral for a loan?
13. When a business firm uses its inventory as collateral for a bank loan, how is the problem of storing and guarding the inventory accomplished for the bank?
14. What is meant by trade credit? Briefly describe some of the possible terms for trade credit.
15. What are the primary reasons for using trade credit for short-term financing?
16. Under what circumstances would a business secure its financing through a commercial finance company?
17. Describe how a factor differs from a commercial finance company in terms of accounts-receivable financing.
18. Why would a business use the services of a factor?
19. How does the Small Business Administration provide financing to businesses?
20. What is commercial paper and how important is it as a source of financing?

PROBLEMS

1. A supplier is offering your firm a cash discount of 2 percent if purchases are paid for within 10 days; otherwise the bill is due at the end of 60 days. Would you recommend borrowing from a bank at an 18 percent annual interest rate in order to take advantage of the cash discount offer? Explain your answer.
2. Assume that you have been offered cash discounts on merchandise that can be purchased from either of two suppliers. Supplier A offers trade credit terms of 3/20, net/70, while supplier B offers 4/15, net/80. What is the approximate effective cost of missing the cash discounts from each supplier? If you could not take advantage of either cash discount offer, which supplier would you select?
3. Obtain a current issue of the *Federal Reserve Bulletin* and determine the changes in the prime rate that have occurred since the end of 1991. Comment on any trends in the data.
4. Compute the effective cost of *not* taking the cash discount under the following trade credit terms:
    a. 2/10 net 40
    b. 2/10 net 50
    c. 3/10 net 50

d. 2/20 net 40
5. What conclusions can you make about credit terms from reviewing your answers to problem 4?
6. Your firm needs to raise funds for inventory expansion.
    a. What is the effective annual rate on a loan of $150,000 if it is discounted at a 12 percent stated annual rate and it matures in five months?
    b. How much must you borrow in order to obtain usable funds of $150,000?
    c. What is the effective annual rate if you borrow the funds computed in part b?
7. Bank A offers loans with a 10 percent stated annual rate and a 10 percent compensating balance. You wish to obtain $250,000 in a six-month loan.
    a. How much must you borrow in order to obtain $250,000 in usable funds? Assume you currently do not have any funds on deposit at the bank. What is the effective annual rate on a six-month loan?
    b. How much must you borrow in order to obtain $250,000 in usable funds if you currently have $10,000 on deposit at the bank? What is the effective annual rate on a six-month loan?
    c. How much must you borrow in order to obtain $250,000 in usable funds if you currently have $30,000 on deposit at the bank? What is the effective annual rate on a six-month loan?
8. Compute the effective annual rates on the following commercial paper offerings (all are sold on a discount basis):
    a. $1 million maturing in 90 days with a stated annual rate of 6 percent. Fees are 0.20 percent of the principal.
    b. $15 million maturing in 60 days with a stated annual rate of 7.6 percent. Fees are 0.35 percent of the principal.
    c. $500,000 maturing in 180 days with a stated annual rate of 8.25 percent. Fees are 0.25 percent of the principal.
    d. $50 million maturing in 210 days with a stated annual rate of 6.5 percent. Fees are 0.125 percent of the principal.

SELF-TEST QUESTIONS

1. Net working capital is defined as:
    a. current assets plus current liabilities
    b. current assets less fixed assets
    c. current assets less current liabilities
    d. current liabilities plus long-term liabilities
2. Permanent current assets are:
    a. accounts receivable that have become bad debts

    b.   inventories that have become obsolete

    c.   the level of current assets equal to fixed assets

    d.   the level of current assets needed to support sales

3. Which of the following are typical financing strategies used by businesses?

    a.   maturity matching, aggressive financing, and conservative financing

    b.   size matching, aggressive financing, and conservative financing

    c.   maturity matching, size matching, and aggressive financing

    d.   maturity matching, size matching, and conservative financing

4. Which of the following operating characteristics affect a firm's short-term financing strategy?

    a.   industry and company factors

    b.   seasonal variation

    c.   sales trend

    d.   cyclical variations

    e.   all of the above

5. A short-term bank loan that is unsecured is referred to as:

    a.   a line of credit

    b.   an accounts-receivable loan

    c.   an inventory loan

    d.   a life insurance policy loan

6. The most important form of short-term business financing is:

    a.   a revolving credit agreement

    b.   accounts-receivable financing

    c.   inventory loans

    d.   trade credit

7. An organization that engages in accounts-receivable financing by purchasing the accounts outright is referred to as a:

    a.   field warehouse firm

    b.   commercial finance company

    c.   factor

    d.   commercial paper house

8. The Small Business Administration assists in the financing of small businesses in which of the following ways?

    a.   by making direct loans to businesses

    b.   by participating jointly with banks in extending loans to businesses

    c.   by guaranteeing bank loans to businesses

    d.   all of the above

9. Large U.S. corporations of high credit quality can issue or sell short-term promissory notes called:

    a.   revolving credit agreements

    b.   commercial paper

    c.   trade credit

    d.   inventory loans

SELF-TEST PROBLEM

Assume that you have been offered cash discounts on merchandise that can be purchased from either of two suppliers. Supplier A offers trade credit terms of 3/15, net/60, while supplier B offers 4/10, net/70. What is the approximate effective cost of not taking the cash discounts from each supplier?

SUGGESTED READINGS

Dickerson, Bodil, B.J. Campsey, and Eugene F. Brigham. *Introduction to Financial Management*, 4e. Orlando, FL: The Dryden Press, 1995. Chap. 11.

Hooks, Linda, and Tim Opler. "What Determines Businesses' Borrowing from Banks?" *Studies*, Federal Reserve Bank of Dallas (August 1994): 15–23.

Kaen, Fred R. *Corporate Finance*. Cambridge, MA: Blackwell Publishers, 1995. Chap. 20.

Marsh, William H. *Basic Financial Management*. Cincinnati, Ohio: South-Western College Publishing, 1995. Chap. 18.

Peterson, Pamela P. *Financial Management and Analysis*. New York: McGraw-Hill Inc., 1994. Chap. 16.

Post, Mitchell A. "The Evolution of the U.S. Commercial Paper Market Since 1980." *Federal Reserve Bulletin* (December 1992): 879–91.

Rao, Ramesh K.S. *Financial Management*, 3e. Cincinnati, Ohio: South-Western College Publishing, 1995. Chap. 23.

Weston, J. Fred, Scott Besley, and Eugene F. Brigham. *Essentials of Managerial Finance*, 11e. Fort Worth, TX: The Dryden Press, 1996. Chap. 12.

ANSWERS TO SELF-TEST QUESTIONS   1. c, 2. d, 3. a, 4. e, 5. a, 6. d, 7. c, 8. d, 9. b

ANSWER TO SELF-TEST PROBLEM

Supplier A:

$$\text{Effective Cost} = \frac{3\%}{100\% - 3\%} \times \frac{365}{60 - 15} = 3.09\% \times 8.11 = 25.09\%$$

Supplier B:

$$\text{Effective Cost} = \frac{4\%}{100\% - 4\%} \times \frac{365}{70 - 10} = 4.17\% \times 6.08 = 25.35\%$$

CHAPTER 17

Capital Budgeting Analysis

AFTER STUDYING THIS CHAPTER, YOU SHOULD BE ABLE TO:

- Explain how the capital budgeting process should be related to a firm's mission and strategies.
- Identify and describe the five steps in the capital budgeting process.
- Identify and describe the methods or techniques used to make proper capital budgeting decisions.
- Explain how relevant cash flows are determined for capital budgeting decision purposes.
- Describe the importance of determining the correct base case from which to estimate project cash flows.
- Discuss how a project's risk can be incorporated into capital budgeting analysis.

As we first discussed in Chapter 13, every firm should have a vision or mission—a reason for being. To successfully implement its mission, a firm needs to have a competitive advantage. A competitive advantage is the reason why a firm's customers are willing to purchase its products or services rather than another firm's. Large corporations spend millions on researching their customers and competitors to gather information they can use to maintain or expand their competitive advantage. Integral to the process of trying to maintain or expand a firm's competitive advantage are its decisions of what products to offer and what markets or market segments to serve.

Capital budgeting is the process of identifying, evaluating, and implementing a firm's investment opportunities. Capital budgeting seeks to identify projects that will enhance a firm's competitive advantage and by so doing increase shareholders' wealth. By its nature capital budgeting involves long-term projects, although capital budgeting techniques also can be applied to working capital decisions.[1] Capital budgeting projects usually require large initial investments and may involve acquiring or constructing plant and equipment. A project's expected time frame may be as short as a year or as long as 20 or 30 years. Projects may include implementing new production technologies, new products, new markets, or mergers. Given their size and duration, the projects undertaken by the firm should reflect its overall strategy for meeting future goals. Given the length of most projects, time value of money concepts should be used to evaluate them.

The typical capital budgeting project involves a large up-front cash outlay, followed by a series of smaller cash inflows and outflows. But the project's cash flows, including the total up-front cost of the project, are not known with certainty before the project starts. The firm must evaluate the size, timing, and risk of the project's cash flows to determine if it enhances shareholder wealth.

The profitability of a firm is affected to the greatest extent by the success of its management in making capital budget investment decisions. A fixed-asset decision will be sound only if it produces a stream of future cash inflows that earns the firm an acceptable rate of return on its invested capital.

capital budgeting
process of identifying, evaluating, and implementing a firm's investment opportunities

MANAGEMENT OF FIXED ASSETS

Fixed-asset management requires financial managers to compare capital expenditures for plant and equipment against the cash-flow benefits that will be received from these investments over several years. When properly adjusted benefits exceed expenditures, these projects will help increase the firm's value.

Investment in fixed assets provides the basis for the manufacturing firm's earning power or profitability. Plant and equipment are employed to manufacture inventories that will be sold for profit, produce cash inflows, and enhance the firm's value. Proper capital-budgeting decisions must be made by the financial manager for this to occur. The types of decisions

---

1.   See Terry S. Maness and John T. Zietlow, *Short-Term Financial Management*, St. Paul, MN: West Publishing Company, 1993; Ned C. Hill and William Sartoris, *Short-Term Financial Management*, 3e, Englewood Cliffs, NJ: Prentice Hall, 1995.

include: whether to replace existing equipment with new equipment; whether to expand existing product lines by adding more plant and equipment similar to that in use; or whether to expand into new product areas requiring new types of fixed assets.

Capital-budgeting decisions can involve mutually exclusive or independent projects. As an example of **mutually exclusive projects,** two or more machines that perform the same function may be available from competing suppliers, possibly at different costs and with different expected cash benefits. The financial manager is responsible for choosing the best of these alternatives since only one can be chosen. Selecting one project precludes the other from being undertaken. **Independent projects** are not in direct competition with one another. They are to be evaluated based upon their expected effect on shareholder wealth. All such projects that enhance shareholder wealth should be included in the firm's capital budget.

mutually exclusive projects
selecting one project precludes others from being undertaken

independent projects
projects not in direct competition with one another

In this chapter we will be able to focus on only a small part of what is a very complex topic. We will present an overview of the capital-budgeting process and some techniques that are used to evaluate potential investments. Then we briefly discuss the process of estimating the cash flows that are expected to occur from a capital-budgeting project. This is followed by a discussion of how a project's risk can affect this evaluation process.

OVERVIEW OF THE CAPITAL BUDGETING DECISION

From Chapter 10, we know that the market value of an investment is the present value of future cash flows to be received from the investment. The net benefit, or the **net present value,** of an investment is the present value of a project's cash flows minus its cost:

net present value
present value of a project's cash flows minus its cost

$$\begin{array}{l}\text{Net present} \\ \text{value}\end{array} = \begin{array}{l}\text{Present value} \\ \text{of cash flows}\end{array} - \begin{array}{l}\text{Cost of the} \\ \text{project}\end{array} \qquad (17.1)$$

Should the net present value be positive (the investor pays *less* than the market value of the investment) the owner's wealth increases by the amount of the net present value. If, for example, the present value of an asset's cash flows is $100 and we can purchase it now for only $80, our wealth rises by $20. If instead we were foolish enough to pay $130 for the investment, our wealth will fall by $30. To maximize shareholder wealth, we need to find assets or capital budgeting projects that have positive net present values.

Where do businesses find attractive capital budgeting projects? Business managers need to search for projects which are related to the firm's present lines of business or future plans. It would be foolish, for example, for a computer manufacturer to consider investing in land and mining equipment to prospect for gold. Despite management beliefs about future trends in gold prices, and despite their confidence in their ability to find gold, such a project is far afield from the firm's current markets, products, and expertise.

Businesses should seek guidance to focus their search for capital budgeting projects. One popular corporate planning tool, **MOGS** (for Mission, Objectives, Goals, and Strategies), develops project plans that fit well with firm plans. A firm should have a MOGS plan, or something similar to it, in place to give direction to company planning and to help the firm's officers identify potential capital budgeting projects.

Over time managers define and redefine the firm's mission, objectives, goals, and strategies. This long-term plan provides a foundation for the next five to ten years of operating planning for the firm. The long-term plan is operationalized, or implemented, in the annual capital budget. To develop the capital budget, managers must find investment opportunities that fit within the overall strategic objectives of the firm; its position within the various markets it serves; government fiscal, monetary, and tax policies; and the leadership of the firm's management. Attractive capital budgeting projects take the firm from its present position to a desired future market position and, as a consequence, maintain or increase its shareholders' wealth.

CAPITAL-BUDGETING PROCESS

The capital-budgeting process involves the preparation and analysis of a business case request for funding, and usually consists of the following five stages:

1. Identification
2. Development
3. Selection
4. Implementation
5. Follow-up

The **identification stage** involves finding potential capital investment opportunities and identifying whether a project involves a replacement decision and/or revenue expansion. The **development stage** requires estimating relevant cash inflows and outflows. It also involves discussing the pros and cons of each project. Development sometimes requires asking what the strategic impact will be of *not* doing the project.

The third **selection stage** involves applying the appropriate capital budgeting techniques to help make a final accept or reject decision. In the **implementation stage,** projects that are accepted must be executed in a timely fashion. Finally, decisions need to be reviewed periodically with a *follow-up* analysis to determine whether they are meeting expectations. If disappointing results occur, it is sometimes necessary to terminate or abandon previous decisions.

MOGS
Mission, Objectives, Goals, and Strategies

identification stage
finding potential capital investment opportunities and identifying whether a project involves a replacement decision and/or revenue expansion

development stage
requires estimating relevant cash inflows and outflows

selection stage
applying appropriate capital budgeting techniques to help make a final accept or reject decision

implementation stage
executing accepted projects

The multinational corporation (MNC) must go through the same capital-budgeting process just described. In addition, however, MNCs need to consider possible added political and economic risks when making their decisions. Risk adjustments may be necessary due to the possibility of seizure of assets, unstable currencies, and weak foreign economies. MNCs also must consider the impact of foreign exchange controls and foreign tax regulations on a project's cash flows in relation to the final amounts that may be paid to the parent firm.

Information generation develops three types of data: internal financial data, external economic and political data, and nonfinancial data. These data are used to forecast financial data which are used to estimate a project's cash flows.

Table 17.1 lists data items that may need to be gathered in the information generation stage, depending on the size and scope of the project. Many economic influences can impact directly the success of a project by affecting sales revenues, costs, exchange rates, and overall project cash flows. Regulatory trends and political environment factors, both in the domestic and foreign economies, may help or hinder the success of proposed projects.

Financial data relevant to the project are developed from sources such as marketing research, production analysis, and economic analysis. Using the firm's research and internal data, analysts estimate the cost of the

TABLE 17.1   Overview of Data Needed in Project Analysis

EXTERNAL ECONOMIC AND POLITICAL DATA

business cycle stages
inflation trends
interest rates trends
exchange rate trends
freedom of cross-border currency flows
political stability and environment
regulations
taxes

INTERNAL FINANCIAL DATA	NONFINANCIAL DATA
investment costs (fixed assets and working capital)	distribution channels
market studies and estimates of revenues, costs, cash flows	quantity, quality of labor force in different global areas
financing costs (cost of capital)	labor-management relations
transportation costs	status of technological change in the industry
publicly available information on competitor's plans, operating results	competitive analysis of the industry, potential reaction of competitors

investment, working capital needs, projected cash flows, and financing costs. If public information is available on competitors' lines of business, this also should be incorporated into the analysis, to help estimate potential cash flows and to determine the effects of the project on the competition.

Nonfinancial information relevant to the cash flow estimation process includes data on the means used to distribute products to consumers, quality and quantity of the labor force, dynamics of technological change in the targeted market, and information from a strategic analysis of competitors. Analysts should assess the strengths and weaknesses of competitors and how they will react if the firm undertakes its own project.

CAPITAL-BUDGETING TECHNIQUES

Appropriate methods or techniques are required to evaluate capital-budgeting projects so proper wealth-maximizing decisions can be made. The techniques used should reflect the time value of money since cash outlays for plant and equipment occur now, while the benefits occur in the future. Four methods—net present value, internal rate of return, profitability index, and the payback period—are utilized widely. Of these four methods, the payback period is the *least* preferable one to use, because it does not take the time value of money into account.

NET PRESENT VALUE

The *net present value (NPV) method* is arguably the best method to use to evaluate capital-budgeting projects. A project's net present value is calculated as the present value of all cash inflows for the life of the project less the initial investment or outlay, as we saw in Equation 17.1. It considers the time value of money and includes all of the project's cash flows in the analysis. It also gives us a measure of dollar impact of the project on shareholder wealth. Thus, projects with positive NPVs are expected to add to shareholder wealth while projects with negative NPVs should be shunned.

In order to apply the net present value method, we need to know the project's required rate of return to discount the cash flow. This required rate, determined by the financial manager, should reflect the cost of long-term debt and equity capital funds for projects with the same risk as the one under consideration. In the following example, we'll assume that the required rate of return, or **cost of capital**, is 10 percent. In Chapter 18 we will review the process of determining the cost of capital.

cost of capital
project's required rate of return

We will apply the net present value technique to projects A and B. Their cash flows are shown in Table 17.2. The cash flows are multiplied by the 10 percent PVIF from Table 2 in the appendix to get the present values shown in Table 17.3. Notice that there is no discount factor for the initial

TABLE 17.2   Cash Flow Data for Projects A and B

YEAR	PROJECT A	PROJECT B
1	5,800	4,000
2	5,800	4,000
3	5,800	8,000
4	5,800	10,000
5	5,800	10,000

TABLE 17.3   Net Present Value Calculations for Projects A and B

	PROJECT A			PROJECT B		
YEAR	CASH FLOW ×	10% PVIF =	PRESENT VALUE	CASH FLOW ×	10% PVIF =	PRESENT VALUE
0	−$20,000	1.000	−$20,000	−$25,000	1.000	−$25,000
1	5,800	0.909	5,272	4,000	0.909	3,636
2	5,800	0.826	4,791	4,000	0.826	3,304
3	5,800	0.751	4,356	8,000	0.751	6,008
4	5,800	0.683	3,961	10,000	0.683	6,830
5	5,800	0.621	3,602	10,000	0.621	6,210
		Net Present Value =	$ 1,982		Net Present Value =	$ 988

outlays because they occur before any time has passed (i.e., in year zero). Positive net present values are shown for both projects. This means that an investment in either project will add to shareholder wealth. However, project A, with the higher net present value of $1,982, is preferable to project B, which has a net present value of $988.

A positive NPV means the project's outflows are sufficient to repay the initial up-front (time zero) costs as well as the financing cost of 10 percent over the project's life. Since their NPVs are greater than zero, each project's return is greater than 10 percent. The following section will show us how to compute a project's return.

A shortcut method can be used to calculate the net present value for project A. Since the cash inflows form an annuity, we could have used the PVIFA at 10 percent for five years from Table 4 in the appendix, which is 3.791. The net present value then can be calculated:

$$\$5,800 \times 3.791 = \begin{array}{r} \$21,988 \\ -20,000 \\ \hline \$\ 1,988 \end{array} \begin{array}{l} \text{PV cash inflows} \\ \text{Initial outlay} \\ \text{Net present value} \end{array}$$

The $1,988 net present value figure using PVIFA differs slightly from the $1,982 using PVIF because of rounding the present-value interest factors in the appendix tables. When cash inflows are not in the form of an annuity,

OIL AND GAS EXPLORATION PROJECTS

Table 17.1 lists some of the information that firms may use to evaluate capital spending projects. For a specific industry example, oil and gas companies ranked the following items, from most important to least important, in affecting capital spending decisions:

1. Forecasts of natural gas prices
2. Forecasts of crude oil prices
3. Forecasted demand for natural gas
4. Forecasted demand for crude oil
5. Availability and cost of outside funds to finance projects
6. Regulatory requirements or constraints on projects
7. Effect of tax considerations.

Natural gas prices and demand and crude oil prices and demand determine company revenues. Higher prices (demand) will result in higher sales revenues, and, all else constant, higher profits. And since oil and gas are substitute products, oil producers will be interested in natural gas price and demand trends and vice versa. With large oil companies spending billions of dollars a year on capital spending, the ability to raise external funds is a consideration should additions to retained earnings be insufficient to finance all of the attractive projects. Because of environmental concerns, oil and gas production is heavily regulated. The intricacies of the tax code also affect oil and gas investment decisions. Not only do U.S. income taxes affect these companies, but so do depreciation and oil and gas depletion allowances, tax codes of the different countries in which they drill, tax credits for taxes paid to different jurisdictions, and so on.

Source: Anne Reifenberg, "Big Oil Opens Capital-Spending Spigot for Overseas Projects Amid Price Slump," *The Wall Street Journal* (January 3, 1996): A2.

as in the case of project B, the longer calculation process shown in Table 17.3 must be used to find the net present value.

Projects with negative net present values are not acceptable to a firm. They provide returns lower than the cost of capital and would cause the value of the firm to fall. Clearly, it is important for the financial manager to make capital-budgeting decisions on the basis of their expected impact on the firm's value.

INTERNAL RATE OF RETURN

While the net present value method tells us that both projects A and B provide expected returns that are greater than 10 percent, we do not know the actual rates of return. The ***internal rate of return (IRR) method*** finds the return that causes the net present value to be zero—that is, when the present value of the cash flows equals the project's initial investment, as seen in Equation 17.2:[2]

internal rate of return (IRR) method
return that causes the net present value to be zero

$$NPV = \sum_{t=1}^{N} \frac{CF_t}{(1 + IRR)^t} - I = 0 \qquad (17.2)$$

A trial-and-error process can be used to find the internal rate of return (IRR), but financial calculators and computer spreadsheets (such as Lotus' @IRR function) provide much quicker means of estimating internal rates of return.

Let's illustrate the IRR process first for project A. Because the cash inflows form an annuity, the IRR is easy to find. We divide the initial outlay (PV annuity) by the cash inflow annuity amount (annual receipt) to arrive at the present value interest factor for an ordinary annuity.

$$PVIFA = \frac{PV\ annuity}{Annual\ receipt}$$

Notice that this is simply a rearrangement of the present value of an annuity Equation 9.9. For project A the PVIFA is 3.448 ($20,000/5,800).

We know this PVIFA of 3.448 is for five years. By turning to Table 4 in the Appendix, Present Value of a $1 Ordinary Annuity, we can read across the five-year row until we find a PVIFA close to 3.448. It falls between 3.605 (12 percent) and 3.433 (14 percent) but is much closer to the PVIFA at 14 percent. Thus the internal rate of return for project A is a little less than 14 percent. Using a financial calculator, the IRR is found to be 13.82 percent:

Financial Calculator Solution:

Inputs   20000   5800   5
          PV   PMT   N
Press   CPT   %i
Solution 13.82

For project B, with its unequal cash flows, a spreadsheet program is perhaps the best to use. But a trial-and-error process can also be used to find the IRR for project B. Discounting the cash flows at a 10 percent rate results in a positive net present value of $988, as we previously calculated. A positive net present value indicates that we need to try a higher discount rate, such as 12 percent, in order to find the discount rate that results in a zero NPV. The 12 percent present-value interest factors are taken from

2.   This method also is used to find the yield to maturity on bonds in Chapter 10.

Table 2 in the Appendix, Present Value of $1. In Table 17.4, we calculate that when the cash flows are discounted at a 12 percent rate, the net present value becomes minus $514. This indicates that the IRR actually falls between 10 and 12 percent. Since minus $514 is closer to zero than $988, the IRR is a little above 11 percent.

Both projects are acceptable because they provide returns higher than the 10 percent cost of capital. However, if the projects are mutually exclusive, we would select project A over project B.[3]

The NPV and IRR methods will always agree on whether a project enhances or harms shareholder wealth. If a project returns more than its cost of capital, the NPV is positive. If a project returns less than its cost of capital, the NPV is negative.

PROFITABILITY INDEX

profitability index (PI)
(benefit/cost ratio)
ratio between the
present values of the
cash flows and the
project's cost

Another discounted cash flow technique for evaluating capital-budgeting projects is the **profitability index (PI)**, also called the **benefit/cost ratio.** The PI method computes the ratio between the present values of the inflows and outflows:

$$PI = \frac{\text{Present value of the cash flows}}{\text{Initial cost}} = \frac{\sum\limits_{t=1}^{N} \dfrac{CF_t}{(1+r)^t}}{I} \qquad (17.3)$$

TABLE 17.4
Net Present Value Calculations for Project B Using a 12 Percent Discount Rate

	PROJECT B			
YEAR	CASH FLOW	× 12% PVIF	=	PRESENT VALUE
0	−$25,000	1.000		−$25,000
1	4,000	0.893		3,572
2	4,000	0.797		3,188
3	8,000	0.712		5,696
4	10,000	0.636		6,360
5	10,000	0.567		5,670
		Net Present Value = $−514		

3.   For several technical reasons, a project with an NPV below that of another project may have a higher IRR than the competing project. That is why it is best to calculate each project's NPV in addition to the IRR. The project with the highest NPV is the one that is expected to add the most to shareholder wealth.

A common misconception is that the internal rate of return represents the compounded return on the funds originally invested in the project. What IRR really measures is the return earned on the funds that remain *internally* invested in the project (hence the name, *internal* rate of return). Some cash flows from a project pay a return on the remaining balance of funds invested in the project. The remainder are used to pay down the principal, or the amount originally invested.

> **WHAT DOES THE IRR MEASURE?**

To show that the IRR measures the return earned on the funds that remain internally invested in a project, we present the following example:

Q: Martin and Barbara have decided to upgrade their business computer system to improve the quality and efficiency of their work. The initial investment is $5,000 and the project will save them $2,010.57 per year. The internal rate of return on the project has been determined to be 10 percent. Show how the IRR represents the return on the unrecovered costs of the project.

A: Below is the cash flow schedule constructed for Martin and Barbara's computer upgrade project.

(1) Year	(2) Beginning Investment Value	(3) Cash Inflow (savings)	(4) 10% Return on the Invested Funds $(2) \times 0.10$	(5) Reduction in the Invested Funds $(3) - (4)$	(6) Ending Value of Invested Funds $(2) - (5)$
1	$5,000.00	$2,010.57	$500.00	$1,510.57	$3,489.43
2	3,489.43	2,010.57	348.94	1,661.63	1,827.80
3	1,827.80	2,010.57	182.78	1,827.79	0.01*

*Value is not 0.00 due to rounding.

This table shows that the yearly cash inflow from the computer upgrade project represents both a return on the funds that remain invested (Column 4) and a reduction in the funds that remain invested in the project (Column 5). The project does *not* earn a 10 percent return, or $500 annually, on the initial $5,000 investment for all three years. The 10 percent IRR represents the return on the funds that remain invested in the project over its lifetime rather than each year's return on the original investment.

The PI measures the relative benefits of undertaking a project, namely the present value of benefits received for each dollar invested. A PI of 2, for example, means that the project returns a present value of $2 for every $1 invested. Since it would be foolish to invest in a project that returns less than a dollar for every dollar invested, the profitability index has a natural decision rule: accept a project that has a profitability index greater than 1.0, reject a project that has a PI less than 1.0.

Using the data in Table 17.3, we calculate the present value of project A's inflows to be $21,982. Since its initial cost is $20,000, project A has a profitability index of $21,982/$20,000 or 1.099. Project B's cash inflows have a present value of $25,988, so its profitability index is $25,988/$25,000 or 1.040.

The relationship between PI and NPV should be clear. Whenever NPV is positive, PI exceeds 1.0. Likewise, whenever NPV is negative, PI is less than 1.0. Thus, the NPV, IRR, and PI always agree on which projects would enhance shareholder wealth and which would diminish it.

PAYBACK PERIOD

payback period method determines the time in years it will take to recover, or pay back, the initial investment in fixed assets

The **payback period method** determines the time in years it will take to recover, or "pay back," the initial investment in fixed assets. Management will choose the projects whose paybacks are less than a management-specified period.

In cases where the cash benefits form an annuity, the payback period is easily calculated:

$$\text{Payback period} = \frac{\text{Initial outlay}}{\text{Annual cash inflow}}$$

For project A we have: payback period = $20,000/$5,800 = 3.4 years.

Cash inflows for project B will total $16,000 ($4,000 + $4,000 + $8,000) for the first three years. This leaves $9,000 ($25,000 − $16,000) still unrecovered. With a $10,000 cash flow expected in year 4, it will take an additional 0.9 of a year ($9,000/$10,000) before the investment is fully recovered. Thus the payback period for project B is 3.9 years. Based solely on the payback-period technique, project A would be chosen over project B because it recoups its investment more quickly.

However, the payback-period evaluation method suffers from two basic drawbacks. First, the technique does not consider the time value of money. The second limitation is that all cash flows beyond the payback period are ignored. Notice that project B will return $10,000 in cash inflow in year five, which is substantially more than project A's fifth year cash inflow. The possible significance of this difference is overlooked by the payback period method.

Thus far, this chapter has presented the basic concepts and techniques of capital budgeting. The capital-budgeting process tries to identify projects that will maximize shareholder value. Using the firm's mission and objectives as a guide, managers seek to identify market or product segments where the firm can build, maintain, or expand a competitive advantage. We have reviewed four capital-budgeting techniques: net present value, internal rate of return, profitability index, and the payback method. The first three use discounted cash flows in order to consider the time value of money.

A large accounting firm conducted a study of store remodelings and renovations. Their findings are disturbing for some retailers: these investments may never pay for themselves.

The study found that large discounters, such as Kmart and Target, have payback periods that average 20 years for renovation projects. The IRR on such projects range from 1 percent to 6 percent. For family-apparel specialty stores (such as Eddie Bauer), it was a different story. Their remodeling IRRs were as high as 67 percent with payback periods that averaged 19 *months*. The participants in the study were not released; the store names used above are only examples of stores in the different retail categories.

REMODELING PAYBACKS

The study concludes that having a good market position is more important than a renovation project. Poor returns on some stores' renovations apparently occurred because stores were trying to modernize in the face of new competition rather than realigning company strategy to respond to a successful competitor.

Source: Christina Duff, "Discount Retailers Get No Quick Fix From Remodeling Stores, Study Says," *The Wall Street Journal* (March 27, 1995): A15C.

The final method, although popular in surveys of corporate practice,[4] ignores time value considerations.

A practical problem when analyzing capital budgeting projects is how to properly estimate project cash flows. We consider how to do this in the following section.

ESTIMATING PROJECT CASH FLOWS

The previous section introduced capital-budgeting evaluation methods. Any attempt to apply those evaluation methods must resolve a practical difficulty: estimating a project's cash flows. This section reviews methods of developing such cash flow forecasts based on input from engineering, economic, and market analyses as well as from examination of the firm's competitive advantages.

ISOLATING PROJECT CASH FLOWS

To properly estimate the cash flows of a proposed capital budgeting project, the project must be viewed separately from the rest of the firm. This

4. See, for example, M. Stanley and S. Block, "A Survey of Multinational Capital Budgeting," *Financial Review* (March 1984): 36–54.

stand-alone principle
analysis focuses on the project's own cash flows, uncontaminated by cash flows from the firm's other activities

stand-alone principle ensures that analysts focus on the project's own cash flows, uncontaminated by cash flows from the firm's other activities.

Influences on Project Cash Flows

The relevant cash flows of a project include its incremental after-tax cash flows, any cannibalization or enhancement effects, and opportunity costs.

Incremental After-tax Cash Flows. The stand-alone principle requires the analyst to examine the after-tax cash flows that occur only as a result of the project. These are the project's **incremental cash flows.** The cash flows are incremental as they represent the difference between the firm's after-tax cash flows *with* the project and its **base case,** or the after-tax cash flows *without* the project. To identify this difference, analysts must try to identify all cash flows that will rise or fall as a consequence of pursuing the project. This includes any expected changes in revenues, expenses, and depreciation as well as investments in fixed assets and net working capital.

incremental cash flows
represent the difference between the firm's after-tax cash flows with the project and the firm's after-tax cash flows without the project

base case
firm's after-tax cash flows without the project

Estimating incremental after-tax cash flows for a project requires more thorough analysis than determining the expected change in cash flows from the firm's current condition. If future strategic moves by competitors are expected to damage or eliminate a firm's competitive advantage, the firm's base case cash flow forecast should reflect this situation. A project's incremental cash flows would then reflect expected changes from this declining trend.

For example, a firm such as Intel must consider competitors' responses when it invests in R&D to develop new computer chips. Intel's base case must include the impact on its sales if it does not develop the next generation of computer chips first. In the fast-moving technology market, being second to market means billions of lost sales.

Intel also is pouring billions in factory improvement and expansion projects to increase Intel's production capacity—$10 billion between 1991 and 1995. The purpose: to maintain and increase Intel's competitive advantage over other chip manufacturers and to sustain cash flow growth. Greater capacity means greater economies of scale, lower costs, and better competitive position in the computer chip market. With forecasted chip demand growing at 39 percent a year, Intel needs additional capacity just to maintain its current market share of 75 percent of the chip market.[5]

cannibalization
a project robs cash flow from the firm's existing lines of business

Cannibalization or Enhancement. **Cannibalization** occurs when a project robs cash flow from the firm's existing lines of business. When a soft-drink firm is thinking about introducing a new flavor or a new diet product, the project's incremental cash flows should consider how much the new offering will erode the sales and cash flows of the firm's other products.

---

5.   Don Clark, "A Big Bet Made Intel What It Is Today; Now, It Wagers Again," *The Wall Street Journal* (June 7, 1995): A1, A6.

Enhancement is less common than cannibalization; it reflects an increase in the cash flows of the firm's other products that occur because of a new project. For example, adding a delicatessen to a grocery store may increase cash flows more than the deli sales alone if new deli customers also purchase grocery items.

Opportunity Costs. From economics, we know that an **opportunity cost** is the cost of passing up the next best alternative. For example, the opportunity cost of a building is its market value. By deciding to continue to own it, the firm is foregoing the cash it could receive from selling it. Economics teaches the TINSTAAFL principle: "there is no such thing as a free lunch." Capital-budgeting analysis frequently applies this principle to existing assets.

If a firm is thinking about placing a new manufacturing plant in a building it already owns, the firm cannot assume that the building is free and assign it to the project at zero cost. The project's cash flow estimates should include the market value of the building as a cost of investing since this represents cash flows the firm *cannot* receive from selling the building.

Irrelevant Cash Flows

Now that we've examined some factors that influence cash flow estimates, let's look at some factors that should be excluded.

Sunk Costs. A **sunk cost** is a project-related expense that is not dependent upon whether or not the project is undertaken. For example, assume a firm commissioned and paid for a feasibility study for a project last year. The funds for the study are already spent; they represent a sunk cost. The study's cost is not an incremental cash flow as it is not affected by the firm's decision to either pursue or abandon the project. Therefore, the cost must be excluded from the project's cash flow estimates.

Financing Costs. It may seem important to account for financing cash flows such as interest and loan repayments, but there is a very good reason for excluding them from cash flow estimates. Capital-budgeting analysis techniques explicitly consider the costs of financing a project in the process of discounting its cash flows. As we shall discuss more fully in Chapter 18, a project's minimum required rate of return, or cost of capital, incorporates a project's financing costs.

APPROACHES TO ESTIMATING CASH FLOWS

The decision of whether to invest in a fixed asset begins with the development of a schedule of relevant cash flows. For many fixed-asset investments, cash outlays occur at the time of purchase. For example, let's assume that a producer will sell you a machine press for $18,000. It will cost you an additional $2,000 for transporting and installing the press. The sum of these expenditures is $20,000 and represents the initial outlay now, which is referred to as time-period zero.

---

enhancement
increase in the cash flows of the firm's other products that occur because of a new project

opportunity cost
cost of passing up the next best alternative

sunk cost
project-related expense not dependent upon whether or not the project is undertaken

Potential after-tax cash inflows to be derived from operating the machine press are more difficult to assess. The producer's specifications about the machine press's output will be helpful. If the firm has previously purchased similar machine presses, it can also use past experiences to assess the cost of producing annual inventories and the resulting before-tax cash benefits from their sale. Adjustments then must be made for tax payments, so that after-tax cash inflows can be directly compared with the initial investment outlays that are payable out of after-tax dollars.

Let's assume that the machine press will have a five-year life and then it will be discarded. Cash revenues from the sale of inventories produced by the machine press are expected to be $12,000 per year. Cash operating expenses associated with the use of the press are estimated at $5,600 per year. The firm also is entitled to write off, or depreciate, the machine press for income tax purposes. Let's assume that $4,000 ($20,000/5 years) can be depreciated each year[6] and that the firm has a 25 percent income tax rate.

The relevant annual after-tax cash earnings for each year can be estimated as seen in Table 17.5. *Cash earnings* is not the same as *cash inflow*. This is because depreciation does not involve actual cash disbursements; it is only an accounting bookkeeping entry for income tax purposes. To figure the cash inflow after taxes, we would start with the $6,400 in cash earnings before depreciation and subtract the $600 in income taxes that were paid in cash. The annual cash inflow after taxes is $5,800 ($6,400 − $600). This can be summarized as:

$$\text{Cash revenues} - \text{Cash expenses} - \text{Taxes} = \text{After-tax cash flow} \quad (17.4)$$

After-tax cash flows can be calculated by other means as well. For example, we can start with the cash earnings after taxes (in this case $1,800) and add back the amount of non-cash expenses such as depreciation ($4,000), giving us the cash inflow, $5,800. This can be summarized as:

$$\begin{array}{l}\text{Cash earnings}\\ \text{after taxes}\end{array} + \text{Depreciation} = \text{After-tax cash flow} \quad (17.5)$$

One other popular method for computing project cash flows is the tax-shield method. It is so called because this method considers the tax consequences of depreciation. Using this method, the after-tax cash flow is computed as:

$$\begin{array}{l}(\text{Cash revenues} - \text{Cash expenses}) \times (1 - \text{Tax rate}) + \\ \text{Tax rate} \times \text{Depreciation expense} = \text{After-tax cash flow} \quad (17.6)\end{array}$$

6. Current income tax laws specify methods for depreciating business assets. These specifications are referred to as the modified accelerated cost recovery system (MACRS). See the box "A Few Words on Depreciation Methods" on pages 574–75 for more details.

TABLE 17.5   Cash-Based Earnings Calculation

Cash revenues	$12,000
Cash operating expenses	−5,600
Cash earnings before depreciation	6,400
Depreciation	−4,000
Cash earnings before taxes	2,400
Income taxes (25%)	−600
Cash earnings after taxes	$ 1,800

From Table 17.5, we see that this is equal to:

$$(\$12,000 - \$5,600) \times (1 - 0.25) + (0.25) \times (\$4,000) = \$5,800,$$

which is the same cash flow we computed using Equations 17.4 and 17.5. As long as they are applied correctly, Equations 17.4, 17.5, and 17.6 will always give the same answer for the after-tax cash flow.

Some explanation of the depreciation tax effect is in order. Since it is deducted as an expense, depreciation helps to reduce taxable income and taxes. Using the above example, the firm will not have to pay taxes on $4,000 of its earnings because of the depreciation expense. Depreciation acts as a tax shield. To see this, let's redo Table 17.5 by omitting the depreciation expense. This is shown in Table 17.6.

Taxes, which must of course be paid in cash, are $1,600 in Table 17.6. In Table 17.5, with depreciation, taxes were only $600. The effect of the $4,000 depreciation expense is to reduce the project's taxes by $1,000. This tax reduction is called the **depreciation tax shield.** It will always equal the amount of the depreciation expense multiplied by the firm's tax rate. In this case, it is:

$$\text{Depreciation tax shield} = \text{Depreciation expense} \times \text{Tax rate} \quad (17.7)$$
$$= \$4,000 \times 0.25$$
$$= \$1,000$$

depreciation tax shield
tax reduction due to depreciation of fixed assets; equals the amount of the depreciation expense multiplied by the firm's tax rate

TABLE 17.6   Cash Earning Calculation Without Depreciation

Cash revenues	$12,000
Cash operating expenses	−5,600
Cash earnings before depreciation	6,400
Depreciation	−0
Cash earnings before taxes	6,400
Income taxes (25%)	−1,600
Cash earnings after taxes	$ 4,800

The depreciation tax shield will affect the project's after-tax cash flows. Without depreciation, the after-tax cash flow from Table 17.6 will be the same as the after-tax earnings, $4,800. As we've already seen, the after-tax cash flow in Table 17.5 is $5,800—exactly $1,000 higher. The reason? The $1,000 depreciation tax shield. Thus, if the project's sales, cash expenses, and depreciation are known, the firm can use its tax rate and Equation 17.6 to directly compute the project's after-tax cash flow.

The after-tax cash outflows and inflows can be combined into the following schedule for the five-year life of the machine press:

YEAR	CASH FLOW
0	$20,000
1	5,800
2	5,800
3	5,800
4	5,800
5	5,800

This example was an annuity—in each year, the sales, cash expenses, depreciation expenses, and tax rate were the same, so the resulting annual cash flows were the same. In general, annual calculations using Equations 17.4, 17.5, or 17.6 must be done if any of these factors vary over the course of the project.

STRATEGIC ANALYSIS AND CASH FLOW ESTIMATION

Proper analysis of a capital spending project must tie together the details of the firm's competitive and strategic analyses to the cash flow estimates of the proposed project. In the end, strategic analysis, marketing analysis, and financial analysis should agree. If they seem to conflict, which may happen when the corporate planners strongly favor a project with a negative NPV for "strategic" reasons, everyone involved in the decision must work together to discover the cause of the conflict. Some common problem areas are:[7]

DETERMINING THE CORRECT BASE CASE

Incremental cash flows were defined as the anticipated changes in cash flow from a base case. The firm's base case projection must assess what the firm's market share and cash flows would be if *no* new projects are implemented. The firm's planners must recognize that if nothing is done, customers *may* start buying competitors' products in response to the marketing, new-product development, and/or quality efforts of the competitors. The base case estimate should reflect these potential declines in cash flow.

OVERVALUING A STRATEGY

Projects may look more attractive than they really are if the analyst ignores cannibalization effects. The project analysis must also consider the effects of competitor retaliation; should you introduce a new product or innovation, your competition will take action to try to blunt the effectiveness of your strategy.

Finally, analysts need to be careful not to lose sight of the assumptions behind the estimates. Too many analysts start changing a few numbers and playing "what if?" games with their computer spreadsheets in order to get a positive project NPV. The spreadsheet output may soon lose any relationship with valid economic assumptions.

DEFINE PROJECT BOUNDARIES AT THE CORPORATE LEVEL

Estimates of revenues and costs should take the corporate view, rather than the business unit view. A project may look attractive to business unit managers because, as either an intended or unintended consequence, it shifts revenues or costs from one part of the company to another. Such projects will most likely fail to enhance shareholder value when total corporate incremental cash flows are properly estimated.

---

7.   This discussion is based upon P. Barwise, P. Marsh, and R. Wensley, "Must Finance and Strategy Clash?" *Harvard Business Review* (September/October 1989): 85–90.

A FEW WORDS ON DEPRECIATION METHODS

IRS tax regulations allow two basic depreciation methods, straight-line depreciation and the modified accelerated cost recovery system (MACRS).

Annual straight-line depreciation expense is computed by dividing the asset's cost by an estimate of its useful life. The annual straight-line depreciation expense for an asset that costs $100,000 and is expected to be used for eight years is $100,000/8 = $12,500.

MACRS depreciates assets by an accelerated method. In essence, MACRS depreciates assets using the double-declining balance method until it becomes advantageous to use straight-line depreciation over the asset's remaining life.

To ensure some uniformity, it assigns assets to classes, as shown below:

DEPRECIATION CLASSES

3-year class	Designated tools and equipment used in research
5-year class	Cars, trucks, and some office equipment such as computers and copiers
7-year class	Other office equipment and industrial machinery
10-year class	Other long-lived equipment
27.5-year class	Residential real estate
31.5-year class	Commercial and industrial real estate

Assets in the 27.5- or 31.5-year classes must be depreciated with the straight-line method over the appropriate number of years. Additionally, with some exceptions, MACRS follows a half-year convention. The asset receives a half-year's worth of depreciation in the year it is acquired, regardless of when it is actually purchased. Thus, assets in the three-year class are actually depreciated over *four* years. The owner writes off a half-year of depreciation in year 1, a full year of depreciation in each of years 2 and 3, and the remaining half-year of depreciation in year 4.

(continued on next page)

RISK-RELATED CONSIDERATIONS

The degree of risk associated with expected cash inflows may vary substantially among different fixed-asset investments. For example, a decision about whether to replace an existing machine with a new, more efficient machine would not involve substantial cash inflow uncertainty. This is because the firm already has some operating experience with the existing machine. Likewise, expansion in existing product lines allows the firm to

(Continued from previous page)

Annual depreciation percentages are given in the chart below. To determine an asset's annual depreciation expense, the cost of the asset is multiplied by the percentage for the appropriate asset class in the appropriate year.

MACRS PERCENTAGES

Year of ownership	Asset class			
	3-year	5-year	7-year	10-year
1	33.33%	20.00%	14.29%	10.00%
2	44.45	32.00	24.49	18.00
3	14.82	19.20	17.49	14.40
4	7.40	11.52	12.49	11.52
5		11.52	8.93	9.22
6		5.76	8.93	7.37
7			8.93	6.55
8			4.45	6.55
9				6.55
10				6.55
11				3.29

For example, for an asset in the three-year class that originally cost $50,000, the first year's depreciation is $50,000 × 0.3333 = $16,665; the second year's depreciation is $50,000 × 0.4445 = $22,225; for the third year, depreciation will be $50,000 × 0.1482 = $7,410; the final year's depreciation expense will be $50,000 × 0.0740 = $3,700.

base cash inflow expectations on past operating results and marketing data. These capital-budgeting decisions can be made by discounting cash flows at the firm's cost of capital because they are comparable in risk to the firm's other assets.

Expansion projects involving new areas and product lines are usually associated with greater cash inflow uncertainty. In order to compensate for this greater risk, financial managers often apply risk-adjusted discount rates to these cash flows as a consequence of the risk/expected return tradeoff. A higher-risk project needs to be evaluated using a higher required rate of return. To use a financial markets analogy, given the current return offered on safe short-term Treasury bills, investors will not want to invest in risky common stocks unless the expected returns are commensurate with the higher risk of stocks. Similarly, managers will not choose to undertake higher risk capital-budgeting projects unless their expected returns are in line with their risks.

The **risk-adjusted discount rate (RADR)** approach does this; it adjusts the required rate of return at which the analysis discounts a project's cash flows. Projects with higher (or lower) risk levels demand higher (or lower) discount rates. A project is expected to enhance shareholder wealth only if its NPV based on a risk-adjusted discount rate is positive.

One way to determine project risk-adjusted discount rates is for the firm's managers to use past experience to create risk classes or categories for different types of capital budgeting projects. Each risk category can be given a generic description to indicate the types of projects it should include and a required rate of return or "hurdle rate" to assign those projects. An example is shown in Table 17.7, which assigns projects of average risk (or those whose risk is about the same as the firm's overall risk) a discount rate equal to the firm's cost of capital. That is, projects of average risk must earn an average return, as defined by the firm's cost of financing. Projects with below-average risk levels are discounted at a rate below the cost of capital. Projects of above-average risk must earn premiums over the firm's cost of capital to be acceptable. Subjectivity enters this process as management must decide the number of categories, the description of each risk category, and the required rate of return to assign to each category. Differences of opinion or internal firm politics may lead to controversy in classifying a project. Clearly defined category descriptions can minimize such problems.

For example, let's use the previously presented data for projects A and B to illustrate the use of risk-adjusted discount rates. Let's assume that

TABLE 17.7   Risk Categories MMWWNN Corporation

Below-average risk:	Replacement decisions which require no change, or only a minor change, in technology. No change in plant layout required. Discount rate = cost of capital −2%
Average risk:	Replacement decisions involving significant changes in technology or plant layout; all cost-saving decisions; expansions and improvements in the firm's main product lines. Discount rate = cost of capital
Above-average risk:	Applied research and development; introduction of new products not related to major product lines; expansion of production or marketing efforts into developed economies in Europe and Asia. Discount rate = cost of capital + 2%
High risk:	Expansion of production or marketing efforts into less-developed and emerging economies; introduction of products not related to any of the firm's current product lines. Discount rate = cost of capital + 5%

> ## "Interest rates were low, so we were able to issue notes at a reasonable cost."

DOUG BARNETT

Corporate Treasurer
Giddings & Lewis, Inc.

*BS Accounting
University of Illinois
MBA Finance/
International Business,
Northwestern University*

Q: *What does Giddings & Lewis produce?*

A: We are the fourth largest producer of machine tools. We sell machine tools to the automotive, aerospace, construction, and other industries.

Q: *What are your responsibilities as Corporate Treasurer?*

A: I am responsible for a number of things including our communications with investors and securities analysts, establishing and maintaining relationships with external sources of capital, and helping our domestic and international locations manage their financial operations.

Q: *When do you need to utilize external sources of capital?*

A: The two main categories would be for working capital needs and for growth. An example of working capital would be a capital improvement. Growth could mean expanding our product line or our customer base via an acquisition.

Q: *You've made a couple of large acquisitions in the last five years. What was your source of capital?*

A: Originally we financed both transactions via bank debt, but since then we have refinanced both transactions. The first one we refinanced through a secondary stock offering and the second we refinanced by issuing ten year notes.

Q: *Why did you choose equity for one and debt for the other?*

A: At the time we refinanced the first acquisition, our stock price was appreciating and the stock market in general was quite strong. We felt that the strong demand for our stock made it a good choice as a source of funds. On the other hand, at the time of the second transaction, the stock market was relatively weak. Interest rates were low, so we were able to issue notes at a reasonable cost. In both cases it was basically a cost-benefit decision.

Q: *Did you work with investment bankers on these transactions?*

A: Yes. We had several firms come in and present options for raising the capital we needed. When we made our selections they were based on the firms' knowledge of our industry, their creativity and our assessment of their ability to get the job done.

Q: *You were an investment banker before you joined Giddings & Lewis. Is that an unusual transition to make?*

A: No, it's really not an unusual move. The things I learned at First Boston have been very helpful to me here. Knowing both sides of the business is a big help.

Q: *What skills are important in your work?*

A: Obviously accounting and finance knowledge are important. People skills and negotiating skills are too. I have a staff which does a lot of analysis and report generation, so I need good managerial skills as well.

project A and B are independent projects. Project A involves expansion in an existing product line, whereas project B is for a new product. The firm's 10 percent cost of capital would be the appropriate discount rate for project A. Recall that this would result in a net present value of $1,982.

In contrast, a higher discount rate for project B's cash flows of possibly 12 percent—the 10 percent cost of capital plus a 2 percentage point risk premium—might be judged appropriate by the financial manager. This would result in a net present value of minus $514. Thus, on a risk-adjusted basis, project A would still be acceptable to the firm, but project B would be rejected. Making adjustments for risk differences is a difficult but necessary task if the financial manager is to make capital budgeting decisions that will increase the value of the firm.

SUMMARY

The firm's long-term success depends upon the firm's strategy and its competitors' actions. The capital budget allocates funds to different projects, usually long-term, that are primarily used to purchase fixed assets to help a firm build or maintain a competitive advantage.

The capital-budgeting process is comprised of five stages: identification, development, selection, implementation, and follow-up. Since the capital-budgeting process involves the analysis of cash flows over periods of time, it is best to examine projects using a selection technique that considers the time value of money. The net present value, internal rate of return, and profitability index are three such methods. A fourth method, the payback period, measures how quickly a project will pay for itself, but ignores time value concerns. Of these selection methods, the net present value is the best, as it measures the dollar amount by which a project will change shareholder wealth.

Estimating cash flows is a difficult part of evaluating capital-budgeting projects. Projected earnings must be converted into cash flows by using one of the methods discussed in this chapter. Depreciation expense acts as a tax shield, because it reduces a project's tax bill and works to increase a project's after-tax cash flows.

By focusing solely on numbers, financial analysts of capital-budgeting projects can lose sight of the strategic importance behind the analysis. On the other hand, strategists need to be made aware of the need for shareholder value-enhancing projects. Analysts must be sure the financial analysis includes the correct base case, includes cannibalization and competitor retaliation effects, and includes proper risk adjustments. As with financial market investments, corporate fixed asset investments should include risk/expected return considerations. Higher risk projects should be evaluated using higher discount rates.

The next chapter will examine how firms can estimate their cost of capital. This is important, as the cost of financing the firm will be used as the discount rate for evaluating average-risk capital budgeting projects.

KEY TERMS

base case	internal rate of return method (IRR)
benefit-cost ratio	MOGS
cannibalization	mutually exclusive projects
capital budgeting	net present value
cost of capital	opportunity cost
depreciation tax shield	payback period method
development stage	profitability index (PI)
enhancement	risk-adjusted discount rate (RADR)
identification stage	selection stage
implementation stage	stand-alone principle
incremental cash flow	sunk cost
independent projects	

DISCUSSION QUESTIONS

1. What is meant by capital budgeting? Briefly describe some characteristics of capital budgeting.
2. Why is proper management of fixed assets crucial to the success of a firm?
3. How do "mutually exclusive" and "independent" projects differ?
4. Where do businesses find attractive capital budgeting projects?
5. Briefly describe the five stages in the capital budgeting process.
6. Identify some capital budgeting considerations that are unique to multinational corporations.
7. What kinds of financial data are needed in order to conduct the analysis of a project?
8. What kinds of nonfinancial information are needed in order to conduct the analysis of a project?
9. What is meant by a project's net present value? How is it used for choosing between projects?
10. Identify the internal rate of return method and describe how it is used in making capital budgeting decisions.
11. Describe the term "profitability index" and explain how it is used to compare projects.
12. Describe the payback period method for making capital budgeting decisions.

13. How is the "stand alone principle" applied when evaluating whether to invest in projects?
14. What are the three types of relevant cash flows to be considered in analyzing a project?
15. What types of cash flows are considered to be irrelevant when analyzing a project?
16. Describe the approaches used to estimate after-tax cash flows.
17. Sometimes strategic analysis and financial analysis of a project may differ. Briefly discuss how this might happen.
18. What is a risk-adjusted discount rate? How are risk-adjusted discount rates determined for individual projects?

PROBLEMS

1. Find the NPV and PI of a project that costs $1,500 and returns $800 in year 1 and $850 in year 2. Assume the project's cost of capital is 8 percent.
2. Find the NPV and PI of an annuity that pays $500 per year for 8 years and costs $2,500. Assume a discount rate of 6 percent.
3. Find the IRR of a project that returns $17,000 three years from now if it costs $12,000.
4. Find the IRR of a project if it has estimated cash flows of $5,500 annually for seven years if its year zero investment is $25,000.
5. For the following projects, compute NPV, IRR, profitability index, and payback. If these projects are mutually exclusive, which one(s) should be done? If they are independent, which one(s) should be undertaken?

	a.	b.	c.	d.
Year 0	− 1000	− 1500	− 500	− 2000
Year 1	400	500	100	600
Year 2	400	500	300	800
Year 3	400	700	250	200
Year 4	400	200	200	300
Discount				
rate	10%	12%	15%	8%

6. A machine can be purchased for $10,500 including transportation charges, but installation costs will require $1,500 more. The machine is expected to last four years and produce annual cash revenues of $6,000. Annual cash operating expenses are expected to be $2,000, with depreciation of $3,000 per year. The firm has a 30 percent tax rate. Determine the relevant after-tax cash flows and prepare a cash flow schedule.
7. Use the information in Problem 6 to do the following:
   a. Calculate the payback period for the machine.

    b. If the project's cost of capital is 10 percent, would you recommend buying the machine?

    c. Estimate the internal rate of return for the machine.

8. The Sanders Electric Company is evaluating two projects for possible inclusion in the firm's capital budget. Project M will require a $37,000 investment while project O's investment will be $46,000. After-tax cash inflows are estimated as follows for the two projects:

YEAR	PROJECT M	PROJECT O
1	$12,000	$10,000
2	12,000	10,000
3	12,000	15,000
4	12,000	15,000
5		15,000

    a. Determine the payback period for each project.

    b. Calculate the net present value and profitability index for each project based on a 10 percent cost of capital. Which, if either, of the projects is acceptable?

    c. Determine the approximate internal rate of return for Projects M and O.

9. Project R requires an investment of $45,000 and is expected to produce after-tax cash inflows of $15,000 per year for five years. The cost of capital is 10 percent.

    a. Determine the payback period, the net present value, and the profitability index for Project R. Is the project acceptable?

    b. Now, assume that the appropriate risk-adjusted discount rate is 14 percent. Calculate the risk-adjusted net present value. Is the project acceptable after adjusting for its greater risk?

    c. Calculate the approximate internal rate of return.

10. Assume the financial manager of the Sanders Electric Company in Problem 8 believes that Project M is comparable in risk to the firm's other assets. In contrast, there is greater uncertainty concerning Project O's after-tax cash inflows. Sanders Electric uses a 4 percentage point risk premium for riskier projects. The firm's cost of capital is 10 percent.

    a. Determine the risk-adjusted net present values for Project M and Project O, using risk-adjusted discount rates where appropriate.

    b. Are both projects acceptable investments? Which one would you choose?

11. The BioTek Corporation has a basic cost of capital of 15 percent and is considering investing in either or both of the following projects. Project HiTek will require an investment of $453,000, while Project LoTek's investment will be $276,000. The following after-tax cash flows (including the investment outflows in year zero) are estimated for each project.

YEAR	PROJECT HITEK	PROJECT LOTEK
0	$ – 453,000	$ – 276,000
1	132,000	74,000
2	169,500	83,400
3	193,000	121,000
4	150,700	54,900
5	102,000	101,000
6	0	29,500
7	0	18,000

a. Determine the present value of the cash inflows for each project and then calculate their net present values by subtracting the appropriate dollar amount of capital investment. Which, if either, of the projects is acceptable?

b. Calculate the internal rates of return for Project HiTek and Project LoTek. Which project would be preferred?

c. Now assume that BioTek uses risk-adjusted discount rates in order to adjust for differences in risk among different investment opportunities. BioTek projects are discounted at the firm's cost of capital of 15 percent. A risk premium of 3 percentage points is assigned to LoTek types of projects, while a 6 percentage point risk premium is used for projects similar to HiTek. Determine the risk-adjusted present value of the cash inflows for LoTek and HiTek and calculate their risk-adjusted net present values. Should BioTek invest in either or even both HiTek and LoTek projects?

12. For a capital budgeting proposal, assume this year's cash sales are forecast to be $220, cash expenses, $130, and depreciation, $80. Assume the firm is in the 30 percent tax bracket. Using each of the three methods discussed in the chapter, determine the project's after-tax cash flow.

13. The Brassy Fin Pet Shop is considering an expansion. Construction will cost $90,000 and will be depreciated to zero, using straight-line depreciation, over five years. Earnings before depreciation are expected to be $20,000 in each of the next five years. The firm's tax rate is 34 percent.

a. What are the project's cash flows?

b. Should the project be undertaken if the firm's cost of capital is 11 percent?

14. Below is a simplified project income statement for Ma & Pa Incorporated. The project is expected to last for eight years. Its up-front cost is $2,000. Its cost of capital is 12 percent.

Sales	$925.00
– cash expenses	310.00
– depreciation	250.00
Earnings before taxes	$365.00
– taxes (at 35%)	127.75
Net income	$237.25

a. Compute the project's after-tax cash flow.

b. Compute and interpret the project's NPV, IRR, profitability index, and payback period.

SELF-TEST QUESTIONS

1. Two or more projects that perform the same function are said to be:
    a. mutually exclusive projects
    b. independent projects
    c. joint projects
    d. dependent projects
2. The capital-budgeting process starts with which one of the following stages?
    a. development
    b. identification
    c. implementation
    d. selection
3. In addition to the standard capital-budgeting process, multinational corporations must also consider added:
    a. domestic follow-up and foreign political risks
    b. domestic development and foreign economic risks
    c. foreign political and economic risks
    d. domestic and foreign selection risks
4. Which one of the following capital-budgeting evaluation techniques requires the use of the project's required rate of return when calculating it?
    a. net present value
    b. internal rate of return
    c. payback period
    d. accounting-based rates of return
5. Which one of the following capital-budgeting evaluation techniques is based on finding a discount rate which causes the net present value to be zero?
    a. net present value
    b. internal rate of return
    c. profitability index
    d. payback period
6. Which one of the following capital-budgeting evaluation techniques does not consider the time value of money in its calculation?
    a. net present value
    b. internal rate of return
    c. profitability index
    d. payback period
7. The relevant cash flows of a project do not include which one of the following?
    a. incremental after-tax cash flows

   b.   cannibalization or enhancement effects
   c.   opportunity costs
   d.   sunk costs
8.   The tax-shield method is used to estimate:
   a.   net income
   b.   after-tax cash flow
   c.   before-tax cash flow
   d.   earnings after taxes but before depreciation
9.   Which one of the following methods should be used to evaluate a project that is more (or less) risky than the firm's average project?
   a.   net present value
   b.   internal rate of return
   c.   payback period
   d.   risk-adjusted discount rate

SELF-TEST PROBLEMS

1.   The Consolidated Company is evaluating a project, code named MXG, for possible inclusion in the firm's capital budget. Project MXG will require a $40,000 investment. After-tax cash inflows are estimated as follows:

YEAR	PROJECT MXG
1	$12,000
2	12,000
3	12,000
4	12,000

   a.   Determine the payback period for the project.
   b.   Calculate the net present value for the project based on a 10 percent cost of capital. Is the project acceptable?
   c.   Determine the approximate internal rate of return for Project MXG.

SUGGESTED READINGS

Barwise, P., P. Marsh, and R. Wensley. "Must Finance and Strategy Clash?" *Harvard Business Review,* September/October 1989, pp. 85–90.

Brigham, Eugene E. *Fundamentals of Financial Management,* 7e. Fort Worth, TX: The Dryden Press, 1995. Chaps. 9 and 10.

Helfert, Erich A. *Techniques of Financial Analysis,* 6e. Homewood, IL: Richard D. Irwin, 1994. Chap. 6.

Peterson, Pamela J. *Financial Management and Analysis.* New York, NY: McGraw-Hill Inc., 1994. Chaps. 8 and 9.

Pinches, George E. *Financial Management,* 5e. New York: Harper & Row, 1994. Chaps. 7 and 8.

Rao, Ramesh K.S. *Financial Management*, 3e. Cincinnati, Ohio: South-Western College Publishing, 1995. Chaps. 8 and 9.

Shapiro, Alan C. *Fundamentals of Multinational Financial Management*, 2e. Boston: Allyn and Bacon, 1994. Chap. 18.

Stanley, M., and S. Block. "A Survey of Multinational Capital Budgeting." *Financial Review*, March 1984, pp. 36–54.

ANSWERS TO SELF-TEST QUESTIONS   1. a, 2. b, 3. c, 4. a, 5. b, 6. d, 7. d, 8. b, 9. d

ANSWERS TO SELF-TEST PROBLEM

1. a.   Payback period for project MXG: $40,000/$12,000 = 3.3 years
    b.   Project MXG PVIFA at 10% for 4 years = 3.170
         $ 12,000 × 3.170 = $ 38,040
                             $\underline{-40,000}$
         Net present value: $ -1,960
         Do not accept Project MXG.
    c.   Internal rate of return for Project MXG: PVIFA = $40,000/$12,000 = 3.333
         Turning to Table 4 in the Appendix and looking along the 4-year row, we find the 3.333 is slightly higher than 3.312 at 8%, indicating the IRR is slightly less than 8%.

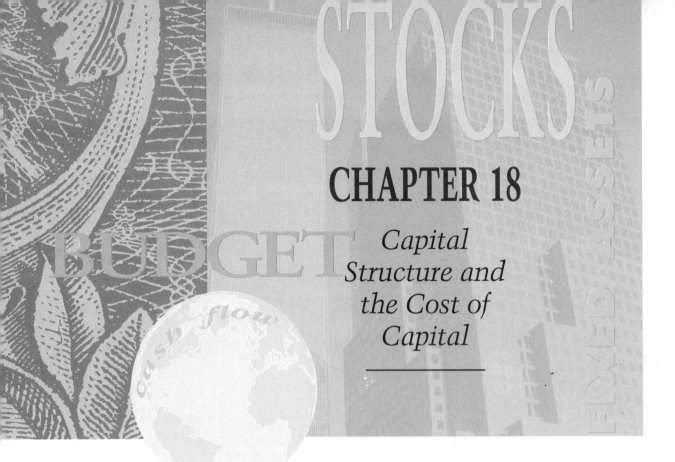

CHAPTER 18

Capital Structure and the Cost of Capital

AFTER STUDYING THIS CHAPTER, YOU SHOULD BE ABLE TO:

- Explain how capital structure affects a firm's capital budgeting discount rate.
- Describe the factors that affect a firm's capital structure.
- Explain how EBIT/eps analysis can assist management in choosing a capital structure.
- Describe how a firm's business risk and operating leverage may affect its capital structure.
- Describe how a firm's degree of financial leverage can be computed and explain how to interpret its value.
- Explain how a firm can determine its cost of debt financing and cost of equity financing.
- Explain how a firm can estimate its cost of capital.

The previous chapter described the capital budgeting process. We learned how to estimate a project's cash flows and how to use techniques, such as NPV and IRR, for evaluating projects. In Chapter 17 we assumed the project's discount rate, or its cost of capital, was given. The purpose of this chapter is to explain how managers can estimate their firm's cost of capital, or the discount rate, the firm will use on its "average risk" projects. This discount rate will be adjusted up or down, as we learned in Chapter 17, depending upon the project's risk. Higher-risk projects will have their cash flows discounted at higher discount rates. Lower-risk projects will use lower discount rates.

Before managers can estimate the cost of capital, two inputs are needed. First, they must determine the appropriate financing mix to use to fund capital budgeting projects. Second, the cost of each financing source needs to be determined. Once the proportions or weights of each financing source are known along with their cost, managers can estimate the firm's weighted average cost of capital. It is this weighted average cost of capital which is the return that should be earned on capital budgeting projects of average risk.

A firm's mix of debt and equity used to finance its assets defines the firm's **capital structure,** as seen in Figure 18.1. In this chapter we will first review the influences that affect a firm's choice of a capital structure. After our discussion of capital structure we review practical means by which managers can estimate the cost of each debt and equity financing source. Finally, we show how the firm's capital structure and the costs of each financing source can be combined to provide an estimate of the weighted average cost of capital.

*capital structure
firm's mix of debt
and equity*

WHY CHOOSE A CAPITAL STRUCTURE?

Obviously, a target capital structure is important as it determines the proportion of debt and equity used to estimate a firm's cost of capital. There is, however, a second, even more important reason. The firm's **optimum debt/equity mix** minimizes the firm's cost of capital, which in turn will help the firm to maximize shareholder wealth.

For example, suppose a firm expects cash flows of $20 million annually in perpetuity. Each of the three capital structures shown in the table below

*optimum
debt/equity mix
minimizes the firm's
cost of capital*

FIGURE 18.1   The Balance Sheet

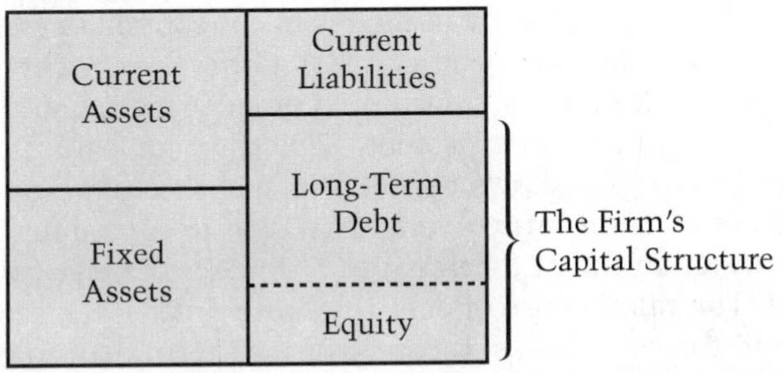

has a different WACC. Following the perpetuity valuation rule from Chapter 9, firm value is computed by dividing the expected cash flow by the firm's cost of capital under each capital structure. Capital Structure 2 in the following table minimizes the cost of capital at 8 percent, which in turn maximizes the value of the firm at $250 million.

	CAPITAL STRUCTURE 1	CAPITAL STRUCTURE 2	CAPITAL STRUCTURE 3
Debt	25.0%	40.0%	70.0%
Equity	75.0%	60.0%	30.0%
WACC	10.0%	8.0%	12.5%
Firm value	$\frac{\$20 \text{ million}}{0.10} \cdot \$200 \text{ million}$	$\frac{\$20 \text{ million}}{0.08} \cdot \$250 \text{ million}$	$\frac{\$20 \text{ million}}{0.125} \cdot \$160 \text{ million}$

A non-optimal capital structure leads to higher financing costs and the firm will likely reject some capital-budgeting projects that could have increased shareholder wealth with an optimal financing mix. For example, suppose a firm has a minimum cost of capital of 8 percent, but poor analysis leads management to choose a capital structure that results in a 10 percent cost of capital. It would then reject an average risk project that costs $100,000 and returns cash flows of $26,000 in years 1 through 5 at a 10 percent cost of capital (NPV = −$1,439.54). This project would be acceptable at the minimum possible cost of capital of 8 percent (NPV = $3,810.46).

There is another, more intuitive way to see the importance of finding the optimal capital structure. A project's NPV represents the increase in shareholders' wealth from undertaking a project. From Chapter 10, we know there is an inverse relationship between value and discount rates (the "seesaw effect"). Thus, a lower WACC gives a higher project NPV and results in a larger increase in shareholder wealth.

TRENDS IN CORPORATE USE OF DEBT

Many firms restructured themselves financially during the 1980s. Some did so in attempts to lower their cost of capital by taking advantage of the tax deductibility of interest by issuing debt to repurchase common stock, thereby increasing their debt/equity ratios. Other firms went private in the 1980s, fought off take-overs, or acquired other firms, financing the transactions with large amounts of debt. The surge in bankruptcies at the beginning of the 1990s shows the folly of such excessive use of debt. As seen in Figure 18.2, the ratio of long-term debt to capital for U.S. corporations meandered in the 21.0 percent to 27.0 percent range from the 1920s until 1960. The relative use of debt then rose until 1989, peaking at 46.8 percent. Into the early 1990s, the ratio of long-term debt to capital fell as firms issued equity to strengthen their balance sheets and to reduce the probability of financial distress due to overborrowing.

FIGURE 18.2   Ratio of Debt to Capital in the United States

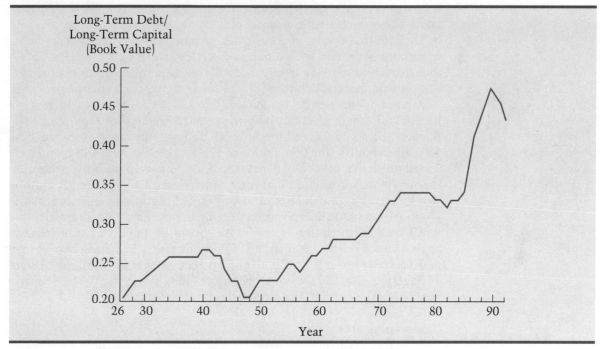

DIFFICULTY OF MAKING CAPITAL STRUCTURE DECISIONS

Examining the various influences that affect a firm's capital structure is not an easy task. Unlike NPV or operating cash flow, there is no formula we can use to determine the proportions of debt and equity a firm should use to finance its assets.

But that doesn't mean we are totally lost. Financial theory and research on firm behavior have given us a set of guidelines or principles by which to evaluate a firm's proper mix of debt and equity. We will also simplify the discussion by referring only to *debt* and *equity* with little distinction between the various types of debt and equity. We will discuss some of the variations in debt and equity later in the chapter.

In the following section, we first examine how different capital structures affect the earnings and risk of a firm in a simple world with no corporate income taxes. We'll use a tool of financial analysis called EBIT/eps analysis.

EBIT/EPS ANALYSIS

EBIT/eps analysis allows managers to see how different capital structures affect the earnings and risk levels of their firms. Specifically, it shows the

EBIT/eps analysis allows managers to see how different capital structures affect the earnings levels of their firms

graphical relationship between a firm's operating earnings, or earnings before interest and taxes (EBIT), and earnings per share (eps). If we ignore taxes, these two quantities differ only by the firm's interest expense and by the fact that eps is, of course, net income stated on a per-share basis. Examining scenarios with different EBIT levels can help managers to see the effects of different capital structures on the firm's earnings per share.

Let's assume the Bennett Corporation is considering whether it should restructure its financing. As seen in Table 18.1, Bennett currently finances its $100 million in assets entirely with equity. Under the proposed change, Bennett will issue $50 million in bonds and use this money to repurchase $50 million of its stock (at a price of $25 a share, Bennett will repurchase 2 million shares of stock). Bennett expects to pay 10 percent interest on the new bonds, for an annual interest expense of $5 million. Assuming that Bennett's expected EBIT for next year is $12 million, let's see how the proposed restructuring may affect earnings per share. For simplicity, we will ignore taxes in this example. As shown in Table 18.2, the scenario analysis assumes that Bennett's EBIT will be either $12 million, or it may be 50 percent lower ($6 million) or 50 percent higher ($18 million). Figure 18.3 graphs the EBIT/eps combinations that result from the scenario analysis of the current and proposed capital structures.

INDIFFERENCE LEVEL

Figure 18.3 clearly shows that the EBIT/eps lines cross. This means that, at some EBIT level, Bennett will be indifferent between the two capital structures, inasmuch as they result in the same earnings per share.

Under Bennett's current capital structure, eps is computed as (EBIT − $0 interest)/4 million shares. Under the proposed structure, eps is (EBIT − $5 million interest)/2 million shares. To find the level of EBIT where the lines cross, we set these two eps equations equal to each other and solve for EBIT:

$$\frac{EBIT - 0}{4} = \frac{EBIT - 5}{2}$$

TABLE 18.1   Current and Proposed Capital Structures for the Bennett Corporation

	CURRENT	**PROPOSED**
Total assets	$100 million	$100 million
Debt	0 million	50 million
Equity	100 million	50 million
Common stock price	$25	$25
Number of shares	4,000,000	2,000,000
Interest rate	10%	10%

TABLE 18.2 Scenario Analysis with Current and Proposed Capital Structures

	CURRENT—NO DEBT, 4 MILLION SHARES (MILLIONS OMITTED)		
	EBIT 50% BELOW EXPECTATIONS	EXPECTED	EBIT 50% ABOVE EXPECTATIONS
EBIT	$6.00	$12.00	$18.00
− I	0	0	0
NI	$6.00	$12.00	$18.00
eps	$1.50	$ 3.00	$ 4.50

	PROPOSED—50% DEBT (10% COUPON), 2 MILLION SHARES (MILLIONS OMITTED)		
	EBIT 50% BELOW EXPECTATIONS	EXPECTED	EBIT 50% ABOVE EXPECTATIONS
EBIT	$6.00	$12.00	$18.00
− I	5.00	5.00	5.00
NI	$1.00	$ 7.00	$13.00
eps	$0.50	$ 3.50	$ 6.50

FIGURE 18.3 EBIT/eps Analysis, Bennett Corporation

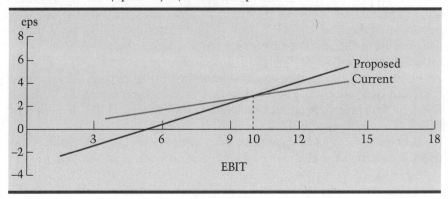

The earnings per share under the two plans are the same when EBIT equals $10 million.[1] When EBIT exceeds $10 million, the proposed, more highly leveraged capital structure will have the higher earnings per share. When EBIT is less than $10 million, the current, less leveraged capital structure will have the higher eps.

1. By cross-multiplying, $2\text{EBIT} = 4\text{EBIT} - 20$. Solving for EBIT, we obtain EBIT = 10.

The indifference level of $10 million in EBIT did not occur by chance. It equals the firm's interest cost of 10 percent multiplied by its total assets ($100 million). In other words, if the firm can earn an operating return on assets (EBIT/TA) *greater* than its interest cost, leverage is beneficial, leading to higher eps. If the firm's operating return on assets is less than its 10 percent interest cost, leverage is harmful, resulting in lower eps. If Bennett strongly believes that EBIT will meet expectations at $12 million, the proposed capital structure change is attractive.

Leverage obviously affects earnings per share. For low values of EBIT, Bennett's current capital structure leads to lower eps than the proposed structure. For higher values of EBIT, debt works to the firm's benefit as eps is higher under the proposed capital structure than under the current structure. Whether the higher level of eps results in a higher stock price depends upon investors and the stock's P/E or price/earnings ratio. In general, firms with better growth prospects and higher quality managers have higher P/Es.[2] If, however, the firm's risk increases to too high a level in the eyes of equity investors—as it may, if too much debt is in a firm's capital structure—the P/E will fall. The firm's stock price will also fall if the decline in the P/E offsets the expected gain in eps from a more highly leveraged firm. A major task of a firm's management is to determine the capital structure that will allow shareholder wealth to be maximized. If the debt level is too low, eps will be lower than it could have been, penalizing shareholders. If, however, the firm's debt ratios are too high, the risk may be such that the firm's P/E ratio will fall, leading to lower stock prices irrespective of the level of earnings per share.

EBIT/eps analysis has several practical implications. First, as seen above, it shows the ranges of EBIT where a firm may prefer one capital structure over another. The firm may decide to increase or decrease its financial leverage depending on whether its expected EBIT is above or below the indifference EBIT level.

Secondly, EBIT is not constant over time; it will change, depending upon sales growth, industry competitive conditions, and the firm's oper-

---

2. In Chapter 10 we learned about the constant dividend growth model:

$$P_0 = \frac{D_1}{r - g}$$

which states that stock price is equal to next year's expected dividend divided by the difference between the shareholder's required rate of return r and the dividend growth rate. This model can be used to estimate a firm's price/earnings ratio by dividing both sides by E, the firm's earnings per share:

$$P_0/E = \frac{D_1/E}{r - g}$$

Using this model, a firm will have a higher P/E ratio if it has a higher dividend payout (D_1/E), higher growth rate g, or lower required return r. The required return r will fall as inflation expectations fall or as the risk premium falls.

ating leverage. Variations in EBIT will produce variations in eps. Should the expected EBIT of the firm lie above the indifference EBIT level, the firm's managers should examine the standard deviation of their EBIT forecast. If there is a relatively high chance that the actual EBIT level may fall below the indifference level, management may decide to play it safe and use a more conservative financing strategy with less debt.[3]

A firm's **business risk** is measured by its variability in EBIT over time. Business risk is affected by several factors, including the business cycle, competitive pressures, and the firm's operating leverage or its level of fixed operating costs. The following section reviews how a firm's business risk is affected by its operating leverage, and how a firm's operating leverage can affect management's choice of a capital structure.

business risk
measured by variability in EBIT over time

COMBINED OPERATING AND FINANCIAL LEVERAGE EFFECTS

The variability of sales or revenues over time is a basic operating risk. Furthermore, when fixed operating costs, such as rental payments, lease payments, contractual employee salaries, and general and administrative overhead expenses exist, they create operating leverage and increase business risk. Since fixed costs do not rise and fall along with sales revenues, fluctuating revenues lead to variability in operating income or EBIT. The effect of operating leverage is that a given percentage change in net sales will result in a greater percentage change in operating income or earnings before interest and taxes (EBIT).

Operating leverage affects the top portion of a firm's income statement, as shown in Table 18.3. It relates changes in sales to changes in EBIT or operating income. The effect of fixed operating costs on a firm's business risk can be measured, as we learned in Chapter 14, by the degree of operating leverage (DOL). In a similar fashion, when money is borrowed, financial leverage will be created as the firm will have a fixed financial obligation—or interest—to pay. Financial leverage affects the bottom half of a firm's income statement. A given percentage change in the firm's EBIT will produce a larger percentage change in the firm's net income or earnings per share.

DEGREE OF FINANCIAL LEVERAGE

A firm's financial risk reflects its interest expense, or in financial jargon, its financial leverage. A quick way to determine a firm's exposure to financial

---

3.   "Relatively high" is subjective, based upon management's risk preferences and past experience.

TABLE 18.3   Effects of Operating and Financial Leverage

Operating Leverage	Sales − Variable costs (such as labor and raw materials) − Fixed costs (such as rent and depreciation expense)
Financial Leverage	EBIT or operating income − Interest expense
	EBT or earnings before taxes − Taxes (a variable expense, dependent upon EBT)
	Net Income
	$\text{eps} = \dfrac{\text{Net Income}}{\text{Number of Shares}}$

degree of financial leverage (DFL)
measures the sensitivity of eps to changes in EBIT

risk is to compute its degree of financial leverage. The ***degree of financial leverage (DFL)*** measures the sensitivity of eps to changes in EBIT:

$$DFL = \frac{\text{Percentage change in eps}}{\text{Percentage change in EBIT}} \qquad (18.1)$$

This definition clearly suggests that DFL represents the percentage change in earnings per share arising from a 1 percent change in earnings before interest and taxes. For example, a DFL of 1.25 means that the firm's eps will rise (or fall) by 1.25 percent for every 1 percent increase (or decrease) in EBIT.

There is a more straightforward method to compute a firm's degree of financial leverage that avoids handling percentage changes in variables. This formula is given in Equation 18.2:

$$DFL = \frac{EBIT}{EBIT - I} = \frac{EBIT}{EBT} \qquad (18.2)$$

DFL equals the firm's earnings before interest and taxes (EBIT) divided by EBIT minus interest expense, or earnings before taxes.

Let's use Equation 18.2 to find the degree of financial leverage when EBIT equals $50 and interest expense equals $10, $20, and $0. When EBIT equals $50 and interest expense equals $10, DFL equals $50/($50 − $10) = 1.25.

When interest expense is $20, DFL equals $50/($50 − $20) = 1.67. Higher interest expense leads to greater financial risk and greater eps sensitivity to changes in EBIT.

When the interest expense is zero, the DFL is $50/($50 − $0) = 1.00. That is, the percentage change in eps will be the same as the percentage change in EBIT. Without any fixed financial cost, there is no financial leverage and there is no magnification effect.

TOTAL RISK

Business risk affects the top half of the income statement. Operating leverage magnifies the effect of changing sales to produce a percentage change in EBIT larger than the change in sales. Financial risk affects the bottom half of the income statement. Financial leverage magnifies the percentage change in EBIT to produce a larger percentage change in earnings per share. Thus, a change in sales, through operating leverage, affects EBIT. This change in EBIT, through the effect of financial leverage, subsequently affects eps.

Total earnings risk, or total variability in EPS, is a combination of the effects of business risk and financial risk. As shown in Table 18.3, operating leverage and financial leverage combine to magnify a given percentage change in sales to a potentially much greater percentage change in earnings.

Together, operating and financial leverage produce an effect called **combined leverage.** A firm's **degree of combined leverage (DCL)** is the percentage change in earnings per share that results from a 1 percent change in sales volume:

> **combined leverage** *effect on earnings produced by the operating and financial leverage*

$$DCL = \frac{\text{Percentage change in EPS}}{\text{Percentage change in sales}} \qquad (18.3)$$

> **degree of combined leverage (DCL)** *percentage change in earnings per share that results from a 1 percent change in sales volume*

There is a straightforward relationship between the degrees of operating and financial leverage and the degree of combined leverage. A firm's degree of combined leverage is simply the product of its degree of operating leverage and its degree of financial leverage:[4]

$$DCL = DOL \times DFL \qquad (18.4)$$

The DCL represents the impact on earnings per share of the effects of operating leverage and financial leverage on a given change in sales revenue.

Let's illustrate this concept with a full income statement for last year and both a 10 percent decrease and a 10 percent increase in net sales for next year, as seen in Table 18.4.

We can estimate directly the individual effects of operating and financial leverage and their combined effects. First, from Chapter 14, the degree of operating leverage (DOL) is estimated as

---

4. Recall that the degree of financial leverage is the percentage change in earnings per share divided by the percentage change in EBIT. The degree of operating leverage is the percentage change in EBIT divided by the percentage change in sales. Multiplying these two formulas gives Equation 18.4:

$$\underbrace{\frac{\text{Percentage change in EBIT}}{\text{Percentage change in sales}}}_{DOL} \times \underbrace{\frac{\text{Percentage change in eps}}{\text{Percentage change in EBIT}}}_{DFL}$$

$$= \frac{\text{Percentage change in EPS}}{\text{Percentage change in sales}} = DCL$$

TABLE 18.4   Effects of Leverage on the Income Statement

	LAST YEAR	NEXT YEAR	
		10% SALES DECREASE	**10% SALES INCREASE**
Net sales	$700,000	$630,000	$770,000
Less: variable costs (60% of sales)	420,000	378,000	462,000
Less: fixed costs	200,000	200,000	200,000
Earnings before interest and taxes	80,000	52,000	108,000
Less: interest expenses	20,000	20,000	20,000
Income before taxes	60,000	32,000	88,000
Less: income taxes (30%)	18,000	9,600	26,400
Net income	$ 42,000	$ 22,400	$ 61,600
Percent change in operating income (EBIT)		−35.0%	+35.0%
Percent change in net income		−46.7%	+46.7%

$$DOL = \frac{Sales - variable\ cost}{Sales - variable\ cost - fixed\ cost}$$

$$= \frac{\$700,000 - \$420,000}{\$700,000 - \$420,000 - \$200,000} = \frac{\$280,000}{\$80,000} = 3.50$$

It should be noted that this is the same as the percentage change in EBIT (35%) divided by the percentage change in sales (10%) in Table 18.4:

$$DOL = \frac{35\%}{10\%} = 3.50$$

The degree of financial leverage (DFL) measures the impact of fixed financial expenses and is estimated as

$$DFL = \frac{EBIT}{EBIT - I}$$

Thus, DFL is equal to:

$$DFL = \frac{\$80,000}{\$80,000 - \$20,000} = \frac{\$80,000}{\$60,000} = 1.33$$

It should be noted that this is the same as the percentage change in eps (46.7%) divided by the percentage change in EBIT (35%) in Table 18.4:

$$DOL = \frac{46.7\%}{35.0\%} = 1.33$$

Finally, the degree of combined leverage (DCL) can be estimated by finding the product of the DOL and the DFL as follows:

DCL = DOL × DFL
DCL = 3.5 × 1.33
DCL = 4.66

Except for rounding, this is the same as the percentage change in eps (46.7%) divided by the percentage change in sales (10%): 46.7%/10% = 4.67.

By knowing the DCL factor, we can now estimate next year's change in net income, assuming no major change occurs in the income tax rate. This is done by multiplying the expected percentage change in net sales by the DCL of 4.67. For example, a 10 percent increase in net sales will result in net income increasing by 46.7 percent (10 percent times the combined leverage factor of 4.67). Of course, combined leverage works in both directions, and a decline in net sales might place the firm in a difficult financial position. A 10.0 percent decline in sales will be expected to reduce net income and eps by 46.7 percent.

The use of both operating and financial leverage produces a compound impact when a change in net sales occurs. Thus, from an overall risk perspective, it is important for the financial manager to use operating and financial leverage so as to form an acceptable combined leverage effect.

For example, if a firm's stockholders do not like large amounts of risk, a firm with a high degree of operating leverage will attempt to keep financial leverage low. In other words, it will use relatively less debt and more equity to finance its assets. Likewise, a firm with low business risk (that is, steady sales and low fixed operating expenses), such as an electric utility can support a higher degree of financial leverage and use relatively more debt financing. There is no evidence that firms adjust their DOLs and DFLs to match some standard degree of combined leverage. But their relationship does, however, imply a potential tradeoff between a firm's business and financial risk.

OTHER INFLUENCES ON CAPITAL STRUCTURE CHOICE

In addition to expected effects on earnings and the firm's degree of operating leverage, several other influences affect a firm's capital structure choices. We review them here.

FLEXIBILITY

Frequently the greatest concern among financial managers is maintaining access to capital. Without the ability to raise funds, a firm may have to pass up attractive investment opportunities, or a temporary cash crunch may push it to the edge of default. Financial flexibility requires financial slack, or unused debt capacity. One way to do this is to try to maintain an investment-grade bond rating over time.

Flexibility is needed when the firm needs to raise funds for either operating purposes or to make strategic capital investments. If such a need arises when stock prices are low, it will be beneficial to the firm if its debt levels are such that it can still borrow funds at reasonable interest rates. Should the firm already have high debt ratios, the firm may not be able to borrow additional funds and it may be forced to issue shares of stock at a time when stock prices are low. Maintaining excess borrowing capacity allows managers to choose between issuing debt or issuing equity. Managers should try to avoid being closed out of debt markets because of previous excessive borrowing.

TIMING

The sale of securities by a corporation and the type of securities sold depend in large measure upon existing conditions in the capital markets. A wise policy for long-term financial planning is to anticipate changing market conditions. For example, during a period of economic recession when business is at a low ebb, interest rates are at typically low levels as are common stock prices. Under these conditions, if additional funds are needed for expansion or to retire maturing debt, it becomes much more attractive to do so through the sale of debt securities rather than through the sale of common stock.

During the early expansion phase of the business cycle, when business opportunities and investment plans are increasing, it is also advantageous to borrow on a long-term basis even though interest rates may be rising somewhat. After a long period of economic expansion, however, pressure on capital resources and on the capital markets is such that interest rates reach very high levels. At these times most common stock prices are typically still high, and thus it is attractive for the corporations to sell new shares of stock.

CORPORATE CONTROL

Although the control of a corporation is usually administered by its board of directors, ultimate control rests with the stockholders, who hold stock with voting rights. Stockholders elect the members of the board of directors, who are in turn responsible to the stockholders. Many stockholders in large corporations do not exercise their voting rights. Thus it is possible and often true that stockholders owning less than a majority of the total stock are able to control the election of the board of directors and, hence, have ultimate control over all activities of the corporation.

A growing firm that has prospered under its existing management may lack the capital necessary to take advantage of available opportunities. Yet management may not want additional stockholders because of the voting privileges the new investors would have. Obtaining the needed financial capital might require selling so much new stock that the existing stockholders would lose control of the affairs of the company. Many firms have avoided expansion rather than risk losing control through the sale of stock.

Corporate bonds and notes, in contrast, provide no voting rights. Therefore, management frequently prefers this form of financing as long as the bond covenants are not too burdensome.

MATURITY MATCHING

In the sections about short-term financial policies in Chapter 16, we saw that one of the important reasons for the use of short-term borrowing is seasonal business change. If a business needs funds for only six or seven months of the year, it may be far cheaper to use short-term borrowing rather than long-term funds on which interest must be paid throughout the year. By the same token, the business cycle itself causes changes in the firm's financial requirements. There are always periods in the life of a business when there are fewer investment opportunities or when the demand for the firm's products may temporarily decrease. A capital structure that allows for change during these periods is a great advantage. A large company with many different debt securities that have staggered maturities may find, during a period of economic contraction, that it is wise to simply pay off a maturing bond. The company can retire the issue out of the increasing liquidity that occurs when working assets move from inventories and accounts receivable into cash.

In other situations the business may engage in temporary ventures that will be ended either at some set future date or at the discretion of management. Here, too, it may be good to have financing that can be eliminated if it is no longer needed. The firm can arrange for debt financing with a maturity matching the expected period of need. For maturity matching, debt holds an important advantage over preferred stock or common stock financing because equity securities do not have a stated maturity that makes it possible to retire them conveniently. We should also note that a lease arrangement for fixed assets is advantageous because the lease term may be set to coincide with the duration of the need for the assets.

MANAGEMENT'S ATTITUDE TOWARD DEBT AND RISK

When push comes to shove, it is people—the management team—who ultimately make decisions about financing policy. Some management teams may be more conservative and hesitant to issue debt, while others may be more aggressive and willing to increase the firm's financial leverage. Their judgment and expectations for the firm's financial future will affect the firm's capital structure.

BEYOND DEBT AND EQUITY

To simplify the discussion in this chapter, we have assumed that the firm faces two basic financing choices: borrow fixed interest-rate debt or sell common equity. Bright Wall Street investment bankers have introduced many variations on these two themes in attempts to market new and different instruments to meet the needs of many kinds of issuers and investors.[5] Today firms can choose among various types of security issues. Consequently many firms have several layers of debt and several layers of equity on their balance sheets.

Debt can be made convertible to equity. Its maturity can be extended, or shortened, at the firm's option. Debt issues can be made senior or subordinate to other debt issues. Coupon interest rates can be fixed, float up or down along with other interest rates, or be indexed to a commodity price.[6] Some bond issues do not even pay interest. Zero-coupon bonds do not pay explicit interest. Investor returns arise from the difference between their face values and discounted selling prices. Other bonds pay "interest" for several years by giving investors additional bonds. Bonds can pay interest in U.S. dollars or other currencies. They can be issued in the United States or overseas. Bonds can be sold alone, or with warrants attached that allow the bond investor to purchase shares of common stock at predetermined prices over time.

Likewise, equity variations exist. Preferred stock has a claim on the firm that is junior to the bondholder claim, but senior to the common shareholder claim. Preferred can pay dividends at a fixed or a variable rate. Preferred equity has gained popularity because it increases a firm's equity without diluting the ownership and control of the common shareholders. It also increases future financing flexibility by expanding the firm's capacity for debt issues. Corporate investors can exempt 70 percent of preferred dividend income from income taxes, paying tax at its marginal tax rate on only 30 percent of the preferred dividend. If the firm is in the 40 percent tax bracket it must pay only \$12 (0.4 × \$30) for each \$100 of preferred dividends. This is equivalent to the firm paying taxes at a 12 percent rate on preferred dividends. Hence corporate investors looking for a tax break tend to invest in the preferred shares of other corporations.

---

5.   Finance is not just finance; it sometimes involves marketing research and analysis. Wall Street firms serve two basic sets of customers: issuers and investors. By designing innovative securities to better meet their customers' needs, investment bankers can exploit market niches by being the first mover in a new product area. Such innovation will attract business, enhance income, and increase the firm's reputation among market players.
6.   For example, a silver-mining firm whose profits and cash flow are quite sensitive to the market price of silver can reduce its financial leverage by issuing bonds that pay interest at a rate that is related to silver price fluctuations.

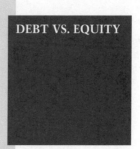

DEBT VS. EQUITY

The decision of how much debt and equity to use in a firm's capital structure is not an easy one to answer. Even the president of the American Finance Association confessed some years ago, "How do firms choose their capital structures? . . . The answer is, we don't know."* There are two main theories that try to explain firm behavior in choosing capital structures.

The first theory is sometimes called the "static trade-off hypothesis." The idea behind this theory is that firms select the proportion of debt in their capital structures in order to balance the benefits of tax-deductible interest payments with its opportunity costs, namely the higher risk premium that investors will demand on a firm's debt and equity as financial leverage rises and the risk of going bankrupt rises. Thus, the firm should have a target debt ratio that will balance these costs and benefits and maximize firm value.

The second hypothesis is called the "pecking order" theory. It states a firm's current capital structure is just the cumulative result of past financing decisions. Adherents to this view argue that firms prefer to use internal financing as much as possible to finance projects. If external financing is needed, the next item on the firm's pecking order is to obtain debt financing as it is less costly (in that it is less risky to investors) for the firm to issue. New equity is sold only as a last resort.

Adherents of each theory can point to evidence which supports their perspective. Additional research will be necessary before this issue is ever settled. In the meantime, this chapter covers basic principles which most practitioners agree can help to guide capital structure decisions.

*S. Myers, "The Capital Structure Puzzle," *Journal of Finance* (July 1984): 575.

Types of common stock can differ. Firms can have different classes of common equity. Some classes can provide holders with higher levels of dividend income. Some classes may have superior voting rights. Firms have issued separate classes of equity to finance acquisitions, distributing part of the acquired firm's earnings as dividends to holders of that particular class of stock. Such was the case with General Motors. It issued its Class E stock to finance its acquisition of EDS; dividends on the Class E shares are determined by the earnings of the EDS subsidiary.

All these variations of debt and equity give the firm valuable flexibility. Corporate financial managers' decisions about the structure of a security issue may be more difficult now, but these choices also can allow them to lower the cost of capital and increase firm value.

Once management decides upon an appropriate capital structure, it must determine the financing costs for its various financing sources. The firm's cost of capital is the weighted average of these financing costs. The remainder of this chapter focuses on how a firm can determine its cost of capital.

cost of capital
minimum acceptable
rate of return to a firm
on a project

The **cost of capital** (sometimes called the hurdle rate) represents the minimum acceptable rate of return to a firm on a project of average risk. Should the project be more or less risky than the average project, its cost of capital can be adjusted so its minimum required return is commensurate with its risk (as discussed in the previous chapter.)

REQUIRED RATE OF RETURN AND THE COST OF CAPITAL

Investors in a project expect to earn a return on their investment. This expected return depends upon current capital market conditions (for example, levels of stock prices and interest rates) and the risk of the project. The minimum acceptable rate of return of a project is the return that generates sufficient cash flow to pay investors their expected return.

To illustrate, suppose a firm wants to spend $1,000 on an average risk capital budgeting project, financing the investment by borrowing $600 and selling $400 worth of common stock. The firm must pay interest on the debt at a rate of 9 percent, while shareholders expect a 15 percent return on their investment. To adequately compensate the firm's investors, the project should generate an annual pre-tax expected cash flow equal to

Lender's interest + Shareholders' return = Annual expected cash flow
= (0.09)($600) + (0.15)($400)
= $54 + $60 = $114

The project's minimum rate of return must then equal

Minimum cash flow/Investment = Minimum rate of return
= $114/$1,000 = 11.4 percent

As another means to determine this, the expected return of each financing source could be weighted by its relative use. The firm is raising 60 percent of the project's funds from debt and 40 percent from equity. This results in a minimum pre-tax required return of

(0.60)(9%) + (0.40)(15%) = 11.4 percent

Thus, the required rate of return on a project represents a weighted average of lenders' and owners' return expectations. Since a cash flow or return to an investor represents a cash outflow or a cost to the firm, *the minimum required rate of return is a weighted average of the firm's costs of various sources of capital.* Thus, the required rate of return on a project is equivalent to the project's cost of capital. It is this number that should be used as a discount rate when evaluating a project's NPV. *Required rate of return, cost of capital,* and *discount rate* are different terms for the same concept.

COST OF CAPITAL

Relevant cash flows are incremental after-tax cash flows. To be consistent, these cash flows must be discounted using an incremental after-tax cost of capital. The firm's relevant cost of capital is computed from after-tax financing costs. Firms pay preferred and common stock dividends out of net income, so these expenses already represent after-tax costs to the firm. Because they pay debt interest out of pre-tax income, however, the cost of debt requires adjustment to an after-tax basis before computing the cost of capital.

A project's incremental cash flows must be discounted at a cost of capital that represents the incremental or marginal cost to the firm of financing the project, that is, the cost of raising one additional dollar of capital. Thus, the cost of debt and equity that determine the cost of capital must not come from historical averages or past costs, but rather from forward-looking projections of future costs. The firm's analysts need to evaluate investors' expected returns under likely market conditions, and then use these expected returns to compute the firm's marginal future cost of raising funds by each method.

Conceptually, investors' required returns equal the firm's financing costs. The following sections use the valuation concepts for bonds and stocks from Chapter 10 to find investors' required returns on bonds, preferred stock, and common stock. It then adjusts these required returns to reflect the firm's after-tax cost of financing.

COST OF DEBT

The firm's unadjusted cost of debt financing equals the yield to maturity on new debt, either a long-term bank loan or a bond issue. The yield to maturity represents the cost to the firm of borrowing funds in the current market environment. The firm's *current* financing costs determine its current cost of capital.

A firm can determine its cost of debt by several methods. If the firm targets an "A" rating (or any other bond rating), a review of the yields to maturity on A-rated bonds in Standard & Poor's *Bond Guide* can provide an estimate of the firm's current borrowing costs. Several additional factors will affect the firm's specific borrowing costs, including covenants and features of the proposed bond issue as well as the number of years until the bond or loan matures or comes due. It is important to examine bonds whose ratings and characteristics resemble those the firm wants to match.

In addition, the firm can solicit the advice of investment bankers on the cost of issuing new debt. Or, if the firm has debt currently trading, it can use public market prices and yields to estimate its current cost of debt. The publicly traded bond's yield to maturity can be found using the techniques for determining the internal rate of return on an investment discussed in Chapters 9 and 10. Finally, a firm can seek long-term debt financing from a bank or a consortium of banks. Preliminary discussions with the bankers will indicate a ballpark interest rate the firm can expect to pay on its borrowing.

The yield estimate, however derived, is an estimate of the coupon rate on newly issued bonds (as bonds are usually issued with prices close to their par value) or the interest rate on a loan. Interest is a pre-tax expense, so the interest estimate should be adjusted to reflect the tax shield provided by debt financing. If YTM is the pre-tax interest cost estimate, the after-tax estimate is YTM times $(1 - T)$, where T is the firm's marginal tax rate. Thus, the after-tax cost of debt, k_p, is

$$k_p = \text{YTM} \, (1 - T) \tag{18.5}$$

Suppose Global Manufacturing has a 40 percent marginal tax rate and it can issue debt with a 10 percent yield to maturity. Its after-tax cost of debt is 10% $(1 - 0.40)$ = 6 percent.

COST OF PREFERRED STOCK

Chapter 10 explained how to model preferred stock as a perpetuity. The investor pays a price, P, for a share of preferred stock, and in return expects to receive $\$D_p$ of dividends every year, forever. Valuing the stock as a perpetuity, the maximum price an investor will pay for a share is $\$D_p/r_p$, where r_p represents rate of return required by investors in the firm's preferred stock. Rearranging the valuation equation to solve for r_p:

$$r_p = \$D_p/P$$

The firm will not receive the full $\$P$ per share; there will be a flotation cost of $\$F_p$ per share. Thus, the cost to the firm of preferred stock financing, k_p, is:

$$k_p = \$D_p/(P - F_p) \tag{18.6}$$

A firm wants to issue preferred stock that pays an annual dividend of $5 a share. The price of the stock is $55 and the cost of floating a new issue will be $3 a share. The cost of preferred stock to this firm is: $k_p = \$D_p/(P - F_p)$ = $5/($55-$3) = 0.0962 or 9.62 percent.

COST OF COMMON EQUITY

Unlike debt and preferred stock, cash flows from common equity are not fixed or known beforehand and their risk is harder to evaluate. In addition, firms have *two* sources of common equity, retained earnings and new stock issues, and thus *two* costs of common equity. It may be clear that there is an explicit cost (dividends) associated with issuing new common equity. But even though the firm pays no extra dividends to use retained earnings, they are not a free source of financing. We must consider the opportunity cost of using funds that could have been given to shareholders as dividends.

Retained earnings are the portion of net income that the firm does not distribute as dividends. As owners of the firm, common shareholders have a claim on all of its net income, but they receive only the amount that the firm's board of directors declares as dividends.

From the shareholders' perspective, the opportunity cost of retained earnings is the return the shareholders could earn by investing the funds in assets whose risk is similar to that of the firm. Suppose, for example, that shareholders expect a 15 percent return on their investment in a firm's common stock. If the firm could not invest its retained earnings to achieve a risk-adjusted 15 percent expected return, shareholders would be better off receiving 100 percent of its net income as dividends. That way they can reinvest the funds themselves in similar-risk assets that can provide a 15 percent expected return.

To maximize shareholder wealth, management must recognize that retained earnings have a cost. That cost, k_{re}, is the return that shareholders expect from their investment in the firm. We will review two methods of estimating the cost of retained earnings. One method uses the security market line, the other uses the assumption of constant dividend growth.

Cost of Retained Earnings: Security Market Line Approach

Chapter 12 developed the security market line, or SML, which can provide an estimate of shareholder required return based upon a stock's systematic risk. The security market line equation,

$$E(R) = RFR + \beta_i(R_{MKT} - RFR)$$

gives the required return as a combination of the risk-free return, R_f, and a risk premium which is the product of a stock's systematic risk, measured by β_i, and the market risk premium $(R_m - R_f)$. The required shareholder return is the opportunity cost the firm must earn on its retained earnings. Thus, an estimate for the cost of retained earnings is:

$$k_{re} = E(R) = RFR + \beta_i(R_{MKT} - RFR) \tag{18.7}$$

For example, assume that the current T-bill rate is 4.5 percent and that analysts estimate that the current market risk premium is slightly above its historical average at 9.0 percent. Suppose also that analysts estimate Global Manufacturing's β to be 1.30. What is Global Manufacturing's cost of retained earnings using the SML approach?

All the information we need to apply Equation 18.7 is presented above:

$$k_{re} = RFR + \beta_i(R_{MKT} - RFR) = 4.5\% + (1.3)(9\%) = 16.2 \text{ percent}$$

Using the security market line, Global Manufacturing's cost of retained earnings is 16.2 percent.

Cost of Retained Earnings: Constant Dividend Growth Model

Chapter 11 presented the constant dividend growth model to estimate a firm's stock price:

$$P = \frac{D_1}{r_{cs} - g} \tag{18.8}$$

where P is the stock's price, g is the expected (constant) dividend growth rate, D_1 is next year's expected dividend (equal to the current dividend increased by g percent) and r_{cs} is the shareholders' required return on the stock. Rather than use the model to determine a price, however, we can substitute today's actual stock price for P and solve for the shareholders' required rate of return, r_{cs}:

$$k_{re} = r_{cs} = \frac{D_1}{P} + g \tag{18.9}$$

The shareholders' required return represents the firm's cost of retained earnings, k_{re}. The ratio D_1/P represents the current income yield to shareholders from their investment of $\$P$. From the firm's perspective, this ratio represents the ratio of dividends it pays to its current market value. The growth rate, g, represents shareholders' expected capital gain arising from dividend growth. From the firm's perspective, g can be viewed as an opportunity cost of raising equity today. It is expected to be able to sell equity at a $g\%$ higher price next year.

Cost of New Common Stock

To estimate the cost of new equity, we must modify Equation 18.9 to reflect extra cost to the firm of issuing securities in the primary market. The costs of issuing stock, or **flotation costs**, include the accounting, legal, and printing costs of offering shares to the public as well as the commission or fees earned by the investment bankers who market the new securities to investors. If the flotation cost is $\$F$ per share, the cost of issuing new common stock, or k_n, is given by Equation 18.10:

flotation costs
costs of issuing stock; include accounting, legal, and printing costs of offering shares to the public as well as the commission earned by the investment bankers who market the new securities to investors

$$k_n = \frac{D_1}{P - F} + g \tag{18.10}$$

Suppose a firm has just paid a dividend of $2.50 a share; its stock price is $50 a share; and the expected growth rate of dividends is 6 percent. The current dividend of $2.50 must be multiplied by a factor to reflect the expected 6 percent growth for D_1, next year's dividend. Using Equation 18.9, the cost of using retained earnings as a financing source is:

$$k_{cs} = \frac{\$2.50(1 + 0.06)}{\$50} + 0.06 = \frac{\$2.65}{\$50} + 0.06$$
$$= 0.053 + 0.06 = 0.113 \text{ or } 11.3 \text{ percent.}$$

If new common stock is to be issued to finance the project and flotation costs are expected to be $4 per share, we need to use Equation 18.10 to estimate the cost of new common equity:

$$k_n = \frac{\$2.50(1 + 0.06)}{\$50 - \$4.00} + 0.06 = \frac{\$2.65}{\$46.00} + 0.06$$
$$= 0.058 + 0.06 = 0.118 \text{ or } 11.8 \text{ percent.}$$

The cost of using new common stock is 11.8 percent.

We learned about the concept of efficient markets in Chapter 12, namely that current market prices and interest rates reflect all known information as well as the market's expectations about the future. Financial managers can do little to "fight the market." If managers feel their financing costs are too high, it is usually the case that the market perceives risk that the managers are ignoring. The efficient market ensures that financing costs are in line with the market's perception of firm's risks and expected returns.

WEIGHTED AVERAGE COST OF CAPITAL

We have seen how to compute the costs of the firm's basic capital structure components. Now we will combine the components to find the weighted average of the firm's financing costs.

The firm's **weighted average cost of capital (WACC)** represents the minimum required rate of return on its capital-budgeting projects. It is found by multiplying the marginal cost of each capital structure component by its appropriate weight, and summing the terms:

$$\text{WACC} = w_d k_d + w_p k_p + w_e k_e \tag{18.11}$$

The weights of debt, preferred equity, and common equity in the firm's capital structure are given by w_d, w_p, and w_e, respectively. As the weighted average cost of capital covers all of the firm's capital financing sources, the weights must sum to 1.0. The firm's cost of common equity, k_e, can reflect the cost of retained earnings, k_{re}, or the cost of new common stock, k_n, whichever is appropriate. Most firms rely upon retained earnings to raise the common equity portions of their financial needs. If retained earnings are insufficient, they can issue common stock to meet the shortfall. In this case, k_n is substituted for the cost of common equity.

weighted average cost of capital (WACC) represents the minimum required rate of return on a capital-budgeting project. It is found by multiplying the marginal cost of each capital structure component by its appropriate weight, and summing the terms

**WHAT DO
BUSINESSES
USE AS THEIR
COST OF
CAPITAL?**

Surveys of U.S. firms find that most (60 percent) use after-tax weighted average costs of capital as their required rates of return for projects. Other methods include management-determined target returns or the cost of some specific source of funds. A survey of U.S.-based multinationals found that 88 percent of them use the WACC as their required rate of return. Over two-thirds of MNCs use the same methods to calculate WACCs for both their U.S. and overseas projects. Nearly half of the respondents use the parent firm's cost of capital to evaluate projects; 32 percent use the specific cost of financing a project as the project's required rate of return.

A third study found that most U.S. and European multinational firms use their WACCs as their project discount rates, although a greater percentage of the U.S. firms (about 60 percent) use WACCs than European firms (46 percent). Many European firms prefer to use the cost of debt as their required rate of return. Most firms in both the United States and Europe adjust their WACCs to compensate for risk differences between projects.

Sources: Marjorie T. Stanley and Stanley B. Block, "A Survey of Multinational Capital Budgeting," *Financial Review* 19, no. 1 (March 1984): 36–54; David F. Scott, Jr., and J. William Petty II, "Capital Budgeting Practices in Large American Firms: A Retrospective Analysis and Synthesis," *Financial Review* 19, no. 1 (March 1984): 111–23; James C. Baker, "The Cost of Capital of Multinational Companies: Facts and Fallacies," *Managerial Finance* (September 1987): 12–17.

CAPITAL STRUCTURE WEIGHTS

The weights in Equation 18.11 represent a specific, intended financing mix. These target weights represent a mix of debt and equity that the firm will try to achieve or maintain over the planning horizon. As much as possible, the target weights should reflect the combination of debt and equity that management believes will minimize the firm's weighted average cost of capital. The firm should make an effort over time to move toward and maintain its target capital structure mix of debt and equity.

MEASURING THE TARGET WEIGHTS

As the firm moves toward a target capital structure, how will it know when it arrives? There are two ways to measure the mix of debt and equity in the firm's capital structure.

One method uses target weights based on the firm's book values, or balance sheet amounts, of debt and equity. The actual weight of debt in the firm's capital structure equals the book value of its debt divided by the book value of its assets. Similarly, the actual equity weight is the book value of its stockholders' equity divided by total assets. Once the target weights are determined, the firm can issue or repurchase appropriate quantities of debt and equity to move the balance sheet numbers toward the target weights.

A second method uses the market values of the firm's debt and equity to compare target and actual weights. The actual weight of debt in the firm's capital structure equals the market value of its debt divided by the market value of its assets. Similarly, the actual equity weight is the market value of the firm's stockholders' equity divided by the market value of its assets. Calculated in this way, bond and stock market price fluctuations, as well as new issues and security repurchases, can move the firm toward— or away from—its target.

Financial theory favors the second method as most appropriate. Current *market* values are used to compute the various costs of financing, so it is intuitive that *market*-based costs should be weighted by *market*-based weights.

The basic capital structure of a firm may include debt, preferred equity, and common equity. In practice, calculating the cost of these components is sometimes complicated by the existence of hybrid financing structures (e.g., convertible debt) and other variations on straight debt, preferred equity, or common equity.[7] A discussion of this advanced topic is beyond the scope of this book.

As an example, let's compute the weighted average cost of capital for Global Manufacturing. Assume that Global Manufacturing has determined that its target capital structure should include one-third debt and two-thirds common equity. Global Manufacturing's current cost of debt is 6.0 percent and its current cost of retained earnings is 15.0 percent. What is Global Manufacturing's weighted average cost of capital, assuming last year's operations generated sufficient retained earnings to finance this year's capital budget?

Since sufficient new retained earnings exist, Global Manufacturing will not need to issue shares to implement its capital budget. Thus, the cost of retained earnings will be used to estimate its weighted average cost of capital. The target capital structure is one-third debt and two-thirds common equity. Using Equation 18.11, Global Manufacturing's weighted average cost of capital is:

$$\text{WACC} = (1/3)(6.0 \text{ percent}) + (2/3)(15.0 \text{ percent})$$
$$= 12.0 \text{ percent}$$

Given current market conditions and Global Manufacturing's target capital structure weights, the firm should use a discount rate of 12.0 percent when computing the NPV for average risk projects.

---

7.   For insights into how to handle these more complex financing structures, see Michael C. Ehrhardt, *The Search for Capital* (Boston, MA: Harvard Business School Press, 1994) and Tom Copeland, Tim Koller, and Jack Murrin, *Valuation: Measuring and Managing the Value of Companies, second edition* (New York: John Wiley & Sons, 1996).

To compare Global Manufacturing's current capital structure with its target capital structure, let's assume that Global Manufacturing has two bond issues outstanding. One is rated AA and has a yield to maturity of 8.8 percent; the other is rated A and yields 9.5 percent. The firm also has preferred stock and common stock outstanding. The table below shows the current market prices and the number of shares or bonds outstanding. How does Global Manufacturing's current capital structure compare to its target?

SECURITY	CURRENT PRICE	NUMBER OUTSTANDING
AA bonds	$1,050	10,000 bonds
A bonds	1,025	20,000 bonds
Preferred stock	40	250,000 shares
Common stock	50	700,000 shares

To begin, Global Manufacturing's target capital structure of one-third debt and two-thirds common equity does not leave any room for preferred stock. Evidently Global Manufacturing's management has decided to reduce its use of preferred stock. Using the given information, let's compute the market values of Global Manufacturing's securities and their current market value weights, and then compare these figures to Global Manufacturing's target capital structure. A security's market value is found by multiplying its market price by the number of bonds or shares currently outstanding. The figures in the previous table give these market values and weights:

SECURITY	MARKET VALUE ($ MILLIONS)	MARKET WEIGHT
AA bonds	$10.50	0.138
A bonds	20.50	0.270
Preferred stock	10.00	0.132
Common stock	35.00	0.460
	$76.00	1.000

Presently, Global Manufacturing's capital structure is comprised of 40 percent debt, about 48 percent common equity, and about 13 percent preferred equity. In order to move toward its target capital structure, Global Manufacturing may want to issue common stock and use the proceeds to purchase outstanding preferred stock and bonds. There is no need for Global Manufacturing to immediately restructure its finances. The flotation costs and administrative fees of such a program would be prohibitive. Some movement toward the target capital structure would occur if Global Manufacturing could identify several positive-NPV projects. Barring a market downtrend, these projects would increase its market value of equity. Also, it could use future additions to retained earnings to repurchase some outstanding debt or preferred equity.

"We definitely have ups and downs with the markets."

JEFF YINGLING

Managing Director—
Corporate Finance
Dean Witter Reynolds Inc.

BBA Finance
University of Notre Dame
MBA Finance
University of Chicago

Q: What is your primary responsibility?
A: My job is to initiate and maintain investment banking relationships with clients in the utility and telecommunications industries.

Q: What do you do for these clients?
A: Our primary role is to help them raise capital through the issuance of equity or debt. We also advise on mergers, acquisitions, and divestitures.

Q: Explain what happens when the client decides to publicly offer common stock.
A: We work with the client to assemble the necessary information to register the offering with the Securities and Exchange Commission, analyze the value of the company to determine the price at which to offer the security, and coordinate a series of "road shows" where we and the client present information to potential investors. These road shows help generate awareness and demand for the upcoming stock issue. We also underwrite the issue which means that Dean Witter buys the stock for an agreed upon price up front. The client gets that money minus our commission. Then it's up to Dean Witter's sales force to sell the stock at the higher public offering price.

Q: What are the major differences between issuing equity as you've just described and selling debt?
A: There are lots of similarities, but one major difference is the time line. A stock issue generally takes a number of weeks. A bond issue can be concluded in a very short time period if necessary. That's because it's much less complicated to determine the value of a bond. Its cash flows, which are a function of the prevailing market interest rates and the credit rating of the company, are known at the time of sale. The value of a common stock issue, on the other hand, is much more subjective because it relates to the value of the company's future earnings and cash flow, which obviously cannot be known in advance. There are many more variables to consider, so it takes longer to analyze.

Q: What is the normal entry-level point in investment banking?
A: Someone with an undergraduate degree would normally start as an analyst. An MBA would normally start as an associate. These positions involve the detail level responsibilities in a transaction such as document preparation, number crunching, and the specifics of the road shows. Each deal is handled by a team of several people, depending on its size and complexity. The work of the analysts and associates is overseen by a more senior person.

Q: Do the fluctuations of the markets affect your success?
A: Very much so. When interest rates are low and equity values are high it is much easier for a company to raise money or complete a merger or acquisition, which means there is more business for us. When the markets are weak, our job is more difficult and the competition is more spirited. We definitely have ups and downs with the markets.

career profiles

611

SUMMARY

The capital structure decision is a very difficult one, but a very important one, for managers to make. An inappropriate mix of debt and equity can lead to higher financing costs for a firm, which in turn will hurt shareholders' wealth. This chapter reviewed several tools that can be used to examine a firm's capital structure, including EBIT/eps analysis and the degree of financial leverage and the degree of combined leverage. A number of other influences affect a management's capital structure decision, including management's desire for financial flexibility, and their risk preferences, as well as their ability to time the financial markets and the feelings of the current shareholders toward maintaining their proportionate control.

Once a target capital structure is selected, the cost of each financing source must be estimated before the weighted average cost of capital can be computed. We review how to estimate the cost of debt, cost of preferred stock, the cost of retained earnings, and the cost of new common equity.

KEY TERMS

business risk
capital structure
combined leverage
cost of capital
degree of combined leverage (DCL)
degree of financial leverage (DFL)

EBIT/eps analysis
flotation costs
optimum debt/equity mix
weighted average cost of capital
   (WACC)

DISCUSSION QUESTIONS

1. What is meant by a firm's capital structure?
2. Explain why determining a firm's optimum debt/equity mix is important.
3. Briefly describe the trends that have occurred in the corporate use of debt.
4. What is EBIT/eps analysis? What information does it provide managers?
5. Describe the term "indifference level" in conjunction with EBIT/eps analysis.
6. Describe how a firm's business risk can be measured and indicate how operating leverage impacts on business risk.
7. How is financial leverage created? Describe how the degree of financial leverage is calculated.
8. Briefly explain the concepts of business risk, operating leverage, and financial leverage in terms of an income statement.
9. What is meant by the degree of combined leverage?

10. Describe how the degree of combined leverage can be determined by the degrees of operating and financial leverage.
11. Briefly explain how the factors of flexibility and timing affect the mix between debt and equity capital.
12. How do corporate control concerns affect a firm's capital structure?
13. What are the implications of "maturity matching" on the capital structure decision?
14. Describe several debt issues that do not have fixed interest rates.
15. What is the relationship between a firm's cost of capital and investor required rates of return?
16. How can a firm estimate its cost of debt financing?
17. Describe how the cost of preferred stock is determined.
18. Describe two methods for estimating the cost of retained earnings.
19. How does the cost of new common stock differ from the cost of retained earnings?
20. What is the weighted average cost of capital? Describe how it is calculated.
21. Should book value weights or market value weights be used to evaluate a firm's current capital structure weights? Why?

PROBLEMS

1. AQ&Q has EBIT of $2 million, total assets of $10 million, stockholders' equity of $4 million, and pre-tax interest expense of 10 percent.
   a. What is AQ&Q's indifference level of EBIT?
   b. Given its current situation, might it benefit from increasing or decreasing its use of debt? Explain.
   c. Suppose we are told AQ&Q's average tax rate is 40 percent. How does this affect your answers to parts a and b?
2. URA, Incorporated, has operating income of $5 million, total assets of $45 million, outstanding debt of $20 million, and annual interest expense of $3 million.
   a. What is URA's indifference level of EBIT?
   b. Given its current situation, might URA benefit from increasing or decreasing its use of debt? Explain.
   c. Suppose forecasted net income is $4 million next year. If it has a 40 percent average tax rate, what will be its expected level of EBIT? Will this forecast change your answer to part b? Why or why not?
3. Stern's Stews, Inc., is considering a new capital structure. Its current and proposed capital structure is given below:

CURRENT AND PROPOSED CAPITAL STRUCTURES
FOR STERN'S STEWS, INC.

	CURRENT	PROPOSED
Total assets	$150 million	$150 million
Debt	25 million	100 million
Equity	125 million	50 million
Common stock price	$ 50	$ 50
Number of shares	2,500,000	1,000,000
Interest rate	12%	12%

Stern's Stews president expects next year's EBIT to be $20 million, but it may be 25 percent higher or lower. Ignoring taxes, perform an EBIT/eps analysis. What is the indifference level of EBIT? Should Stern's Stews change its capital structure? Why or why not?

4. Faulkner's Fine Fries, Inc. (FFF) is thinking about reducing its debt burden. Given the information below and an expected EBIT of $50 million (plus or minus 10 percent) next year, should FFF change their capital structure?

CURRENT AND PROPOSED CAPITAL STRUCTURES FOR FFF, INC.

	CURRENT	PROPOSED
Total assets	$750 million	$750 million
Debt	450 million	300 million
Equity	300 million	450 million
Common stock price	$ 30	$ 30
Number of shares	10,000,000	15,000,000
Interest rate	12%	12%

5. Redo problem 4, assuming that the less leveraged capital structure will result in a borrowing cost of 10% and a common stock price of $40.
6. A firm has sales of $10 million, variable costs of $4 million, fixed expenses of $1.5 million, interest costs of $2 million and has a 30 percent average tax rate.
    a. Compute its DOL, DFL, and DCL.
    b. What will be the expected level of EBIT and net income if next year's sales rise 10 percent?
    c. What will be the expected level of EBIT and net income if next year's sales fall 20 percent?
7. Here are the income statements for Genatron Manufacturing for 1995 and 1996:

INCOME STATEMENT	1995	1996
Net sales	$1,300,000	$1,500,000
Cost of goods sold	780,000	900,000
Gross profit	$ 520,000	$ 600,000
General and administrative	150,000	150,000

Marketing expenses	130,000	150,000
Depreciation	40,000	53,000
Interest	45,000	57,000
Earnings before taxes	$ 155,000	$ 190,000
Income taxes	62,000	76,000
Net income	$ 93,000	$ 114,000

Assuming one-half of the general and administrative expenses are fixed costs, estimate Genatron's degree of operating leverage, degree of financial leverage, and degree of combined leverage in 1995 and 1996.

8. The Nutrex Corporation wants to calculate its weighted average cost of capital. Its target capital structure weights are 40 percent long-term debt and 60 percent common equity. The before-tax cost of debt is estimated to be 10 percent and the company is in the 40 percent tax bracket. The current risk-free interest rate is 8 percent on Treasury bills. The expected return on the market is 13 percent and the firm's stock beta is 1.8.

   a. What is Nutrex's cost of debt?
   b. Estimate Nutrex's expected return on common equity using the security market line.
   c. Calculate the after-tax weighted average cost of capital.

9. The following are balance sheets for the Genatron Manufacturing Corporation for the years 1995 and 1996:

BALANCE SHEET	1995	1996
Cash	$ 50,000	$ 40,000
Accounts receivable	200,000	260,000
Inventory	450,000	500,000
Total current assets	700,000	800,000
Fixed assets (net)	300,000	400,000
Total assets	$1,000,000	$1,200,000
Bank loan, 10%	$ 90,000	$ 90,000
Accounts payable	130,000	170,000
Accruals	50,000	70,000
Total current liabilities	$ 270,000	$ 330,000
Long-term debt, 12%	300,000	400,000
Common stock, $10 par	300,000	300,000
Capital surplus	50,000	50,000
Retained earnings	80,000	120,000
Total liabilities and equity	$1,000,000	$1,200,000

   a. Calculate the weighted average cost of capital based on book value weights. Assume an after-tax cost of new debt of 8.63 percent and a cost of common equity of 16.5 percent.

   b.   The current market value of Genatron's long-term debt is $350,000. The common stock price is $20 per share and there are 30,000 shares outstanding. Calculate the WACC using market value weights and the component capital costs in part a.

   c.   Recalculate the WACC based on both book value and market value weights assuming that the before-tax cost of debt will be 18 percent, the company is in the 40 percent income tax bracket, and the after-tax cost of common equity capital is 21 percent.

10. The Basic Biotech Corporation wants to determine its weighted average cost of capital. Its target capital structure weights are 50 percent long-term debt and 50 percent common equity. The before-tax cost of debt is estimated to be 10 percent and the company is in the 30 percent tax bracket. The current risk-free interest rate is 8 percent on Treasury bills. The after-tax cost of common equity capital is 14.5 percent. Calculate the after-tax weighted average cost of capital.

SELF-TEST QUESTIONS

1. A firm's mix of debt and equity defines the firm's:
   a. capital structure
   b. working capital
   c. net working capital
   d. degree of operating leverage

2. A firm's optimum debt/equity mix:
   a. minimizes shareholder wealth
   b. maximizes the cost of capital
   c. minimizes the cost of capital
   d. maximizes total assets

3. A firm's business risk is measured by the variability in which one of the following over time?
   a. net sales
   b. total assets
   c. operating income (or EBIT)
   d. net income

4. The degree of financial leverage measures the sensitivity of ____ to changes in ____.
   a. net sales to EBIT
   b. EBIT to net sales
   c. EBIT to EPS
   d. EPS to EBIT

5. A firm's degree of combined leverage can be measured as:
   a. degree of operating leverage plus the degree of financial leverage
   b. degree of operating leverage minus the degree of financial leverage

    c. degree of operating leverage times the degree of financial leverage

    d. degree of operating leverage divided by the degree of financial leverage

6. Which of the following affect a firm's choice of capital structures?

    a. flexibility

    b. timing

    c. corporate control

    d. all of the above

7. Which one of the following is not a different term for the same concept?

    a. required rate of return

    b. cost of capital

    c. discount rate

    d. net profit margin

8. Which of the following costs must be adjusted to an after-tax cost?

    a. cost of debt

    b. cost of preferred stock

    c. cost of common stock

    d. cost of retained earnings

9. What percent of U.S. firms use the after-tax weighted average cost of capital as their required rates of return for projects?

    a. 75 percent

    b. 60 percent

    c. 40 percent

    d. 25 percent

SELF-TEST PROBLEMS

1. Without drawing an EBIT/eps diagram, will a firm prefer a more or less leveraged capital structure if it has assets of $30 million, expected EBIT of $4 million, and a debt cost of 12 percent? Would the answer change if the interest cost rose to 15 percent?

2. The current stock price of Trooper Co. is $100. Investors expect the company to pay a $10 per share dividend in the next period. If dividends are expected to grow 5 percent annually into the foreseeable future and flotation costs are 3 percent, what is the cost of retained earnings and the cost of new common stock?

SUGGESTED READINGS

Brooks, Donald E., and Robert H. Hertz. *Guide to Financial Instruments.* New York: Coopers and Lybrand, 1994.

Carey, Mark S., Stephen D. Prowse, John D. Rea, and Gregory F. Udell. "Recent Developments in the Market for Privately Placed Debt." *Federal Reserve Bulletin* (February 1993): 77–92.

Copeland, Tom, Tim Koller, and Jack Murrin. *Valuation: Measuring and Managing the Value of Companies*, 2e. New York: John Wiley and Sons, 1996. Chap. 8.

Dickerson, Bodil, B.J. Campsey, and Eugene F. Brigham. *Introduction to Financial Management*, 4e. Orlando, FL: The Dryden Press, 1995. Chaps. 19 and 20.

Ehrhardt, Michael C. *The Search for Capital.* Boston, MA: Harvard Business School Press, 1994.

Masulis, Ronald W. *The Debt/Equity Choice.* Cambridge, MA: Ballinger Publishing, 1988.

Rao, Ramesh K.S. *Financial Management*, 3e. Cincinnati, Ohio: South-Western College Publishing, 1995. Chap. 15.

Ross, Stephen A., Randolph W. Westerfield, and Bradford D. Jordan. *Fundamentals of Corporate Finance*, 3e. Homewood, IL: Richard D. Irwin Inc., 1995. Chap. 15.

Weston, J. Fred, Scott Besley, and Eugene F. Brigham. *Essentials of Managerial Finance*, 11e. Fort Worth, TX: The Dryden Press, 1996. Chaps. 15 and 16.

Worthington, Paula R. "Recent Trends in Corporate Leverage." *Economic Perspectives.* Federal Reserve Bank of Chicago (May/June 1993): 24–31.

ANSWERS TO SELF-TEST QUESTIONS 1. a, 2. c, 3. c, 4. d, 5. c, 6. d, 7. d, 8. a, 9. b

ANSWERS TO SELF-TEST PROBLEMS

1. The ratio of the firm's expected operating return on assets is ($4 million in EBIT)/($30 million in assets), or 13.33 percent. If the firm's interest rate on debt is 12 percent, the operating return on assets of 13.33 percent exceeds the interest rate, so leverage is beneficial. Another way to answer this would find the indifference level of EBIT at a 12 percent interest rate: (0.12)($30 million), or $3.6 million. Since the expected EBIT of $4 million is greater than the indifference level, leverage is preferred.

   If the interest rate on debt were 15 percent, a capital structure with less debt would be preferred. The operating return of 13.33 percent is less than the 15 percent interest rate, and the indifference EBIT level of (0.15)($30 million), or $4.5 million, exceeds the expected EBIT.

2. Only sufficient information is provided for using the constant dividend growth model. Next year's dividend, D_1, is given as $10. The constant dividend growth rate is 5% and flotation costs are 3%. Substituting this information into Equation 18.9, we have the cost of retained earnings:

   $$k_{re} = \frac{D_1}{P} + g = \frac{\$10}{\$100} + 0.05 = 15 \text{ percent}$$

   The cost of new common equity is given by Equation 18.10. The flotation cost per share is 3 percent of $100 or $3.

   $$k_{cs} = \frac{D_1}{(P - F)} + g = \frac{10}{100 - 3} + 0.05 = 15.3 \text{ percent}$$

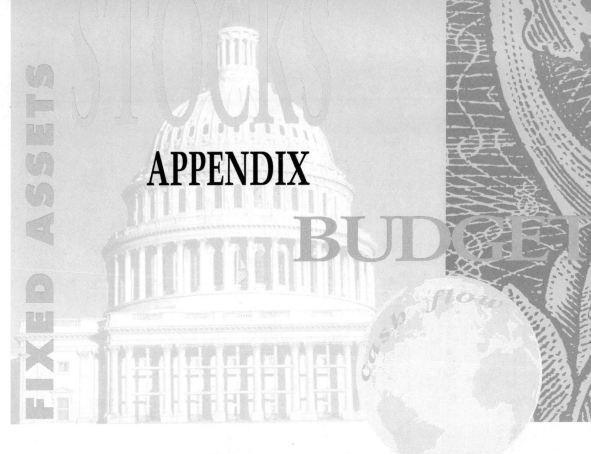

APPENDIX

Table 1
Future Value of $1 (FVIF)

Table 2
Present Value of $1 (PVIF)

Table 3
Future Value of a $1 Ordinary Annuity (FVIFA)

Table 4
Present Value of a $1 Ordinary Annuity (PVIFA)

TABLE 1   Future Value of $1 (FVIF)

YEAR	1%	2%	3%	4%	5%	6%	7%	8%	9%
1	1.010	1.020	1.030	1.040	1.050	1.060	1.070	1.080	1.090
2	1.020	1.040	1.061	1.082	1.102	1.124	1.145	1.166	1.188
3	1.030	1.061	1.093	1.125	1.158	1.191	1.225	1.260	1.295
4	1.041	1.082	1.126	1.170	1.216	1.262	1.311	1.360	1.412
5	1.051	1.104	1.159	1.217	1.276	1.338	1.403	1.469	1.539
6	1.062	1.126	1.194	1.265	1.340	1.419	1.501	1.587	1.677
7	1.072	1.149	1.230	1.316	1.407	1.504	1.606	1.714	1.828
8	1.083	1.172	1.267	1.369	1.477	1.594	1.718	1.851	1.993
9	1.094	1.195	1.305	1.423	1.551	1.689	1.838	1.999	2.172
10	1.105	1.219	1.344	1.480	1.629	1.791	1.967	2.159	2.367
11	1.116	1.243	1.384	1.539	1.710	1.898	2.105	2.332	2.580
12	1.127	1.268	1.426	1.601	1.796	2.012	2.252	2.518	2.813
13	1.138	1.294	1.469	1.665	1.886	2.113	2.410	2.720	3.066
14	1.149	1.319	1.513	1.732	1.980	2.261	2.579	2.937	3.342
15	1.161	1.346	1.558	1.801	2.079	2.397	2.759	3.172	3.642
16	1.173	1.373	1.605	1.873	2.183	2.540	2.952	3.426	3.970
17	1.184	1.400	1.653	1.948	2.292	2.693	3.159	3.700	4.328
18	1.196	1.428	1.702	2.026	2.407	2.854	3.380	3.996	4.717
19	1.208	1.457	1.754	2.107	2.527	3.026	3.617	4.316	5.142
20	1.220	1.486	1.806	2.191	2.653	3.207	3.870	4.661	5.604
25	1.282	1.641	2.094	2.666	3.386	4.292	5.427	6.848	8.623
30	1.348	1.811	2.427	3.243	4.322	5.743	7.612	10.063	13.268

Note: The basic equation for finding the future value interest factor (FVIF) is:

$$FVIF_{r,n} = (1 + r)^n$$

where r is the interest rate and n is the number of periods in years.

TABLE 1   *(continued)*

10%	12%	14%	15%	16%	18%	20%	25%	30%
1.100	1.120	1.140	1.150	1.160	1.180	1.200	1.250	1.300
1.210	1.254	1.300	1.322	1.346	1.392	1.440	1.563	1.690
1.331	1.405	1.482	1.521	1.561	1.643	1.728	1.953	2.197
1.464	1.574	1.689	1.749	1.811	1.939	2.074	2.441	2.856
1.611	1.762	1.925	2.011	2.100	2.288	2.488	3.052	3.713
1.772	1.974	2.195	2.313	2.436	2.700	2.986	3.815	4.827
1.949	2.211	2.502	2.660	2.826	3.185	3.583	4.768	6.276
2.144	2.476	2.853	3.059	3.278	3.759	4.300	5.960	8.157
2.358	2.773	3.252	3.518	3.803	4.435	5.160	7.451	10.604
2.594	3.106	3.707	4.046	4.411	5.234	6.192	9.313	13.786
2.853	3.479	4.226	4.652	5.117	6.176	7.430	11.642	17.922
3.138	3.896	4.818	5.350	5.936	7.288	8.916	14.552	23.298
3.452	4.363	5.492	6.153	6.886	8.599	10.699	18.190	30.288
3.797	4.887	6.261	7.076	7.988	10.147	12.839	22.737	39.374
4.177	5.474	7.138	8.137	9.266	11.974	15.407	28.422	51.186
4.595	6.130	8.137	9.358	10.748	14.129	18.488	35.527	66.542
5.054	6.866	9.276	10.761	12.468	16.672	22.186	44.409	86.504
5.560	7.690	10.575	12.375	14.463	19.673	26.623	55.511	112.46
6.116	8.613	12.056	14.232	16.777	23.214	31.948	69.389	146.19
6.728	9.646	13.743	16.367	19.461	27.393	38.338	86.736	190.05
10.835	17.000	26.462	32.919	40.874	62.669	95.396	264.70	705.64
17.449	29.960	50.950	66.212	85.850	143.371	237.376	807.79	2620.00

TABLE 2   Present Value of $1 (PVIF)

YEAR	1%	2%	3%	4%	5%	6%	7%	8%	9%	10%
1	.990	.980	.971	.962	.952	.943	.935	.926	.917	.909
2	.980	.961	.943	.925	.907	.890	.873	.857	.842	.826
3	.971	.942	.915	.889	.864	.840	.816	.794	.772	.751
4	.961	.924	.888	.855	.823	.792	.763	.735	.708	.683
5	.951	.906	.863	.822	.784	.747	.713	.681	.650	.621
6	.942	.888	.837	.790	.746	.705	.666	.630	.596	.564
7	.933	.871	.813	.760	.711	.665	.623	.583	.547	.513
8	.923	.853	.789	.731	.677	.627	.582	.540	.502	.467
9	.914	.837	.766	.703	.645	.592	.544	.500	.460	.424
10	.905	.820	.744	.676	.614	.558	.508	.463	.422	.386
11	.896	.804	.722	.650	.585	.527	.475	.429	.388	.350
12	.887	.788	.701	.625	.557	.497	.444	.397	.356	.319
13	.879	.773	.681	.601	.530	.469	.415	.368	.326	.290
14	.870	.758	.661	.577	.505	.442	.388	.340	.299	.263
15	.861	.743	.642	.555	.481	.417	.362	.315	.275	.239
16	.853	.728	.623	.534	.458	.394	.339	.292	.252	.218
17	.844	.714	.605	.513	.436	.391	.317	.270	.231	.198
18	.836	.700	.587	.494	.416	.350	.296	.250	.212	.180
19	.828	.686	.570	.475	.396	.331	.276	.232	.194	.164
20	.820	.673	.554	.456	.377	.312	.258	.215	.178	.149
25	.780	.610	.478	.375	.295	.233	.184	.146	.116	.092
30	.742	.552	.412	.308	.231	.174	.131	.099	.075	.057

Note: The basic equation for finding the present value interest factor (PVIF) is:

$$PVIF_{r,n} = \frac{1}{(1 + r)^n}$$

where i is the interest or discount rate and n is the number of periods in years.

TABLE 2   *(continued)*

12%	14%	15%	16%	18%	20%	25%	30%
.893	.877	.870	.862	.847	.833	.800	.769
.797	.769	.756	.743	.718	.694	.640	.592
.712	.675	.658	.641	.609	.579	.512	.455
.636	.592	.572	.552	.516	.482	.410	.350
.567	.519	.497	.476	.437	.402	.328	.269
.507	.456	.432	.410	.370	.335	.262	.207
.452	.400	.376	.354	.314	.279	.210	.159
.404	.351	.327	.305	.266	.233	.168	.123
.361	.308	.284	.263	.225	.194	.134	.094
.322	.270	.247	.227	.191	.162	.107	.073
.287	.237	.215	.195	.162	.135	.086	.056
.257	.208	.187	.168	.137	.112	.069	.043
.229	.182	.163	.145	.116	.093	.055	.033
.205	.160	.141	.125	.099	.078	.044	.025
.183	.140	.123	.108	.084	.065	.035	.020
.163	.123	.107	.093	.071	.054	.028	.015
.146	.108	.093	.080	.060	.045	.023	.012
.130	.095	.081	.069	.051	.038	.018	.009
.116	.083	.070	.060	.043	.031	.014	.007
.104	.073	.061	.051	.037	.026	.012	.005
.059	.038	.030	.024	.016	.010	.004	.001
.033	.020	.015	.012	.007	.004	.001	.000

TABLE 3 Future Value of a $1 Ordinary Annuity (FVIFA)

YEAR	1%	2%	3%	4%	5%	6%	7%	8%
1	1.000	1.000	1.000	1.000	1.000	1.000	1.000	1.000
2	2.010	2.020	2.030	2.040	2.050	2.060	2.070	2.080
3	3.030	3.060	3.091	3.122	3.152	3.184	3.215	3.246
4	4.060	4.122	4.184	4.246	4.310	4.375	4.440	4.506
5	5.101	5.204	5.309	5.416	5.526	5.637	5.751	5.867
6	6.152	6.308	6.468	6.633	6.802	6.975	7.153	7.336
7	7.214	7.434	7.662	7.898	8.142	8.394	8.654	8.923
8	8.286	8.583	8.892	9.214	9.549	9.897	10.260	10.637
9	9.369	9.755	10.159	10.583	11.027	11.491	11.978	12.488
10	10.462	10.950	11.464	12.006	12.578	13.181	13.816	14.487
11	11.567	12.169	12.808	13.486	14.207	14.972	15.784	16.645
12	12.683	13.412	14.192	15.026	15.917	16.870	17.888	18.977
13	13.809	14.680	15.618	16.627	17.713	18.882	20.141	21.495
14	14.947	15.974	17.086	18.292	19.599	21.015	22.550	24.215
15	16.097	17.293	18.599	20.024	21.579	23.276	25.129	27.152
16	17.258	18.639	20.157	21.825	23.657	25.673	27.888	30.324
17	18.430	20.012	21.762	23.698	25.840	28.213	30.840	33.750
18	19.615	21.412	23.414	25.645	28.132	30.906	33.999	37.450
19	20.811	22.841	25.117	27.671	30.539	33.760	37.379	41.466
20	22.019	24.297	26.870	29.778	33.066	36.786	40.995	45.762
25	28.243	32.030	36.459	41.646	47.727	54.865	63.249	73.106
30	34.785	40.568	47.575	56.805	66.439	79.058	94.461	113.283

Note: the basic equation for finding the future value interest factor of an ordinary annuity (FVIFA) is:

$$\text{FVIFA}_{r,n} = \sum_{t=1}^{n} (1 + r)^{t-1} = \frac{-(1 + r)^n - 1}{r}$$

where r is the interest rate and n is the number of periods in years.

Future Value of a $1 Annuity Due (FVIFAD)

The future value interest factor of an annuity due (FVIFAD) may be found by using the following formula to convert FVIFA values found in Table 2:

$$\text{FVIFAD}_{r,n} = \text{FVIFA}_{r,n}(1 + r)$$

where r is the interest rate and n is the number of periods in years.

TABLE 3   *(continued)*

9%	10%	12%	14%	16%	18%	20%	25%	30%
1.000	1.000	1.000	1.000	1.000	1.000	1.000	1.000	1.000
2.090	2.100	2.120	2.140	2.160	2.180	2.200	2.250	2.300
3.278	3.310	3.374	3.440	3.506	3.572	3.640	3.813	3.990
4.573	4.641	4.779	4.921	5.066	5.215	5.368	5.766	6.187
5.985	6.105	6.353	6.610	6.877	7.154	7.442	8.207	9.043
7.523	7.716	8.115	8.536	8.977	9.442	9.930	11.259	12.756
9.200	9.487	10.089	10.730	11.414	12.142	12.916	15.073	17.583
11.028	11.436	12.300	13.233	14.240	15.327	16.499	19.842	23.858
13.021	13.579	14.776	16.085	17.518	19.086	20.799	25.802	32.015
15.193	15.937	17.549	19.337	21.321	23.521	25.959	33.253	42.619
17.560	18.531	20.655	23.044	25.733	28.755	32.150	42.566	56.405
20.141	21.384	24.133	27.271	30.850	34.931	39.580	54.208	74.327
22.953	24.523	28.029	32.089	36.786	42.219	48.497	68.760	97.625
26.019	27.975	32.393	37.581	43.672	50.818	59.196	86.949	127.91
29.361	31.772	37.280	43.842	51.660	60.965	72.035	109.69	167.29
33.003	35.950	42.753	50.980	60.925	72.939	87.442	138.11	218.47
36.974	40.545	48.884	59.118	71.673	87.068	105.931	173.64	285.01
41.301	45.599	55.750	68.394	84.141	103.740	128.117	218.05	371.52
46.018	51.159	63.440	78.969	98.603	123.414	154.740	273.56	483.97
51.160	57.275	72.052	91.025	115.380	146.628	186.688	342.95	630.17
84.701	98.347	133.334	181.871	249.214	342.603	471.981	1054.80	2348.80
136.308	164.494	241.333	356.787	530.312	790.948	1181.882	3227.20	8730.00

TABLE 4   Present Value of $1 Ordinary Annuity (PVIFA)

YEAR	1%	2%	3%	4%	5%	6%	7%	8%	9%	10%	12%
1	0.990	0.980	0.971	0.962	0.952	0.943	0.935	0.926	0.917	0.909	0.893
2	1.970	1.942	1.913	1.886	1.859	1.833	1.808	1.783	1.759	1.736	1.690
3	2.941	2.884	2.829	2.775	2.723	2.673	2.624	2.577	2.531	2.487	2.402
4	3.902	3.808	3.717	3.630	3.546	3.465	3.387	3.312	3.240	3.170	3.037
5	4.853	4.713	4.580	4.452	4.329	4.212	4.100	3.993	3.890	3.791	3.605
6	5.795	5.601	5.417	5.242	5.076	4.917	4.767	4.623	4.486	4.355	4.111
7	6.728	6.472	6.230	6.002	5.786	5.582	5.389	5.206	5.033	4.868	4.564
8	7.652	7.325	7.020	6.733	6.463	6.210	5.971	5.747	5.535	5.335	4.968
9	8.566	8.162	7.786	7.435	7.108	6.802	6.515	6.247	5.995	5.759	5.328
10	9.471	8.983	8.530	8.111	7.722	7.360	7.024	6.710	6.418	6.145	5.650
11	10.368	9.787	9.253	8.760	8.306	7.887	7.499	7.139	6.805	6.495	5.938
12	11.255	10.575	9.954	9.385	8.863	8.384	7.943	7.536	7.161	6.814	6.194
13	12.134	11.348	10.635	9.986	9.394	8.853	8.358	7.904	7.487	7.103	6.424
14	13.004	12.106	11.296	10.563	9.899	9.295	8.745	8.244	7.786	7.367	6.628
15	13.865	12.849	11.938	11.118	10.380	9.712	9.108	8.559	8.061	7.606	6.811
16	14.718	13.578	12.561	11.652	10.838	10.106	9.447	8.851	8.313	7.824	6.974
17	15.562	14.292	13.166	12.166	11.274	10.477	9.763	9.122	8.544	8.022	7.120
18	16.398	14.992	13.754	12.659	11.690	10.828	10.059	9.372	8.756	8.201	7.250
19	17.226	15.678	14.324	13.134	12.085	11.158	10.336	9.604	8.950	8.365	7.366
20	18.046	16.351	14.877	13.590	12.462	11.470	10.594	9.818	9.129	8.514	7.469
25	22.023	19.523	17.413	15.622	14.094	12.783	11.654	10.675	9.823	9.077	7.843
30	25.808	22.397	19.600	17.292	15.372	13.765	12.409	11.258	10.274	9.427	8.055

Note: The basic equation for finding the present value interest factor of an ordinary annuity (PVIFA) is:

$$\text{PVIFA}_{r,n} = \sum_{t=1}^{n} \frac{1}{(1+r)^t} = \frac{1 - \dfrac{1}{(1+r)^n}}{r}$$

where r is the interest or discount rate and n is the number of periods in years.

Present Value of a $1 Annuity Due (PVIFAD)

The present value interest factor of an annuity due (PVIFAD) may be found by using the following formula to convert PVIFA values found in Table 4:

$$\text{PVIFAD}_{r,n} = \text{PVIFA}_{r,n}(1+r)$$

where r is the interest or discount rate and n is the number of periods in years.

TABLE 4 *(continued)*

YEAR	14%	16%	18%	20%	25%	30%
1	0.877	0.862	0.847	0.833	.800	.769
2	1.647	1.605	1.566	1.528	1.440	1.361
3	2.322	2.246	2.174	2.106	1.952	1.816
4	2.914	2.798	2.690	2.589	2.362	2.166
5	3.433	3.274	3.127	2.991	2.689	2.436
6	3.889	3.685	3.498	3.326	2.951	2.643
7	4.288	4.039	3.812	3.605	3.161	2.802
8	4.639	4.344	4.078	3.837	3.329	2.925
9	4.946	4.607	4.303	4.031	3.463	3.019
10	5.216	4.833	4.494	4.193	3.571	3.092
11	5.453	5.029	4.656	4.327	3.656	3.147
12	5.660	5.197	4.793	4.439	3.725	3.190
13	5.842	5.342	4.910	4.533	3.780	3.223
14	6.002	5.468	5.008	4.611	3.824	3.249
15	6.142	5.575	5.092	4.675	3.859	3.268
16	6.265	5.668	5.162	4.730	3.887	3.283
17	5.373	5.749	4.222	4.775	3.910	3.295
18	6.467	5.818	5.273	4.812	3.928	3.304
19	6.550	5.877	5.316	4.843	3.942	3.311
20	6.623	5.929	5.353	4.870	3.954	3.316
25	6.873	6.097	5.467	4.948	3.985	3.329
30	7.003	6.177	5.517	4.979	3.995	3.332

GLOSSARY

A

acceptance receivable from the sale of merchandise on the basis of a draft or bill of exchange drawn against the buyer or the buyer's bank

administrative inflation the tendency of prices, aided by union-corporation contracts, to rise during economic expansion and to resist declines during recessions

advance factoring factor pays the firm for its receivables before the account due date

aftermarket period of time during which members of the syndicate may not sell the securities for less than the initial offering price

agency costs tangible and intangible expenses borne by shareholders because of the actual or potential self-serving actions of managers

agents hired by the principals to run the firm

American depository receipt (ADR) receipt which represents foreign shares to U.S. investors

amortized loan a loan repaid in equal payments over a specified time period

annual percentage rate (APR) determined by multiplying the interest rate charged per period by the number of periods in a year

annual report contains descriptive information and numerical records on the operating and financial performance during the past year

annualize a return stating the return as the annual return that would result in the observed percentage return

annuity a series of equal payments that occur over a number of time periods

annuity due exists when the equal payments occur at the beginning of each time period

arbitrage 1. buying commodities, securities, or bills of exchange in one market and immediately selling them in another to make a profit from price differences in the two markets 2. operation that takes place if there is a mispricing between two different markets for the same asset that leads to a risk-free profit

ask price price for which the owner is willing to sell the security

asset management ratios indicate extent to which assets are used to support sales

assets financial and physical items owned by a business

at-the-money an option's exercise price equals the current market price of the underlying asset

automatic stabilizers continuing federal programs that stabilize economic activity

average tax rate determined by dividing the taxes paid by the taxable income

B

balance of payments a summary of all economic transactions between one country and the rest of the world

balance of trade the net value of a country's exports of goods and services compared to its imports

balance sheet statement of a company's financial position as of a particular date

bank holding company company that holds voting power in two or more banks through stock ownership

bankers' acceptances a promise of future payment issued by a firm and guaranteed by a bank

banking system commercial banks, savings and loans, savings banks, and credit unions

barter exchange of goods or services without using money

base case firm's after-tax cash flows without the project

bearer bonds have coupons that are literally "clipped" and presented, like a check, to the bank for payment. The bond issuer does not know who is receiving the interest payments

best-effort agreement agreement by the investment banker to sell securities of the issuing corporation; assumes no risk for the possible failure of the flotation

beta measure of an asset's systematic risk

bid price price that the buyer is willing to pay for the security

bimetallic standard monetary standard based on two metals, usually silver and gold

blanket inventory lien claim against a customer's inventory when the individual items are indistinguishable

blue-sky laws protect the investor from fraudulent security offerings

bond rating assesses both the collateral underlying the bonds as well as the ability of the issuer to make timely payments of interest and principal

branch banks bank offices under a single bank charter

break-even analysis used to estimate how many units of product must be sold in order for the firm to break even or have a zero profit

broker one who assists in the trading process by buying or selling securities in the market for an investor

budgetary deficit occurs when expenditures are greater than revenues

budgets financial plans utilized in sales forecasts

business risk measured by variability in EBIT over time

buying on margin investor borrows money and invests it along with his own funds in securities

bylaws rules established to govern the corporation; they deal with how the firm will be managed and the rights of the stockholder

C

call deferment period specified period of time after the issue during which the bonds cannot be called

call option contract for the purchase of a security within a specified time period and at a specified price

call price price paid to the investor for redemption prior to maturity, typically par value plus a call premium of one year's interest

call risk risk of having a bond called away and reinvesting the proceeds at a lower interest rate

callable bonds can be redeemed prior to maturity by the issuing firm

callable preferred stock gives the corporation the right to retire the preferred stock at its option

cannibalization a project robs cash flow from the firm's existing lines of business

capacity ability to pay bills

capital adequacy of owners' equity relative to existing liabilities

capital account balance foreign government and private investment in the United States netted against similar U.S. investment in foreign countries

Capital Asset Pricing Model (CAPM) states that expected return on an asset depends on its level of systematic risk

capital budgeting process of identifying, evaluating, and implementing a firm's investment opportunities

capital consumption allowances estimates of the "using up," or depreciation of, plant and equipment assets for business purposes

capital formation 1. process of constructing residential and nonresidential structures, manufacturing producers' durable equipment, and increasing business inventories 2. the creation of productive facilities such as buildings, tools, and equipment

capital gains gains or losses on capital assets held for more than one year

capital markets markets for longer-term debt securities and corporate stocks

capital structure firm's mix of debt and equity

cash budget tool the treasurer uses to forecast future cash flows and estimate future short-term borrowing needs

cash conversion cycle time between a firm's paying its suppliers for inventory and collecting cash from customers on a sale of the finished product

central bank federal government agency that facilitates operation of the financial system and regulates money supply growth

central limit order book limit "book" in which the specialist keeps unexecuted limit orders

certificates of deposit (CDs) time deposits with a stated maturity

character ethical quality upon which one can base a judgment about a customer's willingness to pay bills

charter provides the corporate name, indicates the intended business activities, provides names and addresses of directors, and indicates how a firm will be capitalized with stock

chartists (technicians) study graphs of past price movements, volume, etc., to try to predict future prices

chief financial officer (CFO) responsible for the controller and the treasury functions of a firm

clean draft a draft that is not accompanied by any special documents

closed-end mortgage bond does not permit future bond issues to be secured by any of the assets pledged as security to it

coefficient of variation measures the risk per unit of return

collateral whether assets are available to provide security for the potential credit

collateralized bonds pledge securities to protect the bondholders against loss in case of default

combined leverage effect on earnings produced by the operating and financial leverage

commercial finance company organization without a bank charter that advances funds to businesses

commercial letter of credit statement by a bank guaranteeing acceptance and payment of a draft up to a stated amount

commercial paper 1. short-term promissory note sold by high-credit-quality U.S. corporations; notes are backed solely by the credit quality of the issuer 2. short-term unsecured promissory notes

commission brokers act as agents to execute customers' orders for securities purchases and sales

common stock represents ownership shares in a corporation

compensating balance requirement that 10 to 20 percent of a loan be kept on deposit at the bank

compound interest interest earned on interest in addition to interest earned on the principal or investment

compounding an arithmetic process whereby an initial value increases at a compound interest rate over time to reach a future value

conditions current economic climate and state of the business cycle

contractual savings savings accumulated on a regular schedule by prior agreement

contribution margin contribution of each unit sold that goes toward paying fixed costs

controller manages accounting, cost analysis, and tax planning

conversion ratio number of shares into which a convertible bond can be converted

conversion value stock price times the conversion ratio

convertible bond can be changed or converted, at the investor's option, into a specified number of shares of the issuer's common stock

convertible preferred stock has special provision that makes it possible to convert it to common stock of the corporation, generally at the stockholder's option

corporate equity capital financial capital supplied by the owners of a corporation

corporation legal entity created under state law with unending life that offers limited financial liability to its owners

correlation statistical concept that relates movements in one set of returns to movements in another set over time

cost of capital 1. project's required rate of return 2. minimum acceptable rate of return to a firm on a project

cost-push inflation occurs when prices are raised to cover rising production costs, such as wages

cost-volume-profit analysis used by managers for financial planning to estimate the firm's operating profits at different levels of unit sales

coupon payments interest payments paid to the bondholders

covenants impose additional restrictions or duties on the firm

credit bureaus source of credit information about business firms and individuals

credit money money worth more than what it is made of bimetallic standard monetary standard based on two metals, usually silver and gold

credit risk (default risk) the chance of nonpayment or delayed payment of interest or principal

cross-sectional analysis different firms are compared at the same point in time

crowding out lack of funds for private borrowing caused by the sale of government obligations to cover large federal deficits

cumulative preferred stock requires that before dividends on common stock are paid, preferred dividends must be paid not only for the current period but also for all previous periods in which preferred dividends were missed

current account balance the flow of income into and out of the United States during a specified time period

current assets cash and all other assets that are expected to be converted into cash within one year

D

dealer satisfies the investor's trades by buying and selling securities from its own inventory

dealer system depends on a small group of dealers in government securities with an effective marketing network throughout the United States

debenture bonds unsecured obligations that depend on the general credit strength of the corporation for their security

debt management various Treasury decisions connected with refunding debt issues

default risk premium compensation for the possibility of the borrower's failure to pay interest and/or principal when due

deficit financing how a government finances its needs when spending is greater than revenues

deficit reserves the amount that required reserves are greater than total reserves

degree of combined leverage (DCL) percentage change in earnings per share that results from a 1 percent change in sales volume

degree of financial leverage (DFL) measures the sensitivity of eps to changes in EBIT

degree of operating leverage measures the sensitivity of operating income to changes in the level of output

demand-pull inflation occurs during economic expansions when demand for goods and services is greater than supply

depository institutions commercial banks, savings and loan associations, savings banks, and credit unions

depreciation devaluing a physical asset over the period of its expected life

depreciation tax shield 1. tax reduction due to depreciation of fixed assets; equals the amount of the depreciation expense multiplied by the firm's tax rate 2. tax reduction due to noncash depreciation expense. It equals the depreciation expense multiplied by the tax rate

derivative deposit deposit of funds that were borrowed from the reserves of primary deposits

derivative security value determined by the value of another investment vehicle

development stage requires estimating relevant cash inflows and outflows

deviations computed as a periodic return minus the average return

direct financing involves use of securities that represent specific contracts between the savers and borrowers themselves

dirty float intervention by central banks to control exchange rates in the foreign exchange market's flexible exchange system

discount bond bond that is selling below par value

discounted loan borrower receives the principal less the interest at the time the loan is made; the principal is repaid at maturity

discounting an arithmetic process whereby a future value decreases at a compound interest rate over time to reach a present value

disintermediation periods of significant decrease in funds moving through depository institutions to the credit markets

dissave to liquidate savings for consumption uses

diversification occurs when we invest in several different assets rather than just a single one

documentary draft draft that is accompanied by an order bill of lading and other documents

draft (bill of exchange) an unconditional order for the payment of money from one person to another

Du Pont analysis technique of breaking down return on total assets and return on equity into their component parts

due diligence detailed study of a corporation

E

EBIT/eps analysis allows managers to see how different capital structures affect the earnings levels of their firms

effective annual rate (EAR) measures the true interest rate when compounding occurs more frequently than once a year

efficient market market in which prices adjust quickly after the arrival of new information and the price change reflects the economic value of the information

electronic funds transfer systems (EFTS) electronic method of receiving and disbursing funds

eligible paper short-term promissory notes eligible for discounting with Federal Reserve Banks

enhancement increase in the cash flows of the firm's other products that occur because of a new project

equipment trust certificate gives the bondholder a claim to specific "rolling stock"(movable assets) such as railroad cars or airplanes

equity funds supplied by the owners that represent their residual claim on the firm

equity capital investment made by the owner into the company

Eurobonds bonds denominated in currencies other than that of the country where they are sold

Eurocurrencies all non-U.S. currencies held by banks outside their country of origin

Eurodollar bonds dollar denominated bonds sold outside the United States

Eurodollars U.S. dollars placed in foreign banks

ex-ante expected or forecasted

excess reserves the amount that total reserves are greater than required reserves

exchange rate value of one currency in terms of another

exchange rate risk fluctuating exchange rates lead to varying levels of U.S. dollar-denominated cash flows

exercise price (strike price) price at which an underlying asset can be traded

expectations theory states that shape of the yield curve indicates investor expectations about future inflation rates

Export-Import Bank bank established to aid in financing and facilitating trade between the U.S. and other countries

extendable notes have their coupons reset every two or three years to reflect the current interest rate environment and any changes in the firm's creditworthiness. The investor can accept the new coupon rate or put the bonds back to the firm

F

factor engages in accounts-receivable financing for business; purchases accounts outright and assumes all credit risks

Fed Board of Governors seven-member board of the Federal Reserve that sets monetary policy

federal funds temporary excess reserves loaned by banks to other banks

Federal Reserve float temporary increase in bank reserves from checks credited to one bank's reserves and not yet debited to another's

Federal Reserve System (Fed) U.S. central bank that sets monetary policy and regulates banking system

federal statutory debt limits limits on the federal debt set by Congress

fiat money legal tender proclaimed to be money by law

field warehouse enterprise establishes a warehouse on the grounds of the borrowing business establishment

finance study of how institutions, markets, and individual firms operate within the financial system

financial assets 1. claims against the income or assets of individuals, businesses, and governments 2. claims against the income or assets of others 3. claims in the form of obligations or liabilities issued by individuals, businesses, financial intermediaries, and governments

financial intermediaries firms that bring about the flow of funds from savers to borrowers

financial leverage ratios indicate the extent to which borrowed funds are used to finance assets, as well as the ability of a firm to meet its debt payment obligations

fiscal agent role of the Fed in collecting taxes, issuing checks, and other activities for the Treasury

fiscal policy government influence on economic activity through taxation and expenditure plans

flexible exchange rates a system in which international exchange rates are determined by supply and demand

floor brokers independent brokers who handle the commission brokers' overflow

flotation initial sale of newly issued debt or equity securities

flotation costs 1. comprised of direct costs, the spread, and underpricing 2. costs of issuing stock; include accounting, legal, and printing costs of offering shares to the public as well as the commission earned by the investment bankers who market the new securities to investors

foreign exchange markets electronic network that connects the major financial centers of the world

fourth market large institutional investors arrange the purchase and sale of securities among themselves without the benefit of broker or dealer

fractional reserve system reserves held with the Fed that are equal to a certain percentage of bank deposits

full-bodied money coins that contain the same value in metal as their face value representative

futures contract obligates the owner to purchase the underlying asset at a specified price on a specified day

G

generally accepted accounting principles (GAAP) set of guidelines as to the form and manner in which accounting information should be presented

global bonds generally denominated in U.S. dollars and marketed globally

global depository receipt (GDR) listed on the London Stock Exchange; facilitates trading in foreign shares

Gordon Model (constant dividend growth model) a means of estimating common stock prices by assuming constant dividend growth over time

greenbacks money issued by the U.S. government to help finance the Civil War

gross domestic product (GDP) measures the output of goods and services in an economy

gross private domestic investment (GPDI) investment in residential and nonresidential structures, producers' durable equipment, and business inventories

H

hedge reduce risk

I

identification stage finding potential capital investment opportunities and identifying whether a project involves a replacement decision and/or revenue expansion

implementation stage executing accepted projects

income statement reports the revenues generated and expenses incurred by the firm over an accounting period

incremental cash flows represent the difference between the firm's after-tax cash flows with the project and the firm's after-tax cash flows without the project

independent projects projects not in direct competition with one another

indirect financing financing created by an intermediary that involves separate instruments with lenders and borrowers

industry comparative analysis compares a firm's ratios against average ratios for other companies in the industry

inflation 1. a rise in prices not offset by increases in quality 2. occurs when an increase in the price of goods or services is not offset by an increase in quality

inflation premium average inflation rate expected over the life of the security

initial margin 1. initial equity percentage 2. required deposit of funds for those who are purchasers and sellers of futures, usually 3 to 6% of the contract

initial public offering (IPO) initial sale of equity to the public

interest rate price that equates the demand for and supply of loanable funds

interest rate risk 1. fluctuating interest rates lead to varying asset prices. In the context of bonds, rising (falling) interest rates result in falling (rising) bond prices 2. possible price fluctuations in fixed-rate debt instruments associated with changes in market interest rates

intermediation the accumulation and lending of savings by depository institutions

internal rate of return (IRR) method return that causes the net present value to be zero

International Monetary Fund (IMF) provides means for United Nations' countries to borrow money

in-the-money option has a positive intrinsic value; for a call (put) option, the underlying asset price exceeds (is below) the stroke price

investment bankers (underwriters) assist corporations by raising money through the marketing of corporate securities to the securities markets

L

legal tender money backed only by government credit

liabilities creditors' claims on a firm

limit order maximum buying price (limit buy) or the minimum selling price (limit sell) specified by the investor

limited liability company (LLC) organizational form whose owners have limited liability; the firm can have an unlimited number of shareholders; income is taxed only once as personal income of the shareholders

limited partners face limited liability; their personal assets cannot be touched to settle the firm's debt

limited partnership has at least one general partner who has unlimited liability; the liability of the limited partners is limited to their investment

line of credit loan limit the bank establishes for each of its business customers

liquidity how easily an asset can be exchanged for money

liquidity preference theory states that investors are willing to accept lower interest rates on short-term debt securities which provide greater liquidity and less interest rate risk

liquidity premium compensation for securities that cannot easily be converted to cash without major price discounts

liquidity ratios indicate the ability of the firm to meet short-term obligations as they come due

loan amortization schedule a schedule of the breakdown of each payment between interest and principal, as well as the remaining balance after each payment

loanable funds theory states that interest rates are a function of the supply of and demand for loanable funds

M

maintenance margin minimum margin to which an investment may fall before a margin call will be placed

margin minimum percentage of the purchase price that must represent the investor's equity or unborrowed funds

margin call investor faces the option of either closing the position or investing additional cash to increase the position's equity or margin

marginal tax rate rate paid on the last dollar of income

market maker one who facilitates market transactions by selling (buying) when other investors wish to buy (sell)

market order open order of an immediate purchase or sale at the best possible price

market portfolio portfolio that contains all risky assets

market segmentation theory states that interest rates may differ because securities of different maturities are not perfect substitutes for each other

market stabilization intervention of the syndicate to repurchase securities in order to maintain their price at the offer price

market value added (MVA) measures the value created by the firm's managers

market value ratios indicate the value of a firm in the market place relative to financial statement values

marketable government securities securities that may be bought and sold through the usual market channels

maturity factoring firm selling its accounts receivable is paid on the normal collection date or net due date of the account

maturity matching approach financing strategy that attempts to match the maturities of assets with the maturities of the liabilities with which they are financed

maturity risk premium compensation expected by investors due to interest rate risk on debt instruments with longer maturities

medium of exchange the basic function of money store of purchasing power when money is held as a liquid asset

merchandise trade balance the net difference between a country's import and export of goods

mission statement statement of a firm's reason for being; sometimes called a vision statement

MOGS Mission, Objectives, Goals, and Strategies

monetary base banking system reserves plus currency held by the public

monetary policy formulated by the Fed to regulate money supply growth

monetizing the deficit the Fed increases the money supply by purchasing government securities

money anything that is generally accepted as payment

money markets markets where debt instruments of one year or less are traded

money multiplier the ratio formed by 1 divided by the reserve ratio, which indicates maximum expansion possible in the money supply

mortgage bonds backed or secured by specifically pledged property of a firm (real estate, buildings, and other assets classified as real property)

mutually exclusive projects selecting one project precludes others from being undertaken

N

negative correlation two time series tend to move in opposite directions

negotiable certificates of deposit debt instruments of $100,000 or more issued by banks that can be traded in the money markets

net present value present value of a project's cash flows minus its cost

net working capital dollar amount of a firm's current assets minus current liabilities

nominal interest rate interest rate that is observed in the marketplace

nonbank financial conglomerates large corporations that offer various financial services

non-cumulative preferred stock makes no provision for the accumulation of past missed dividends

nonmarketable government securities issues that cannot be transferred between persons or institutions but must be redeemed with the U.S. government

O

odd lot sale or purchase of less than 100 shares

off-budget outlays funding for some government agencies that is not included in the federal budget

offer price price at which the security is sold to the investors

open market operations buying and selling of securities by the Federal Reserve to alter the supply of money

open-end mortgage bond allows the same assets to be used as security in future issues

operating cycle time between ordering materials and collecting cash from receivables

opportunity cost cost of passing up the next best alternative

optimum debt/equity mix minimizes the firm's cost of capital

option financial contract that gives the owner the option or choice of buying or selling a particular good at a specified price on or before a specified expiration date

option premium price paid for the option itself

option writer seller of option contracts

order bill of lading document given by a transportation company that lists goods to be transported and terms of the shipping agreement

ordinary annuity exists when the equal payments occur at the end of each time period (also referred to as a deferred annuity)

out-of-the-money option has a zero intrinsic value; for a call (put) option, the underlying asset price is below (exceeds) the strike price

P

par value (face value) principal amount that the issuer is obligated to repay at maturity

par value stated value of a stock; accounting and legal concept bearing no relationship to a firm's stock price or book value

partnership form of business organization when two or more people own a business operated for profit

payback period method determines the time in years it will take to recover, or pay back, the initial investment in fixed assets

personal consumption expenditures (PCE) expenditures by individuals for durable goods, nondurable goods, and services

pledge obtain a short-term loan by using accounts receivable as collateral

poison pills provisions in a corporate charter that make a corporate take-over more unattractive

political risk actions by a sovereign nation to interrupt or change the value of cash flows accruing to foreign investors

portfolio any combination of financial assets or investments

positive correlation two time series tend to move in conjunction with each other

precautionary motives holding funds to meet unexpected demands

pre-emptive rights right of existing shareholders to purchase any newly issued shares

preferred stock equity security that has preference, or a senior claim, to the firm's earnings and assets over common stock

premium bond bond that is selling in excess of its par value

primary deposit deposit that adds new reserves to a bank

primary market original issue market in which securities are initially sold

primary securities market market involved in creating and issuing new securities, mortgages, and other claims to wealth

prime rate 1. interest rate on short-term unsecured loans to highest quality business customers 2. interest rate the bank charges its most creditworthy customers

principal-agent problem conflict of interest between the principals and agents

principals owners of the firm

private placement sale of securities to a small group of private investors

profitability index (PI) (benefit/cost ratio) ratio between the present values of the cash flows and the project's cost

profitability ratios indicate the firm's ability to generate returns on its sales, assets, and equity

program trading technique for trading stocks as a group rather than individually, defined as a minimum of at least 15 different stocks with a minimum value of $1 million

progressive based on the concept that the higher the income the larger the percentage of income that should be paid in taxes

proprietorship business venture that is owned by a single individual who personally receives all profits and assumes all responsibility for the debts and losses of the business

prospectus highly regulated document which details the issuer's operations and finances and must be provided to each buyer of a newly issued security

public offering sale of securities to the investing public

put option contract for the sale of securities within a specified time period and at a specified price

putable bonds (retractable bonds) allow the investor to force the issuer to redeem the bonds prior to maturity

R

random walk prices appear to fluctuate randomly over time, driven by the random arrival of new information

ratio analysis financial technique that involves dividing various financial statement numbers into one another

real assets 1. include ownership of land, buildings, machinery, inventory, commodities, and precious metals 2. land, buildings, machinery, inventory, and precious metals

real rate of interest interest rate on a risk-free debt instrument when no inflation is expected

registered bonds the issuer knows the names of the bondholders and the interest payments are sent directly to the bondholder

registered traders buy and sell stocks for their own account

reinvestment rate risk (rollover risk) fluctuating interest rates cause coupon or interest payments to be reinvested at different interest rates over time

representative full-bodied money paper money fully backed by a precious metal

repurchase agreements short-term loans using Treasury bills as collateral

required reserves the minimum amount of total reserves that a depository institution must hold

reserve ratio the percentage of deposits that must be held as reserves

revolving credit agreement legal obligation of the bank to provide up to the agreed-upon borrowing limit

risk-adjusted discount rate (RADR) adjusts the required rate of return at which the analyst discounts a project's cash flows. Projects with higher (or lower) risk levels require higher (or lower) discount rates

risk-free rate of interest interest rate on a debt instrument with no default, maturity, or liquidity risks (Treasury securities are the closest example)

round lot sale or purchase of 100 shares

S

savings income that is not consumed but held in the form of cash and other financial assets

savings deficit occurs when investment in real assets exceeds current income

savings surplus occurs when current income exceeds investment in real assets

secondary market market in which securities are traded among investors

secondary securities market market for transferring existing securities between investors

secured loan loan backed by collateral

selection stage applying appropriate capital budgeting techniques to help make a final accept or reject decision

semi-strong form efficient market market in which all public information, both current and past, is reflected in asset prices

settlement price determined by a special committee that determines the approximate closing price

shelf registration allows firms to register security issues (both debt and equity) with the SEC, and have them available to sell for two years

short sale sale of securities that the seller does not own

sight draft draft requiring immediate payment

simple interest interest earned only on the principal of the initial investment

sinking fund requirement that the firm retire specific portions of the bond issue over time

sinking fund payments periodic bond principal repayments to a trustee

Special Drawing Rights (SDRs) international reserve assets created by the International Monetary Fund that can be drawn upon by member nations

specialists assigned dealers who have the responsibility of making a market in an assigned security

speculative inflation caused by the expectation that prices will continue to rise, resulting in increased buying to avoid even higher future prices

speculative motives holding funds to take advantage of unusual cash discounts for needed materials

spot market cash market for trading stocks, bonds, or other assets

spread difference between the offer price and the price paid by the investment bank

stand-alone principle analysis focuses on the project's own cash flows, uncontaminated by cash flows from the firm's other activities

standard deviation square root of the variance

standard of value a function of money that occurs when prices and debts are stated in terms of the monetary unit

statement of cash flows provides a summary of the cash inflows (sources) and cash outflows (uses) during a specified accounting period

stock certificate certificate showing an ownership claim of a specific company

stock options allow managers to purchase a stated number of the firm's shares at a specified price

stop-loss order order to sell stock at the market price when the price of the stock falls to a specified level

store of purchasing power when money is held as a liquid asset

street name 1. allows stock to be held in the name of the brokerage house 2. an investor's securities are kept in the name of the brokerage house to facilitate record keeping, settlement, safety against loss or theft, and so on

strong-form efficient market market in which prices reflect all public and private knowledge, including past and current information

subchapter S corporation has fewer than 35 shareholders, none of which is another corporation. Its income is taxed only once, as personal income of the shareholders

subordinated debenture claims of these bonds are subordinate or junior to the claims of the debenture holders

sunk cost project-related expense not dependent upon whether or not the project is undertaken

syndicate group of several investment banking firms that participate in underwriting and distributing a security issue

systematic risk (market risk) risk that cannot be eliminated through diversification

T

tax policy setting the level and structure of taxes to affect the economy

term structure relationship between interest rates or yields and the time to maturity for debt instruments of comparable quality

third market market for large blocks of listed stocks that operates outside the confines of the organized exchanges

thrift institutions savings and loans, savings banks, and credit unions

time draft draft that is payable at a specified future date

time value of money the mathematics of finance whereby interest is earned over time by saving or investing money

token coins coins containing metal of less value than their stated value

tombstones announcements of securities offerings

total reserves deposits held in Federal Reserve Banks and cash in depository institutions

trade credit credit extended on purchases to a firm's customers

trade discounts provided to purchasers as an incentive for early or prompt payment of accounts

transactions motive demand for cash needed to conduct day-to-day operations

transfer payments government payments for which no current services are given in return

traveler's letter of credit issued by a bank to banks in other countries authorizing them to cash checks or purchase drafts presented by the bearer

treasurer oversees the traditional functions of financial analysis

Treasury bills federal obligations that bear the shortest original maturities

Treasury bonds obligations of any maturity but usually over five years

Treasury notes federal obligations issued for maturities of one to ten years

trend or **time series analysis** used to evaluate a firm's performance over time

trust indenture contract that lists the various provisions and covenants of the loan arrangement

trust receipt 1. an instrument through which a bank retains title to goods until they are paid for 2. lien against specific identifiable items in inventory

trustee individual or organization that represents the bondholders to ensure the indenture's provisions are respected by the bond issuer

U

underpricing represents the difference between the aftermarket stock price and the offering price

underwriting agreement contract in which the investment banker agrees to buy securities at a predetermined price and then resell them to the investors

unsecured loan loan that is a general claim against the borrower's assets

unsystematic risk risk that can be diversified away

V

variance derived by summing the squared deviations and dividing by $n - 1$

velocity of money the rate of circulation of the money supply

voluntary savings financial assets set aside for future use

W

warehouse receipt inventory is placed in a bonded warehouse for safekeeping; items are removed as they are paid for

weak-form efficient market market in which prices reflect all past information

weighted average cost of capital (WACC) represents the minimum required rate of return on a capital-budgeting project. It is found by multiplying the marginal cost of each capital structure component by its appropriate weight, and summing the terms

working capital assets needed to carry out the normal operations of the business

World Bank provides loans to developing countries

Y

Yankee bonds dollar denominated bonds issued in the United States by a foreign issuer

yield curve graphic presentation of the term structure of interest rates at a given point in time

yield to maturity (YTM) return on a bond if it is held to maturity

INDEX

This index uses several conventions to help you find information. If the page number appears in boldface (for example, **120**), the citation refers to a definition in the margin of the text page. If the page number appears in italic *(120)*, the citation refers to an illustration. The letter *n* after a page number (120n) refers to a footnote on the cited page.